The Monied Metropolis

Social classes, like fortunes, are made and remade, and invariably the two are linked. Tracing the shifting fortunes and changing character of New York City's economic elite over half a century, this book brings to light a neglected – and critical – chapter in the social history of the United States: the rise of an American bourgeoisie.

How a small and diverse group of New Yorkers came to wield unprecedented economic, social, and political power is a story that Sven Beckert pursues from 1850 to the turn of the nineteenth century. Blending social, intellectual, and political history, his book reveals the central role of the Civil War in realigning New York City's economic elite, as merchants began to shed their old allegiances to slavery and the Atlantic economy and to cede a greater share of economic power to industrialists. We then see how in the wake of Reconstruction the New York bourgeoisie reoriented its ideology, abandoning the free labor views of the antebellum years for laissez-faire liberalism. Finally, in the 1880s and 1890s, we observe the emergence of a fully self-conscious and inordinately powerful New York upper class.

Drawing on a remarkable range of sources – from tax lists to personal papers, credit ratings to congressional testimony – *The Monied Metropolis* provides a richly textured historical portrait of society redefining itself. Its reach extends well beyond New York, into the most important issues of social and political change in nineteenth-century America.

Sven Beckert is Dunwalke Associate Professor of History at Harvard University.

Map of New York City in 1859. Arabic numerals indicate the ward numbers. Map courtesy of Harvard Map Collection.

The Monied Metropolis

New York City and the Consolidation of the American Bourgeoisie, 1850–1896

SVEN BECKERT

Harvard University

CAMBRIDGE
UNIVERSITY PRESS

PUBLISHED BY THE PRESS SYNDICATE OF THE UNIVERSITY OF CAMBRIDGE
The Pitt Building, Trumpington Street, Cambridge, United Kingdom

CAMBRIDGE UNIVERSITY PRESS
The Edinburgh Building, Cambridge CB2 2RU, UK
40 West 20th Street, New York, NY 10011-4211, USA
10 Stamford Road, Oakleigh, VIC 3166, Australia
Ruiz de Alarcón 13, 28014, Madrid, Spain
Dock House, The Waterfront, Cape Town 8001, South Africa

http://www.cambridge.org

First published 2001

Printed in the United States of America

Typeface Sabon 10/13.25 pt.   *System* QuarkXPress®   [GH]

A catalog record for this book is available from the British Library.

Library of Congress Cataloging in Publication Data
Beckert, Sven, 1965–
    The monied metropolis : New York City and the consolidation of
the American bourgeoisie, 1850–1896 / Sven Beckert.
        p. cm.
    Includes bibliographical references.
    ISBN 0-521-79039-5
        1. New York (N.Y.) – Economic conditions.   2. New York (N.Y.)
    – Social conditions.   3. Middle class – New York (State) – New
    York – History – 19th century.   4. Elite (Social sciences) – New
    York (State) – New York – History – 19th century   I. Title.

    HC108.N7 B343 2001
    305.5'5'09747109034 – dc21   00-058605

    ISBN   0 521 79039 5   hardback

For my parents,

Uta and Ulfert Beckert

Contents

Maps, Graphs, and Illustrations

Illustrations

Following page 97

The core of the bourgeois world: The family, 1897.
Forging new identities: Daughters of the American Revolution,
1898.

Following page 195

Social Life

Escaping the city: Partying in the country, 1863.
Lavish meals: The Harrison Grey Fiske dinner, 1900.
Aping the artistocracy: The Bradley Martin ball, 1897.
Equestrian pastimes: Riding in Central Park, 1860.
Going to the theater: The Park Street Theatre in 1822.
Churches as social clubs: Grace Church, 1845.

Encountering the City

The monied meet the people: Union Square.
The heart of immigrant life: The Lower East Side, ca. 1890.
The other half: Life in a tenement, 1898.

Politics

The elite 7th Regiment leaves for the war, 1861.
Marching for the gold standard: Sound money parade, 1896.
The old armory of the 71st Regiment, 1850s.
"Defensible from All Points," the Armory of the 71st Regiment, 1880s.

Conquering a World

Investing abroad: Guano production in Peru.
Capturing a continent: Park Avenue at 105th Street, 1860.
Winning foreign markets: Singer Sewing Machines conquer the world.

Acknowledgments

Writing this book was a journey of discovery. It took me to places I had not been, introduced me to people I would not have met, and allowed me to read books that would have otherwise escaped my attention. It has brought me also to a deeper appreciation and understanding of the city that I love above all others – New York. Though history is distinctly not its business, its very position as the quintessential modern city invites inquiries into its past and rewards its historians generously; not least, New York has taught me to put capital and capitalists closer to the center of modern history. In this discovery of New York, I have been aided by the writings of a marvelous group of historians who have devoted their scholarly lives to this wonderful city. Though our visions may not always coincide, I would not have been able to write this book without their scholarship.

As anybody who has ever written a book knows, rather than being any one solitary endeavor, writing involves numerous people and institutions. It is with great pleasure that I am able to thank them publicly for their support, their ideas, and the countless hours they gave to debating the issues that this work raises.

When this book was still on its way to becoming a dissertation, I was fortunate to have a group of challenging advisers. Eric Foner accompanied the conception and initial writing with sharp analytical comments and an extraordinary grasp of the world of the nineteenth-century United States. Elizabeth Blackmar shared her broad knowledge of New York City and spent more hours than she probably cares to remember discussing issues ranging from the idiosyncrasies of the New York Chamber of Commerce to the relationship between legitimacy and power. Charles Tilly reminded me persistently, and I hope to good effect, of the importance of confronting big questions; his broad sociological vision and love for history make him an extraordinary teacher. I thank them all for their support.

Along the way of conceptualizing, researching, and writing this study, other scholars also generously contributed their insights from a diversity of perspectives. At first I had the good fortune to receive counsel and help from Richard Bensel, Barbara Fields, Joshua Freeman, Atina Grossmann,

Michael Hanagan, Eric Hobsbawm, Kenneth Jackson, Jürgen Kocka, and James Shenton. At later stages, they and others have read parts or all of the manuscript and shared their knowledge with me, especially Pam Brown, Kathleen Dalton, Page Delano, Jörg Deventer, Tom Ertman, Leon Fink, Charles Forcey, Tami Friedman, Walter Friedman, Lawrence Glickman, Andrew Hahn, Robert Johnston, Ira Katznelson, Marion Kaplan, Allen Kurzweil, Deborah Levenson-Estrada, Bruce Levine, Rebecca McLennan, Behrooz Moazami, Dieter Plehwe, Julia Rodriguez, Julie Rosenbaum, Manisha Sinha, Jonathan Soffer, Anders Stephanson, Cyrus Vesser, and two readers for Cambridge University Press. And at the very end of writing this book, I was fortunate to benefit from the wisdom of my editor, Frank Smith. This book is considerably better for all their insights, and I thank them for their help.

In a variety of ways, all of them important, I also have benefited from discussions with audiences on three continents, who have led me to confront an astounding range of issues. I most particularly thank those who engaged my work at meetings of the American Historical Association, the Organization of American Historians, the Social Science History Conference, the European Social Science History Conference, the International Conference in Urban History, the Business History Conference, the North American Labor History Conference, and the International Congress of Historical Sciences. Moreover, audiences at the Charles Warren Center for Studies in American History in Cambridge, Massachusetts, the Aby Warburg Foundation in Hamburg, Germany, Bilkent University in Ankara, Turkey, and the Proseminar on State Formation and Collective Action at the New School for Social Research in New York engaged in lively and instructive debates, on subjects ranging from the relationship between capitalism and democracy to the role of the opera in the constitution of a bourgeois cultural sphere. What I found most remarkable in these discussions is that New York's history raises issues that are relevant to people who live far from the city and will probably never see it.

This is also an opportunity to thank publicly the many people who have encouraged my interest in history and helped me to realize it, not least by providing me with the resources to embark on my studies. Among them are Klaus von Dohnanyi, Dieter Galinski, Arno Herzig, Günter Moltmann, and Fritz Stern. I thank them for their faith in me. The Studienstiftung, Columbia University, the MacArthur Foundation, the Center for Labor–Management Policy Studies in New York, and Harvard University's Clark Fund and C. Boyden Gray Career Development Fund provided essential financial support. An extraordinary year at the Harvard Business School in the company of a most energetic group of historians, most particularly Alfred D. Chandler Jr., Nancy Koehn, Thomas McCraw, David Moss, and Richard Tedlow, allowed me to think through many of the issues raised in this book. At a later stage, Harvard University's Charles Warren Center for Studies in American History and the Center for Scholars and Writers at the New York Public Library provided me with valuable time to finish my writing. And all along, my colleagues at Harvard University's Department of History have provided an intellectually stimulating environment: I most particularly thank David Blackbourn, Lizabeth Cohen, Bill Gienapp, Akira Iriye, James Kloppenberg, and Charles S. Maier for discussing parts of the manuscript with me. Special thanks also to William Kirby, for making the department a hospitable place to work.

Last but not least, I am happy to acknowledge the support of the librarians and archivists at Columbia University, the Library of Congress, the New-York Historical Society, the New York Public Library, the Huntington Library, Widener Library, and Baker Library who have given me access to the materials on which this study is based. I am particularly grateful to the archivists at the Division of Old Records of the New York County Clerk, who went out of their way to give me access to census records. These librarians and archivists also kindly allowed me to quote from materials in their holdings, as did Henry Z. Steinway, who has generously granted me permission to quote from William Steinway's diary. Along the way, moreover, I was fortunate to have the support of a particularly able group of research assistants, among them Ned Arnsby, Nancy Elam, John-Paul Giugliano, JuNelle Harris, Eileen O'Pray, Rachel Hindin, Jared Shirck, and Lois Smith. Thanks to all of them.

Many people helped in the process of bringing this book into being, but nobody played a more important role than Lisa McGirr. She not only has been the greatest influence in shaping this work, but she has also made its writing vastly more enjoyable. This study was born alongside our treasured relationship. I thank her with all my heart, for everything. At the end of my journey, she is the greatest discovery of all.

Cambridge and New York
November 2000

Abbreviations

American Historical Review	AHR
American Railroad Journal	ARJ
Commercial and Financial Chronicle	CFC
Harper's Weekly	HW
Hunt's Merchants' Magazine and Commercial Review	Hunt's
Iron Age	IA
Journal of American History	JAH
Journal of Commerce	JoC
Library of Congress	LOC
The Merchants' Magazine and Commercial Review	MMCR
The Nation	Nation
New-York Association for Improving the Conditions of the Poor	AICP
New York Commercial Advertiser	NYCA
New-York Daily Tribune	NYDT
New York Herald	NYH
New York Public Library	NYPL
New-York Historical Society	NYHS
New-York Historical Society Quarterly	NYHSQ
New York Times	NYT
Radical History Review	RHR
Railway World	RW
Scientific American	SciAm
United States Economist and Dry Goods Reporter	USEconomist

The Monied Metropolis

Introduction

On February 10, 1897, at the tail end of the most severe economic depression the United States had experienced in the nineteenth century, 700 merchants, industrialists, bankers, and professionals assembled at New York's Waldorf-Astoria Hotel for a costume ball. Invited by lawyer Bradley Martin and his wife Cornelia, the guests arrived in fancy historic costumes. Fifty celebrants impersonated Marie Antoinette, while others, according to the *New York Times,* came dressed as "Kings and Queens, nobles, knights, and courtiers whose names and personalities take up pages of history."[1] Real estate mogul John Jacob Astor, wearing a Henry of Navarre costume, brandished a sword decorated with jewels; Ruth Hoe, daughter of printing press manufacturer Robert Hoe, "appeared in a dainty Louis XIV"; banker J. P. Morgan donned a Molière costume; and Caroline Astor had gems worth $250,000 sewn into her dress.[2] Cornelia Martin, not to be outdone, wore a necklace once owned by none other than Marie Antoinette herself.[3] To receive her guests, Cornelia Martin sat on a raised platform resembling a throne, her husband, Bradley Martin, standing next to her, wearing a "Court dress of Louis XV., white and pink brocaded satin, knee breeches, white silk hose, diamond buckles on low, red-heeled shoes; powdered wig."[4] Furthering such aristocratic pretensions, the rooms themselves were decorated to resemble the great hall of Versailles, and the guests dined on such delicacies as "Terrapene decossée à la Baltimore" and "Sorbet fin de Siècle."[5] It was, as the *New York Times* continued to comment only one day after the ball, "the climax in this form of entertainment thus far reached in the metropolis."[6]

Indeed, the ball was so lavish and ostentatious that it galvanized all of New York, making it the "universal and engrossing subject of interest and discussion."[7] Cornelia Martin had justified the extravaganza as helping the country overcome the depression, arguing that it would "give an impetus to trade."[8] Many New Yorkers, if we are to believe the *New York Times,* objected to such rationalizations in the midst of economic crisis, and threats of bombs kept not only New York's police but also a hired army of Pinkerton detectives on alert, watching "for thieves or for men of socialistic tendencies."[9] As a further precaution, the first-floor windows of the Waldorf Hotel were nailed shut.

This "most elaborate private entertainment that has ever taken place in the history of the metropolis" pointed to a dramatic departure from the past.[10] The event and the frame of mind that inspired it were part of a series of transformations that had remade the city's economic elite between 1850 and 1890, economically, socially, ideologically, and politically. Forty years earlier, New York's wealthy citizenry, steeped in the country's republican heritage and the moral imperatives of frugality and thrift, would have looked with disdain upon the ostentatious displays of wealth and conspicuous consumption that flourished at century's end.[11] Championing northern society as the land of liberty and equal opportunity in opposition to Europe and the American South, they could not have imagined a world of such deep class hostilities evident in bomb threats, boarded windows, and Pinkertons. And in contrast to the armed-camp setting in which bourgeois New Yorkers of the 1890s displayed their social position to the world, New York's "respectable classes" forty years earlier had proudly paraded up and down Broadway each afternoon exhibiting their status to one another and to the city, a ritual in which they shared public space with other social groups. Indeed, the Martins' ball was far removed from a time when Alexis de Tocqueville observed that "in the United States the more opulent citizens take great care not to stand aloof from the people; on the contrary, they constantly keep on easy terms with the lower classes: they listen to them, they speak to them every day."[12] The ball symbolized other changes as well: Forty years earlier, manufacturers and merchants would hardly ever have assembled at the same social occasions. And while forty years earlier "society" events usually brought only upper-class New Yorkers together, now the Martins' ball was national in scope, with "people [coming] from distant cities to attend."[13] The ostentatious display of riches, the depth of class conflict, the national reach of social networks, and the unification of New York's upper class across economic sectors evident at the ball symbolized a significant departure from antebellum times.[14]

This book tells the story of the consolidation of a self-conscious upper class in New York City in the second half of the nineteenth century, and with it the genesis of the world represented by the Martins' 1897 ball. It is the history of a small and diverse group of Americans who accumulated unprecedented economic, social, and political power, and who decisively put their mark on the age. The book explores how capital-owning New Yorkers overcame their distinct antebellum identities, rooted in the ownership of different kinds of capital, to forge in the wake of the Civil War dense social networks, to create powerful social institutions, and to articulate an increasingly coherent view of the world and their place within it. Actively engaging with a rapidly changing economic, social, and political environment, these merchants, industrialists, bankers, real estate speculators, rentiers, and professionals metamorphosed into a social class.

This book, then, is about the making of a social class: New York City's bourgeoisie. It is also, however, about the tremendous power upper-class New Yorkers amassed during the second half of the nineteenth century and how they employed this power. This is the second story the book will tell. On a journey that will take us from the factory floor to the opera house, from the family parlor to Congress, I will show how bourgeois New Yorkers dominated the drama of production, culture, ideas, and politics. I will, for example, examine how their capital helped to revolutionize the way most Americans worked and lived, effectively forging their firms into the most powerful institutions of nineteenth-century America.[15] I will also explore their central part in the spectacle of the Civil War and Reconstruction. And I will inquire into their active role in making the trajectory of American labor "exceptional."[16]

In this book, in short, I investigate how bourgeois New Yorkers in the course of the nineteenth century became "structurally dominant."[17] It is striking, indeed, that nowhere else in the world did an economic elite emerge as powerful as that of New York City, effectively making the United States the most bourgeois of all nineteenth-century societies.[18] Upper-class power was such that more than a hundred years later, it is not presidents but prominent bourgeois New Yorkers, such as John D. Rockefeller and J. P. Morgan, who still symbolize the age to most Americans. Consequently, understanding the history of this economic elite in the nation's greatest metropolis is critical to understanding the history of the United States in the last half of the nineteenth century.[19] Unlocking the history of upper-class Americans, the central social actors of the quintessential bourgeois century, provides one important key to understanding the dynamics of economic, social, and political change between 1850 and 1900 and with it the emergence of modern America.[20]

It was in New York that these developments unfolded most dramatically and from there had the greatest impact on the rest of the nation. Capital and capitalists gather in cities, and nowhere did economic, social, and political power coalesce more than in New York City.[21] New York's bourgeoisie dominated the nation's trade, production, and finance and served as the gatekeeper of America's most important outpost in the Atlantic economy.[22] The city's merchants, bankers, and industrialists staged the most elaborate social events anywhere, setting the bourgeois standard for the nation. And their economic, social, and political power reverberated from California to South Carolina, from the factory to the farm, from City Hall to the White House.[23] For these reasons, no other site of inquiry promises such rich insights into when, how, and why an upper class formed as a cohesive group with a shared identity, as well as the place of this emerging economic elite in the political, social, and economic context of the nation.[24]

Throughout the Western world, the nineteenth century saw the rise of the bourgeoisie and bourgeois society. As a result of the unfolding of capitalist economies and the emancipation of society from the state, owners of capital decisively shaped economic change and the newly emerging societies. As the first elite not to derive its status from the accidents of birth and heritage, the rising bourgeoisie worked hard, lived in modest comfort, and celebrated individual accomplishment. Accumulating ever more capital and power, this new social class gained the upper hand over an older, feudal, social elite and eventually shaped the economy, ideology, and politics of all Western nations.[25]

In the United States, the history of this social class was exceptional.[26] In the absence of an aristocracy or a feudal state, both bourgeois society and the bourgeoisie burst more powerfully onto the scene than anywhere else. By the end of the American Revolution, a socially distinct group of merchants had gained ever more prominence in the cities of the eastern seaboard. During the second quarter of the nineteenth century, these traders were joined by a group of artisans who had recently turned into manufacturers, and who were accumulating capital in production, not commerce. Unlike in Europe, where conflicts with an entrenched aristocracy at times drove bourgeois citizens to articulate shared identities as early as midcentury, the economic elite of the United States did not forge such bonds. While both merchants and industrialists developed social networks, cultural orientations, and institutions, as well as ideas and politics that diverged from those of farmers on the one side and workers on the other, even by as late as the 1850s they remained divided, articulating sharply different identities, creating competing social networks, and envisioning very different kinds of political economies.[27]

By the 1870s and 1880s, however, bourgeois New Yorkers articulated a consciousness of separate class identity. In a process that accelerated during the depression of the 1870s, upper-class social life and politics increasingly manifested a new and greater distance from other groups – especially from workers, whom the economic elite perceived as a double threat to their economic and political power. As a result of these fears, many elite New Yorkers abandoned their belief in a socially cohesive society without deep class divisions and their reluctant wartime support for a state-sponsored social revolution in the South. Instead, they advocated the unquestioned primacy of unregulated markets and, most dramatically, restriction of suffrage rights in municipal elections.

Proletarianization and the overthrow of slavery drove the process of bourgeois class formation. The overthrow of slavery and the destruction of the political power of slaveholders sped the economic development of the North, benefiting industrialists and bankers while increasing the political power of the northern bourgeoisie over the federal government. It also provided the basis upon which different capitalists could find common ground. Before the war, the city's industrialists, in particular, had embraced the emancipatory promises of republicanism, seeing in the eradication of slavery, or at least its limitation, the possibility for preventing the emergence of a permanent proletariat.[28] Merchants, in contrast, aimed at building a paternalist relationship to the city's workers, supported by the profits derived from a slave-based plantation economy. When the war destroyed slavery, it also destroyed the grounds for these arrangements.

The destruction of slavery, in effect, moved the process of proletarianization to center stage. During the war and its aftermath, those segments of New York's economic elite who based their economic activities on wage labor – namely, industrialists and financiers – became the dominant segment within the bourgeoisie itself. A coincidental challenge from the increasingly militant workers in the North compelled merchants, financiers, and industrialists to unify in defense of property rights, and to become more ambivalent about democracy, in fact, challenging some of their older assumptions about the nature of society. Many of them also increased the amount of capital they controlled, thus sharpening social inequality. As a result, the emancipatory vision of many antebellum bourgeois New Yorkers, with its universalist preoccupations, gave way to an articulation of class identities. Their political ideas focused ever more nar-

rowly on the guarding of their own elevated social position. A new industrial liberalism replaced the producerist liberalism of antebellum manufacturers and the communitarian liberalism of merchants. New York's bourgeoisie was made and had made itself.

But before we embark on the epic story of New York City's bourgeoisie a
word about terminology. The term "bourgeoisie" was not frequently
employed by capital-rich New Yorkers during the nineteenth century, who
preferred to refer to themselves at first by the specific line of business they
engaged in and, later, as "taxpayers," or "businessmen." Similarly, historians have employed various other terms to describe the group under review
here, such as "elites," "aristocracy," "plutocracy," "ruling class," and
"middle class."[29] I believe, however, that the term bourgeoisie grasps more
precisely the historical formation with which I am concerned. "Elite," for
example, while a useful term, does not sufficiently distinguish the bourgeoisie as a fundamentally different kind of elite from other elites who
have come before or after.[30] Aristocracy, while used derogatorily by nineteenth-century workers and lower-middle-class citizens resentful of the
wealth and power of the bourgeoisie, is problematic because it is the distinguishing feature of United States history that no true aristocracy
emerged.[31] Plutocracy, in turn, insufficiently grasps the totality of the
bourgeoisie, calling to mind only fat, cigar-smoking robber barons who
reigned tyrannically over their enterprises and the government.[32] Ruling
class assumes the political power of the bourgeoisie instead of investigat-
ing it. The term middle class (or middle classes), in contrast, by referring
to a distinct elite based on the ownership of capital rather than heritage
and birth, as the "estate" situated between inherited aristocracy on the
one side and farmers as well as workers on the other side, describes the
group this book is concerned with quite well. Its usage, however, has
become so overwhelmed with present-day concerns that it lacks sufficient
analytical clarity. Today, "middle class" can stand either for all Americans, past and present, who are neither extremely wealthy nor homeless,
or for a distinct social group that corresponds somewhat with the European notion of the "petite bourgeoisie" – artisans, shop owners, and lesser
professionals.[33] For these reasons, the term that best fits the group of
people I am looking at is bourgeoisie, which I use interchangeably with
"upper class" and "economic elite." It refers to a particular kind of elite
whose power, in its most fundamental sense, derived from the ownership
of capital rather than birthright, status, or kinship. Bourgeoisie, moreover,
focuses our attention squarely on the relationships between members of

the city's economic elite, allowing us to put into the center of our investigation the question of what they did and did not share.[34]

In order to come to a workable definition of the term, we have to acknowledge that its meaning will always be somewhat ambivalent, because it is the essence of modern societies that boundaries between social groups are imprecise and to a certain degree porous. Still, for the purposes of this book, the bourgeoisie most prominently and unambiguously includes the city's substantial merchants, industrialists, and bankers, along with rentiers (people who lived off investments they did not manage themselves), real estate speculators, owners of service enterprises, and many professionals. Taken together, this was the entrepreneurial or economic bourgeoisie par excellence.[35] They shared a specific position in New York's social structure in that they owned and invested capital, employed wage workers (or, at the very least, servants), did not work for wages themselves, and did not work manually.[36]

Since, as I have argued, social boundaries in the nineteenth-century United States were open, we need to acknowledge that many nineteenth-century New Yorkers were on the margins of the city's bourgeoisie. For one, there were the small shopkeepers and artisans. They, just like the more substantial industrialists and merchants, owned capital and frequently employed others, but in contrast to their wealthier neighbors, participated actively in the production process or stood behind their retail store's counter. Artisans, in particular, defined themselves less by the control of capital than by their skills. Their independence, moreover, was more tenuous as they were easily wiped out by the smallest of economic misfortunes, their capital so limited that it needed monthly replenishment in order to guarantee its owners even the most marginal of bourgeois lifestyles. Yet because this group provided the most important reservoir of people rising into the bourgeoisie and because they shared some of the social and political sensibilities of their betters, artisans and shopkeepers, especially in the earlier years of the century, were not sharply divorced from the city's economic elite.[37]

The second group with a complicated relationship to the city's bourgeoisie were the professionals, experts, and intellectuals. Many of them were clearly part of the bourgeoisie in their role as rentiers or landowners. As the century went on, however, some also found access to bourgeois networks and bourgeois institutions solely based on the educational capital they controlled.[38] This book, however, while interested in the relationship between economic elites and professionals, as well as the lower middle classes, decisively focuses on the *economic* or *entrepreneurial*

bourgeoisie. It was unambiguously at the center of New York's bourgeoisie, distinguishing the city's bourgeoisie sharply from that of many
European cities, where high-ranking civil servants, military officers,
church officials, and state-employed professors often constituted an
important part of this class.

The diverse entrepreneurial bourgeoisie that is at the center of this work
was deeply divided and notoriously unstable. It was unstable for the simple reason that it was not based on accidents of birth. It was also unstable
because bourgeois New Yorkers were committed to social mobility. Therefore, the boundaries of this social class, while real, were in constant flux.[39]
Moreover, the bourgeoisie was marked by deep internal divisions. Certainly, one of bourgeois New Yorkers' defining characteristics, the ownership of capital, drove them apart as market competition and divergent
demands on the state threw them into constant struggles. They, moreover,
owned different kinds of capital, its cultural and political imperatives
sharply diverging. And they were diverse in other ways: They had different religious beliefs, they had deeply rooted and conflicting loyalties to
different political parties, they were born in many places all over the
world (thus lacking a shared history), and the amount of their wealth dif-
fered sharply, as did its relative "age." This book poses the questions
when, how, and why the coherence between these different groups became
dominant over their differences.

To speak of the bourgeoisie in a meaningful way, then, the term must be
more than a merely descriptive term defining an economically heteroge-
neous group. One needs to look beyond social structure to discover if, at
certain points, something more than the shared ownership of capital held
this group of New Yorkers together.[40] Indeed, it is only in this specific
sense that this social class, like any other, has a history. Bourgeois defines
not only a certain space in the social structure but potentially also a
shared culture and identity.[41] And because social identities often emerge in
conflict with other social groups, it was in the process of distinguishing
themselves from others, especially from workers, but by the late century
also from the lower middle class or the petty-bourgeoisie, that bourgeois
New Yorkers came to an understanding of themselves as a class and at
times were able to act collectively upon this identity.[42]

In the emergence of this identity, culture in the broadest sense played a
central role.[43] Especially by the late nineteenth century, a common cultural
vocabulary increasingly defined bourgeois New Yorkers, transcending
divisions rooted in economic competition, the ownership of different

kinds of capital, and ethnic and religious differences.[44] This class culture emphasized rationality, discipline, and individual effort. It expressed itself in shared habits and manners (such as rituals of eating at the dining room table), preferences in interior design, definitions of "high culture," and gender roles (women occupying a "separate sphere" from men).[45] The bourgeois family, in particular, was central to the definition and production of this bourgeois cultural world. Eventually, all these identities and inclinations were institutionalized in clubs, debutante balls, voluntary associations and museums, and, in exceptional circumstances, even in political mobilizations.[46] These institutions, in effect, bound different segments of the city's (and the nation's) bourgeoisie together. By emphasizing culture as well as conflict, this book allows us to see the creation of a bourgeoisie as the result of an active process of class formation, not as the automatic or necessary outcome of a shared position in the social structure.[47] It also allows us to talk about class without falling into the trap of teleology.[48]

Considering the central role of the nineteenth-century bourgeoisie in the most bourgeois of all countries, the United States, recent historical scholarship has produced few in-depth discussions on the nation's merchants, industrialists, and bankers. Historians have shied away from a comprehensive analysis of the formation of the United States bourgeoisie, except in portraits of hinterland towns where its members exercised only local power, or in studies on isolated aspects of bourgeois life, especially social networks.[49]

On the one hand, this lack of interest is hardly surprising, as bourgeois Americans, especially in the twentieth century, denied the existence of classes – most particularly their own.[50] The economic elite's position in society, moreover, was so hegemonic that their interests, ideas, and passions seemed to be those of most Americans and, thus, hardly the stuff of historical inquiry.

On the other hand, however, the dearth of interest in the American bourgeoisie is surprising, considering that class and power have played a central role in the writing of social and political history over the past three decades.[51] Social historians have shown persuasively how during the first half of the nineteenth century, a working class began to emerge in the United States. While emphasizing the uneven trajectory of its development, and the wide variation between regions, cities, ethnic groups, and industries, they have demonstrated that workers embraced a culture, ideas, and at times organizations and politics distinctly stamped by their class position. These historians, moreover, suggested sophisticated methods for the study of social groups. They emphasized the openness of the process of class formation, regional variation, and, especially, the relational nature of class.[52] In the process of writing the history of labor, they have also persuasively established that American society, especially during the second half of the nineteenth century, was socially stratified. And, while disagreeing about their meaning, they have shown that class institutions, class ideologies, and class politics emerged.[53]

Yet despite the focus on class stratification and working-class formation, and despite one perceptive observer's comment that "[c]lass consciousness is not equally characteristic of all levels of American society: it is most apparent in the upper class," few studies have undertaken to trace the history of the formation of the nation's economic elite as a class.[54] One reason for this omission is certainly that many social historians desired to uncover the once-hidden history of "common people" and to de-emphasize those who for so long had dominated historical narratives. Moreover, these scholars found it easier to write about people with whom they could identify and whose struggles they viewed sympathetically. Yet in their desire to rescue the historical agency of the downtrodden, social historians often ignored the balance of social power and relocated the struggles over social power into the sphere of culture.[55] As a consequence, they neglected the most powerful social group in the nineteenth-century United States – the bourgeoisie.[56] Many business historians, who resisted the new methods of social history and therefore failed to make business people relevant to modern historiographical concerns, exacerbated this lack of attention.[57] While they made the important point that business as an institution and business people as historical actors are significant to understanding United States history, they often looked at them in isolation from society and the state.[58]

Both consensus and progressive school historians, writing from the 1930s through the 1950s, on the other hand, had been more cognizant of the nation's upper class. Louis Hartz, for example, thought of Americans as "a kind of national embodiment of the concept of the bourgeoisie," but saw the "bourgeois class passion [as] scarcely present." He made the very hegemony of the bourgeoisie responsible for its absence as a social analytical category.[59] Richard Hofstadter, too, conceptualized the United States as a largely middle-class society and thus, by default, gave the country's bourgeoisie a central place in its national story.[60] While both Hartz and Hofstadter identified one of the central facts of American history – the absence of feudal structures in opposition to a bourgeois way of life – their stress on consensus undermined their ability to see the bourgeoisie not as a representation of all (or most) Americans, but as a specific and limited social group that had its own history. Progressive historians, such as Charles and Mary Beard, were more attuned to the historically and sociologically specific nature of the bourgeoisie and, indeed, gave conflicts between different groups of capitalists a central place in their account of the eighteenth and nineteenth century. They failed, however, to go beyond economistic reductions of complex social, ideological, and political processes.[61] Nevertheless, the scope of the questions addressed by both progressive and consensus school historians have inspired my work, though its methods and conclusions are very different.

Because social and business historians by and large have not taken up the broad questions about the bourgeoisie posed by progressive and consensus historians, the upper class remains the most neglected social group in United States historiography.[62] Across the Atlantic, in contrast, European historians have pursued the social history of the bourgeoisie with enormous élan. Particularly in France, Great Britain, and Germany, the last two decades have seen an outpouring of research on the European bourgeoisie, often in comparative perspective. This body of work has outlined, at times brilliantly, not only the internal history of the Western bourgeoisie as a social class but also the place of the bourgeoisie in the emergence and development of bourgeois society.[63] These historians have emphasized the importance of culture to the emergence of bourgeois identities and also found the European bourgeoisies, in general, more powerful than previously believed. The European literature, moreover, provides a valuable model for how the new methods of social history can be usefully employed in studying the bourgeoisie and how the history of the bourgeoisie can help explain the trajectories of different national histories.[64] Most important for the purposes of this book, these works help us understand what is unique about New York City's economic elite and what is not.

In the United States, the absence of modern research on such central questions has hampered not only our understanding of the formation of the northern economic elite, but also our understanding of nineteenth-century American history.[65] Indeed, Barrington Moore noted more than three decades ago that "an adequate study of the political attitudes of Northern industrialists remains to be written," and not much has changed since.[66] The goal of this book is to restore New York's merchants, manufacturers, bankers, real estate speculators, rentiers, and professionals to the central place in the nation's history that they deserve. They were certainly not the only ones who mattered, but for better or for worse, the history of the nineteenth-century United States remains incomplete without them.

≈ ≈ ≈

To grasp fully the dynamics of the emergence of an economic elite in New York City, this book employs a class-formation approach, an approach that has been used fruitfully in the study of workers. Critical to understanding the emergence of the bourgeoisie is the notion that class occurs on distinct but related levels. These levels, broadly speaking, are the structure of the economy and the place of bourgeois New Yorkers within it, the social organization and culture of the economic elite, their dispositions, and, lastly, their collective actions.[67] With this broad approach, courting practices at balls are as significant to understanding the formation of a bourgeoisie as changes in incorporation law; the mustering of arms of the elite Seventh New York Regiment in April of 1861 is as important as changes in the marketing of manufactured goods.

The formation of a bourgeoisie as a class, I argue, was neither historically necessary nor irreversible.[68] Rather, class identities were historically contingent: Merchants, bankers, and industrialists, for example, only expressed them once identities based on the ownership of a particular kind of capital had moved to the sidelines. They did so for specific reasons, most importantly their encounter with the social polarization of Gilded Age America. Furthermore, class identities expressed on one level, for example in the emergence of a shared class culture, did not necessarily have to articulate themselves in other spheres, such as politics, which is why the degree of class identity and class solidarity could change over time. And the relationship between bourgeoisie and bourgeois society, despite Marx's assertion to the contrary, was fraught with tensions: Bourgeois New Yorkers were ambivalent about extending the benefits of bourgeois society to African Americans in the South during the era of the "last bourgeois revolution" (the Civil War) and later, during the 1870s, they articulated a powerful critique of liberal democracy in the North.[69] By emphasizing contingency and change, structure as well as agency, this book will illuminate the dynamics of upper-class formation as a specific historical process unfolding in the second half of the nineteenth century.[70]

Studying New York's economic elite, in turn, tells us about class formation more generally. The book shows empirically that the different levels of social reality in which class can be expressed are not linked in a direct and straightforward manner, but instead can, to a certain degree, be autonomous.[71] Also, the book tells us about the relational nature of class formation, in this case the importance of working-class formation to bourgeois class formation. While bourgeois New Yorkers developed a certain sense of classness independent of outside challengers, especially in the emergence of shared manners, habits, and social institutions, it was only the confrontation with other mobilized social groups (such as the slaveholders of the South and workers in the North) that encouraged them to act collectively in the realm of politics. Furthermore, this book allows us to see clearly the fundamental difference between bourgeois and working-class formation, namely, the distinct relationship between class formation and power. Workers, usually, can only exert power when they overcome divisions and act collectively, either in trade unions or in politics, whereas bourgeois New Yorkers exerted extraordinary power even without engaging in collective action, thanks to their control of capital.[72]

Last but not least, it is important to remember that the emergence of a more cohesive bourgeoisie, the rise of a social group with shared identities, ideas, and at times politics, did not eliminate economic conflicts, social distinctions, and political quarrels. While I disagree with accounts that put ethnic and cultural divisions at the center of their analysis of New York's economic elite, these demarcations still mattered.[73] What changed, instead, was the balance between division and cohesion. And this change, in turn, had a tremendous impact on the power of New York's bourgeoisie and, thus, on the history of the United States in the late nineteenth century.

This book is organized in three parts. While analysis of the process of bourgeois class formation structures all of them, they generally follow a chronological order, divided by significant political or economic breaks, such as the onset of the Civil War in 1861 and the beginning of the depression of 1873. The first part paints a broad picture of the economic, social, ideological, and political world of New York's merchants, industrialists, and bankers in the decade before the Civil War – emphasizing the diversity of different segments of capital and how this diversity resulted in sharp political conflicts. The second part begins with an analysis of the dramatic changes that the Civil War brought to the city's upper class and how they influenced the war effort. It portrays the "golden age" of New York's entrepreneurial elite, years when many of them embraced, if with some hesitation, a coalition with working-class New Yorkers in local politics and the limited engagement of the federal government in the defeated southern states. The most important break in the history of New York's bourgeoisie, I argue, came with the depression of 1873, and the years between 1873 and 1896 are the subject of the third part of the book. It was during these decades that conflicts with the city's working class, as well as a restructuring of economic power relations among bourgeois New Yorkers, led to an increasing articulation of separate identities, socially, ideologically, and at times politically. Social networks coalesced, class institutions mushroomed, and bourgeois New Yorkers captured cultural institutions. Also during these years, bourgeois disenchantment with democracy emerged, with dramatic effects on local as well as national politics. The last chapter explores how the greater coherence of New York's upper class translated into unprecedented political power, and with it, why J. P. Morgan, Caroline Astor, and others attended the 1897 Bradley Martin ball in the costumes of "Kings and Queens, nobles, knights, and courtiers."[74]

Our journey will begin during the 1850s, at the core of the city's economic elite, New York's merchant community.

PART I

Fortunes, Manners, Politics

It must be added that, though she had the expectation of a fortune – Doctor Sloper for a long time had been making twenty thousand dollars a year by his profession, and laying aside the half of it – the amount of money at her disposal was not greater than the allowance made to many poorer girls. In those days, in New York, there were still a few altar fires flickering in the temple of republican simplicity, and Doctor Sloper would have been glad to see his daughter present herself, with a classic grace, as a priestess of this mild faith. It made him fairly grimace, in private, to think that a child of his should be both ugly and overdressed. For himself, he was fond of the good things in life, and he made a considerable use of them; but he had a dread of vulgarity, and even a theory that it was increasing in the society that surrounded him. Moreover, the standard of luxury in the United States thirty years ago was carried by no means so high as at present.

Henry James, *Washington Square* (1881)

1

Accumulating Capital

In the fall of 1857, August and Caroline Belmont sailed into New York harbor, his four-year assignment as United States ambassador to The Hague complete. As their boat passed the Narrows between Brooklyn and Staten Island, the steeples of Trinity Church appeared on the horizon, followed by the merchant houses of South Street and the banks just north of the Battery. On the calm waters before them, dozens of ships crisscrossed the port, ferry boats shuttling between lower Manhattan and Brooklyn, canal sloops loaded with wheat arriving from Albany via the Erie Canal, ocean-going clippers unloading barrels stamped "Liverpool," and coastal brigs lying low with their heavy load of cotton bales. As it unfolded before the Belmonts, New York radiated material bounty. Indeed, August himself had thrived in the city in the short twenty years after first setting foot on the North American continent as a representative of the banking house of Rothschild.[1] Now, he was one of the richest and most powerful Americans. Within days of the Belmonts' return to their mansion on Fifth Avenue and 18th Street, they had exhibited their exquisite art collection, "containing paintings of most of the first living masters," and given lavish dinners that featured the delicacies of a chef brought back with them from Europe.[2] By giving back to this nascent world capital some Old World culture, the Belmonts were reasserting their prominent position.

By the year of the Belmonts' return, New York and the nation had risen on a great, fast-moving swell of economic growth.[3] In the course of this boom, the city, the nation, and the relationship between the two had changed radically. During the short span of seven years before 1857, American coal production had more than doubled, railroad mileage nearly tripled, and pig-iron shipments expanded fully thirteen times. At the helm of this expanding economy was New York. Already the most important port in the Americas, New York in these years saw exports – especially of cotton, wheat, and corn – increase by 139 percent and imports – especially of textiles and iron goods – rise by 97 percent.[4] By 1860, a full two-thirds of the United States' imports and one-third of its exports went via New York.[5] Its chief rivals, Boston, Philadelphia, and Baltimore, could not compete: Together they traded in goods only one-quarter the value of those which passed through the port of New York.[6] Trade, in turn, supported the city's burgeoning factories, and during the decade of the 1850s, capital invested in manufacturing grew by 60 percent, making it the New World's most important manufacturing location.[7]

Such rapid expansion reshaped the very face of the city: Returning citizens marveled at the growing number of docks and wharves, thickening forests of masts and steam pipes in the harbor, and sprawling warehouses and dry goods stores. A short walk from these powerful testimonies to the city's enormous trade they found evidence of New York's industry: Northward along the East River they encountered large iron factories, among them the Morgan, Allaire, and Novelty Works. Strolling through the streets of lower Manhattan they ran into workshops small and large, which churned out shirts, shoes, newspapers, and hundreds of other goods. At the tip of Manhattan, around Wall Street, new Renaissance-inspired palazzi ennobled the city's banks, insurance companies, and expanding financial and commodities markets – the fount of capital for the trade and manufacturing of the city and the nation. By midcentury the Western world knew few cities like it; its wealth dwarfed that of all but London and Paris.[8]

New York outpaced its rivals through good fortune and determination. It was blessed by geography: A large, protected port that remained free of ice throughout most of the year, its closeness to the open sea, and a river that provided it with easy access to a vast hinterland gave it a privileged start. New York's merchants, capital rich and risk taking, used these endowments to good advantage by dredging shallow passages in the harbor, and by forging canals and railroads that enlarged the city's hinterland ever more. But more important in the story of New York's rise than geography or even infrastructure were the commercial enterprises that its merchants built. Here, where the Hudson meets the Atlantic, they fashioned trading houses that connected the British industrial economy to the cotton plantations in the American South.[9] New Yorkers bought cotton in the South for transport to Liverpool, returning in their sailing vessels the bountiful goods of Britain's industry to equip and clothe western farmers, northern workers, and southern plantation owners. Once they drew this trade into their port, it was all but impossible for others to compete. Advantages in trade, in turn, could be translated into other enterprises. Drawing labor from the densely inhabited streets along the East River, manufacturers large and small produced ever more printing presses, carriages, books, and ready-made clothing, supplying not only New York's unrivaled urban market but also much of the rest of the nation. Along the fine boulevards of southern Manhattan just north of the Battery, bankers, insurance agents, and lawyers set up shop and lubricated the machinery of trade and production. Strategically placed at the center of a rapidly growing economy, New York's bankers, manufacturers, and merchants reaped proceeds from the cotton fields of Louisiana, the iron works of Pennsylvania, the sugar plantations of Cuba, and the railroads extended throughout the nation.

The merchants' activities, in turn, strengthened the city's position ever more, making it the center of the nation's trade, information, and transportation networks. Indeed, in contrast to all other urban areas in the United States, New York dominated not only its hinterland and the northeastern region but also the nation as a whole.[10] Thanks to the merchants' resolve to take advantage of the privileged position of New York, the city sat like a spider in the web of the American economy, drawing resources into the metropolis, transforming them, and sending them to places near and far. Moreover, as a central outpost of the trading networks of the Atlantic world that stretched from the coasts of Europe and Western Africa to North and South America, the city connected the southern plantation economy to the factories of Great Britain. Few cities in the world owed as much to capitalists and capital than New York at midcentury, and in 1857, such capitalists as August Belmont were poised to reap the harvest of all their activity.

These capitalists stood out in dramatic relief against a city that was mostly artisanal and proletarian.[11] In 1856, 9,000 individuals, about 1.4 percent of New York's inhabitants, or 5 percent of the city's economically active, owned assets exceeding $10,000 each – a sum that provided them well-furnished living quarters and the help of servants, and thus the essential attributes of respectability.[12] Though small in number, these capitalists, together with their families, controlled a significant share of the city's and nation's resources. At midcentury, they owned roughly 71 percent of the city's real and personal wealth.[13] This was a concentration of assets made all the more remarkable considering that 84 percent of the city's economically active citizens owned no personal or real wealth of consequence at all.[14]

These propertied New Yorkers represented the largest and most diverse segment of the nation's economic elite, surpassing in wealth, power, and diversity of their business undertakings the merchants of both Boston and Philadelphia. While Boston and Philadelphia had their long-established merchant elites, and Pittsburgh would eventually have a well-defined group of industrialists, New York City had all this and more. Already at midcentury, its economic elite was extraordinarily diverse. Most strikingly, in a city built by merchants, a full 20 percent of substantial taxpayers had accumulated their capital in an entirely different kind of undertaking, manufacturing. The city on the Hudson, so it seemed, was a springboard for capital and entrepreneurial vision of every kind. Indeed, by the 1850s, New York enjoyed an influx not just of trade but also of the merchants themselves, drawn, like August Belmont, by its seemingly unlimited opportunities. New York was different. New York was the future.

≈ ≈ ≈

Despite New York's almost unbridled growth and increasing diversity, its traditional mercantile elite still bestrode the core institutions of the city's economy. They were, for one, the oldest and most numerous segment of the city's economic elite. Ever since the arrival of the first settlers on Manhattan island in 1625, the city had prided itself on its trade. The merchant community thrived throughout the centuries, and by 1855, despite the rise of competing economic elites, they still constituted approximately 40 percent of all taxpayers assessed on personal and real wealth above $10,000.[15] They were not only the most numerous segment of the city's economic elite but also by far the wealthiest. This small group of about 3,600 merchant families owned roughly 28 percent of the city's total real and personal wealth.[16] Even more dramatic was their concentration among the very richest New Yorkers: Merchants, auctioneers, brokers, and agents constituted an estimated 70 percent of the 300 wealthiest New Yorkers in 1845.[17]

For these merchants, moreover, the 1850s were a golden age, a flowering of decades of intense investment and planning. By offering reliable shipping at competitive rates, by advancing credit to cash-hungry planters, by providing buyers with the greatest selection of goods available anywhere in the Americas, by supplying ready markets for huge quantities of agricultural commodities, by furnishing legal expertise, and by arranging insurance, these merchants had turned themselves into a vital link between producers and customers in a new nation building its transportation, communication, and banking facilities. The ships that regularly left New York for ports close and far, the canals and railroads that radiated from the city, and the market information that traveled through its newspapers and telegraphs further solidified their position.[18] The ever-expanding cotton kingdom, and the slave-labor system that produced it, remained the primary engine of profits for merchants as it had since the early nineteenth century. Indeed, it was, above all, New York's intense commitment to cotton that helped it decisively leave Philadelphia, Baltimore, and Boston behind.[19]

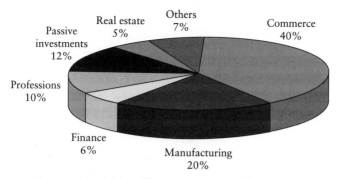

Economic activities of bourgeois New Yorkers, 1855.
Source: Sample of 324 New Yorkers assessed on real and personal property of more than
$10,000 in 1855.

Despite their long history in New York and their privileged position in
the urban, national, and international economy, the world of these merchants remained challenging, risky, and volatile, demanding great vigilance. They constantly needed to adapt to the rapid expansion and growing complexities of trade. In response, many of New York's merchants
specialized their lines of business and diversified their investments. And
they intensely cultivated social, cultural, and personal networks that were
the bone and sinew of their businesses. While the 1850s were a decade for
harvesting huge gains, they were also a decade of rapid and sometimes
unsettling change.

Merchants made the most dramatic and consequential changes to their
ways of doing business. By the 1850s, few New York merchants remained
the generalists of an earlier generation who had traded in a wide range of
goods and provided an integrated array of services. The increased volume
of trade and competition forced them to specialize – by either commodity
or function.[20] At midcentury, some houses exclusively traded certain commodities such as cotton, whereas others provided services such as shipping
or financing. This specialization was imprinted on the face of the city.
While most merchant activity was concentrated in the southernmost area
of Manhattan, different lines of business clustered on specific streets.
Importers and shipping merchants located next to the port on South
Street, commission merchants and wholesale grocers set up shop on Water
Street and Front Street, jobbers and auctioneers concentrated their activities on Pearl Street, and large retailers erected their shopping emporiums
on the lower reaches of Broadway.[21] Specialization not only segregated

merchant businesses from one another but also began to loosen the ideological and political ties that once had reliably held the merchant community together. It set a small but growing number of traders free from the political economy of Atlantic trade and, thus, free of the powerful dependence on slavery and low tariffs.

For a majority of the city's merchants, however, specialization meant ever tighter embrace with New York's traditional strength: the cotton trade. Cotton, the fuel of the industrial revolution, remained at the center of the city's trade relationships, and a growing number of merchants committed themselves to this line of business. Many New York traders made their fortunes buying cotton in the South, advancing credit to planters, and shipping the raw material to Liverpool and a few other European ports. The Leverich Brothers, for example, bought cotton and sugar in the South and exported them to Great Britain. Charles Morgan covered another aspect of the trade, running numerous ships between New York City and Charleston, New Orleans, and Texas ports.[22] These and other merchants earned remarkable profits because their capital was so desperately needed in the South and because they had a hand in each step of the trade, most notably a virtual stranglehold on the regularly scheduled ships shuttling between northern, southern, and European ports.[23] Even if cotton was shipped directly from New Orleans or Charleston to Europe and did not touch New York, the city's merchants still profited from commissions, interest on loans, shipping charges, insurance payments, and, ultimately, the import of manufactured goods to the South.

Often associated with the cotton trade but soon transcending it in importance was the dry goods and hardware commerce. Merchants specializing in this line of business acquired manufactured goods from Europe and the United States and sold them to retailers in the South, the Northeast, and the expanding West. Many cotton-bearing ships returned from Liverpool with the fruits of British industry, especially such materials as textiles and iron, for which Britain's advanced factories lacked serious competition in the North American market. In 1860 alone, fully 904 ships disgorged European goods to New York warehouses; that is, on any given day, an average of nearly three ships arrived from Europe loaded with Manchester cloth, Sheffield iron, or Lyon silk.[24] Once stevedores landed these goods, New York merchants disposed of them in a variety of ways. Auctioneers usually put dry goods under the hammer, to be sold to the city's numerous jobbers. Jobbers, in turn, delivered them wholesale to retailers all over the United States. Commission merchants, who, in contrast to the jobbers, never took ownership of the goods they traded, specialized in bulkier products, such as machines and iron rails.[25] They also at times marketed textiles to retailers or to New York wholesalers.

Wholesalers played a particularly important role in the distribution of imported and domestic manufactured products. Their presence in such great numbers was another factor that set New York apart from all other American cities. These jobbers received shopkeepers from the most remote parts of the United States in their stores on Pearl Street, especially during the retailers' annual summer sojourn to the city. They offered their visitors the opportunity to stock up their entire stores in Manhattan, stressing the vast array of goods available and the convenient transportation of them back home.[26]

For decades, a steady stream of southern customers had lavishly spent their cotton money with these New York City jobbers, further solidifying the merchants' links to the plantation economy of the South. By the 1850s, however, a trickle of retailers from the trans-Appalachian West had become a flood at their stores. Western commerce began in the 1850s to challenge the exalted role of trade with the South, a slow-moving shift whose political repercussions were only just being felt on the eve of the Civil War. This change was partly the result of the merchants' own exertions: Since 1825, the Erie Canal, built on their urging, had connected New York to western hinterlands, and by 1857, the canal was moving goods worth $218 million to and from the city. Merchants had also financed new railroad connections to complement the canal, and by 1853, the New York Central stretched all the way to Buffalo. These new links led to a rapid expansion of capitalist agriculture in the West. Farms, in turn, became new markets for manufactured goods, markets served by a swelling stream of western retailers pouring into the city. During the 1850s, moreover, the California gold rush created new business opportunities in the Pacific West. Some merchants saw bright opportunities for profit in this western trade: The firm of Schuyler, Hartley, and Graham, for example, bought sporting guns and small arms in Europe and sold them in the West.[27] Similarly, Isaac Sherman, who had migrated in 1854 from Buffalo to New York City, traded barrel staves in the West.

This transformation of the West also gave rise to a group of merchants who would specialize in the trade in wheat and corn. They purchased grains from rural store owners who had accepted provisions as payment by farmers. These merchants transported the grains to New York City and then sold them to the Caribbean, and to Europe, as well as to other places in the United States itself.[28] So rapid was the increase in their line of business, that in 1851, the provision merchants founded the Produce Exchange to rationalize and organize their trade.[29]

Another group of traders specialized in long-distance trade. They sent ships to the remotest corners of the world – from India they bought tea, from China silk, and from Brazil rubber, exchanging it for American flour, textiles, and manufactured products such as carriages and furniture, as well as furs.[30] Prominent among them was Abiel Abbot Low, owner of a fleet of ships, who imported tea and silk from the Far East, and George Griswold, who exported flour to the West Indies, from whence he imported rum and sugar.[31] The expanding economy provided an ever-larger number of Americans with the resources to purchase these luxury goods from faraway places. And with the growing volume of trade, specialization became possible for long-distance merchants, despite the fact that their ships were in transit for many weeks.

If Abiel Abbot Low and George Griswold made their fortunes in trading with distant places, New Yorkers such as Alexander T. Stewart and Rowland Macy understood that money was to be made by selling at retail to the new metropolis. They opened up gigantic shopping emporiums with an unmatched variety of goods, at a stroke capturing the imagination and pocketbooks of well-off consumers, who traditionally had shopped at a host of small retailers. Alexander T. Stewart launched this revolution in the city's retail culture when he opened A. T. Stewart's, his large "marble palace," in 1846.[32] He was emulated twelve years later by Rowland Macy, whose store would eventually advertise itself as the largest department store in the world.[33] In addition to New York's huge urban market, visitors flocked to their stores to acquire the goods that would make them look "smart" upon returning to their home towns.

Whereas in the 1850s some merchants specialized in a limited number of products such as tea or cotton, or concentrated on relationships that involved mostly one section of the United States, others sensed an opportunity to diversify into growing auxiliary segments of the merchant economy. The most important of these was banking, both the American branches of European houses and a growing number of domestic banks. This shift from the world of trading goods to the world of finance came easily since one of the central functions of merchants had always been to advance credit. Merchants' willingness to extend credit to farmers for crops not yet harvested and to traders for goods not yet sold was the keystone of New York's booming economy. The nation's hub for goods thus also became the nation's center for the trade in money. With the first commercial bank having been founded in 1784, New York dominated the nation's banking industry by 1830 and expanded rapidly, especially after the closure of the Second Bank of the United States in 1836.

Earlier in the century, general merchants had supplied the bulk of this credit. By the 1850s, however, banks had taken on this role. The most important innovation of banks was to allow merchants to discount promissory notes, and thereby considerably enlarge the pool of capital they could lend.[34] If a merchant, for example, delivered dry goods to a South Carolina retailer and was paid with a ninety-days note, he could take this note to a bank and have it discounted, receiving the face value of the note, less interest for ninety days. As the flow of trade into New York surged to record levels, demand for capital and banking services expanded proportionately. In 1851 alone, twelve new banks opened their doors in Manhattan, and of the fifty-four banks conducting business in 1858, merchants had founded twenty-eight in the previous eight years.[35] Together, these institutions controlled fully one-fifth of the banking capital in the United States.[36]

A growing number of New York merchants found banking so profitable that they ceased merchandising.[37] Six percent of those New Yorkers who paid taxes on assets of more than $10,000 in 1856 engaged primarily in banking and insurance.[38] On average, they were the richest New Yorkers, their real and personal wealth averaging $59,580, compared to the typical merchant's $39,350.[39]

Although an unprecedented share of the capital fueling the growth of banking was generated domestically, during the 1850s New York's banks directed primarily British and Continental capital into American agriculture and trade. Fittingly, the two most important bankers of the city were the chief agents for European capital: George Cabot Ward of London's Baring Brothers and August Belmont of the house of Rothschild.[40] They provided their respective houses access to American investment opportunities, as well as market information, shaping the immense flow of French, British, and to some degree German capital into the up-and-coming American economy.

More typical of the rising American financiers than either Ward or Belmont, however, was James Brown. By 1850, he had built one of the most influential private banking houses in the United States. His father, an Irish-born linen merchant, had migrated to Baltimore in 1800. There he extended the scope of his business to include the import and export of a broad range of goods from and to Britain, and the discounting of bills on British merchant houses. In 1825, his son James was sent to New York to open a branch of the Baltimore firm. Nine years later, after his father's death, James Brown sold the dry goods business in order to concentrate on providing credit and foreign exchange. Although in the 1850s the house still engaged in shipping as well as commission merchandising of cotton, the focus of their enterprises was firmly centered on banking.[41]

Another merchant scion, Moses Taylor, also found profits and a calling in banking. At his birth in 1806, his father was a business manager for the fur trader and land speculator John Jacob Astor. Apprenticed in the merchant house of G. C. & S. S. Howland, a leader in the Cuba trade, Taylor, at age twenty-six, founded his own firm for importing Cuban sugar and rose quickly to become one of the city's most successful merchants and the nation's leading sugar trader. In 1837, he served as director of City Bank, a small merchant bank that ran into frequent trouble when the participating merchants too generously supplied themselves with credit.[42] Unlike his predecessors, Taylor brought the bank under his close direction, sharpening its practices and embarking on a plan for rapid growth. Its strength rested on its close association with dynamic New York City entrepreneurs, especially the city's traders in sugar, metals, and cotton, as well as businessmen who invested in coal mines, gas companies, and railroads.[43] Taylor assumed the presidency of the bank in 1856, all the while remaining active in his wholesale business.

Like Brown and Taylor, Levi Parsons Morton had started his career in trade before moving into finance. Born in 1824 into a well-known New England family, he had joined, in 1849, J. M. Beebe, Morgan & Co., a Boston merchant firm, for whom he opened a branch house in New York City five years later, before moving on to become a partner of Morton, Grinnell & Co., a large wholesale dry goods merchant. Despite a stunning career in trade, Morton remained intrigued by the world of finance, and in 1863 set up shop as an international banker.[44] He sold many millions of federal government bonds in Europe, raised money for states on credit markets, and facilitated international exchanges, turning himself into one of the Gilded Age's major financiers.[45]

Banking, in turn, drew these figures into more distant and innovative adventures, particularly railroads, but also factories, mines, and utilities.[46] Indeed, with the rise of national markets and industry in the 1850s, bankers began to channel capital into promising new ventures well outside their traditional realm of expertise in trade and agricultural commodities. Wealthy merchants had always recognized the importance of railroads, but at midcentury, the scale of their investment shifted radically upward. Between 1850 and 1860, New Yorkers contributed to a capital fund sufficient to finance a threefold expansion of the railroad net, or another 20,000 miles of roadbed.[47] The total investment for the decade reached as much as $1 billion.[48]

The railroads' appetite for capital far exceeded the average banker's resources and tolerance for risk, and into this gap stepped professional stockbrokers in the 1840s and 1850s.[49] In 1848, for example, J. F. D. Lanier formed, with Richard H. Winslow, a banking house whose first six years of transactions nearly exclusively involved railroad securities.[50] Their firm, Winslow, Lanier & Co., sold the first western railroad securities ever – the Madison and Indianapolis Railroad – on the New York market and for a few years enjoyed a virtual monopoly in this trade.[51] The staggering profits earned by some of these deals were obvious by the 1850s, so obvious, indeed, that one of New York's leading merchants, William Aspinwall, retired from international trade to concentrate entirely on railroad development.[52]

The growing size and, hence, risks of the American economy also drove another group of merchants to specialize in insurance. Merchants had long since learned to share the risks associated with trade and instinctively moved to a more institutionalized structure of risk sharing in the form of insurance companies. By 1860, New York housed twelve marine insurance companies (with total assets of more than $21 million) and ninety-five fire insurance companies (with a total capital of more than $20 million), seventy-one of which were founded in the preceding decade.[53] At the same time, eleven life insurance companies competed for business in the city, more than in the rest of the nation taken together.[54] So great was the market for insurance that most of these new firms grew rapidly. The Mutual Life Insurance Company of New York, for example, which had written its first life insurance policy in 1843, counted more than 12,000 contracts on its books seventeen years later.[55] Along with banks, insurance companies represented the largest concentration of capital in the United States, enjoying a lively trade on Wall Street.[56] Moreover, as voracious consumers of capital, they provided rentiers with an ideal investment for their inheritance.[57]

Investing in insurance, just like railroads and banking, was, for the city's merchants, another important way to diversify their investments. As insurance was directly related to trade, it was at first only a small departure from traditional mercantile pursuits and interests. Eventually, however, this diversification could be expected to weaken their links to trade, as insurance firms could and eventually did employ their capital by insuring a whole range of risks not directly linked to trade itself. The merchants' move to diversify their investments also began to diversify their interests – with dramatic political consequences.

The majority of New York's economic elite, hence, had made their fortunes in trade and finance. As aggressive investors, however, many of them realized that opportunities for profit also beckoned elsewhere, perhaps at no time more than during the 1850s. The real estate of the new metropolis was one such opportunity, not least because of New York's emergence as the central port city of the Americas. During the 1850s, and for several decades earlier, speculating in the development of the city was nearly a sure bet, and most merchants leapt at the chance. Not only did they purchase their own residences but they also regularly acquired land or rental properties in the city or its surrounding areas.

They followed a path laid down by a generation of wealthy New Yorkers. Throughout the first half of the century, the Astors, Beekmans, Schermerhorns, and Rhinelanders had invested a large share of profits they had accumulated in trade in vast tracts of land and numerous houses. Their families had bet correctly on the seeming stability of real estate and spectacularly right on the potential of the island of Manhattan. Most prominently, John Jacob Astor had used capital accumulated in the fur and China trade to buy vast tracts of Manhattan land. At the time of his death, in 1848, these holdings made him the richest American citizen.[58] Similarly, James Beekman, a New York state senator in the early 1850s and heir to a large real estate fortune, returned in 1856 from an extended sojourn in Europe and found, to his astonishment, that his wealth had actually increased.[59] This was the more remarkable for the heavy tax burdens on his property for the construction of Central Park. Some merchants also sought to capitalize on the rapid economic growth of the nation beyond the city, and they invested widely in the new towns and cities of the West.[60]

Merchants' investment in real estate, though on a larger scale in the 1850s, was a traditional way of diversifying and limiting their great exposure to the risks inherent in trade. During the same period, however, a number of merchants were also closely watching the profitability of domestic manufacturing. Though most merchants were reluctant to get involved with the unrefined world of production, and rested content under the common stricture that "a merchant ought not to be a manufacturer," a few understood early on that manufacturing provided another path toward diversification.[61] Moreover, they knew firsthand how industrial capital had mushroomed in Europe, with some industries producing astonishing profits. Their own networks of trade made clear the growing and ever more accessible markets for domestic manufacturers.[62] As a result, merchant capital began in the 1850s to trickle into manufacturing, typically through partnerships or closely held stock companies.

Merchants were drawn especially to investments in factories that manufactured the particular product they were trading. Pearl Street apparel wholesalers, for example, frequently invested in and managed clothing manufacturing firms. Other merchants favored different industries: Metal trader Anson Phelps invested in copper- and brassware factories in the Connecticut Valley, despite his son-in-law's warning not to leave the traditional world of trade.[63] The New York copper merchant Uriah Hendricks similarly supplemented his thriving copper-importing house with a copper mill in 1813. By 1850, this mill had grown into one of the largest of its kind.[64] In the wholesale grocer trade, Jeremiah Milbank invested funds to start the Borden Condensed Milk Company.[65] And Robert Stewart Buchanan, a New York belting merchant, financed the research and patents of a Richard Montgomery, who invented new kinds of corrugated boilers and iron bridges, doors, rafters, and beams. In 1855, Montgomery received a patent for "a new and useful improvement in the manufacturing of sheet metal beams," and Buchanan, using this invention, incorporated the Lamina Beam Machine Manufacturing Company the following year.[66] In other cases, merchant and industrial undertakings were joined through kinship ties, as, for example, when New York merchant John Talcott sold the products of his brother's Connecticut hosiery and knit goods factory.[67]

These merchants, by moving into manufacturing, were at the leading edge of diversification, especially considering that at midcentury, manufacturing lacked either the financial security or the dignified reputation that came along with the more gentlemanly trade. These early forays into manufacturing, however, brought some merchants into closer proximity with the industrialists, a group of well-off New Yorkers who had accumulated their capital in ways utterly alien to the mercantile elite. Suddenly, for some merchants-cum-manufacturers, southern trade became less important, internal improvements mattered substantially more than before, and even the traditional bête noire of traders, tariffs, might be countenanced.

❧ ❧ ❧

Accumulating capital in an ever greater number of different economic undertakings, New York's merchant community by the 1850s had decisively left the well-ordered world of the colonial port behind. The community itself had expanded rapidly as wave after wave of capitalists set up businesses in the city. Each year dozens, if not hundreds, of new entrepreneurs arrived, making New York's economic elite truly international. August

Belmont, when he migrated in 1837 from Frankfurt, Germany, to represent the banking house of Rothschild in the New World, had been one of them. Like him, about 26 percent of New Yorkers assessed at more than $10,000 were born in foreign countries; of the rest, 43 percent were born in other parts of the United States and only 31 percent in the city itself.[68] Significantly, the number of merchants, bankers, and industrialists born overseas nearly equaled the number of those born in New York City, most of them arriving from Great Britain (10 percent), Ireland (6 percent), and Germany (6 percent). Even the majority of native-born businessmen had migrated to the city from elsewhere in the United States: 16 percent from New York State, 15 percent from New England (particularly Connecticut and Massachusetts), and 6 percent from New Jersey. Altogether, these migrants followed closely the national and international flows of capital and goods, and, in turn, many of them facilitated these flows in their function as bankers, agents, and importers.

But no group among New York's economic elite was as mobile as the merchants. At midcentury, a full 25 percent of them had migrated from New England, and an astounding 39 percent had been born overseas, many of whom, such as the German-born importer James Benkard or the Swiss-born watch merchant Jacques Guedin, had accumulated significant resources in their home countries before embarking for the United States.[69] New York's booming port attracted foreign merchants whose cosmopolitan connections, in turn, strengthened the port's worldwide reach. Merchant and banking houses in ports all over the world sent relatives to New York to look after their interests, many of whom enjoyed long careers there and significant independence from their ports of origin.[70] New England traders, capital rich and sensing greater opportunity in the metropolis to the south, came to play an important role in New York trade, among them such families as the Griswolds (from Old Lyme), the Lows (from Salem), and the Grinnells (from New Bedford).[71]

It would be difficult to envision a mercantile elite more mobile, more ethnically diverse, and more specialized than the one of New York during the 1850s. Although neither mobility nor ethnic diversity as such were a new phenomenon, the scale of the transformation of the world of the city's merchants and bankers was unprecedented, giving their community a fluidity entirely lacking in the tight-knit world of colonial days. For merchants, it was ever more difficult to know their peers and to be known to them, as the old networks of personal contact strained under the pressure of expansion and specialization.

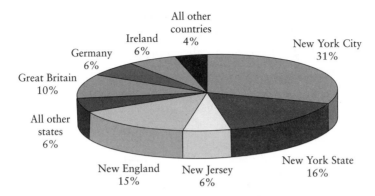

Place of birth of bourgeois New Yorkers, 1855.
Source: Sample of 191 New York City taxpayers who were assessed on real and personal property of $10,000 or more in 1855.[72]

While few begrudged the profits of the new metropolis, most merchants reacted to the disruption of their social world by shoring up their traditional kinship and social networks, by building institutions, and by articulating shared habits, manners, and values that helped create a sense of collectivity. It was in the family parlor, not the counting house, that New York's merchant elite worked hardest to remain a community. The parlor's importance resulted from the very nature of midcentury businesses. Merchant houses, after all, were nearly always family enterprises. They were usually small, encompassing only a few trusted partners – often relatives – and some clerks, frequently the sons of friends and business partners. Indeed, with access to capital and contacts, starting out in business was not difficult. Normally, a small number of merchants formed partnerships, with each party paying in a set amount of capital. In return, each person could sign for the firm, thus gaining a share in the work as well as in the profits and losses. There was no limit to the active partners' liability, which certainly helped ensure that all partners vigilantly guarded their businesses' operations.[73] State charters, so important for insurance companies, banks, and transportation enterprises, never incorporated merchant houses, because, in the eyes of the legislature, they were not endowed with sufficient public purpose.[74] If merchant houses desired to enlarge the reach and scope of their operations, they would create a web of interlocking partnerships, especially with traders in distant ports, allowing for transactions to remain in the hands of those they knew and trusted.[75] The goals of most partnerships, however, were quite limited, so much so that even single voyages of ships were held by a number of merchants who each owned a share in the risk and profits of the endeavor.[76] While such small and close-knit businesses allowed for enormous flexibility and rapid adjustments to changing conditions, they also made firms unstable. At any time, a partner might die, move away, or look for new business opportunities, bringing the partnership arrangements to an end. If a firm was to persist, owners had to allow younger members to join, and the choice of these partners was of crucial importance to the firm's continued prosperity.

A brief examination of merchant origins illustrates the nature of these firms and the importance of individual owners to their survival. Charles Howland Russell, a wholesale dry goods merchant and importer, had started out as an apprentice to a merchant in Providence, Rhode Island. When he turned twenty-one, in 1817, he joined his employer's firm as a partner, and eight years later went to New York City to open a branch of the Providence firm. Sensing business opportunity, however, Russell dissolved the partnership and went into business for himself. When he retired, his brother, together with a mutual friend, continued the same line of business, but again under a new partnership agreement. Russell's firm, typical for midcentury merchants, depended for its existence entirely on its owner. Should the owner die, or move his capital elsewhere, the firm itself would come to an end. As a result of this personal form of business organization, the success of a firm rose and fell with the capital and talents of its proprietors, making their social standing, their family connections, and their "character" crucial elements of the relative standing of the firm itself.[77]

This web of partnership agreements, personal relations, and family contacts also characterized the career of William E. Dodge, who by midcentury was the nation's most important metals merchant. He was born in Hartford, Connecticut, in 1805, to a moderately successful trader who sent his son to work at age eighteen as a clerk for a wholesale dry goods dealer. In 1825, William joined his father's dry goods business in Manhattan and, two years later, took it over. An ambitious young man, he married Melissa Phelps, a daughter of merchant Anson G. Phelps, one of his father's friends. Not long afterward, in 1832, Dodge joined his new father-in-law in a partnership, forming Phelps, Dodge & Co. They imported tin plate, sheet iron, copper wire, and other metal goods from Great Britain, paid for with cotton exported from New Orleans. They were the first house to institute regular shipping service between New York and Charleston.[78] Although they, like most merchants, specialized in one commodity – metals – the inability of many of their customers to pay in cash led Dodge eventually to trade also in rugs, cloth, shoes, beeswax, and fruit. When the senior Phelps died, in 1853, the firm's capital was redistributed, giving Anson G. Phelps, Jr., Dodge, and Daniel James, a brother-in-law to both, a stake of 25 percent each, the rest held by various other relatives. The company grew rapidly, and by 1857, annual profits amounted to $455,177. Yet all the partners also engaged in business ventures separate from their partnership. Dodge, for example, invested heavily in railroads, Pennsylvania timberland, Michigan copper mines, and real estate.[79] Phelps, Dodge & Co., like most merchant houses, was essentially a family firm that adjusted its ownership structure according to family strategies and market conditions. This typical structure allowed it the flexibility to integrate newcomers and assimilate their skills and capital into new ventures.

Considering that the focus of the typical firm was still to an important degree the family, as it had been for centuries, it was not surprising that merchants and bankers, together with their wives, expended extraordinary effort to maintain and strengthen these relationships, both among relatives and among larger social networks. Kin and friends, after all, helped to mobilize capital, skills, and information. And in the absence of powerful educational institutions, it was also through the family that social and business skills were passed to the next generation.

Central to these networks were marriage links. Because marriages allowed for the fashioning of new alliances that made additional capital, information, and expertise available, they were ritualized in forms strikingly similar to those of market exchanges.[80] Members of New York's mercantile and financial elite frequently chose marriage partners for compatibility of status, wealth, and even the specific line of business.[81] Though the concept of romantic love was important, the marriage market itself had developed social norms and institutions that practically guaranteed the "right" romantic choices. Balls and rounds of visiting brought the sons and daughters of well-to-do families together in a controlled, yet potentially intimate, environment. When William E. Dodge, for example, set his eyes on young Melissa Phelps, he proposed to her during a carriage ride to Coney Island, but later asked permission of her father, who granted it, emphasizing the "long and uninterrupted friendship subsisting between your family and ours."[82] Although part of a "society" marriage, love had a meaning quite distinct from its modern-day usage. It did not necessarily include sexual attraction, as exemplified by the widespread use and general acceptance of prostitutes by wealthy New Yorkers.[83] (As Walt Whitman noted, "the custom is to go among prostitutes as an ordinary thing" among the "best classes of men.")[84] Marriage was first and foremost an economic venture; indeed, it was one of the most important business decisions of any career.

Numerous biographies attest to this link: Merchant William E. Dodge, as we have seen, married Melissa and became a partner in the Phelps metal business.[85] Three of Melissa's sisters also married to their family's economic advantage: Elizabeth took the hand of merchant Daniel James (who eventually came to run the business's Liverpool branch), Caroline wedded the merchant James Stokes, and Olivia the merchant B. B. Atterbury.[86] And the Phelpses were no anomaly. In the 1830s, the newly arrived Tobias family, dry goods merchants, established themselves by marrying two of their daughters to the sons of a prominent copper merchant, Harmon Hendricks.[87] Indeed, some of New York's dynastic marriages have become legendary. William Backhouse Astor's 1853 marriage to Caroline Webster Schermerhorn connected, at one stroke, Astor's "new" real estate wealth to the "old" landed and mercantile wealth of the Van Cortlandts, Bayards, Beekmans, Suydams, and Joneses. The wedding of newcomer August Belmont, a Jew, to Caroline Slidell Perry, daughter of an established (and Protestant) Japan trader, in 1849 symbolized the entry of recent immigrant Belmont to the inner circles of New York society.[88]

Good marriage deals were considered so important that the Dun credit-reporting agency even mentioned them in its assessments of enterprises.[89] When manufacturer Robert S. Buchanan married, Dun remarked approvingly that he had aligned himself with a "young lady of lavish fortune."[90] Not surprisingly, the choice of an "unworthy" marriage partner, in turn, was cause for serious concern. Charles Haswell disapproved of the 1857 marriage of Mary Ann Baker, daughter of a "very much esteemed citizen," to John Dean, her father's coachman, ruminating that "the public was much surprised. . . . So distasteful was the marriage to her father that he essayed to remove her from the country, and also to have her declared a lunatic."[91] As a result of this connection between business and marriage strategies, 37 percent of the wealthiest New Yorkers in 1856 were directly related to one another.[92]

Once a match had been made, it fell to the wife to solidify further these kinship networks by writing to relatives, inviting them to family affairs, or by visiting them. Women, in effect, spun the threads that held these families together, both emotionally and economically, constituting what was one of the most important links of mid–nineteenth-century businesses.[93] And not only did they maintain contact among relatives; they also raised the next generation whose exertions would eventually become central to the very survival of the family's businesses. While the public face and economic institutions of this influential group of capital-owning New Yorkers was overwhelmingly male, their power was drawn in substantial ways from a much broader intergenerational network of kin and social contacts, forged by their wives and daughters.

The enormous attention paid to the forging of these kinship links and their maintenance was the direct result of the importance of these networks to business enterprises. Family ties gave access to business contacts, partnerships, and credit, thus making them central to business success. Moreover, in a world of underdeveloped communication facilities and weak impersonal institutions, trust was essential to the conduct of business. Since mail service was slow, for example, merchants and bankers had to allow their distant representatives significant leeway in making decisions. The advance of credit, which was part of every business transaction, was also based on the reputation of individuals. Consequently, trustworthy conveyors of information were essential for making investment decisions, and family members were the best and sometimes only partners in business, because they could normally ensure "trust" most effectively. When, for example, the banking house of Brown Brothers opened new branches in Philadelphia, Baltimore, Boston, and Liverpool, they were all headed by James Brown's brothers. In retrospect, John Crosby Brown, the son of James, remembered that the "business of the firm . . . was a purely family affair, and when in later years the growth of the business required additional help, the junior partners taken in were usually relatives." He attributed their firm's success to the "mutual confidence" among family members.[94] The textile entrepreneurs Talcott took a similar path. When John Talcott wanted to sell the products of his Connecticut hosiery and knit goods factory in the New York market, he sent his brother James to the city.[95]

Kinship networks similarly facilitated the constant supply of labor and expertise into businesses and, as a result, contributed to social and regional mobility. Relatives and friends in the metropolis helped aspiring youngsters from smaller towns or the countryside to find employment as clerks in merchant firms. They employed the sons of business partners and supervised them until they could stand on their own or – perhaps – until marriage with one of their daughters strengthened the social and economic bonds. Shepherd Knapp, for example, moved from Massachusetts at a young age to New York to work in the office of his cousin, a leather merchant. Soon, he became a member of the firm.[96] Moses Taylor's father, who was a real estate broker aligned with John Jacob Astor, used his contacts to apprentice his fifteen-year-old son to the merchant J. D. Brown.

Many years later, after Taylor had set up his own business, he took Percy R. Pyne as a partner, a tie that six year later was cemented by his daughter's marriage to the new partner.[97] William E. Dodge's route into trading, as we have seen earlier, was similarly eased by his parents.[98]

Not only did parents provide access to businesses but they were also a prominent source of capital. Inheritance normally followed kinship lines and provided for the accumulation of capital over long periods. Indeed, by the mid-1850s, 71.1 percent of all New York households assessed at more than $100,000 had inherited their wealth from the preceding generation.[99] Among the numerous examples of such continuity are Moses H. Grinnell, Robert B. Minturn, Samuel Shaw Howland, and Abiel Abbot Low, all of whose parents had left them significant resources.[100]

The sons of merchant families, their wealth established, also began by the mid–nineteenth century to take up careers in the emerging professions, especially law and medicine. Indeed, the surging economy of the 1850s and its ever more numerous and anonymous relationships demanded that merchants diversify not only their capital but also their skills. Professions represented an opportunity for sons who did not take an active part in the family business to remain connected to elite social networks and, at times, to live off the proceeds of prior generations' labor in a respectable manner. If in the past the sons of well-off families might have considered careers in politics or among the clergy, by the 1850s new opportunities in law and medicine marked bright and clear paths to respectability and utility. By 1855, a full 10 percent of all Manhattan taxpayers assessed at more than $10,000 were professionals.[101]

Professions themselves, such as law and medicine, however, conferred no particular status on the practitioner. In contrast to the later decades of the nineteenth century, the lack of proper training, standards, and organization, indeed the absence of their "professionalization," made these occupations ill defined. People of lesser means easily turned themselves into "experts" in law or medicine since they did not need to fulfill any specific set of educational requirements. But such a step did not lead to riches or prestige. George Templeton Strong, himself a lawyer, saw most of his colleagues "by appearance, diction, or manner as belonging to a low social station," an opinion widely shared about medical practitioners as well.[102]

Nor was it education that made successful professionals, as would be the case later in the century. Indeed, education played only a marginal role in the training of upper-class professionals. Most of the small number of students who graduated from Columbia College in the 1850s (in 1851 there were only twenty-one), for example, considered its curriculum less a path to social mobility than a means to refine character and to acquire useful skills to manage the business they were about to inherit.[103] John Ward, one of them, who studied law in the late 1850s, knew that the skills he was about to learn could be usefully employed in his family's banking firm. And men like Robert B. Minturn, Francis Hendricks, and John Crosby Brown went to Columbia as much for "refinement" as for study.[104] Education for most merchants and bankers, however, was received at home and in the counting houses themselves, under the oversight of parents or close friends. Merchants, reported *Hunt's Merchants' Magazine,* lived a life "absorb[ed] . . . in unimportant material details." For this reason, their "faculties . . . are best developed in the counting house."[105]

What it took to be a proper lawyer or doctor, instead, was family capital and family connections.[106] By and large, well-off and respectable lawyers and doctors were the sons of wealthy merchants. They had gone into law or medicine with considerable resources at their disposal, and their wealth derived to a significant degree from capital investments, often inherited capital, and not from the mostly modest fees that a professional career provided.[107] When the lawyer Samuel B. Ruggles died, the Chamber of Commerce noted that "his associations were . . . with the great merchants of the City."[108] The lawyer William Peet, the Dun credit-reporting agency asserted in 1853, had "clients of a very respectable class, merchants," which was not surprising, considering that his father was one of them.[109]

Law was an especially attractive pursuit for the sons of wealthy merchants, since the practice of law provided useful skills for managing the family business. Frederic DePeyster, for example, a mid–nineteenth-century New York lawyer, brokered deals with the real estate he had inherited from his parents and had estimated assets of several hundred thousand dollars.[110] State Senator James Beekman had studied law for similar reasons: He had embarked on the career, according to his biographer, "not with the idea of practicing, but merely to acquire that general knowledge of its principles which should be possessed by every gentlemen."[111] Having a background in law would also be a valuable skill for managing the newly emerging bureaucratic corporations, such as railroads and insurance companies.

Medicine, in contrast to law, did not prepare for managing family wealth, but it was a possible career choice for merchant sons and, with the right kinds of social connections, lent itself to accumulating a modest fortune. Again, just as for lawyers, "[a] physician's standing," according to one historian of medicine, "depended as much on his family background and the status of his patients as on the nature of his occupation."[112] The experience of Horace Green, a prominent Manhattan doctor, can testify to this link: Green was born into a prosperous Vermont family, which had enabled him to study medicine in Rutland, Middlebury, Philadelphia, and Paris.[113] He made money from his practice, or so at least believed Dun's credit reporter, but also, quite typically, had "means of his own." Indeed, in 1856 his combined wealth was assessed at a full $35,500.[114] Similarly, surgeon John Beekman was deeply rooted in the elite social networks of midcentury Manhattan, which was hardly surprising considering that he was the cousin of State Senator and real estate investor James Beekman.[115]

Some sons went even further astray from the business world and followed artistic or intellectual inclinations. This was a path only open to those sons whose families gave them a secure economic hold. Born into wealthy merchant families, such writers as Washington Irving or such artists as Frederic Edwin Church and Sanford Robinson Gifford procured their income primarily from capital investments, not books and paintings, and had close family ties to the city's merchants and bankers.[116] Irving's niece Julia Irving, for example, married the merchant Moses H. Grinnell.[117] (Irving was also a welcome guest at the mansions of such notables as August Belmont.)[118] Their writings and paintings depicting the world of New York's mercantile elite were often extraordinarily perceptive – not least because it was their own world they portrayed. And their works also served as powerful testimony to the leisure, wealth, and growing cultural maturity of the city's mercantile elite – an elite, which by the mid-1800s, was making the first tentative steps to legitimize its power through cultural achievements.

Family held this rapidly growing and diverse group of people together, and it balanced powerful centrifugal economic forces, ethnic diversity, and mobility. Indeed, the imperatives of capital accumulation, the specific structure of enterprises, and the weak development of impersonal financial institutions continually moved merchants, bankers, and industrialists toward the strengthening of these networks.

But there were other, more subtle, collectivities. Dry goods merchants and Pearl Street jobbers, Wall Street bankers and uptown real estate developers, gentlemen rentiers and China merchants also shared a social world with distinct values and practices – a world that advertised their distinguished economic position and revealed who amid the burgeoning populace of New York belonged to the "respectable classes."

Here again, the family took center stage, its private economic function matched by its public symbolic power, for families were the bedrock of individuals' claims to respectability. Central to the maintenance of proper appearance was a system of distinct gender roles.[119] Merchant men and women lived distinct roles, even inhabiting what some historians have called "separate spheres."[120] While men bought and sold cotton, negotiated loans, and acquired railroad securities, women fashioned themselves as guardians of the home, a space they and their husbands increasingly defined as being fundamentally different from the outside world. In a world in which most women worked manually, often for wages, merchant women organized the household, maintained emotional ties among family members, raised the children, and presented the family to the public. Organizing proper meals and entertainments, seeing to the appropriate decoration of the home, and displaying themselves in fashionable costume projected their family's standing to the wider world. It also underlined the fundamental importance of distinct gender roles to the mercantile elites' identity – an ideology of gender difference peculiar to their class.

Beyond these distinct gender roles, merchants defined their shared world by the design of the family dwelling. Its layout served to create the illusion of a sphere removed from the harsh realities of the market – a world in which "gentlemen" could recover from the world of exchange. Thick carpets, heavy curtains, and ornate wallpaper insulated the abode from the outside world, offering a physical retreat from the noises, odors, and visual blur of the metropolis.[121] Portraits of living or deceased family members lined its walls, denoting continuity, tradition, and stability. Artfully carved furniture, neo-Grecian sculptures, crystal lights, and memorabilia from trips to exotic places served as testimony to material wealth.[122] Public and private spaces were strictly separated; bedrooms and the kitchen remained invisible to visitors.[123] Though modest by later standards, the merchant home of the 1850s served as an effective stage to display the material wealth and good taste of its inhabitants, and to set them decisively apart from other New Yorkers who had neither the resources nor inclination to forge such an abode.[124]

In order to craft a home and a family on a level prescribed by standards of respectability and business necessities, women, in charge of the household, employed servants. Indeed, the employment of servants came very close to defining the city's mercantile elite itself. When banker John Crosby Brown looked back to his adolescent years in their house on University Place in the 1850s, he remembered distinctly the army of servants:

There was the housekeeper, . . . in the kitchen the black cook, and the scullery maid, in the dining room the colored butler, and his assistant, another colored man. . . . The upstairs maids were all white, and consisted of the old nurse, a parlormaid, a house maid, and a seamstress, who was my mother's maid.[125]

Though Brown remarked in 1909 on the "simplicity of life" in the 1850s, his parents' household, with a total of eight resident servants, employed an exceptional amount of household help. In 1855, the average upper-class New York household (that is, among those assessed at more than $10,000) paid wages to only 2.3 servants.[126]

Servants and tutors not only guaranteed a certain minimum level of comfort for adults, but they also played a crucial role in the upbringing of the family's children.[127] Particular ways of raising children became a hallmark of the "gentleman's" household inasmuch as the heirs to the business had to be socialized in elite manners and values and to learn the business itself. Characteristically, well-to-do families protected their children from the disorderly world unfolding on the streets of Manhattan and provided them with careful attention and schooling, at home and in private academies. Exposure to table manners, conversation styles, and dress codes, as well as to classical literature, philosophy, and the sights of Europe, further helped to transmit the culture of their parents.[128] Children learned to be "well mannered" and to behave according to strict rules of public performance. This reassertion of a complex web of behavior, tastes, and taboos provided them with the symbolic capital that proved to be a major asset in navigating their world.[129]

If the evolving patterns of the mercantile household sought to delimit an ordered world away from the chaos of the urban metropolis and provide a sense of community with other wealthy New Yorkers, more subtle rituals, shared manners, and institutions built a sense of "moral collectivity" among the city's gentleman capitalists. One of the most important articulations of a shared ethos of gentlemanly respectability was the relationship of New York's business elite to work itself. Though most wealthy New Yorkers were not self-made in the sense of having risen from poverty, money still provided only a precarious foundation for social status. Risks were often great, and the nature of most businesses exhibited a pronounced dependence on the owners' efforts, which made "the American merchant . . . a type of a restless, adventurous, onward-going race of people."[130] Supported by religious beliefs that promised redemption for worldly engagements, and not unlike Benjamin Franklin's and Max Weber's prescriptive theories of capitalism, banker Moses Taylor considered "hard work and prudence [as] governing principles."[131] He attributed his success to "work[ing] late."[132] Banker Levi Parsons Morton similarly perceived "slackness akin to sin."[133] "[B]usiness means *habit*," editorialized *Hunt's Merchants' Magazine*, a leading voice of the city's merchants, "the soul of which is regularity."[134] "Strict punctuality" and "economy of time," asserted the *American Merchant,* were a trader's most valuable traits.[135] Another propertied New Yorker, Henry Moore, in 1857, noted that he "[c]ould not sleep last night . . . think[ing about] the money crisis and panic."[136] Money demanded constant vigilance, a lesson instilled early on, when many young gentlemen began keeping personal account books that tracked their expenses.[137]

A key component in this devotion to work among the city's gentleman capitalists was the steering of the myriad personal relationships in which business endeavors were embedded. An account of merchant William E. Dodge's work patterns represents this world well: Typically, Dodge would leave his house on Madison Avenue and 36th Street, taking a carriage to his office on Cliff Street. There he began his day, at about 8:30 in the morning, by reading the mail and by instructing his personal secretary. "Then [Dodge] outlined matters for the day, leaving to the juniors the task of giving his directions definite shape."[138] After signing checks, Dodge usually received a stream of visitors, some asking him to participate in projects, others requesting loans, and still others suggesting philanthropic endeavors. He next walked to Wall Street to inquire into exchanges, visit banks, have a chat at the Chamber of Commerce, and get a business update at the office of his Lackawanna Iron and Coal Company. After lunch, Dodge would typically attend meetings of boards on which he was a director and then return to his office to draft more letters. At about 4:00 P.M., the day would wind down at the National Temperance Society or at the American Bible Society. Two hours later, Dodge usually returned home.[139] The world Dodge inhabited interwove business, religion, and philanthropy, all of them governed by the same evangelical zeal and facilitated by dense social networks.

In a world based on trust and personal contacts, "character" proved critical. "Integrity of character and truth in the inner man are the prerequisites for success," counseled *Hunt's Merchants' Magazine,* emphasizing the importance of "honesty," "[m]utual confidence," "honor," "sincerity," "integrity," "strict morality," and "endurance."[140] The editors advised their readers that "[s]elf-reliance, conjoined with promptness in the execution of our undertakings, is indispensable to success."[141] In a society that knew of no formal system of ranking and mutual obligation, it was no great surprise that the first systematic efforts at reporting the creditworthiness of individuals focused, to a large degree, on character. Dun's credit-reporting agency described some of the city's entrepreneurs as "worthy," "honorable," "of good moral character," "a man of family,"

and referred to others in less favorable terms, as for example, when it concluded about one businessman that "his habits are free – he is not what
might be called strictly temperate."[142] Indeed, "character," according to
Hunt's Merchants' Magazine, "to a man of business . . . is as dear as life
itself."[143]

While an intense commitment to work was, in many ways, at the core of
capital-rich New Yorkers' identities, they also shared particular patterns
of consumption. Consumption helped strengthen shared identities and
simultaneously displayed them to a larger public. Although earlier generations of merchants had lived in material comfort, displays of luxury had
for a long time been considered unrepublican. But by the 1850s, New
York's mercantile elite slowly began to replace their relatively simple
dress, decor, and food with more overt displays of riches. Their greater
wealth allowed for such a departure, but even more decisive was their
desire to delineate the boundaries of their world and appropriate some of
the strategies of social distinction of the elites who had come before them,
most particularly of the European aristocracy. Women especially participated in very public forms of consumption.[144] When Alexander T. Stewart
opened his department store on Broadway and Chambers Street in 1846,
the *New York Herald* praised him for having "paid the ladies of this city a
high compliment in giving them such a beautiful resort in which to while
away their leisure hours of the morning."[145] The store displayed goods on
mahogany counters and marble shelves in grand halls decorated with fres-
coes and paintings, stressing the imaginative quality of goods and the contribution their consumption made to the self-definition of its bourgeois
customer.[146] It marked a revolution in retailing in New York. Though
notions of modesty and "dignified simplicity" still resonated among
wealthy New Yorkers, they increasingly gave way to more elaborate displays of taste and fashion.[147]

Part of this greater willingness to display one's wealth and social standing were new forms of self-presentation in public. More so than ever
before, well-to-do New Yorkers displayed their confidence by presenting
themselves in a self-consciously theatrical manner to the public. New ways
of dressing and new kinds of manners slowly undermined a once-preva-
lent culture of sentimentality among upper-class New Yorkers.[148] As historian Karen Halttunen remarked, "[w]hereas the sentimental woman had
been slim, pale, and vaguely transparent, the fashionable woman of the
1850s was ample, brilliant, and decidedly opaque."[149] The wives and
daughters of New York City's gentlemen capitalists displayed artfully dec-

orated hoop dresses, embroidered or decorated with raised velvet figures, and protected their heads from view with bonnets of satin, silk, or lace.[150] The staging of public appearances turned into an art in itself. Even a properly and successfully conducted funeral demanded familiarity with the numerous rules of a complex public ritual: Appropriate "mourning apparel," an elaborately decorated hearse, a well-dressed corpse, and proper pallbearers were all essential to a successful funeral.[151] These rituals self-consciously drew boundaries around the proper world of the mercantile elite, as participating in them demanded access to leisure, money, and knowledge about how to do things the "right" way – a combination of assets only accessible to capital-rich New Yorkers.[152]

Travel, another form of consumption, further delineated the boundaries of this society. In a world in which most people moved only because of wars, persecution, or poverty, many well-to-do New Yorkers left their homes for places close and far in a predictable rhythm: Summers dictated a move to the country, young adulthood a trip to the American West and to Europe, and sickness a trip to the spas of Europe. Summer travel was by far the most common, and by the 1850s, railroad lines brought New York's mercantile elite to fashionable places, such as Saratoga, the Catskills, Cape May, Niagara Falls, and Newport.[153] Postadolescent sons of well-to-do New Yorkers saw travel as an important "rite of passage."[154] Robert B. Minturn, for example, set sail to India in 1856 at age twenty and published upon his return many months later a book entitled *From New York to Delhi*.[155] He followed in the footsteps of his well-traveled father, who had frequently spent months at a time in Europe and North Africa.[156] And nineteen-year-old Theodore Roosevelt, a glass importer and father of the future president, went west in June 1850, exploring the country as well as renewing his father's business contacts.[157] In the following summer, Roosevelt began an eighteen-month tour of London, Paris, Rome, Ireland, and Russia, shopping in London and Paris, climbing mountains in the Alps, and admiring ruins in Rome.[158] To be "cultured" required exposure to Europe, which was, in the minds of the city's gentlemen capitalists, the original source of refinement and tradition. And just as upper-class New Yorkers were in the process of revolutionizing the world and building empires of their own, Europe provided them with impressions of empires long gone – Egypt, Athens, and Rome.[159]

Traveling, just like consumption, had the dual purpose of allowing New York's mercantile elite to display their social capital while at the same time acquiring more of it. This flaunting of social capital found its regular audience on the city's streets, in parks, and in public buildings. With their rising wealth and growing numbers, by the 1850s merchants, bankers, and elite professionals proudly began to display their accomplishments to the public. Their most public ritual was the promenade: Since the late 1820s, the city's "gentry" had walked along Broadway during the later afternoon, greeting one another in a prescribed manner.[160] Over the next three decades, this promenade had become larger and more entrenched as a public affirmation of status, a confident assertion of a shared identity. The parade, featuring "pavements . . . full of well-dressed persons," exhibited "no contemptible show of millinery and dry goods, whalebone, and crinoline."[161] In a society that knew little of aristocratic deference, such forms of communication, as historian David Scobey has argued, created a sense of "moral collectivity" among the participants.[162]

The annual New Year's Day visit further strengthened the sense of moral collectivity. On January first of each year, New York's gentlemen capitalists crisscrossed the city's streets from morning till night to pay New Year's visits to the wives and daughters of those they acknowledged or by whom they wanted to be acknowledged. The caller carefully selected and noted those to be visited ahead of time, strategically orchestrating the schedule to include all addresses of importance. John Crosby Brown recalled this occasion in vivid detail, in his memoirs of 1909:

> The great festival day in New York, greater than Christmas, was New Year's Day. One of the earliest recollections of my boyish days in University Place was preparing my own special list of calls for New Year's Day. It was my father's custom to take all the younger boys with him, for some special calls, but we had in addition our own lists. . . . The ladies of the houses at both the north and south ends of the town were expected to be ready to receive visitors by ten o'clock in the morning. Otherwise it would have been impossible to cover the ground in one day. The list of calls sometimes numbered 250 to 300. It was made carefully by streets, and the time for a call varied from two to three minutes. . . . The region just north and south of University Place was filled with houses of the very best people in New York, and it was in this region progress was very slow. It was often nine or ten o'clock before the day's work was finished.[163]

Similarly, twenty-two-year-old banker John Ward made thirty-three calls in 1861 – beginning with the Astors, and including the Beekmans, Fisches, Joneses, Minturns, Grinnells, and Blatchfords.[164] Thus, year after year, networks that proved so important for business and politics were reaffirmed. In contrast to the promenade, New Year's Day visits were more selective, with the 250 to 300 visits of James Brown or the 90 calls of the lawyer Frederick DePeyster including a very large segment of the city's rich and powerful.[165] Though May King Van Rensselaer may have exaggerated when she claimed that a boundary had emerged "between [society] and the rest of the world . . . as solid and as difficult to ignore as the Chinese Wall," gentlemen capitalists had created a social world quite separate from that of the majority of the city's population.[166] Political equality, an advice book stated perceptively, "did not extend to the drawing-room. None are excluded from the highest councils of the nation, but it does not follow that all can enter into the highest ranks of society."[167] Living this class culture, with its consumption of specific goods and sights, increasingly became a shared experience for New York's mercantile elite.

The almost absurd number of visits James Brown made on a typical antebellum New Year's Day, however, pointed toward the strains that a rapidly growing city put on these traditional social networks. The networks that held the city's merchants and bankers together had rested essentially on personal contacts among families, a structure of social life that worked well in a world in which people shared common experiences and lived in close proximity to one another. However, the streets that the merchants claimed as theirs were becoming increasingly filled by people far removed from the social world of the economic elite – sailors, workers, the poor, many of them immigrants. Even the city's economic life was hardly stable, as merchants specialized and as a new group of capital owners, unconnected to their social networks and inhabiting a very different economic, social, and ideological world, emerged – the manufacturers. The city's mercantile elite responded to these challenges by creating new public institutions and new organizations that they hoped would protect their world and project their power over the city's public spaces, and the nation's political destiny.

2

Navigating the New Metropolis

Emboldened by New York's emergence as a center of world trade and finance, New York's merchants and bankers moved to project their economic power into the city. There, however, they collided with the disconcerting sights, sounds, and smells of life below the decks of merchant respectability. They met there a citizenry, by no means all poor or powerless, unafraid to contest their claims to stewardship. Indeed, the very economic boom that had transformed their economic prospects, enriching them beyond all expectations, had also undermined their relatively stable, deferential, and manageable port city. Especially the city's public spaces were an affront as the city's merchants and bankers had built few bourgeois cultural institutions and had to fight for control over the handful of cultural venues that existed. Their visible and boisterous adversaries came from the urban masses, whose labor was necessary to their enterprises and whose admission tickets financed New York's predominantly commercial cultural institutions. But the 1850s also marked the gradual yet fateful emergence of a powerful new social group: the artisans turned manufacturers. While often beholden to merchant capital, these men were gaining sufficient wealth and power in the 1850s to strain the age-old association of respectability with merchant gentility. And while they may have shared merchants' providential belief in material progress, they were coming to their own divergent, unsettling conclusions about the direction, the agents, and the obstacles in the path of America's destiny. Without a shared ideology, a shared map of the social landscape of their city or nation, New York's merchants and manufacturers marshaled little strength to shape their own city.

New York's rapid economic growth made and remade fortunes, but it also set the landscape of population swirling. The thousands of hopeful newcomers who filled the abundant jobs available in Manhattan, many of them poor Irish and German immigrants, transformed the face of the city, pushing the urban boundary ever farther into the Manhattan countryside and transforming neighborhoods in the lower parts of the city into ghettos of the poor. Each year, thousands of people stepped off boats, railcars, and wagons to try their luck in the city. Manhattan's population grew by leaps and bounds. In 1845, the city had 371,000 inhabitants, ten years later it numbered 630,000 citizens, and another five years later, in 1860, the number had skyrocketed to 814,000.[1] In a short fifteen years, the city's size had more than doubled. Whole areas of the city were densely populated by new arrivals, who brought with them alien customs, unfamiliar languages, and miserable poverty.

Living at the tip of an island, the city's merchants, bankers, speculators, and professionals encountered the full spectrum of the city's inhabitants. On their daily rounds from their homes to their banking houses and trading floors, they encountered the poorest of the poor, who scavenged the city for means of survival, dressed in ragged clothes, and living in squalid quarters. "[A] few moments walk from salons superbly furnished in the style of Louis XIV," reported the writer Lydia Child in 1845, was a world of "dreary desolate apartment[s] where shivering urchins pay a cent apiece for the privilege of keeping out of the watchmen's hands, by sleeping on boards ranged in tiers."[2] They interacted with wage workers: servants cleaning their homes and raising their children, and workers in New York's burgeoning industries and ports. Some workers, like the printers, blacksmiths, and machinists, could be fiercely independent and proud of their craft. Others, such as the coal haulers, the seamstresses, and the day laborers on the docks struggled to survive in unskilled occupations with little prospect for advancement. The city's mercantile elite also met the small shopkeepers, minor professionals, and artisans who might aspire to respectability but lacked the means to achieve it.

The overwhelming impression the city left on the minds of its upperclass citizens was one of incomprehensible chaos. As the *New York Herald* complained, the "swearing, drinking, silly boors" of the Bowery had "destroyed all enjoyment" of carriage drives along city streets.[3] The city was noisy, it stank, and it permanently threatened encounters with its most undesirable inhabitants. This perception of the loss of control over their environment would occupy New York's economic elite throughout the century – decisively shaping their ideas and their politics.

This environment of toil, exertion, and sweat was more than an aesthetic affront; it symbolized the unprecedented openness and democratic dynamism of the city's shared spaces. Indeed, as nowhere else in the mid–nineteenth-century world, all social groups vied for the control of

New York's public space and public sphere. In Europe, the bourgeoisie, together with the aristocracy, dominated both. In New York, however, individuals and groups, without regard to class, shaped public spaces and built "public" institutions they claimed as their own. Indeed, the city and its public spaces were not sharply segregated.[4] On streets and in parks, but also at public ceremonies such as July Fourth celebrations, the city's rich and poor, native and foreign born, Protestant and Catholic, would meet.[5] And the process of institution building was similarly open to all: "I confess I had no previous notion," Alexis de Tocqueville admitted to his readers, that Americans "of all ages, all conditions, and all dispositions constantly form associations . . . of a thousand . . . kinds, religious, moral, serious, futile, general or restricted, enormous or diminutive." Indeed, he asserted, in "no country in the world has the principle of association been more successfully used or applied to a greater multitude of objects than in America."[6] In the hurly-burly atmosphere of New York, the merchants and bankers were, often to their great displeasure, jostled and circumvented in controlling the central institutions of the public sphere, such as museums, orchestras, theaters, and even opera houses, just as the city's public spaces slipped out of their sway.[7]

The commercial origins of midcentury cultural institutions made them resistant to the financial control and aesthetic vision of the city's mercantile elite. Museums, for example, which would later in the century become leading pillars of bourgeois self-definition, remained at midcentury socially inclusive institutions driven by profit. Most prominent in Manhattan were commercialized curiosity museums, such as Scudder's or Barnum's, which exhibited bearded ladies, legless wonders, live mud turtles, and bed curtains belonging to Mary, Queen of Scots.[8] Barnum's alone claimed to display 600,000 such curiosities by 1849.[9] These artifacts, along with themed exhibits on such topics as the "missing link" between men and apes, featuring "Mademoiselle Fanny" (an orangutan), attracted an audience ranging from manual workers to millionaire manufacturer Peter Cooper.[10] "Tasteful" art collections were to be found, if at all, only in fashionable homes, as for example the remarkable collections of George T. Strong, William Aspinwall, August Belmont, William B. Astor, and Cornelius Vanderbilt. The public display of such art, however, proved difficult: The pioneering New York Gallery of Fine Arts closed its doors in 1854, "plagued by chronic debts."[11] The modest gallery had grown out of the wholesale grocery merchant Luman Reed's private collection, which he had consolidated on the third floor of his home on Greenwich Street and made accessible one day a week.[12] Three years later, in 1857, the New-York Historical Society opened a small art gallery, whose somewhat defensive mission was "to prove to mankind that in art the present is not inferior to the past, or the New World to the Old World."[13] Despite these small efforts, New York would not see a major public fine arts institution until the late 1870s.

In a similar manner, commercial orchestras dominated the performance of music and welcomed a socially inclusive paying audience. The New York Philharmonic Orchestra, which would later in the century turn itself into a leading bourgeois cultural institution, was in the 1850s a discordant cultural battlefield where New York's mercantile elite struggled to make it into a sanctified space for the enjoyment of "high culture" music. Giving "public concerts of high-class instrumental music," however, was difficult to achieve because "[t]he people of New York . . . did not [have] a refined appreciation of instrumental music." Instead, according to the Philharmonic Society's historian, the "people" flocked to commercial entertainments with an enthusiasm that "was not the child of intelligent appreciation."[14] Indeed, by the late 1850s, the society, in its flyers, insisted "upon musical good manners [since] the inattention and heedless talking and disturbance of but a limited number of our audience are proving a serious annoyance."[15] This audience "had to be cautioned not to stand on chairs at a reception, and . . . was rebuked for their habit of resting their boots on the cushioned rails of the theaters." They had, in short, a "rude taste."[16]

The city's major theaters and opera houses, which in Europe were prominent spaces of aristocratic self-display and bourgeois pretensions, likewise remained socially inclusive spaces outside of elite control. While wealthy audiences did attend plays at Wallack's Theater, for example, its 1,000 seats also attracted the city's lesser sorts.[17] Sounding a common refrain, French banker Salomon Rothschild declared New York theaters "not worth much."[18] After a few months' exposure to New York's cultural life, Rothschild concluded, "I have rarely seen such depraved tastes; they applaud only the feeblest dramas or low-grade farces worthy of the St. Cloud fair," and, he went on, "[t]his low taste is to be seen everywhere, in the arts as well as in letters."[19]

Distaste for the masses turned into fear and loathing when the lower classes insisted on control of what was exhibited or performed. This cultural competition, combined with a dose of anti-British sentiment, came to a spectacular head in the 1849 riots over casting at the Astor Place Opera

House. On the eve of a much-publicized performance, a brawl flared up between working-class supporters of popular Shakespearean actor Edwin Forrest and the police, who protected a more upscale audience supporting an elite actor of British heritage, William Charles Macready. Troops called out to restore order, with heavy artillery at their disposal, killed twenty-two people. The city's merchants and bankers had won the battle, but they lost the war: The Opera House subsequently faltered and finally closed its doors in 1852.[20]

This sense of loss of control over the public spaces of the city was a key factor in the ground breaking of Manhattan's grandest public park – Central Park. In 1850, a group of wealthy New York merchants, centered around trader Robert Minturn, saw in such a project not only a chance for capital accumulation through rising real estate prices, but also a way to create a space removed from the disorderly city. The park would symbolize the material wealth of the city, a space equal to the grand public spaces of European cities. It would also be a haven in which bourgeois New Yorkers could flaunt their wealth without being harassed by Bowery "boors."[21] Indeed, the *New York Evening Post* editorialized that a "new park [must] be secured at once," because well-off women were "stared out of countenance by troupes of whiskered and mustachioed chatterers."[22] By the late 1850s, Central Park began to take shape.

Faced with such a tumultuous public, many among New York's mercantile elite at midcentury looked with envy at the more powerful assertions of their social equals in Paris and London, and even those of the French, British, and German provinces.[23] A city with such promise for future greatness, they believed, deserved well-ordered public spaces and world-class cultural institutions. They were eager to disprove Alexis de Tocqueville's assertion two decades earlier that "in few of the civilized nations of our time have the higher sciences made less progress than in the United States; and in few have great artists, distinguished poets, or celebrated writers been more rare."[24] New York's merchants and bankers began, in this decade, to struggle for the creation of cultural institutions worthy of their rich, dynamic, and important city. They hoped, moreover, that such institutions would endow them with a new sense of stability, permanence, and control. Appropriating the "high culture" of past ruling classes promised to crown their own claims to power with legitimacy. It would also allow them to anchor their new wealth in history and cultural achievement, and to set themselves apart from others.[25] Last but not least, it could serve as a basis for social power. New York's mercantile elite faltered, however, on the shoals of a furiously democratic metropolis.

As the mercantile elite of the city began their battle for control over the city's public spaces and public sphere, they faced a more subtle, but ultimately more significant challenge from "a rising industrialist class."[26] This class had accumulated capital in novel ways and largely outside of the kinship and social networks of New York's mercantile elite. Merchants and bankers remained the most important group of the city's businessmen, to be sure, but by 1850 manufacturers were joining the upper ranks of the tax rolls at a remarkable rate. The majority of manufacturers were artisans who had expanded their shops, transforming themselves into entrepreneurs.[27] As one historian observed, by midcentury "they were knocking at the doors of political power and social prestige so long guarded by their commercial brethren."[28]

New York led the nation in manufacturing, just as it had in trade. In 1856, 20 percent of New York's economic elite produced goods. By 1860, the city housed 4,375 manufacturing establishments, employing 90,204 workers.[29] One of every fifteen workers employed in manufacturing in the United States was hired on the island of Manhattan. Yet, New York's industry belied the stereotype of large-scale factories whose huge workrooms bristled with machinery. As Sean Wilentz has described it, New York was a "labyrinth of factories and tiny artisan establishments, central workrooms and outworkers' cellars, luxury firms and sweatwork strapping shops."[30] Large and small, new and old coexisted, making for an astoundingly varied system of enterprises that produced the widest spectrum of goods in the Americas. Indeed, the city may very well have been the most rapidly industrializing area in the world.[31] Thirty-two Manhattan shops churned out expensive carriages and coaches. Four hundred and ninety-one made fine shoes and rough boots. Dwarfing all others was the men's clothing industry, in which 21,568 workers in 303 shops produced an annual product valued at more than $17 million. Book printing came in a distant second, followed by sugar refining, newspaper printing, machinery, and piano making. Most factories were small; the average number of employees was under six, and many of their owners artisans, deeply involved in manual labor. A full one-third of all workers, however, toiled in shops with more than 100 employees, albeit in a variety of physical settings.[32] The city's largest private employers, the Novelty Works and the Morgan Works, both producing iron, each employed more than 1,000 workers, as did the Allaire Works and the clothing manufacturers of Hanford & Brother, which had 2,000 workers on its payroll.[33]

New York's predominance in trade fundamentally shaped the size and structure of its manufacturing.[34] Trade procured the raw materials necessary to produce refined sugar, iron, or pianos. New York merchants also controlled the most important national distribution networks by which manufactured goods could be sold to America's widely dispersed markets. Not least, the metropolitan region provided a peerless urban market for consumer goods, such as furniture or ready-made clothing. Local markets were especially crucial, given the expense of shipping before the spread of railroads. New York's mercantile machine itself fostered massive enterprises capable of turning copper, iron, and lumber into ships.

Merchants, moreover, were a vital source of capital for New York's fledging industrialists. By 1860, more than $61 million had been invested in the city's manufacturing sector. Although more and more artisans earned sufficient profits to expand production, most did not.[35] The financing of industrial undertakings through the sale of securities was, with the exception of railroads, largely unknown. Banks granted loans only if secured by real estate, not by future sales of a product.[36] Consequently, no one was better situated to supply needed capital than merchants, some of whom were willing to risk investments in the new factories.[37] In one prominent case, merchant-banker James Brown injected capital into the bankrupt iron manufacturer Stillman, Allen & Co. and installed Howard Potter, his brother-in-law, as secretary of the renamed Novelty Iron Works. It took the deep pockets of Brown to sustain an enterprise that, according to the Dun credit-reporting agency had "not paid any dividends."[38]

However dependent on merchant capital and services, the industrialists were not part of the same social class. Their artisan backgrounds alone set them apart from the close-knit and venerable merchants. Richard March Hoe, for example, the largest maker of printing presses, had inherited his company from his father, who had come to New York as a skilled carpenter in 1803.[39] Theodore Low DeVinne, who in 1858 became a junior partner in the printing house of Francis Hart, had been an apprentice printer at the *Gazette* in Newburgh, New York.[40] Robert Edwin Dietz, a maker of lamps, had first learned carpentry and then experimented in his "leisure hours, striving to burn various hydro-carbons which were at that time introduced for artificial lighting." Once successful, he "purchased with [his] small savings, a lamp and oil business" in 1840. By 1855, he owned a large lamp factory in New York City.[41] And Isaac Singer, by the mid-1850s a successful maker of sewing machines, had learned the machinist trade in Auburn, New York, and spent more than a decade as a traveling mechanic and inventor before producing the machine that brought his name into households throughout the world.[42] Immigrant manufacturers, in particular, according to historian Robert Ernst, often started out "as journeymen or master craftsmen and gradually accumulated enough money to acquire plants and become big employers."[43]

In this age of inventions, artisanal ingenuity could lead to economic advancement and even a limited emancipation from merchants. Printing-press maker Richard Hoe, Etna Iron Works owner John Roach, Delamater Iron Works proprietor Cornelius Delamater, and iron manufacturer George Quintard all controlled their manufacturing enterprises without the direct involvement of merchants in the ownership or operations of the firm, albeit depending on mortgaging their land and buildings to merchant-dominated banks.[44] John Roach worked for fourteen years, at a dollar a day, in the molding department of the New York Iron Works, educating himself in his free time about the principles of marine engines. In April 1852, he combined his carefully accumulated savings of $1,000 with $8,000 from his brother-in-law and acquired the Etna Iron Works, a tiny iron shop in Manhattan. One year later, Roach secured a mortgage on the small foundry building, bought out his brother-in-law, and received a favorable review from the normally skeptical Dun credit-reporting agency.[45] Closely supervising the actual work of building machines, he secured enough contracts to expand his works, until, in 1859, he employed forty workers.[46] While his best days lay ahead, when he would become a major supplier of the navy during the Civil War, Roach successfully leveraged his mechanical skills and modest family capital to become one of the city's premier industrialists. He had won his independence from old wealth by seizing opportunity in a new realm of production, and by managing his factory so well that it returned sufficient profits for expansion.

In a similar vein, Peter Cooper, one of the major industrialists in mid–nineteenth-century New York, had started out as a coachmaker's apprentice in the early 1800s. A self-educated inventor, the youthful Cooper once remarked that he "was always fussing and contriving, and was never satisfied unless [he] was doing something difficult – something that had never been done before."[47] He was a regular at curiosity museums such as Scudder's or Barnum's, looking for inspiration among the exhibited "wax works, historical relics, dwarfs, giants as well as living and stuffed animals."[48] During the 1810s, he dabbled in machines for shearing cloth, and later set up a grocery business in New York. By 1821, he had purchased a glue factory in the city for a modest $2,000, determined "to make the best glue that could be produced."[49] The enterprise proved enormously successful because of Cooper's close supervision, his commitment to improving product and production processes, and the rapidly expanding market for glue.[50] Cooper, now a shrewd businessman, diversified, investing in the first American railroad and, in 1837, in a Manhattan wire factory. A few years later, he set up a large iron works in Trenton, New Jersey. By the 1850s, Cooper's entrepreneurial activities had made him one of New York's few millionaire manufacturers, though he still saw himself "essentially [as] a master craftsman."[51]

Manufacturers also followed the leads of merchants and diversified into real estate.[52] For them, acquiring land and housing was less often an attempt to aggrandize their families' social position as it was to seek profit and security.[53] Real estate was also the standard basis for raising capital for other endeavors, as when Roach mortgaged his property to gather capital for new manufacturing equipment. Uptown residential development was a particularly promising investment and attracted many manufacturers. Robert S. Buchanan of the Lamina Beam Machine Manufacturing Company, for example, owned ten lots on 105th Street and Third Avenue.[54] Similarly, the Hoe brothers purchased the St. James Hotel in 1856.[55]

A significant 5 percent of the city's substantial taxpayers made their fortunes entirely in the building industry.[56] Builders such as Peter Bogert and contractors such as John P. Cumming amassed remarkable fortunes. Because construction required only small capital outlays for builders and contractors, it allowed for rapid social mobility.[57] John D. Crimmins, who became an important Manhattan contractor, had been the gardener at the estate of Thomas Addis Emmet until 1849.[58] Alexander Masterson, who came from Scotland to the United States on borrowed funds in 1797 and started his career as a journeyman, later acquired his own stone yard and erected large public and private buildings, such as the New York Customs House and the Old Exchange on Wall Street. When he retired in 1855, his fortune was estimated at more than $200,000.[59] William S. Dudley, a successful contractor who himself had accumulated a fair number of houses and lots, did not have "any property when he first began; but by correct habits and good management . . . raised [him]self to independence," according to the Dun credit-reporting agency.[60] Rapid social mobility and close involvement with production put builders and contractors in the same ambiguous economic and social world as the city's manufacturers.

Manufacturers, including builders and contractors, thus inhabited a very different environment from the city's mercantile elite. They had joined the ranks of the city's upper class only recently, and many had achieved a distinct status and a degree of autonomy from the merchants. While many manufacturers remained essentially artisans, a small but significant group had freed themselves from the toil and sweat of the workshop. They had utilized the opportunities provided by the emergence of integrated national markets, advances in transportation technology, and large-scale capital accumulation to emancipate themselves from their dependence on merchant capital.[61] As we will see later, their focus on production, not trade, also rooted them in different institutions, and, more importantly, in a distinct political economy, both of which would have far-reaching political consequences. Their relationship to labor, to the position of the federal government in American economic development, and to slavery, were all at odds with the mercantile elite's political economy.

❧ ❧ ❧

The social world of New York's merchants and bankers was rocked by the emergence of this new group of rising manufacturers, and a broader sense that the urban masses these industrialists employed were taking control of the city. Despite the great new economic opportunities of the 1850s, the city's merchants and bankers were on the defensive. They reacted by moving more closely together and farther apart from the rest of New York's inhabitants. They did so, first and foremost, by creating socially exclusive neighborhoods. By century's end, this impulse would transform the city into a place dramatically more socially segregated than it had ever been before. Increasingly, a family's address imparted status as a member of the "better classes." An earlier migration had already completed the separation of workplace and home for elite New Yorkers; for the city's merchants and bankers most especially, the need to be close to the wharves and warehouses in the southern parts of Manhattan no longer dictated residential location.[62] As a result, New York's mercantile elite had started to move north beginning in the 1820s.

In subsequent decades, the growth of the economy simultaneously increased the value of real estate in commercial neighborhoods and made them unpleasant areas to live in for opulent New Yorkers. The sailors, workers, and vagrants flowing into these wards were now perceived as a distinct threat to their well-being, and the substandard housing they inhabited as an aesthetic indignity. Merchants made subsequent migrations to new neighborhoods, away from the city's social ills, and into closer exclusive proximity to one another.[63] James Brown's family exemplifies this exodus. In 1846, the banker's house in lower Manhattan became unsatisfactory, because "the character of Leonard Street and the adjoining streets had greatly changed, and boarding houses and undesirable neighbors were creeping in."[64] The Browns moved uptown to what was then the city's most fashionable neighborhood, University Place in the fifteenth ward. Similarly, the merchant Charles H. Russell left his house on White Street in 1833 and moved to Broadway and Great Jones. Twenty-nine years later, in 1862, he relocated to 417 Fifth Avenue, just up the street from August Belmont's new mansion at the corner of 18th Street.[65]

As a consequence of this emphasis upon the importance of one's address to impart status, exclusive neighborhoods emerged in the city: In 1856, the streets around Washington Square and Union Square became home to the most homogeneous neighborhood in Manhattan. In the four adjacent wards to this area – the ninth, fifteenth, eighteenth, and twenty-first – 57 percent of all taxpayers assessed at more than $10,000 made their homes. In one ward, the eighteenth – between 14th and 23rd Street east of Fifth Avenue – 25 percent of all of the city's economic elite lived. Another 15 percent resided on the urban frontier, north of 23rd Street. By 1856, very few of the city's upper class lived south of Houston Street, a kind of border between "respectable" and working-class neighborhoods. Only around South Street and along the Hudson River did some merchants remain, 7 percent of the total. This evolving residential pattern, while still in its infancy, was new to a city in which for a long time rich and poor had lived in close proximity.[66] Yet it was far from complete: One in four well-to-do New Yorkers still lived spread out throughout the city, often with working-class neighbors.

Not only did the mercantile community try to isolate itself from the rest of the city, but it also created institutions to encourage concerted social action as much as to sustain business networks. Merchants and bankers had created, in the first half of the century, a number of stable associations and social clubs that enhanced their solidarity and their distinctiveness.

Places of residence of bourgeois New Yorkers, 1855.
Source: Sample of 261 New York taxpayers who were assessed on $10,000 or more of real and personal property in 1855. Map courtesy of Harvard University Map Collection.

The most important of these and the most closely tied to the merchant political economy was the Chamber of Commerce, a body of merchants and bankers founded in 1768. The organization had expanded so rapidly during the 1850s that by 1858, 70 percent of its 424 members had joined during the prior eight years.[67] Presided over by William E. Dodge, the Chamber of Commerce was pledged to the creation of a physical and political environment conducive to trade, the safeguarding of shipping, the construction of canals, and the minimization of tariffs – in short, the political economy of Atlantic trade. "Its chief function," writes one historian, "seems to have been the facility with which it gave co-ordinated expression of the views of the merchants."[68] The Chamber of Commerce was strikingly homogeneous – 71 percent of its members were engaged in trade and another 18 percent in banking. The number of industrialists in its ranks was negligibly small, totaling only six (2 percent), all of whom had joined after 1850. Three of the six were shipbuilders.[69]

Overshadowing these traditional economic associations was a relatively new phenomenon: social clubs. The oldest, the Union Club, had been formed in 1836 by "gentlemen of social distinction." It organized the merchant and financial elite of the city and counted among its members such New Yorkers as August Belmont, Samuel Tilden, and Alexander T. Stewart.[70] Membership was strictly regulated and limited to 1,000 individuals.[71] The club firmly established itself when it moved in 1855 into a new building on Fifth Avenue and 21st Street where members enjoyed a parlor, a library, a reception room, a billiard room, and a dining room with "carved black walnut paneling, and . . . beautiful paintings of game over the chimney pieces."[72] The building was the first in the city used solely as a club, testifying to the increasing importance of socially segregated spaces. Here, gentleman capitalists took their meals in a dignified atmosphere in the company of their peers instead of at the family table.

Three similar social clubs of importance existed in the 1850s, all of which had split from the Union Club: the New York Club, which was most like the Union Club; the small New York Yacht Club, founded in 1844 and dedicated to the "cultivation of naval sciences," pleasure outings, and boat races; and the Century Club, founded in 1847 to bring together writers and artists with their wealthy benefactors, among them John Jacob Astor and James W. Beekman.[73] Though ancestry played some role in membership admittance to these four clubs, identification as a "gentleman," a term in the 1850s applied mostly to merchants, bankers, and professionals and not to industrialists, determined who could join. For example, 72 percent of the members of the New York Club were engaged either in trade or finance, with manufacturers constituting a meager 2 percent. At the Union Club, 55 percent of members were engaged in trade and finance, 23 percent were lawyers and other professionals, and about 3 percent were manufacturers.[74] Ethnic and religious backgrounds did not play an overarching role: The Union Club offered membership to Jewish New Yorkers August Belmont and members of the Hendricks family.[75] The clubs, just like the Chamber of Commerce, instead provided the glue that bound one segment, but only one, of New York's economic elite firmly together.

Elite churches and synagogues further strengthened the networks of the mercantile elite.[76] "Almost every one went to church in those days," reported the Union Club, and indeed the club itself remained closed on Sunday evenings until 1856.[77] The predominant Protestant denominations were Episcopalian and Presbyterian; their social exclusivity providing the basis for these congregations' strength among opulent New Yorkers. For example, when Moses Taylor moved in 1852 from Clinton Place to 18th Street and Fifth Avenue, he changed his church membership, leaving behind his pew at the Dutch Reformed Church on Washington Square and purchasing a new one "for $700 in the more fashionable St. George's Episcopal Church on Stuyvesant Square."[78] Similarly, James Beekman, though a lifelong member of the Church of Holland, quite regularly attended services of Presbyterian or Episcopal churches.[79] Even August Belmont, though Jewish by birth and upbringing, attended an Episcopal church.[80]

The city's merchants and bankers clearly dominated some congregations, their buildings, and personnel financed from the profits derived from trade. The well-off within the Jewish community worshipped at Temple Emanu-El, and provided for its resources. Monied Christians of the mercantile elite attended the Presbyterian Church on 10th Street and University Place (steered by the banker James Brown), the Episcopal St. Mark's Church, as well as Grace Church, where high pew rents excluded all but the city's wealthiest.[81] Keeping churches and synagogues socially homogeneous was important to well-off worshippers: When St. George's, for example, moved uptown, it "scrapped" the idea of providing "free seats" and instead sold its pews.[82] With a good sense for business, the church estimated the value of its "two hundred pews on the groundfloor, ... at $94,650 and [its] ninety-three [pews] in the gallery, ... at $21,200," and sold them for prices ranging from $100 to $700 each, plus an additional "ground rent" of 8 percent yearly.[83] Not surprisingly, Grace Church was filled with what one journalist called "one of the most beautiful and fashionable congregations we ever saw gathered together," combining "[y]outh, elegance and jewelry."[84]

These churches' dependence on the wealth of their congregants was most glaringly demonstrated by the desire of ministers to keep their places of worship close to the city's ever-shifting center of wealth. If elite churches wanted to remain fashionable, that is, "filled with gay parties of ladies in feathers and moussleine-de-laine dresses," they had to move with their congregations, and this principally meant relocating farther uptown.[85] The Episcopal Grace Church – "the most fashionable and exclusive of our metropolitan 'courts of Heaven,'" according to worshiper Isaac Brown – packed up its belongings on Rector Street in 1846 to move to 10th Street and Broadway.[86] By 1853, the Fourth Avenue Presbyterian Church similarly considered its location on Bleeker Street as "too far down-town" and opened a new building on 22nd Street and Fourth Avenue.[87] And the Episcopal St. George's Church closed its old location on Beekman Street in 1846 and relocated to 18th Street, where Peter Stuyvesant had donated land for a new edifice.[88] The relocation, church administrators could not help but notice, was successful, because the amount of money collected during the weekly services increased sixfold in the ten years following the move.[89] For what had been for many years the most elite church in Manhattan – Episcopal Trinity Church – moving was more difficult, because its large edifice and important landholdings bound it to its downtown location. But eventually, the desertion of its main building by the city's wealthy motivated it, in 1855, to open "Trinity Chapel" on 25th Street.[90] Trinity, like other churches, moved with its parishioners because of its dependence on their support.[91]

While churches that catered to the city's well-to-do sought to maintain their social exclusivity, they also pointed to the distance between merchants and manufacturers. More than half of Trinity's vestrymen and wardens in 1850 were professionals or rentiers, and the other half were engaged in trade or finance, yet not a single industrialist made it into the inner circle of this church during the 1850s.[92] Similarly, St. George's vestrymen and wardens were all from the mercantile elite of the city, a full 82 percent engaged in trade or finance, again with no manufacturer included in the flock.[93]

Geography and institutions increasingly bound New York's mercantile elite together. They also set them apart, not only from the city's lower classes but also from the city's manufacturers. While controlling new forms and sometimes substantial amounts of recently acquired capital, these manufacturers lived in a different world from New York's gentlemen capitalists. Their working-class backgrounds, their often rough manners and lack of genteel education, their dearth of kinship links to the city's mercantile elite, and the nature of their work itself marked the manufacturers as upstarts. As one industrialist observed in 1845, "There is much complaint that mechanics [as many manufacturers called themselves] are not received evenly with merchants and professional men."[94] This divide was especially relevant because the manufacturers' different economic as well as cultural location led them to articulate sets of beliefs and embrace policies frequently at odds with those of the merchants.

The fault line between the social world of industrialists and that of merchants and bankers is best seen when looking at the city's richest manufacturer, Peter Cooper. Cooper was far from a typical manufacturer, since his enormous wealth easily matched that of all but the very wealthiest bankers and merchants. Yet in many ways, Cooper and his family were different from the typical merchant family of his time. At a moment when capital-rich New Yorkers increasingly embraced more lavish forms of public consumption, Cooper disdained any ostentatious display of riches. Despite his wealth, he employed for most of his life only two servants (after his death, his son-in-law would employ fourteen servants in the same house).[95] When his wife bought an elaborate carriage, he exchanged it for a more frugal model.[96] He dressed simply and allegedly had to be convinced to purchase a dress suit when he joined the reception committee welcoming the Prince of Wales to the city.[97] He had built the bed he slept in with his own hands. Only in the 1850s did Peter Cooper fill the gaps in his education and begin to train himself in grammar and spelling.[98] Though Cooper had moved into the respectable Gramercy neighborhood in 1850, he had lived before at 28th Street and Fourth Avenue near his glue factory and directly next to the tracks of the New York & Harlem Railroad. When he moved, he avoided the city's most fashionable living quarters on and around Fifth Avenue. And though his new home was large, it was simple. After he died, his son-in-law completely redecorated the house – adding marble stairways, stuffed peacocks, copper-lined bathtubs, and a clock mounted on a bust of Napoleon, all things Cooper himself would have scorned.[99] Cooper also provided his children with vocational training – handicrafts for the boys and housekeeping, cooking, and sewing for his daughter Amelia – which most merchants would not have dreamed of doing. Sharing Cooper's philosophy, publisher Horace Greeley quite paradigmatically asserted, "[y]outh should be a season of introduction in Industry and the Useful Arts, as well as in Letters and Sciences mastered by their aid. Each child should be trained to skill and efficiency in productive Labor, Study, and Recreation."[100] Nothing of this sort crossed the minds of most merchants. Not surprisingly, Cooper's daughter Amelia did not marry into a merchant family, but instead took the hand of her father's business partner, ironmonger Abram Hewitt, with her father's blessing.[101] Cooper's extraordinary position among the city's producers foreshadowed not only the material possibilities of manufacturing but also the ways in which the attendant social independence allowed for a new kind of ideology and, eventually, the building of institutions that reflected the manufacturers' way of thinking.

While some industrialists, such as Isaac Singer, had different social aspirations, Cooper, despite his extraordinary wealth, was quite typical of the manufacturers of New York City.[102] Manufacturers generally lived in more mixed neighborhoods than the city's merchants. Instead of congregating around Washington Square, they preferred the sixteenth and twentieth wards, an area west of Fifth Avenue between 14th and 40th Streets where many of their workshops and factories were situated.[103] Characteristically, sugar refiner Alexander Stuart lived right next to his "enormous refinery," as did all three Steinways, who built brownstones adjacent to their piano factory (on 52nd Street and Lexington Avenue), Heinrich Steinway's back door even opening directly onto the factory's courtyard.[104] Manufacturers inhabited a world quite distinct from the one of the mercantile elite, a distinction directly rooted in their different route to wealth and the different imperatives of the particular capital they accumulated.

The city's mercantile and financial elite looked warily on those industrialists. George T. Strong, a powerful and wealthy lawyer, derided Cooper as a "self-made millionaire glue-boiler."[105] When Cooper received the Prince of Wales, he was chided for "playing the patriarchal Beau Nash with an assiduity at least as agonizing to its unaccustomed object as it was amusing to all the world besides."[106] Tellingly, the credit-reporting agency Dun remained quite skeptical about manufacturers. In 1860, they described industrialist John Roach as a "rough illiterate kind of man," pointing out that he "has made all he is worth."[107] And despite Roach's phenomenal prosperity during the Civil War, Dun reported a "lack of confidence in his final success."[108] Even the extremely successful maker of printing presses Richard Hoe was still a "machinist" for Dun.[109] It was not unusual to see industrialists, such as the iron master John Roach, described as "poorly educated, rugged, brusque and bold."[110] Industrialists, in turn, often scorned the city's "Wall Street Gentry."[111] When banks failed in September of 1857, Peter S. Hoe announced that he had "no sympathy" for "Brokers or Gamblers" and hoped that "they and others will have to seek a more legitimate calling."[112]

There are many reasons for this distance: For one, most manufacturers had acquired their wealth recently. Peter Cooper, John Roach, and Isaac Singer all had accumulated their riches during their own lifetimes. Although many had used kinship ties to gain access to capital, their rapid social mobility had been largely of their own making. New wealth did not easily support claims to social exclusiveness. Yet the newness of their wealth alone cannot account for their distance from the city's mercantile elite. Quite a number of merchants and bankers had, in fact, also accumulated most of their capital in their own lives – August Belmont is one example.

Merchants shunned industrialists because manufacturing involved the dirty, smelly, and decidedly unrefined world of the factory and a day-to-day struggle with its workers. Industrialists, by contrast, often saw, beneath the grime and grit, a mechanical world that fascinated them.[113] Cooper, for example, strongly believed in the possibilities of science and invested in many inventions, some of them preposterous.[114] He shared this interest in technology with his son-in-law, Abram S. Hewitt, who always kept abreast of the newest developments in mining, studied manufacturing processes, and experimented with innovative ways to make iron.[115] Similarly, the Steinways continually improved their pianos, in the process becoming increasingly familiar with their skilled workers. The Steinways and Hoes, as well as Cooper and Hewitt, saw themselves as producers first and foremost.[116] Using technology, they molded the material world alongside their workers; their profits derived from what they perceived to be a most legitimate source – productive labor.

Excluded from the social universe of the city's mercantile and financial elite, industrialists also created their own institutions. "[M]echanics and manufacturers," as one of them observed, "found rallying points in the American and Mechanics' Institutes."[117] Since 1830, the Mechanics' Institute, dominated by masters of their craft, offered lectures on "natural and mechanical philosophy," classes in mechanical drawings and mathematics, and "Meetings, Debates, and Discussions for the benefit of its members."[118] It boasted a library holding a large number of volumes on the natural sciences and engineering, as well as on philosophy and history, ranging from *Newton's Mathematical Principles of Natural Philosophy* to *The Natural History of Insects,* and from François-Marie Arouet Voltaire to Adam Smith.[119] In typical fashion, the institute provided a forum for exchanging technical expertise and opportunities to train apprentices – two central concerns of industrialists.[120]

Similarly, the American Institute, founded in 1829, organized industrial-ists (such as clothing manufacturer William H. Dikeman, printing-press maker Robert Hoe, and builder James N. Wels, Jr.) for "the purpose of encouraging and promoting domestic industry in this State."[121] Represent-ing those "citizens who enjoy that extraordinary genius for originality of thinking and invention so distinguishing this new world," they exhibited the products of America's manufacturers, provided training in engineering and mathematics, and discussed "philosophical subjects."[122] These institu-tions were the nurseries of a different elite sensibility from that of the mer-chants, a sensibility that often translated into a distinct set of politics.

The world of gentlemen capitalists, inhabited by the likes of James Brown, August Belmont, and Robert B. Minturn, was poles apart from that of the manufacturers.[123] As we have seen, they grew up in different kinship net-works, experienced a different kind of education, frequented different social clubs, and enjoyed different kinds of work. Most important for their self-definition, merchants and bankers were only indirectly involved in production processes, thereby creating a distance from both machines and workers. Seeking to maintain an image as arbiters of the market, as risk-taking but conservative traders, they did not directly concern them-selves with how a product came into being, but with its exchange.

Removed from the day-to-day efforts in factories and involved instead with negotiating myriad personal relationships, merchants considered themselves gentlemen, even "statesmen."[124] They were "bound to know something about the policy of foreign nations and of political economy," observed manufacturer James J. Mapes.[125] More so than the industrialists, they were destined to benefit from striking up friendships in social clubs and marrying their children to the "right" partners, thus favoring social characteristics that merged a gentlemanly ideal with economic success. *Hunt's Merchants' Magazine* emphasized that "[j]udgment of expediency, insight into character, tact, quickness of comprehension, and acquaintance with the present history of the world, are perhaps the main essentials of a business education."[126] Trading gave people a degree of personal indepen-dence and free time, an opportunity to mingle with their own kind while advancing their economic interests, an opportunity absent from the world of the Coopers and Steinways. "Commerce," as a result, advanced to the "most honorable of employments," socially superior to manufacturing.[127] Preeminent in the economy, "the merchants of the United States compose the true aristocracy of the country," proclaimed *Hunt's Merchants' Maga-zine*: "They really rule, whoever may seem to hold the reins of power."[128]

If the ownership of particular kinds of capital informed the identities of bourgeois New Yorkers, it was not surprising that this spectacularly diverse economic elite also organized itself along ethnic and religious lines. As noted earlier, only a minority of the city's major capitalists had been born locally. Hundreds of wealthy migrants came to the city each year, many from neighboring regions of New England and New York, others from England, Germany, and other distant countries. And like their poorer counterparts, these migrants often banded together, forming the German Society, the Society of the Friendly Sons of St. Patrick, the St. Andrew's Society (organizing the Scottish-born elite), and the Hebrew Benevolent Society.[129] Since regional identities ran almost as strong as national ones in the new republic, traders from Connecticut and Massachusetts had founded the New England Society of New York in 1805. And fearful of being swept aside by all these newcomers, old residents of the City of New York and their descendants, many of them of Dutch ancestry, united in 1836 in the St. Nicholas Society, presided over by James Beekman.[130]

While these organizations institutionalized the great ethnic diversity of the city's upper class, they were in other ways harbingers of the potential rapport between merchants and industrialists. Under the umbrella of a particular ethnicity or heritage group, such societies brought together men of means from both merchant and manufacturing worlds, while excluding their less-well-off ethnic compatriots. The German Society, for example, included lawyer Friedrich Kapp, banker August Belmont, piano manufacturer Charles Steinway, shipping merchant Gustav Schwab, railroad speculator Henry Villard, pencil manufacturer Eberhard Faber, and sugar refiner, banker, and railroad speculator William Havemeyer.[131] In similar fashion, the Friendly Sons of St. Patrick comprised mostly merchants, but also builders, lawyers, and the owners of a drydock.[132] And the Hebrew Benevolent Society organized apparel manufacturers, dry goods merchants, and physicians, among others.[133]

Vibrant and prescient these organizations may have been, but they were never to become the dominant form of social organization for the city's economic elite. Indeed, like all other Americans, New York's economic elite embraced multiple identities. The ethnic diversity of merchants as well as industrialists was a point of pride, not contention. And it was easily transcended: Elite social clubs, neighborhoods, commercial associations, and cultural institutions, as well as political mobilizations, were all ethnically diverse. Ethnic identities did not become dominant, because social, economic, and political interests and inclinations did not express themselves predominantly along ethnic lines. Indeed, as one historian has argued, "[s]ome of the European commercial and financial magnates were associated only incidentally with the immigrant communities."[134] Merchants, bankers, and manufacturers might have been members of the German Society (such as August Belmont, for example), but they socialized, negotiated business deals, and mobilized politically with other wealthy New Yorkers of different backgrounds. In a world of global capitalism, of which New York was an important part, it would have been difficult, and usually unprofitable, to do otherwise.

Yet in order to understand the overlapping as well as distinct identities of the city's merchants, bankers, and manufacturers as common members of an economic elite, we must look not only at their social worlds and the institutions and clubs they built but to their broader system of beliefs, values, prejudices, and mores – in short, their ideology. Their ideology provided them with a road map of the city's and nation's social terrain, reflecting both their diverse, conflicting interests and the potential basis for a shared understanding. Often, their convictions were open-ended, rooted in their deeply held faith in the dynamic, promising, and integrative nature of modern bourgeois society. Almost always, their diverse social and economic milieus led them to sharply different assessments of the nature and direction of the world they had helped create. But despite these disagreements, their ideology had within it the seeds of collective identities and purposeful social action. And indeed, some of these beliefs brought upper-class New Yorkers together and enabled them at times to act collectively.

≈ ≈ ≈

Of course, New York's merchants, bankers, rentiers, professionals, and manufacturers, and, for that matter, most northerners, shared a number of common assumptions. A commitment to progress, markets, and democracy was common to all. Well-to-do New Yorkers took pride in the world they had helped create and the institutions that had facilitated the economic development of the past half century.[135] When the manufacturers' American Institute opened its annual exhibition in 1855, it proudly asserted that the displayed products "nourish . . . the pride of national independence."[136] Columbia College junior John Ward expressed a similar sentiment with youthful optimism in 1857 when he marveled at

Canals & railroads intersecting the broad surface of our fertile land & pouring the treasures of the far West into the lap of our proud city. . . . The hum of the steam engine resounding in almost every village. A treasury overflowing with money &

last not least a happy people in every sense of the word. When we compare the flourishing state of affairs with the condition of downtrodden Europe a glow of pride swells every American bosom & a secret conviction steals over the mind that government under whose protection such prosperity continues, must be sound at heart.[137]

Optimism about the boundless opportunities of the future infected all, manufacturers as well as merchants, builders as well as bankers.

Though rapid change created some anxieties, the city's economic elite saw it first and foremost as a validation of the republican experiment. Economic prosperity was, in their minds, the accomplishment of free individuals in a democratic society. The New-York Historical Society, a bastion of the mercantile elite, understood its mission exactly in documenting the connection between freedom and prosperity.[138] In similar ways, the manufacturers' American Institute proudly proclaimed that in the United States "are enthroned the precious things of the earth, instead of dynasties of the old world."[139] The United States had succeeded economically because it allowed its citizens, the "freest people on earth," without despotic interference, to follow their natural inclination to maximize profits.[140]

Combining Protestant ethics with classical liberal economic ideas, New York's economic elite by the 1850s accepted markets as the primary institutions for regulating production, distribution, and consumption.[141] As Elisha P. Hurlbut, a New York City attorney, lectured in 1845, no political authority had a right to interfere with markets: "Just government will confer no special privileges; its power will be exerted only in the vindication and defense of human rights."[142] In these markets, God had made people responsible for their own fate; creative engagement with the material world brought success on earth and acknowledgment in heaven. There was opportunity because nonmarket forms of domination – so prevalent in Europe and the American South – had given way to freedom. Departing from earlier mercantilist ideas and dismissing working-class notions of a moral economy, New York's men of property saw people as responsible for their own fate.[143] "[S]uccess," they proclaimed, "springs from no condition of birth or accident."[144] As the Association for Improving the Conditions of the Poor (AICP) observed in the wake of the economic crisis of 1857, in the United States, "all are peers, and every citizen is a sovereign. . . . All being parties to the social compact, and on footing of perfect equality in respect to rights, no one man has rights which are not common to all, consequently no one has a right to demand work and wages from another."[145] Such views went well with a belief in the fundamental harmony of interests among different social groups. Emphasizing the fluidity of social divisions and the prevalence of social mobility, New York's upper class made the denial of the very existence of any kind of meaningful class divisions in American society the cornerstone of their world view.[146]

In a society structured by markets and social mobility, free individuals created free institutions that, in turn, facilitated economic initiative. This relationship between republicanism and progress made wealthy New Yorkers of the 1850s supportive of democratic institutions. While democratic revolutions were being suppressed all over Europe, New York's merchants, bankers, and manufacturers defended the right of people to govern themselves. Sugar merchant and manufacturer William Havemeyer, for example, actively supported the Hungarian Revolution of 1848, and when its leader, Louis Kossuth, arrived in New York City, he "was received by unbound enthusiasm."[147] Manufacturer Charles Haswell saw the "thousands of skilled workmen" in the shipyards of Manhattan as "the sturdiest foundations of our civil government."[148] To be sure, questions persisted as to the wisdom of universal male suffrage, reservations that came to the fore in the context of the nativist movement of the 1850s, with its calls for the disenfranchisement of immigrants (one proponent proclaimed, "I am no democrat"). But even then, the calls for disenfranchisement were not formulated as a class issue. As rabid a nativist as Thomas Whitney thought moderate intelligence, morality, and "unwavering patriotism" to be sufficient qualifications for suffrage.[149] And others, such as the *New York Journal of Commerce,* balanced these voices, believing that it would be wrong to "interfere with the qualifications of voters."[150] Alexis de Tocqueville had been right when he observed two decades earlier that in America, opponents of suffrage rights "hide their heads."[151] Optimistic about the future of the republic, most well-to-do New Yorkers did not see a conflict between universal male suffrage and the sharpening social tensions engendered by a dynamic capitalism, in contrast to some visiting Europeans who felt (despite their liberal inclinations) that in "this country of exaggerated liberty . . . universal suffrage confers authority on persons who are not worthy."[152]

Though capital-owning New Yorkers by and large shared this pride in economic progress, markets, and democratic institutions, merchants and manufacturers articulated quite divergent views on other matters, their very different cultural, social, and economic worlds infusing distinct and even mutually hostile beliefs. Merchants first and foremost desired stability and predictability. Rooted in the world of trade, they shunned disruptions of any kind, desiring a society orderly in its domestic relations and peaceful in its relations to the larger world. To them, order still depended, to some extent, on social hierarchies, and thus they struggled to maintain their position as stewards of the community.

Merchants and bankers, the oldest segment of the city's economic elite, saw themselves as the central characters in the country's rapid economic development. It was merchants who had built a large cotton trade, sent clippers to China to bring back tea, and raised the capital for the railroads' conquest of the continent. As trader Pelatiah Perit remarked proudly about the city's merchants: "Of their enterprise you have evidence in the crowded shipyards and wharves of our city, and in the countless sails which whiten every ocean."[153] "Commerce," seconded Charles King, president of Columbia College, "is the interpreter of the wants of all other pursuits, the exchanger of all values, the conveyor of all products."[154] Merchants saw commerce and trade as central to both the past and future growth of the American economy, in sharp contrast to industrialists, who emphasized the ingenuity and inventiveness of America's mechanics as the basis for that development.[155] Confidently, *Hunt's Merchants' Magazine* asserted that "[t]he influence of the Feudal Lord has passed into the Merchant's hands. . . . The fate of nations is now decided at the Bourse and Exchange."[156] Commerce brought not only wealth and power but also "a vast humanizing and beneficent system, [a] handmaid of religion, of civilization, of philanthropy, of the arts, and of every good influence."[157] "This city," in short, "is the creation of Commerce."[158]

Because merchants saw trade as central to the unfolding economic progress, they emphasized the securing of its continued expansion. Nothing was more important to this goal than peace. The relationship between trade and peace had already been articulated by liberal thinkers, who had predicted that as market relationships replaced the need for domestic coercion, they would have the same effect on relationships among states. Thomas Paine and Immanuel Kant, for example, had argued that monarchy and war went hand in hand, as did trade and peace, a view New York's merchants shared.[159] "Peace," exclaimed Charles King on the occasion of the opening in 1858 of a new building of the New York Chamber of Commerce, was the "first necessity of Commerce – the vital breath of liberty! – the highest obligation of Christian civilization."[160] According to the city's merchants, commerce's "enlightened and liberalizing spirit . . . harmonizes conflicting interests and reconciles even national antipathies."[161] They saw not war, but trade as the "great concern of society, and the very pivot of power."[162] Embracing internationalist outlook, merchants perceived themselves as the bearers of a fundamentally cosmopolitan spirit, a view undoubtedly strengthened by the memory of the devastating impact of the war of 1812. "Mercantile pursuits," argued the *American Merchant*, "discourag[e] physical conflicts between nations."[163] Without despotic rulers, enlightened free trade among free nations would create a common interest in preventing war.[164] This desire for peace extended, of course, to their own nation, and would eventually bring many merchants into conflict with the city's manufacturers.

The merchantile elite's interest in order and stability also fostered their claim to moral stewardship of their community.[165] "You owe duties to society as a man, a citizen, and a millionaire," lectured *Hunt's Merchants' Magazine,* and suggested that a merchant respond to claims of charity "most nobly."[166] The magazine counseled its readers that ["s]uccess should induce liberality. . . . How pitiable is the condition of that sordid wretch who has amassed a fortune," yet gives nothing "to reach the poor and needy."[167] Benevolent activities revealed merchants' belief in social hierarchies, hierarchies that placed on the stewards of the community the burden of demonstrating their moral leadership with deeds.[168]

Merchants' attitudes toward the ever-growing number of wage workers in the city and beyond reflected their sense of stewardship. Because merchants and bankers derived profits largely from exchange, instead of from production, they easily embraced a paternalist relationship to those in their employ, "exercis[ing] . . . a watchful care over them."[169] On a larger scale, with the production and export of agricultural commodities central to the mercantile elite's vision of the American political economy, they anticipated that industrial wage work would remain marginal to the nation, and that northern workers, the "bone and sinew of our population," would indirectly benefit from the profits derived from trade.[170] These profits, in effect, allowed merchants to embrace a sense of political and moral obligation toward society, to believe that they "do now exert . . . a greater amount of influence for good or evil than any other class."[171] Most telling, in the immediate aftermath of the 1857 economic crisis, they repeatedly expressed sympathy for the misery suffered by the large number of unemployed, blamed the crisis and not the poor themselves for their fate, and actively supported public works as well as private charity.[172] "We are a Christian people," editorialized the *Journal of Commerce,* "and must do as we might reasonably wish to be done by, were we in the place of those actually in want for the necessaries of life."[173] Not surprisingly, then, merchants also saw strikes as rooted less in economic grievances than in "brooding hate" they blamed on both employers and workers. Because of "superior intelligence and the advantage of their position," employers bore the major responsibility to alleviate these conflicts, so that "both classes learn that their interests are one."[174] Such attitudes, however, did not preclude hostility to strikes if they created unacceptable levels of social upheaval. Indeed, the mercantile elite's relationship to workers was not so much a question of profits as it was a question of order.

Yet order and free markets were somewhat of a contradiction, and this created anxiety among some of the city's merchants. Older traders, having witnessed the destruction of the contained mercantile world of the 1820s and 1830s, felt threatened by the influx of new merchants and, most especially, by those who accumulated their capital in entirely new endeavors – the manufacturers. The rise of manufacturers brought with it a transformed and seemingly more dangerous metropolis. The city had changed rapidly; its population, for example, had quadrupled in the past thirty years, and the fastest-growing segment were the workers who powered industrial enterprises. The lawyer William Betts expressed the resulting anxiety well when he lectured to the members of New York's St. Nicholas Society that "[y]ou present the singular spectacle of being strangers in your native home. So rapid has been the growth of this crowded metropolis; . . . so constant and increasing have been the changes; that an absence of five and twenty years, would render the recognition of the place of your nativity, no easy task."[175] And the lawyer Edwards Pierrepont, on the occasion of the death of his colleague Theodore Sedgwick, expressed similar fears:

I ask, if you do not find the rich dissatisfied that they are governed by the ignorant and poor? – the poor dissatisfied that they are not rich? – the laborer dissatisfied with the wages of honest toil, and striving to get into some office? – those in office dissatisfied to perform their duties for the allotted pay, and seeking more gain by the shameless plunder of the public? And the North and South dissatisfied with each other. . . . I have said this much, . . . being well aware that I speak in advance of the times; but I leave the times to overtake these fleeting words.[176]

Pierrepont's words were quite prescient. His concerns spoke to a growing animosity between rich and poor in the antebellum city that was deepened by a strong correspondence between class position and national origin. These tensions were expressed in the fledging labor and worker movements that dotted the city's landscape, the violent confrontations between police and the urban masses that flared up in the Astor Place riots of 1849, and elite preoccupation with "corruption" and state spending. Yet these developments presaged a far deeper hostility that would mark the class relations of Gilded Age America and leave a deep mark on the sensibilities, ideas, activities and politics of the city's economic elite in the latter years of the nineteenth century.[177]

Whereas the city's merchants and bankers saw their own and the nation's future in a society characterized by commerce, stability, and peace, manufacturers embraced a different vision. Indeed, manufacturers often harbored pronounced hostility toward the city's merchants and bankers, whom they saw as nonproducers living off the labor of others, agitating for free trade, importing cheap goods from Europe, and providing credit only on harsh terms. American industry, they believed, is a "widespread elm, with scores of parasites clinging to its trunk"– with the city's merchants prominently represented among those parasites.[178] Manufacturers were superior, they asserted, because "[u]nlike commerce," manufacturing did not merely consist in the exchange of goods, but in "giving them a new form and greatly increased value. . . . As an agent of civilization, all other pursuits fade before it."[179] Manufacturers saw themselves as part of the "producing classes" or just as "labor," drawing a dividing line between themselves and the commercial or financial bourgeoisie. Indeed, while Sean Wilentz correctly notes that "the defense of the 'producing classes' [included] an amalgam of 'honorable' anticapitalist small masters and wage earners," it also allowed more substantial manufacturers to rally under the banner of an ill-defined but deeply rooted producerism.[180] This set manufacturers clearly apart from the mercantile elite of the city. Not surprisingly, in turn, merchants complained that "[a]s a class [they] rarely have justice awarded to them by writers and speakers. If a preacher wishes to depict any evil practices in the community, he most generally selects the mercantile profession to illustrate his theory. . . . It is time, we think, that this constant tirade against merchants should cease."[181]

The city's manufacturers, however, had no intention of embracing the cultural, ideological, and political impetus of the city's merchants. They believed that they alone were forging America's future. It was a future that was to be even more glorious because of Americans' "extraordinary genius for originality of thinking and invention."[182] Believing in the promise of science, they thought of "man [as] the maker of things left unmade by his Creator."[183] Whereas merchants ascribed human progress to commerce, the industrialists ascribed it to "the mechanics of the world," without whom people would still be "stripped stark naked, with neither house, nor bed, nor bread, – naked as an earth-worm."[184] Central to the manufacturers world view was a positive attitude toward labor. Glorifying the "mechanic arts," they argued that "[t]he dignity of labor is in its results, and not in the form of employment."[185] Peter Cooper, quite typically, was known to be "passionately fond of his work."[186] According to one of his biographers, he "profoundly realized that temperance, industry, frugality, and patience were the necessary preliminaries to any longed-for achievement."[187] Cooper's son-in-law, Abram Hewitt, often slept only four or five hours a day, never took a vacation, and was said to lie awake at night planning his next day's activities.[188]

As employers of a large number of wage workers, industrialists were more concerned with the problems of labor than their mercantile counterparts. The success of industrialists' business undertakings, after all, related directly to the wages they paid, as well as to their employees' productivity. There was an immediacy in their relationship to workers that was entirely lacking from the horizon of merchants.[189] Labor concerns were strengthened by the fact that by 1850, the old trade organizations had fallen apart; workers had organized into unions and were increasingly experienced in the use of strikes.[190] Throughout the decade, a variety of workers – coachmen, pianoforte makers, cartmen, firemen, house painters, carvers, marble polishers, journeymen ironmolders, box makers, cigar makers, tailors, printers, carpenters, and coopers – demanded higher wages and better working conditions, with mixed but notable success.[191]

Despite these limited challenges, most manufacturers, like merchants, believed in the mutual interest of capital and labor, a belief that came naturally to a group of employers in close contact with their workers.[192] They expected that for skilled, temperate, and native-born workers, wage labor was to be merely a way station en route to economic independence. If jobs were lacking, agricultural expansion in the West would provide a new route to realize their independence.[193] As long as there was opportunity, there would be no permanent proletariat and, correspondingly, no permanent poverty. Opportunity, as industrialists saw it, was a right of the citizens of the republic. This view contrasted with merchants' assumptions of a paternalist responsibility toward the "deserving" poor, a responsibility that grew out of their "duty" as stewards of the community.

For these manufacturers, free labor was the basis of the Republic, and in order to secure opportunities for all, the prospects for industry and agriculture had to be promising. Horace Greeley, the publisher of the *Tribune* and a leading spokesman for this position, wanted to guarantee "each man . . . an assured chance to earn, and then an assurance of the just fruits of his labors."[194] Greeley believed "that there need be, and should be, no paupers."[195] Even during the crisis of 1857, the *Tribune* argued that "a true and rightly constituted state could take care that none of its members were forced to steal or doomed to starve for want of work."[196]

The free-labor ideology of these manufacturers stressed the preservation of individual opportunity. Yet in sharp contrast to workers, who embraced such discourse to empower their collective struggles, manufacturers had hardly any tolerance for strikes and assertive unions. The free-labor *Tribune*, for example, showed little patience with demonstrating workers in the wake of the 1857 crisis.[197] Workers, in the eyes of industrialists, had to be molded to assume their position among the respectable working class, many employers going to some lengths to teach them frugality and good work habits. The maker of printing presses Richard Hoe, for example, instituted an evening school, requiring his apprentices to study mechanical drawing and mathematics.[198] He also instituted the "Mutual Relief Society of Richard Hoe and Company's Works," providing insurance benefits to workers and educating them in a "Prevention of Sickness Committee."[199] While such measures were at times motivated by the desire to circumvent unionization, at first they arose more generally from an earnest desire to make proletarian work only a stop on the path to true independence and, thus, republican citizenship.

Nothing better symbolized the industrialists' worldview than Peter Cooper's grandest project, Cooper Union. Cooper laid the cornerstone for his school in 1853, opening it five years later.[200] Like the efforts put forth by the merchants, the Union symbolized the industrialists' desire for stewardship of the community, yet its primary emphasis was quite distinct: to educate the city's working people in natural and social sciences, with a particular weight on practical education.[201] It included an astronomical observatory and rooms for women to study "practical and natural sciences."[202] Emerging from Cooper's fundamental belief in the mutual interests of entrepreneur and worker, the project expressed how closely he still linked himself to the city's workers. The Union, as he saw it, was to provide the city's youth with means to "enable [them] to improve and better their conditions."[203] Cooper Union stood in some contrast to the project that merchants and bankers planned at the same time, the establishment of Central Park, which was to be built in upper Manhattan, too far for most workers to be in easy reach. Whereas the Union invited the many to study the basics of mechanics, Central Park was intended to give the "better sorts" a public space fit for their own recreation, a pastoral retreat removed from the disorderly city.[204]

At the heart of the manufacturers' project, therefore, was a desire to bring the benefits of frugality, learning, and work to a large segment of the population. Though many of these efforts had repressive characteristics, they were employed to draw workers into the fold of the manufacturers' particular form of bourgeois morality. This universalism was most clearly expressed in the industrialists' efforts to reform the city's working class outside of their workshops. In these reform efforts, manufacturers would find common ground with some of the city's merchants. It was, hence, in the interaction with workers that merchants and manufacturers could overcome, though still only tentatively, the divide that stood between them.

Though disagreeing on the precise meaning of proletarianization, both manufacturers and the mercantile elite saw themselves as stewards of the community and sensed their increasing lack of control over the city and its inhabitants. In response, they asserted their authority over the public sphere and over the city's poorer inhabitants by creating, financing, and running vigorous reform movements – movements that were part of a wave of religiously inspired reform efforts that swept the United States for more than three decades.[205] Combining their belief that salvation was to come from industry, sobriety, and piety with a new evangelical fervor, they found multiple ways to involve themselves in the material and spiritual life of New York's laboring classes.[206] They worked with the Sabbatarian reform and temperance movements.[207] They formed and financed numerous benevolent associations. Some, such as the American Home Missionary Society, dispatched preachers, spread the gospel, or advocated temperance; others, such as the Association for Improving the Conditions of the Poor (AICP), distributed charity. Still others demanded the abolition of slavery.[208] The religious concern for souls helped justify radical, far-reaching efforts to remold the lives of their less-well-off brethren. In New York, specifically, their most important goal was the reform of the city's working class and poor, and many of these organizations concentrated on building institutions to rescue the "worthy poor" – by building asylums for widowed women or orphans, for instance. "God," said James Beekman, "is doubtless to be glorified by active duty."[209] Elite women played a central role in such efforts; as guardians of morality in the home, they appropriated the role of guardians of society.[210]

The most important vehicle for elite reform efforts in the 1850s was Robert B. Minturn's AICP, founded in 1843 to eradicate poverty and elevate the poor, and it was the AICP that drew significant numbers of manufacturers to its fold. The association tried to rationalize the previously erratic system of charity by developing an elaborate system of home visitors who allocated relief to those who had fallen into distress. Of the twenty-four original subscribers to the 1848 incorporation of the AICP, seventeen can be identified: eight were merchants, three bankers, five professionals, and one the owner of a large industrial enterprise, Horatio Allen, who steered the New York Novelty Works.[211] In the 1850s, other manufacturers, such as the molding-mill owner A. T. Serrell, the carriage builders John Stephanson and James Brewster, and the iron founder Noah Worrall, joined the AICP leadership.[212] Those who funded the organization's activities represented a cross section of the city's well-to-do, 41 percent engaged in trade and 24 percent in manufacturing.[213] These activist merchants, bankers, and manufacturers exuded an extraordinary confidence in the value of their work. Seeing that "marked changes are transpiring in the social conditions of the people [and that the] laboring population, constituting a large part of the community, appear not to obtain a proportionate share of the growing prosperity around them," they announced confidently that "pauperism is an anomaly in our country, an exotic to our soil."[214] These reformers sincerely believed that poverty could be eradicated.[215]

Upper-class New Yorkers widely shared this belief. Indeed, the reform movement, and especially the AICP, was one of the few institutions to transcend the divide between the mercantile elite and the manufacturers. In their common position as members of the city's economic elite, they saw themselves as the moral center of the community with duties to their fellow men. They worked together to ensure harmonious class relations by seeking to instill proper bourgeois morals and habits in the urban masses. It was their agreement, indeed, that enabled them to act collectively. This common concern with class relations evident in the AICP foreshadowed the emerging bourgeois solidarities of the postbellum years. In the 1850s, however, bourgeois women and men did not run these organizations in the name of their class, but in the name of God. They believed it possible to redeem souls, a responsibility that came naturally to a group of New Yorkers who felt obliged to impose their values on all of the city's citizens. The universalism inherent in the evangelical project stood in stark contrast to attitudes in later years, when bourgeois New Yorkers would see most workers as beyond redemption, would paint them as racially inferior, and would justify their reform efforts increasingly in terms of the protection of their own property.

During the 1850s, however, this universalism would motivate a few bourgeois New Yorkers to face the one institution that so flagrantly violated the most fundamental bourgeois right to self-ownership – slavery. The ensuing struggle between North and South over this issue was replicated in a struggle between various segments of New York City's economic elite. In this conflict, the distinct identities, beliefs, and interests of manufacturers and merchants would find their clearest expression, demonstrating that social and ideological differences mattered a great deal. And it was here, in the realm of politics, that they would matter most for the future of American society.

3

The Politics of Capital

Challenged by the city's working class and its rising manufacturers, New York's merchants and bankers struggled to maintain their political power. Since the American Revolution, they had enjoyed great influence over the agenda of the national government, often in coalition with the slaveholders of the South, as well as a controlling position in municipal administration. By the 1850s, however, this once seemingly stable world had given way under the combined strains of proletarianization and elite differentiation. New interests had come to the fore. Urban workers advocated an activist local government, and the rising manufacturers demanded an end to the domination of national politics by slaveholders and their merchant allies.

As the traditional relationship between economic might on the one side and political power on the other side became ever more tenuous, all segments of the city's economic elite experimented with new forms of political mobilization. During the 1850s, they struggled over two core issues: the future shape of the nation's political economy, especially the future of slavery, and control over the city. Because upper-class New Yorkers could not agree on the former, however, moments during which common approaches to the latter could have brought them together were extremely rare. Instead, disagreements about how to respond to the ever more aggressive policies of southern slaveholders brought different groups of bourgeois New Yorkers into bitter conflict with one another. These conflicts revealed and deepened fault lines that were marked by the kind of capital individuals controlled, by religious convictions, and by political party allegiances – most importantly, the mercantile elite on the one side and the rising manufacturers on the other. As a result, the vast majority of the city's economic elite, while still powerful, was on the political defensive throughout the 1850s. And eventually, most of them experienced the secession winter of 1860/61 as their most devastating political defeat ever.

Engaging in politics, of course, was nothing new to upper-class New Yorkers. Though they spent most of their days running their businesses, attending to their families, and socializing with their peers, affairs of state were never far from their minds. After all, the conflict over the control of the policies and institutions of state directly affected their business interests. Although the American state of the 1850s was weak in comparison with contemporary European states, capital accumulation was still in numerous ways based on the power of local, state, and national governments:[1] courts enforced contracts; Congress determined tariffs; the federal government registered patents; state legislatures passed incorporation laws, built canals, and gave railroad grants; state militias forced Indians out of western territories; and the local police enforced social order.[2] Consequently, many merchants, industrialists, bankers, builders, real estate speculators, lawyers, and rentiers felt compelled to involve themselves in politics. Indeed, commented an annoyed Salomon Rothschild in 1860, "[p]eople are concerned here with virtually nothing but politics."[3]

The mercantile elite's political involvement had been spectacularly successful. For nearly two centuries, they had dominated the politics of the city and played an important role in state and national affairs. Partly, they had succeeded because of the nation's dependence on them. The city's merchants, bankers, and industrialists provided indispensable resources and expertise. Customs duties, for example, generated by the trade of New York merchants, paid for most of the operations of the federal government.[4] Property taxes funded the budgets of City Hall. Indeed, any "statist" project, such as territorial expansion, depended ultimately on resources mobilized by economic elites. The city's upper class and the state, then, were closely linked, a relationship that was strengthened by the fact that the United States, in contrast to contemporary European states, never experienced the emergence of strong state structures independent of bourgeois society.

By the 1850s, however, as a result of rapid economic growth and its attendant social changes, the mercantile elites' claims to leadership were increasingly contested both by the city's burgeoning working class and by the rising artisans-turned-manufacturers. Not only on the streets or at the Philharmonic but also in politics, merchants faced an assertive citizenry who made their voices heard. Indeed, it was the increasing economic dominance of the city's upper class that drove many working-class people into politics in the first place. By the 1840s and 1850s, these lesser citizens were enjoying some success. They were beginning to influence the city's Democratic Party, finding the party responsive to their demands for the abolition of the contract system and for housing reform.[5] Trade unions and working-class political organizations also moved their candidates onto Democratic Party tickets.[6] And by the 1850s, the figure of the party "boss" would emerge, who would negotiate the political demands of workers and lower-middle-class citizens.[7]

The shifting social origins of the holders of political offices demonstrate this slow but steady erosion of the once-towering position of the city's mercantile elite. Not that the mercantile elite of the city abandoned all political offices. Indeed, the venerable Union Club, testifying to its members' political involvement, counted in its ranks a former secretary of the navy, a United States senator, two governors of New York State, and four mayors of New York City, as well as a governor of Rhode Island. Just as strikingly, during the 1850s all mayors of New York City were businessmen – a merchant, a shipbuilder, a merchant shipper, and a paint manufacturer.[8] Still, the number of upper-class New Yorkers holding political office declined.[9] Among 103 politically active wealthy New Yorkers, only twelve ran for office in the years between 1850 and 1863, compared to thirty-two who had been candidates between 1828 and 1840.[10] And of 1,052 Democratic Party activists in 1844, 38 percent were professionals or businessmen, while 33 percent were skilled workers, a substantial number that was probably unprecedented in the Western world at large.[11] Increasingly, professional politicians of lower-middle-class or even working-class background occupied political offices.[12]

Most worrisome to the city's mercantile elite, the changing character of local politics encouraged the Democratic Party, which enjoyed unquestioned dominance in municipal politics, to raise the city's tax rate to fund patronage-intensive public construction projects beneficial to the city's workers. Not that upper-class New Yorkers opposed infrastructure improvements; to the contrary, many agreed on the need to build canals, roads, and railroads, as well as to improve the city's harbor and enhance its defense installations. They favored subsidies for ocean-going steamers carrying mail, as well as state support for railroad construction, such as the granting of federal land in the South and West.[13] Nonetheless, as taxpayers, merchants as well as manufacturers were suspicious of what they perceived as excessive spending by local government. They desired to control these projects, but control proved ever more elusive as mobilized and enfranchised workers entered onto the political stage.

Both the city's mercantile elite and its rising manufacturers worried about the loosening of elite control over municipal politics. While the *New York Herald,* closely aligned with banker August Belmont, complained about the "atrocious tyranny of ruffian plunderers," publisher Horace Greeley found the city "fearfully misgoverned and despoiled."[14]

At meetings, they decried high taxes, corruption, and municipal waste, the "despotism in [the city's] midst."[15] Many believed "that our metropolis is the worst governed city in Christendom."[16] The erosion of control over municipal parties, it seemed to upper-class New Yorkers, was a further element in the demise of their control over the city. But how should they respond to such challenges?

The answer lay in the economic elite's embrace of several strategies to exert power in the new era of mass politics. It is important to note that they understood what many historians have failed to see, that office holding was not the only form of political influence.[17] Solidifying their hold over party organizations offered another route. Parties, after all, needed not only votes but also money, and during the 1850s, no party had yet come up with ways to raise resources without recourse to the city's wealthy. Both Whigs and Democrats, in fact, had developed a division of labor between professional politicians (who focused their activities on office holding, as well as grassroots organizing) and wealthy party members, who funded the organizations, formulated party policies, and maintained ties to state and national bodies.[18] One of the most prominent among these party activists was financier August Belmont, who, as the head of the Democratic National Committee, played a large role in formulating the organization's policies and bankrolled various presidential campaigns.[19] Locally as well, wealthy citizens continued to serve as chairmen of party meetings and on party committees.[20]

Furthermore, even though bourgeois New Yorkers did not hold the same number of political offices as they had earlier in the century, they still enjoyed extraordinarily good access to people in power. Their expertise, as well as their financial capacity for rewarding politicians, facilitated a fine-spun network of personal relationships to people in elective office. These relationships probably proved most effective in the struggle over specific issues, issues they often disagreed about with one another. Should a large city park be built on the banks of the East River, where it would enhance the value of the Beekman family's adjacent real estate holdings but diminish the value of those of the Schermerhorn family, or should it be built in the center of Manhattan?[21] Should the New Haven Railroad be allowed to construct a bridge across the Harlem River, or should the Harlem River north of the planned bridge remain accessible to tall ships, as Edgar Ketchum demanded in 1852?[22] Should the Pennsylvania Coal Company be permitted to build a railroad from its coal fields to the Hudson River, or should the Delaware & Hudson Canal Company keep its monopoly on transport?[23] Should the Crystal Palace exhibition be supported by the State of New York? Who should become harbormaster? Which streets should be graded?

The influence of upper-class New Yorkers on political decisions through these networks was subtle but powerful: Concerned about the passage of a bill in Albany, Frederick DePeyster contacted State Senator and lawyer J. Winthrop Chauler, who assured DePeyster that "[w]hen the Bill reaches the Assembly I will endeavor to put the matter in a true light."[24] In a conflict over tax assessments in Manhattan in the early 1850s, soap and candle manufacturer Eben Meriam wrote to Senator James Beekman, "I hand you a memorial in relation to assessments, which please present to the Senate. . . . The Community will sustain you in this against the Corporation."[25] When in 1851 a group of investors planned to build the Madison Hotel and sought support from New York State, they contacted Senator Beekman: "You may act as you please with reference to your own interests, but I do think that citizens and property-holders in the 16th, 18th, 19th and 21st Wards have a right to look at you as their natural representative."[26] And stave dealer Isaac Sherman was reassured in February 1859 by State Assembly member G. Tucker of Albany, "I will bring the question of toll upon staves before the Board, as you desire, and urge a reduction, when your memorial comes up."[27] This is not to say that requests of these kinds were always granted, but New York's merchants, bankers, and manufacturers enjoyed access to all levels of government, not least because the government perceived the well-being of commerce and industry as essential for the well-being of the city, the state, and the nation.

While these networks allowed upper-class New Yorkers to exert influence over state and national politics that continued to go well beyond their numbers, it became ever more difficult to exert power in local government. It was in the city, after all, that workers represented a majority of the voters, giving upper-class New Yorkers a decisive disadvantage. A majority of these workers, moreover, were immigrants, often of Catholic persuasion, allowing many (though not all) bourgeois New Yorkers to combine their fear of the disorderly city with fears of the religious and cultural "other." The expansive and expensive municipal politics favored by these immigrant workers called for a response by the city's upper class.

Reasserting control, however, proved difficult. For some among the city's economic elite, an anti-immigrant policy suggested itself, and during the early 1850s, the "Know Nothings" attracted substantial upper-class support for their goal of excluding immigrants, especially Catholics, from access to political power. But in the end it was difficult to win elections on the basis of hostility to immigrants in a city that had so many of them.

Another solution to the problem of elite influence in the era of mass politics was to mobilize outside of traditional party channels, and here the city's economic elite gained a few victories: In 1853, for example, a bipartisan "reform movement" was the vehicle of choice. Concerned about high municipal spending, crime and corruption, and an increase of the tax rate from 0.92 percent of assessed value to 1.23 percent during the preceding two years, a broad-based coalition drawn from the ranks of the city's economic elite, including both merchants and manufacturers, united in a "reform movement" and organized "the largest meeting ever held in this City in regard to Civic Affairs." They decried the "absence of all economy in the expenses of the city – the disposition to add to its permanent debt . . . – and the evidence of extravagance, abuse of power, favoritism, and mismanagement."[28] In the 1853 elections, they prevailed; candidates whom they endorsed won thirteen of twenty-two elections for aldermen.[29] In turn, they temporarily succeeded in reducing the tax rate and successfully lobbied for a new charter for the city.[30] The reform impulse resurfaced again in 1857 when in the wake of a serious economic crisis, Mayor Fernando Wood embraced some of the demands of protesting workers, spurring upper-class New Yorkers to mobilize outside of traditional party channels.[31] The bipartisan reform coalition they created victoriously ran the wealthy paints and oil manufacturer Daniel F. Tiemann for mayor.[32]

Eventually, however, both these reform movements disintegrated. There were two reasons for the movements' failure: First, despite efforts by the activists to include nonpropertied citizens, especially skilled workers, in their ranks (the 1853 "City Reform League" had among its supporters workers from the Novelty Works and some shipyards), they still essentially presented themselves as a movement of the city's propertied classes. Mobilizing on the basis of a shared class position, however, made it difficult to achieve widespread and durable popular support. In a democracy, gentlemen needed voters, and an appeal on the basis of class could not produce a sufficient number of them.[33] It was a dilemma that eventually undermined their ability to act politically outside of the established party channels.[34]

Second, and more importantly, these reform movements foundered on the shoals of sectional conflict. The 1853 reform movement's support, for example, evaporated rapidly because its elite backers split along party lines. Many of its supporters moved into the Democratic Party, which, they hoped, would guarantee sectional reconciliation. As a result, in 1854 the reform movement gained only 26 percent of the mayoral votes and, in 1855, an insignificant 5 percent.[35] The 1857 reform movement sputtered for the same reason, as many of its wealthy backers attached themselves to one or the other political party. With their economic interests diverse and contradictory, their social institutions weak and divided, and their visions for the future sharply at odds with one another, bourgeois New Yorkers failed to muster the strength to imprint their claims on New York City in the era of mass politics. And the incentives to overcome deep political divisions in national politics in order to enable a collective political project in New York City were limited: The threats posed by the local working class and its politics were too slight during the 1850s to strike true fear into the hearts of capital-owning New Yorkers.

Conflicting loyalties in the national political arena made it difficult for the city's mercantile elite and its manufacturers to leave established parties behind. As the sectional crisis deepened, Democrats and Republicans claimed their loyalty, making bipartisan local political mobilization all but impossible. As a result, the city's mercantile elite, drawn to the politics of sectional reconciliation and thus the Democratic Party, found itself embracing the machine politicians of Tammany, thus undercutting its own reform efforts.[36] While the number of wealthy Democrats in the early 1850s had been small ("[t]he Democratic merchants could have easily been stowed in a large Eighth Avenue railroad car," observed Walter Barrett with slight exaggeration),[37] their ranks grew throughout the decade, especially once the Whig Party (the traditional political home of many among the city's economic elite) began to disintegrate at midcentury.[38] This growing number of wealthy Democrats could not give up the party that guaranteed to them the preservation of the Union.[39] Hence, ultimately, local reform efforts failed because the conflict over the territorial expansion of slavery was what was of greatest importance to large segments of the city's economic elite – hardly surprising, considering their deep involvement in the cotton economy.

Maybe more important, however, was the small but growing number of upper-class New Yorkers who moved into the Republican Party during the second half of the 1850s. The emerging strength of the Republican Party truly seemed to endanger the interests of the city's mercantile elite, a more substantial threat than assertions of working-class citizens in municipal politics. By 1856, the Republicans had even gained (with strong support from upstate farmers) the governorship, and they immediately proceeded to weaken the power of New York City's Democratic Party, not least by making the significant patronage spoils of the city available to loyal Republicans.[40] It seemed only a question of time before their influence on national politics would be felt. And it was often the city's manufacturers who supported the new party – challenging in the political sphere the pre-eminence and power of New York's mercantile elite.

⌣ ⌣ ⌣

By the 1850s, mounting tensions about slavery and the future shape of the Union had driven a deep wedge between different upper-class groups, overshadowing all other political conflicts. For largely economic reasons, but also on other grounds, the future of the Union was the most signifi-cant political issue of the day for businessmen acting in national and inter-national markets. This future seemed more controversial and uncertain with each passing year.

The majority of bourgeois New Yorkers wanted to accommodate the South, which meant acceding to its political interests. This was particu-larly true of the merchants and bankers. They sought to preserve the Union and throughout the 1850s were willing to compromise with south-ern slaveholders, politically as well as ideologically, on nearly every issue: from the Compromise of 1850 to the Fugitive Slave Act and even Dou-glas's Kansas-Nebraska Act.[41] Their ultimate interest in peace and union transcended all other political loyalties, and they exerted their power inside and outside the party system to promote compromise. "The peace . . . of the country," they believed, secured their own prosperity.[42]

As the sectional conflict intensified during the 1850s, merchants and bankers mobilized politically to an astounding degree.[43] Though politics was decidedly not their business, they realized that without political engagement, their central position in the American economy was in dan-ger.[44] Rallies, meetings, petitions, journeys to Washington, D.C., the cre-ation of political movements, and the endorsement of candidates were all part of the mercantile elite's political repertoire during these eventful years. Partly out of desperation about their inability to end sectional ten-sions, merchants and bankers were driven further and further into the arms of the southern slaveholders. Already by 1850, they were willing to accede to a major expansion of slavery.[45] Yet ten years later, after a decade of struggle, many of them began to realize that the world they had fought to preserve was beyond rescue. Lincoln, they now feared, would "disrupt . . . or destroy . . . vast interests."[46]

Throughout the 1850s, preserving the status quo, and with it slavery, became central to the politics of the city's economic elite. "[T]he slavery question is the pivot upon which all interests of the country turn and . . . it is through [the slavery issue] that all political questions derive their mean-ing," argued Wall Street lawyer Friedrich Kapp.[47] Sharing Kapp's sense of urgency, the city's merchants, bankers, and industrialists struggled to find ways to secure their national political influence. This was a difficult task, considering the turmoil among political parties, which, most significantly, slowly tore apart the old political home of the city's mercantile elite – the Whig Party. While a small minority of upper-class New Yorkers began to embrace the emerging Republican Party, the vast majority tried first to rescue the Whig Party as a voice for reconciliation, then mobilized in ad-hoc political movements for compromise and flirted with the nativist American Party, before finally moving into the arms of the Democrats.

For the city's mercantile elite in particular, their failure to forge the New York State Whig Party into an effective voice for compromise set them on a torturous search for a new political home. Already in 1850, when New York Whigs, strongly influenced by William H. Seward and Thurlow Weed, refused to endorse the Compromise of 1850, the largely elite-dominated New York City faction of the party split off and united with pro-compromise Democrats to form a "Union State Ticket," which elected Horatio Seymour as Governor. Thousands of capital-owning New Yorkers had signed a petition to support the campaign, and the banker James Brown had even donated $1,000 toward it, hoping that strengthening the pro-Union forces in New York State would strengthen them in the nation at large.[48] Following a similar pattern, in 1851 New York State Senator and real estate speculator James Beekman deserted his party, the Whigs, and voted against the nomination of Whig antislavery advocate Hamilton Fish for the U.S. Senate, to the applause of many of the city's merchants.[49] Despite this weakening of older party loyalties, however, most of the city's merchants and bankers struggled to the end against the splintering of the party system along sectional lines, looking "with apprehension and aversion upon the organization of parties on a sectional basis.[50] Merchant Hiram Ketchum already feared in 1850 that if the Whig Party were to turn into a sectional party, the secession of the South could not be far off.[51] And tellingly, when in 1855 New York State's Whigs fused with the newly organized Republican Party, only five of 128 delegates opposed the move – all from New York City.[52]

With the Whigs disintegrating, the city's pro-compromise mercantile elite searched for new political channels. Ad-hoc political mobilization outside of traditional parties became an important part of their political repertoire. In 1850 and 1851, the upper-class Union Safety Committee nominated a "Union Ticket" for statewide elections, and thousands of merchants signed pledges that they would vote for pro-compromise candidates only.[53] "It is time," they proclaimed, that "the trammels of party subjugation were thrown off, and our intelligent business men . . . stand up for the protection of their true interests. . . ."[54] Yet their "true interests" seemed to be represented increasingly by the Democratic Party, and during the 1852 presidential elections, a large number of merchants and bankers again deserted the Whig Party and its candidate Winfield Scott and helped elect pro-compromise Democrat Franklin Pierce President, taking the first step in approaching the Democratic Party as one of their new political homes.[55] The 1856 elections solidified this reorientation.[56] But even then, ad-hoc political mobilizations remained important: In 1859, 100 leading merchants organized the "Union Safety Committee" to propagandize pro-Union politics in upstate New York, and during the 1860 presidential elections, merchants urged a vote for the candidates endorsed by the Union Committee of Fifteen.[57] In the end, however, the frantic efforts and the multiple and rapidly shifting channels the city's mercantile elite chose to exert their influence only showed that they faced an uphill battle in their struggle to preserve the status quo between the sections.

The reason so many of New York's merchants and bankers mobilized so consistently and energetically for compromise with the South was not that they thought slavery as such was desirable, nor that they believed it was morally justifiable. While some sought to defend slavery by arguing that African Americans were "an inferior race" in need of "masters," most in fact opposed the expansion of slavery and hoped that it would eventually die.[58] George Templeton Strong, for example, considered slaveholders "a race of ignorant, coarse, sensual, swaggering, sordid, beggarly barbarians," and in October 1850 a large rally of New York merchants in support of the Compromise of 1850 affirmed that slavery was immoral and should eventually be abolished.[59] Nonetheless, a large number of bourgeois New Yorkers advocated compromise with the South in order to protect their overwhelming economic interest in the continuation of cotton production, and to prevent any disruption in the South's system of labor. Even Whig merchant William E. Dodge, who would eventually join the Republican Party, declared pragmatically throughout the 1850s that the South had a constitutional right to maintain slavery.[60] As Dodge's biographer remarked, "[i]n this matter, the merchant dominated the Christian."[61]

As we have seen, most merchants, the dominant segment of the city's upper class, rooted their economic activities in the existing arrangements of the Atlantic economy, especially the export of agricultural commodities and the import of manufactured goods. Trade in cotton was their most important business, and its sale enabled southerners, in turn, to purchase manufactured goods from the city's merchants. The export of cotton also secured the nation's credit on the European money markets and thus kept the city's banks afloat.[62] As *Hunt's Merchants' Magazine* observed in

1855, "the whole Commerce of the world turns upon the product of slave labor."[63] No other segment of the nation's upper class was as rooted in the old structures of the Atlantic economy as New York's mercantile elite, and not surprisingly, no other segment of the nation's upper class was as willing to compromise with the South. Demonstrating a striking inability to imagine a different political economy, the *Journal of Commerce* editorialized quite characteristically, "We cling to the Compromise (of 1850) as long as there is hope."[64]

Once the connection to the South seemed threatened, merchants and bankers became even more aware of that section's importance to their economic well-being. Southerners reminded New York's merchants repeatedly of their mutual dependence by threatening boycotts of services and goods from New York.[65] These threats became even more meaningful when, after the Panic of 1857, the West sank into a long depression, and the South became economically more significant to New York as a haven of relative stability.[66] The South had to be accommodated because, they believed, "the Union [is] the great source of our dignity, the great spring of our prosperity, and the street-anchor of our safety."[67] By 1857, the city's mercantile elite was willing to accept "the right of the people alone of any State or Territory, to regulate their institutions and frame their own government."[68]

But it was not only a defense of southern slaveholders for the sake of unity that motivated New York's merchants and bankers. The political underpinnings of the Atlantic economy itself also seemed threatened by the newly emerging Republican Party's program of tariffs, homesteads, and containment of slavery, endangering the modus vivendi under which they had thrived economically.[69] Merchants saw very little need for the activist government many Republicans envisioned, and which they rightly feared would result in a political economy fundamentally different from the existing one, a political economy that would undermine their central role in it.[70] What was at stake for them was the future position of the United States in the world economy, and the control of the federal government mattered a great deal in shaping this future.

The city's mercantile elite struggled hard to maintain the existing structures of the Atlantic economy, building the future of commercial capitalism on slavery. The international banker August Belmont, for example, believed that the coexistence of slavery in the South and capitalism in the North was unproblematic. He saw the harvesting of the enormous agricultural potential of the United States by slave labor as a route to prosperity that ultimately would also benefit the working class.[71] A rapidly expanding but socially stable society could be forged by combining slavery, free trade, territorial expansion through the construction of railroads and the annexation of Cuba, government restraint in religious matters, and a paternalist attitude toward the white poor.[72] August Belmont and his political allies strove for the classic coalition between the upper class and the landed gentry of the South, with the peculiar twist of integrating some urban workers into the fold.[73] The political economist and editor of the New York-based *United States Economist and Dry Goods Reporter,* Thomas P. Kettell, made the argument even more bluntly, reasoning that cotton produced by slave labor "sustain[s] the rates of labor and capital, and secure[s] the prosperity of our country."[74] In the 1860 pamphlet *On Southern Wealth and Northern Profits,* written in New York, native southerner Kettell succinctly argued that merchants, bankers, and manufacturers, as well as artisans and northern farmers, enjoyed their prosperity only thanks to the South's "peculiar institution."[75] Indeed, he observed (correctly) that the South's riches accumulated in the North.[76] And no place, according to Kettell, benefited more from these political and economic arrangements than New York: "If the South produces this vast wealth, she does little of her own transportation, banking, insurance, brokering, but pays liberally on those accounts to the Northern capital employed in those occupations."[77] "The history of the wealth and power of nations," he concluded, "is but a record of slave products."[78]

This vision of Thomas P. Kettell, August Belmont, and the *Journal of Commerce* was not shared, however, by all northerners, including a small but growing group of well-to-do New Yorkers. While, as we have seen, most took an essentially conservative view of sectional conflict, an important minority was confident that new and profitable arrangements could be forged in opposition to southern planters. They were at first few in numbers, composed largely of religiously motivated abolitionists, such as the merchant brothers Arthur and Lewis Tappan, who had made New York a center of antislavery organization by establishing the American Anti-Slavery Society a good twenty years earlier. The increasingly aggressive stance of the South, especially in the wake of the introduction of the Kansas-Nebraska Bill in the Senate, however, convinced growing numbers that the status quo was impossible to maintain.[79] To their eyes, the westward expansion of slavery was a threat both to their own economic well-being and to the Republic, and it was necessary to take "united, deliberate, persistent and persevering action" that "such men no longer possess the Government," as the president of the Bank of Commerce, John A. Stevens, proclaimed in May 1856.[80] In its most moderate form, this upper-class opposition to southern slaveholders countered the expansion of the slaveholders' political power while still accepting the persistence of slavery. In its more radical versions, this upper-class opposition to Southern slaveholders outlined a future that included slave emancipation and state-sponsored industrialization in a protected American market. Whatever the exact motives behind the willingness to stand up to southern elites and to destroy the political status quo, the struggle over the federal government moved to center stage.

Nothing was as important to the emergence of these new voices than the dramatic economic developments of the 1840s and 1850s. American industry had experienced rapid growth, and railroads, together with increased immigration, had helped settle the West, resulting in an expansion of prairie agriculture based on free labor. The advent of new economic structures facilitated the emergence of new segments of the economic elite, who based their businesses not on the export of agricultural commodities produced by slave labor but instead on domestic industrialization, import substitution, and the export of agricultural commodities (especially wheat) grown by free farmers. Consequently, during the 1850s, some upper-class New Yorkers were already rooted in a different political economy than that inhabited by most, while others, though still embedded in the Atlantic economy, could see alternative arrangements emerging on the horizon.[81] They all believed that a different political economy not only could secure prosperity but could also preserve social stability by providing workers with an opportunity to turn themselves into propertied farmers, furnishing them with an alternative to their status as wage earners.[82]

According to these upper-class New Yorkers, the political power of southern slaveholders over the federal government was nothing less than a threat to the development of the United States and to their own economic well-being. Free labor needed free soil, a political program that brought these businessmen into increasing conflict with an expansionist South and into coalition with other social groups in the North. It was not only the spread of slavery as such but also the perception that the expansion of slavery would undermine the republican project, and especially threaten social stability in the North, that made them wary about the aggressive stance of southern slaveholders.[83] Peter Cooper, an iron manufacturer and lifelong Democrat who by 1856 found himself moving closer to the Republican Party, thought that several hundred thousand men with a material interest in slavery should not be allowed to "continue to control" the government.[84] George T. Strong, a wealthy lawyer who had left the Whig Party and voted Republican in 1856, advocated an end to the expansion of slavery into the territories, though he thought "slavery is not wrong per se," and that its main damage was to be found in "demoraliz[ing] and degrad[ing] the slave-owner."[85] Moreover, the political power of southern slaveholders, these businessmen began to argue, prevented necessary reforms in the banking, currency, credit, and transportation systems.[86] William E. Dodge, moving closer to the Republican Party, believed that there were "more important interests to advance as a nation than to spend our time in agitating the everlasting slave question."[87]

Those manufacturers, merchants, and bankers who were willing to stand up to the South were convinced of the superiority of the North's economy and system of labor. The clothing manufacturer George Opdyke, who ventured into economic and political theorizing with his 1851 *Treatise on Political Economy* and who was one of the city's early Republicans, saw slavery as the root cause of southern economic backwardness. Capital bound in humans, he argued, could not be profitably employed otherwise, and the driving force of economic development – the motivation to work hard – was lacking in slaves for whom "the hope of gain and the fear of want are both extinguished by the deprivation of freedom." This, in Opdyke's mind, was in stark contrast to the striving and economically successful freemen of the North, including its wage workers.[88] Stave trader and railroad investor Isaac Sherman took a similar stand. As one of the early members of New York's Republican Party and a strong supporter of John C. Frémont's 1856 presidential campaign, he was committed to free labor: "[S]ooner or later," he wrote in April 1856, "the masses of this country will see that the real issue is the rights of men, the rights of labor. . . . Democracy consists in the people ruling through justice, and in harmony with the great principles of equity, and that an attack upon the inalienable right of even a minority, is an aggression on the individual rights of the whole." Although Sherman did not advocate interference with slavery in the South, he strongly opposed its extension.[89]

Tentatively, and to varying degrees, a growing number of upper-class New Yorkers saw a future nation without slaveholders and a city that solved its social conflicts by providing opportunity for deserving workers. They acknowledged the growing contradiction between the forces unleashed by rapid capitalist development and the persistence of slavery, and they saw the persistence of coerced labor, as well as the attendant political power of slaveholders over the federal government, as damaging to their own interests, which they had begun to identify with the national interest. They proposed, in effect, to further the promises of bourgeois revolution. In contrast to the majority of New York's wealthy, they were able to see beyond the sectional and class arrangements of the antebellum years. They were the ideological and political innovators of the economic elite, and, in effect if not in intention, its revolutionary wing.[90]

Those who were least entrenched in old arrangements could most easily challenge them. Merchants, such as Isaac Sherman or Samuel Willets, for example, who focused on trade with the West, stood up against the South. But most consistent and vocal in their opposition to the southern slave-holders were the city's manufacturers. Horace Greeley, publisher of the *New York Daily Tribune,* spoke for many of them when he demanded no "concession to slavery." Like a number of New York manufacturers, Greeley moved early into the Republican Party.[91] He was attracted to the pro-gram of the Republican Party not only for its opposition to slavery but also for its broader vision of political economy. For one thing, the promotion of free and capital-intensive agriculture in the West promised to create grow-ing markets for manufactured goods. The annual fairs of the American Institute best exemplified this perspective by exhibiting not only farm prod-ucts but also the numerous agricultural implements that formed the main-stay of early American manufacturing.[92] Moreover, the expansion of free farming in the West promised to provide workers in the city with access to property and an escape from permanent proletarian status.

Even more important, however, were the industrialists' different demands on the state. The "fostering hand of government" was to protect America's manufactures from overseas competition and to provide an infrastructure for technical advance. Indeed, industrialists saw the state's support of manufacturing as the key variable in the development of domestic industries.[93] In this alternative vision of a political economy, quite distinct from the interests and inclinations of most merchants, "[t]he products of the manufacturer, mechanic, and artisan, must be exchanged for the products of the cultivator, and these exchanges should form within our Union an internal commerce such as no nation has before exhib-ited."[94] Higher tariffs in particular would "promote the increased prosper-ity of American manufactures."[95] To fulfill this vision and to unlock the potential expansion of their own particular form of capital, these industri-alists collided ever more with the political economy of the city's mercantile elite. It was in this context that the Republican Party provided a political basis for building a very different American society.

New York's Republican Party was founded on September 1, 1855. At first, few New Yorkers joined.[96] In the 1855 state elections, only 6,000 citizens in the city cast their votes for the Republican Party, while 49,301 voted for other parties.[97] But even early on a fair number of Republican voters were of elite backgrounds: In the November 1856 election, the Republicans secured more than 25 percent of the vote in the bourgeois fifteenth ward.[98]

While New York City in general proved inhospitable terrain for Republicans, some upper-class New Yorkers found their way into the new party early on. The manufacturers Peter Cooper and John Roach, the wholesale grocer and importer of sugar and coffee Edwin D. Morgan, the clothing manufacturer George Opdyke, the dry goods merchant John A. C. Gray, the silk merchant Henry C. Bowen, the banker Simeon Draper, the importer S. B. Chittenden, the flour and tea merchant George Griswold, and the lawyers David Dudley Field, Joseph Blunt, and James W. Nye all joined the Republican Party soon after its founding.[99] The merchant Moses H. Grinnell, a former Whig, followed suit the same year.[100] Though weak, the Republican Party radiated a confidence about the future that a small but growing number of upper-class New Yorkers began to share and that was entirely absent from the proclamations of the accommodationist mercantile elite. In an October 1856 meeting, the party leaders proclaimed:

There will be to witness [the nation's] glorious advances in all areas . . . and the general diffusion of intelligence and virtue among its citizens of all conditions of life. . . . The republican party is but an infant, but, like Hercules, it is capable, if its energies are exerted, of struggling against the monsters sent to destroy its existence.[101]

In 1860, there was a strong correlation between economic position and support for the Republican Party. The upper-class supporters of the city's Republican Party were overwhelmingly manufacturers, lawyers, and western merchants who had little to lose from a conflict with the South – or at least much less than the majority of merchants.[102] An analysis of 109 supporters of the Republican Party who served in 1860 as vice presidents or secretaries of a party meeting, only weeks before Lincoln's election, finds that manufacturers were represented in far greater proportion than merchants. Merchants represented 23 percent of the people present at the meeting – only slightly more than half of their share of the city's economic elite.[103] Manufacturers, on the other hand, who comprised only 20 percent of the city's substantial taxpayers, represented 36 percent of all those supporting the Republican Party. To put it differently, a New York manufacturer was four times more likely to be involved in Republican politics than was a merchant. Professionals, who made up 10 percent of the city's taxpayers assessed in 1855 on more than $10,000 worth of real and personal property, constituted another 23 percent of the supporters. Most of them were lawyers, who in general had a greater propensity to participate in politics than anybody else.

Considering their corresponding political visions, it was hardly surprising to find so many manufacturers in the Republican camp. But what
about the merchants? Those merchants who publically agitated for the
Republican Party and its presidential candidate Abraham Lincoln were
part of a small and tightly knit network of traders not centrally invested in
the South. Some traded in silk (Henry C. Bowen and Eliot C. Cowdin),
others in Latin American coffee or Chinese tea (James Galatin, Moses H.
Grinnell, Abiel A. Low, and Jonathan Sturges), and still others supplied
California with hardware (Samuel Willets). Relative distance to trade with
the South thus characterized the merchants who supported the Republican
Party in 1860, even if they saw in Lincoln essentially a conservative pre-
server of the Union against southern extremism.[104] Blood or marriage,
moreover, related many of the Lincoln supporters to one another.[105]

Economic incentives alone, however, cannot explain why some of New
York's merchants took a more aggressive stance against southern power
and slavery.[106] Rather, for some traders, including even a few who were
engaged in trade with the South, a commitment to the values of liberal
individualism – most especially to self-ownership – meshed with religious
convictions about the evil character of slavery and motivated them to join
the crusade against the "peculiar institution." Not surprisingly, two of the
most prominent Republicans supporting Lincoln in 1860 were the merchants William E. Dodge and Pelatiah Perit, who had both been extraordinarily active in the evangelical movement.[107] Yet that only 5 percent of
Phelps Dodge & Co.'s sales went South probably contributed to Dodge's
decision to join the Republicans.[108]

Dodge and Perit, just like George Opdyke, leather manufacturer Jackson S. Schultz, and iron works owner Thomas B. Stillman, were willing to
challenge the ruling class of the South. That this would have serious consequences was obvious by 1856 – and it was precisely these consequences
that frightened the majority of New York's mercantile elite. However,
because farmers, workers, and artisans enjoyed the franchise in the
mid–nineteenth-century United States, a movement at odds with the most
powerful social groups of the nation – the southern slaveholders and the
majority of New York City's upper class – eventually did gain national
political power and succeeded in destroying the basis of an alliance
between slaveowners and merchants.

In 1860, however, the majority of New York's economic elite struggled to
the end for compromise with the South. Merchants trading with the South
sent private appeals to their customers to oppose secession.[109] Others

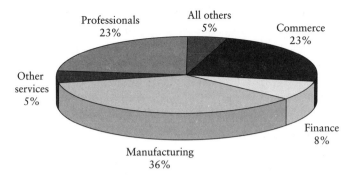

Upper-class supporters of New York City's Republican Party, by economic sector, 1860 (N = 109).
Source: Vice presidents and secretaries of the "Great Republican Rally" in New York City on September 13, 1860 (*New York Times,* 14 September 1860, p. 1). Of 178 vice presidents and secretaries, 109 (or 62 percent) could be located in *Trow's New York City Directory.*

spoke out publicly at meetings, demonstrations, and in delegations, for example in the Democratic Vigilance Committee, which worked for the fusion of all forces opposed to the Republican Party. In August of the same year, August Belmont's Volunteer Democratic Association of New York met to call for the unification of all anti-Republican forces. In September, upper-class New Yorkers held a "meeting of gentlemen opposed to the election of ABRAHAM LINCOLN."[110] The same month, William F. Havemeyer, William B. Astor, Moses Taylor, and August Belmont presided over a rally called to oppose the Republican Party.[111] And on December 15, 1860, a large crowd of merchants and bankers gathered in front of the office of the merchant Richard Lathers, appealing to the South not to leave the Union.[112] Accommodating themselves to southern interests, the attendees resolved that all laws that prevented the return of fugitive slaves should be repealed; in addition, slavery in the territories should be protected until the territories attained statehood and their citizens could decide if they wanted theirs to be a slave or free state. So constant had political mobilization become that Democrat and lawyer Samuel Barlow felt "perfectly overwhelmed" by his political exertions for compromise.[113] Some merchants even suggested by late December that a peaceable separation of the South was desirable.[114] It was, according to the *New-York Daily Tribune,* a "complete triumph of the dry goods Southerners."[115]

While it was hardly surprising that the Democratic merchants would do everything in their power to support last-ditch efforts for compromise, the

Republican elite joined in the pleading as well. They did so mainly because of their fears of what secession and possibly war would mean for the future of the nation and their business enterprises. In mid-December, a bipartisan group of wealthy New Yorkers, including August Belmont, William B. Astor, William H. Aspinwall, Moses H. Grinnell, Hamilton Fish, and Richard M. Blatchford, journeyed to Washington, D.C., to discuss with the administration further possibilities for compromise. In late January 1861, Abiel A. Low, Peter Cooper, William H. Aspinwall, William E. Dodge, Thomas Phelps, Wilson G. Hunt, Apollos R. Wetmore, and James Gallatin left New York City on a special train, delivering a memorial to the administration signed by thousands of merchants, bankers, manufacturers, and professionals pressing for further concessions to the South to rescue the Union. A group of upper-class Republicans separately ventured to Washington to make the same argument before the administration. The persistent demands for sectional reconciliation by Republicans, such as that of William E. Dodge, who pleaded dramatically in February that his "heart is filled with sorrow at the dangers threatening [my country]," demonstrated impressively how committed upper-class New Yorkers were to compromise. Despite their increasing isolation in the North, some of the city's wealthy were so determined to save the Union at all costs that they even talked about using their collective financial power to block a new tariff bill, which increased duties substantially. This bill, they feared, would make a southern Confederacy potentially viable by channeling the western trade away from New York City and into the South, where western products could be exchanged for low tariff imports.[116] "It is said that certain capitalists have addressed leading Republicans in Washington in terms more forcible than elegant," reported the *Journal of Commerce* in February 1861.[117] Even as late as March 1861, a bipartisan group of merchants, industrialists, and bankers, among them William B. Astor, Robert B. Minturn, James Brown, Peter Cooper, and William F. Havemeyer, formed the "American Society for Promoting National Unity."[118] Yet that New York's bourgeois Republicans failed to persuade Lincoln to appease the South stood as powerful testimony to the limited influence they enjoyed in a party dominated by farmers in general and westerners in particular.

As the sections drifted further apart in the winter of 1860/61, however, more courageous dissenting voices came slowly to the fore. Some upper-class New Yorkers, fearful that the Confederacy's lower tariff would draw business away from New York City to the South, demanded that the new tariff also be enforced in southern ports.[119] Others advocated a firmer stance in order to collect their southern debts. And still others favored an end to talks of compromise because they feared for the value of the large amounts of government securities they had bought throughout the winter of 1860/61.[120] As banker Sheppard Knapp argued, "if the Government is not sustained we shall not be good for long."[121] It was this constellation of shifting interests that brought a number of merchants, industrialists, and bankers together in early March 1861 to demand a more assertive policy towards the South. As David Dudley Field would recount two years later, this was the moment when some bourgeois New Yorkers began to see that "the day of argument is gone" and that "it is by the sword alone in Freedom's right hand that we can conquer a peace."[122]

Yet neither the policy of reconciliation nor assertiveness could convince the southern states to remain in the Union. South Carolina seceded on December 20, 1860. Mississippi, Florida, Alabama, Georgia, Louisiana, and Texas followed in rapid succession. By the end of March 1861, the Union was effectively destroyed; the federal government in Washington had lost its ability to coerce and tax the population of the southern states. When on April 12, 1861, General Anderson refused to surrender at Fort Sumter in Charleston Harbor, Confederate troops opened fire. The gunfire announced one of the greatest political defeats ever for upper-class New Yorkers.

⁓ *Faces* ⁓

Peter Cooper, iron manufacturer.
Source: Allan Nevins, *Abram S. Hewitt,
With Some Account of Peter Cooper*
(New York: Harper, 1935), p. 33.

August Belmont, banker.
Source: 1883 photograph by W. Kurtz,
courtesy of the Museum of the City
of New York.

Caroline Astor, socialite.
Source: Portrait by Charles Emile Auguste
Carolus-Duran, reproduction courtesy
of The Metropolitan Museum of Art,
Gift of Orme Wilson
and R. Thornton Wilson, 1949.

98

Regina and William Steinway, piano manufacturers,
with their children, 1874.
Source: Courtesy of the Steinway Collection, LaGuardia and Wagner Archives,
LaGuardia Community College, the City University of New York.

Making Money

Shipping agricultural commodities and manufactured goods: A view of the port of New York.
Source: *Harper's Weekly*, 4 September, 1869, reproduction courtesy of Harvard University.

⟁ *Making Money* ⟁

Financing America's railroads, insurance companies, and utilities:
The New York Stock Exchange, 1863.
Source: Diorama model by Ned J. Burns, photograph courtesy
of the Museum of the City of New York.

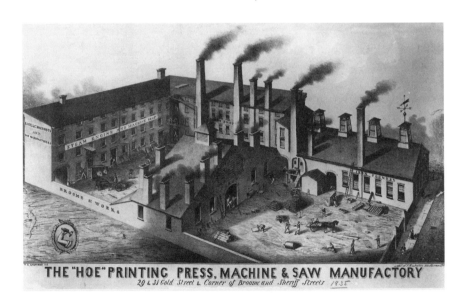

Manufacturing in the city:
Hoe & Company, manufacturer of printing presses, 1835.
Source: Gift of George W. Hickman, courtesy of the Museum of the City of New York.

The factory in the backyard: The Steinways on 52nd Street, 1861.
Source: Courtesy of the Steinway Collection, LaGuardia and Wagner Archives,
LaGuardia Community College, the City University of New York.

Displaying wealth and culture:
Cornelius Vanderbilt's mansion on Fifth Avenue, 1891.
Source: Courtesy of the Museum of the City of New York.

⌇ *Interiors* ⌇

The practical manufacturer:
Peter Cooper's bed,
built by himself.
Source: Allan Nevins,
*Abram S. Hewitt, With Some
Account of Peter Cooper*
(New York: Harper, 1935), p. 34.

Acquiring culture, with a vengeance: Alexander T. Stewart's private art gallery.
Source: Artistic Houses, Part 1,
courtesy of the Collection of the New-York Historical Society, 73290.

☞ *Spending Money* ☜

Men go shopping: Hoffman's Cigar Store.
Source: Advertisement, reproduction courtesy of the
Collection of the New-York Historical Society, 29603.

Women's first palace of consumption: A. T. Stewart's Department Store, 1850.
Source: Lithograph published by Henry Off, courtesy of the
Collection of the New-York Historical Society, 878.

⌁ Spending Money ⌁

Summering in the country: Packing up the essentials.
Source: A Fifth Avenue Belle Superintending the Packing of Her Saratoga
Trunk in Her Dressing Room. *Frank Leslie's Illustrated Newspaper,* 19 July 1879,
reproduction courtesy of the Museum of the City of New York.

Consuming a world, conquering a world:
The Morgans travel to the seats of fallen empires, Karnak, Egypt, 1877.
Source: Courtesy of the Archives of the Pierpont Morgan Library, New York.

Forging a new generation: Students of an exclusive private school promenade through the city.
Source: Harper's Weekly, 8 March 1868, reproduction courtesy of Harvard University

☞ *Bourgeois Women* ☜

The core of the bourgeois world: The family, 1897.
Source: The Byron Collection, courtesy of the Museum of the City of New York.

Forging new identities: Daughters of the American Revolution, 1898.
Source: The Byron Collection, courtesy of the Museum of the City of New York.

PART II

Reluctant Revolutionaries

Civil War and Reconstruction

4

Bourgeois New Yorkers Go to War

On April 20, 1861, the dreadful news of war that had arrived in the city on the Hudson only a few days earlier began to sink in. Throughout the day, New Yorkers, hungry for information, wandered through the streets, and debated heatedly with friends, neighbors, or strangers about what was to come. By afternoon, between 100,000 and 250,000 citizens of the metropolis streamed into Union Square to join a demonstration expressing their outrage at southern aggression and to mobilize for war. The spacious square was so crowded with people that the rally spilled over into adjacent streets, with "Broadway from Fourteenth-street almost to the Battery . . . a surging mass of human beings."[1] Rich and poor alike assembled, as stores and factories closed and even the Stock Exchange shut down to allow attendance by its members.[2] "Union Square was a red, white and blue wonder," reported an awestruck *New York Times,* the demonstrators listening to speeches "in tones of thunder for the Union, the Constitution and the enforcement of the laws."[3] When Major Anderson, who had just arrived from Charleston Harbor, appeared, he was welcomed by "an outburst of applause seldom, if ever, equaled."[4] It was the biggest demonstration the United States had seen in its young history.

At the very center of the rally, in front of the statue of George Washington, and in the midst of thousands upon thousands of citizens, stood the organizers of the event: the city's economic elite. The area was "crowded to excess with the wealth and talent of the city," observed the *New York Times,* and indeed, upper-class New Yorkers were the driving force behind the rally.[5] Since they had received the news that Fort Sumter had been attacked, they had mobilized for war and the Union Square demonstration was the crowning success of their exertions. During the days leading up to the rally, already convinced that immediate action was called for, members of the Merchants, Corn, and Produce Exchanges had met to announce their firm support of the government. A special meeting of the Chamber of Commerce on April 19 had followed suit, resolving that "policy and humanity alike demand that [the secession of the South] should be met by the most prompt and energetic measures . . . a policy so vigorous and restless that it will crush out treason now and forever."[6] Pelatiah Perit, the Chamber's president, had declared on the occasion that "peculiar emergencies" justified the unusual step to "intermeddle with the political questions which agitate the country," and had appealed to its members to "forget all party distinctions, and, with unanimity and warm hearts, rally in support of a constitution and government the best in the world."[7] They did so decisively: Lawyer Joseph Hodges Choate reported that "[t]he war is all that we think or talk of now."[8]

As a first step, upper-class New Yorkers organized political support for the government, and it was for that purpose that they had chosen the rather unusual form of a mass political demonstration on April 20. When huge crowds heeded their call that Saturday, the city's merchants, bankers, and manufacturers ascended the various stands that had been built throughout Union Square to rally the people behind their cry for reuniting the nation by force. The speakers, among them William Havemeyer, Moses H. Grinnell, and Hiram Ketchum, confirmed the need to overcome political divisions so that the Union and constitutional government could be restored. Resolving that "it is the duty of all good citizens, . . . to contribute by all the means in their power, to maintain the Union of the States," they expressed fear that secession undermined the United States' economic power and that it could ultimately threaten the whole republican experiment.[9] "If we do not now stop at this threshold," thundered merchant Robert J. Walker to the assembled multitudes, "this Government cannot be maintained, but we shall fall into universal anarchy, and become the scorn and scoff of the civilized world."[10]

Though for the thousands who attended the rally it was not immediately obvious, near the statue of George Washington something unusual was happening. Upper-class New Yorkers, who throughout the past years had been at odds with one another over the big political questions of the day, assembled together. Indeed, what was most striking about the demonstration was not the large number of people who had come, but that all segments of New York's economic elite supported the rally, regardless of party affiliation and economic position. Democrats Alexander T. Stewart, Moses Taylor, and William B. Astor shared the leadership with Republicans William E. Dodge, Moses H. Grinnell, and Abiel A. Low. Merchants, among them Robert B. Minturn, manufacturers, including Peter Cooper, and bankers, such as Joseph Seligman, sat on the podium. They agreed, as merchant Hiram Ketchum put it on the occasion of the rally, that "our first duty . . . should be to banish all thoughts of difference among ourselves, to forget that we even had any controversies."[11] This group of bourgeois New Yorkers remained highly mobilized throughout the next four years of war, sharing a "universal determination . . . to settle the great question now forever."[12]

The upper-class sponsorship of the Union Square demonstration signified an important departure. Throughout the 1850s, merchants, industrialists, and bankers had dreaded the possibility of military conflict with the South and quarreled with one another about how to best approach the South. But now that the volleys of Confederate cannons were pounding the walls of the federal fort in Charleston Harbor, the economic elite's political discourse changed abruptly, allowing them to move decisively into the forefront of mobilization for war. "I have prayed for a peaceful solution of our national difficulties," explained lawyer John Lorimer Graham, "but the purposes of Providence are to me evident and I am convinced that reason has fled the southern mind, fomented & misled by traitors."[13] Realization that the nation was divided beyond peaceful compromise was certainly painful, yet "now that it is upon us," wrote Senator James Dixon to James W. Beekman, "I am for using every means in the power of the Government to crush the rebellion. . . . Let it cost what it may, in blood & treasure."[14] This determination to stand up to the Confederacy and the sense of urgency marked a dramatic departure. Peter Cooper, who only a few weeks earlier had pleaded for reconciliation, noted that "[i]t is impossible for us to overestimate the importance of the life and death struggle now going on in our country. . . . [T]he confederacy with its pretended right of secession, must die."[5] Although a very small minority of New Yorkers proposed that the city itself could secede from the Union, the idea had little support from upper-class citizens who preferred – as August Belmont suggested – "to leave to my children instead of the gilded prospects of New York merchant princes, the more enviable title of American citizens."[16]

Such altered political discourse allowed bourgeois New Yorkers in late April 1861 to come together and mobilize collectively as never before. This unprecedented move marked the – albeit temporary – cessation of a decade of political conflict within the upper class about their relationship to southern slaveholders. Elite New Yorkers who had overwhelmingly supported compromise and accommodation suddenly united to restore the territorial integrity of the United States. While many of the city's manufacturers and some of its merchants had advocated a more assertive policy toward the South for some years, most merchants and bankers, particularly those with intimate social and economic relations to the South, had done everything possible to prevent sectional war. Now, however, even August Belmont helped mobilize for battle.[17]

They came together because, for the first time in almost seventy-five years, a serious challenge to the power of northern economic elites had materialized, one that could not be reversed solely by political means. Secession was a direct attack on the basis of upper-class power. The division of the nation diminished, for example, the economic opportunities of New York's merchants and bankers. Although some of them had at first hoped that New York City could keep its place as the nation's premier center of trade with the South, the passage of a Confederate bill to impose a tariff on all goods imported into its territory blocked this possibility.[18] Moreover, bankers worried that secession threatened the stability of the monetary system, which, backed by the Bank of England, relied on the export of agricultural commodities to Europe, most of which grew in the South. Industrialists, ironically, had fewer economic reasons to see the nation reunited, although for some, such as the clothing manufacturers, markets had contracted since April 1861.

Yet narrow economic interests alone did not account for the rapid and decisive mobilization for war. Secession also threatened the long-term goal of territorial expansion of the Union by creating a serious military contender on the North American continent. Moreover, secession challenged central ideological tenets of New York's upper class, who feared that the first democratic constitutional government would be unable to maintain national unity. As Hiram Ketchum warned during the Union Square rally, "We must resist to the death, if necessary, all who attempt to destroy the principle of popular liberty."[19] The war, according to Howard Potter, a partner in the banking firm of Brown Brothers & Co., was "but a duty, so clear, so imperative, that to have shrunk from it would have not only covered us with infamy, but have resulted in the certain destruction of everything dear to humanity in these States."[20] "We are," J. Cooper Lord commented, "in fact, engaged in a struggle for nothing short of our existence, and we must, and will carry our point if we fail in everything else and lose all our possessions in the effort."[21]

Threatened to such a degree, New York's economic elite cast aside their political, economic, and ideological differences and united around a program for the restoration of the Union. This unity evinced a new degree of political mobilization, a mobilization unknown in times of less drastic challenges. But despite the move of large segments of the city's upper class away from prior compromise policies, the mobilization of the spring of 1861 was essentially conservative, aimed primarily at restoring the antebellum status quo.[22] The sudden change in opinion on the sectional crisis was less of a radical departure than it seems at first glance. Both the earlier compromise policy and the more assertive stance towards the South shared essentially the same goal – to unify the nation without attacking the institution of slavery. How economic elites sought to attain this goal, however, changed in the spring of 1861, when war replaced compromise.

Despite these initial hopes, the war would shatter the world upper-class New Yorkers had struggled so hard to preserve. When Confederate soldiers fired on Fort Sumter, the shots ushered in dramatic social transformations, most notably the freeing of nearly four million slaves and the destruction of the southern ruling class.[23] They also ushered in profound changes for New York City's economic elite. The war, which most merchants, industrialists, and bankers first had seen as a defense of the status quo, turned into a revolutionary war. It was, as Barrington Moore has argued, a "bourgeois revolution" – violently transforming the South in the image of the North. In what can be considered a historical irony, however, the most powerful segments of the northern bourgeoisie joined the revolution only late and reluctantly.[24]

The war was revolutionary because it resulted in the destruction of the central social institution of the southern states – slavery – and with it the national political power of slaveholders. But the war was also revolutionary because it facilitated changes in the businesses, politics, and beliefs of the city's economic elite. Economically, the position of industrialists and bankers was strengthened, while the relative position of many merchants declined. Politically, the removal of slaveholders as a significant force in national politics opened the way to greater influence for New York City's upper class over the federal government. Ideologically, the war seemed to complete (and in this sense also end) the revolutionary promises of American republicanism while at the same time undermining the social base for free-labor ideology, as well as mercantile stewardship. The city's upper class, in effect, to a large extent, made itself in and through the Civil War.

In April 1861, in the midst of unprecedented upheaval and uncertainty, only the most perceptive among the city's economic elite would understand how fundamentally the war would reshape the nation and their own class. For most of those who lived through the early days of the war, more urgent problems called for immediate solutions and it was here that the collective mobilization of upper-class New Yorkers went well beyond words. After all, no other group of Americans controlled as much capital and as many productive resources as the city's merchants, industrialists, and bankers, and no other group of Americans was able to support the federal government to a similar degree. Consequently, they mustered some of their assets for the fight. Cornelius Vanderbilt, for example, offered his ships to the War Department.[25] The banker J. F. D. Lanier raised $400,000 to arm and equip the troops of his native Indiana.[26] And William E. Dodge purchased arms and ammunition for the army.[27] Providing these assets was not only patriotic but quite profitable as well, as the federal government often paid inflated prices for these desperately needed resources.

Central to the war mobilization of upper-class New Yorkers, however, were the numerous activities of the Union Defense Committee, which they had organized within days of the start of fighting and which consisted at first of twenty-six eminent businessmen, approximately half Democrats and half Republicans.[28] During the first twenty-eight days of the war alone, the members of the committee met forty-eight times. On April 21, only one day after the large Union Square rally, they committed troops and equipment to President Lincoln to defend Washington, D.C.[29] Three days later, the committee sent workers to Annapolis to restore the rail link between New York and Washington that had been destroyed by southern sympathizers in Maryland. They immediately raised several regiments, and by the end of the war had helped to organize a total of sixty-six regiments. On the home front, they aided poor families of soldiers who had left to fight.[30] At first, the money for such activities came largely from the committee's members, who donated $179,413 for purposes of mobilization (the largest payment of $15,000 made by John Jacob Astor), supplemented by $22,969 from the Chamber of Commerce.[31] Later, public monies found their way into the coffers of the organization as well.

To a degree not seen before, elite New Yorkers directly usurped governmental functions: The Union Defense Committee was at once an organization of New York's bourgeoisie and simultaneously a quasi-governmental agency. The line between the state and private citizens was blurred and represented a unique assertion of governmental authority by private citizens. Some members of the committee received power of attorney from the War and Treasury Departments. They raised troops on their own account, and their committee was the only institution in New York City that had authority to issue passes for travel into such war zones as Washington and Baltimore.[32] Even a member of the Union Defense Committee, Charles Russell, remarked that it was "extraordinary, that a committee of citizens, not holding office, . . . should have taken in hand such important public measures."[33]

A similar merging of private and state activities occurred in the realm of foreign policy. International bankers, such as August Belmont, who enjoyed exceptional access to the politically powerful in Europe – especially in France and Great Britain – took center stage in efforts to convince European governments not to recognize the Confederacy. As early as the spring of 1861, Belmont, encouraged by the administration, wrote to his high-placed European friends defending the cause of the Union. His private diplomacy sent him that July to Great Britain, Germany, and France, where he consulted with Lord Palmerston, the British prime minister, and officials close to Louis Napoleon, the French emperor, about the war and about possibilities of raising funds for the United States government in Europe.[34] Although he did not think it likely that European powers would recognize the Confederacy, Belmont doubted that funds could be raised in Europe so long as the Union lacked military success and did not repeal its new tariffs, tariffs which he had opposed while in New York. Using the administration's dependence on his diplomatic contacts, he pressured Secretary of the Treasury Salmon P. Chase to remove a cornerstone of Republican economic policy, the Morrill Tariff, arguing that "I consider the repeal of the Morrill Tariff worth more to our Cause than the most brilliant victory which our arms could achieve over the rebels."[35]

Although Belmont was unsuccessful in pressuring for lower tariffs, the war, in effect, had given capital-rich New Yorkers enormous bargaining power vis-à-vis the state.[36] Especially during the first months of fighting, the insufficient administrative capacity of the federal government allowed bourgeois New Yorkers to virtually appropriate state functions.

In no other area did material support by the city's wealthy become more important than in raising money for the federal government. "The problem of providing money to carry on . . . a great war," recognized Senator John Sherman, is "next in importance to the conduct of armies, and those who [are] engaged in solving this problem [are] as much soldiers as the men who . . . [carry] muskets, or [command] armies."[37] Extraordinary financial resources had to be mobilized: The federal government in the fiscal year ending June 30, 1861, had spent $67 million, but it spent approximately seven times as much during the first year of the war and nearly twenty-two times as much by 1865.[38] And since the war undermined the flow of international capital into the United States, new sources of domestic capital needed to be unlocked. No one but bourgeois New Yorkers could muster these kinds of resources.

New York's banks in particular were an enormous source of money for the federal government. Throughout the war, the federal government sold bonds and negotiated loans in the city, increasing the national debt forty-two-fold, from $65 million in 1860 to $2.75 billion by 1866.[39] When in the summer of 1861 Secretary of the Treasury Salmon P. Chase was in desperate need of money, he personally traveled to New York to negotiate a loan. Chase offered 7.3 percent interest, substantially more than the 5 or 6 percent that financially sound railroad bonds yielded. Yet despite this tempting offer, Shepherd Knapp of the Mechanics Bank and John A. Stevens of the Bank of Commerce objected to the terms.[40] Though Chase eventually succeeded in selling the loan and New York's banks bought $35 million of the total $50 million, he had in effect been forced to negotiate its terms with New York City's banking community, which was the only plausible source of capital.[41]

New York City's wealthy also helped pay for the war in other ways. With the outbreak of hostilities, the federal government instituted an income tax for the first time in its history. Since only incomes over $800 were taxed (at the moderate rate of 3 percent), the charge hit mainly well-off New Yorkers. Although the tax broke with tradition, it passed without significant resistance, in large part because it was understood to be a temporary measure. Additionally, all consumers were simultaneously burdened with new excise taxes, which put a levy on the manufacture, distribution, and purchase of most goods made in the United States.[42]

While financing the war was the most important contribution of upper-class New Yorkers to the war effort, some of them also fought as soldiers, albeit seldom in the trenches. Their participation, however, gave credence to their calls for national sacrifice. As early as April 19, 1861, the 7th New York Regiment, an elite military unit of wealthy New Yorkers, left the city supported by a $1,000 contribution made by the board of the New York Stock Exchange.[43] Although Lincoln had called for volunteers to serve three months, the members of the 7th returned from Washington after thirty uneventful days because "in the urgency of the moment [they] had not sufficient time to arrange personal business."[44] The regiment itself stayed home for the rest of the war. A full 662 of its members, however, served in the Union Army, 84 percent of them as officers.[45] Other children of upper-class families also fought. James Brown's youngest son Clarence enlisted, for example, as did Charles C. Dodge, son of the merchant William E. Dodge (though his father's personal intervention with Governor Morgan ensured him high rank – first commissioned as major, he was soon promoted to brigadier general, despite a very undistinguished record in the field), and Albert Steinway, brother of the piano manufacturer, who saw battle in Pennsylvania.⁴⁶ Military assignments, mostly somewhat removed from the front lines, were sought after, and were often considered a badge of honor: John Jacob Astor II, for example, after having contributed significant funds to the Union cause, was commissioned as a colonel on the staff of General McClellan.⁴⁷

Paying for and equipping the war effort increased the dependence of the state on New York's bourgeoisie and the bourgeoisie's dependence on the state. Their important material role and their assumption of governmental functions during the first months of the crisis strengthened their relationship to the federal government; the relatively weak American state became, to a large extent, dependent on the material support of those who controlled capital. At the crux of the modern American state thus stood upper-class northerners, particularly those of New York City. As a result, private investment decisions became more and more entangled with the fate of the nation, and the defeat of the South became a question of economic survival. "[W]e uphold the Government in order that the institutes of commerce may be sustained," explained Abiel Abbot Low to the members of the Chamber of Commerce.⁴⁸ Financial support for the government, confirmed the *American Railroad Journal,* was "dictated by a wise regard to their own interests, [because the] first condition of property is a stable government."⁴⁹

The mutual dependence of state and economic elite enabled "a vast realignment of forces in the national economy."⁵⁰ The war presented the federal government with an opportunity to forge a new and different kind of political economy, including strengthened forms of state intervention – from tariffs to immigration laws, from land grants to banking regulations. Though the federal government needed to bargain with all segments of New York City's upper class to gain access to the resources necessary to equip huge armies, the influence of these different segments varied widely. The power of the merchants who invested in trade with southern agricultural commodities and in the import of manufactured goods from Europe declined vis-à-vis the central state because their most important political allies, the southern slaveholders, had disappeared from the halls of power in Washington. Industrialists and some bankers, however, strengthened by a political coalition with western farmers, gained considerable influence to help shape the newly emerging political economy. If the war provided the federal government with new opportunities to intervene in existing economic arrangements, it also gave important segments of the upper class substantial bargaining power to influence this political economy.

Manufacturers in particular benefited tremendously from the mobilization for war, while at the same time, the government's new economic policy linked them solidly to the state. Demands for military equipment led many manufacturers, in particular makers of iron, textiles, and boots, to produce at capacity. At the same time, the newly enacted Morrill Tariff Act of 1861, as well as subsequent tariff increases (which by 1864 had doubled the 1857 duties on a wide range of goods), protected American industrialists from foreign competition. Homestead laws and land grants to railroads, moreover, benefited commercial agriculture in the West and increased demands for agricultural implements produced by domestic industries.[51] Joseph Seligman, mindful of these connections, concluded in September of 1864 that if the Republicans would win the November elections, "I would be in favor of investing in manufacturing as in that case the tariff would hardly be lowered during nearly 5 years."[52] The *American Railroad Journal* went even further, and predicted that the government's need for revenue would keep the tariff in place for at least twenty years.[53]

Industrialists, indeed, saw the war early on as a decisive and irreversible break with the antebellum political economy.[54] The war "has released us from the bondage to cotton," opined the *American Railroad Journal,* "which for generations has hung over us like a spell, destroying all freedom of commercial or political action, and rendering us slaves to the most absurd delusions."[55] With the "the old channels of business" gone, trade with the West, in combination with high tariffs and the provision of an abundant labor supply through immigration, spelled a bright "future of our manufacturing interests."[56] And these new arrangements, forged by war, were to last, since "[t]emporary war measures," such as higher tariffs, have "brought into existence business interests largely dependent on the continuance of" them.[57] Many industrialists were clearly aware that the war had the potential for revolutionizing not only the South but also the political economy of the North, and they welcomed this revolution.[58]

Bankers, however, saw the new political economy emerging in the war years with considerably more ambivalence. Their business activities had traditionally focused on financing trade as well as the transfer of foreign capital to the United States, and both these activities were now disrupted by the conflict. Moreover, their tight economic and social links to the city's merchant community made it difficult for them to embrace wholeheartedly the newly arising economic policy of the federal government, which impeded the developmental trajectory of Atlantic trade. As if this was not enough, the war also endangered the delicate balance of state regulation and self-policing that had given a semblance of stability to the nation's monetary and banking system. Indeed, the war years decisively recast the nation's banking system, and New York's bankers could not help but feel ambivalent about such rapid change.

Ambivalence about change, however, did not equal unforgiving hostility to the newly emerging political economy. For bankers, winning the war and forcefully reuniting the nation was of tantamount importance, since the stability of the nation's monetary and banking systems, and therefore, the stability of their enterprises, rested on subjugating the South. More immediately, the federal government owed huge and ever-growing amounts of money to them, and its ability to serve on principal and interest depended on victory in the war.[59] Because their business interests, in effect, depended on capturing the Confederacy, they provided the government with ever more resources, making a victory in war ever more urgent.[60] The federal government, in turn, desperately sought the resources of New York's banks, giving the bankers enormous influence over central areas of government policy.[61]

The federal government hence depended on New York City's bankers, and vice versa. It was a dependence fraught with tensions. At their core was the question of how to restructure the nation's monetary and banking systems. The rapid mobilization for war put the old institutional framework under such tremendous strains that it effectively broke down. As early as December 1861, New York banks had suspended specie payment because of high demand for gold from the government and speculators. In obvious ways, the old system was not capable of sustaining the necessary war mobilizations.

Open conflict surfaced as early as February 1862, when Congress responded to the banks' suspension of specie payment by issuing legal tender notes worth $150 million.[62] Many, but not all, of the city's bankers opposed this bold new assertion of federal powers. George S. Coe of the American Exchange Bank, Jacob D. Vermilye of the Merchants' Bank, David R. Martin of the Ocean Bank, and James Gallatin of the National Bank all spoke out against the bill.[63] As creditors and old-fashioned merchant bankers, they feared the inflationary impact of such a move. Other bankers, however, supported the measure, among them Moses H. Grinnell, Moses Taylor of City Bank, and the president of the Bank of Commerce, John A. Stevens.[64] Their move was certainly politically motivated, as both Stevens and Grinnell were leading Republicans in New York, but they also expressed willingness to experiment with new forms of monetary policy to advance the Union's military position.

The split in the city's banking community on monetary politics allowed Lincoln and Congress to proceed with the planned issuance of greenbacks. However, when New York's bankers stood as a phalanx against reform, the federal government lacked the power to effect change. This effective veto power of New York's bankers came into sharp focus in the winter of 1862/63 when Chase pushed for the creation of national banks, which, regulated by the federal government, would create a secure market for federal bonds and integrate the new greenbacks into the financial system.[65] The measure promised to revolutionize the United States banking system, creating the position of Comptroller of the Currency, who could charter "national" banks.[66] In return, these banks would receive national bank notes in the amount of 90 percent of the market value of the bonds. These national banks would have to keep reserves of greenbacks and specie of at least 25 percent of their outstanding notes and deposits.[67]

New York's bankers opposed this reform unequivocally. Distrusting federal regulation, they feared that the reserve requirements would keep a larger share of very profitable funds away from New York City banks.[68] This would effectively strengthen non–New York banks. As a result, by November 1863, only three national banks had organized in New York City.[69] Yet without national banks organizing in sufficient numbers in New York, national banks in other states could not keep some of their reserves as bankers' balances in the city, thus undercutting the viability of the system as a whole. In fact, New York's bankers opposed the new law to such a degree that they collectively decided to resist its implementation. In September 1863, banker Augustus Ely Silliman went as far as to call upon members of the New York City Clearing House to refuse cooperation with the federal government.

The pressure of the city's bankers, undercutting the aims of the banking bill, was so powerful that by November, Comptroller of the Currency Hugh McCulloch proposed changing the law in order to accommodate the protesting banks.[70] The new banking act reduced reserve requirements from 25 percent, as legislated in the first bill, to 15 percent, of which three-fifths could be kept as bankers' balances in eighteen designated redemption cities, including New York. Banks in these eighteen cities were then required "to redeem their notes in New York; in return, these banks were permitted to keep one-half of their twenty-five percent required reserves on deposit in New York City banks."[71] The upshot of these complicated regulations was that the city's banks would be able to draw the very profitable bankers' balances into their vaults. Moreover, a special provision in the act was made solely for Stevens's Bank of Commerce, exempting it from the double liability rule, thus inducing a political friend of the Republican administration to convert to the national system. According to Charles Russell, who at that time was a director of the Bank of Commerce, "the administration and the leaders of the majority in Congress were anxious to meet the wishes of the Bank of Commerce."[72]

The revised act was now successful; by October 12, 1864, twelve national banks were doing business in New York City, and by mid-November, the important Bank of Commerce had become a national bank.[73] Through their determined struggle, New York City's bankers had influenced the nation's new banking structure and succeeded in concentrating ever more financial resources in the city. Most remarkably, even in times of war, the United States had opted against creating a central bank, and though for the next forty years conflicts over monetary politics would focus on the relative importance of the state vis-à-vis the market, it was the latter that remained dominant.[74]

As a further result of this twisted path toward reform, the war catapulted bankers into the center of the newly emerging political economy. Bankers had pledged a good deal of their future on the survival of the Union, and they eventually agreed to a strong role for the federal government in financial policy making. They also agreed to and paid for a vast expansion of the state apparatus. These attachments to the nation would bring them into close contact with the federal government and its particular developmental vision for many decades to come.[75] The institutionalization of national bank regulations, and the issue of a national currency, in particular, linked the city's bankers to the state to a degree before unknown, while simultaneously emancipating them as a group from the tight grip of the traders in southern agricultural commodities. By virtue of their importance to the war, their eventual openness to change, and their ability to shape financial policy, bankers were among the greatest beneficiaries of the conflict.[76]

The emancipation of many of the city's bankers from the city's merchant community and its developmental vision was made all the easier because of the ever more prominent role played by a generation of bankers who only came into their own during the Civil War. It was the Morgans and Seligmans, linked to the national government and the newly emerging industries, not the Belmonts and Wards, who became the most powerful bankers of the postbellum United States.[77] Indeed, some bankers got their start only as a result of the war. George F. Baker, as we have seen, was one of them, and Levi Parson Morton another. The Seligmans also began their career in finance during the Civil War when they sold treasury bonds in the European market, eventually giving up their clothing business and turning themselves into important international bankers.[78] By 1865, as a result, the makeup of New York's banking community, its links to the state, and its developmental vision had all changed dramatically.

Even more ambiguous than the position of the bankers was the relationship of the city's merchants to the war. Although they profited from the conflict, their position was weakened relative to other segments of New York's upper class. Many of their trade links were disrupted, and attacks by the Confederate navy on 150 Union merchant vessels during the first three years of the war alone damaged the United States shipping industry severely, as insurance premiums skyrocketed.[79] Rising tariffs, a cornerstone of Republican economic policy, further threatened to undermine the merchants' foreign trade. Although the Chamber of Commerce opposed the passage of new tariff laws, it did so largely without success, drawing into stark relief the merchants' weakened political power.[80]

A minority of merchants, however, began to adjust themselves to the dynamics of the new age, and it was these who blossomed most during the war. Their trade and other business activities moved them away from dependence on the South. Republican William E. Dodge, for example, with his investments in railroads and metals rooting him firmly in the country's newly emerging political economy, ran successfully for Congress in 1864, mostly with the help of his constituents in the wealthy Murray Hill section of Manhattan. Seeing himself as the representative of the "commercial interests of the city," he still embraced the high tariffs of his Republican colleagues, envisioning a political economy in which merchants would flourish, "promoted by the prosperity of the agricultural and manufacturing interests, and by the ability of the country, which alone can come from that prosperity, to buy and pay for the vast amounts of import."[81]

Like merchants, builders and contractors showed ambivalence about the effects of the war on the nation's political economy. Because they did not forge strong links to the federal government, and because they depended on local political connections for public construction projects, they remained sensitive to the concerns of working-class voters and politicians who fought for local autonomy, an allegiance which would come into sharp focus during the conflict over conscription in 1863.[82]

Still, for these local capitalists, as for the merchants, bankers, and manufacturers, the importance of the federal government increased tremendously, not least because it was only through a strong state that the Union could be reunited. Never before in United States history had the federal government played such an important role in domestic economic life, and never before had upper-class Americans been so thoroughly linked to this government. As a result, the economic elites' stakes in the war increased as the fighting continued. By 1863, the Chamber of Commerce had added to its reasons to "unite in putting the rebellion down" the "vast pecuniary obligation" that the war itself had created. Not only would the defeat of the Union make the collection of $200 million in private debt in the South impossible, but "it now puts in jeopardy one thousand millions or more of public debt."[83]

The more New York City's merchants, manufacturers, and bankers were materially, politically, and ideologically invested in the war effort, the more urgent a military victory over the South became. Accomplishing this goal meant defining what the war was actually being fought over. In April 1861 they had united behind the effort to defend the status quo. At first, the pro-war movement sustained its unity because bourgeois New Yorkers, like the rest of the nation, were confident that the Confederacy would not survive for long. August Belmont, for example, was certain that the southern "nation" would soon collapse financially.[84] Samuel Barlow, similarly, expected "a decisive victory at an early day."[85]

But contrary to expectations, the Confederacy proved to be astonishingly resilient and militarily quite successful. The defeat of the northern armies on July 21, 1861, in the Battle of Bull Run came as a complete surprise to northern observers and posed troubling questions about the future direction of the war effort. Bull Run ignited a process that on the one hand fragmented the city's upper class and on the other hand radicalized growing numbers of the city's merchants, industrialists, and bankers.[86] The longer the fighting lasted, the more some believed that the restoration of national unity without a social revolution in the South would be neither possible nor desirable.

The military setbacks in the summer and fall of 1861 shattered the unity upper class New Yorkers had exhibited some months earlier, creating conflicts over the war – its prosecution, its meaning, and its goals. The significance of the split should not be overemphasized: The "mainstream" of the pro-war movement at first remained intact and encompassed Republicans as well as Democrats, united around a program of the military reunification of the nation without disturbing the institution of slavery. Democrats, such as William Havemeyer and Charles P. Daly, continued to support Lincoln's administration, while Republicans, such as William Evarts and Henry Whitney Bellows, continued to distrust antislavery ideas.[87] Even Belmont continued to support the administration, "warmly defend[ing] its course, . . . though my convictions have certainly not approved the course pursued by Mr. Lincoln."[88] However, as the war stalemated, an increasing number of merchants, manufacturers, and bankers drifted into opposing camps – both offering different solutions as to how to unify the nation.

On the one side were those who demanded a radicalization of war goals. This radicalization was at first formulated as a critique of the military strategies of General McClellan. "Yes! I think too that the fighting has got to be pushed on our side," exclaimed the young banker George F. Baker.[89] Republican George T. Strong agreed: "McClellan's repose is doubtless majestic, but if a couchant lion postpones his spring too long, people will begin wondering whether he is not a stuffed specimen after all."[90]

Faulting McClellan for the unfortuitous progress of the war, these upper-class New Yorkers demanded a more aggressive conduct of the Union army, a demand that led them to embrace the strategies of General John C. Frémont, who had declared military emancipation in Missouri. The stave trader and railroad speculator Isaac Sherman, for example, was personal friends with the general and in frequent contact with him.[91] Not surprisingly, then, the radicals' first big political project developed in support of General Frémont. When, in the aftermath of a huge pro-Union meeting in City Hall Park on August 27, 1862, the National War Committee was formed, its goals were to aid the vigorous prosecution of the war and to raise troops for Generals Frémont and Mitchell, as well as to equip Unionists in western Texas.[92] The committee, directed by thirty-three upper-class New Yorkers, among them Isaac Sherman, banker John A. Stevens, Jr., iron manufacturer Peter Cooper, and clothing manufacturer and mayor George Opdyke, represented the radical wing of the city's upper class, who saw the war as an all-out struggle between two different social systems. According to George Opdyke, the rebellion had "assumed the character of a life-and-death struggle between two antagonistic forms of social organization" – democracy pitted against a slaveholding oligarchy.[93] "For what are we fighting?" he asked rhetorically. "It is for nothing less than national existence and the cause of civil liberty everywhere. An aristocracy, grounded on human servitude has rebelled against a democratic government."[94]

In the fall of 1862, however, the National War Committee and its support for a more vigorous prosecution of the war met resistance from the moderate forces among the city's economic elite. The committee was soon refused the continued use of rooms in the Chamber of Commerce.[95] It was also deserted by many of its original subscribers, partly because of a tactical blunder: The organizers had not asked them for permission to use their names and also left them in the dark as to the committee's goals. August Belmont, Alexander T. Stewart, John Austin Stevens, Nelson Waterburg, Samuel Sloan, Jonathan Sturges, Edwards Pierrepont, and Andrew Carrigan all resigned immediately, some under protest. "[F]rom what I have heared of the action of the Committee," wrote Moses H. Grinnell, "it seems to me that some of its proceedings are incompatible with the purposes of its creation and would embarrass rather than assist the action of the government in its efforts to reduce the rebellion."[96] August Belmont, not surprisingly, requested the return of money he had pledged to the committee, provoking the scorn of its chairman.[97] But other bourgeois New Yorkers were already edging toward more radical positions without quite having the courage to articulate them in public. William B. Astor, for example, donated a thousand dollars to the National War Committee but instructed them not to use his name in association with the undertaking.[98]

While an increasing number of merchants, manufacturers, and bankers advocated a radicalization of the war effort, McClellan's strategy of building military strength without engaging in combat seemed attractive to another group of bourgeois New Yorkers, organized around August Belmont, the powerful international banker and head of the Democratic Party.[99] Samuel Barlow, who was closely linked to Belmont politically, wrote approvingly in November of 1861 that "McClellan cannot be driven into a battle until he is fully prepared."[100] Belmont and Barlow, along with others, such as importer George Bancroft and lawyer Samuel Tilden, supported the war effort, yet advocated a negotiated peace with the South, including a compromise on emancipation, until very late in the war.[101] Distancing themselves from those who sympathized with secession, they demanded that the Union be restored "by every *constitutional* means, which the government can employ."[102] The war as such was not at issue for them, but "the principles and means on which to prosecute it."[103] For this group, McClellan's posturing was preferable to aggressive military engagement. Their strategy was to bully the South into a settlement that would bring the sections together and allow for the continuation of slavery.

Fear of a radical transformation of the southern economy was the guiding motive of the circle's activities. Though they couched their arguments in paternalistic language that emphasized that for African Americans "servitude was comfort and plenty, [while] freedom is misery and starvation" (emancipation thus was cruel and inhumane), their underlying motives were more straightforward.[104] Belmont and his political friends clearly saw that emancipation would fundamentally alter the economic and political landscape of the nation. In their view, only slavery would guarantee the continued production of agricultural commodities for export so central to their economic interests and to the monetary stability of the country.[105] They hoped against mounting evidence that the social effects of the war could be contained while still restoring a unified nation.[106] Moreover, they thought that only stable social relations in the South would prevent political as well as constitutional changes that could result in the enfranchisement of African Americans and ultimately threaten the viability of the Democratic Party. Despite their anxiousness to limit the meaning of the war, however, they remained committed Unionists: August Belmont, the leader of this group, had disdain for "the secessionist leaders who have brought the terrible calamities of civil war upon once so happy a country."[107] And in November 1862, after the Democrats succeeded in electing Horatio Seymour as governor of New York State, Belmont confirmed that "the Democrats will not accept any compromise which has not the reconstruction of but one government over all the thirty-four states for its basis."[108]

Considering the conservative pro-Union stance of Belmont and his friends, it was only logical that when Lincoln fired General McClellan in November 1862, the general moved to New York City to be in close proximity to August Belmont. Politically sympathetic and with complementary assets – Belmont had money and contacts, McClellan had impeccable pro-Union credentials – the two publicly exhibited their alliance at frequent joint visits to the city's opera.[109] They would later challenge Republican power in the presidential campaign of 1864.

The growing anticompromise wing of the upper class, however, pushed for a radicalization of the war. They related the North's failure to prevail over the South to its unwillingness to attack more directly the institution of slavery. Slavery, they understood, helped the South to maintain its military strength. Peter Cooper, who became an ever more outspoken supporter of this position, concluded early on that the war could only be won if the North "use[d] the negroes as a power."[110] He and others saw southern military might to a large degree resting on slave labor, slaves who would demonstrate – given the opportunity – the determined desire to become free and join the Union's fight.[111] To them, the relationship between Union victory and emancipation became increasingly evident.

Indeed, as early as late 1860, Samuel Barlow feared that the southern states harbored "an enemy in their midst, and they cannot escape . . . from insurrections."[112]

The lack of northern military victories, together with the ever-increasing resources the city's economic elite had committed to the struggle, pushed the question of revolutionizing the South to the fore and converted a growing number of bourgeois New Yorkers to support emancipation. This changing orientation was furthered by long-time abolitionists among the ranks of the city's upper class, such as Abram Wakeman, Sinclair Tousey, Hiram Barney, Lewis Tappan, and Henry C. Bowen, who were strategically placed to move the question of the eventual fate of slavery from the margins to the center of bourgeois discussions about the war.[113] Partly as a result of their exertions, by November 1861, banker George F. Baker was calling slavery the "mainspring of rebellion," a view now also preached at the elite St. George's Church.[114] In the same year, Peter Cooper supported the raising of black troops.[115] By the summer of 1862, Henry Ward Beecher similarly began to embrace emancipation as a legitimate goal of the war, since "slavery has become a military question."[116] Robert Hoe, more tentatively, saw "gradual Emancipation" as a necessary outcome of the war.[117] And in the summer of 1862, George Templeton Strong, not an abolitionist before the war, anxiously awaited the moment the Lincoln administration would attack slavery directly.[118]

Lincoln's promise of emancipation on September 22, 1862, and its realization on January 1, 1863, coincided with and helped to foster this decisive reformulation of war goals among large segments of New York City's economic elite. Indeed, one can argue that 1863 was a revolutionary moment for bourgeois New Yorkers, a year in which many moved from a defense of the status quo to the embrace of emancipation in the South. This turn of opinion was so decisive, as historian Paul Migliore has argued, that the "issue of emancipation could no longer be used to distinguish radicals from moderates or conservatives."[119] Mayor George Opdyke, maybe somewhat too optimistically, asserted that "a large majority of the whole people of the United States subscribe heartily and earnestly to the President's proclamation of emancipation," and John W. Phelps noted that blacks were seen differently after Lincoln's proclamation.[120]

So rapid and deep was the embrace of emancipation that by February 1863, wealthy New Yorkers, including Columbia College President Charles King and banker John A. Stevens, Jr., had formed the Loyal Publication Society, which pushed these views aggressively. They published "journals and documents of unquestionable and unconditional loyalty" on subjects such as "Emancipation is Peace," "Patriotism," and "No Party now, but all for our country."[121] Peter Cooper began writing circulars on "the Defeat of Slavery" and "Slave Emancipation," asserting that the "act of causeless war, committed by States now in open rebellion, has relieved our country and Government from all obligations to uphold or defend an institution so at war with natural justice and all the dearest rights of a common humanity."[122] Supporting Lincoln's Emancipation Proclamation, he argued that "by making war for the destruction of the Union and Constitution," southerners "have made it necessary, right and proper, for the government to abolish slavery upon the same principles that it would be right to destroy a city in order to save the nation."[123] The Emancipation Proclamation, he concluded, "has done more to weaken the rebellion than any other measure that could have been adopted."[124] As Salmon P. Chase reassured merchant William H. Aspinwall in March of 1863, "The policy of the Proclamation, faithfully pursued, seems certain to secure to the National Government that most important element of strength, the earnest good-will and support of the black population of the rebellious States."[125] By August of 1863, even the *Journal of Commerce,* which a few month earlier had called the emancipation proclamation a "miserable sham," promised to "labor for the removal of slavery from the land," albeit envisioning a future of race relations solidly built upon its belief that "[e]quality is impossible."[126]

This spreading sentiment gained its most powerful expression in the founding of the Union League Club.[127] The Union League Club gave form and structure to the demands of the radical bourgeoisie – the forceful unification of the nation, emancipation, and the strengthening of the nation state. Founded in late 1862 by a group of elite New Yorkers, the club had as its purpose "to cultivate a profound national devotion, . . . to strengthen a love and respect for the Union, . . . to elevate and uphold the popular faith in republican government [as well as] to enforce a sense of the sacred obligation inherent in citizenship."[128] By May 1863, 350 merchants, industrialists, bankers, and professionals had joined.[129] The impressive expansion of the radical wing of the upper class showed in the rapid growth of the exclusive club: By 1865 it counted 800 members. Powerful and wealthy New Yorkers presided over it during the war years, among them merchant Robert Minturn, shipping merchant Charles H. Marshall, and financier and lawyer John Jay.[130]

The Union League Club became an important meeting place for New York's radical bourgeoisie, a place to welcome similarly minded people from other cities, politicians and state officials, as well as foreign visitors.

It facilitated and strengthened national networks among the economic elite and with representatives of the state. Many of the club's members enjoyed extraordinary access to Congress and the Cabinet, journeying frequently to Washington, D.C., to consult on policies.[131] The club also supported the rights of African Americans in New York City, for example, by advocating the desegregation of the city's railroads.[132] And it helped create the Loyal Publication Society, the Loyal National League, and the Loyal League of Union Citizens, all of which organized broad segments of the city's bourgeoisie and put out propaganda material in support of the war, emancipation, and the Union, distributing a staggering 900,000 pamphlets by the end of 1865.[133]

The reorientation of many bourgeois New Yorkers that expressed itself in the rapid growth of the Union League Club was aided by central tenets of republican thought. Now that slavery did not contribute to their economic power but instead undermined it, ever more bourgeois New Yorkers made good on their abstract commitment to the principle of self-ownership of the person and compromised on the sanctity of property rights. And the legitimization for the violation of property rights came easily to this group of propertied New Yorkers: Southern slaveowners had lost their rights to the protection of property by turning against the nation. "[T]raitors against the Government forfeit all rights of protection and of property," members of the Loyal Publication Society wrote in January 1863.[134]

Moreover, by 1863 the former reliance on slavery seemed anachronistic to many bourgeois New Yorkers. The rapidly emerging political economy of domestic industrialization, import substitution, and capitalist agriculture saw no place for bonded labor and put considerably less emphasis on the production of southern agricultural commodities.[135] Even for agriculture, slavery became less important: The *Merchants' Magazine and Commercial Review* remarked as early as 1862 on the stunning fact that the "sovereignty of cotton certainly appears to be disputed by corn . . . in a remarkably direct competition."[136] Moses Taylor, who had fought to the end for compromise with the South, now became an avid defender of aggressively pursuing the military reunification of the nation, even if this was to have revolutionary consequences. His former allegiance to the political economy of Atlantic trade, which he had exhibited in his years as a sugar merchant, became much less compelling in his new role as director of City Bank, as well as the owner of utility companies, iron mills, railroads, and mines. Taylor, like so many others, left behind the economic arrangements that had once made him rich and instead embraced the manufacturers' vision of domestic industrialization.[137] Similarly, William E. Dodge, who in 1861 had faced the specter of war with great anxiety, now argued that emancipation would go hand in hand with the rapid growth of agriculture in the West, rising exports of wheat to Europe, and the development of natural resources, as well as of industries that processed them, the spread of railroads, increasing immigration, and the export of manufactured goods to England. "Prosperity" was now the word that came most frequently to his mind when he described the effects of the Civil War.[138]

Such a revolutionary spirit, however, had its limits. Although many or even most bourgeois New Yorkers embraced emancipation by 1863, they did not intend to turn freedpeople into full citizens or right the inequities of the past.[139] Peter Cooper, writing in support of Lincoln's Emancipation Proclamation, did not once mention suffrage rights and even expressed his expectation that "as soon as the South is secured to freedom, the colored people of the North will rapidly emigrate to the South and furnish an abundance of cheap labor of all kinds."[140] Hence, in 1863 and 1864, most merchants, industrialists, and bankers interpreted emancipation to mean slaves' freedom from bondage, but not their admittance as equal citizens of the republic. Even less so did their embrace of emancipation imply support for a redistribution of the economic resources of the South.[141]

Meanwhile, August Belmont and his conservative peers were finding themselves increasingly isolated politically. Such isolation encouraged them to become more vocal and more vehement in their critique of the Republicans' project for the South. Their political strategy now focused entirely on antiabolitionism.[142] Belmont suggested that as part of a settlement with the South, Lincoln should rescind the Emancipation and Confiscation Acts. Samuel Barlow advocated a negotiated compromise with the South, including compromise on the question of slavery, a compromise that included the reunification of the nation on "fair terms" and the continued enslavement of those African Americans not "actually freed" at the moment of reunifcation.[143] Manon Marble's *New York World,* which Belmont had financed since August 1862 and which had considerable influence over public opinion, advocated a similar position.[144] August Belmont, Henry Grinnell, James Brown, and others desired "a vigorous prosecution of the present war" but not the "overthrowing or interfering with the rights and established institutions of the states."[145] By early 1863, they agitated against abolition through the newly founded "Society for the Diffusion of Political Knowledge."[146] While they remained committed Unionists, they explicitly feared the revolutionary nature of the changes the war seemed to engender.[147] But as a minority among the city's upper class, their position was weak, a weakness that forced them to ally themselves with Democratic machine politicians, some of the city's workers, and even with those who openly sympathized with the Confederacy.

While the Democratic bourgeoisie around August Belmont were supporting the war, a small group of capitalists mostly active in local markets were advocating a diplomatic settlement with the Confederacy, a settlement that would allow not only for the persistence of slavery but also – possibly – for the continued independence of the southern states. These "peace Democrats" emphasized the "sovereignty of the States" and demanded "that a Convention of the States composing the Confederate States, and a separate Convention of the States still adhering to the Union, be held to finally settle and determine in what manner and by what mode the contending sections shall be reconciled."[148] Fearing the social results of the war, particularly the emancipation of slaves, they stressed that "[t]he negro race are not entitled and ought not to be admitted, to political or social equality with the white race," not least because they might migrate to the North and compete with white workers.[149] They saw the government of the United States as "a government of white men . . . established exclusively for the white race," arguing that "the right of the several States to determine the position and duties of the race is a sovereign right."[150] These "peace Democrats," however, enjoyed only marginal elite support: When "peace Democrats" convened in June 1863, the entire contingent of wealthy New Yorkers consisted of Fernando Wood, coachmaker Peter Fullmer, and congressman, lawyer, and former South Carolinian C. Winthrop Chauler.[151]

These reactionary "peace Democrats" were significant, however, because they posed a difficult political problem for August Belmont and other elite pro-war Democrats. On the one hand, they enjoyed considerable strength in the party and attracted a large number of voters – particularly in New York City – while on the other hand, they could not be trusted to support the project that was, after all, dearest to Belmont: the unification of the nation. The resulting problems of navigating the shrinking political space between the pro-emancipation bourgeoisie and the radical peace advocates came into sharp focus during the 1864 presidential campaign. Belmont, chairing the Democratic Party, together with Barlow and Marble, successfully organized the candidacy of General McClellan.[152] They had overcome inner-party resistance against a war Democrat but failed to prevent the inclusion of a peace plank in the party's platform, "hurting us badly."[153] Belmont had urged McClellan to come out strongly for the Union, advising him that "[i]t is absolutely necessary that in your reply of acceptance of the nomination you place yourself squarely and unequivocally on the ground that you will never surrender one foot of soil and that peace can only be based upon the reconstruction of the Union remained identified with the peace plank."[154] Yet McClellan's uncertain course in the campaign, hampered as much by his political ineptness as by the peace plank in the party's platform and the Union's improved military position, resulted in a last devastating blow to the conservative bourgeois circles and a victory for Abraham Lincoln.[155] So small had the group around Belmont become that even a number of wealthy Democrats came out in support of Lincoln, among them banker Moses Taylor, who chaired the Union Campaign Committee in 1864.[156]

On the other side of the divide among upper-class New Yorkers, the shift in war goals resulted in bold political steps that would have been all but unthinkable only a year before. "The air generally is very suggestive of freedom," wrote printing press manufacturer Robert Hoe II, exuberant about the likely outcome of the war.[157] In early 1863, the New York Association for Promoting Colored Volunteering was founded by, among others, Horace Greeley, William C. Bryant, Parke Godwin, Peter Cooper, William Noyes, and Morris Ketchum.[158] The association successfully recruited into the army large numbers of African American New Yorkers, who had long been willing to join in a struggle of liberation for southern slaves. These efforts became more pronounced in the wake of the Draft Riots in 1863, when the Union League Club formed a committee to recruit black volunteers, counting among its leaders Henry J. Raymond, David Dudley Field, and Peter Cooper. This committee later joined forces with the Association for Promoting Colored Volunteers, and by December 19, a regiment one thousand soldiers strong was ready for departure.[159] Several other African American regiments followed.[160]

That large segments of New York's bourgeoisie now supported a step that two years earlier would have been proposed only by the most radical circles was demonstrated impressively on March 5, 1864: The 20th Colored Regiment marched through the city to Union Square, where the Union League Club sent them off, the flag being presented by Columbia College president Charles King, who lauded the black troops: "You are in arms not for the freedom and law of the white race alone, but for universal law and freedom, for the God implanted right of life, liberty, and the pursuit of happiness in every being."[161] Who would have thought in

March 1861 that three years later, 135 upper-class women, among them the wives and daughters of John Jacob Astor, James W. Beekman, James Brown, Robert B. Minturn, and R. L. Stuart, would help raise a regiment of black soldiers? Who would have thought that they would hand over a flag to these men with the reminder that the flag "is also an emblem of love and honor from the daughters of this great metropolis to her brave champions in the field, and that they will anxiously watch your career, glorying in your heroism, ministering to you when wounded and ill, and honoring your martyrdom with benedictions and with tears?"[162]

By the end of the war, most wealthy New Yorkers had embraced emancipation. "Peace without liberty assured for all," commented printing press manufacturer Robert Hoe II, would be a defeat.[163] It was a change that had come only slowly and had derived from a combination of war emergencies, as well as from the evident determination of slaves to gain their freedom. In some sense, the city's upper class had been compelled to embrace the completion of bourgeois society: Only the destruction of slavery would win the war, and this destruction could only be effected with the help of former slaves themselves. Embracing radical social change in the South was a big gamble, since nobody could tell how far freedpeople would press for change once they had been mobilized to help in the project dearest to the hearts of all bourgeois New Yorkers: the reunification of the nation. In 1863, it was entirely unpredictable whether bourgeois New Yorkers would be able to limit these upheavals to emancipation itself. But despite these limitations, bourgeois New Yorkers embraced social change, the likes of which the United States had not seen before.

The economic boom of the war years greatly facilitated this decisive break with the antebellum world. But it also sharpened economic disparities between rich and poor. Manufacturers, merchants, and financiers dramatically profited from the war, and as early as the fall of 1861, after the short recession of 1860/61, business in New York was prospering as the government's demand for goods and capital made its impact felt. "The business of this port since the war commenced has exceeded the expectations of the most sanguine," commented the *New York Times* on this unexpected prosperity.

Military procurement created the boom. Demand by the army and navy for copper, for example, surpassed all earlier demand and as a result, the Hendricks Brothers Copper Rolling Mills worked at capacity throughout the war.[164] The gun merchant Marcellus Hartley, appointed special agent by the United States for the acquisition of guns in Europe, shipped no fewer than 200,000 stands of arms to the United States in nine months (from July 1862 to April 1863). After his return home his business prospered, not least because of his contacts with the government.[165] And George W. Quintard's Morgan Iron Works built forty-three war steamers for the navy, making "money fast."[166] "The country at large was never in a better condition," reported the *American Railroad Journal* in July 1861, and it predicted quite correctly that "for the manufacturing and railroad interests an era of prosperity is about to open."[167] Most of New York's merchants even recovered from the blow to the cotton trade, especially when the failed European harvest of 1861 offered a new export market for American traders.[168] All told, according to banker Moses Taylor, the war years were "highly profitable."[169]

For some small manufacturers, the war proved a watershed event, turning them into major industrialists.[170] By 1865 John Roach, the iron manufacturer who had started his small enterprise in the 1850s, and who at the beginning of the war had counted forty workers on his payroll, was building engines for war ships and merchant vessels and employing 500 workers in a factory that he had converted "into an efficient plant."[171] The Novelty Iron Works, as well, "made money fast during the war."[172] And James Talcott, the New York clothing merchant and owner of a textile mill, profited from the rapid expansion of demand for textiles, making "enormous profits" clothing Union troops. Filling government orders, his business grew rapidly, indeed so rapidly that in 1863 and again in 1864 he had to relocate his factory to accommodate production.[173] By the end of the war, he had joined the small group of New York millionaires.[174]

Manufacturers, in particular, did exceedingly well and came into their own – not only vis-à-vis European producers but also vis-à-vis American merchants. While this trend had already begun prior to 1861, the war greatly accelerated it.[175] War-time profits permitted manufacturers to repay debts to wholesale merchants and provided the means for a self-financed expansion of factories.[176] George Quintard's iron works did so well that he did "not ask much cr[edit] in this Market, buying mostly for cash or short term."[177] At the same time, manufacturers' need for capital decreased, as the introduction of greenbacks and the accompanying strong currency fluctuations resulted in an increased reliance on cash payments.[178] Manufacturers who in the past had only been paid with one-month or even three-month notes now received their money immediately upon delivery. As a result, the Civil War helped to mold an enduring relationship between industrialists and capital markets, the government raising funds through bonds on the capital markets and buying manufactured goods with the proceeds. So beneficial was this relationship that the *American Railroad Journal* concluded that "[n]ever before in this country was there a more useful currency."[179] Merchants, in contrast, who had formerly been the sole suppliers of capital, saw their functions reduced to the distribution of goods. In their place, bankers began to make loans to industrialists, eventually enabling factory owners to raise capital on the New York Stock Exchange. Manufacturers, in the process, gained a new respectability, symbolized by such small gestures as John Roach beginning to wear a black stovepipe hat during the war years.[180]

The material well-being of upper-class New Yorkers translated into the blossoming of their social life during the war years – balls and dinners, the opera, and theater were well attended and opulent.[181] The *Journal of Commerce,* tellingly, thought that the "cutting off of the Chesapeake oyster trade [was] one of the incidental curses inflicted upon the North by secession."[182] Indeed, life was so good that some wealthy New Yorkers felt slightly uncomfortable. The lawyer Joseph Choate wrote to his wife in August 1862 that they should "in some way or other sacrifice a little of our abundance to the great cause to which we are sincerely devoted." The suggestion he made, however, was a modest one: "Maybe," he wrote, one could help "some poor family who have given their father. . . . We must struggle against selfishness in our great love – and don't you think it does tend slightly that way?"[183] If it were not for the "crowds of soldiers you see about the streets," remarked a stunned William E. Dodge, "you would have no idea of any war."[184]

A war this profitable undoubtedly helped many bourgeois New Yorkers to embrace the new political economy that it forged, including the destruction of slavery. Yet the wealth New York's upper class derived from the war stood in stark contrast to the deteriorating living standards of large segments of the city's working class, especially unskilled workers and independent craftsmen, who experienced an erosion of their wages through high inflation.[185] Often, they responded with strikes. Indeed, "work stoppages," reported immigrant manufacturer Karl Wesslau to his parents in Germany, "are a daily occurrence."[186] At the same time, some employers became more assertive, such as when in 1863 Charles Steinway, together with twenty-two other piano manufacturers, organized the Pianoforte Manufacturers' Society of New York to resist their workers' demands.[187]

It was on July 12, 1863, that the social conflicts in the city finally exploded. White working-class New Yorkers took to the streets in response to the implementation of the Conscription Act of March 1863, which enabled the federal government to draft any male between the age of twenty and thirty-five and all unmarried men between age thirty-five and forty-five who did not procure an acceptable substitute or pay $300 for an exemption.[188] Despite the fact that the act suggested to many working-class New Yorkers that they, and not the city's well-off, were to bear the brunt of the fighting, the registration process had been peaceful, many workers still believing that the Democratic state government would prevent a draft in New York City. But when on July 11 the conscription lottery began, discontent boiled over, and two days later, crowds of workers, many of them Irish immigrants, attacked draft officers with stones and fire. Symbols of bourgeois power, such as St. George's mission chapel on the Lower East Side, were "attacked and gutted."[189] By late afternoon on July 13, the first black New Yorkers were assaulted. The riot lasted for five days, changing its character after the first day to one increasingly directed by white workers against African Americans, symbols of the Republican government and federal institutions. Black women and men were murdered and often mutilated by white rioters. The Colored Orphan Asylum, a symbol of Republican reform as much as of the African American presence, was destroyed. Rioters fought the police and military on barricades. At week's end, an estimated 105 people lay dead.[190]

The riot was the most spectacular uprising the city had ever seen. It presented New York's upper class with a variety of unprecedented challenges, in particular how to contain explosive social tensions and simultaneously pursue the war in the face of widespread working-class dissatisfaction with its conduct and its goals. There was urgent and at times panicky concern about urban disorder. The *American Railroad Journal,* finding the city's "[c]apitalists . . . feverish and excited," saw the city "pretty much in possession of a mob."[191] "The situation," it noted, "was of hair-trigger tenseness."[192] George Templeton Strong observed "these wretched rioters" in close view, and by July 13 was commenting: "God knows what tonight or tomorrow may bring forth."[193] William Steinway, the piano manufacturer whose diary was largely devoid of political comments, wrote of the "terrific excitement" the riots produced and feared "the prospect of having the factory destroyed." He personally stayed until 1:00 A.M. at his workshop, together with father Charles, who calmed the "mob" by handing over $40 in cash and a check for a further $30. So tense was the moment that Steinway reported that "I have been unable to eat for the last 3 days except bread & drinking water for excitement."[194] As wealthy New Yorkers, hearing cries of "Down with the rich," saw threatening crowds assemble in front of their homes, John Parker observed that "a feeling of uneasiness" was spreading.[195] Fear that the crowds might attack the "great banking-houses and moneyed institutions" permeated upper-class talk.[196] It was in the context of this fear that Samuel Barlow expressed relief when Governor Seymour declared a state of insurrection, freeing "the fire power of the state to put down the terrible riot."[197] Joseph Hodges Choate agreed that "this mob" could only "be quelled . . . by slaying them like sheep."[198]

Elite New Yorkers were so shaken by the violence that they organized protective associations equipped with guns, the "Stuyvesant Square Home Guard" and the Merchants Volunteer Brigade among them.[199] The Union League Club even prepared itself for an extended battle as they "put shutters or shields of unpainted pine, bullet proofed and pierced for musketry" into their windows. "Here," the *New York Times* wrote, "united in an institution devoted to loyalty, they have both the will and the means to guarantee that . . . the rights of property & opinion will not be violated with impunity."[200]

Fear crossed all political divisions among the city's economic elite – from August Belmont to George Opdyke. On the night of the first day of the riot, some wealthy and powerful New Yorkers, among them mayor and manufacturer George Opdyke, lawyer George T. Strong, and the maker of nautical instruments George W. Blunt, as well as bankers John Jay and John Austin Stevens, Jr., consulted with General John E. Wool and Colonel Frank E. Howe in one of the city's hotels, "all urging strong measures."[201] Just as in April 1861, bourgeois New Yorkers found common ground – this time combining in defense of their property.

Although upper-class New Yorkers agreed on the urgent need to suppress the riot and its attacks on property, there was less unity on how this should be accomplished. After all, the rioters' assault on the increasingly radical goals of the war was quite compatible with the political interests of some. The members of the ad hoc committee at the hotel were divided about how to respond, as George Templeton Strong reported disappointedly: "Much talk, but no one ready to do anything whatever, not even to telegraph to Washington."[202]

In the following days it became increasingly clear that New York's economic elite could not agree on much beyond the need to restore order. As historian Iver Bernstein has shown, distinct responses to the riot emerged, disagreements once again rooted in very different perspectives on the war. Those upper-class New Yorkers who favored an aggressive pursuit of the war, many of them Republicans, agreed with George T. Strong that martial law should be declared and federal troops deployed to restore order, enforce the draft, and protect government property, as well as black New Yorkers, from the violence unleashed by some of the city's immigrant workers. This response crystallized particularly among the members of the Union League Club.[203] Their support for federal intervention often went hand in hand with a strong nativist outlook, defense of African Americans, and calls for paternalist reform.[204] This pro-war elite saw the Draft Riots as first and foremost a struggle over the meaning and consequences of the war. They were politically, materially, and ideologically invested firmly in the nation, and their commitment to emancipation eventually merged with their commitment to the physical safety of black New Yorkers.

This group of the city's economic elite was confronted with a more conservative – and mostly Democratic – elite who proposed an alternative solution to the crisis. Opposing federal intervention and the declaration of martial law, these upper-class New Yorkers, some of whom tacitly supported the antidraft movement, wanted to reintegrate the rioting white working class with a combination of concessions and repression, while leaving the black riot victims to themselves. The *Journal of Commerce,* advocating this strategy, expressed understanding for the rioters and suggested peaceful means of settling their grievances.[205] Maria Daly, wife of Democratic Judge Charles Patrick Daly, sympathized with these sentiments: Although she feared for property in the city and supported the restoration of order, she hoped the riot "will give the Negroes a lesson, for since the war commenced they have been so insolent as to be unbearable."[206] Contractors, such as Peter Masterson and Terence Farley, whose close connections to the Democratic Party gave them a strong incentive to build a coalition with the rioters, supported such an approach, suggesting that the city provide a substitute payment of $300 for each New Yorker called to serve.[207]

Ironically, the Draft Riots had played into the political efforts of this more conservative segment of the city's economic elite around August Belmont. They had based their political power on a coalition with white immigrant workers, and the Draft Riots provided them with a long looked-for opportunity to challenge the Republicans' war. But most of them saw that the rioting working class endangered their own property as well. Therefore, they sought ways to suppress the riots without harming their political alliances with the white working class, a strategy that drove them further into the arms of Tammany Hall, which provided them with an institutional tie to the city's workers while still enforcing order. Eventually, this strategy strengthened Tammany itself, and one rising politician in particular, William M. Tweed.

The solution to the conflict between these elite groups and to the crisis itself, then, was a compromise that expressed primarily the seriousness of the threat. Lincoln, as well as Opdyke, knew he had to compromise with Governor Seymour and the Democratic elites of the city, who, their property threatened, saw no alternative other than agreeing to the repression of the riot by military means. Federal troops were brought to the city, but General Butler did not, as Republicans had demanded, command them; instead it was General Dix, a Democrat loyal to Lincoln. Seymour declared New York to be "in a state of insurrection," enabling him to put down the riot without having to declare martial law.[208] This compromise restored order. And weeks later, conscription laws were successfully enforced.[209]

In the end, however, the Draft Riots had another significance for the city's economic elite. They strengthened the distinct impression of many merchants, manufacturers, bankers, and professionals that they were being confronted by the "dangerous classes." One decade later, in 1873, J. T. Headley published a book on *The Great Riots of New York, 1712–1873, Including a Full and Complete Account of the Four Day's Draft Riot of 1863* in which he compared the rioters to the "mobs of Paris," and argued that "these riots assume a magnitude and importance that one cannot contemplate without a feeling of terror."[210] Upper-class New Yorkers learned that the masses in general and democracy in particular bred danger, and they went to work after the riots to "reform" local government in order to reduce working-class power. At the moment when most of them had finally decided on crushing the basis of power of the southern slaveholders and establishing their firm control over the North American continent, at a time when enormous profits made them look optimistically into the future of a united and rapidly industrializing country, they witnessed the first glimpse of the confrontations that were to accompany their rise for years to come. And it was in these conflicts that they would overcome their deep divisions of the era of slavery.

But before new challenges arose, a triumph was to be celebrated. Most of New York's merchants, manufacturers, bankers, and professionals recognized by mid-1863 that the North would eventually subdue the southern Confederacy.[211] Toward the end of the war, at a moment when military victory became certain, most of New York's economic elite advocated a nationalist program and supported the determined fight to capture Richmond.

It was then hardly surprising that during the 1864 presidential elections, few wealthy New Yorkers came out for the Democrats.[212] While August Belmont stubbornly clung to the party, even such Democrats as Moses Taylor, Edwards Pierrepont, and Francis B. Cutting mobilized in public meetings "to adopt measures to sustain the present administration."[213] An October 1864 meeting of bankers and merchants for McClellan was so poorly attended that even one of its organizers, Samuel Barlow, admitted that the attendees "knew nothing about such matters, so that we were compelled to engineer it in every respect."[214] August Belmont's campaign for McClellan in fact isolated him from his peers, reducing people around him to political outcasts from respectable circles. George T. Strong remarked sarcastically in his diary that now even "Barlow & Belmont, O'Connor & Betts will soon be sending in their names" to join the Union League Club.[215] And indeed, the *Journal of Commerce* found that "[a]ll questions relating to the object and conduct of the war were settled by that election, and they were no longer subject of discussion."[216]

In early 1865 the mood in the city was celebratory. On March 6, after the announcement of decisive Union victories, a seven-mile-long parade snaked through the city to a rally at Union Square.[217] George T. Strong remembered the atmosphere of the day as "splendid" and recalled that "it took me an hour to work my way uptown through the crowded streets."[218] At the rally, Democratic Judge Charles P. Daly applauded the resoluteness of the northern troops and celebrated military victories. His party friend Edwards Pierrepont rejoiced "at the many brilliant successes over the enemies of Liberty." And William E. Dodge compared the ruins of Charleston with the vibrant metropolis of New York City.[219]

When on April 3 the news came to New York City that Richmond had been captured, ten thousand New Yorkers poured again into the streets.[220] On Wall Street, a spontaneous meeting ended with the singing of the Doxology and the 100th Psalm.[221] "Never before did I hear cheering that came straight from the heart," wrote George Templeton Strong in his diary on the same day.[222] "The deliverance is so signal, sudden and complete that we are lost in astonishment, admiration and thankfulness," reported Robert Hoe II.[223] At the Union League Club a large crowd assembled later in the day, and even Hamilton Fish, remarked Strong, was "beaming and gushing."[224] Flags were everywhere. On April 4, celebrations continued and two days later New York's Chamber of Commerce celebrated the Union victories, thanking all soldiers for their participation in the restoration of national unity, and resolved shortly afterward that "the victories of the Republic shall endure to the honor of free institutions, to the lasting good of humanity, and to the total extinction of slavery."[225] When on April 10 news of Lee's surrender reached the city, the Stock Exchange moved to acquire "the best and most beautiful" American flag to "adorn the room of the Board of Brokers."[226] Strong found "sleep . . . difficult."[227]

The city planned its official victory celebrations for April 20. They would never happen. When the news came that Abraham Lincoln had been assassinated, Helen Grinnell observed that "the nation is paralyzed."[228] "I am stunned as by a fearful personal calamity," wrote George T. Strong in his diary.[229] John Ward confided to his diary in similarly emotional terms that upon hearing the news he "could not restrain my grief."[230] Even Samuel Barlow, no friend of the administration, spoke of the "terrible calamity."[231] Businesses closed down in mourning; the Chamber of Commerce asked its members to resort "very generally to houses of public worship."[232] On April 24, Lincoln's body arrived in the city, and thousands congregated around his casket.

During these April days of 1865, nearly all upper-class New Yorkers celebrated the restoration of the Union and the decisive defeat of the southern slaveholders. The *American Railroad Journal* expressed its "gratitude to that Omnipotent power which has reached from its highest dwelling place" to make victory possible.[233] And John Austin Stevens, Jr., celebrated the "glorious triumph of universal freedom."[234] The symbolic reappropriation of the nation was best expressed by the frequent trips wealthy New Yorkers took to the South. Abiel Abbott Low, for example, traveled to Hilton Head, Charleston, and Fortress Monroe in April 1865. From Charleston he embarked with a group to Fort Sumter, and there "raised the Flag amid cheers & shouts & crying. . . . There was a great looking for relics. . . . I had the good fortune to find a cannon ball just the convenient size to bring home."[235]

The victory of April 1865 can be considered one of the great triumphs of New York's bourgeoisie, a triumph which gave them increased power and promised even more rapid economic development. Banker John A. Stevens, Jr., expressed this sentiment in retrospect: "[T]he great principles which underlie the structure of our Government . . . received their triumphant vindication in the utter overthrow of the most formidable rebellion that ever strained the power or tested the strength of any government."[236] The *American Railroad Journal* proudly asserted that the "model republic" had "purified itself of its last deepest guilt" and now stood as "the most enduring defense of religious, civil and political liberty."[237] How the North would employ its might in the subjugated South and how the newly created power of the national government would be altered in the postwar period, however, were open to contest.

The war, by demolishing the political economy of Atlantic trade, had also removed one of the fundamental divisions among bourgeois New Yorkers. Slavery was dead and with it important elements of the economic and political structure of the antebellum United States. Beginning in 1865, neither merchants nor manufacturers could continue to see the social conflicts of the North through the lens of their particular relationship to slavery. The perception of the ever-growing working class henceforth had to be newly negotiated. This struggle would solidify the ranks of New York's upper class and increasingly set them apart from other social groups, whom they began to view as a threat to their power.

5

The Spoils of Victory

As the institutional, social, and ideological arrangements of the ante-bellum world gave way in the spring of 1865, bourgeois New Yorkers had to find their bearings. Though the city's well-to-do had hesitantly helped to revolutionize the nation, few had anticipated or desired the ways in which the Civil War had changed the United States. Perhaps most significantly, the war had encouraged popular claims to state power and resources – ranging from freedpeople's demand for land to workers' insistence on an eight-hour day – claims that frequently ran counter to the interests of capital-rich New Yorkers. After the dust of the victory celebrations had settled, they assessed, struggled over, and nego-tiated the consequences of the transformations of the past years.

Navigation of this transition was aided by the exuberant optimism that they came to share about the future of the United States and New York City's place in it, an optimism that was the direct outcome of victory. Quite typically, Horace Greeley predicted that New York was on its way to becoming "the centre [sic], as she should be, of industrial as well as commercial greatness in the New World and ultimately in the whole world."[1] Such hopes helped bourgeois New Yorkers to master the upheavals of the postwar years and to adjust not only to fundamental changes in the nation's political economy but also to a further revolution-izing of southern society.

The enormous economic growth in the wake of the war, especially the spread and deepening of industrialization, fueled such confidence. In 1869, the number of factories in the United States had nearly doubled from one decade earlier, and by 1873, $400 million of capital was invested into manufacturing, or four times as much as in 1865.[2] These factories mechanized rapidly; the horsepower produced by their machines was augmented by 46 percent during the 1860s.[3] Most striking was not only the tremendous expansion of the United States economy but also the transformation of its character. New industries came into their own. Telegraphs spanned the continent, and in 1866 a cable put London and New York City in nearly instant contact.[4] The oil industry –

after the first discoveries in Pennsylvania in 1859 – grew by leaps and bounds.[5] Other important technological innovations, such as mechanical reapers, sewing machines, leather and textile machines, new mining processes, and rolling mill and cattle-slaughtering systems, led to enormous productivity gains. And the most important industry of the age, railroads, transformed every aspect of the nation's life. Railroad mileage doubled in only eight years – from 35,085 miles in 1865 to 70,268 miles in 1873.[6] In no other year in the nineteenth century were as many tracks laid as in 1872 – 7,439 miles, or nine times more than in 1865. In May 1869 the transcontinental railroad was joined, and for the first time, a truly national market emerged.[7] Indeed, between 1850 and 1900 railroad investments exceeded investments in all other industries combined.[8] This economic growth was accompanied by a surge in population, as between 1865 and 1873 another three million immigrants reached the shores of the United States, helping to boost the total population by 22.6 percent.[9] Manhattan was an important magnet to these immigrants, and by 1873 the city counted close to one million inhabitants, or nearly twice as many as two decades earlier, while the number of families who controlled assets of more than $15,000 increased to more than 12,500.[10] Many people with capital and skills joined in this move, so that by 1870, a full 43 percent of all upper-class New Yorkers had been born overseas, compared with only 26 percent fifteen years earlier.[11] So rapid were these transformations that the *Commercial and Financial Chronicle* found that "[t]he movements of time seem to have quickened," observing that "it would be impossible to find in the annals of mankind ten years in which such momentous changes have taken place."[12]

These were the golden years of the age of capital, and not surprisingly, it was an age of exuberant optimism among bourgeois New Yorkers. Yet no segment of the city's upper class represented the dynamics of the age better than did the industrialists. Though in 1870, as in 1855, industrialists were only the second largest group of the city's economic elite, they had come into their own, expanding the manufacturing capacity of the city and the nation at breathtaking speed.[13] Between 1860 and 1870, the number of factories in Manhattan rose from 4,375 to 7,624, the invested capital increased by 34 percent, and the number of workers employed grew by 39,373, to 129,577.[14] Clothing manufacturers, producers of iron goods, and printers all expanded their operations.[15] Though the expansion of the city's industrial capacity was slightly less rapid than that of the nation as a whole, by 1870 one in thirty-three U.S. factories still operated in Manhattan,

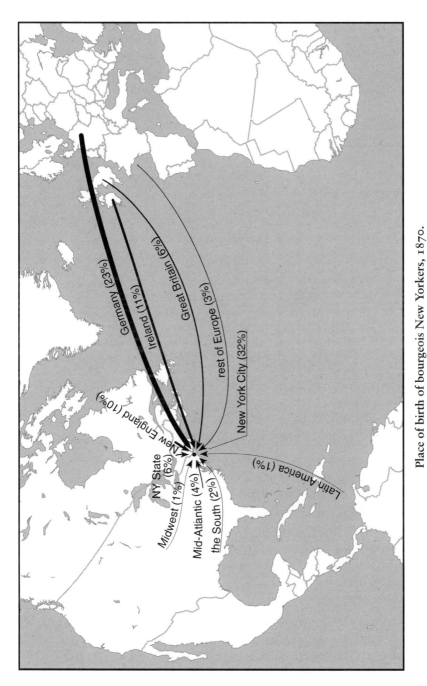

Place of birth of bourgeois New Yorkers, 1870.
Source: Sample of 1,571 New Yorkers assessed on real and personal wealth of $15,000 or more in 1870. Map courtesy of Harvard University Map Collection.

one dollar out of sixteen was invested in its manufacturing enterprises, and one out of sixteen workers was employed there. While manufacturing in the city remained labor intensive, some manufacturing companies also increased in size: A few of Manhattan's clothing firms, for example, employed up to 3,000 workers.[16] And even traditionally small firms, such as those engaged in construction, were increasingly dominated by such builders as John Conover, who employed between 50 and 100 workers.[17]

Manufacturing in Manhattan expanded essentially for the same reasons it had taken such a strong hold in the first place: The city itself provided the single largest market in the United States, labor was abundant, and raw materials were readily available. New York was at the center of a huge emerging transportation network, making national markets easy to reach. Moreover, essential secondary services – insurance companies, banks, auction rooms, and stock as well as commodity exchanges – were in close proximity. These conditions were especially beneficial for the city's largest industries. The clothing industry needed accessible markets and cheap labor. The same factors favored the production of iron goods, especially machinery. Although makers of heavy iron goods increasingly left for cheaper locations closer to the sources of iron, Manhattan remained a prime place for the manufacture of carriages, sugar molds, sewing machines, cutlery, and printing presses (New York's Hoe brothers were the leading manufacturer of presses in the world).[18] The city's iron manufacturers also supplied the beams used in construction, thus benefiting from the physical growth of the city.[19] Publishers and printers profited from the plethora of writers, journalists, and intellectuals who worked in the economic capital of the nation. Manufacturers prospered not only because markets expanded but also because the enormous profits of the Civil War years allowed them to gain greater independence from capital-rich merchants. In turn, they became more assertive, as when Horace Greeley argued in 1867 that because "production is primary to and more important than distribution, . . . commerce should be the servant or ally, not the master, of industry. . . ."[20] In a city that had stood as a symbol of the power of trade, this was a courageous assertion.

The most significant industry to come into its own after the Civil War was railroads. Railroad building consumed staggering amounts of capital, and most were built and controlled by upper-class New Yorkers who either invested their own capital or channeled that of Europeans.[21] (Junius Morgan's London banking house, for example, employed the contacts of his son's New York City bank to sell American railroad bonds on the European markets.) The number of upper-class New Yorkers who restricted themselves solely to this sector was small, but those who did, such as Cornelius Vanderbilt and Jay Gould, became enormously wealthy and powerful. Many more New York merchants, industrialists, and bankers invested a share of their wealth in railroads, leading in turn to a rapid expansion of the New York Stock Exchange, which listed more than 300 different companies after the war, most of them railroads. The railroad fever was a huge windfall for New York's economic elite, not least because they reaped the profits from the tremendous postwar land giveaway by the federal government, which between 1862 and 1871 turned over more than 100 million acres of federal land to the railroads.[22] When in 1866 Illinois Lieutenant Governor William Bross spoke to New York's merchants, he predicted correctly that "the men who have built the road will . . . be the richest men in America."[23]

Economically and politically, the rise of railroads, in turn, benefited another group of New Yorkers, lawyers. They defended railroads in courts, lobbied for land grants, and managed the day-to-day operations of the roads. Lawyer Richard Blatchford, for example, was the director of the New York Central Railroad from 1861 to 1867, lawyer Edwards Pierrepont was officer and director of the Texas & Pacific Railroad until 1870, and David Dudley Field represented Jay Gould.[24] Many of these attorneys also took important positions in government, lobbied in Albany and Washington, and helped to draft bills. They bridged the worlds of business and the state as did no other sector of the city's economic elite, translating the railroads' economic might into unrivaled political influence.

Along with the rise of railroad owners and industrialists, New York witnessed the emergence of a new group of financiers, distinct from the old merchant bankers, in the postwar years. Though they accounted for only 6 percent of the city's upper class, they moved into a central position in the national economy.[25] The reorganization of the nation's banking system during the war had proved to be a boost to their dominance. Between 1860 and 1870, the profitable "bankers' balances" had increased by a staggering 250 percent. As a result, by 1870, 24 percent of all banking resources in the United States were concentrated in New York City – and 87 percent of these assets were in national banks.[26] The rapid increase of industrialization and domestically accumulated capital helped the United States banking system to become ever more independent; by 1870, while foreign direct investments in the United States boomed, some capital was already being exported to Europe.[27] So rapid was the growth of banks that John Crosby Brown complained in February 1871 that his banking house enjoyed "too much prosperity."[28] Further indicating the rapid

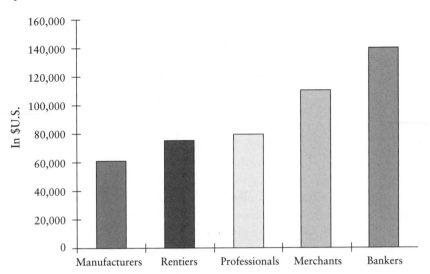

Average combined real and personal wealth of bourgeois New Yorkers, by economic sector, 1870 (N = 1571).
Source: 1870 sample.

ascendancy of financiers, this group had on average accumulated the most capital and could afford to hire the largest number of servants among upper-class New Yorkers.[29]

While some antebellum merchant bankers, such as August Belmont and James Brown, managed well the transition to this new kind of banking, others were replaced in importance by a generation of aggressive financiers who saw that the future lay with industry, in particular railroads, and not in the financing of trade.[30] As a result, the top ten banks in 1870 included five that had not even existed in 1860.[31] Those bankers who had accepted the national banking system and who saw the opportunities of America's industries were the most successful. Prominent among those who had a clear vision was J. Pierpont Morgan, who invested systematically in the country's industries and who symbolized the new fusion of finance and industrial capital when in 1870 he joined the board of the Albany & Susquehanna Railroad, which he had helped finance.[32]

Economic boom times also gave a boost to the small but important segment of the city's upper class who concentrated on real estate. Real estate experienced a particularly rapid expansion after the Civil War. Between 1868 and 1872, no fewer than 11,223 new building plans were filed in

Manhattan as the wealthy built more houses and population growth demanded new residential areas.[33] Land values soared in fashionable districts, particularly along Fifth Avenue and the east side of Central Park, augmenting the assessed value of the city's land by 341 million dollars between 1865 and 1871.[34] Sometimes, the increase in value was truly stunning: A lot bought in 1868 by the YMCA at Fourth Avenue and 23rd Street for $75,000 was sold a few months later for $125,000.[35] This residential construction boom was accompanied by a rapid improvement of the city's infrastructure – the expansion of gas, water, and sewage systems, as well as the grading of streets, especially in wealthy neighborhoods, all of which offered untold opportunities for the city's builders and land speculators.[36]

The ascendancy of industrialists and financiers continued to chip away at the once overwhelming dominance of merchants. Although they remained the single largest group among bourgeois New Yorkers (approximately 38 percent) and their trade expanded rapidly – exports skyrocketed by 130 percent and imports by 115 percent between 1865 and 1873 – they began to lose their commanding position in the economy.[37] The advent of the telegraph and regularly scheduled steamships made their services less important because the telegraph helped customers to order directly from producers, reducing their dependency on the market knowledge of merchants.[38] Moreover, some manufacturers (for example, in the iron and steel industry) began to deliver goods directly to their customers, as well as to raise their own capital. Those merchants who did not or could not adjust to the changing times, especially the shipping merchants, experienced economic duress.[39]

The postwar boom thus saw a shift of economic power away from merchants and toward manufacturers and financiers. The changing importance of different segments of capital, however, did not necessarily entail, in each and every instance, a change in individuals. Some bourgeois New Yorkers changed the emphasis of their businesses instead, for example the firm of Brown Brothers, which discontinued its merchant business and focused entirely on banking. They now referred to themselves as "Exchange Dealers and Bankers" and not, as they had done before the war, as "Merchants, Factors and Bankers."[40] Moreover, the primary occupation of merchants, industrialists, or bankers at times only poorly reflected their actual economic interests. The attraction of profits in distinct economic sectors was great for anyone with capital to spare – and bourgeois New Yorkers constantly looked for new investment opportunities.

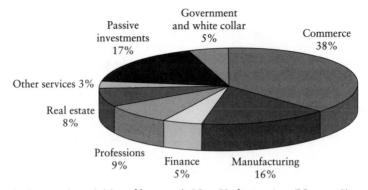

Economic activities of bourgeois New Yorkers, 1870 (N = 1428).
Source: Sample of 1,571 New Yorkers assessed for a combined real and personal wealth of more than $15,000 in 1870 federal census. 143 individuals (9 percent) had either no entry in category "occupation" or the entry was unreadable. See 1870 sample.

The gun merchant Marcellus Hartley, for example, used his profits from supplying northern troops with guns to acquire the Union Metallic Cartridge Company in Bridgeport, Connecticut, where he profitably manufactured cartridges to enormous profit.[41] By the end of the war, Edwin D. Morgan, the owner of a wholesale grocery business and wartime New York State governor, added to his business investments in two banks, nine insurance companies, four railroads, two gas companies, and two telegraph companies.[42] Horace Greeley, the publisher, invested $20,000 in Jay Cooke's transcontinental railroad and acquired 500 shares in the Globe Gold and Silver Mining Company, located in California.[43] Henry Ward Beecher, the pastor, put $15,000 into the same railroad.[44] Elisha Riggs, Jr., who until 1865 was engaged mainly in banking, left business and invested his possessions of more than one million dollars in railroads, the oil industry, and land in the West, as well as in textile stocks.[45] And copper manufacturer Uriah Hendricks diversified his holdings to a significant degree, investing more than half of his capital in other sectors of the economy, especially New York City real estate. Boundaries between different segments of the city's upper class thus were porous, especially because capital markets allowed for a diversification of investments into railroads.[46]

In a further departure, rapid economic development expanded horizons and boosted ambitions among all upper-class New Yorkers. This enormous confidence expressed itself best as they saw their sphere of interest expand much beyond what it had been before the Civil War. For one thing, there were the vast spaces of the American West to carve up. Now

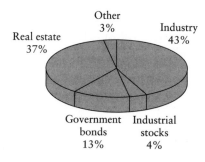

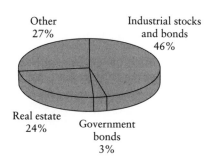

Distribution of Capital of
Uriah Hendricks at the
Time of his Death, May 1, 1869

Elisha Riggs, Jr.,
Ledger Balances as of
March 31,1872

Diversification of investments.

Source: New-York Historical Society, Hendricks Papers, Case 22, "Hendricks Brothers, 1831–1926," and "E. Riggs Ledger Balances March 31, 1872," in Riggs Family Papers, Box 56, Library of Congress. Elisha Riggs' holdings in industrial stocks and bonds were concentrated in the oil industry and railroads, his real estate investments outside of New York City. Uriah Hendricks' investments in industry were concentrated in the copper industry; his real estate was located mostly in New York City.

that railroads made the West accessible and federal troops were herding Native Americans into ever shrinking reservations, the region's lands and minerals captured the imagination of the city's economic elite (the art dealers around Union Square did a brisk business in painters' depictions of the West).[47] When in January 1866 William Bross, lieutenant governor of Illinois, delivered a glowing account to "many of the oldest and most distinguished New York merchants" on the "Resources of the Far West and the Pacific Railroad," he asserted that "now that the war is over, it is the duty . . . of the American people to inquire how they can most rapidly develop the resources of their vast country."[48] The western plains he saw as "the great meat-producing section of the continent," and Colorado, Idaho, Nevada, and Montana as the great new mining areas, a vision his elite audience shared.[49]

The merchants and bankers of New York City, however, saw as their mission not only the commercial exploitation of their own continent but of others as well. As the head of the Bank of Commerce, John Austin Stevens, Jr., said in 1869, "The flag, which it aided to carry in triumph through the war, must take the news of our victories to every country, and float on every sea."[50] Not surprisingly, the Chamber of Commerce paid attention to developments around the globe, from Italy and Morocco to

Argentina, Japan, and China.[51] In 1864 they had pressured Lincoln to exert his influence more strongly in the Western Hemisphere, especially with Venezuela, which was to be made "tributary to the commerce and wealth of the United States."[52] The Chamber lobbied for regular mail communications between the United States and Brazil in 1865, supported a National Exposition of Agricultural Machines in Rio Janeiro in 1866, discussed the benefits of annexing San Domingo "to the territory of the United States" in early 1871, and in 1872 invited a Japanese delegation to a banquet.[53]

New York City's future seemed splendid because it was here that the "Atlantic washes its feet, the tropics pour their riches into its lap, the Arctic brings its products, the vast interior of our own country fills its warehouses, while by the Pacific railroad the regions of China, Japan and the East Indies are brought onto its door."[54] When Abiel Abbot Low returned from a "Voyage round the World" in 1867, he reported to his merchant colleagues about the spectacular opportunities awaiting American entrepreneurs.[55] Infected by this optimism, Simeon B. Chittenden wondered, "if any of us fully comprehend the coming power and splendor of our city."[56]

᷎ ᷎ ᷎

Nothing quite expressed the confidence of the city's merchants, industrialists, and bankers better than the blossoming of social life among the economic elite's wealthiest ranks after the Civil War. In a distinct departure from the antebellum years, social events of this select and powerful group became more elaborate and more public than ever before. The social season following the war – one historian has estimated – saw 600 balls, and the amount spent on dresses and jewelry for these affairs ran to about $7 million.[57] Teas, receptions, intimate dinners, parties, balls, and cotillions kept upper-class New Yorkers busy.[58] In this "golden age of New York society," some women would order forty gowns from Worth in Paris each season – at a cost of $2,500 a dress.[59] Meals would consist of seven to ten courses. At a legendary dinner organized by Leonard Jerome at Delmonico's, each woman found a gold bracelet hidden in her napkin.[60] Boxes at the Academy of Music were prized possessions.[61] "Year by year," commented May King Van Rensselaer, an astute observer of New York's social life, "the love of luxury, and the taste for excitement increased."[62] Some of these entertainments bordered on the bizarre, as Mrs. Stuyvesant Fish would on occasion throw a "lavish tea party" for her friends' dogs or even seat an ape in the "place of honor at the dinner table."[63]

The new conspicuous display of wealth contrasted with the more staid mores and manners of the antebellum mercantile elite and explains the obsession of upper-class New Yorker with social events. To become part of the social scene of the city, one had to have enough money to pay for elaborate dinners, fashionable dresses and suits, and plush carriages. The setting itself, of course, also had to be acceptable. Though brownstones would still do, some bourgeois New Yorkers set their sights far beyond such modest dwellings.[64] Alexander T. Stewart's marble mansion on 34th Street and Fifth Avenue, finished in 1869, was ornamented in the most elaborate fashion along its 150-foot facade. The financier Leonard Jerome, August Belmont's cousin, lived in a house on Madison Avenue and 26th Street that included a 600-seat private theater and carpeted stables paneled in walnut.[65] The interiors of these homes were decorated ever more elaborately. It became de rigueur to have at least one receiving salon, "furnished with piano, paintings, crystal chandeliers, and every nook and cranny filled with cast statuary, clocks and clutter, underlined and muffled by draperies, doilies and cushions."[66] Vases and hangings further crowded rooms.[67] To remain up to date with the latest fashions, some upper-class households even commissioned professional interior designers.[68] "Oh, . . . I see Cottier [a famous interior designer] has been with you," says a fictional character in Clarence Cook's contemporary tour of fashionably decorated bourgeois homes.[69] Even manufacturer Richard Hoe II considered presenting his brother with a marble bust of himself to be put on display.[70]

The location of the home was as important as its interior, and fashionable neighborhoods came and went in rapid succession. By 1870, the center of bourgeois life had moved well above 14th Street to Fifth Avenue and adjacent avenues.[71] James Brown's family, for example, moved in 1868 from the fifteenth to the twenty-first ward – away from University Place, where they had located only a decade earlier, "because of the changes in the neighborhood, similar to those which occurred in Leonard Street." They built a new house on 37th Street and Park Avenue.[72] Tellingly, the restaurant Delmonico's also packed up and moved from its old location on 14th Street to 26th Street.[73] In 1855, only 15 percent of bourgeois New Yorkers had lived north of 23rd Street, but in 1870, about 56 percent had moved into the uptown wards, with a full 23 percent inhabiting the Upper East Side between 40th and 86th Street.[74] On the other hand, the eighteenth ward stretching around Union Square, which in the fifties had been home to one in four bourgeois New Yorkers, now only provided a home for every tenth merchant, industrialist, or banker. Except for a scattering of upper-class New Yorkers in the twelfth, sixteenth, seventeenth and twentieth wards, there were few merchants, industrialists, or bankers living in the other neighborhoods of the city.[75] This was quite a significant change from fifteen years before, when one-fourth of New York's bourgeoisie resided in the eighteenth ward but scarcely anyone lived above East 40th Street in the nineteenth ward. Moreover, the fifteenth ward, the area around Washington Square, once the most bourgeois neighborhood in town, had lost its elite character.

In unprecedented ways, addresses themselves imputed social standing. Other rituals of bourgeois self-identification and distancing also moved evermore into the public eye. In antebellum New York, social events generally had not been publicized in the press, but now society reporters filled the columns of the dailies with elaborate accounts of the festivities of the wealthy.[76] Balls, which had always been given in private homes, were now moved into public spaces, such as the debutante ball Archibald Grace King gave for his daughter in the early 1870s at Delmonico's.[77] It became also much more acceptable to flaunt one's wealth publicly, for example, by having diamonds sewn into a dress.[78] In effect, the old merchant tradition of modesty and privacy gave way to ostentatious display.

Yet the swelling of the ranks of the city's merchants, industrialists, and bankers also created considerable problems for those who were part of the inner circles of bourgeois sociability. What were the boundaries of society to be? While in the 1850s the social rituals of the upper class had clearly been dominated by the city's mercantile elite, who were also economically the controlling force, by the late 1860s and 1870s new individuals were accumulating large amounts of capital in such undertakings as railroads, banks, or even industry. "In the decade following the Civil War, there came a great change," observed May King Van Rensselaer; "all at once [society] was assailed from every side by persons who sought to climb boldly over the walls of social exclusiveness."[79]

Though under assault in the 1860s and early 1870s, New York's old-guard mercantile elite was still able to dominate the social life of their peers. But this domination did not come easily and required conscious organizational efforts, including the inclusion of some segments of "new wealth." The most elaborate effort for such domination was Caroline Astor's and Ward McAllister's "Society of Patriarchs." Both Astor and McAllister lamented the fragmentation of "society" and hoped to alleviate it by creating a circle of elite New Yorkers at the top of the city's social hierarchy. For that purpose they appointed twenty-five "patriarchs" – among them Eugene E. Livingston, Royal Phelps, and William C. Schermerhorn – who each could invite five women and four men to the balls and dinners organized by Caroline Astor. Though old and new wealth were integrated in the circle, the relatively old New York merchant families clearly set the tone.[80] According to Van Rensselaer, the "patriarchs" were "instilling a new and dignified gaiety into the ranks of the old aristocracy."[81]

Although the "patriarchs" dominated New York society in the sense that invitations to their events were considered to be of great importance, in other areas of upper-class social life it was money and money alone that determined who could enter into the orbit of bourgeois sociability. The daily carriage parade in Central Park, for example, was open to all with sufficient resources to buy an appropriate carriage.[82] The New York Yacht Club, similarly, was accessible to most wealthy New Yorkers and, hence, it attracted many of the war profiteers, some of whom sported huge boats of more than 200 tons.[83]

No matter how and when capital-rich New Yorkers had accumulated their capital, moreover, they presented themselves as the proud representatives of a city and a nation riding on the crest of a new age. In May 1871, when preparations were made for the reception of the Grand Duke Alexis of Russia, such old timers as merchants Jonathan Sturges and John Jacob Astor served alongside railroad entrepreneur William H. Vanderbilt, banker August Belmont, publisher Elliot L. Godkin, and financier J. Pierpont Morgan on the reception committee.[84] They and others presented New York City – from its firefighters to the carriage parade in Central Park – proudly to "Our Imperial Guest."[85] But the high point of the Grand Duke's visit was a ball, which "kept all the aristocracy and respectability of this good city in a fever of expectation for weeks."[86] Hundreds of upper-class New Yorkers attended, while hundreds more had to be excluded because of the limitations of space in the Academy of Music. The room was lavishly decorated with silks and flowers. When the Grand Duke entered, New York's wealthy promenaded over the dance floor, showing off their expensive getups before the critical eyes of His Majesty. "More brilliant [a moment] was never witnessed within the walls of the Academy," asserted the *New York Times*.[87] Two painted banners hung from the ceiling, one depicting Czar Alexander abolishing serfdom and the other Abraham Lincoln holding the Emancipation Proclamation in his hand and "at his foot a family of liberated slaves."[88] Upper-class New Yorkers were proud of the nation they had helped create, at long last the equal of the powers of Europe.

⤵ ⤵ ⤵

Such fundamental optimism expressed in their social life also guided upper-class New Yorkers' relationship to the conquered southern states, firmly committing them to the revolutionary accomplishments of the war.

Both the city's mercantile elite and its rising manufacturers celebrated the defeat of slavery, believed that free labor was to guide the southern states to prosperity, and concluded that the former slaveholders were not to enjoy dominant national political power again.[89] "[S]lavery has met its eternal doom!" exclaimed the New England Society of New York proudly; this "disgusting, . . . hideous birth-mark which had blotted the fair face of this young Republic from her cradle" had "been absolutely burned out."[90] With the death of slavery, the end of the enormous political influence of the southern elite was to come as well: Even the *United States Economist and Dry Goods Reporter,* at the forefront of the demand to end federal involvement in the South, lost no love on former slaveholders. Warning of an "overflowing sentiment of generosity" that might lead northerners to embrace an amnesty for secessionist leaders, the journal pleaded that "for the sake of public quiet, and upon every ground of political interest, it is of the most paramount consequence that the leaders of the rebellion should be at least deprived of the rights of franchise and excluded from holding any position of national, State or civic office."[91] In the same spirit, the Chamber of Commerce, once the slaveholders' most important political ally in the North, demanded that cotton confiscated by Union troops in the South be used to cover debts southerners owed to New York City merchants and bankers and that bankruptcy laws be rewritten to help with "the sequestration of property for the purpose of discharging such indebtedness."[92] The defeated southern elite should transfer their remaining assets to their northern debtors and should stay politically subordinate to them.

The South, the city's economic elite believed, should be rebuilt in the image of the North. Free labor was the beacon to guide this reconstruction. Though upper-class New Yorkers disagreed on how "free" free labor would be, they held a deep-seated conviction that free labor was more productive than slave labor. Quite typically, the *American Railroad Journal* asserted that "it will be seen that free labor in tropical climates is competent to an increasing and profitable production. . . . [A]s the negroes are unquestionably particularly adapted to labor in those climates, we shall now have the immense advantage of stimulating their industry by the boon of freedom and the possession of their own earnings." They would become "an industrious and thriving race."[93]

Not only did bourgeois New Yorkers believe in the future of free labor, but some also invested considerable ideological, political, and economic resources in helping freedpeople make the transition from bondage. As early as 1862 they had begun to support freedpeople in areas captured by the Union army by founding and financing the National Freedmen's Relief Association.[94] Throughout the war and the early Reconstruction years, they sent clothing and teachers south.[95] Some involved themselves even more directly, such as William E. Dodge, who financed schools in the South and paid for the training of southern teachers in the North.[96] Hoping to transform the freedpeople into their image of frugal, well-behaved northern workingmen and women, they saw as their goal to "mold this mass of human beings . . . into a regular community."[97]

In these specific ways, all upper-class New Yorkers committed themselves to the results of the "bourgeois revolution." They saw these commitments, however, through the lens of powerful economic interests, most basically their desire to overcome the upheavals of war and occupation as rapidly as possible. "All that is now required is confidence and security," editorialized the *Merchants' Magazine and Commercial Review,* a stability that would allow for the accumulation of capital in the states of the former Confederacy, as well as in the nation as a whole.[98] "[I]nsecurity," they feared, "is the death of enterprise."[99] Only political stability would enable New York's merchants, industrialists, and bankers to trade with the South, invest in its railroads, and resume cotton production.[100]

As a result of these interests and inclinations, most bourgeois New Yorkers favored a rapid end to federal involvement in the South.[101] It was, in particular, the city's mercantile elite, those who had fought to the end for compromise with the southern states before the war, who were now at the forefront of demands for reconciliation.[102] With emancipation achieved, and the former slaveholders removed from national political prominence, they argued, no reason for extensive federal meddling remained. Freedom, as they saw it, meant first and foremost self-ownership and the right to participate in markets, both of which seemed to have been accomplished in the states of the former Confederacy. It was not surprising, then, that Andrew Johnson's policy of reconciliation with the South – his pardoning of former Confederates, his support for the reconstitution of political bodies in the southern states dominated by planters, and his ultimate rejection of black suffrage – at first won their endorsement.[103] The merchants especially demanded in the early fall of 1865 that "the restoration of civil government should not be delayed till the social problem is solved," since "[s]ocial questions must be left . . . to adjust themselves."[104] They favored a "more generous policy" toward the South and desired to give white southerners "every facility for an immediate resumption of the various avocations of peaceful life."[105] The Chamber of Commerce, voicing these preferences, worked "unceasingly [for] the restoration of friendly relations between the two sections," and advocated as early as May 1865 to "relieve the loyal citizens and well-disposed persons residing in the insurrectionary states, from unnecessary commercial restriction to encourage them to return to peaceful pursuits."[106]

Johnson, who promised to implement many of the Chamber of Commerce's desired policies, secured powerful and much-needed support from the city's economic elite. In August 1866, he received a triumphant reception in New York City. Welcoming Johnson, Alexander T. Stewart, the dry goods merchant, expressed his "deep conviction that it is the true interest of the country, through kind and conciliatory measures, to extend to the whole Union the blessings of active, social, political and commercial intercourse."[107] Banks put banners on their buildings declaring support for the president. Johnson himself, sharing a table at a banquet at Delmonico's with William B. Astor, Alexander T. Stewart, and Moses Taylor, defended his policies, interrupted only by the frequent applause of the approximately 200 wealthy guests.[108] Republican James Brown and Democratic leader August Belmont cheered Johnson on, as did Cornelius Vanderbilt and Abiel Abbot Low.[109] A similar group had already in February 1866 celebrated Johnson's veto of the continuation of the Freedmen's Bureau and had ventured to Washington to back him.[110] To the liking of many upper-class New Yorkers, Johnson seemed to be rapidly ending the destabilizing aftershocks of the war. "The time for peace has come, and the duty of the hour is restoration," announced the *Commercial and Financial Chronicle*. Johnson's "kindness and benignity" showed the way.[111]

At the core of this orientation was the hope of a substantial group of bourgeois New Yorkers, especially the city's mercantile elite, to restore the political economy that they had left behind in 1861, save for slavery. Expressing this sentiment, lawyer Charles P. Kirkland thought "reconstruction" the wrong term for describing the relationship between North and South, favoring "restoration" instead, since legally the seceding states had never left the Union. The southern states, he argued, should immediately regain their sovereignty and make all decisions regarding their internal affairs themselves.[112] Kirkland and others hoped to return to the antebellum economic relations between the sections, especially the resumption of the production of cotton, rice, and sugar in the South, exported in exchange for manufactured goods from the North and from abroad. For them, the war had been an unwelcome disruption of their profitable business transactions with the South, and they now desired first and foremost the restoration of "unrestricted commercial intercourse" between the sections.[113] These links included the export of agricultural commodities, mainly cotton, but also the provision of manufactured goods to southern customers and the resumption of debt payments by southerners, as well as investments in railroads.[114] Indeed, the *Journal of Commerce,* at the forefront of such debates, found that "the old questions of political economy resume their primary importance now in the eyes of wise citizens."[115]

The profitable production of cotton, rice, and sugar, however, required an abundant supply of cheap labor. At the core of the interests of merchants, investors in southern plantations, and textile manufacturers was, therefore, the creation of a stable system of labor relations in the South, an interest which was fundamentally at odds with the programs of land reform demanded by many freedpeople.[116] Freedom, in effect, could endanger cotton production, as George H. Brown noted with concern in a May 1865 letter to his brother, John Crosby Brown, written from Mobile, Alabama: "The negroes are frenzied by their freedom. They are all going to housekeeping; get together, with a table [and] a frying pan, a pot and chair and Government rations, and think themselves made. They will wake up to dreadful reality. Their notion of freedom is idleness and when want comes they will feel it."[117]

This relationship between the organization of labor and the production of agricultural commodities explains the striking attention bourgeois New Yorkers paid to the "labor problem" in the South. The cotton merchants of Tobias, Hendricks and Co., for instance, speculated on the effects emancipation would have on cotton prices: "[P]rices will yet be much higher. If the Sea Islands are given to the negroes for three years, then Contracts will be broken and the Freedmen will flock to the 'land of promise.'"[118] The cotton crop, they were informed on January 8 of the same year, "is solely a question of *labor.* . . . [N]o one expects the same amount of work from them [the freedpeople] as was obtained before the war."[119] Those, like the Leverich family, who, as cotton merchants, had invested directly in plantations, were especially concerned about labor availability and discipline, but reports in New York City's business press spread knowledge of the problem more widely.[120] These papers described freedpeople as "idle," and voiced complaints about the "exorbitant" wages of black cotton workers.[121] "Much of the prevailing indolence of the colored people is due to their foolishly imagining that a millennium of idleness has dawned upon them," asserted one writer.[122] Another business paper found that "[t]he liberated negroes appear to be absorbed in the celebration of an idle and lawless jubilee," and might, therefore, not work with sufficient diligence in the cotton fields.[123] The labor situation, in the eyes of bourgeois New Yorkers, remained volatile throughout the 1860s. In 1866 the *New York Commercial Advertiser* expressed great relief when freedpeople were willing to contract for a year's service since the "improving aspect of the labor question has an important bearing upon the prospects of the next cotton crop."[124] But three years later, the *Merchants' Magazine and Commercial Review* found freedpeople still "idle," engaged in "the vicious habits of life," and "frequently unreliable."[125]

Not surprisingly, the city's mercantile elite saw the control of labor as a crucial element in reestablishing the antebellum economic relations between New York City and the South. This connection between labor discipline on the one hand and cotton, sugar, and rice production on the other hand drove many merchants into a coalition with southern planters to resist a revamping of the South's social structure, in particular by opposing the making of freedpeople into land-owning, independent yeomen. A mass conversion of cotton lands to subsistence agriculture, they feared, would endanger cotton exports (and the stability of the monetary system), and, moreover, would set a dangerous example for the northern working class by putting into question the sanctity of property in the United States, a theme that would become particularly prominent after 1873 (see Chapter 7).[126]

While the need for a stable supply of labor did not settle the question of how the North should approach the South, it did limit what many merchants and bankers saw as viable options. In similar ways, direct investments in the southern states also profited from calm social relations and again suggested to many bourgeois New Yorkers a conservative approach to "what is called 're-construction.'"[127] Though manifold new investment opportunities had opened up by 1865 – from western railroads and mines to industrial enterprises in the North – the South reemerged as an outlet for capital as well, not least because the region lacked resources of its own.[128]

For many upper-class New Yorkers, such investments confirmed much older economic ties to the region. Isaac Sherman, for example, enlarged his interests in southern railroads: By May 1870, he listed his holdings in the region as worth $125,000 – made up of stocks of the Mobile & Ohio, Louisville & Nashville, Memphis & Charleston, and the East Tennessee Road.[129] William E. Dodge similarly expanded his commitment to the South by adding to his railroad investments and buying extensive tracts of lumber lands in Georgia, in what came to be known as Dodge County.[130] Samuel Barlow speculated in southern bonds and Virginia lands.[131] Moses Taylor moved, after 1865, a significant share of his investments into southern railroads, especially the Central Railroad of Georgia and the

South Carolina Railroad.[132] Not surprisingly, Taylor, Barlow, Dodge, and Sherman all advocated reconciliation with the South. Their economic links indicated to them that the retreat of the federal government from the South and the restoration of southern planters to some of their former regional prominence could guarantee political and economic stability, benefiting their particular economic interests.

This approach toward Reconstruction, moreover, suggested to the city's mercantile elite a restoration of other elements of the antebellum political economy, especially a return to low tariffs, a weak central state, and the gold standard. "For ourselves we confess freely," argued the *Journal of Commerce,* "that we have more interest in knowing what are President Johnson's views on the tariff question, and on national banks, than what he would do with Jeff Davis."[133] These members of the city's mercantile elite envisioned policies that would correct a condition in which "the war has left us with an undue proportion of the capital and labor of the country employed in manufactures, and an inadequate proportion engaged in the culture of the soil."[134] Conceptualizing the exchange of southern agricultural commodities with British manufactured goods as the core of the American economy, they not only found that "the commerce of the whole country and our command over the trade of Europe are supremely dependent upon the planting interest being restored to the relative position it occupied before the war," but also saw it necessary to resume the gold standard, to contract the federal government as rapidly as possible, and to end legislation "to create departments of industry."[135] In short, to regain a "preponderance in the commercial system of the world," federal involvement in the South had to be curtailed as rapidly as possible.[136] This, they argued, would have broader political ramifications as well, because once "the Southern States shall return to their position in the Union as coequal participators in the hall of national legislation, the agricultural interests of the republic, especially combined with its commercial interests, will be entirely irresistible."[137]

In the eyes of bankers, brokers, insurance owners, and merchants, an important step in rebuilding the antebellum political economy was the resumption of specie payments.[138] They feared that without resumption, the government would use an inflationary currency to pay back the vast amounts of money it owed to private investors, most of whom were to be found in New York's financial community. Merchants, moreover, saw the disadvantage of a fluctuating currency on "our intercourse with foreign nations," since a premium on gold made imports more expensive.[139] The reform of monetary policy was so urgent that the Chamber of Commerce's president, Abiel Abbot Low, linked foes of specie payment to foes of the Union who had waged war on the integrity of the United States.[140] "[M]easures that were justified by the emergencies of war will not be tolerated now that peace is restored," he argued.[141] For him as well as for most of the city's merchants and bankers, resumption was the "only hope of rescue from impending evil."[142] A return to the gold standard was that much more urgent because "important interests are being daily founded upon [greenbacks]," making future resumption more difficult to effect.[143]

Quite apart from short-term interests, bankers opposed greenbacks out of concerns about the stability of the financial system itself.[144] As it was, greenbacks not guaranteed in gold gave the federal government an enormous power over the regulation of financial markets. As Richard Bensel has shown, the Treasury proved, in the eyes of the nation's bankers, unable to fulfill this task so central to the larger economy.[145] Hence, bankers concluded, control over the currency should be left to markets (or to the Bank of England, which regulated the world gold market), and not to the United States government, with its vulnerability to myriad political influences.[146] These fears of a democratically controlled monetary policy, together with their specific economic interests in resumption, helped create a powerful movement, indeed so powerful that someone who had different views on the subject, such as iron manufacturer Peter Cooper, could be considered "a traitor to his class."[147]

Conflicts over tariffs further alienated many merchants and bankers from a more radical approach toward Reconstruction, since its proponents were also ardent protectionists.[148] New York's merchants and bankers protested frequently against new tariff bills, eventually organizing the American Free Trade League, most of whose members were New Yorkers.[149] In a twisted way, that struggle motivated a conservative approach toward Reconstruction because renewed political influence for the former southern elites, some hoped, would limit "the power of New England and Pennsylvania to force high tariffs upon the country."[150]

Hence, throughout 1865 and 1866, a large majority of New York's economic elite shared interests and inclinations that suggested the rebuilding of economic ties between North and South, the return to central elements of the antebellum political economy, and an early end to Reconstruction. Yet despite the prominent and powerful support of this position by New York City's upper class in general, and President Johnson's policies in particular, Johnson himself did not survive politically. And when his presidential Reconstruction collapsed in the face of widespread resistance in Congress against the reassertion of the powers of the former Southern ruling class, it opened the political space for the rise of Radical Republicans.

With few exceptions, New York's economic elite wanted nothing to do with the Radicals. Though by the fall of 1866 many among the city's upper class had also become critical of Johnson's policies, they continued to oppose the measures implemented with the help of Radical Republicans, especially the Fourteenth Amendment, establishing equal rights under the law, and the Reconstruction Act of 1867. Business papers warned on a daily basis that Radical Republicans threatened the prosperity of the nation.[151] "[P]olitical agitation in the South," according to the fearful *United States Economist and Dry Goods Reporter,* would endanger the cotton crop.[152] The *Commercial and Financial Chronicle* agreed: "What the country needs is peace and rest, and our legislators greatly mistake the temper of the people if they think they will much longer endure unnecessary agitation."[153] Tellingly, William E. Dodge, a Republican representing the wealthy uptown wards of Manhattan in the House, and himself a member of the Chamber of Commerce, fought determinedly against the Radicals' policy – but to little avail. In 1867 he asserted that suffrage rights for freedmen were out of the question: "The country is anxiously looking at us now as the focal point from which is to emanate something that shall give peace, harmony, and prosperity to the country and perpetuity to the Government."[154] Dodge wanted to "secure quiet and better feeling" and urged House members "not to look simply to the immediate enfranchisement of the negro race, overlooking all the other great interests of the country which are dependent upon the legislation we may adopt."[155] He wanted to leave "the question of suffrage where it has always been left" – with the States.[156] Even the Republican *New York Commercial Advertiser* complained about the "harsh" policies of the North toward the southern states, a policy it called "simple despotism." It opposed the expansion of the Freedmen's Bureau in 1866 and the Civil Rights Bill of 1866, as well as the congressional reconstruction plan.[157]

The powerful opposition of upper-class New Yorkers, in particular the city's mercantile elite, to the politics of Radical Reconstruction, however, came to naught, demonstrating conclusively that their sway on federal policies was greatly reduced.[158] Abiel Abbot Low acknowledged as much in 1866 when he explained to the members of the Chamber of Commerce that "the influence exerted by the Chamber in the Legislative halls of the country in former years is no longer felt to the same extent."[159] Regaining influence and bringing an end to the upheavals of Reconstruction was difficult, with Radicals setting the agenda of the Republican Party and the Democratic Party too entangled with southern elites, and with dangerously powerful advocates of "soft" monetary policies among its ranks.

In 1868, however, the presidential candidacy of Republican Ulysses S. Grant pointed a way out of their political problems.[160] Grant had already been wined and dined by the city's economic elite after the Civil War, and there were widespread expectations that he would bring an end to the upheavals of Reconstruction by advocating policies much more moderate than those of the Radicals, but not quite as accommodationist as those of Johnson. Both Republicans, such as William E. Dodge, Cornelius Vanderbilt, Henry Ward Beecher, and Peter Cooper, and wealthy Democrats, such as Moses Taylor and John Jacob Astor, enthusiastically backed him.[161] Indeed, Grant's presidency accomplished what bourgeois New Yorkers demanded most vehemently: "Finishing up Reconstruction."[162]

Yet Grant assisted in ending Reconstruction only by embracing some of the policies of the Radicals. Most significantly, he helped settle the vexing problem of suffrage rights for freedmen. In 1870, the Fifteenth Amendment, which prohibited racial discrimination at the polls but allowed for poll taxes, literacy tests, and property qualifications, was ratified.[163] Although the city's economic elite had in 1865 opposed such a radical departure, by 1869 they embraced it.[164] Now even Democrat Richard Lathers demanded "[e]qual right under the law and at the polls for Every Citizen regardless of nationality, Color or religion," and the *New York Commercial Advertiser* stated unequivocally: "We demand Suffrage for the Colored People in the Southern States."[165] Equality before the law and full voting rights hence were "no longer matters of controversy in the mainstream of American political life," as historian David Montgomery has observed.[166]

For some bourgeois New Yorkers, the enfranchisement of African Americans could even be translated into novel ways of gaining political influence, such as for William E. Dodge, who channeled funds into a congressional race in Georgia (which covered his lumber lands), using the money to pay African Americans' poll taxes in the hope that a candidate friendly to his interests would move into Congress.[167] In effect, upper-class New Yorkers followed Grant in accepting a more thorough revamping of southern society than they ever would have conceived of in 1865. As during the war, their interest in stability and the assertiveness of other social groups forced many of them to adjust their political visions. Yet even then they saw their own radicalization as an essentially conservative step that favored stability by ending the upheavals and uncertainties of Reconstruction.

In fact, there are a number of reasons that help account for the radicalization of the city's economic elite. First was the fundamental optimism that characterized upper-class New Yorkers during these years. The promises of bourgeois society shone bright; the possibilities for capital accumulation seemed endless. Once rapid economic expansion followed victory in war, anxiety about radical change in the South diminished. Second, the situation in the South itself suggested to many merchants, industrialists, and bankers the need for a more active involvement of the federal government. They realized that the political dynamic of the Reconstruction years had created expectations among freedpeople and among many northerners that could not be reversed.[168] Third, after 1866, a growing number of bourgeois New Yorkers came to believe that Johnson's policies had created an unacceptable level of upheaval in the South. As southern elites once more threatened stability and peace, some wealthy New Yorkers became convinced that the federal government had to intervene in the South.[169] They were concerned about the "outrages and wrongs perpetrated upon the liberated blacks," especially when Ku Klux Klan violence reared its head.[170] "We are afraid to fill any requirements from the South, while the country is so excited," argued Robert Hoe.[171] The Union did not win the war, they reasoned, in order to lose the peace.

The interest in stability, which had at first led most bourgeois New Yorkers to hope for a rapid end to federal involvement in the South, ironically turned out to be double-edged. Although they continued to dismiss freedpeople's claims on economic resources and demands for political change, they also opposed southerners' violent resistance to Reconstruction. Once enfranchisement had been accomplished, upper-class New Yorkers defended it against southern and Democratic Party attacks because such attacks threatened the peaceful settlement of Reconstruction.[172] By the late 1860s, it was the southern elites who were threatening the cherished "stability" once again.

It was in this context that some merchants, industrialists, and bankers also accepted the enfranchisement of freedmen as a strategy for building the electoral strength of the Republican Party. Aware of the unrelenting hostility of most white southerners to the Republican Party, and with it the most fundamental interests of large segments of northern capital, they realized that black southerners were the only large block of loyalists who might provide the basis for continued Republican power in the South, as well as in the nation.[173]

This belated embrace of a more active involvement in the South was furthered by those few upper-class New Yorkers who had seen strong federal intervention in the South as necessary all along. The industrialist Peter Cooper, for example, as well as the editors of *Iron Age,* had supported the congressional Radicals from the beginning, Cooper warning that those "who once levied war against [the Union] with bullets . . . now seek to overthrow it with ballots."[174] Sharing this opinion, manufacturer Robert Hoe was certain that Johnson "is more of the type of *Pharaoh* then of *Moses* . . . destitute of either high moral or religious principle."[175] Similarly, some of the members of the powerful Union League Club, which had helped radicalize so many of the city's bourgeois citizens during the war, had by June 1865 demanded universal manhood suffrage regardless of color, and had supported congressional Reconstruction in the spring of 1866, most importantly by attempting to secure the passage of the Civil Rights Act and by supporting expanded funding for the Freedmen's Bureau.[176] A sufficient number of the club members had even backed the congressional Radicals' goal of impeaching Andrew Johnson to have the issue debated, although the divisions among the members were so persistent that no resolution was passed.[177]

The desire of the radical wing of the city's bourgeoisie to revolutionize southern society expressed a firm commitment to transcend the economic and political arrangements of the antebellum years. The vision for an entirely new political economy, a political economy born out of the war, animated the wealthy supporters of radicalism. At the industrialists' American Institute, speakers looked "to the development of this great internal enterprise, aided by cheap and rapid railway communication, and by the most ingenious machinery, for the life of our home market, for the revival and support of our commerce, and for our financial success."[178] The opening of lands, the building of mills and railroads, the development of mineral resources, and the embrace of free labor, as well as human equality, they believed, "opens the way for a brilliant future."[179] Tellingly, in an 1865 Union victory parade in New York City, a float by the oil manufacturers proclaimed that "Oil is King Now, not Cotton."[180] Firmly linked to a strengthened federal state, they saw the Radical Republicans' project as conducive to their interests.

These upper-class New Yorkers, dominated by the rising group of manufacturers, had also, from the beginning, embraced a set of monetary and tariff policies quite different from those of the majority of the city's mer-

cantile elite. They opposed rapid resumption, because it threatened defla-
tion.[181] The circulation of greenbacks made imports more expensive and
thus functioned as a protectionist barrier.[182] The greenback, in effect,
amounted to a devaluation of the U.S. currency.[183] George Opdyke, a
leader of the opposition against resumption, argued that contraction
would "depress prices, . . . paralyze industry, and . . . transfer a portion of
the wealth of the debtor class to the creditor class."[184] Peter Cooper was a
similarly outspoken advocate of greenbacks, opposing those whose "pecuniary interests, as importers, agents, and merchants, are directly and
deeply identified with those of the manufacturers of Great Britain and
Continental Europe."[185] Cooper's and Opdyke's was a minority position
in New York City, yet a position strengthened by support from industrialists elsewhere.[186] *Iron Age,* for instance, the voice of the nation's iron and
steel manufacturers, opposed contraction, as did the National Manufacturers' Association.[187]

Along with an inflationary currency, high tariffs were the cornerstone of
this political economy. In May 1867, Peter Cooper, Henry C. Carey, and
John A. Griswold had formed the American Industrial League to combat
free-trade sentiment (making Peter Cooper president), lending support to
the protectionist policies of congressional Republicans. These New Yorkers, in contrast to the majority of merchants and bankers, had demanded
all along the "protection of every branch of American industry against
foreign competition."[188]

This group of mostly manufacturers, who favored a more substantive
revamping of southern society, by 1869 found increasing support among
the conservative majority, who themselves had grown disenchanted with
the southern elites and their policies.[189] By 1868, the *New York Commercial Advertiser,* once an avid foe of the Freedmen's Bureau, thought of it as
"a triumph of human forethought and discernment."[190] These bourgeois
radicals, in effect, forged a political discourse on Reconstruction that
became ever more compelling as their more conservative colleagues began
to understand that their goal of southern social and economic stability
might be accomplished only with the help of more drastic policies. Equally
important, the power of radicalism at times seemed so great in the North
that embracing some (but not all) of the Radicals' political goals suggested
itself as one of the ways to put an end to the upheavals of Reconstruction.

Most striking was the tentative embrace of new policies in regard to
monetary matters. By the late 1860s and early 1870s, a growing number
of merchants and bankers embraced the idea of postponing resumption,

since they saw that an inflationary currency had helped propel economic growth.[191] Banker George S. Coe opposed "quick redemption," as did former redemptionist Simeon B. Chittenden, who thought that "paper money may possibly be a great blessing," and related to the great postwar prosperity.[192] One result of this reorientation was that George Opdyke gained substantially more support for his positions among members of the Chamber of Commerce, the Chamber resolving in 1871 that "the legal tender money now in use has proved a convenient and acceptable circulating medium."[193] Even the *Commercial and Financial Chronicle* had second thoughts, seeing that "[s]udden resumption means, the taking by force from the debtor class to give to the creditors," a move that it opposed because of the "individual suffering" and "universal bankruptcy" which would result: "[T]he imagination shrinks back appalled at its terror."[194] By February 1869 the journal was arguing that "[i]t is out of the question to suppose that we could safely resume specie payments under such a condition of commercial affairs as now exist; and much less that we could do so without business interests suffering."[195]

This slowly evolving position in regard to monetary politics went along with a growing number of bourgeois New Yorkers' embrace of protectionism. Merchant William E. Dodge explained how he came to support high tariffs, arguing that "I am impressed with the conviction that the commercial interests of the city which I in part represent will be promoted by the prosperity of the agricultural and manufacturing interests, and by the ability of the country, which alone can come from that prosperity, to buy and pay for the vast amount of imports which I am confident, notwithstanding this tariff, will continue to flow to this country."[196] Dodge celebrated the strengthening of domestic industries that had been one of the results of the war and high tariff legislation, a development he saw as the precondition of the nation's glorious future.[197] A position such as Dodge's moved increasingly into the center of the discourse of the city's economic elite, and quite tellingly, Dodge himself was elected president of the Chamber of Commerce in 1867, a position he was to hold until 1875.

While the majority of the city's merchants, industrialists, and bankers were slowly shifting toward a fundamentally new vision for the economic development of the United States and their place within it, another wing of the upper class continued to oppose this new orientation and demanded the abandonment of Reconstruction. The Democratic merchants and bankers around August Belmont, who had refused to accept to the end the social revolutionary implications of the war effort, insisted that southern states immediately be readmitted into the Union. "The erring members of our political family should be allowed to resume their wanted places in the social circle," argued Belmont. "Let them be welcome as was the prodigal son in the parable and received back with all their rights and privileges unabridged."[198] By June 1865, he was preparing the reentry of southern delegates into the National Committee of the Democratic Party.[199] The enfranchisement of freedmen remained this group's bête-noir. As late as 1869, Belmont's collaborator, Samuel J. Tilden, rejected black suffrage "as we would reject the doctrine that an African or a negro has a right to marry our daughter without our consent." This opinion was shared by the *Merchants' Magazine and Commercial Review*, which suggested limiting the franchise of black men to those who had served in the Union army or had personal wealth of at least $250.[200] These Democrats perceived that only a political coalition with white southerners could restore the party's former power, and black enfranchisement threatened such a vision.

But, as during the war, by the late 1860s the conservative forces around August Belmont were isolated among the city's economic elite. Hence, Grant's bid in 1872 for a second term again won the support of large segments of the city's upper class, including Democrats such as Moses Taylor and Edwards Pierrepont.[201] Typically, James Beekman supported Grant even though he had lost his earlier enthusiasm for him.[202] By 1872, the major questions of Reconstruction, in the eyes of the city's merchants, industrialists, and bankers, were settled. They again enjoyed access to the economic resources of the South and had successfully helped to move the Republican Party away from radicalism. Their desire for stability and the limits of their political power had, however, also created a new political space for the freedpeople of the South, a political space that depended on the continued commitment of the North to its protection.

While the city's economic elite acquiesced to an expansion of democratic rights in the South, they were never committed to their protection. Their support for suffrage rights remained tenuous, especially as they became increasingly concerned about the implications of democracy in the North. A wave of strikes, radical labor agitation, the passage of eight-hour laws by Radical Republican state legislatures, and eventually the collapse, in 1871, of the Tweed regime in New York City made many of them skeptical about the political power of citizens who did not and would probably never own property.[203] The social revolution that they had been forced to forward in the South should not, they believed, endanger the stability of social relations in the nation as a whole.

6

Reconstructing New York

When President Andrew Johnson signed the Thirteenth Amendment to the Constitution in 1865, and slavery was outlawed in North America, the major political and social fault line of the United States suddenly disappeared. Emancipation removed what until then had been the most important reference point for the political discourse of northern society. Though New York's economic elite had been aware of the social changes fostered by economic expansion in the antebellum North, they had linked the problem of proletarianization in one way or another to slavery: Some had believed that an expanding slave economy would provide for prosperous employment of northern wage workers while others had held that the destruction of slavery would reinvigorate social and geographical mobility for temporary proletarians.[1] Yet by the late 1860s and early 1870s, both the republic of independent producers, envisioned by Abraham Lincoln along with New York manufacturers, and the commercial capitalism based on slavery championed by August Belmont and many of the city's mercantile elite were rapidly faltering on the shoals of industrialization.

Indeed, social tensions arising from the blossoming of capitalism sharpened considerably in the wake of the Civil War. During the 1860s, rapid economic development and novel political arrangements mitigated these strains, but workers' collective action eventually forced upper-class New Yorkers to come to terms with the emerging new world. This reorientation was at first careful and tentative, but by the early 1870s, New York's merchants, industrialists, and bankers began to reconsider the meaning of proletarianization and the role of the state in society, with dramatic results not only for class relations in the North but also for Reconstruction and the fate of the freedpeople in the South.

Proletarianization was a central fact of life in the city, the direct result of its relentless growth. As economic opportunity beckoned, manufacturers searched for ever-increasing numbers of wage workers, workers who arrived from the American countryside and Europe, as well as from the ranks of the city's artisans.[2] By 1870, Manhattan alone counted close to 130,000 laboring women and men among its inhabitants, and was adding new workers at a rate of about 340 a month. Each morning, thousands of toilers streamed into the factories along the East River, into the myriad clothing workshops in lower Manhattan, and to the building sites farther uptown. These workingmen and women now decisively stamped the character of large areas of the city, particularly below 14th Street on the east side of Manhattan, a section inhabited by laborers and their families, many of them recent immigrants from Ireland and Germany. Here lived the "elements," according to the *New York Times,* "who possess . . . no property and can get none."[3]

As never before in the history of New York City, many of these workers, especially those with skills, organized into unions and engaged in strikes. Whereas in 1861 there had been only about fifteen unions in the city, the number exploded to 157 three years later.[4] In June 1864, the Workingmen's Union formed, assembling different trades into one body.[5] This degree of organization translated into novel collective challenges to employers: According to the estimates of one historian, 249 tradewide strikes occurred in New York between 1863 and 1873, some of them – like the 1868 bricklayers strike – involving several thousand workers.[6] Though most disputes focused on wages, the length of the workday motivated an increasing number of conflicts. This new emphasis was particularly encouraged by the passing of an eight-hour bill in the New York State legislature by Radical Republicans, symbolizing how the reconstruction of the southern states suddenly seemed to open new political opportunities in the North, as the boundaries of the antebellum political world fell apart.[7] The successful outcome of many of these strikes inspired workers in late 1868 to organize a labor party.[8] By 1870, New York's skilled workers had achieved a degree of mobilization and organization they had never sustained before.

Indeed, the newfound power of workers was indirectly reflected in the local political arrangements that emerged toward the end of the war. According to historian Iver Bernstein, in 1865 the exuberant confidence of well-to-do New Yorkers, along with the resources made available by the booming local economy, provided them with a way out of the local political crisis that had unfolded in the wake of the Draft Riots. The city's merchants, manufacturers, and bankers came to accept a political compromise that was negotiated by William M. Tweed and his Tammany Hall faction of the Democratic Party. Tweed delivered social peace and extracted, in return, a comprehensive system of public aid and patronage jobs for the city's working class.[9]

William Tweed, who had become an influential politician in the city's Democratic Party by 1864, celebrated his first citywide electoral victory in December 1865, carried the state in 1869, and dominated the political life of the city until 1871. Tweed's Tammany Hall derived its strength from a coalition of working-class New Yorkers, particularly Irish immigrants, along with large segments of the city's economic elite, both of which benefited from the urban expansion fostered by his deficit-spending program. Though Tweed decreased taxes, he increased per capita expenditure by more than 50 percent between 1860 and 1869 – from $17.99 to $28.12 (in 1869 dollars).[10] The resulting social stability was so apparent to upper-class New Yorkers that the city's Republican Party was said to be aligned with Tammany Hall, with even so staunch a Republican as George Templeton Strong voting, albeit reluctantly, for Tammany.[11]

While Tweed's Tammany Hall was certainly not their ideal of urban rule, the city's economic elite accommodated themselves to its policies. Among bourgeois New Yorkers, support for Tweed came at first mainly from bankers and real estate developers.[12] International financiers profited from selling municipal bonds in domestic and overseas markets, bonds that were used to finance the city's expansion. Between 1867 and 1871, the city's debt increased nearly threefold – a windfall for local bond dealers such as August Belmont, John A. Dix, Augustus R. Schell, and Moses Taylor.[13] One of the voices of the city's bondholders, the *Commercial and Financial Chronicle,* hence saw little reason to be concerned about Tweed's spiraling expenditures, arguing that "the whole debt is well secured."[14]

The other elite group supporting William Tweed was comprised of those who capitalized most directly on urban expansion – builders, uptown landowners, and investors in utilities. With the physical growth of Manhattan northward, especially of residential districts along Central Park, property holders had organized in the West Side Association (1866), the East River Improvement Association (1868), and the East Side Association and stood ready to defend the policy of urban expansion.[15] The president of the West Side Association, the lawyer and developer William R. Martin, proudly proclaimed that Tweed was "by our aid, firmly seated."[16] When Tweed obtained a new city charter in 1870, one that restored to the city much of the power that had been assumed by Albany in 1857, thus concentrating authority over infrastructure improvements in New York itself, he could count on the backing of large segments of the city's upper class.[17]

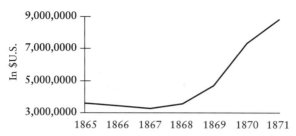

Net bonded debt of New York City, 1865–1871.
Source: Edward Dana Durand, *The Finances of New York City*
(New York: Macmillan, 1898), p. 375.

Indeed, so pervasive was this support that in 1870, upon an investigation of the comptroller's books, John Jacob Astor, Moses Taylor, Edward Schell, and others found nothing wrong with Tweed's financial dealings.[18]

Tweed's form of rule was attractive to elite New Yorkers, not only because of the particular material benefits they derived from his administration but also because his policies won the allegiance of large segments of the working class, and helped to bolster their commitment to the nationalism that the Union League Club had pioneered during the war years. The price of this alliance – public relief and city patronage jobs – seemed affordable during economic boom times. In this age of exuberant confidence, support for Tweed reflected economic elites' continued belief in stewardship and a shared polity, while indirectly acknowledging the strength of labor.

The emergence of a large wage-earning class, however, confronted capital-rich New Yorkers not only in city politics but also in all other spheres of their lives, from the streets to the workshops. Manufacturers faced conflicts over the terms of employment most directly.[19] But merchants had to come to terms with this new world as well. While most of them did not have a large number of employees on their payrolls, nor profits derived directly from production, massive stakes in real estate involved them with the city's construction workers, and investments in railroads and mines exposed them to the organizing efforts in these industries.[20] Moreover, as we have seen, the rise of a new agricultural proletariat in the South fundamentally changed the ways agricultural commodities were planted and harvested. Slowly but persistently, the relationship to wage workers moved to the center of attention for all of the city's property owners, including merchants.

How did both merchants and manufacturers negotiate the sudden expansion of the city's working class? Politically, as we have seen, they found, at first, a workable solution facilitated by Tweed's activist state, a solution that in many ways harked back to the politics of stewardship characteristic of the antebellum world. Ideologically, however, the problem was of considerably greater scope. Americans were unaccustomed to think of their country as possessing a permanent working class. Before the Civil War, merchants had hoped to limit proletarianization and address its social effects with the profits derived from a prosperous southern plantation economy. Manufacturers, in turn, believed in the promise of social and geographical mobility enabled by westward expansion. For merchants, wage work had been ephemeral to the American economy; for industrialists, it had been only a temporary condition in life.

Despite the challenges of the postwar years, most manufacturers, having grown up in an ideological world entrenched in free-labor thought, held onto their older beliefs. Prominently representing this outlook, Horace Greeley stuck determinedly to his credo, telling and retelling the tale of free labor, protectionism, and agricultural prosperity.[21] He and other industrialists saw free-labor ideology validated and strengthened by the experience of the war.[22] As Greeley pointed out, "[r]ecent events have opened the Southern States to settlement and cultivation by free labor," which, according to the *Manufacturer and Builder,* "is stimulating the Southern people."[23] Free labor, now generalized throughout the nation, could contain the potentially divisive effects of industrialization. As a speaker at the annual fair of the industrialists' American Institute argued, the world needed to learn that "free, self-reliant, well paid labor, the citizenship of a republic of human equality, lies at the foundation of national greatness."[24] In such a society, *Iron Age* concluded optimistically, "there is much less apparent danger . . . than in any other of the great producing countries of the world of a conflict of classes."[25]

Validated by the war, free-labor ideology flowered once more during the second half of the 1860s. It also flowered because the war had vastly strengthened the political economy of the industrialists. The new economic and political arrangements promised to guarantee future social mobility so essential to free-labor thought. "The America of the future must differ greatly from the America of the past," argued one manufacturer, pointing to a system in which high tariffs protected rapidly expanding American industries and in which the resulting prosperity created bountiful markets for American farmers.[26] This vision, now turned into governmental policy, put industrialists and free-labor ideology squarely at the center of the American political economy.[27]

Ironically, the growing dominance of the manufacturers' political economy also undermined the future of free-labor ideology. It undermined it for two reasons: First, it helped create a larger working class, as an ever-smaller percentage of workers became independent entrepreneurs or farmers. And, second, because northern victory in the Civil War had created the conditions industrialists thought to be sufficient to the unfolding of a free-labor society, the legitimacy of further state intervention diminished. Permanent proletarianization, despite being much more widespread now, could be seen by manufacturers as the result of individual failure, not large-scale social change. Horace Greeley, typically, held workers responsible for their status, arguing that "they might be their own employers if they chose."[28]

Free-labor ideology prepared industrialists to blame workers for their social standing and to see workers' collective action as a threat to their core beliefs. As proletarianization widened, workers organized, and the social distance between manufacturers and their employees increased; commitment to a shared social contract centered on social mobility became more difficult to maintain. With notions of a mutuality of interest between workers and their employers diminishing, industrialists eventually would recast their relationship to the people in their employ.[29] This new orientation emerged most forcefully, as we will see shortly, among large-scale employers, especially the railroads, but in due time affected ever larger numbers of the city's manufacturers. As an expression of this reorientation and the solidarities it enabled, by the early 1870s *Iron Age* and the *New-York Commercial Advertiser* appealed to manufacturers to organize against the power of trade unions.[30]

Yet throughout the 1860s, it was difficult for industrialists to come to terms with their workers' greater assertiveness. The Hoe brothers, for example, on the one hand tried to blame strikes on "outside influences," or even "a society of Communists . . . who advocate the wildest theories, such as the division of property etc."[31] On the other hand, however, they also took note of their changing relationship to the people in their employ: "I am persuaded," wrote Robert Hoe II, "that there has been too little attention paid during the last 10 or 15 years to recruiting the shops with foremen of character and ability and filling the shops with workmen upon whom we can depend. . . . All these things have weakened our influence directly and indirectly over the minds of the men."[32] Hoe did "not feel disposed to waste much sympathy" on the workmen. "I do not believe in any system of cooperation such as is being tried," he asserted, since "it is very fair to let the natural law of supply and demand alone."[33]

Merchants and bankers were even less prepared than manufacturers for navigating the new world that resulted from the Civil War. Their notions of paternalist stewardship became more difficult to maintain in the face of a massively enlarged group of wage laborers. Moreover, while the political economy of industrialists, and with it their free-labor ideology, had been validated by the war, that of the merchants had experienced a defeat.

The political and economic ideas of merchants made it difficult for them to come to terms with the massive wave of proletarianization. "It is one of the misfortunes of the times that . . . antagonism has arisen between capital and labor in place of the feeling of identity of interests which should exist," expounded the *United States Economist and Dry Goods Reporter*.[34] China merchant Abiel Abbot Low concurred, asserting that the only real dangers to "the prosperity of our port and our city . . . appear to be . . . the combinations of men who seek continually to advance the prices of labor beyond what employers can afford to pay."[35] But what should be done about it? Thinking of strikes as "against reason, and opposed to that community of interest which Providence has instituted between the workmen and the employer," merchants persistently appealed to the "intellectual and moral elevation of the working class."[36] Yet this "community of interest" was threatened, as "industrial society . . . during the past ten years has been . . . broken down among us into the two great classes of rich and poor – capitalists and their employes [sic]," making it more difficult for the "man of small means" to "begin business for himself."[37] In fact, workingmen "were deprived of the facility for rising as rapidly and easily to be masters."[38] But what should be done about the growing number of wage workers and the increasing social conflict remained unclear.[39]

Slowly, however, the old merchant paternalism weakened. Especially once the Tweed regime had unraveled and workers had shown their collective power in the streets and workshops of New York in the early 1870s, the merchants' concern with order, along with their traditional embrace of a weak state, made them fall easily into a new ideological orientation of laissez-faire individualism. This orientation denied the state's responsibility for addressing social inequality and allowed for the repression of citizens of the Republic if they were seen as endangering order. Adjusting themselves to the new order of things, the *Merchants' Magazine and Commercial Review* found that "[s]ociety is divided into two classes, the laborer and the capitalist. . . . A certain amount of suffering and misery will always exist; and no amount of benevolence on the part of the capitalist, nor of the philanthropist, can materially lessen it."[40] Here, the merchants joined the ideological universe of the city's industrialists, forging an ideology that made the defense of the prerogatives of property the centerpiece of their shared beliefs.

This halting ideological reorientation went along, as we have seen, with the social and geographic retreat of ever-larger segments of New York's upper class from other social groups. But the more bourgeois New Yorkers tried to gain control of their physical surroundings, the more removed the working class became from the paternalist control of earlier times. "The boy is now left to run at large," declared the Association for Improving the Conditions of the Poor (AICP) in a report mourning the decline of the paternalist apprenticeship system.[41] And as workers moved farther away from the field of vision of their betters, the fear of them increased exponentially. Not surprisingly, journalists responded to the worries of their upper-class readers by reporting on the mysterious lower ranks of society, sometimes with a kind of anthropological curiosity. "It is very difficult for a journalist who knows the condition and feelings of the working classes throughout the world to make readers of the comfortable classes understand how they regard their relations to capitalists and to society at large," remarked the *New York Times*.[42] From 1866 onward, the AICP published yearly reports on "Labor Movements and Strikes."[43] And the *Atlantic Monthly* in May 1871 printed a detailed study on "Organization of Labor: Its Aggressive Phases," focusing in particular on the International Workingmen's Association.[44] Slowly but persistently, workers were cast as "the other."

Anxiety, bordering on fear, was the clearest expression of the decay of antebellum ideological certainties. For this reason, around the early 1870s there was an increasing discrepancy between what workers and unions actually did and how upper-class New Yorkers interpreted their actions. Skilled workers fought for improvements in their living conditions to enable them to live a dignified life. Workers recognized that a condition of permanent wage labor clouded the fundamental ideological pillars of American society. After all, a republic of independent producers was the basis of republican democratic theory – a man's economic independence guaranteed his political independence and, most importantly, a shared interest in the defense of private property. Many if not most skilled workers did not accept the permanence of their proletarian station, and for them, unions were just one way to improve their standing. Employers, however, saw the same kind of activities increasingly as interference with property rights they held to be sacred, and their concerns about the collective power of workers in improving their shop conditions easily turned into hysteria.

Employers, more attuned to the permanence of proletarianization than many workers, feared the consequences of non–property owners becoming a majority of the voting citizenry. After all, there was no example in history for a republic based upon unequal distribution of property and a simultaneously enfranchised working class. The British, German, and French bourgeoisie all had lost their enthusiasm for a broad-based suffrage in the face of growing working-class militancy. Consequently, as the importance of slavery and sectional conflict retreated in the political discourse of the city's merchants, industrialists, and bankers, the existence of a large, permanent proletariat began to permeate ever more debates. Prophetically, silk merchant Elliot C. Cowdin remarked in 1871 that the "relations between Capital and Labor now raise questions which have assumed colossal magnitude."[45]

Events abroad magnified the fears of the city's economic elite. In March 1871, Parisian workers and sympathetic National Guard soldiers took control of Paris and, in the words of the *New York Times,* "declared war . . . against art, property, and religion – against civilization itself."[46] For the first time ever, the lower classes had taken control of the government of one of the world's premier cities. Propertied citizens everywhere woke to the potential of the working classes to seize political power and to threaten private property.[47] In this moment, upper-class New Yorkers articulated many of their greatest fears about the direction in which their society was headed. According to *The Nation,* the Commune gave "an air of practicalness to what all the rest of the world sneered at as unpractical": that "a great crowd of persons" could seize the "government of a great capital and administer it."[48] "This demonstration against capital . . . may prove as memorable as the first organized and violent move of any importance toward great changes," confided lawyer George Templeton Strong to his diary.[49] And *The Nation* editorialized:

On the whole, the reign of the Commune must be pronounced the most extraordinary episode of modern times, and strikingly illustrates the truth of observation that the barbarians whose ravages the modern world has to dread, live not in the forests, but in the heart of our large cities.[50]

With great determination, bourgeois New Yorkers tried to persuade themselves that the European situation was fundamentally different from that in the United States. In America, "[t]here is no pressure on the *prole-taire* class beyond the necessary inequalities of life," wrote the *New York Times.*[51] Social mobility and westward migration would distinguish America's workers from those of Europe. "In our own happy country," explained the *New York Herald,* workers were equal before the law, were better paid, and had access to land as well as political rights; therefore they showed less revolutionary inclination.[52] The silk merchant Elliot Cowdin, in an address on the Commune delivered at Cooper Union, thought conditions in the United States "no . . . longer dangerous" and hoped that common schools, a free press, free speech, free religious worship, and an open Bible, "would prevent another Commune."[53]

Despite such beliefs in American exceptionalism, uneasiness prevailed. The *New York Times* predicted direly that the "great revolution of labor has yet to come," and saw dangers lurking close at home: "[T]he dangerous and seething materials . . . are to be found in every large capital . . . [where] the thousands of wretched creatures . . . hide in attics and cellars, poor, slovenly and hard-pressed."[54] The AICP agreed, warning that communism in the United States "found a soil so congenial to its growth that it is already formidable in numbers."[55] Indeed, it was such thinking that led to comparisons between the Commune and the Draft Riots of 1863. "For a few days in 1863, New-York seemed like Paris under the Reds," remarked the *New York Times* retrospectively. "Our Communists had already begun towards the houses of the rich, and the cry of war to property was already heard."[56] If not for the resistance of the "better classes . . . we should have seen a communistic explosion in New-York which would have probably left the City in ashes and blood."[57] The experience of Paris even encouraged one author, J. T. Headley, to pen down an account of all riots that had occurred in New York's history, furnishing "a sort of moral history of that vast, ignorant, turbulent class which is one of the distinguishing features of a great city, and at the same time the chief cause of its solicitude and anxiety, and often of dread."[58] It was hardly surprising, then, that George Templeton Strong expressed relief when the Commune was finally repressed and "[t]he foot of the [French] bourgeoisie is on the neck of the dreaded and hated Rouges at last, and it will stay there till they are made powerless for mischief on any large scale, if anything short of extermination can render them innocuous."[59]

In the weeks following the Paris Commune, the Tweed regime unraveled in New York City. The relationship between the two events was only symbolic, but the experiences in France had probably encouraged the city's economic elite to act boldly, and indeed the *New York Daily Tribune* had already editorialized in April that "[u]nless we succeed in the political reform we shall not need to look abroad to inquire whether republican government is a failure."[60] It was a confluence of factors that made Tweed's regime collapse. In July 1871, the first accusations of fraud became public. Manhattan newspapers revealed corruption on a scale unheard of before. As a result, international bondholders cut off the city's credit.[61] In the same month, bloody riots (the so-called "Orange Riots") pitted Catholic and Protestant Irish immigrants against one another, the city's bourgeoisie nearly unanimously siding with the Orangemen. Urban disorder on a scale not seen since the Draft Riots threatened New York, and in the eyes of the city's wealthy, Catholics and workers were the cause of it. Tweed, identified with both, now drew the wrath of upper-class New Yorkers.[62]

On September 3, 1871, hundreds of merchants, industrialists, bankers, and professionals assembled at Cooper Union to force a retreat of the Tweed faction and a restructuring of city government. Called by the newly founded "Committee of Citizens and Taxpayers for the Financial Reform of the City and County of New York," the meeting witnessed a bipartisan condemnation of Tweed by the likes of sugar manufacturer William Havemeyer, banker James Brown, publisher Oswald Ottendorfer, financier Jesse Seligman, and printing press manufacturer Robert Hoe II.[63] The demands of the first meeting – which were for the next year articulated by the Committee of Seventy, so named for the number of members on the executive board – were twofold: First, they pressed for an immediate inquiry into the corruption and fraud of the Tweed Ring and the prosecution of its members. Second, they wanted to secure "good" government by reforming the political structure of the city's administration. They resolved to "give to the City of New York a form of government such as shall be devised . . . by our wisest and best citizens."[64]

At the center of the storm was New York City's financial community and, in particular, James Brown, who presided over the first meeting and whose son, James M. Brown, also joined the group. Shortly after the first meeting, Charles O'Conor, the special deputy attorney general for the State of New York, along with lawyers prosecuting Tweed (who were hired by the committee), located their offices in the building of Brown Brothers.[65] In effect, the offices of Brown Brothers became City Hall. From here, the committee controlled the city's accounts and decided over expenditures.[66] They pressured city officials to step down in order to make space for the committee's members. They pressured the mayor to nominate one of their own, Andrew H. Green, as the new comptroller.[67] For a few weeks, the committee ruled the city. It was a municipal coup d'état.

⤳ ⤳ ⤳

The suddenness with which the Committee of Seventy organized may at first glance be surprising. Yet most of the individuals, ideas, and strategies associated with the committee had been articulated before 1871. Of the older organizations that had formulated a critique of Tammany rule, the Citizens' Association had been the most important. In the wake of the Draft Riots and a failed attempt to form a reform party, a bipartisan group of merchants, industrialists, and bankers – among them Hamilton Fish, Morris Ketchum, Peter Cooper, and James Brown – had come together in December 1863 to advocate "a reduction of our taxes, the protection of our homes and business."[68] Though the association they founded was a class-based organization ("Bankers, Merchants, Capitalists and Manufacturers are cordially invited to become members . . ."),[69] it appealed in its early years for support from skilled workers, in line with some antebellum reform organizations.[70]

The goal of the association, chaired at first by the banker James Brown and in later years by the manufacturer Peter Cooper, was "to organize the highest intelligence of society represented by the better classes of merchants, manufacturers, capitalists, bankers and others to oppose corruption and promote reform and progress in all matters that interest the citizen."[71] It advocated a reduction in taxes and government expenditures, lower wages for city employees, housing reform in working-class districts, and improvement of the city's docks.[72] In contrast to later reform movements, however, the Citizens' Association still operated very much in a paternalist mold that embraced the activist state, asserting that its reforms would create a city in which "streets [are] carefully graded and paved, swept and cleaned daily; comfortable, clean and cheap public conveyances [are run] so that the poorest might enjoy them, . . . model dwellings for the laboring and poorer classes [are provided]; and presiding over all a Mayor, Common Council, and other city officials, chosen from among well-known and universally esteemed citizens."[73] The Citizens' Association had great hopes for its reforms as it saw New York City politics as important to the nation as a whole: "Great cities have always wielded a moral sovereignty in human affairs. Thebes, Nineveh, Babylon, Palmyra, Rome gave laws and manners to ancient times. London, Paris, Vienna, Constantinople, St. Petersburg, sway nations now and advance or depress the standard of civilization, freedom and social economy. As are its great cities, so is Europe, so is Christendom."[74] Hence, "imperial New York [must] fulfill a like destiny to the States and territories which commerce, science, and other interests shall attract towards her bosom."[75]

Implementing these lofty goals, however, was difficult. After the war, once William Tweed's Tammany Hall had entrenched itself firmly in the politics of the city, the Citizens' Association lost the support of workers, and many of its wealthy backers. In response, it radicalized its demands. The much smaller organization now focused increasingly on the way New York City was governed, searching for ways to limit popular influence over local politics.[76] Although this antidemocratic impulse of the Citizens' Association was not entirely new among the city's mercantile elite and rising manufacturers, its organized expression was without precedent.[77] As early as 1860, for example, Samuel P. Dinsmore (who later would join the association) had demanded that a board, elected only "by actual taxpayers," be created, one which would approve all expenditures of the city, with the effect that "the numerical limit to the franchise . . . should secure the worthiest of our citizens."[78] In the second half of the 1860s, the Citizens' Association translated an argument like Dinsmore's into concrete reform proposals. They organized meetings, printed pamphlets, and developed plans for changes in the government of the city.[79] Arguing that a clique of professional politicians had subverted republican government, they called Tweed's domination of local politics a "[f]oul and Monstrous Conspiracy."[80] The city had to be rescued from the "dregs of Europe," from the "rascality of the old world" that flowed into it.[81]

Although their analysis was still couched in an earlier nativist mold that feared the subversion of the Republic from the outside, the conclusions they drew did not suggest a limitation of immigration. Indeed, the opinion of the *Commercial and Financial Chronicle* that immigration was "the most fruitful source . . . of the rapid material progress of the country" was widely shared.[82] A limitation of political rights was not to be based on nativity, but rather on economic status.

Organizing those who stayed outside of Tweed's growth coalition, the Citizens' Association, in effect, sought to reform the way New York City was governed. An opportunity to embark upon such reform came in 1868, when the New York Constitutional Convention worked on rewriting the constitution of the state, including those parts that governed its cities. The Citizens' Association's main mission was to limit suffrage rights: They warned that "[t]he advocates of the unrestricted use of the ballot-box must . . . have forgotten the fearful scenes enacted in the July riots of 1863 [when] the thousands and tens of thousand . . . came forth from lanes, alleys, cellars and slums, and from dark holes and corners," and argued that "[i]t is not safe to place the execution of the laws in the hands of the classes against which they are principally to be enforced."[83] Having "abandoned all hope" for reform by the city itself, they instead appealed to the State of New York to give the city a new charter that

would exclude "political parties and cliques from the control of interests
. . . and selecting from our citizens men of character, intelligence and thorough knowledge of public duty to which they may be assigned."[84] A new
state constitution was to secure that elections should be few, and "held to
fill the highest offices only," with other posts, such as judgeships, filled by
gubernatorial appointments only.[85] Suffrage was to be restricted by educational requirements, one branch of the Common Council elected only by
"tax-payers," and a system of "minority representation" devised.[86] Furthermore, a board of 24 taxpayers – selected by lot from a group of 250
taxpayers assessed at more than $20,000 – "SHALL DETERMINE . . . THE
SUMS NECESSARY TO BE RAISED FOR ALL LOCAL PURPOSES," thus enjoying
practical veto power over all local decisions.[87]

The reform plans of the Citizens' Association, however, came to naught,
and the association slowly disintegrated.[88] Despite the organization's frantic publicity efforts, their positions found only minority support among
New York's upper class. While it had gained backers in the wake of the
Draft Riots, many well-to-do citizens eventually found a comfortable
arrangement with the Tweed regime and left the association.[89] August Belmont, the international financier benefiting from the sale of New York
City bonds in international credit markets, for example, was not mentioned in relation to the Citizens' Association after 1864, and banker
James Brown was replaced as president by manufacturer Peter Cooper.
Ironically, by 1870, Tweed even succeeded in drawing Cooper into his
ranks by advocating some of the very same reforms the Citizens' Association had demanded. He and his associates lowered taxes and passed a new
charter in the legislature, which, while not limiting the franchise, radically
increased the power of the mayor and provided for the improvement of
the docks.[90] Hence, in March 1871, the Citizens' Association advocated
the passage of "An Act to provide the Government of the City and
County of New-York" – the very charter the once-despised William Tweed
supported.[91] By 1870, the Citizens' Association was only a shadow of its
former self.

Tweed had been so successful in weakening the Citizens' Association
that in the spring of 1870 a group of upper-class New Yorkers established
a new reform organization – the New York City Council of Political
Reform – to drum up opposition to Tweed.[92] This council, moderate in its
demands, expressed anxiety about government spending and corruption at
the national, state, and local levels.[93] It was dominated by a group of
lawyers, bankers of lesser stature, and prominent manufacturers – among
them printing press manufacturer Robert Hoe II and sugar refiner William

F. Havemeyer. Relatively few merchants joined. In the fall of 1871, however, William F. Havemeyer, in close cooperation with the railroad lawyer
Samuel Tilden, bypassed both organizations and absorbed many of their
original supporters into the newly formed Committee of Seventy. They
were out to prove what the Citizens' Association had optimistically
declared three years earlier: "Any government the capitalists and merchants may determine to have in New-York can be established."[94]

In early September 1871, the Committee of Seventy began its work where
the Citizens' Association and the Council of Political Reform had left
off.[95] In addition to activists of the two precursor groups, many merchants, industrialists, and bankers who had stayed away from such organizations before joined the Committee of Seventy. Indeed, the first meeting
in Cooper Union was so crowded that George Templeton Strong found it
"beyond endurance."[96] The Committee of Seventy was entirely bourgeois;
no worker, not even a lesser shop owner, was among its 239 vice presidents and secretaries.

By far the most important group supporting the movement was the
merchants, who made up a full 42 percent of the organization's leadership. Among them were traders, such as Simeon B. Chittenden, Marshall
O. Roberts, and Thomas Sturges, importers, such as Joseph Blumenthal,
and dry goods dealers, such as Howbett Scudder and William L. Pomeroy.
Financiers constituted the next largest group; with 26 percent of all members, they were significantly overrepresented, as they accounted for only 6
percent of the city's upper class. Among them were bankers, such as James
Brown, Joseph Seligman, and Washington R. Vermilye. Thirteen percent
of the leadership were professionals – for example, the lawyers Samuel B.
Ruggles, Edgar Ketchum, and Charles P. Kirkland. Manufacturers made
up 11 percent of the leadership, including the city's most important industrialists, such as the printing press maker Robert Hoe II, the paint manufacturer Julius W. Tieman, and sugar refiner Henry Havemeyer.[97] (William
Steinway, though not in the leadership of the organization, donated $100
to the committee and attended its meetings regularly.)[98] Owners of small
workshops, retail traders, and real estate interests were significantly
underrepresented, which was not surprising considering that they had
been closest to Tweed and took a generally subordinate role in the leadership of bourgeois political mobilization. In contrast, professionals – especially lawyers – had become, to some extent, the spokesmen of their class,
its "practical theorists," as they represented fully 36 percent of the secretaries of the Committee of Seventy – the small group that actually ran its

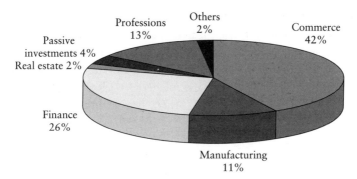

Committee of Seventy, vice presidents and secretaries
by economic sector (N = 191).
Source: *New York Times*, 15 September 1871, supplement, p. 1.
The occupations of the activists were culled from *Trow's City Directory* (1871).

day-to-day operations.[99] Altogether, the Committee of Seventy represented one of the very few classwide political mobilizations, its scope comparable only to the mobilizations for war in April 1861.

As with the mobilizations of April 1861, the members of the Committee of Seventy agreed on certain essentials, while differing on the ultimate goal of the fight on which they were embarking. They agreed to remove William Tweed and his associates from office and to reform city government. Yet the relationship of reform to the working class remained controversial. While Democrats, such as Oswald Ottendorfer and Robert B. Roosevelt, tended to stress the rescue of popular democracy and the working class from Tweed's corruption, Republican members articulated a vision of restricting the political power of workers. Thus, while Edwards Pierrepont sought to appeal to workers by blaming "high rents" as well as expensive food, clothes, and fuel on "your rulers [who] defraud you," the Republican *Nation* argued that "[t]he first remedy which any sane mind would suggest to correct these abuses would be to place the funds of the city under the control of the men who contribute them."[100] But limiting suffrage was, in 1871, not a step most upper-class New Yorkers were willing to take, as they remained committed to democratic solutions.[101]

Despite these divisions, the Committee of Seventy succeeded in usurping municipal power at a moment of grave crisis. This momentum carried into the electoral campaign for the State Assembly and the Common Council in the fall of 1871, when the committee successfully endorsed candidates and financed their campaigns.[102] By the end of 1872, the committee had reached its first goal, purging Tweed's supporters from local politics and capturing political power in the city. In 1872, the chairman of the committee, William F. Havemeyer, was elected mayor of New York. He proceeded immediately to implement an important element of the committee's program by laying off city workers, thus helping in "the retrenchment in the extravagant customs that existed everywhere."[103] Robert Hoe II reported that as a result of these measures, "there is a feeling of relief as to the financial affairs of the City especially among those Savings Banks who are full of the City and County Bonds."[104]

Despite these victories, their second goal, to rewrite the charter of the city of New York, failed. Opposition in Albany and the internal disunity of the Committee of Seventy on the question of the relationship of reform to the working class broke the coalition apart. While some more radical members sought to curtail the number of elections, and reorganize the governmental structure of the city by, for example, merging the Police, Fire, and Health Department into a "Department of Public Safety," the opposition of those more optimistic about democracy blocked them.[105]

Most importantly, the more radical members failed to implement their scheme for "minority representation," a euphemism for electoral mechanisms designed to give "respectable" bourgeois citizens a permanent foothold in city government.[106] According to this plan, proposed by the committee to the legislature of New York State, the legislative board of the city was to include those who did not receive the majority of votes in an election. Similarly, losing mayoral candidates (presumably those supported by the city's upper class) should become first and second assistant mayors.[107] No "party majority" should govern the city but "all classes of citizens."[108] Reflecting the fear that bourgeois politicians would not be able to win a majority of votes, minority representation seemed to guarantee at least some bourgeois influence in local politics, in turn making class-based political movements more viable. Indeed, the idea had floated around the city's elite circles since 1865, when the Personal Representation Society under the leadership of the young lawyer Simon Sterne began its agitation, and it would surface again in the North and South throughout the last decades of the century as a way to "prevent the swamping of the more intelligent classes and of the property interests of the community."[109]

A charter drafted on these principles passed the state House and Senate, but it was vetoed by Democratic Governor Hoffman, who maintained that it was unconstitutional.[110] The dreams of a segment of New York City's upper class for structural reforms foundered on the shoals of political democracy. Not surprisingly, they could not convince popularly elected politicos entrenched in the system to rearrange the democratic institutions of American local politics in order to guarantee elite power. An even more radical plan to limit suffrage rights, proposed by the Constitutional Commission's Committee on Municipal Reform (chaired by none other than Committee of Seventy member George Opdyke), similarly failed.[111]

The committee's political weakness resulted, to a large degree, from clashes among its members. When more radical activists succeeded in December 1871 in pushing through a draft charter that stated that "the common council shall be elected by a system of representation which shall insure to minorities of citizens in proportion to their numerical strength, a pro-rata share of the seats in that body," and that the Common Council "should be invested with a supervision of all the departments," Peter Cooper, who was still chairing the Citizens' Association, opposed the move and resigned from his position eleven days later.[112] Though Cooper, the Citizens' Association, and the Committee of Seventy all agreed that the "main object of the passage of this Charter is . . . to take the Government out of the hands of professional politicians . . . and to entrust it to those substantial citizens who have other than political avocations," they disagreed on how to accomplish this goal.[113] *The Nation,* on the forefront of an ideological reorientation of the city's upper class, called for the most radical steps – the formation of a vigilance committee (because "the revolution of force must sooner or later follow") and the disenfranchisement of propertyless voters from city politics, as municipal democracy was a "ridiculous anachronism."[114] Though, undoubtedly, many bourgeois New Yorkers agreed with this assessment in 1871, many more were still committed to democratic institutions and believed that a reformed working class might be educated to use its political power wisely, as defined by respectable citizens. A further reason for the collapse of the committee was increasing political strains. The Democratic Party still had a firm hold on New York City, and its upper-class members were not necessarily keen to share this power with a minority Republican Party. Thus, on December 20, 1872, a resolution to cooperate with the Republican Party of New York in writing a new charter failed.[115] The committee in early 1873 moved away from its classwide and bipartisan character and became increasingly an organ of elite Republicans, publicly identified as such in the press.[116] In October 1873, the Committee of Seventy – now torn by intensifying infighting – disbanded.[117]

Despite its failure to implement structural reforms in city government, the Committee of Seventy realized the central aim of bourgeois New Yorkers to reclaim political power, which in itself made structural reform less urgent. It also successfully narrowed the scope of urban politics with its advocacy of retrenchment.[118] Not surprisingly, the New York Council of Political Reform reported in 1876 that after 1871, "good government has been two-thirds accomplished."[119] Not only did this assertion of bourgeois political power decisively end the rule of Tweed, but it also ended the politics of compromise that had characterized New York since the war, a form of politics that had mitigated social conflict via a redistributive state.

≈ ≈ ≈

During this ideological reorientation among bourgeois New Yorkers, a number of intellectuals rose to prominence by formulating a theory of society that clarified the sometimes unsystematic ideas emanating from upper-class circles. While merchants, industrialists, and bankers were not silent on these questions – indeed, they articulated important elements of this theory of individualism and laissez-faire liberalism – most did not venture to formulate a theory of society. Instead, such journalists as Elliot Godkin and George William Curtis, together with such lawyers as Samuel Tilden and Simon Sterne and such economists as David A. Wells, all of whom had come of age during the Civil War, elaborated an account of and justification for postwar American society. By the early 1870s, they pushed aside the prewar generation of free-labor ideologues, such as Horace Greeley, who became increasingly isolated among the city's owners of property. Godkin, Curtis, Tilden, Sterne, and Wells were the ideological vanguard of the city's economic elite, as they sought to refashion elite ideology at a time when many of the city's merchants, industrialists, and bankers still supported Tweed's activist state and a somewhat less drastic departure from the mutuality of free-labor paternalism and stewardship.

Despite being somewhat ahead of bourgeois New Yorkers' ideological reorientation, these self-styled "reformers" were in close social, political, and economic contact with the city's owners of capital. At social occasions, for example during the reception for the Grand Duke Alexis of Russia in May 1871, they would mingle with the city's merchants, industrialists, and bankers. Elliot Godkin had most of his contacts among the "moneyed aristocracy of the eastern Seaboard."[120] His magazine, *The Nation,* had at first been financed by bankers, including James Brown and Brown's son-in-law Howard Potter, and was, according to historian Thomas Bender, "written by gentlemen for gentlemen."[121] Politically as well, intellectuals and bourgeois New Yorkers worked closely together in the reform movement; Curtis, Godkin, Tilden, and Sterne all were connected at one point or another to the Committee of Seventy.[122] And because these liberal intellectuals were the most articulate defenders of bourgeois privilege and power, the city's economic elite admitted them to their social circles and financed many of their intellectual endeavors. Though these intellectuals were in many ways on the radical edge of bourgeois discourse and somewhat of a vanguard, these "reformers," as they styled themselves, were the organic intellectuals of New York's bourgeoisie.[122]

The ideologues' main contribution was a theoretical justification for the weakening of the power of the state versus the market and the limitation of democracy, combined with a justification for social inequality. In their most radical moments, they advocated the disenfranchisement of the working class and poor as a way to protect private property; indeed, Godkin supported a national literacy test to decide who would be eligible to vote for Congress.[124] Their hostility to working-class political power implied nothing less than a "fundamental revision of the democratic tradition."[125]

Although the reformers, together with some powerful merchants, industrialists, and bankers, failed in their fight for suffrage restrictions, they much more successfully advocated the retreat of the expansive Civil War state from economic and social regulation, a theme on which nearly all bourgeois New Yorkers would agree by the mid-1870s.[126] This was a distinct departure from the 1860s, when many bourgeois New Yorkers had come to embrace or at least accept an expansive public policy that lavished city funds on urban improvements and public schools, as well as on public health and a municipal government deeply involved in urban planning.[127] The move away from such policies was supported by the liberal reformers' agenda of interpreting laissez-faire economics as a system of natural laws beyond human interference, and they now included in their interpretation not only the protection of private property but also minimal taxation, a stable currency, and a reduction in state spending.[128] They believed that it was the market that had to regulate all economic activity, a system of thought that attracted those who controlled markets. The resulting extreme inequality was naturalized by references to the increasingly popular ideas of Herbert Spencer and morally justified by innovators of the interpretation of Christian religious doctrine like Henry Ward Beecher.[129] Indeed, Beecher, exemplifying the ideological ties between bourgeois and clergy, became a crude apologist for inequality, arguing at one point that higher wages were not called for since "[w]ater costs nothing; and a man who cannot live on bread is not fit to live."[130]

The relationship between ideas articulated by reform intellectuals and bourgeois ideas about public policy was close: *The Nation,* for example, reasoned for an end to public relief on the grounds that it violated the primacy of markets.[131] The AICP similarly argued that "[p]overty, under the constituted order of things, is one of its essential conditions . . . whose universality [is] certain."[132] "It is," according to those elite welfare specialists, "the order of Divine Providence that a large proportion of the population should be poor."[133] The greatest good, they reasoned, is "rendered to the community when each man is left to consult and labor for his own particular advantage."[134] The Citizens' Association seconded this line of thinking: "Nature has wisely ordained that man, through labor, wins from her all that is necessary for his comfortable support."[135] In close cooperation, bourgeois intellectuals and intellectualizing bourgeois New Yorkers had moved the locus of democracy from the political rights of the many to economic freedom.[136]

⁀ ⁀ ⁀

The ideas of Godkin, Curtis, Tilden, Sterne, and Wells also began to permeate the ways in which all segments of the city's bourgeoisie thought about themselves and the world. In 1871, during the mobilizations against Tweed, the ideas of these reformers had informed the thinking of a large number of the upper-class activists. In 1872, during a massive strike of the city' workers, the ideas spread even further among the ranks of the economic elite.

The biggest strike the city had ever witnessed began in May 1872. During its eight weeks, it involved approximately 100,000 workers, two-thirds of all those engaged in manufacturing.[137] What amounted practically to a general strike was initially quite successful, as a number of entrepreneurs, especially the owners of small shops, capitulated in the face of the strong movement. The bricklayers, joiners, carvers, upholsterers, and plumbers succeeded against employers who lacked the resolve and resources to resist their demands.[138] They "yielded to the storm which they could not resist," wrote the *New York Times.*[139] Some of the manufacturers, especially in the building trades, even showed sympathy to the workers' demands, "having, with hardly an exception, been workmen themselves."[140] Encouraged by the success of their movement, other groups of workers, such as the piano makers and the 15,000 iron and metal workers of the city, joined the walkout.[141]

There was a difference, however, between taking on the multiple small capitalists in the building trades and such large factory owners as William Steinway, Isaac Singer, or John Roach.[142] These employers expressed an increasing willingness to oppose their workers' demand and the "iron despotism" of union leaders, first and foremost by organizing in employers' organizations that coordinated their approach.[143] Singer, the manufacturer of sewing machines, announced defiantly that he could do without his 2,500 workers, as he had thousands of machines in stock.[144]

William Steinway, formerly known for his paternalist labor policies, took the lead in resisting the workers' advances by strengthening his pianoforte manufacturers' association. Steinway & Sons had settled most of its previous labor conflicts by compromise. When on May 27, 1872, the journeymen piano makers of Steinway joined the eight-hour movement, William Steinway at first hoped for another fast settlement with his employees: If they would deal directly only with him (and not through a union), he in turn would give them either the nine-hour day or a 10 percent wage increase.[145] His workers, however, rejected the offer. In response, Steinway called a meeting of all the city's piano manufacturers, who expressed their resolve to hold out.[146] Collective determination, however, proved insufficient as workers mobilized large demonstrations in front of his factory. Now the new control over city government worked to the advantage of Steinway and other manufacturers, who succeeded in getting the city's police deployed to escort strikebreakers to their workplaces.[147] Steinway frequently called the police to dispel demonstrating workers in front of his factory. "We immediately sent for Captain Gunner," he noted in his diary on May 29, 1872, when he faced angry workers in front of his factory's gates. The police responded promptly: "I tell Captain Gunner to drive away the crowd which is done without force."[148] On June 15, "Captain Gunner arrives with about ten men, charges at the strikers and club them over arms and legs, they running as fast as their legs can carry them."[149] Sometimes more than 300 policemen remained stationed around the piano factory.[150] With the help of the police, William Steinway, as well as other employers, were able to recruit sufficient numbers of strikebreakers to resume production.[151] Not surprisingly, the strike ended in total defeat for the piano workers. The close cooperation of organized employers with the police eventually proved too powerful for the city's workers.[152] The piano manufacturers were "exultant over their success."[153]

Emboldened by these victories, employers moved closer together to coordinate their relationship to labor.[154] On June 18, 300 to 400 of them met to take "concerted action on the question of maintaining the principles of ten hours for a day's work" – among them such large manufacturers as the owners of the Morgan Iron Works, the Delmater Iron Works, and the Singer Sewing Machine Company.[155] Collectively, one journal estimated, these employers had 45,000 workers on their payrolls, or about 35 percent of all "hands employed" in New York's industry.[156] This meeting was a first, as it united manufacturers of different trades into the "Executive Committee of the Employers of the City and County of New-York and its Vicinity," led by machine manufacturer A. S. Cameron, engine builder John Roach, carriage manufacturer John W. Britton, the maker of soda water apparatuses John Matthews, and bedding manufacturer George Heyman.[157] Though still appealing to the mutuality of interest between labor and capital, they left no doubts that their position had to prevail. Turning away from an earlier form of paternalism toward workers – a carriage maker was "sorry to say his missionary labors were of no avail" – some employers now saw "behind all this the specter of Communism." "Our duty," one of them proclaimed, "is to take it by the throat and say it has no business here."[158] Adam S. Cameron, a manufacturer of steam pumps, saw it as "the duty of employers to have labor as cheap as they could," and was horrified by the "tyranny exercised by some of the trades of New-York."[159] The Molders' Union, he had to report, enjoyed more influence in the shops than the owners themselves. So urgent had the problem become, that machine builder John Roach concluded that "the question of the strike was more important than the result of the Presidential Campaign."[160] The "temper of employers," observed *Iron Age* aptly, "has . . . changed."[161]

Merchants went along with the manufacturers' perception of the strike as a threat to public order, warning that the strike would undermine New York City's locational advantages for industrial enterprises. They argued that "a few discontented, artful men have organized the present strike. . . . By means of a minority, like-minded with themselves, these leaders rule the whole body of the workingmen with an iron despotism, which is compacted, united, and riveted by the affiliated trades-unions, and is worked by secret, irresponsible agents."[162] The merchants were puzzled about this new world, observing that "the existing strike differs so much from similar events in the past, that it scarcely seems to have originated with the same men."[163]

By the end of June, workers could not resist the employers' determined opposition and most went back to work – defeated. The employers' association's aggressive posture against unions and workers had moved to center stage in the employers' camp in 1872, the association thanking the police "for the measure of protection we have thus far received."[164] The 1872 strike was a decisive break with employers' reaction to labor con flicts in prior decades, when the owners of small shops articulated a dominant vision of paternalism, social mobility, and self-improvement, which frequently had allowed some space for labor organizing. Not that paternalism as such disappeared from the scene, but it increasingly became a tool in the arsenal of containment of workers' collective action, not a shared belief in social mobility. The printer Theodore Low De Vinne, for example, had believed in harmony between labor and capital and conceptualized his company as a "family." Until 1864 he had claimed that labor and capital were not in opposition; as long as unions focused on self-improvement, they would be a positive influence.[165] By 1872, however, faced with the massive movement for the eight-hour day, he argued that "it is from the apostles of the International and the Commune that American mechanics have been unwittingly receiving teachings and orders," and he approved of another employer's step of "thrusting out every union man."[166]

By the early 1870s, not only manufacturers but also merchants, bankers, and professionals were experiencing a full-fledged crisis of their older ideological certainties. The conflict with labor had moved toward the center of their political world. As paternalist strategies seemed to fail and as free-labor ideology provided little guidance in the social universe of the early 1870s, many bourgeois New Yorkers sought new explanations for the world they lived in and new ways to safeguard their exalted economic and social status.

These lessons did not bode well for the support of an activist state in the Reconstruction South. When in 1873 the nation's economy collapsed, upper-class New Yorkers pushed for even more radical retrenchment. It was during these years that the merchants, bankers, manufacturers, and professionals of New York City would abandon support for the reconstruction of the southern states, would become ever more ambivalent about democracy, and would formulate important elements of an identity as a class distinct from other social groups.

Escaping the city: Partying in the country, 1863.

Source: Party at the house of Mr. and Mrs. George R. Satterlee, Grimes Hill, Stapleton, Staten Island, photographer unidentified, reproduction courtesy of the Museum of the City of New York, gift of Herbert L. Satterlee.

Lavish meals: The Harrison Grey Fiske dinner, 1900.
Source: The Byron Collection, reproduction courtesy of the Museum of the City of New York.

Aping the aristocracy: The Bradley Martin ball, 1897.
Source: Engraving by Harry McVickar, from *Harper's Weekly* (20 February, 1897), courtesy of the Collection of the New-York Historical Society, 64281.

Equestrian pastimes: Riding in Central Park, 1860.
Source: Engraving from *Harper's Weekly* (15 September, 1860), courtesy of the Collection of the New-York Historical Society, 73291.

**Going to the theater:
The Park Street Theatre
in 1822.**
Source: Watercolor by
John Searle, courtesy of the
Collection of the New-York
Historical Society, 229.

**Churches as social clubs:
Grace Church, 1845.**
Source: Engraving by
J. E. E. Prudhomme, printed by
W. Bayley, courtesy of the
Collection of the New-York
Historical Society, 73290.

The monied meet the people: Union Square.
Source: Harper's Magazine (January 1878), reproduction courtesy of Harvard University.

Encountering the City

The heart of immigrant life: The Lower East Side, ca. 1890.
Source: Hester Street looking west from Clinton, unidentified photographer, courtesy of the Collection of the New-York Historical Society, 33534.

The other half: Life in a tenement, 1898.
Source: Old Mrs. Benoit, in Her Hudson Street Attic, Jacob A. Riis Collection, courtesy of the Museum of the City of New York.

☞ *Politics* ☜

The elite 7th Regiment leaves for the war, 1861.
Source: Oil on paper, by Thomas Nast, courtesy of the New-York Historical Society, accession
number 1946.174, negative number 7394.

Marching for the gold standard: Sound money parade, 1896.
Source: The Great Sound Money Parade, Broadway, South from Murray Street,
The Byron Collection, courtesy of the Museum of the City of New York.

⌒ *Politics* ⌒

The old armory of the 71st Regiment, 1850s.
Source: Official Souvenir, Celebration of the Opening of the New Armory, 71st Regiment
(New York: n.p., 1894), p. 53. Reproduction courtesy of Harvard University.

"Defensible from All Points," the Armory of the 71st Regiment, 1880s.
Source: Official Souvenir Celebration of the Opening of the New Armory, 71st Regiment
(New York: n.p., 1894), p. 17. Reproduction courtesy of Harvard University.

Investing abroad: Guano production in Peru.
Source: Alexander Gardner, "Loading Cars With Guano at the Great Heap, Chincha Islands," print in *Rays of Sunlight from South America* (Washington, D.C.: Philp & Solomons, 1865), courtesy of Photography Collection, Miriam and Ira D. Wallach Division of Arts, Prints and Photographs, The New York Public Library, Astor, Lenox and Tilden Foundations.

Capturing a continent: Park Avenue at 105th Street, 1860.
Source: Courtesy of Milstein Division of U.S. History, Local History, and Genealogy, The New York Public Library, Astor, Lenox and Tilden Foundations.

Winning foreign markets: Singer Sewing Machines conquer the world.
Source: Singer trade card, "Denmark," courtesy of The New York Public Library, Astor, Lenox and Tilden Foundations.

PART III

A Bourgeois World

Meanwhile the holidays had gone by and the season was beginning. Fifth Avenue had become a nightly torrent of carriages surging upward to the fashionable quarters about the park, where illuminated windows and outspread awnings betokened the usual routine of hospitality. Other tributary currents crossed the main stream, bearing their freight to the theatres, restaurants or opera; and Mrs. Peniston, from the secluded watchtower of her upper window, could tell to a nicety just when the chronic volume of sound was increased by the sudden influx setting toward a Van Osburgh ball, or when the multiplication of wheels meant merely that the opera was over, or that there was a big supper at Sherry's.

Edith Wharton, The House of Mirth (1905)

7

Democracy in the Age of Capital

On the eve of the 1873 depression, many among the city's mercantile elite and its rising manufacturers had moved away from their universalist belief in a society without class divisions and from their competing and antipathetic particularist identities rooted in the distinct kinds of capital they owned. But it was only when the years of plenty came to a sudden halt in September 1873 that upper-class New Yorkers began to consolidate their class institutions and to see themselves and at times act as a class. In the next half decade, the city's economic elite formulated a collective identity whose main elements were a theory of (often racial) hierarchy, a recast relationship between state and economy, and ambivalence about democracy.

The end, in 1873, of the years of plenty set the scene for this reorientation and accelerated it by sharpening social conflicts and by furthering reorganization of businesses. The depression that began in September of that year was the most severe economic crisis the United States had experienced in its short history, a crisis that later historians would term the "Great Depression."[1] On September 8, 1873, the New York Warehouse and Security Company failed. Five days later, Kenyon, Cox & Co. went out of business, and on September 18, Jay Cooke & Co., the banking house which had symbolized the rise of financiers during the Civil War like no other, went bankrupt. A day later, Fisk & Hatch stopped business, and on September 20, the New York Stock Exchange, for the first time in its history, closed.[2]

For the next twenty-three years, the U.S. economy would swing between periods of retrenchment and stunted growth.[3] The first period of retrenchment did not end until 1879. During the previous six years, 414 banks suspended business.[4] In the first four months of the crisis alone, New York's banks reduced their specie holdings by 67 percent to meet the demands of depositors.[5] Whereas between 1865 and 1873 railroad mileage had doubled in the United States, it grew only 9 percent in the following five years.[6] Three years into the crisis, 50 percent of all railroads were in the hands of receivers.[7] Consequently, the production of rails dropped by 22.4 percent.[8] With the market for iron largely gone, half of all iron furnaces in the United States lay cold by the end of 1874.[9] Bankers, merchants, and manufacturers all suffered.

To contemporaries, it seemed that the depression arrived without warning, though in hindsight ominous signs had foretold its coming. The immediate stumbling block was the inability of Jay Cooke & Co. to sell millions of Northern Pacific Railroad bonds, but the structural reasons for the crisis lay deeper. Ever since the Civil War, the nation had been gripped by a reckless railroad fever, a fever fueled by speculative dreams of rapid economic development along the new western lines. When these expectations failed to materialize, the nation's railroads, representing by far the largest capital outlays of any industry, brought down with them banks that had provided the capital for expansion, as well as those industries that had built their fortunes on railroads, such as iron factories and coal mines.[10] With the fall of these core industries, the country sank into deep depression.

The six years of depression hurt all segments of the city's economic elite. "Everything looks dark," noted a distraught August Belmont. "I have met with greater losses . . . than I have ever known in the many years of my mercantile experience." He confided to his son that he could not "imagine the utter prostration of all business."[11] Gloomily, William E. Dodge reported to the annual banquet of the Chamber of Commerce on May 7, 1874, that "[s]ince last we met, the commercial interests of the country have been called upon to face another . . . financial crisis."[12] In its review of the iron trade of the same year, the Chamber of Commerce was "unable to record any thing satisfactory. . . . It is probable that never in the history of the trade . . . has a darker cloud rested over its prospects than now."[13] Even as late as 1878, New York Mayor Smith Ely was alarmed that "vacant shops, stores and manufactories . . . stare at us in every street."[14]

Like merchants, manufacturers felt the impact of the crisis. Alarmed, printing press manufacturer Peter S. Hoe wrote to his brother Robert that "[b]usiness is just about as dull as it is possible to make it. We don't get any order for any thing."[15] William Steinway, the producer of nonessential luxury goods, agonized in his diary over the effects of the depression. "I feel very sad on acc. of the financial troubles," he noted on October 1, 1873, adding later that "business seems to be perfectly dead," that it "seems to grow still worse," and, by the end of October 1873, that "[b]usiness [is] at a standstill . . . not a single order coming in."[16] By October 24, Steinway was making plans to incorporate his business in order to limit his personal liability.[17]

While August Belmont had to call in loans and William Steinway was unable to sell pianos, six years of depression meant much greater suffering for the city's workers. By 1874, an estimated 25 percent of all workers in New York City had lost their jobs.[18] Those who managed to hold onto their positions saw their wages decline.[19] "[L]abor can now be had on terms exceedingly favorable," commented the *Manufacturer and Builder,* and, indeed, wage cuts were one of the chief ways employers dealt with the crisis.[20] August Belmont, for example, saw "no reason why laborers' wages should not be reduced in times of depression" – and in 1876 curtailed the remuneration of his employees at his Long Island farm from $2 to $1.50 per day.[21] Worst off were the thousands of newly jobless who were in search of employment. In the winter of 1873/74, mass gatherings of the unemployed assembled in cities throughout the nation, demanding public relief and work. In New York, 7,000 unemployed workers gathered in Tompkins Square Park to demand help from the city – to no avail.[22] Sixteen years earlier, during the crisis of 1857, the city's mercantile elite, along with its rising manufacturers, had offered relief and public jobs in response to the mobilization of the poor in times of crisis, but now they rejected responsibility for the less fortunate and instead devised new ways to protect their property. *Iron Age* went so far as to argue for the beneficial results of the depression: "[T]he power of the trade unions for mischief is weakened."[23]

The depression not only sharpened social conflicts, and thereby helped propel upper-class New Yorkers toward the articulation of collective identities, but also led to the reorganization of many businesses, creating in its wake accumulations of capital on a scale unimaginable in earlier times, removing its owners ever further from other social groups. As the depression bankrupted many companies, it gave birth to new ones, its powerful forces battering and transforming the city's economic elite. Many merchants, bankers, and manufacturers were wiped out, especially those who had extended themselves most – bankers whose loans were not paid back, builders whose large credits were called in, or industrialists whose markets evaporated.

Into this vacuum, however, stepped others such as George F. Baker, who took advantage of the depression to buy out the frightened majority shareholder of the First National Bank.[24] J. Pierpont Morgan, in similar ways, benefited from the downfall of Jay Cooke by taking over his share of government business.[25] For Morgan, the depression was moreover an opportunity to consolidate; he reorganized many failed railroads and secured seats on their board of directors for his own house.[26] The New York Central, for example, passed into his control in 1879, after he had brokered the sale of 250,000 of its shares owned by Commodore Vanderbilt's heirs.[27] Morgan, in the process, converted – according to his biographer Ron Chernow – "financiers from servants to masters of their clients."[28] John D. Rockefeller similarly undertook a stupendous reorganization of one industry, drastically expanding his control over oil production, refining, and distribution, culminating in 1882 in the formation of the Standard Oil Trust.[29] While during the 1870s these consolidations were still the exception, it was the destructiveness of the depression that paved the way and would enable more entrepreneurs to build companies of a scale and scope unknown in earlier times. Manufacturers and bankers who took advantage of the changes of the depression years accumulated a degree of power and operated on a scale that had little in common with the mercantile elite of antebellum New York, and ever less so with the rising manufacturers of the 1850s. They eventually would come to represent the age.[30]

The depression disrupted not only businesses but also the social and cultural institutions of New York's upper class. George T. Strong, who was the comptroller of the elite Trinity Church, became acutely concerned about meeting its bills and was relieved when, on October 2, 1873, he "[s]aw Shepherd Knapp of the Mechanics Bank, who says Trinity Church shall have all the 'accommodation' necessary to keep her afloat."[31] August Belmont stepped down from all of his club functions.[32] The trustees of the Museum of Natural History had great trouble raising funds.[33] Boxes at the Academy of Music remained unsold.[34] The income of the New York Philharmonic fell by 50 percent between the 1872/73 and the 1874/75 seasons.[35] And the Church Music Association was so weakened by low attendance at its concerts that it reduced the pay of its musicians, hoping this would alleviate the problem.[36]

The depression also had effects on the city's bourgeoisie that were more difficult to measure but nonetheless profound. For a whole generation of upper-class New Yorkers, the crisis was the first experience of serious economic problems. It shattered their postwar dream of unending prosperity. The great mobilizations of workers in the winter of 1873/74 and again in 1877 reminded them of the Draft Riots of 1863 and the fragility of their power.

≈ ≈ ≈

In the face of these experiences, the city's bourgeoisie moved closer together. In the economic sphere, they organized a growing number of employers' associations (see Chapter 9). In the social sphere, they built institutions that would stabilize their collective power. While times were hard for most Americans during the 1870s, bourgeois New Yorkers, after recovering from the first shock of the depression, continued the building of organizations, among them boarding schools, museums, and clubs to promote "the culture and solidarity of the elite."[37] These institutions, as Nicola Kay Beisel has argued, were directed toward exclusion of other social groups and promotion of a "bourgeois world"[38] (see Chapter 8). In retrospect, the social life of the 1850s now seemed staid, modest, and restrained. During the 1870s, the 1,317 member-strong Union League Club "showed a disposition to fortify itself in the aesthetic direction against any losses it might be called to bear from the decline in political zeal."[39] Fancy balls, lavish houses, daily rounds through Central Park, and the hunt for genealogical legitimacy through marriage to European aristocrats became ever more prominent.[40] In 1875, in the midst of depression, August Belmont gave a debutante ball for his daughter at Delmonico's that was reportedly "more splendid than the famous one given the previous year in London by the Prince of Wales."[41] Bourgeois New Yorkers self-consciously advanced their solidarity, with their numerous organizational efforts transcending ever more the particularist identities of different segments of the city's economic elite. The depression, in effect, separated "classes more than ever."[42]

The depression, moreover, accelerated the ideological reorientation among upper-class New Yorkers. The universalist antebellum traditions of stewardship and free labor slowly gave way to notions of the unfettered rights of property and the social or even racial superiority of the holders of wealth. Wage workers were no longer perceived as being the temporary dependents of free-labor times, but as the "dangerous classes" who threatened the inalienable rights of property holders. The Union League Club reported in 1875 on the "antagonisms between capital and labor," a notion that would have been alien to the antebellum upper class.[43] The free-labor manufacturers of the 1850s and 1860s, in particular, with their vision of an expansive democracy and near-universal social mobility, as well as their deeply held belief in the exceptional character of the American experiment, now retreated by choice and by necessity to the dogmatic defense of their property rights and a narrowly conceived economic liberalism. The republicanism that had informed some of their ideas and politics in the antebellum years and that still guided the assumptions of many workers had run its course. While free-labor ideology had allowed for the essential equality of employers and temporary proletarians as producers, the new acceptance of an "antagonism" between the two had dramatic ideological and political implications.

Yet inequality remained a most pressing ideological problem for the city's economic elite. Iron manufacturer Abram S. Hewitt observed perceptively that "[t]he problem . . . presented to systems of religion and schemes of government is, to make men who are equal in liberty . . . content with that inequality in its distribution which must inevitably result from the application of the law of justice."[44] Since many employers believed that a lifelong status as wage laborer was the result of some peculiar fault of one's own, explanations for proletarianization were sought and found in the character of workers themselves. As Antonio Gramsci has argued, elites have almost always seen subordinate groups as displaying "barbaric and pathological" features, and it was thus not surprising that the city's upper class legitimized inequality by referring to differing physical and mental endowments.[45] No other ideology answered their needs better than the application of Charles Darwin's theories of natural selection to an analysis of society by the likes of Herbert Spencer. Supporting some central notions of liberal individualism and free exchange, while contradicting liberalism's less convenient universalist elements, social Darwinism captured the imagination of bourgeois New Yorkers.[46]

By the early 1870s, according to Richard Hofstadter, "the transmutation of species and natural selection dominated the outlook of American naturalists," and became popular among the city's bourgeoisie.[47] Appropriating Darwinist ideas to help understand the emerging spectacular social inequality, the president of the New York Central, Chauncey Depew, asserted that the social elite of New York represented those who are "the survival of the fittest." They had won in the struggle for dominance because they were endowed with "superior ability, foresight and adaptability."[48] Railroad investor James J. Hill agreed, contending that "railroad companies are determined by the law of the survival of the fittest."[49] Andrew Carnegie and John D. Rockefeller seconded such notions, as did reformers E. L. Godkin and George W. Curtis.[50] As Carnegie put it: "Before Spencer, all for me had been darkness, after him, all had become light – and right."[51] Elite New Yorkers' embrace of these ideas was undoubtedly furthered by the immigrant nature of much of the working class, allowing for a correspondence between class and "race." Testifying to such racialized thinking, the *Manufacturer and Builder* announced that "[t]here is more difference between a Caucasian and the lowest type of Australian than between such an Australian and the highest type of monkeys."[52] Social Darwinism became a convenient tool for understanding and legitimizing the world of Gilded Age New York. Spencer, whose influence in the United States was much greater than that of Darwin himself, indeed became so popular among the city's economic elite that they arranged a grand banquet at Delmonico's to welcome him to the United States in 1882. Cyrus W. Field, Perry Belmont (son of August), E. L. Godkin, Andrew H. Green, John Quincy Ward, Andrew Carnegie, Abram S. Hewitt, Samuel J. Colgate, George P. Peabody, and Chauncey M. Depew all applauded him at the occasion.[53] In such a climate it was hardly surprising that New York's premier antisuffrage activist, Simon Sterne, sought the fellowship of Herbert Spencer, and Spencer himself called Andrew Carnegie his best friend in the United States.[54]

Old free-labor manufacturers, such as Horace Greeley and Peter Cooper, now increasingly became curiosities, a surviving species of an earlier age. By the early 1870s, Greeley had lost his earlier standing among the city's working class, and his quixotic presidential campaign in 1872 alienated him from the city's upper class, who had come to dislike intensely his policy of class compromise.[55] In a similar fashion, Cooper's inflationist opinions on greenbacks, while bringing him the respect of labor organizations, isolated him from his peers.[56] Despite or perhaps because of his isolation, Cooper was in many ways the most perceptive observer of the changes among his class. What he saw moved him to speak out publicly against the "money powers," who represented in his eyes "a dangerous class."[57] He railed against the selfishness of other manufacturers who hired labor for the "smallest consideration for which it can be obtained."[58] He warned that "[t]here is fast forming in this country an aristocracy of wealth – the worst form of aristocracy, that can curse the prosperity of any country."[59] Not only did he fear for labor, but he also feared for the Republic, which was being threatened by the "class legislation of Congress since the war."[60] Peter Cooper went so far as to amend his old free-labor beliefs (which had seen little role for the state) and ask for state intervention to provide government regulation of the economy, state ownership of railroads, and public employment programs for infrastructure improvements.[61] But now well into his eighties, Cooper was ignored by his peers.

꙳ ꙳ ꙳

Just as upper-class New Yorkers questioned their universalist belief in a society without fundamental social divisions, they were becoming ever more wary about political intervention into markets. Motivated by their own squeeze in profits, they saw in the depression an opportunity to succeed in demanding drastic fiscal retrenchment.[62] Though appeals for spending cuts and lower taxation had a long history, they had never been articulated as aggressively before. Fiscal retrenchment – the abandonment of stewardship – was another sign of the distance that merchants, manufacturers, and bankers had traveled from their earlier beliefs and practices.[63]

The demand for fiscal retrenchment, as we have seen earlier, was first articulated in the early 1870s by the city's bondholders, who feared for the security of their investments. During the depression, however, all segments of the upper class came to favor this position. Economically vulnerable, they were unwilling to pay taxes to maintain the "extravagances" of relief and public works. Edwards Pierrepont declared in May 1876 that the economic decline of New York was the result of investments in "costly parks[,] . . . unnecessary boulevards [and] costly ornaments," and a similar sentiment led the president of the Chamber of Commerce, Samuel D. Babcock, to call for the "great principles of integrity, self-reliance and industry."[64] The Chamber itself saw the "evils of the day" increasingly in "excessive legislation."[65] Samuel Tilden, the railroad lawyer, politician, and New York governor from 1875 to 1877, wanted to solve the country's economic problems by "trusting to the people to work out their own prosperity and happiness," and indeed as governor, he cut taxes dramatically, along with reducing spending on public work.[66] Expressing similar sentiments, the Council of Political Reform, throughout the seventies, repeated the mantra of retrenchment, advocating lower city taxes, the sale of most of the city's property, a reduction of state taxes by one-third, and an end to all public improvements in the city.[67] Even the building and real estate interests, at one time chief supporters of Tweed's expansionist policies, demanded "the exercise of the sternest economy and the wisest adaptation of means to the end in view."[68] Beyond short-term economic rationales for retrenchment, bourgeois New Yorkers also perceived political dangers from public works. As employers of wage workers, they correctly saw that the employment programs of the municipal government limited their ability to cut wages and indirectly supported the power of trade unions.

The foremost plea for retrenchment was articulated in municipal politics, where the crisis further radicalized bourgeois New Yorkers' demands for lower expenditures and lower taxes. They were successful in their demands, not least because the political regime of Mayor William Havemeyer and Comptroller Andrew Green, which the Committee of Seventy had helped to install in 1872, gave them great control over the city's response to the depression. The depth of the change in municipal politics that Havemeyer represented, however, became clear only in 1874, when the Democratic Party regained the mayoralty, thanks to voters enraged by the unwillingness of the city to help the victims of the depression, yet still proving unwilling or unable to change the thrust of municipal policy. It was not least this commitment to retrenchment that guaranteed the new Tammany mayor, William H. Wickham, a diamond merchant, enjoyed political support from the city's economic elite.[69] His successor, John Kelly, also a Tammany Democrat, followed in his footsteps, albeit aiding the poor to some extent through the party machine.[70] During the 1870s, in many ways the control of the city's economic elite over local politics increased – mainly through their influence on political parties. John Kelly, who commanded Tammany Hall after Tweed's fall, enjoyed the support of such wealthy Democrats as Samuel Tilden, Abram Hewitt, Sanford Church, Wheeler Peckham, Augustus Shell, and Horace Clark throughout most of the decade, and was widely accepted by the business community.[71] Ironically, it was Tammany that oversaw the retrenchment of the municipal government in the 1870s and, thus, the implementation of one of the most important goals of the city's upper class.

Retrenchment affected every area of municipal government.[72] Though tax rates and city debts rose until the fiscal year 1875/76, due to a decline in property values in the wake of the depression, both tax rates and municipal debt fell from 1876 until the 1890s. (In 1875 the tax rate in New York City was 2.94 percent. By 1895 it had fallen to 1.72 percent.)[73] Between 1876 and 1886, the city's debt decreased by 25 percent.[74] To attain this goal, Comptroller Andrew Green implemented, according to historian Jerome Mushkat, "tight-fisted" budgets that "harmed vital city services."[75]

The demand of the city's economic elite for retrenchment also included hostility to public relief. The large number of desperately poor citizens increasingly lost public support. While in 1871 the Department of Public Charities and Correction distributed $2.23 per person on public relief, by 1875 only 93 cents was available.[76] In 1875, the city finally eliminated all public relief, except for the distribution of coal to the needy and donations to the blind.[77]

Not only did the city's public relief disappear but also any significant public works programs that might have employed thousands of desperate New Yorkers. Even after mass demonstrations by working people in the winter of 1873/74, the city refused to institute public works – which had been one of the responses to the crisis of 1857.[78] Mayor Havemeyer told the *New York Times* in November 1873 that "[h]e could not see why the property of those who, by thrift and industry, had built up their houses, should be confiscated [by] men who had . . . by strikes or the like, contributed to the present state of things themselves."[79] "Care has been taken not to diminish the terror of this last resort of poverty," exclaimed Myer Stern, commissioner of charities and correction, "because it has been deemed better that a few should test the minimum rate at which existence can be preserved, than that the many should find the poor-house so comfortable a home that they would brave the shame of pauperism to gain admission to it."[80]

So dominant had the discourse of retrenchment become, that the city went even further and cut its workers' wages. In 1876, the city's public works commissioner laid off many of its employees and hired day laborers through private contractors instead, resulting in a drastic reduction of wages, perhaps by as much as 65 percent.[81] One of the rationales for such cutbacks was the need to facilitate wage cuts in the private sector. "The whole settlement of the labor question was postponed by the over-generous charity of the city," argued Robert T. Davis in the *Journal of Social Science,* hoping specifically that the "crisis would bring down the wages of female servants."[82] The Union League Club, for its part, again demanded in January 1877 that public workers should be paid at rates "which would govern an honest and discreet citizen in securing labor and supplies in his private business."[83]

In combination with their rejection of public relief, the city's merchants, manufacturers, and bankers embraced private charity.[84] Arguing that private giving would be superior to public giving because a sharper line could be drawn between the "deserving" and "undeserving" poor, by 1876 they had succeeded in monopolizing relief. Faced with the exigencies of the depression, private charities had already met at Cooper Union in 1873 to rationalize their charity efforts, but focused their attention mainly on how to "detect and expose imposition and fraud."[85] "Charities should follow and not precede want," these bourgeois welfare activists proclaimed, since a "worse evil to the poor than poverty is the spirit of pauperism."[86] It would be a "bounty to pauperism [to] call the poor to a public office, to clothe, feed, and help them," argued Robert T. Davis, justifying the harsh limits private charities put on the funds they distributed.[87] Because these upper-class New Yorkers believed that there was a clear-cut distinction between "poverty and pauperism," with paupers having chosen poverty "by preference, or very often by inheritance," they saw it as their central task to "root [paupers] out by resolute treatment."[88] The bottom of the social ladder, they claimed, was inhabited by people who "reached that condition by idleness, improvidence, drunkenness, by some form of vicious indulgence."[89] Consequently, the AICP, whose income had fallen as a result of the depression, concluded in its 1874 report that those who either "refuse to labor or waste its proceeds in profligacy should suffer the just retribution which God has attached to indolence and vice."[90]

Sharply distinguishing between the "deserving" and undeserving" poor, private benevolence was now a far cry from the paternalist expressions the AICP had uttered in the 1850s, when it still believed that organizations like itself, as stewards of the community, could eradicate poverty from the United States.[91] Now, these activists instead spoke of the "perpetuity" and "universality" of the condition of poverty.[92] Though private benevolence continued (Moses Taylor, for example, gave a substantial $270,000 in 1882 for the construction of a hospital for his railroad workers in Scranton, Pennsylvania), such beliefs explain why public and private relief remained starkly insufficient to address the severe social dislocations that rapid industrialization had brought about.[93]

The source of the remaining bourgeois concern for the poor in the 1870s was fear of the dispossessed, where earlier it had been sympathy for the material welfare of the community. In 1875, the New York AICP warned that the depression might encourage the "socialistic element" in the city to "advance its interests" and pointed out that "[t]here is a dangerous class in New York quite as much as in Paris."[94] There was no "greater social and economic concern than that relating to the industrial classes, which numerically embrace more than two-thirds of the City population," they warned, praising themselves in the same breath for having "done more for the security of person and property" than any other organization in the city.[95] Benevolent activists who in the 1850s had seen their work as an effort to rescue society from evil influences, now saw their rationale increasingly as the protection of their own class.[96] Charity, the New York Charity Organization Society argued, provided "insurance, terrestrial and celestial" for the property of the rich "at easy rates."[97]

Realizing that their pitiful relief was grossly insufficient to quiet the "dangerous classes," however, the city's economic elite also called for stronger police forces, national guards, and strict legislation. They applauded when the police dispersed the demonstration of unemployed workers in 1874 in Tompkins Square Park, and when new vagrancy laws were hastily enforced.[98] In 1878, a group of bourgeois New Yorkers founded the Society for the Prevention of Crime to "aid in the enforcement of the laws of this State."[99] Later, during the 1877 railroad strike, large segments of the upper class supported the military repression of strikers.

The depression, in effect, in hurting the city's merchants, industrialists, and bankers economically, helped turn their former optimism into severe anxieties about the future. They were "pervaded by an uneasy feeling that they were living over a mine of social and industrial discontent," observed a British visitor to the city in 1877.[100] For all their power, wealthy New Yorkers seemed uncertain whether a democratic society characterized by such severe social inequality could remain stable for long.

≈ ≈ ≈

Although upper-class New Yorkers successfully implemented their program of government retrenchment, they were far from solving the larger problem of political rule under the conditions of popular suffrage and extreme social inequality.[101] Indeed, despite their continued influence on local politics, they saw their position as unstable and subject to the whims of powerful machine politicians, an instability that eventually would move them to address the problem of municipal political rule in a more fundamental way. Indeed, the depression brought to full flower the earlier critique of universal white male suffrage articulated by the Citizens' Association, the Council for Political Reform, and the Committee of Seventy. While some liberal intellectuals, such as Godkin and Curtis, went so far as to demand restriction of suffrage rights in national elections, the most virulent manifestation of bourgeois ambivalence about democracy was the movement for a constitutional amendment limiting voting rights in the cities of New York State.[102] Suffrage restrictions, in the eyes of many upper-class New Yorkers and liberal reformers alike, promised to resolve their political problems once and for all.

These well-to-do antisuffragists saw the city as belonging to its propertied citizens, ridiculing notions that citizens would derive political rights qua their status as citizens and not as that of taxpayers. Their "implicit distaste for a democracy of the masses," as one historian observed, "was calculated to remove all but their own kind from the political arena."[103] By the 1870s, some of them were already looking back upon distinguished careers as outspoken opponents of universal suffrage. Simon Sterne, as one of the intellectual leaders of the movement, spoke as early as 1865 in front of a distinguished audience in London about "the dangers of universal suffrage."[104] He claimed that universal suffrage in municipal elections would lead to "communism, confiscation, and threatened bankruptcy."[105] Conceptualizing the city as a "corporative [sic] administration of property interests," he argued that just as in a bank the depositors would have no right to "take part in the election of the officers of the bank," propertyless citizens, "the paupers and criminals," should have no right to vote for municipal officials. The ballot, in effect, had become an "element of aggression" of the poorer classes against the well-off.[106] As a result of such inclinations among bourgeois New Yorkers, the 1870s became a turning point in American democratic thought. Economic liberty was elevated as an end in itself, and not, as before, an integral part of the democratic republic.[107] In turn, the critique of democracy that emerged in the North effectively destroyed any hope for the enfranchisement of women and endangered the hard-won rights of freedmen in the South.[108] "Universal suffrage," according to Francis Parkman, "is applicable only to those peoples, if such there are, who by character and training are prepared for it."[109]

The opinion that the city was a corporation that only its stockholders should control now spread like wildfire among the city's upper class.[110] Focusing their efforts on municipal government, because it was there that workers' political power was most pronounced, the antisuffragists argued that "[i]t is in the cities that the diseases of the body politic are gathered to a head, and it is here that the need of attacking them is most urgent."[111] "It would be a great gain," the *New York Times* editorialized in 1878, if "our people could be made to understand distinctly that the right to life, liberty, and the pursuit of happiness involves, to be sure, the right to good government, but not the right to take part, either immediately or indirectly, in the management of the State."[112] The "masses" now were conceived of as being outside the bounds of political citizenship.

Liberal intellectuals like E. L. Godkin, Simon Sterne, and George W. Curtis not only agitated for suffrage restrictions but, in tandem with well-to-do New Yorkers, organized to make disenfranchisement of the lower classes a real political possibility. The personnel and the ideas of these organizational efforts were directly linked to prior elite reform efforts, and retained the traditional program of a limitation of the franchise by wealth. In contrast to the 1860s, however, these ideas enjoyed very broad, if not universal, support from the city's upper class by the mid-1870s.

The movement for municipal disenfranchisement peaked in 1875 when the Democratic governor of New York State, railroad lawyer Samuel Tilden, created a bipartisan commission to propose reforms in the structure of municipal government in the state.[113] The commission consisted of twelve men, among them Wall Street lawyer William M. Evarts, editors E. L. Godkin and Oswald Ottendorfer, and lawyer Simon Sterne. It deliberated for nearly two years. When it published its final report, it presented a stunningly antidemocratic document, asserting "the fruitlessness of any effort for improvement through the regular instrumentality of popular election," and demanding, "that the excesses of democracy be corrected."[114]

The commission expressed its dissatisfaction with the traditional system of urban rule. Specifically, it located the city's problems in high debts, excessive expenditures, and high taxes.[115] The origins of these ills were seen in the election of "incompetent and unfaithful" municipal officials and the prevalence of parties in municipal politics.[116] But how to improve municipal rule? After dismissing a whole range of reform ideas that had been traditionally articulated – the prosecution of corrupt officials, the strengthening of the position of the mayor, or civil service reform – the commission concluded that only an attack on the roots of the problem could save the cities.[117] They questioned "whether the election by universal suffrage of the local guardians of the financial concerns of cities can be safely retained," concluding that "the choice of the local guardians and trustees of the financial concerns of cities should be lodged with taxpayers."[118] By distinguishing between national and state government on the one side and municipal government on the other, they rationalized the limitation of the most central right of the American political system, arguing that "[a]ll true friends of the system [of universal suffrage] should unite in rescuing it from such perils."[119]

To effect the desired outcome, the commission recommended that New York State amend its constitution, because only such an amendment would guarantee "stability."[120] The constitutional amendment they suggested stipulated that appointed commissions, instead of elected officials, should do much of the work of municipal administration.[121] Moreover, it made the borrowing of money by cities unconstitutional except for tightly regulated emergencies.[122] But at the heart of their proposal was the creation of a board of finance, its members elected by those residents of the city who "have paid annual tax on property owned by them, and officially assessed for taxation in such city, of the assessed value of not less than five hundred dollars," or those who paid yearly rent of at least $250.[123] These were substantial sums in a city in which skilled workers could hope to take home between $400 and $600 annually, of which they would not spend more than 20 percent on rent. The board of finance was to be endowed with all powers regarding taxation, expenditures, and debt – including the allocation of city expenditures to specific projects.[124] As a result, the mayor, as well as the Board of Aldermen, though still elected by popular suffrage, would have lost most of their powers.

An estimate by the *New York Times* concluded that of a total electorate of about 140,000 New Yorkers, 60,000 to 65,000 would retain the right to vote as taxpayers, with another 35,000 to 40,000 as rent payers.[125] These numbers suggest that about 29 percent of the city's voters would have lost their right to participate in the choosing of the "financial guardians of the city." This, however, is a conservative estimate, since the 100,000 New Yorkers who would have still been allowed to vote constituted only 31 percent of the total number of men twenty-one years or older who lived in Manhattan in 1880.[126] As many as 69 percent of all voters, hence, would have been disenfranchised.

The commission's plan was a dramatic reconceptualization of the way in which New York City would be ruled, albeit one that harkened back to the venerable ideas of propertied republicanism. That it eventually failed was not as surprising as the broad support it received from upper-class New Yorkers. The Chamber of Commerce called a special meeting in March 1877 (with an "unusually large number of members assembled") to consider the amendment, and it unanimously declared its backing.[127] James M. Brown, Henry F. Spaulding, Royal Phelps, George S. Coe, Seth Low, and Joseph Seligman were among those who expressed their support at the meeting, the lawyer William Allen Butler praising in particular the proposed board of finance, because it excluded "the irresponsible, floating and shiftless vote, which never has any but a mischievous and indefensible relation to the exercise of the right of suffrage."[128] A member of the commission that drafted the amendments praised the work with the argument that "[m]erchants will no longer find themselves in contest with the loafer element, which would eventually outnumber and beat them."[129] More control, merchant and future mayor of the city Seth Low argued at the same meeting, would mean lower taxes.[130]

Not only the Chamber of Commerce but also the New York Stock Exchange, the Produce Exchange, the Importers' and Grocers' Board of Trade, the Council of Political Reform, the Union League Club, the Municipal Society, the New-York Board of Trade, and the Cotton Exchange passed resolutions in support of the amendment.[131] Indeed, all the major business groups of New York City endorsed the constitutional change and mobilized in support of it, the *New York Times* noting that it "is warmly supported by the entire commercial and tax-paying interests of the City."[132] The New York press endorsed the amendment; the *New York Times*, the *New York Herald*, the *Commercial and Financial Chronicle*, the *New York Daily Tribune*, *Harper's Weekly*, and *The Nation* all came out enthusiastically for it.[133] The city's Taxpayers' Association went even further; its members demanded that large rent payers also be excluded from the electorate for the board of finance.[134]

Upper-class New Yorkers and their institutions had found a political project around which they could mobilize: "If we really want relief," editorialized the *Commercial and Financial Chronicle,* "we must bestir ourselves vigorously and at once."[135] And they did, indeed so vigorously that when the former Governor of New York State Hoffman spoke out against the suffrage restrictions at the annual banquet of the Chamber of Commerce, he ended his defense with the words, "Now, gentlemen, I did not expect that that sentiment would receive much applause here."[136] Such a collective political mobilization of elite New Yorkers had not been seen since September 1871, when they rebelled against the Tweed regime. Overwhelming support came from all segments of the city's wealthy, including Joseph Seligman, Henry Havemeyer, William E. Dodge, Jr., Peter Cooper, Cornelius Vanderbilt, and John Jacob Astor.[137] Where six years earlier the Committee of Seventy had failed to accomplish long-term structural changes because its members could not agree on how to structure the relationship of the city's working class to local administration, in 1877 these divisions had evaporated, replaced by widespread agreement that reform was only feasible by disenfranchising a large number of New Yorkers.

When in the spring of 1877 the passage of the constitutional amendment seemed possible, upper-class New Yorkers mobilized a powerful movement in its support. As the *New York Times* reminded its readers, such a chance would "not return for years to come."[138] On April 7, 1877, a large meeting in Chickering Hall was "filled with merchants, bankers, and business men," who resolved that "cities should be run on business principles."[139] A speech by William Evarts set the tone with the argument that the proposed reform would "separate . . . us at once from that continual change of persons which makes anything like permanent and useful administration utterly impossible."[140] Simon Sterne followed at the lectern, reasoning that the idea that "a mere majority should direct how the public expenses . . . should be regulated [was] preposterous."[141] The meeting "received with enthusiastic cheers . . . every reference to the cutting down of salaries and dismissal of superfluous employees" by the city, a retrenchment, which, after all, was the political goal of disenfranchisement.[142]

At first, these mobilizations in favor of disenfranchisement were successful: The constitutional amendment passed the legislature in Albany. In order to be put to a vote by the people of the State of New York, however, it had to pass a second legislature, a legislature that was to be newly elected in November 1877. The electoral campaign in the fall of 1877 thus focused on the reform of municipal government in general and suffrage rights in particular, bringing the "tax-payers" movement once more into public view.[143] The support that the movement now derived from the city's propertied voters was so immense that even its initiators were surprised, finding that "a much greater interest had been developed in the movement than had been anticipated by the most sanguine of gentlemen."[144] Channeling their political impulse, they called another "mass meeting" in early October, just like the one they had summoned in April.[145] Though a "party of Communists . . . attempted to make a disturbance," the atmosphere was generally upbeat, not least because the alleged Communists' efforts were "futile" and "several of them were arrested."[146] The speakers called upon bourgeois New Yorkers to "combine," because of the "necessity for property-owners to secure control of the Municipal Government."[147] "[I]f property did not get power," thundered one of them, "power would take property."[148] So dominant was the theme of disenfranchisement in the election campaign that the *New York Times* noted after the elections that "a good many voters were yesterday and last night actually looking for ballots on the constitutional amendments."[149]

Despite the exceptional degree of mobilization of bourgeois New Yorkers, however, the election saw a defeat of the supporters of suffrage restriction. The amendment failed to pass the legislature in the spring of 1878. Instrumental in the defeat of the antisuffrage forces was a coalition of professional politicians, upstate farmers, and working-class New Yorkers. Tammany politicians, such as John Kelly and ex-Governor Hoffman, opposed the amendment, which was hardly surprising, considering that they derived their political power from the to-be-disenfranchised workers.[150] In a similar way, upstate farmers mobilized against the Tilden Commission's amendment. But most articulate and most consistent in its defense of democratic politics was the city's labor movement, including the nascent Workingmen's Party. Seeing the amendments correctly as a threat to their political influence, they mobilized against candidates supporting the amendment, and even founded a "Universal Suffrage Club."[151] A "Workingmen's Mass Meeting," called by the party two weeks after the businessmen's meeting in Chickering Hall, mobilized against the amendments, whose measures it called "infamous in character, revolutionary in principle, and an insult to every honest citizen."[152] A radical journalist close to the party, George McNeill, made the point most succinctly when he argued that "the elective franchise is a privilege and power that must be retained by the wage labor class even at the cost of bloody revolution."[153] The experience of the summer of 1877, when the state's military power had helped quell a railroad strike, made it that much more urgent for labor to secure continued access to state power.

In 1877, the antidemocratic fervor of New York's economic elite peaked, yet despite its vocal strength it came to naught. That their project failed and, hence, that democracy was sustained in New York State was not because well-to-do New Yorkers had not tried hard enough, but because other social groups rose to the defense of one of the most fundamental rights of a liberal democracy. Because these defenders of suffrage enjoyed access to resources and institutions (such as political parties, trade unions, and newspapers), they could put up powerful resistance. In fact, once democratic rule had been established in New York City, the institutional and political forces to maintain it were too strong to allow for a limitation of suffrage rights through a constitutional process. As the *Sun* remarked, it was rather unlikely for "universal suffrage to commit suicide by destroying universal suffrage."[154] This was the lesson upper-class New Yorkers learned in 1877, a lesson that would not diminish their antidemocratic convictions but would end their struggle for institutional changes.[155] The problems that the city's merchants, manufacturers, and bankers faced with municipal rule were not significant enough to justify a step entirely out of the bounds of the political-constitutional framework of the United States, a step that southern elites took later in the nineteenth century.[156] As Simon Sterne remarked resignedly, "political power, once granted, cannot be modified."[157]

While municipal democratic institutions persisted in the North, the depression and its accompanying social conflicts spelled the end of upper-class support for interventionist policies in the Reconstruction South. The emancipatory mission some bourgeois New Yorkers had embraced, albeit reluctantly, during the Civil War and after, gave way to an unremitting focus on protecting the rights of property. Now that the rule of the market seemed to have been established also in the South, freedpeople had to look out for themselves, a notion that meshed well with ever more popular social Darwinist beliefs. Increasingly, the discourse on the problems of political rule in the North informed the discourse on Reconstruction and vice versa, resulting in the formulation of a coherent "taxpayers" point of view, which focused the fear of the political power of citizens without property. In a review of the situation in the South, the *New York Tribune* expressed this sentiment, asserting that as a result of Reconstruction, the "control of several of the States has been secured by the colored race.

They have occupied the bench and the jury-box, made the laws, collected the revenue, voted the appropriations, handled the money – done everything except pay the taxes."[158] This, after all, was exactly what bourgeois New Yorkers saw as wrong with lower-class influence in municipal politics in the North. Quite symbolically, it was Samuel Tilden's presidential campaign in 1877 that awakened hope among southerners that an end to Reconstruction was in sight – the very same Samuel Tilden who had enabled elite New Yorkers to bring forward a constitutional amendment to abridge suffrage rights in the state's cities.

Even more so than before the onset of the depression, upper-class New Yorkers wanted to bring economic and political stability to the South. While before 1873 some bourgeois New Yorkers had defended federal involvement in the South in order to contain the counterrevolutionary intimidation and violence of the region's white elite, such a policy became increasingly controversial after the onset of the crisis.[159] In 1874, moreover, an "electoral tidal wave" changed the North's political balance – it was in this year, for instance, that Democrat Samuel Tilden won New York's gubernatorial election.[160] Not only did the northern Republican Party lose political power but it also turned increasingly conservative and sounded a general retreat from Reconstruction under President Grant's leadership.[161] In addition, federal courts limited the scope of the Fourteenth Amendment to federal regulations, excluding the greater and more significant body of state regulations.[162] Though the Civil Rights Act of 1875 guaranteed a number of rights independent of race, its enforcement was left mostly to black litigants.[163] By 1875, Grant had proven himself unwilling to protect black voters from the terror unleashed by southern whites, who were emboldened by the early signs of the waning commitment of the North.[164]

More so than most northerners, New York's economic elite welcomed the abandonment of interventionist policies.[165] Upper-class Republican Party activists, such as William E. Dodge, worked feverishly for a reorientation of the party away from radicalism. Iron manufacturer and Democratic member of the House Abram Hewitt campaigned in the Appropriations Committee for a drastic reduction of funding for the army, "which would make it impossible to use the troops in sustaining Republican claimants in South Carolina and Louisiana."[166] And Republican George T. Strong, who had voted in 1872 for Grant, now became increasingly dissatisfied with the administration.[167] "The governments of South Carolina and Louisiana are, I fear, mere nests of corrupt carpet baggers upheld by a brute nigger constituency," he noted in September 1874. In Strong's eyes,

New York City's "Celtocracy" had become linked to the South's "niggero-cracy."[168] It was the experience of Reconstruction itself that fueled the growing ambivalence about an activist and democratically legitimated state among bourgeois New Yorkers.

Although this retreat from Reconstruction was driven by a desire for political and economic stability in the South, its impetus derived from the ideology of retrenchment and absolute property rights that captured the imagination of the city's upper class after 1873. Quite tellingly, those bourgeois New Yorkers who had come to embrace the greenback a few years earlier, jumped by 1873 on the bandwagon of gold standard resumption, hoping that it would help resolve the economic crisis, as well as limit any possible political intervention into markets. In November 1873, just weeks after the crisis hit the stock market, the Chamber of Commerce called a special meeting and anxiously resolved once more to return to specie payment.[169] By 1876, the Chamber was unanimous in its position, save for the lone voice of Peter Cooper.[170] Bankers followed suit.[171] The *Commercial and Financial Chronicle*, which had during the late sixties and early seventies at times voiced sympathy for a currency not backed by gold, now consistently advocated resumption.[172] Indeed, the weekly went so far as to deny that "among the solid, conservative, intelligent masses of our citizens, there has [ever] been any temporary conversion to paper money heresies such as is in some quarters affirmed."[173]

More significant than the merchants' reorientation, however, was that of the manufacturers: Robert Hoe II now found the reasons for the economic troubles in the "excessive use of paper money," and even such a quintessential manufacturers' journal as the *Shoe and Leather Reporter* embraced the gold standard.[174] By July 1875, *Iron Age*, along with manufacturing interests everywhere, supported contraction and the Resumption Bill, a major departure from their earlier embrace of greenbacks.[175] In March 1874, a meeting at Cooper Union brought together such former advocates of greenbacks as clothing manufacturer George Opdyke and iron manufacturer George W. Quintard (as well as importer Simeon B. Chittenden and banker George S. Coe) to oppose the Inflation Bill, which would have authorized a limited issuance of additional greenbacks.[176] Three thousand businessmen signed a resolution to the same effect. This meeting pointed powerfully to the emergence of a shared view on monetary matters by bourgeois New Yorkers, an important change from the late 1860s.

After 1873, it was mostly workers and farmers who supported an inflationary currency, while owners of capital moved nearly completely into the hard-money camp. The debate on monetary politics, in effect, had split along class lines.[177] Tellingly, when in 1878 banker Levi P. Morton ran successfully on the Republican ticket for a congressional seat in the eleventh district of Manhattan, he appealed to his mostly elite voters by basing his campaign on a pro-specie platform.[178]

Retrenchment was the call of the hour, accelerating the demise of Reconstruction, as the debate on Reconstruction took on a similar vocabulary as the debate on the problems of political rule in cities. What bourgeois New Yorkers did, in effect, was to formulate a "taxpayer" view on political rule, a view that eventually merged the inclinations and interests of propertied white southerners with those of propertied white northerners. Economic elites in both sections of the country increasingly spoke a similar political language, with dramatic political effects. "Southern States have been fearfully robbed by their rulers," asserted the *Financial and Commercial Chronicle,* a position that also informed its discourse on northern local politics.[179]

Southern elites, in turn, felt greatly encouraged by this reorientation among the northern upper classes. In fact, the increasing prominence of taxpayer movements in the North encouraged them to appropriate northern taxpayer ideology and politics for their own ends. In 1871, for example, South Carolina elites held a "Tax-Payers Convention" to demand a redistribution of political power in the state. Three years later, in 1874, they filed "Taxpayers" candidates for state elections.[180] The ideological themes of this taxpayers' revolt in the South were the same as those in the North, among them the "tyranny of a majority," "rights of property," "retrenchment," "taxation without representation," "fraud," "extravagant spending," and "the right of revolution."[181] Redemptionists in New Orleans chose to call themselves the "Committee of Seventy," and saw their goal as fighting "Tweedism."[182] Even esoteric schemes, such as those proposed by Simon Sterne on "minority representation" and cumulative voting, made their way into the political repertoire of elite South Carolinians.[183] Perceptively, the disempowered southern planters speculated that the appropriation of the political lingo of northern elites would provide them with urgently needed political support.

Their expectations were met: Even Horace Greeley's old free-labor and antislavery *New York Daily Tribune* began to sympathize with southern elites, stating that "[t]he intelligent people of the State have no voice in public affairs . . . and are obliged to submit to the rule of a class just released from slavery," a class of "ignorant, superstitious, semi-barbarians."[184] With great consternation, the *Tribune* remarked not only that the freedmen had gained political rights but that "they have absolute political supremacy."[185] The connection between North and South was made explicit, as the paper "decidedly disagrees . . . [with] those who hold Ignorance a qualification for political franchises, whether in South Carolina or New-York."[186] Comparing "such voting as we now average in the lower Wards of this City" with that "in the Sea Islands and in many of the lower Counties of South Carolina," the *Tribune* concluded that neither "did and never can result in wise, capable, provident, frugal rule."[187] If such things would happen in the North as had transpired in the South, the paper's writer observed, "a tax-payers league" would be organized.[188] Such ideas entered into the mainstream of bourgeois discourse and, indeed, New York drug manufacturer and merchant Samuel B. Schieffelin warned explicitly of the dangerous connection between democracy in the North and the rights of freedmen in the South.[189] He advised southern states to write constitutions that would limit suffrage rights, thus saving themselves from "future danger and evil."[190] Universal suffrage, he bluntly asserted, "is a curse to any community, whether white or black, until fitted for it."[191]

While northerners as well as southerners began to speak in aggressively racist ways, elite southerners often framed the question of who would wield political power in terms of class, not race, presumably expecting to find greater commonality with elite northerners.[192] And their calculations were justified: The *Commercial and Financial Chronicle* had already stated in 1868 that it "is not a question of negroes as negroes with which we have to deal [in regard to suffrage rights] but a question of a vast number of ignorant human beings degraded by long years of slavery, and suddenly clothed with power to control the property and the interests of great communities."[193] And when in 1873 the *New-York Daily Tribune* sent James S. Pike, the former abolitionist and Republican from Maine, to South Carolina to report on its politics, he returned with a similar portrait of the political rule of African Americans, seeing South Carolina as a "society suddenly turned bottom-side up," a place in which "the dregs of the population, . . . asserting over them the rule of ignorance and corruption [govern] through the inexorable machinery of a majority of numbers. It is barbarism overwhelming civilization by physical force."[194] For Pike and many elite northerners, the government of South Carolina was a revolutionary force, "a huge system of brigandage," which threatened the "future peace and prosperity of the country": "[T]hey are the classes who have never yet in history exercised the functions of government."[195] This was a language bourgeois New Yorkers understood as it allowed them to sympathize and support southern elites in their project of first undermining and eventually destroying democracy in the South. The *Commercial and Financial Chronicle* stated this position conclusively when it linked the efforts at restricting the suffrage in New York City in 1877 with the situation in the South, asserting that "[t]hey have there an ignorant class to deal with, as we have here."[196]

Not only did the emergence of a "taxpayers' viewpoint" create a unifying ideology of propertied northerners and southerners, but it also helped undermine the project of state expansion and federal involvement in the South in material ways.[197] By the early 1870s, bourgeois New Yorkers were mobilizing forcefully for an end to the federal income tax, a tax that they had accepted as a war measure but which had become decidedly unpopular by 1865. For George Templeton Strong, it was "iniquitous, unconstitutional, demoralizing, infernal"; the *American Railroad Journal* thought of it as "repugnant to the feelings of men."[198]

The center of antitax mobilization was New York City, and its foremost spokesman was the politicized stave dealer Isaac Sherman. Sherman and his cohorts campaigned for a repeal of the income tax by organizing, petitioning, and calling for acts of civil disobedience.[199] They publicly urged their fellow New Yorkers to pay the tax only under protest or not at all, and Sherman helped organize a campaign of refusal to file returns in order to challenge the income tax in the Supreme Court.[200] In the spring of 1871, leading bourgeois New Yorkers, including Sherman, formed a bipartisan "Association to take steps to oppose the levying and collecting of the Income Tax." Its president was William E. Dodge, and among its vice presidents were such illustrious figures as Jonathan Sturges, William Astor, Henry E. Stebbins, John Jacob Astor, Horace Greeley, James M. Brown, August Belmont, J. Pierpont Morgan, and William E. Dodge, Jr.[201] By early April, the organization, which was now named the "Anti-Income Tax Association of New York," had opened an office.[202] By December 1871, thirty-seven wealthy New Yorkers had challenged the constitutionality of the income tax in the U.S. Supreme Court.[203] Their combined pressure eventually proved successful; the tax was at first reduced and finally discontinued in 1873.[204]

Although Reconstruction did not hinge primarily on federal spending – land reform and the enfranchisement of blacks, as such, were not especially costly – bourgeois New Yorkers linked the undesirable level of taxation to the activist state. William E. Dodge, the metal importer, iron manufacturer, and president of the Chamber of Commerce who was elected to Congress on the Republican ticket, stressed this connection when he argued that army occupation of the South would be expensive and thus make high taxes necessary.[205] "The commercial, the manufacturing, and the agricultural interests of this country," he said, "will see in it a continuance of taxation necessary to support this military array sent to these ten States."[206] State activism, hence, became linked to taxation, which had proven unpopular, to say the least, among the city's wealthy. And state activism also led to further upheaval, which again seemed to limit investment opportunities in the South.[207]

Thus, as a consequence of the coalescing of a northern taxpayers' viewpoint, the city's merchants, manufacturers, and bankers employed their considerable political influence to mobilize against Reconstruction. This mobilization was part of the greater political assertiveness that they exhibited during the 1870s, an assertiveness that gained its impetus from their efforts to limit the political influence of those social groups that had been mobilized during the Civil War, most particularly northern workers and southern freedpeople.

The catalyst for agitation against Reconstruction in a public manner came in January 1875, when President Grant ordered troops into the New Orleans State House to block the Democrats' attempt to seat five of their candidates whose elections were disputed. Almost immediately, a large bipartisan assembly of bourgeois New Yorkers protested against this "most marked attack upon the rights of American citizenship which has been made since the establishment of our Government."[208] August Belmont, James M. Brown, Edward Cooper (Peter Cooper's son), Abram S. Hewitt, Simon Sterne, Robert B. Minturn, and William E. Dodge, among many others, used the opportunity to demand an end to federal intervention in the South. The Chamber of Commerce, the Stock Exchange, the Produce Exchange, the Corn Exchange, the Gold Board, the Cotton Exchange, the Maritime Exchange, and the "various clubs" all collected signatures in support of the meeting.[209] It was predictable that Democrats like August Belmont, who saw the future of his party in an alliance with the white population of the South, would condemn Grant's step, but now many bourgeois Republicans joined him in the appeal for an end to federal intervention.

William E. Dodge, a Lincoln supporter in 1860, best explained what motivated him to leave behind the period of federal intervention in the South: "Ten years have now passed since the close of the war," he argued, "and there is a very general feeling that the time has come when we should all . . . say 'Let us have peace.'"[210] Dodge saw Reconstruction's main mission as accomplished: Despite a "radical change in the social system of the South," freedpeople worked and produced large crops of cotton. Critical of the political coalition Radical Republicans had built with the freedmen of the South, he concluded his eulogy for Reconstruction with a cry for leaving the South to itself:

Many of us feel that the General Government has made a mistake in trying to secure the peace and quiet of the South by appointing many Northern men to places of trust in the South, who have in their turn been active in securing the votes of the freedmen, and making them feel that the United States Government was their special friend. . . . [N]ow let the South alone; let them work out their own problem, understanding that, only in case of oppression or insurrection, which the State cannot control, will the General Government interfere. As merchants, we want to see the South gain her normal position in the commerce of the country.[211]

The South eventually did "gain her normal position," albeit one subordinated to the North and northern capitalists, such as William E. Dodge. Already by 1875, however, bourgeois New Yorkers were seeing their position of leaving the South to itself largely vindicated.

With Reconstruction effectively buried, one more threat to peace and stability arose in the wake of the contentious presidential elections of 1876. The well-documented conflict over the result of the election – Democrats claimed a majority of the Electoral College for Samuel Tilden, Republicans for Rutherford B. Hayes – greatly worried the city's economic elite.[212] Transcending party loyalties, they called for a peaceful solution to the conflict.[213] "[T]he business interests of New York (democrats and republicans) made themselves felt . . . and demanded some action that should snuff out the violent talk of the mob element," observed one perceptive contemporary.[214] Chambers of Commerce throughout the nation urged compromise (including the New York Chamber of Commerce), and even a zealous pro-Tilden supporter like Abram Hewitt "personally" preferred "four years of Republican administration based upon fraudulent returns than . . . four years of civil war."[215]

The fears of upper-class New Yorkers were allayed when Hayes took the presidency and, in turn, ended the intervention of federal troops in southern politics.[216] "There is a general feeling of relief," opined Samuel Barlow.[217] Even as rabid a supporter of Tilden as Samuel Ward announced in March that "I think well of Hayes' intentions," and Samuel Barlow's business partner William Shipman, fearing civil war as an alternative, declared that "a settlement . . . is better than to have left matters adrift."[218] "And now all this is ended, and for ever," proclaimed secretary of state and Chamber of Commerce member William M. Evarts to the annual banquet of the New York Chamber of Commerce, for which he was treated to prolonged applause.[219] Symbolizing the renewed close connection between the city's bourgeoisie and the federal government, for the first time ever an acting president, secretary of state, and secretary of the interior attended the event.

By that moment in early 1877, the city's upper class had abandoned their beliefs that all citizens shared equal rights and that a strong nation-state could enforce them.[220] Instead, they applauded the virtue of unrestricted markets and the Darwinian struggle in which African Americans would find their "rightful" place.

꙳ ꙳ ꙳

The shape social relations were to take was most clearly foreshadowed in July 1877 when workers of the Baltimore & Ohio Railroad, angered by a second round of wage cuts in one year, went on strike. What began as a wage dispute erupted into a nationwide uprising. Militia troops, sent to quell the walkout in Martinsburg, West Virginia, refused to fire on the strikers. The strike extended to other cities, and in Baltimore ten workers were shot and killed, yet in Pittsburgh the local police again disobeyed orders. Demonstrations in Chicago and St. Louis drew tens of thousands of workers into the streets, and throughout the United States, battles between workers and law-enforcement agents erupted.

The strike was like nothing the young nation had ever seen before; it exhibited a degree of anger and determination that most observers had thought to be limited to Europe. Most upper-class New Yorkers still believed the American working class to be somehow different from the one in Europe, a belief which lost credence in these July days. William Steinway found the news of the strike "most exciting" and expressed relief when Governor Robinson of New York called out the entire militia.[221] On Wall Street and in the New York Stock Exchange, "great anxiety" prevailed.[222] Railroad tycoon William Vanderbilt, refusing to negotiate with his workers, asserted that rioters "belong to the communistic classes."[223] Silk merchant Elliot Cowdin concurred, linking the strike to the Paris Commune, as did *Railway World,* which saw the strikers "virtually and actually as wicked and wanton as the portion of Paris which formed and created the Commune."[224] The outcry over the strike and the broad agreement about how to deal with the strikers stood in stark contrast to the reaction to the Draft Riots of 1863, when some among the city's upper class had counseled restraint on the side of authorities, hoping to exploit working-class discontent for their own political ends. Now, bourgeois

New Yorkers articulated an "uneasy feeling that these people can be masters of the city if they choose."[225]

Respectable circles noted with great relief that the national strike wave only lightly rocked the city itself. Though "business in the metropolis [was] completely paralyzed," and the "entire National Guard of the State was under arms," New York's workers demonstrated only once in Tompkins Square Park, albeit "arous[ing] all good citizens to be prepared for the worst."[226] These good citizens feared the potential social conflicts the severe social inequality among the city's inhabitants could generate.

Yet what was new about bourgeois New Yorkers' reaction to the strike was not their hostility to the cause but rather the radical answers they found to the conflict. Suffrage restrictions, which had just been passed by the New York legislature, were of course seen as part of the solution.[227] But by far the most prevalent cure proposed by observers was violence. Indeed, in a dramatic departure from their belief in a united polity, the *Tribune* recommended that it "is time to understand that a great country like ours cannot be governed by the force of public opinion alone; it must have material muskets at its disposal."[228] *Railway World,* similarly, called for repression, arguing that workers' collective action threatened to reintroduce "slavery" to the United States (slavery here defined as workers forcing a corporation to pay certain wages to its employees). Therefore, they saw it as "one of the highest and most imperative duties of all governments . . . to enforce this principle at all times and places, even if the drums must beat, the glittering bayonets advance, the breech-loading rifles pour forth death-dealing volleys in quick succession, the Gatling guns mow down crowds of the new champions of slavery, and if heavy artillery must batter down whole towns that become citadels of folly and crime."[229] This embrace of military force went hand in hand with a radical departure from any sense of responsibility for the welfare of the larger community, *Railway World,* for example, insisting that "[i]t is no part of the duty of the railway company to support the population of West Virginia."[230] And in a further departure from free-labor thought, the journal argued that capital, not labor, was the true foundation of the nation's economic well-being.[231]

Deeds followed words, and on July 23, the New York City National Guard units were called to duty. The 12th, 21st, and 22nd Regiments mobilized in the city, while the 9th New York State Regiment moved to Albany to attend to the "usual duties incident to a railroad strike."[232] Most significantly, however, more than 500 members of the elite 7th Regiment assembled by nightfall, many having rushed to the city from their summer homes in Newport, Long Branch, Lake George, and Saratoga.[233] So urgent was the situation that "telegrams were dispatched" to bring back to the city the members who were "at the mountains or the sea-side, fishing, hunting or yachting."[234]

The scene in front of the armory was described in terms quite similar to the scenes before the opening of a new opera at the Academy of Music: "[C]oupés and carriages flew around the corner, and drew up at the door of the armory with a crash."[235] Young bourgeois New Yorkers, under arms (each member had been issued forty rounds of ammunition), camped out at the armory that night in expectation of battle, yet more conventional fare came their way: "When dinner time arrived, Delmonico's waiters came hurrying in with big baskets and trays, and long tables were set in the large drill-room, and the men were marched in to a cold lunch of meats and bread and iced coffee."[236] While the meal might have been lighter than usual, it was still served on "the finest French china and cut glass."[237] Dinner at the armory remained the high point of the mobilization, however, as the city's police were easily able to control the demonstrators who had turned out in solidarity with the strikers. The elite soldiers of the 7th Regiment were a bit disappointed about the lack of opportunity to fight, venturing to stage a mock strike in the armory to build morale. While not engaged in combat, the very presence of the regiment boosted morale among the propertied of Manhattan, as "the people of the city . . . began to have a returning confidence in the speedy triumph of the law, when it was backed by bayonets."[238]

With the widely held belief among bourgeois New Yorkers that the solution to social conflict lay in the repression of discontent, it was only natural that merchants, manufacturers, and bankers would express concern over the relative strength and reliability of the militia units and federal troops. While the 7th Regiment, solidly upper class, was beyond distrust, they viewed citizen soldiers from proletarian families with great concern.[239] Indeed, J. T. Headley concluded that citizen soldiers were potentially dangerous, since "the members are taken out from the mass of the people, between whom there might be a strong sympathy in some particular outbreak, which would impair their efficiency, and make them hesitate to shoot down their friends and acquaintances."[240] The *New York Times* deduced from such an analysis that a "free country" needs a "standing army."[241] Because "[m]ilitias [are] not to be relied on for serious emergencies," the editors of *The Nation* concurred, "the necessity of greater force at the command of the authorities will hereafter be universally recognized."[242] And indeed, discussion of the rebuilding of American military power and the professionalization of its army after the retrenchment in the wake of the Civil War was framed by the exigencies of class conflict.[243]

While calls for repression were widespread, there were still some among the city's economic elite who retained a different vision of class relations: Abram Hewitt strongly opposed the use of the army for domestic social conflict, for reasons rooted in antebellum free-labor ideas. Similarly, the *Commercial and Financial Chronicle,* one of the voices of the city's Democratic merchants, doubted the necessity of more troops, warning that physical force alone could not keep the country together.[244] Though perhaps a vestige of traditional mercantile ideas about stewardship (and merchants' much more limited exposure to workers), such sentiments were also based on fundamental hostility toward maintaining a large standing army, which, after all, gave the federal government the ability to intervene in southern affairs as well.

The demand by most bourgeois New Yorkers for a larger army to protect private property in the North was indeed ironic, since they had just called upon the federal government not to intervene in the contentious relations between freedpeople and white southerners. While freedpeople – with their very limited social power – were left alone to preserve their civil rights, powerful northern bourgeois demanded federal intervention to protect their property from strikers. Unregulated property rights, if necessary defended by the policing power of the federal government against the claims of other social groups, were now at the center of bourgeois discourse and politics.

Despite these qualms and contradictions, the 1877 strike stood at the beginning of the most violent phase of American class relations.[245] The strike of 1877 and the reaction of bourgeois New Yorkers to it were harbingers of a militarization of class relations that would last until the end of the century.[246] In big cities throughout the nation, armories were built to house national guard troops, close at hand to quell urban conflict.[247] Junius S. Morgan, the American banker in London, sent $500 to the building fund of the new armory for the 7th New York Regiment, as he looked to them "as a sure guarantee for the future."[248]

That the city's upper class now saw an armory located in the center of Manhattan as the guarantor of their future was the most telling symbol of the ideological and political changes of the three prior decades. The shift toward industrial and finance capital and away from trade in agricultural commodities, as well as the increasing distance of these industrialists from their workers, had fundamentally altered the relationship of the city's bourgeoisie to other social groups. The universalist belief in a society without fundamental social divisions, which they all had shared in the 1850s, as well as the distinct, competing, and antipathetic identities of merchants on the one hand and manufacturers on the other, now gave way to class consciousness, most dramatically symbolized by a disenchantment with democracy. This transition consolidated the economic, social, and political power of the city's upper class – yet, as the next chapters will show, did not succeed in creating stable social and political relations.

8

The Culture of Capital

By the 1880s and 1890s, New York's merchants, industrialists, and bankers had transformed themselves more than ever before into a self-conscious class. They saw themselves and were seen by others as a distinct social group, a collective identity they articulated in numerous ways as class position and class identity corresponded to a degree unknown before. Though divisions of a cultural and political kind persisted, they did not rival those that had had their roots in slavery and the Civil War. The conflicts of the antebellum years had now finally been left behind, replaced by widespread agreement on the fundamentals of the political economy of a free-labor United States. At the same time, however, rapid industrialization deepened social cleavages, and the combined effects of rising inequality and proletarianization created tensions that, as we have seen, at times drove workers and farmers to mobilize collectively, in turn motivating upper-class New Yorkers to define themselves against these "dangerous classes." This greater sense of class identity, as well as the overcoming of the deep divisions that had characterized the age of the Civil War, enabled wealthy New Yorkers to translate their ever-growing economic power into unprecedented influence on the institutions and policies of the state. Indeed, by the last quarter of the century, their power was such that not presidents but prominent New York entrepreneurs – such as John D. Rockefeller, J. Pierpont Morgan, and Andrew Carnegie – came to represent the age.[1]

At the core of the altered character of the city's upper class lay a number of structural changes. Important among them was the tremendous increase in the number of bourgeois New Yorkers.[2] This expansion was partly the result of the rapid economic growth of the United States, as well as the continuing importance of New York in the nation's economic life. The city grew by leaps and bounds and by 1880 Manhattan alone counted 1.2 million inhabitants; ten years later there were 1.4 million (with another one million inhabitants in Brooklyn, the Bronx, Queens, and Staten Island), a small percentage of whom came to start new businesses or to invest capital they brought from somewhere else. This expansion of

the economic elite was supported by an economy that by 1880 had overcome the severe crisis of 1873. New York was one of the most dynamic
places in the world, and its ability to attract capital and capitalists set it
apart from its former rivals, Boston and Philadelphia.[3] As a consequence,
New York fortified its position as the American capital of capitalists: By
1892 a staggering 27 percent of all the nation's millionaires lived in the
city on the Hudson.[4]

This expansion of the city's economic elite, however, went along with
the persistence of old capital. Two of three 1892 millionaires had inherited
their fortunes, and half of those even had to thank their grandparents for
their material bounty.[5] Many of the city's old merchants, such as the
Astors, Roosevelts, and Dodges, blossomed in this new age. One historian
has found that 61 percent of New Yorkers who had been among the
wealthy in 1828 and 43.2 percent who had been similarly well-off in
1856/57 reappeared among the city's 1892 millionaires – either personally
or via their descendants.[6] Assuming that some wealth was divided by
inheritance and that some upper-class New Yorkers did not have heirs,
these numbers testify to the vitality of the mercantile elite in the first half
of the century. Not surprisingly, 60 percent of the leadership of New York
City's national corporations, investment banks, and railroads in 1890
came from the ranks of the old mercantile elite.[7]

Persistence, however, did not equal stagnation. The single most important shift was the emergence of a national upper class. Two distinct but
related developments stood for this nationalization: For one, there was a
growing divergence between the location of capital investments and management. Whereas the wharves of New York's antebellum merchants and
the factories of its manufacturers had been located in and around the city,
in the 1880s some of New York's industrialists, as well as many of its
bankers, controlled enterprises in entirely different areas of the country,
such as southern railroads, Illinois factories, and Colorado mines. Milo
Merrick Belding, for example, who by the end of the century was the
largest manufacturer of silk goods in the world, employing more than
3,000 workers in his factories in Massachusetts, Michigan, Connecticut,
California, and Canada, steered his emporium from the company's headquarters in Manhattan.[8] In aggregate, these investments outside the city
were significant: According to historian David Hammack, in 1880, 11 percent of New York manufacturers, wholesalers, and bankers assessed by
R. G. Dun & Company at a value of a million dollars or more owned
branches outside the city; fifteen years later the number had nearly doubled, a tendency that certainly continued into the new century.[9]

At the same time that a small but growing number of capital-owning New Yorkers were investing in locations remote from the city, other upper-class Americans were moving to Manhattan during the 1880s and 1890s after having made their fortunes elsewhere. The Armours, who accumulated their riches in meatpacking in Chicago, came to live in the city (in 1864), as did Collis P. Huntington, the California railroad magnate (1864), Andrew Carnegie, the Pittsburgh steel industrialist (1867), John D. Rockefeller, the Pennsylvania oil entrepreneur (1884), and Meyer Guggenheim, the Colorado mine operator (1889).[10] Many lesser-known industrialists joined in this migration. The cottonseed oil manufacturer Edmond Urquhart, who had built his American Cotton Oil Trust mostly in rural Arkansas, relocated in 1887 to New York City "owing to the magnitude of his interests."[11] Similarly, in 1880, John H. Shoenberger removed himself from Pittsburgh, where he owned a furnace and had banking and railroad interests, to live in Manhattan. Three years later, yeast manufacturer Maxmillian Fleischmann from Cincinnati joined him.

These men, along with many others, were drawn to the city by its dense networks of business contacts and specialized experts, but their relocation, in turn, increased the need for experts – especially lawyers, who became more central to the economic relations of the city's bourgeoisie, architects, and engineers, but also musicians, artists, and journalists. Indeed, it was to some extent the social life of the city that attracted the "provincial" upper class. Maxmillian Fleischmann, for example, immediately upon his arrival in New York "took a deep interest in social and business affairs," joining the Produce Exchange, the Liederkranz, and the Republican Down Town Club.[12] The draw of the social life of the city was such that even entrepreneurs who continued to reside in other cities joined the cultural institutions of New York's upper class: Iron manufacturers from Wheeling, Pennsylvania, for example, joined the Union League Club, the Lotos Club, and the New York Yacht Club.[13]

As a result, upper-class social institutions and networks became more national in scope. Educational institutions were important pillars of this "nationalization."[14] The few bourgeois New Yorkers who had attended college in the 1850s usually had enrolled at Columbia, but now many went to institutions in more remote locations, most particularly the citadel of Boston's economic elite, Harvard University.[15] Jack Morgan, son of J. P., was the first in his family to obtain a college degree, from Harvard, in 1889.[16] Even the Roosevelts and Fishes, who had traditionally attended Columbia, now studied in the halls of Harvard and Yale, alongside the Vanderbilts and Astors.[17] These institutions, in turn, had become more national themselves: Harvard alumnus and New York lawyer Joseph Hodges Choate spoke in 1882 of the "radical change" that Harvard had undergone, as it "today presents . . . to the world a great and national university, and the national features and relations of Harvard are now its most striking and attractive ones."[18] Similarly, private boarding schools, such as rapidly expanding St. Paul's, Phillips Exeter Academy, and Phillips Academy in Andover, served as breeding grounds for bourgeois Americans from all regions of the country, to be joined by such newly founded elite schools as the Taft School (1890), the Hotchkiss School (1897), St. George's School (1896), Choate (1896), Middlesex School (1902), and the Kent School (1906).[19] These colleges and schools constituted networks in which national elites not only could transcend their particularistic economic interests rooted in the specific kind of capital they owned, but could also overcome localism and even build lasting ties to university-trained experts who eventually joined their firms as lawyers, managers, or engineers.[20]

Institutions other than schools and universities supported this nationalization. Employers' associations frequently transcended localities. The Hardware Club of New York, for example, included among its ranks 700 manufacturers and merchants, 115 of whom did not live in New York, but instead resided in New England, the mid-Atlantic states, and the Midwest.[21] The American Institute, in similar ways, now perceived of itself as "national in its aims and influence."[22] Organizations such as the American Protective Tariff League and the Daughters of the American Revolution created further links across cities and towns, as did such financial institutions as the New York Stock Exchange.[23] Even the reform organizations that had mushroomed in northern cities now organized into a "National Municipal League."[24]

Possibly most important in the creation of links among cities was the changing form of capital itself. The explosive growth of joint-stock companies effectively brought together investors from places large and small, east and west, and linked them to single economic undertakings. As control over enterprises became more mediated, geographical distance between owner and firm mattered less, and production as well as trade were supervised by people specifically hired for this purpose. Now, bourgeois New Yorkers had business interests in Chicago and San Francisco, while members of the Chicago and San Francisco economic elite held investments in New York.

The increasingly national scope of bourgeois class formation, strengthened by educational and cultural institutions as well as social networks, was conducive to ideological and political sensibilities that transcended the regional base of economic power and instead embraced the nation as a whole. Obviously, the degree to which elite New Yorkers were entangled in these national networks varied, and small manufacturers, retail merchants, and builders among others, were still deeply rooted in the city itself. Still, because New York had become the headquarters of the national economy, tensions between a national and a local elite were much weaker than in other towns and cities. Even bourgeois New Yorkers who seemed to be rooted in the city alone enjoyed numerous economic and social ties to the national upper class. And it was the rising national bourgeoisie that set the social, ideological, and political tone for the class at large.

This increasing dominance of the national bourgeoisie was also the result of fundamental changes in the structure of American businesses. During the 1880s and 1890s, industrialists like Andrew Carnegie and John D. Rockefeller used their enormous profits and the weakness of many of their competitors to integrate production vertically as well as horizontally, building businesses that combined access to raw materials, transportation capabilities, and production facilities, as well as distribution and marketing.[25] Bankers like J. Pierpont Morgan expanded their control over the various enterprises they financed, and railroad families like the Vanderbilts acquired new lines and integrated them into national systems.[26] The visions of these families, like the businesses they built, were national in scope. Their way of conducting business increasingly dominated the United States economy.

Increases in the scope of capital were directly related to the growing scale of businesses. The new transportation network, together with the application of the latest production technologies by capital-rich industrialists, encouraged the concentration of capital. Tobacco, crude oil, and grain-processing industries, for example, successfully employed continuous-process production technologies, and the resulting profits enabled their owners to acquire an increasing number of their competitors as well as suppliers and distributors.[27] Vertical integration was particularly attractive to manufacturers who engaged in mass production, as well as manufacturers whose products required special handling, such as meat or complex machinery. Many of these firms then moved into the distribution of their goods, diminishing, in the process, the importance of merchants as intermediaries. When James Buchanan Duke, the New York City tobacco manufacturer, employed new cigarette-making machines, for example, he found existing marketing channels insufficient and began instead to sell directly to small shops.[28]

No industry aggregated the same staggering amounts of capital and

power as did railroads. Truly national in scope, railroads had consolidated
during the 1870s by forming cartels, their owners agreeing on market
shares and the distribution of traffic, albeit with mixed success.[29] During
the 1880s, they undertook a more determined effort to limit competition
as the Pennsylvania Railroad, the Baltimore & Ohio, and the Vanderbilt
family's New York Central were successfully built into large integrated
systems.[30] These new railroad corporations were often formed with the
help of investment bankers such as J. Pierpont Morgan, investment
bankers who took on an ever more central role in the economy.[31]

By the turn of the century, consolidation spread to other industries,
including steel, rubber, and sugar. Large corporations now increasingly
determined how Americans worked and how they brought their products
to market. The headquarters of these national corporations moved to
New York to be near the array of specialists the city provided, as well as
its social and cultural institutions, giving New York an even more overwhelming dominance in the national economy and its entrepreneurs an
ever increasing national orientation. Suddenly, in turn, strikes in Colorado
silver mines or Homestead steel mills, the removal of Native Americans
from western lands, and the contentious politics of Chicago or California,
mattered just as much to the city's capitalists as conflicts closer to home.

The increasing nationalization of the city's upper class went hand in hand
with the transcendence of the deep divide between merchants and manufacturers that had characterized the antebellum economic elite, and constituted second major structural change of the 1880s and 1890s. Economically, this divide was abetted by the growing importance of industrialists
to the national economy and the tendency of merchants to spread capital
accumulated in trade into other economic sectors, especially railroads,
mining, and manufacturing, a move facilitated by the newly emergent
financial intermediaries. Merchants, moreover, lost their central role as the
providers of capital. And, testifying to the great flexibility of merchant
capital, they also increasingly dealt in industrial goods, not agricultural
commodities, which in turn linked them more firmly to the nation's manufacturers.[32] In 1860, crude materials (especially cotton) had accounted for
27 percent of all exports from New York City, a number that fell to only
11 percent forty years later, while the export of manufactured goods
increased its share from 24 to 38 percent.[33]

As a result, manufacturers, not merchants, now set the framework in
which national economic development took place. "In nothing is the
change greater than in the vast progress and extent of our manufactures,"

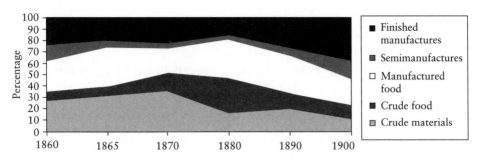

Exports from New York City by category of products, 1860–1900.
Source: Jean Heffer, *Le Port de New York et le Commerce Extérieur Americain, 1860–1900*
(Paris: Publications de la Sorbonne, 1986), p. 93.

remarked merchant William E. Dodge, looking back to the past half century of his life.[34] Dodge, though himself benefiting enormously from this change, still viewed it with considerable anxiety: "Our rapid growth in population and wealth, . . . the great variety of incorporated companies, . . . the immense power of capital invested in our railways . . . all these have engendered a spirit of speculation most dangerous to regular business. The fearful increase of defalcations has tended to weaken that principle of mercantile honor which has heretofore been the pride of our city and country."[35] Acknowledging the abdication of merchant capital, Frederic J. DePeyster, whose ancestors had been deeply rooted in the New York merchant community, now complained that "[t]he mighty city of today knows little or nothing of our traditions."[36]

The emergence of nationally integrated companies, however, not only moved industrialists to center stage but also gave investment bankers an ever more important role in the economy. Though few in number, banking houses such as Drexel, Morgan & Co.; Morton, Bliss & Co.; Seligman Brothers; Lehman Brothers; Kuhn, Loeb & Co.; Manufacturers Trust Co.; Chase National Bank; National City Bank; First National Bank; Farmers' Loan & Trust; and the Guaranty Trust Co. became powerful intermediaries between investors and industrialists.[37] Firmly linked to industry, not trade, these banks captured an ever more powerful position in the economy, especially as railroads and insurance companies (both of which once had been funded and controlled by the city's merchants) came under their sway.[38] The bankers' position was further strengthened by the maturing financial institutions, notably the New

York Stock Exchange, which became for the first time a major instrument for raising capital; mining and petroleum stocks, for example, traded in unprecedented numbers.[39]

Investment bankers, controlling vast amounts of capital, transcended the interests of individual entrepreneurs, and by virtue of the capital they controlled, they could organize chaotic industries, such as railroads, and impress their vision upon them. In striking contrast to the antebellum merchants or manufacturers, they had much less of a commitment to a specific economic sector, and instead were driven by the impetus of capital accumulation in the economy as a whole. Hence, they decisively overcame particularist identities that had been articulated by earlier bourgeois New Yorkers rooted in distinct sectors of the economy. They also helped further this process for the economic elite as a whole as they assisted others in diversifying their holdings.

Indeed, it was this diversification of investments that diluted particularist identities most decisively. Capital accumulated in one sector of the economy flowed via the financial intermediaries into many different areas. Even someone like John D. Rockefeller, who clearly focused his activities on the oil business, diversified his holdings: In 1890 he held (apart from his Standard Oil, natural gas investments, and real estate) investments of more than $23 million, nearly $14 million of that in railroads, $2.8 million in mining, $2.1 million in various other industries, and $1.2 million in banks and investment companies.[40] Rockefeller owned mines, paper mills, nail factories, timber mills, bank and insurance companies, orange groves, soda factories, steamship lines, and real estate companies.[41]

Other large capitalists, including Andrew Carnegie and J. P. Morgan, built dense networks of capital that strung together many sectors of the economy. In a more modest but fundamentally similar way, tobacco manufacturer Edwin Augustus McAlpin invested some of his profits from his factory on Avenue D on Manhattan's Lower East Side into railroads, banks, and a hotel.[42] As a result of this diversification, the formerly pronounced hostility of many manufacturers toward merchants diminished. By 1880, even the quintessential manufacturers' journal the *Shoe and Leather Reporter* could see nothing immoral in merchants' speculative business activities. Though calling excessive speculation an unwise business strategy, the journal saw it as a "sure guarantee against famine in the land," and added that merchants' "eagerness to trade prompts them to alacrity in ministering to the wants of the public."[43]

Industrialists' and financiers' economic ascendancy went hand in hand

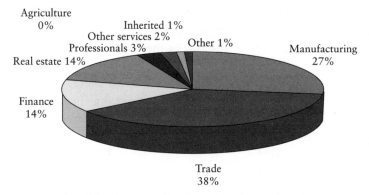

Source of wealth of New York City millionaires, 1892 (N = 1103).
Source: "American Millionaires, The Tribune's List of Persons Reputed to be Worth
a Million or More," in the *Tribune Monthly* 4 (June 1892), p. 90. For the purposes of this
table, the categories used by the *Tribune* have been consolidated. Manufacturing includes
manufacturing, brewing, distilling, tanning business, sugar refining, protected mines, coal,
iron, etc., shipbuilding, making patented and proprietary articles, silver and gold mines,
railroads, local gas, railroad, ferry and kindred business, oil refining, publishing, bakery
business. Trade includes merchandising, coasting vessels, ocean ships, freighting and foreign
trade, mercantile agency business. Finance includes banking and investments, brokerage, and
insurance. Real estate includes real estate, contracting, and building. Professionals include
lawyers and doctors. Agriculture includes cattle raising, West India plantations, livestock
raising. Other services include hotel and restaurant business, storage and warehousing, river
and harbor boats, express business, telegraph and telephone business, ice business, and
pawnbroking.

with their social rise. Manufacturers for the first time became integrated
in the social and cultural institutions of the city's merchants.[44] Even the
Chamber of Commerce, which had been an institution of the city's merchants, by 1886 had a significant number of industrialists and financiers
among it members. Approximately 12 percent of its members were primarily engaged in manufacturing, still a minority, but a substantially
larger share than in the 1850s, when only 2 percent of its members had
been manufacturers. Now, in 1886, the Chamber of Commerce included
among its ranks the manufacturer of printing presses Robert Hoe (who
had joined in 1872), the shipbuilder John Roach (1881), railroad entrepreneurs Cornelius Vanderbilt (1881) and Chauncey Depew (1885), as
well as iron manufacturers George W. Quintard (1865) and John M. Cornell (1881).[45] In 1889, John D. Rockefeller joined, and in 1897 Charles H.
Steinway followed suit.

This integration spilled over into other areas of bourgeois social life: Wardens and vestrymen of elite St. George's Church had mostly been merchants (76 percent) in the 1850s, but by the 1880s their number had fallen to only 27 percent, replaced by industrialists and bankers.[46] In 1898, Edward Cooper became president of the venerable Union Club, an organization his father Peter never had joined.[47] Merchant, financier, and industrialist families also forged marriage alliances, such as when in 1887 Pittsburgh industrialist Andrew Carnegie married Louise Whitfield, the daughter of a New York City merchant, or when J. Pierpont Morgan took the hand of Amelia Sturges, daughter of merchant Jonathan Sturges.[48] Printing press manufacturer Robert Hoe III followed suit when he married Olivia Phelps James, daughter of Daniel James, a partner in the trading firm of Phelps, Dodge and Company, as did Peter Cooper's grandson Peter Cooper Hewitt, who took in 1887 the hand of Lucy Work, daughter of New York dry goods merchant and banker Frank Work.[49] John D. Rockefeller's sons solidified their father's banking relationship to the long-established National City Bank when they both married daughters of its president, James Stillman.[50]

Manufacturers also joined the most elite social clubs of the city, including the Union Club, the Union League Club, and the St. Nicholas Society. By the 1880s, brewers, appliance manufacturers, clothiers, hatmakers, and iron manufacturers walked in their refined halls. Of 143 New York industrialists listed in *America's Successful Men of Affairs,* at least thirty-six were members of the Union League Club, seven of the Union Club, and six of the Century Club, with others being on the roster of a wide range of additional organizations.[51] Bolstered by their ascendancy to the higher echelons of bourgeois social networks, manufacturers indeed were now becoming so confident that they asserted that the material bounty of the city was due to them and not the merchants.[52] "[P]roductive industry," they exclaimed, had "principally caused [the country's] astonishing growth."[53] Even manufacturer John Roach (who once had been described by the Dun credit agency as a "rough illiterate kind of man") was now wined and dined at Delmonico's, hosted by none other than Mayor Havemeyer and a wide assortment of prominent merchants.[54]

Because an important reason for the economic elite's creation of cultural institutions was the demarcation of a particular upper-class cultural sphere, the effort of the newly rich to enter this world was bound to create conflicts. Yet the fundamental openness of the city's upper class eventually enabled capital-rich New Yorkers to force entrance. Three events symbolized this conflict between demarcation and openness, three events that marked the end of the old mercantile elite's rule over entrée to the most exclusive social circles.

The first occurred in 1874, when Commodore Vanderbilt organized a ball at Delmonico's, to which "prominent bachelors in old New York Society" were invited together with "men and women heretofore not considered among the socially elect."[55] Old and new wealth thus transcended the boundaries that had heretofore kept them apart. "This ball made the old regime appreciate that its time of absolute dominion was past," remembered May King Van Rensselaer, one of the old guard, but she added: "No social group ever abdicated supremacy in more sumptuous surroundings."[56]

Next came the struggle over the control of the opera, demonstrating how industrialists and financiers forced access to "society" from which they once had been excluded. The New York Academy of Music, which had provided an exclusive space for opera performances since 1854, was a stronghold of the old mercantile elite of the city: The Belmonts, Stuyvesants, Roosevelts, Rhinelanders, and Astors monopolized its eighteen private boxes.[57] When railroad entrepreneur William H. Vanderbilt, despite offering $30,000, was refused a box in the early 1880s, he, together with seventy others who strove for social acceptance, built their own opera house instead. The Goulds, Vanderbilts, Morgans, Whitneys, Bakers, and Rockefellers all contributed $10,000 each to incorporate the Metropolitan Opera House Company, which boasted 122 private boxes.[58] In a major victory for the new industrialists and bankers, the Academy of Music was unable to face the competition and had to close its doors in the spring of 1885, its owner stating that "I cannot fight Wall Street."[59] Although the *New York Times* had called the conflict a "social war of extermination," the old elites eventually also moved to the Metropolitan Opera, symbolically acknowledging the new power relations.[60] From then on, the newly wealthy Rockefellers and Vanderbilts rubbed shoulders with the city's older wealth.[61] The Metropolitan Opera, in effect, absorbed the forces that had supported the Academy of Music, creating an elite cultural institution that was steered by a wide assortment of bourgeois New Yorkers, some of old money background – such as the Astors and Belmonts – and some of new money background – such as the Morgans and Rockefellers.[62]

A third event underlined the triumph of the industrialists and bankers over the old mercantile elite. When Alva Vanderbilt finished her $3 million mansion on Fifth Avenue in 1883, she invited 750 New Yorkers to her housewarming party, at which the guests dressed in costumes representing the likes of Queen Elizabeth, Mary Stuart, and Louis XIV. The Vanderbilts used this leverage to force social recognition from the Astors.[63] In exchange for inviting socialite Caroline Astor to the party, the Vanderbilts would be added to Caroline Astor's exclusive 400 list.[64] The ball, according to one author, was a "triumph" for the Vanderbilts.[65]

Not every segment of the bourgeoisie retained influence, however. While financiers and industrialists were determining the economic dynamism of the age and could force social recognition, merchants and local manufacturers were losing influence. Although New York retained numerous merchant houses, their relative importance in the national economy declined.[66] Wholesalers, who had served western and southern customers for so long, often lost out to large manufacturers or to new retailers who arranged shipments of goods directly from the factory to the final consumer.[67] John D. Rockefeller, for example, who had relied until the early 1880s on merchants to sell his products in international markets, established his own selling agencies in 1882, making merchant intermediaries obsolete.[68] Similarly, in the 1890s Andrew Carnegie began to sell his steel directly to consumers, instead of to commission merchants.[69] *Iron Age* spoke of the "gradual disappearance of middlemen," a change that was so severe that a group of merchants advocated the "formation of a national protective association" in order to combat the "evil" of manufacturers selling directly to customers.[70]

Also undermining the importance of merchants was the new ability of manufacturers to expand production on the basis of retained earnings, emancipating them from their earlier dependence on credit provided by merchant intermediaries. Furthermore, commodity exchanges increasingly took over the market mediation that had once been facilitated by the city's merchants. When in December 1889 Robert B. Minturn, the old Republican merchant, died, the *New York Times* reported that "owing to the decline in American shipping and other changes wrought in the business, the firm had lost, at the time of Mr. Minturn's death, much of its old-time prominence."[71]

Having lost their once dominant position, merchants began to realize that prosperity in this new political economy depended on their adaptability to change. Many of them were spectacularly successful. Horace Claflin, for example, turned himself from a dry goods jobber into an importer, manufacturer, and distributor. The gun merchant Marcellus Hartley became a multifaceted entrepreneur. He not only added manufacturing operations to his business but also invested in the Equitable Life

Assurance Society, the Manhattan Railroad Company, the Western Bank, the Lincoln Bank, the German American National Bank, the Mercantile Trust Company, the Fifth Avenue Trust Company, the Audit Company, the American Surety Company, and the International Banking Company.[72] Similarly, by the late 1870s, Roosevelt & Son had given up on its business of importing and distributing plate glass and instead was focusing its activities on banking.[73] And Meyer Guggenheim, once a successful embroideries trader, in the early eighties invested massively in silver mining in Colorado; by 1886 he had integrated production forward into smelting and expanded operations into the silver mining regions of Mexico. By 1895, he had made profits from these operations estimated at $1 million a year.[74] Hence, while merchant capital became less central to the city's (and the nation's) economy, old merchant families themselves could thrive in this new age.

Besides the merchants, the second segment of the city's upper class that experienced a relative weakening of their position were those manufacturers whose factories were located in the city itself. While local manufacturer Peter Cooper was the quintessential industrialist of the 1850s, Andrew Carnegie, who operated on a national scale, represented the industrialists of the 1880s and 1890s. This shift, however, was a relative one and not due to the failing of industrial enterprises in Manhattan. Instead, it was a result of developments that made these enterprises seem small compared to the giant new firms of the second industrial revolution.

Indeed, less spectacularly and less noticed, local manufacturing firms did thrive, and their number increased quite dramatically in the last decades of the nineteenth century.[75] In 1880 a staggering 11,273 manufacturing firms operated in the city, a number that more than doubled by 1890 – much of it small shops, many of which were run by subcontractors.[76] In step with such an expansion, the number of manufacturing workers in New York City had increased from 129,577 in 1870 to 227,352 in 1880 and to 354,291 in 1890. In consequence, New York remained the most important manufacturing center of the nation. These shops stitched together 60 percent of all American women's clothing and baked more bread in Manhattan than in any other city in the country.[77] Capital intensity of production also grew: Taking 1850 as the base year, capital invested per worker increased to $139 in 1860, to $172 in 1880, to $279 in 1890, and to $388 in 1900.[78] Capital invested per establishment also rose, especially between 1880 and 1900, when it nearly doubled. Yet despite this increase, Manhattan factories were still different from those of the rest of the nation, especially because they were unusually labor intensive. In contrast, Pittsburgh factories represented, on average, more than three times the capital investment of Manhattan factories, and their products were much less labor intensive than those of New York.[79]

Although skyrocketing real estate prices and the distance from bulky natural resources drove the capital-intensive industries of the second industrial revolution out of the city, two different kinds of firms thrived in New York, those that served the needs of the urban market (such as pianos and printing presses), and those that tapped the huge supply of cheap immigrant labor (especially clothing, printing, and publishing, as well as specialty and luxury goods).[80]

An apt example of an industry that used immigrant labor, and a symbol of the particular structure of New York's industry, was its most important branch, the apparel industry. Seventeen percent of all capital invested in Manhattan manufacturing in 1890 was bound up in this industry, compared to only 5 percent in 1855.[81] As a result, the number of workers in the industry had increased dramatically from 15,969 to 114,619, making up a stunning 32 percent of all wage workers in New York, compared to only 23 percent in 1855. The clothing industry grew because its markets in ready-made clothing (first for men, than for women) expanded and because New York City provided what seemed like an inexhaustible supply of cheap labor.[82] Capital intensity remained low; the average apparel manufacturing firm had invested slightly less than $10,000 and employed only 15 workers, because the bulk of the work was contracted out to sweatshops (by 1900, between 50 and 66 percent of all workers in the industry worked in sweatshops).[83] Yet despite the small size of many firms, huge profits could be derived by the few companies that were at the top of the industry, such as Devlin & Co., Brooks Brothers, and H. B. Claflin & Co., whose owners played significant roles in the social, cultural, and political organizations of the city's upper class. In turn, the economic relationships they developed to the myriad smaller clothing manufacturers linked the industry as a whole firmly together.

Besides these labor-intensive industries, serving both local and national markets, there were those local industries that thrived because of their proximity to the largest urban market in the Americas. These industries were also major employers. Makers of food products, for example, counted 19,792 wage earners among their ranks, the printing and publishing industry another 33,617, the metal-working firms 36,927, and the construction industry 14,522.[84]

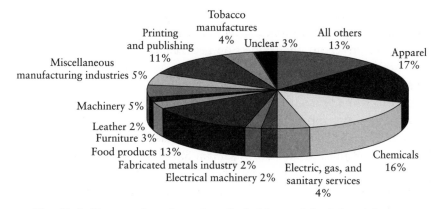

New York City manufacturing, 1890: Capital invested, by industrial sector.
Source: "Manufactures in 165 Principal Cities by Specified Industries – NY, NY," United States Bureau of the Census, *Eleventh Census of the United States, 1890*, vol. 12, *Manufacturing Industries*, Part 2 (Washington, D.C.: Government Printing Office, 1895), p. 390. Industries are arranged by the Standard Industrial Classifications. See Executive Office of the President, U.S. Office of Management and Budget, *Standard Industrial Classification Manual* (Washington, D.C.: GPO, 1972). *Note:* "All others" includes miscellaneous repair services; personal services; rubber; petroleum; transportation equipment; measuring; analyzing and controlling instruments; building construction; primary metals industry, textile mill products; paper; construction – special trades, stone, clay, and glass; and lumber and wood products.

The relationship between the large urban market and economic success is best exemplified by the metal industry. Because of high real estate costs, the metal entrepreneurs shied away from the heavy iron production and shipbuilding that had characterized such antebellum firms as the Novelty Iron Works or the Delameter Iron Works. Instead, metal firms came to specialize in products that linked them to other manufacturing industries in the city, most especially construction (i.e., architectural iron), printing (printing presses), and clothing (sewing machines).[85] Entrepreneur John M. Cornell, for example, expanded his father's business that made architectural iron, entering a market that expanded rapidly thanks to the prevalence of new construction techniques, which required elevators and iron frames.[86]

Some entrepreneurs succeeded in accumulating large fortunes in these local industries, enabling them to join the elite social circles of the city earlier dominated exclusively by merchants. The thousands of other New Yorkers who controlled the numerous small workshops, however, were in no meaningful way part of the city's economic elite. While they were nominally independent entrepreneurs, they remained physically involved with production, preserving the connection between labor and ownership that characterized artisans, but not the bourgeoisie. Most subcontractors in the apparel industry, for example, were still deeply involved with manual labor, which made it all but impossible to join the social and cultural world of the city's upper class.

There were also, however, plenty of local industrialists who transcended physical labor and artisan status, William Steinway, John B. Cornell, and George William Quintard among them. Most prominent was probably Robert Hoe, who had taken over his father's factory on Grand Street, where he employed about 2,500 workers. Making what arguably were the best printing presses in the world, he considered New York City, the nation's publishing capital, the perfect location for his enterprise. In turn, the profits derived from the undertaking gave him a secure standing in the city's social scene, enabling him to play an important role in the founding of the Metropolitan Museum of Art, as well as in clubs such as the Union League, and in institutions such as the Chamber of Commerce.[87]

Such industrialists as Hoe and Steinway, though they manufactured locally, were not principally removed from the "national bourgeoisie," nor were they hostile to it. On the contrary, they were intimately linked to the industrial growth of the new national economy, not least because the emerging national corporations provided for the economic dynamism of the city, which was the precondition of local manufacturers' well-being. Steinway sold pianos only if middle-class families prospered, John B. Cornell only marketed his architectural iron if construction in New York was thriving, and Robert Hoe delivered his printing presses to expanding publishers all over the United States. Even such a quintessential local business as real estate (and its attendant branches, such as iron works and construction) was tightly linked to and dependent upon the railroads, insurance companies, national banks, and national manufacturers, who were the real engines of New York's growth. In this early dominance of a national bourgeoisie, New York City stood out from other American cities.[88]

While industrialists and bankers who operated on a national scale left room for local and small capitalists and even created new markets for them, it was they who set the terms of the nation's political economy. In the 1880s and 1890s, notwithstanding Robert Wiebe's assertion to the contrary, there was no systematic development of a distinct "class geared to national institutions and policies," facing another class "dominating local affairs."[89] Shared cultural preferences along with shared concerns about the power of labor further drove capitalists operating in local markets close to those who dominated the national economy, as in the summer of 1892, when Carnegie faced his striking workers in Homestead and the *Manufacturer and Builder* related his troubles there to a "recent strike of the union workmen against the employers in the building trades in this city."[90] The national bourgeoisie was clearly and decisively the driving force among the city's upper class, setting the terms of debate and its ideological and political projects.

There was yet another fundamental change in the structure of the city's economic elite. The 1880s also saw the emergence of a group of managers, experts, and professionals who increasingly took control of the day-to-day operations of enterprises. Symbolizing the new bureaucratization of business structures, company headquarters, employing large numbers of salaried workers, expanded skyward: Between 1875 and 1900, 300 buildings of more than nine stories were erected in the city.[91] For the first time in history, secular structures towered above houses of religious worship. These buildings sheltered the new group of experts who came to dominate the operations of many companies.

Concentration of capital in single firms, integration of production and distribution, technologically advanced production processes, and the resulting complex organizational problems all called for more expertise than merchant, manufacturer, and banker families could provide.[92] Consolidated railroads, large retailers, and insurance companies, among others, required expertise in the management of complex organizations and hired salaried managers to run operations.[93] Though the ownership structure of firms was not necessarily affected by the rise of non-family members in the management of day-to-day operations, the importance of family networks to the economic projects of the city's upper class certainly declined.[94] Increasingly, ownership and control of enterprises were divided. By the 1880s these new professionals strengthened their position even further by institutionalizing their professions through creation of their own organizations and journals, translating their authority into unique market chances.[95] No group of professionals became more important than lawyers. They expertly created the new large organizations and steered them through a complex web of relationships to the institutions and personnel of the state. Lawyers, managers, and engineers furthered the processes that had brought them about in the first place.[96] As a result, according to Alfred D. Chandler, a "new business class" emerged.[97]

Strikingly, despite their lack of capital, these experts joined the social and cultural world of the city's bourgeoisie. In 1899, *King's Notable New Yorkers* listed 753 professionals, a substantial percentage of whom had made their way into the circles of the socially elect: Fifty-seven percent of all lawyers, 58 percent of all physicians, 33 percent of all architects, 25 percent of all clergymen, and 41 percent of all artists were also listed in the *Social Register.*[98] Quintessentially bourgeois organizations, such as the New York Genealogical and Biographical Society, counted among their members an extraordinary number of lawyers, physicians, and even artists and professors.[99] These professionals dressed like other bourgeois New Yorkers, decorated their homes in similar ways, joined clubs, and consumed conspicuously, thus appropriating the cultural values of the city's economic elite. Those highest in the new bureaucratic ranks found themselves in closest social contact with the actual owners of firms. For the first time, a large number of Americans joined the bourgeois world without being owners of substantial amounts of capital.

As a result, cultural identifications would increasingly provide the glue that kept an expanded bourgeoisie together. This was a change of major importance, as until then, access to the social networks of the upper class was limited to those New Yorkers who owned substantial amounts of capital. One of the reasons for the admittance of nonproperty owners into the bourgeois world was that for the first time in American history, a few employees earned sufficient salaries to share the lifestyle of the owners of capital. Moreover, capital-owning New Yorkers admitted experts and managers to their social networks and cultural institutions because these networks and institutions themselves were central to their economic projects and could not exclude those who played important roles in running factories, merchant houses, and banks. Experts, in turn, identifying with the corporations they increasingly came to run, moved ideologically and politically close to the owners of capital.

Although some managers and experts joined the world of the city's bourgeoisie, the high-ranking military officers, church officials, civil servants, state-employed professors, and cultural experts who were such indispensable members of the European bourgeoisie were largely absent. The relative weakness of the American state, especially of its bureaucracy, its army, and its educational and cultural institutions, along with the absence of a dominant church, all undermined the emergence of what Europeans have called an *educated bourgeoisie*. New York's bourgeoisie, in contrast, continued to be unquestionably dominated by businesspeople.

~ ~ ~

Thus, by the 1880s and 1890s, upper-class New Yorkers had overcome the divisions between different segments of capital, had boosted industrialists and financiers into dominance, and were operating in increasingly national networks, while strengthening their cultural bonds. These structural changes weakened the particulartist identities of the city's merchants, industrialists, and bankers. Once the prerogatives of a specific line of business became less central to the formation of collective identities (as was the case for workers, who increasingly moved away from craft consciousness), and once the economic elite's universalist, revolutionary, and emancipatory ideology began to weaken in the social conflicts engendered by proletarianization and rising social inequality, class identities came to the fore.[100] "The gulf between employers and the employed is constantly widening, and classes are rapidly forming," argued President Cleveland astutely in 1888.[101] Both contemporary observers and historians agree that a "perception of social distances" spread during the 1880s and 1890s, with the result that these years saw "the deepest awareness among Americans of the classes that divided them."[102] "Class lines have become more rigid," observed labor economist John R. Commons in 1894.[103] Indeed, "[n]o observing person can help being aware of an increasing tendency toward a strong *demarcation of classes* in this country," reported writer and former abolitionist Lydia Maria Child as early as 1877.[104] "Antagonism," was the word that came to mind when Albert Bolles reflected upon *The Conflict Between Capital and Labor* in 1876.[105] And seven years later, William Graham Sumner concurred: "It is commonly asserted that there are in the United States no classes. . . . On the other hand, we constantly read and hear discussions of social topics in which the existence of social classes is assumed as a simple fact."[106] This was especially the case in reference to New York, and indeed, it became one of the central motifs of descriptions of the city.[107] As if to prove these observers right, bourgeois New Yorkers themselves enacted these class lines: Starting in 1898, annual Christmas feedings for the poor in Madison Square Garden attracted the rich and powerful, who would sit in the galleries and private boxes staring down at the city's lower sorts (a full 20,000 of them) who ate below them.[108]

European observers, who were used to their own share of inequality and class conflict, concurred with the observation of many Americans who came to see the United States in general and New York in particular as drifting toward a pronounced articulation of class distinctions. By the 1880s, for example, British travelers writing about the United States consistently observed class divisions, writing of "plutocracy," "class wars," "love of caste distinctions," and "the aristocracy of wealth."[109] One such traveler, James Bryce, wrote in his *American Commonwealth* that "those who deem themselves ladies and gentlemen draw just the same line between themselves and the multitude as is drawn in England, and draw it in much the same way."[110] British journalist George Steevens concluded from such an analysis in 1896 that "[o]pen warfare between capital and labour will be earlier and bitterer in the United States than in Europe."[111] And German observers agreed: One self-identified socialist wrote in his *Sozialistische Briefe aus Amerika* of an America he called the "Bourgeoisierepublik" – the republic of the bourgeoisie – and of the unlimited power of "money capitalism," a power "nowhere as strong as in America."[112] Even Friedrich Engels, despite his great respect for the might of the European bourgeoisie, stood in awe of the radical power of this new American class: "Nowhere in the whole world do they come out so shamelessly and tyrannically as over there," he contended in 1886 just after the Knights of Labor had seen their spectacular rise and fall.[113] Though all these commentators might have overemphasized the two-class nature of the United States by overlooking the emergence of a lower middle class, the fact that class distinctions became the object of widespread comment suggests the increasing currency of class in those decades and stands in striking contrast to the antebellum years.[114]

Bourgeois class identities came to the fore in several different ways. Most prominent was the construction and articulation of a class culture. Manners, networks, and institutions showed a new degree of "classness" in general and an overcoming of the divide between merchants and industrialists in particular. But class identities articulated themselves also in a sense of social distance to other social groups, especially workers. In these ways, bourgeois New Yorkers participated in a larger transatlantic process of refashioning their own class. The international nature of this change, in turn, magnified it, as capital-rich New Yorkers asserted their prominence not only vis-à-vis the city itself but also vis-à-vis the upper classes of Paris, London, and Berlin.

Most basically, new class identities expressed themselves in language. Language serves as a marker of social distinction as well as self-description, and during the 1880s and 1890s, bourgeois New Yorkers began to refer to themselves in ways distinctively different than before. While in the 1850s they had regularly alluded to themselves by the specific line of business they were engaged in, such as "merchant" or "iron manufacturer," by the 1880s self-depictions as "business man" or "capitalist" had become more frequent.[115] The *North American Review, Atlantic Monthly,* and Mark Twain all spoke of "business men" as a group of people engaged in commerce, production, and finance.[116] In the pages of the *Commercial and Financial Chronicle,* the term "business men" now came into frequent use, replacing the term "merchant" that had regularly appeared in the pages of one of its predecessor publications, *Hunt's Merchants' Magazine.*[117]

While "business men" turned into a generic term describing people who were engaged in manufacturing, commerce, or banking, terms such as "the better classes" and "taxpayers" entered the vocabulary to depict members of one's own class in political discourse, in contrast to the less respectable "masses" and "dangerous classes."[118] The reform movements of the last third of the nineteenth century, as we have seen, regularly and consistently appealed to the solidarity of taxpayers.[119]

Language, however, only expressed changes of a far-reaching kind. Upper-class social networks, habits, and institutions increasingly constructed a shared culture that overcame the divisions of the antebellum years and decisively set bourgeois New Yorkers apart from other social groups. While this bourgeois culture, with few exceptions, was predicated on access to resources that only the ownership of substantial amounts of capital made possible (that is, "culture" does not explain itself), it provided the glue that constituted the upper class and helped it to transcend the numerous economic fault lines that market competition generated.[120] "Clothing, housing, furniture, gestures, and language, as well as opinions and beliefs" were consciously and unconsciously regulated.[121] As Andrew Carnegie put it: "I began to pay strict attention to my language, and to the English classics, which I now read with great avidity. I began to notice how much better it was to be gentle in tone and manner, polite and courteous to all – in short, better behaved."[122]

The bourgeois home, social clubs, food, and ways of personal interaction all helped to define the realm of the bourgeoisie. It was a realm in which bourgeois New Yorkers set rules and created boundaries, both of which were essential for the self-definition of a group that lacked legal status. Yet as the result of the principally open nature of bourgeois culture, conflicts over whom to admit and how to draw lines between different subsets were frequent, and in themselves an integral part of this bourgeois culture. Cohesion and differentiation were made from the same cloth.

The emergence of collective identities and the distancing from other social groups normally went hand in hand. Consumption was a prime example of this correspondence: Especially the richest bourgeois New Yorkers were, by late century, displaying their wealth as never before, and thus emphasizing the social gap that set them apart from the lower sort. Houses of a size and opulence unknown to earlier generations, for instance, sheltered the railroad tycoons, financial wizards, and empire-building industrialists. J. Pierpont Morgan's mansion on Madison Avenue was spacious enough to give employment to twelve servants, more than any bourgeois New Yorker had employed in the 1850s.[123] William Vanderbilt, the son of Commodore Vanderbilt, built a mansion at Fifth Avenue and 51st Street; the interior decoration by Christian Herter alone was said to have cost $800,000.[124] For this kind of money, Vanderbilt got a Pompeian vestibule, a Japanese parlor, and a Renaissance dining room.[125] Alva Vanderbilt, wife of William, shortly afterward built a castle-like structure on the next block north, at a rumored cost of $3 million.[126] Not to be outdone, George Washington Vanderbilt constructed a castle in North Carolina – including forty bedrooms, a library of 250,000 volumes, and a garden designed by Frederick Law Olmsted.[127] The wealth and abundance of New York's bourgeoisie in the 1880s and 1890s, in turn, pervaded all forms of popular culture – ranging from novels, such as Mark Twain and Charles Ardley Warner's *Gilded Age,* to theater plays, such as *The Henrietta.*[128]

Searching for a cultural repertoire appropriate to a rising elite, bourgeois New Yorkers increasingly turned toward European aristocratic culture. Fashion, for example, was derived from the tastes of European monarchs (truly wealthy New Yorkers had the same tailors as European rulers). Quite tellingly, when in 1897 Cornelia and Bradley Martin organized their fancy dress ball, their guests attended in the costumes of the aristocracy of yesteryear.[129] Tiffany & Co. opened a heraldry department in the 1870s to design coats of arms.[130] Recreational hunting, one of the favorite pastimes of the European aristocracy, found aficionados among upper-class New Yorkers, who were particularly fond of slaughtering the buffalo herds of the West.[131] Elaborate country seats, sometimes of a size matching European castles, attracted the city's elite to the country. In these years, Newport, Rhode Island, came into its own, sporting a large number of enormous summer homes.[132] Though August Belmont owned one of them, he also purchased more than a thousand acres in Babylon, Long Island, in the late 1860s, and built a twenty-four room house, stables, and greenhouses, as well as a one-mile racetrack.[133]

August Belmont, like many upper-class New Yorkers, had developed a fascination for horses, another interest they shared with the European aristocracy. Since the opening of the drives in the newly built Central Park, carriage and horse riders had become the predominant users.[134]

More elaborate than the earlier promenade of the 1850s and more removed from the increasingly disorderly city, each afternoon a good number of bourgeois New Yorkers rode through the park, acknowledging each other's presence and basking in the stares of lesser spectators passing below them.[135] Another equine pastime, albeit faster paced, was horse racing. In 1865, Leonard Jerome, August Belmont, and William Travers had formed the "American Jockey Club," and a year later, "Jerome Park" in Fordham opened, where the likes of August Belmont and Henry Ward Beecher raced their horses.[136] On race days, New York's merchants, industrialists, and bankers took their carriages through Central Park to the tracks, the destination of "[d]ashing four-in-hands, filled with beautiful women and their attending cavaliers."[137] The working-class public was outraged at the high entrance fees at the track that excluded poor and middling folk, but August Belmont maintained haughtily that "[r]acing is for the rich."[138]

Collecting works of art, particularly those of European origins, further recalled the habits of ruling classes throughout history, including those of the aristocracy. After all, as sociologist Pierre Bourdieu reminds us, "[m]aterial or symbolic consumption of works of art constitutes one of the supreme manifestations of *ease*," and a life not dictated by economic necessities was one of the central attributes of the bourgeoisie.[139] Edwin D. Morgan, the Civil War governor of New York State, described his Fifth Avenue home characteristically: "We find our Parlors, Rooms, Halls & Bed rooms so full that we have no room for more."[140] When Morgan died, 152 art items from his estate were sold.[141] Similarly, William Henry Vanderbilt's mansion on Fifth Avenue was crowded with paintings valued at $1.5 million.[142] Sugar refiner Henry O. Havemeyer and his wife accumulated a huge art collection (later to be donated to the Metropolitan Museum of Art), and in their drive to acquire old European masters, unwittingly decorated their home with a number of fake Rembrandts.[143] J. Pierpont Morgan stationed agents throughout Europe to acquire paintings, etchings, and statues.[144] In many ways, the flow of art from Europe to the United States expressed the new economic power relations that began to evolve during these years.

Some bourgeois New Yorkers, especially of recently acquired wealth, went so far in their admiration of the aristocracy that they married their daughters to cash-poor or simply impoverished European aristocrats.[145] The deal was straightforward: social honor in return for financial support. The trail of "dollar princesses" began in the 1870s, and by 1915 there were forty-two American princesses; seventeen duchesses; thirty-three viscountesses; thirty-three marchionesses; forty-six ladies, wives of knights, or baronets; sixty-four baronesses; and one hundred and thirty-six countesses.[146] Jennie Jerome, daughter of Leonard Jerome, married Lord Randolph Churchill in 1874, after he had proposed to her in 1872. Prior negotiations between the families had nearly broken off when the Churchill family demanded a higher dowry from the Jeromes.[147] Two years later, in a similar deal, Consuelo Yznaga married the Eighth Duke of Manchester, Lord Mandeville.[148] Even Helen Stuyvesant Morton, daughter of banker and Republican Governor Levi Parsons Morton, married an aristocrat, the Comte de Perigord, Duc de Valencery. These efforts to assimilate the cultural norms of the European ruling classes of past centuries expressed the enormous confidence, power, and wealth of upper-class New Yorkers.[149]

Even for bourgeois who were less fabulously wealthy, certain forms of consumption became essential to their status. The parlor, with its elaborate references to learning, art, nature, and family continuity, may have been the most powerful symbol of this set of shared cultural values.[150] Since midcentury, the parlor had significantly changed, evolving from an essentially private space used by the family to one increasingly resembling a museum.[151] In the process, it also lost its simple sternness. Earlier parlors had been largely devoid of the ornaments that now covered every surface: "textile furnishings, door curtains . . . and myriad additional forms of semi-permanent drapery – piano covers, mantel lambrequins, and tables having permanently affixed fabric coverings; forms of 'scarf drapery'; and mountains of elaborately decorated sofa pillows."[152] According to *Scribner's Monthly,* in the parlor "no merely useful thing is permitted, [it] is always overcrowded . . . everything bought for show goes there."[153]

Testifying to the importance of interior design as a marker of class identity, historians have found that the houses of the bourgeoisie had an eerie resemblance to one another, "as if they were created at the same moment, according to agreed-upon decorative criteria, by designers who had taught one another."[154] This, of course, was partly true, because a new kind of professional – interior designers – had taken charge of creating the right kind of home, transforming the living quarters themselves into a fashion statement. When self-identified "capitalist" Bradley Martin (the son-in-law of Isaac Sherman) redecorated his house in 1883, for example, he hired designer Leon Marcotte, who purchased furniture (including chandeliers in Paris) for more money than many New Yorkers could hope to earn in a lifetime.[155] Antique furniture, or replicas of such, were especially desirable, since "things from the past" implied the mastery of time, a mastery only available to people with substantial resources.[156] While undoubtedly the truly wealthy decorated their much larger homes in a much more elaborate fashion than less well-off upper-class households, the principal elements of reference remained the same and were distinctly different from those of householders who lacked the time and resources to fashion such kinds of living quarters.[157] Indeed, the notion of "my home is my castle" was hardly one shared by workers, who often spent their spare time in public spaces. In effect, where to live and in what kind of home, but also which church to attend, what to wear, and which kinds of amusements to enjoy were tightly regulated, often quite consciously.[158]

Just like the parlor, food and its consumption also became strong indicators of bourgeois culture. What was on the table and how it was ingested clearly set bourgeois New Yorkers apart from other social groups. Simply the management of the vast number of utensils that typically decorated bourgeois tables, including such exotic tools as "sugar tongs, Saratoga chips servers, ice cream knives, lemon forks, grape shears, oyster ladles, sardine tongs and salt spoons," was a skill that demanded training, helped along by the study of etiquette books, such as Clara Jessup Moore's *Sensible Etiquette of the Best Society*.[159] Dinners, typically, consisted of multiple courses, and it was not unusual for a meal to include not only an assortment of appetizers but also main courses of fish, beef, and poultry. At public events, menus in French became the fashion of the day, even for such ancestor-conscious organizations as the New England Society of New York, groups of mostly small manufacturers like the printers (who enjoyed on the occasion of their 1887 convention in Chicago such delicacies as "potatoes a la Parisienne"), and the metal manufacturers and merchants who dined in 1896 on "Filet of Beef à la Moderne."[160] Even the choice of dinner conversation demanded training in the cultural rules of one's class, which called for the evasion of such topics as "political or sectarian controversies, sicknesses, sores, surgical operations, dreadful accidents, shocking cruelties or horrible punishments."[161] These preferences, tastes, and shared manners created boundaries that were the more important since they could not always be attained in schools and colleges.

Women as well as men were to be trained in these social skills, though this cultural capital had a significantly greater importance to women, as it was often their principal contribution to the family business. Because they had the time, inclination, and support from servants necessary to forge this class culture and transmit it to the next generation, women played dominant roles in organizing the household's social life, and it was thus not surprising that a woman, Caroline Astor, stood at the pinnacle of New York society. Bourgeois women, in effect, shaped the institutions of society, and served, as Elizabeth Blackmar and Roy Rosenzweig have argued, "as emblems of their husbands' wealth and judges of their own and others' status."[162]

Since class formation was tightly linked to family reproduction, bourgeois women also took center stage in the transfer of this culture to their children.[163] Though upper-class children were normally born into the material bounty of their parents' world, they still had to acquire its cultural attributes in an active process of learning. Indeed, bourgeois life was difficult to master, and the inability of most Americans to acquire these skills was one of the major lines of demarcation and one of the principal functions of this class culture. Appropriating social capital, again, was particularly important to girls. The principal goal of their education was to make them socially competent to negotiate the bourgeois world, an education, as historian Maureen Montgomery has argued, that was largely "ornamental," providing the skills to secure the right kind of husband, which, in turn, was "an important means of establishing a family's social ranking."[164]

Schools helped out in this project: Laura Celestia Rockefeller's three daughters, for instance, were sent to the Rye Female Seminary.[165] Barbara Guggenheim's daughters, Cora and Rosa, attended a Catholic finishing school in Paris.[166] Diverse schools in the city itself, such as the Spence School for Girls ("pupils come from wealthy families of all sections") and the Comstock School for Girls (among its alumnae were "many of New York's most prominent society women," including Theodore Roosevelt's sister Corinne and his future wife Edith Kermit Carow) trained many of the city's daughters of wealthy families in forms of appropriate behavior, including table manners.[167] This, in turn, helped their mothers place them well on the marriage market.[168]

For boys, the emphasis of their upbringing was on the ethic of work. Even someone as rich and powerful as John D. Rockefeller put great weight on imbuing his children with the values and culture of his class. When at their summer home, Rockefeller's children were set to tasks such as pulling weeds from the lawn or chopping wood. Each task was paid for by the family patriarch; a wage of a penny was paid for every ten weeds pulled, at a time during which Rockefeller's Standard Oil alone would pay out dividends of nearly $14 million a year. "All home activities," remarked one of Rockefeller's biographers, "were carried on with an eye to character-building."[169] Similarly, Joseph H. Choate told his son George early on that "the only way any man ever got on in any business . . . [is] by hard work, and sacrificing everything else to it."[170]

How important the maintenance of social capital really was became clear when upper-class New Yorkers turned into avid supporters of Anthony Comstock's Society for the Suppression of Vice, which was founded in 1872 with the support of J. Pierpont Morgan, as well as the Colgate, Cornell, and Dodge families.[171] The society's goal to keep pornography out of the hands of children appealed to Comstock's elite sponsors because they believed, as sociologist Nicola Beisel writes, that "[o]bscenity endangered elite children because moral corruption threatened to topple them from the peak of the social hierarchy, rendering them unfit for respectable society."[172] Social capital, it seemed to them, was an integral part of what it meant to be bourgeois, and the consumption of pornography was a direct threat to this social capital.

This new class culture also provided the underpinnings for various institutions. Social clubs were the most prominent among them, and by the 1880s, dozens of exclusive clubs littered the scene, among them the Union Club, the Union League, the Manhattan Club, the Knickerbocker Club, the Calumet, the Metropolitan, the Tuxedo, the New York Yacht Club, and the Racquet Club, many of recent vintage.[173] While their numbers had increased substantially since the 1850s, their character had not changed:

In one corner [of the Union Club] may be seen the solid men, who have passed the age of frivolities, calmly discussing stocks, bonds, railroads, real estate, and business, failures, and defalcations. Further on politics, elections, and municipal affairs are treated from a taxpayer's standpoint. Another group again are deep in horse racing, yacht racing, pigeon shooting, mail stage coaching, and of late fox hunting.[174]

Clubs provided institutionalized networks that now transcended the specific interests of a single economic sector.[175] This was a major departure from the 1850s. The Union Club, once merchant dominated, for example, by late century counted among its members appliance manufacturer Thomas B. Burnham, iron manufacturers James A. Abercombie, and Dudley B. Fuller, and cordage manufacturer James M. Waterbury.[176] The Union League Club, once the home mostly of merchants and bankers, by the 1880s had among its ranks manufacturers of oil, clothing, tobacco, hats, cotton thread, iron, machinery, and silks.[177]

As a result, different segments of the city's economic elite were integrated into the rapidly growing number of clubs. Despite multiplying in numbers, however, these institutions did not create new boundaries of the kind that had kept capital-owning New Yorkers apart in the antebellum years. There are several reasons that the diversity of institutions went along with an increasing sense of cohesion: For one, membership in these organizations overlapped, because many if not most bourgeois New Yorkers joined more than one club. J. P. Morgan was said to have belonged to nineteen social clubs, and while this number was exceptional, membership in multiple and varied clubs was not: A sample of 128 bourgeois New Yorkers whose club affiliations could be established (all of them attended an 1891 dance organized by Mrs. Havemeyer) shows a total of 681 club memberships, or about 5.3 a person.[178] These affiliations overlapped in ways that bound all of their members to one another: For instance, while Union Club members E. D. Morgan and Cornelius Vanderbilt were not members of the Calumet Club, they encountered Calumet members J. Arden Harriman at the Racquet Club and James Waterbury at the Knickerbocker Club, organizations to which both Morgan and Vanderbilt belonged. In aggregate, such overlapping affiliations created dense connections among members of these clubs.[179]

These connections were furthered by a commitment to shared cultural forms. All clubs, for example, encouraged the same forms of bourgeois socializing. Moreover, clubs were not the only form of bourgeois socializing, as wedding receptions, debutante balls, political mobilizations, and commercial associations again brought people together from a wide variety of different club memberships. And no matter if the Seligmans, the Morgans, the Roosevelts, or the Steinways organized a ball or a reception, the events themselves looked very much the same. Even restaurants could emphasize this trend towards cohesion, as Delmonico's, "the great meeting ground of business men," prided itself on its "infinite variety" of guests, as the "trysting [sic] place of men from the Union, Knickerbocker, Calumet and Manhattan Clubs."[180]

For these reasons, it is best to think of the diversity of these bourgeois associations as the result of the sheer size of the city's upper class and their desire to keep their institutions small enough to facilitate personal contacts. The social institutions of bourgeois New York were structured like a spider web; not each point on the web was joined with every other point, but taken together they were all connected. While society "is so large and complex a system that to determine its component parts, its many intersecting circles and relations, would require the time and the skill, almost, of the astronomer who would map out the heavens," it represented in totality an effort of upper-class New Yorkers to set themselves apart. And, indeed, despite the prevalence of many social circles, "one person may belong to nearly all of those circles, if he is versatile in social qualities."[181] The vast array of bourgeois institutions allowed for distinction as well as for cohesion.[182]

By the 1880s and 1890s, balls, children's parties, dinners, musicales, receptions, and, of course, weddings, among others, provided an unremitting series of social occasions to draw boundaries between those who belonged to the bourgeois world and those who did not, while transcending former divisions rooted in the ownership of a particular kind of capital. Simultaneously, public markers of belonging to the "right" social circles became more important, since the small bourgeois world of antebellum New York, based on personal contact, had given way to a world in which people were less familiar with one another. Tellingly, in 1883, *The Season – An Annual Record of Society* was published, serving as a record for society's social occasions by providing its readers ("those personally interested") with comprehensive lists of guests at these events.[183] And in 1886, the *Social Register* began publishing a list of New Yorkers who were considered among the socially elect, including their various club memberships.[184] Increasingly, class formation became a conscious "project."

While class identities became increasingly important to bourgeois New Yorkers, other identities persisted, especially those based on religious beliefs and heritage. Just as during the 1850s, these identities also formed the basis of institutions. A German immigrant such as William Steinway might attend the ethnic Liederkranz Society, while the Seligmans and Loebs participated in Jewish organizations such as the Harmonie Gesellschaft, the Beekmans and Depeysters celebrated with the St. Nicholas Society, and the Morgans and Griswolds fervently supported the New-England Society.[185] Some of these organizations were in the business of inventing traditions, such as the Knickerbocker Club, which was devoted to the celebration of a long family history in New York, but included such recent arrivals as August Belmont and Bradley Martin.[186]

The most significant of these identities, however, was a negative one – anti-Semitism. Elite anti-Semitism had sharpened by the late nineteenth century, and its strongest articulation was the partial exclusion of Jewish New Yorkers from the social world of which they once had been a part.[187] By the 1890s, upper-class anti-Semites had driven Jewish members out of the Union Club, closed Saratoga hotels to Jews, and banned the mentioning of Jewish organizations in the *Social Register*.[188]

Elite anti-Semitism spread in the 1880s and especially in the 1890s for a number of reasons. For one, economic competition, especially in the world of investment banking, gave Protestants a strong incentive to isolate their Jewish competitors from some of the social networks that were the lifeblood of their particular line of business. Moreover, the influx of thousands of unskilled workers from the ghettos of eastern Europe to New York in the late nineteenth century helped to link the bourgeois fear of workers to the fear of Jews, especially because Jewish workers showed an exceptional tendency to embrace trade unions and socialism. And, last but not least, the embrace of racialist ideas that became prevalent in the late nineteenth century throughout American society (in distinct departure from a prior bourgeois universalism) easily translated into the view that Jews were inferior. These things, taken together, resulted in a heightened isolation of bourgeois Jewish New Yorkers from their gentile peers. In comparison with anti-Semitism elsewhere, however, it was relatively mild (especially when contrasted to Germany and France), because it "was never officially sanctioned or politically institutionalized" in the United States.[189]

Anti-Semitism, along with other ethnic and religious identities, captured the imagination of bourgeois New Yorkers. Yet, they did not overwhelm class identities. For one, associations based upon ethnic and religious loyalties were, in the form of their activities, very much classic examples of bourgeois socializing.[190] They were, in effect, societies within a society, alternative forms of the archetypal bourgeois association.[191] Moreover, none of these identities and affiliations prevented frequent contact across lines of religion and nativity. For example, throughout the 1880s, even after elite anti-Semitism had sharpened, it was more likely that Jewish bourgeois New Yorkers would mingle with the Protestant elite in their homes and in their places of assembly than with any of their lower-class Jewish co-ethnics, who inhabited the less desirable areas of town. Thanks to *The Season, The Annual Report of Society*, we know of such encounters: When in March 1883, the Metropolitan Club gave a "calico hop" at Delmonico's, for instance, guests included Seligmans, Rothschilds, and other illustrious Jewish New Yorkers alongside the Protestant elite.[192] That same year, banker Jesse Seligman was invited to attend a reception at the house of William E. Dodge, together with a crowd that included the ex–California Governor Leland Stanford, Cyrus W. Field, Albert Bierstadt, and Walter Phelps, as well as Helen Day Gould, Jay Gould's wife, and Russell Sage.[193]

The same mixing of different ethnic groups occurred during political mobilizations, such as the 1874 meeting against the Inflation Bill, a rally which included among its vice presidents not only the who's who of New York's Protestant elite but also several Seligmans, Isaac Bernheimer, and Oswald Ottendorfer.[194] Moreover, organizations ranging from the Philharmonic Society to the Hardware Club and the Republican Party counted, among their members, merchants as well as industrialists of native Protestant, Catholic, and Jewish background.[195] Also, neither employers' associations nor trade associations, elite Democratic circles nor elite Republican circles were divided on the basis of ethnicity, nor did bourgeois New Yorkers mobilize politically across class lines on the basis of shared ethnicity or religion. Perhaps most importantly, the Chamber of Commerce not only organized merchants as well as manufacturers, but also included immigrant capitalists, such as banker Henry Clews, financier John S. Kennedy, and fur merchant Frederick Gunther; Catholic businessmen, such as bankers Adrian Iselin and Eugene Kelly, as well as real estate developer James Lynch; and Jewish entrepreneurs, such as Emanuel Spiegelberg and tobacco merchant Isaac Rosenwald, as well as bankers Isaac Ickelheimer and Jesse Seligman.

In fact, common interests, experiences, and values united bourgeois New Yorkers across all ethnic boundaries. Even if they did not marry one another across religious or ethnic divides, when it came to the defense of their common interests, they could transcend religious, ethnic, and other cleavages. Indeed, in the early 1880s, with broad upper-class backing, an Irish Catholic immigrant, William R. Grace, even ascended to the mayoralty of the city.[196] This does not mean that non–class identities did not matter, yet it does suggest that their importance was limited to creating the numerous and finely distinct social circles of the bourgeoisie.

This became most obvious when upper-class New Yorkers ventured to create a class-segmented public sphere, an effort in which they were spectacularly successful, in contrast to their more tentative and essentially ineffectual efforts of the 1850s.[197] By the 1880s, they had created a set of cultural institutions they clearly dominated and in which they set class-specific aesthetic standards, most prominently at the Metropolitan Museum of Art, the Metropolitan Opera, and the New York Philharmonic.[198] These institutions were financially dependent on bourgeois New Yorkers, derived their programmatic ideas from them, and principally catered to the city's economic elite. In turn, they became the focus of bourgeois philanthropy.[199]

All these institutions served to define a particular set of works as high culture. The Metropolitan Museum of Art, which had originated from a

1869 meeting of the Union League Club and had opened its doors in 1880, for example, displayed the works of ancient as well as more recent European painters and sculptors, thus classifying them as legitimate forms of art. It acquired most of its collection through donations from wealthy New Yorkers (William Henry Riggs, for example, was already busy spending his father's money on the old European armaments that he would donate to the Museum in 1913).[200] This was a great departure from the kinds of museums that had dominated the cultural landscape of midcentury New York, such as the commercialized showrooms of Phineas T. Barnum, with their eclectic collections and diverse audience. The definition and appropriation of a high culture served to distinguish the city's economic elite from the lower classes, as well as to exert cultural hegemony over middle-class New Yorkers who strove to live up to the cultural standards of their betters.[201] Though the museum claimed an "educational" role, it effectively kept working-class New Yorkers out. Until 1891, the museum remained closed on Sunday, the one day workers could have actually enjoyed its collection, and even then, the museum harassed lower-class visitors. In 1897, for example, it turned away a plumber who came to view the exhibit, the director of the museum arguing that "[w]e do not want, nor will we permit a person who has been digging in a filthy sewer or working among grease and oil to come in here, and by offensive odors emitted from the dirt on their apparel, make the surroundings uncomfortable for others."[202]

Defining and appropriating high culture, the Metropolitan Museum also brought different segments of New York's upper class together, again transcending earlier divisions. Among the Metropolitan's trustees was a whole range of bourgeois New Yorkers, some of whom represented the old mercantile elite, others the newly made industrial fortunes. Old-time merchants, such as William H. Aspinwall, William H. Astor, and Theodore Roosevelt, along with newcomers, such as printing press manufacturer Robert Hoe, Jr., banker J. Pierpont Morgan, and railroad entrepreneur Cornelius Vanderbilt, had heeded Joseph Choate's call to convert their "railroad shares and mining stocks . . . into the glorified canvas of the world's masters."[203] Among the fifty-nine trustees who served on the museum's board between 1870 and 1896, at least thirty-eight of them (64 percent) also were members of the much older New-York Historical Society, demonstrating that the Metropolitan Museum integrated the old mercantile elite with new segments of the city's upper class into a classwide cultural institution.[204]

The struggle to create a class-segregated public sphere, a prominent motif of the Metropolitan Museum's founding, was replicated by the Philharmonic Society of New York. The society, just like the museum and the Metropolitan Opera, was largely an organization that institutionalized high culture, characterizing its audience tellingly in 1892 as "untouched by those freaks of fashion . . . of the majority of popular entertainments."[205] It saw "its purposes diametrically opposed to those of the itinerant virtuoso." With "its resolute refusal to yield . . . to the demands of an unformed taste," it staked out a separate ground for high culture, and wrested control of the public sphere from the raucous audiences that had been typical of concerts in earlier times, setting itself self-consciously apart from the "advertising-managers of the Barnum stamp."[206]

This state of things, however, had come about only after decades of struggle. The society's purpose, to give "public concerts of high-class instrumental music," had been difficult to achieve in the antebellum years because "[t]he people of New York . . . did not [have] a refined appreciation of instrumental music."[207] Only after the Civil War did things change, and the Philharmonic Society evolved from an organizationally and financially fragile institution run by and for its musicians to an elite institution codifying high art, as well as the manners for its enjoyment. Such illustrious New Yorkers as George Templeton Strong, Henry G. Stebbins, and E. H. Schermerhorn now rose to the presidency of the society.[208] As a result, "the audiences soon came to represent the choice spirits of the social world," and the atmosphere at concerts was, finally, "orderly" and "respectful."[209] During the 1867/68 season, a new president of the society "invoked all the social and fashionable forces in behalf of the concerts, and soon made the Society's concerts the sensational features of the season." This strategy proved successful, as the income of the society nearly tripled in four short years between 1866 and 1870.[210]

While the Philharmonic Society defined and segregated a realm of culture, it integrated diverse segments of the city's bourgeoisie, just as the Metropolitan Museum of Art and the Metropolitan Opera did. Merchants and industrialists, Jews and Gentiles, immigrants and natives, local manufacturers and the heads of large national corporations, all rubbed shoulders listening to the music of Mozart and Beethoven. The Carnegies, Goulds, Hoes, Hewitts, Harrimans, Morgans, Rothschilds, Rockefellers, Roosevelts, Seligmans, Steinways, Swifts, and Sturgeses all subscribed to the Philharmonic's concerts.[211]

Forging new and powerful cultural institutions helped define the realm of the bourgeoisie, brought the economic elite together, and projected their claims to leadership into the wider society. An even more self-conscious effort by upper-class New Yorkers to set themselves apart was their search for genealogical legitimacy. Even if constructed more or less of whole cloth, heritage was important because a distinct line of ancestors legitimized their powerful position and went well with the social Darwinist beliefs that many had come to share. Societies like the Sons of the American Revolution (1889) and the Daughters of the American Revolution (1890) emerged, creating imaginary communities of shared heritage.[212] Simultaneously, bourgeois New Yorkers became obsessed with family trees, often going back hundreds of years to prove their distinct heritage: Levi Parsons Morton, a future governor of New York State, traced his family lineage to the year 1066; the Belknap family engaged in genealogical research to enable Robert Belknap to join the Sons of the American Revolution; and John Jacob Astor traced his wife's line of ancestry to 1377 (following the male line up to the point of the marriage of Charlotte Augusta Gibbs [his wife], when, presumably, the "blood" became part of the Astors).[213] Elizabeth Roosevelt, distant relative of Teddy Roosevelt, even claimed descent from William the Conqueror. "The bourgeoisie buckled History around themselves like moral armor," one historian has observed.[214] A class that once had shaped its identity and sense of self in opposition to the degenerated European aristocracy now defined itself increasingly by "blood."

The New York Genealogical Society exhibited, in a striking manner, the astonishing sense of separateness that a very significant segment of New York's bourgeoisie had developed by the last decades of the century. The object of the society, one of its members proclaimed, was not "the mere purpose of a hunt for ancestors to gratify personal or family pride." Instead, he argued, the society "is for the purpose, primarily, in my opinion, of forming a true and firm foundation on which those who are to come after us can establish the fact that they are the descendants of the original settlers and founders of civilized life upon this continent, not of the hordes of the foreigners." He claimed that those "original settlers and founders" are "primarily entitled to rule this country." Another of the society's activists asserted that "the descendants of well-mated husbands and wives . . . will be . . . morally and physically superior to those of the ill-mated, feeble and indifferent."[215]

Inequality, which traditionally had been explained in bourgeois political discourse as the result of individual exertion in the marketplace, now came to be seen in racial terms. This, in turn, provided a convenient explanation for the social conflicts of these decades, as immigrants indeed played a prominent role in them. The Genealogical Society, in a further ironic twist, did not object to foreigners per se, counting among its members such illustrious immigrants as Andrew Carnegie (from Scotland), Jose Francis Di Navarro (from Spain/Cuba), and William R. Grace (from Ireland). Fearing the political influence of the lower classes, its real project was the creation of a bounded bourgeois world. Such sentiments were so broadly shared that between 1869 and 1894, the society attracted 478 members, among them such central figures as J. Pierpont Morgan, Collis P. Huntington, William W. Astor, Russell Sage, and Theodore Roosevelt. Even Isaac Sherman, the Republican manufacturer and railroad investor, joined.[216]

Expressing a similar orientation but in a more public manner, the newly created Museum of Natural History, which had opened its gates in 1871 on the west side of Central Park, represented the economic elite's pride in scientific accomplishments, global domination, and biological hierarchy. Established by the likes of J. Pierpont Morgan, Alexander T. Stewart, James Brown, William E. Dodge, and Theodore Roosevelt, the museum collected a wide range of artifacts: At first, ten thousand butterflies from Europe and the United States, six thousand shells from the Spice Islands, and four thousand mounted South American birds decorated the walls, later to be joined by lions, elephants, and tigers, as well as the cultural artifacts of Asian and African peoples.[217] It was especially the latter that made it obvious that the museum's creators saw their own as the highest form of civilization. Whereas the Metropolitan Museum of Art represented the economic elite's claim to parity with its counterparts in the capitals of Europe, the Museum of Natural History celebrated the domination of the natural world and non-Western peoples by the Western bourgeoisie.

By the 1880s, thus, bourgeois New Yorkers had forged a shared class culture, along with social networks and institutions, that held their world together. However, such cohesion did not preclude divisions nor competing identities. Because New York's economic elite continued to grow in numbers and change in composition during the last two decades of the nineteenth century, problems of social demarcation remained high on their agenda. As a result, those who had inherited their capital and position kept drawing lines between themselves and those who had made their wealth in their own lifetimes, even though these boundaries were undermined by marriages across those demarcations. The onslaught of new wealth was felt particularly painfully in the post–Civil War years because it went hand in hand with the replacement of mercantile capital. And it was felt nowhere more than in New York City. As a result, boundaries had to be constantly renegotiated, and the balance of inclusiveness versus exclusiveness had to be struggled over. In this encounter, old wealth expressed ambivalence toward new wealth, precisely because newly rich New Yorkers had often not been socialized into the culture of their class. Old wealth also tended to object to the greater visibility of the uglier sides of capital accumulation as exhibited by the newly rich, the very real struggles of a Guggenheim or Rockefeller with competitors as well as with labor. Older wealth, in contrast, especially if clouded in claims to a distinct heritage and the appropriation of European culture, could claim greater legitimacy than those who had accumulated their fortunes after the war.

Yet, as we have seen, despite this enormous dynamism and constant recomposition of New York's upper class, their efforts to stabilize their own class were amazingly successful, not least because of their ability to absorb newcomers rapidly. New York's economic elite had joined the mainstream of the bourgeois Atlantic. While the organizational patterns and ideas of American workers might have made them "exceptional," bourgeois New Yorkers built a world that was very much like the one that emerged in other Western cities during the last decades of the century. Indeed, at the very moment when socialists everywhere were appealing to the internationalism of their respective working classes, bourgeois citizens increasingly talked a common language and inhabited a common universe.

This was a major departure from earlier years, a departure driven by large-scale structural changes, most importantly the diminishing economic and social chasm between the old mercantile elite and the rising industrialists. But it was also a departure propelled by sharpening conflicts with other social groups – most notably with workers. It was they, after all, who seemed to threaten bourgeois economic, social, and political power most decisively. And if push came to shove, bourgeois New Yorkers had much in common with one another.

9

The Rights of Labor, The Rights of Property

While bourgeois New Yorkers had forged a shared culture, and had amassed unprecented economic power by the 1880s, their assertion of this power, their conspicuous consumption, and the striking inequality of wealth within the city and the nation propelled other social groups, particularly workers, to challenge them at the workplace and the polls.[1] This mobilization, in turn, drove the city's economic elite even closer together and enabled them to act at times collectively. Bourgeois class formation thus developed in relation to working-class formation; bourgeois class identities were sharpened by workers' collective action. This relationship was new, a result of the emerging dominance of industrial over merchant capital after the Civil War.

During the 1880s and 1890s, with the strife over slavery and Reconstruction left behind, concerns about wage labor moved to the center stage of bourgeois discourse.[2] "The silver question is a bubble of insignificance," and the "tariff issue . . . of minor importance," compared to the "relation that prevails between labor and capital," wrote a perceptive reader to the editors of *Iron Age*.[3] *The Nation* seconded this notion, observing that "the labor problem [received] an amount and kind of discussion from all classes such as it never received before."[4] Indeed, *Iron Age,* the journal of iron manufacturers, discussed the "labor question" regularly and in great detail, as did the *Oil and Paint Manufacturer* and the *National Bottlers' Gazette,* and aside from discussions of new technologies and the economic outlook of the trade, it was the most important topic in their pages. A stream of more substantial publications considered the relationship between "capital and labor" as well, with titles such as *The Wage-Workers of America and the Relation of Capital to Labor; Labor, Capital and a Protective Tariff; The Duty of the Church in the Conflict Between Capital and Labor; Social Struggles;* and many more.[5] In 1882 a journal even began to circulate with the title *Capital and Labor,* "the organ of the manufacturers on the labor question."[6] Indeed, so fully did the conflict between workers and employers move to center stage that when the widow of department store owner Alexander T. Stewart died, the *New York Times* discussed her will in terms of its implications for class relations, noting that its provisions would spread her wealth broadly enough so that "there is nothing . . . to make a case for the Communists."[7]

Labor took center stage in the political discourse of the economic elite because they were confronted by a larger and more mobilized working class.[8] Whereas the antebellum merchants had normally employed only a few wage workers, the newly powerful industrialists depended on a large number of employees. New Yorker Meyer Guggenheim, like many others, had personally experienced this transition when he left the calmer days of trade behind and invested in Colorado silver mines, where he employed thousands of workers.[9]

Not only were there more workers but they also struck more frequently. Indeed, just like the city's merchants, industrialists, and bankers, who had organized and become more class conscious by the 1880s, the city's workers, after the devastation of the depression, began to rebuild their organizations. The somewhat more prosperous early 1880s and the hostility of employers encouraged them to organize collectively. The number of strikes in the nation increased from fewer than 500 a year in the early 1880s to approximately 1,500 in 1886.[10] In New York City alone, it has been estimated that between 1881 and 1900, 5,090 strikes involved 33,161 factories and 962,470 workers.[11] These walkouts were often successful; nationwide, workers won 46.5 percent of the strikes between 1881 and 1905.[12] And not only was the number of strikes large; American labor relations, compared to those of western Europe, also turned exceptionally violent.

Industrialists faced strikes especially frequently. William Steinway, for instance, was constantly battling his workers throughout the 1880s, conflicts he faithfully chronicled in his diary. In November 1878 there was a "[r]evolution at our factory"; in September 1879 the casemakers, machine men, and blockers successfully struck for a 10 percent raise; in early 1880 all of Steinway's workers walked out (after a bitter lockout, the strike ended in a compromise settlement); in October 1882 workers went on another four-week-long strike, during which Steinway refused to give in and discharged the strike leaders (noting on November 20, 1882, that "strike broken, feel greatly elated"); and in May 1886 Steinway defeated a strike of his workers for the eight-hour day.[13]

Steinway's handling of strikes, quite typically, became increasingly confrontational. While he had tried in the 1860s to seek compromise, by the 1880s he battled his workers directly. During the 1880 strike he initiated a decision, backed by the Boss Piano Makers of New York, to lock out all piano workers throughout the industry.[14] In 1882 he gave the strike leaders "a fearful talking" and planned to "in toto discharge them all."[15] On November 10, 1882, he served "dispossess warrants . . . on the Astoria Strikers."[16] Again, in 1883 during another strike, Steinway hired detectives to spy on his employees, paid the local police more than $2,000 for support during the conflict, and expelled the strike leaders from company housing in Astoria. "Our victory is complete, and the men are very much cowed down," he proclaimed triumphantly.[17] During the 1886 eight-hour strike, he again refused to compromise.[18] These steps, according to Steinway, brought him great support: "[A]m downtown. I am greeted everywhere," he noted in his diary in October 1882 in the wake of one strike.[19] Though Steinway explicitly approved of the legitimacy of unions and strikes, and saw himself as a paternalistic employer, his attitude toward workers hardened. He justified his actions by blaming the "entrance of the socialistic and the communistic element in the labor unions" for the new level of hostility, a hostility he termed "terrorism" in 1883.[20]

There was widespread agreement among bourgeois New Yorkers that the relationship between capital and labor had changed for the worse. Witnesses who appeared before the Senate Committee on Education and Labor described "a very thorough change . . . within the last ten or fifteen years" as employers and employees "look at each other now more or less as enemies."[21] In somewhat exaggerated fashion, the New York machine builder John Roach even claimed that "90 per cent. of all the successful men in business at the present time would be willing to go out of it now . . . owing to this unsettled condition of things and this feeling which is working up between capital and labor."[22] His colleague, the iron manufacturer Abram Hewitt, agreed: When in 1878 he headed a congressional commission to inquire into the relationship of labor and capital and find ways to improve it, the *New York Times* ridiculed his hearings ("curious specimens of thought"),[23] and Hewitt admitted that "the feeling of mutual respect and confidence and good will was rapidly diminishing."[24] As printer Theodore Low De Vinne bemoaned, "friendly intercourse between employers and employed outside the office is becoming more restrained."[25]

Such musings were the direct result of the precarious instability of labor relations, which easily turned into panic about the great threat that unions and workers represented. The mobilizations of 1886 especially struck fear into the hearts of upper-class New Yorkers because it was in this year that they were challenged both at the workplace and at the polls. At the core of these threats stood the Knights of Labor. Though this union's ideology still was rooted in the artisan republicanism of earlier times, its comprehensive organizational strategy and its political efforts gave it a presence no other union had ever enjoyed before.[26] When in May 1886 the Knights called out hundreds of thousands of workers throughout the nation to demand the eight-hour day, among them Manhattan trolley car conductors, piano makers, and furniture makers, bourgeois New Yorkers closed ranks against any kind of compromise.[27] So great was their concern about the movement that even the Chamber of Commerce, which had in prior years not taken a public position on specific strikes, called a special meeting to discuss the eight-hour movement. No fewer than fifty-seven of the Chamber's members requested the meeting, which must have originated among the city's dry goods merchants (fourteen of the twenty-three dry goods merchants who belonged to the Chamber of Commerce were present), to consider "what action . . . the chamber may appropriately take, with a view of sustaining and enforcing existing laws for the protection of all classes of our citizens in the peaceful pursuit of their business, and the prevention of illegal interference therewith."[28] They resolved that "under the circumstances now existing, [the Chamber] considers it the paramount duty of every American citizen to uphold and strengthen the hands of the constituted authorities."[29] When in early May 1886 a bomb exploded in Chicago's Haymarket, killing eight policemen during a rally held by anarchists, anxiety reached fever pitch. The *New York Times* drew a fearful portrait of a widespread plot of workers, who placed "responsibility for their poverty upon the bourgeoisie," drilling with rifles and building bombs throughout New York City, with plans to overthrow the "ruling class."[30] From then on, "[t]he radical specter," according to historian T. Jackson Lears would, "[continue] to haunt the bourgeois imagination."[31]

Such exaggerated fears were further fed when in the fall of 1886 the mobilization of labor – in reaction to the government's involvement in the strikes of the summer – moved into the sphere of politics. In New York City, as elsewhere, policemen during these months had escorted strikebreakers to work, had clubbed workers who tried to keep trolleys from running, and had used conspiracy laws to undermine the workers' most powerful weapon in the competitive local economy, the boycott as its "very strength . . . made it necessary to forbid its use."[32] Far from solving the conflicts that gave rise to the Knights in the first place, however, this heavy-handed response sharpened the crisis even further.[33]

Although labor had not built a class movement in municipal politics since after the Civil War – in contrast to bourgeois New Yorkers who had organized along class lines in the early 1870s – by 1886 the Central Labor

Union (CLU), which united about 200 of the city's unions, called for the organization of a new political party that would advocate public works, limits on police intervention in strikes, municipal control of public transportation, and abolition of private ownership of land.[34] The CLU's deep roots in the city's working-class districts enabled it quickly to mobilize 34,000 voters to sign a petition supporting the candidacy of Henry George, a reformer and critic of America's growing class polarization. Drawing a sharp dividing line between "earned" and "speculative" profits, George made monopolists who appropriated "unearned" profits from land ownership responsible for social ills. The separation of "productive" versus "nonproductive" property harked back to old republican beliefs and resonated among many working-class and lower-middle-class New Yorkers, attracting a wide range of supporting organizations, ranging from the Irish Land League to social reformers.[35] Contemporaries correctly saw the ensuing electoral campaign as the most serious challenge to the dominance of the city and its politics by bourgeois New Yorkers, and as a break in the power arrangements of the city.[36] It symbolized, even more than the constant struggles in the factories, a crisis of legitimacy for the city's upper class.[37]

The prospect of seeing a mayor elected by a broad-based working-class movement was hardly welcomed by the city's merchants, industrialists, bankers, and professionals. There was "a feeling of uneasiness amounting almost to alarm [among] many excellent citizens" when they considered what a George victory might mean for the city and the country.[38] The *Financial and Commercial Chronicle*, "[r]epresenting the industrial and commercial interests of the United States," reported that "[t]he coming election has . . . absorbed attention, and uneasiness has been felt in some quarters respecting the contest for the Mayor of this city and its possible effect on speculation."[39] Most remarkable, observed *Bradstreet's*, was that a "new element" had entered politics, which "has in its power to derange the calculation hitherto made by political managers."[40] Something had to be done, resolved the Union League Club after one of its "largest and most enthusiastic meetings," as the "present revolt of the working men of this city . . . has . . . become a matter of the first importance."[41] In a series of talks at the Young Men's Democratic Club, J. Bleecker Miller, lawyer and one-time secretary of the Bar Association of New York, tried to formulate such a "property-owners answer" to George but did not get much beyond debunking George's ideas.[42] While some upper-class New Yorkers prophesied that "the French Revolution . . . is about to repeat itself here," merchants, industrialists, and bankers feared most that George, if elected, could shift the balance of power between workers and employers at the workplace, by allowing workers to proceed with boycotts, for example, the very issue that had inspired George's campaign in the first place.[43] *The Nation* direly anticipated that "[a] large vote for George will undoubtedly diminish the value of the law as a protection for non-union men and for employers in all parts of the country."[44] A George victory, predicted Samuel Barlow, would almost certainly precipitate a conflict between "order and disorder and between labor and idleness, between the madness engendered by German philosophy, French Anarchism and beer on the one side and common sense conservatism on the other."[45]

Bourgeois New Yorkers took up the challenge. A wide range of individuals and organizations campaigned zealously against George, ranging from William Steinway and the Union League Club to the Dry Goods Merchants and the Committee of One Hundred, as well as the Business Men's Cleveland Association.[46] While they shared a mutual opposition to George, they faced a real dilemma: If the Democratic Party did not overcome its divisive factionalism in local politics of the prior twenty years, a victory for George lay on the horizon. Only a unification of Tammany and the elite County Democracy, the two dominant groups within the party, could defeat George.[47] And indeed, the two factions cooperated, nominating Abram Hewitt as their candidate for mayor. Even *The Nation,* which normally refused to support a candidate endorsed by Tammany, called upon Republicans and Democrats to close ranks behind the "candidate friendly to property and order" – Abram Hewitt.[48] Many Republicans heeded the call as well.[49]

After a bitter campaign, the outcome of the election was ambiguous for the city's merchants, industrialists, and bankers. Although Hewitt won more than 90,000 votes, Henry George received 68,000 votes, significantly more than Theodore Roosevelt, the Republican candidate.[50] A third-party challenge, though defeated, had thus been extraordinarily successful. William R. Grace wrote to Hewitt with great relief that "the real danger" was averted, although he predicted that "this whole business brings up a new force in politics which will not be easy to handle."[51] To Grover Cleveland he dropped a note contending that "the labor vote . . . surpassed my calculations + will be a difficult force to handle in the future."[52]

George's campaign was the local manifestation of a national crisis. The juncture between an unprecedented mobilization of workers for the eight-hour day, the Haymarket bombing, and the spectacular rise of a third-party mayoral candidate in New York City (and also in other towns and

cities throughout the nation) pointed not only to a challenge to the bourgeoisie's economic and political power, but also to the lack of legitimacy of
their claims to a reformulated republican legacy. It is only in the context of
this multifaceted challenge in the fall of 1886 that the noisy panic of the
owners of capital makes sense. As J. Bleecker Miller observed, "Anyone
who looks back upon the last few years and sees how rapidly this discontent has spread and organized for political action, must realize that it is not
a matter which this generation can afford to disregard."[53] And, indeed, it
became this generation's most troublesome political problem.

From 1886 onward, the alarm engendered by the rise of working-class
political movements, strikes, and unions would become a regular feature
of bourgeois discourse.[54] Upper-class New Yorkers feared that American
exceptionalism had come to an end – that a permanent proletariat had
arisen quite like that of Europe, and that these workers might embrace
dangerously radical ideas or even follow the example of the people of
Paris. The *Commercial and Financial Chronicle* clearly recognized that the
root cause of this frightening spectacle was that the relationship between
employers and workers had changed fundamentally:

> The old relation has been completely destroyed, and that which has taken its place
> is something far different and much less satisfactory. No longer does the farmer's
> "hired man" live in the house of his employer, and sit at his table; the journeyman
> carpenter or shoemaker, living on terms almost of equality with the slightly more
> prosperous or enterprising journeyman who paid him wages, has disappeared. The
> causes of the change which these examples illustrate are well known. They are,
> first, the magnitude of modern industrial undertakings, which has led to a minute
> subdivision of labor; second, the substitution of corporate for individual employers;
> third, the growth and adoption of the spirit of modern political economy, which
> logically inculcates the treatment of labor with the same consideration, and no
> more, that is accorded to any other of the raw materials or tools of manufacture.[55]

The world had changed dramatically and bourgeois New Yorkers had
to come to terms with it. The rapidly expanding business press played an
especially important role in this conversation about the nature of workers
and trade unions. These publications took a central role – not only
because they formulated coherent ideological positions but also because
they helped employers find out what other employers where doing and
thinking. In effect if not in intent, they were a central tool for collective
mobilization.[56] And these publications increasingly came to formulate
"class" positions instead of those rooted in the specific exigencies of their
trade. It was indeed in their discussions of the relationship to labor that

they transcended most decisively older particularist identities. This was a dramatic change. In the 1850s, for example, the industrialists' free-labor position still had been most prominently articulated by a paper, the *New-York Daily Tribune,* that counted Karl Marx among its contributors. Such proximity between bourgeois and socialist thinkers was all but unimaginable during the 1880s and 1890s.

By the 1880s, notions of a mutuality of interests based on commonly experienced social mobility and transgression of the line between employers and employees, which once had dominated the discourse of manufacturers, had diminished.[57] As the moral economy that had informed social relations in the artisanal workshop of midcentury crumbled, manufacturers increasingly saw labor as "a marketable commodity – quite as much as wheat," its price to be determined by the law of "supply and demand."[58] So great was the distance industrialists had traveled from the free-labor ideology of antebellum times that in 1893 *Iron Age* quoted approvingly a pamphlet by a Chicago manufacturer, who asserted that "[a]ggregations of capital are beneficial to society, as they reduce the cost of production," and concluded that because "[c]apital and labor are partners, but capitalists and laborers are not . . . [t]he obligations of capital to share profits with labor are no greater than those of others to share their surplus with the needy."[59] Classical liberalism now guided the city's economic elite in their understanding of the freedom of labor, a freedom that they defined as the right to enter or refuse to enter into a contract with an employer. Capitalists, they argued, "have an unquestionable right to make such contracts, rules, and regulations as may be necessary to promote the best interests of their business, as well as for the maintenance of good order."[60] Tellingly, in 1877 the American Institute, renowned for its free-labor thinking during the 1850s, invited the silk merchant (and Republican) Elliot Cowdin to speak at its semicentennial celebration, an occasion Cowdin took to explain that workers should not envy the "seemingly wealthy man of business" because a businessman is "[l]ashed to his task by the exigencies of his business, harassed by anxieties, [a state] ruinous to his peace of mind." As a result of these trials and tribulations, Cowdin argued, businessmen were about ten times more likely to commit suicide than workers.[61]

During the 1850s, manufacturers and others had seen propertied independence as the prerequisite of republican citizenship, but now bourgeois New Yorkers redefined republicanism itself as endorsing permanent proletarianization: while laborers still saw wage work as destroying the "independence" essential to workers as citizens, and "wage slavery" as its outcome, elite New Yorkers emphasized "freedom of contract" as the principal freedom of the Republic.[62] For them, the "law of supply and demand" was to structure the relationship between employers and employees a "law as invariable as those of the universe."[63] That labor refused to accept the denigration of citizens to permanent dependence was for *The Nation* the result of a peculiar "mental mood."[64]

Mystifying the laws of the market into laws of nature allowed upper-class New Yorkers to account for their own exalted position. They explained to themselves and others that they had risen to the top of society because of their own superior intelligence, hard work, and diligence.[65] As John D. Rockefeller put it: "It is my personal belief that the principal cause for the economic differences between people is their difference in personality."[66] In this light, workers' collective action appeared as an effort by those with less beneficial endowments to redistribute income and power by force, undermining the pillars that kept society from sinking into anarchy and chaos. The economic elites' vision of their own beneficial role in society, in effect, allowed them to characterize challengers as threats not only to their own private wealth and power but also to the well-being of American society. Large industrialists in particular, such as Andrew Carnegie and John D. Rockefeller, assumed that natural hierarchies had put them into an elevated position from which they should steer their undertakings without outside interference.[67] They believed, after all, that at the center of American society was the right to control and accumulate property without interference, either from the state or the propertyless. In Smithian fashion they held that what is best for the individual is best for society. Upper-class New Yorkers effectively brushed aside questions of productive versus unproductive labor, the importance of independence to republican selfhood and citizenship, and the corrupting influence of large accumulations of capital, which had been such dominant tropes in antebellum discussions, and replaced them with an emphasis on the civilizing mission of business. As Andrew Carnegie argued, inequality today guaranteed prosperity tomorrow.[68] During the 1880s and 1890s, however, bourgeois New Yorkers failed to universalize this particular vision, encountering firm resistance from workers, farmers, and even the lower middle classes.

This vision of American society also structured their approach to trade unions: On the one hand, employers held unions as well as strikes to be legitimate institutions, though in a highly restricted fashion.[69] In their eyes, unions could help educate workers and protect them against mishaps, while strikes were an accumulation of numerous individual deci-

sions to withhold labor to negotiate a better price for it.[70] According to
Iron Age, "[o]ne of the fundamental principles of the so-called rights of
labor is the absolute right of every man to sell his services to the best
advantage to himself."[71]

On the other hand, the belief in the "laws of supply and demand" also
provided an ideology that lent itself to aggressive hostility to trade unions
and indeed American employers, it has been argued, were unusually hostile to unions.[72] Especially during the 1880s and 1890s they conceived of
workers' collective action as an essentially illegitimate interference with
markets.[73] In 1882, *Iron Age* succinctly formulated this position by claim-
ing that strikes were a struggle against "the state of the market," a struggle "[t]he market will win every time."[74] If economic conditions were
poor, a decline in wages was "inevitable," no matter what workers did.[75]
Jay Gould seconded this thought, arguing that unions were a positive
good so long as they focused on providing mutual benefits and education
to their members, but not on tinkering with "the law of supply and
demand."[76] Because market laws were presumed to regulate all economic
activity, higher wages or better working conditions were independent of
either the collective pressures of workers or the goodwill of manufacturers. Therefore, strikes expressed a conflict not between employers and
workers but of "labor against labor," that is, striking workers against
strikebreakers.[77] Wages were entirely a result of supply and demand.[78]
"No trades-unions, or riotous strikes, or leveling legislation, can suspend
the operation of the inexorable law that has determined that labor . . .
must be sold for what it will bring," contended Elliot Cowdin.[79]

It was at this point that employers limited the legitimate sphere of collective action by workers. As they conceived of markets as an aggregation of
individual decisions, unions could dangerously alter market outcomes by
organizing the individual decisions of the many into one collective voice.
Quite typically, the New York Chamber of Commerce, while reaffirming
the right to join unions and to strike, resolved in 1886 that the full power
of the state should be employed against those who prevent "any other man
from working whenever and wherever the latter may choose."[80] By keeping strikebreakers out and by coercing workers to join unions, "workingmen . . . are violating the laws made for the government of the community," a violation that leaves "the officers of the law no choice but to
proceed against them, even if it be necessary to invoke the aid of the military."[81] In effect, this interpretation, by making the replacement of striking
workers into a fundamental right of employers, limited unions' power to a
very narrow scope. As *Iron Age* explained: "It is every man's right to sell

his labor and . . . any man or any set of men who take it upon themselves to be the guardian of his conduct in this matter are as great tyrants as ever lived on the face of the earth."[82] Workers' organizations and collective action thus were represented as a direct threat to the workings of the market, a convenient assertion that neglected to account for the power of aggregations of capital represented by single entrepreneurs, and moreover, by entrepreneurs who were acting collectively. In this concept of things, workers were to have little power. This, the *New York Times* remarked laconically, was "the misfortune of their position."[83]

Bourgeois New Yorkers built their limited acceptance of unions and strikes on an assumption that legitimate unions and legitimate strikes embraced the "principles of political economy," principles that left de facto little power to trade unions.[84] Not surprisingly, they saw any effort of workers to assert their power as stepping out of the bonds of this legitimate sphere, in turn allowing employers to call on the state to enforce the violated "laws of supply and demand."[85] Such employers considered unions that did not follow these "laws" to be "essentially un-American" and "unnatural, founded on no principle of right or justice," and they questioned, "How long is society or a free community going to tolerate such an institution?"[86] The greater the degree of mobilization by workers, the greater the collective outcry of employers against such "tyrannical" orders.[87] Respectable circles viewed these strikers as the "dangerous classes," the "vagabond class," "the idle and vicious class," a "mass of envious discontent," or even a "wild beast."[88] In 1886, during the strikes of the Knights of Labor against Gould's railway system, *Iron Age* went so far as to compare the strike to the final months of the sectional crisis of 1860, and warned that "toleration will not be carried beyond the point of safety. . . . No tyranny was ever so absolute and irresistible as that which organized labor seeks to exercise over those who work without first paying it tribute."[89] Such "tyranny," asserted the journal, called for a response: "By resorting to [the argument of force] the working man at once antagonizes the whole machinery of Government, local, State and Federal, bringing upon himself certain defeat."[90]

Employers feared most those unions that stepped out of the traditional bounds of craft unionism, organizations employers called the "socialistic" or "communistic element."[91] It was these unions that truly struck fear into the hearts of the city's bourgeoisie.[92] While we might think of their reaction as overdrawn hysteria, from the vantage point of 1886 or 1892, this seemed less of an exaggeration because the conflict between labor and capital was continually sharpening, and its outcome was unpredictable.

The celebration of the rule of the market and its presumably atomized individuals, packaged as an explicitly antiunion ideology, however, went along with the persistence of a certain form of paternalism. "[A] good understanding . . . is of benefit to both parties," suggested *Iron Age* in 1884, and the *Commercial and Financial Chronicle* editorialized that "by kindliness, by considerate treatment, b‚ a disposition to improve his lot, the laborer may be made to feel that his interests are identical with those of his employer."[93] At times, deeds followed words, such as when William Steinway, who employed 400 piano workers in 1883 at his factory in Astoria, "carried out our ideas of improving the conditions of the workingmen by giving them light and air and good houses to live in, building them public baths, and laying out a public park."[94] Paternalist articulations ranged from the construction of company housing to ideas about profit sharing and suggestions such as the one *Iron Age* forwarded in 1894 that employers should "[t]ry stopping [when encountering workers] to cheerfully inquire after their welfare."[95]

This paternalism, however, was quite distinct from the shared belief in social mobility of the 1850s. That *Iron Age* felt compelled to advise its readers to talk to their employees was in itself a sign of the growing distance between owners and workers. By the 1880s, paternalism was centrally concerned with undercutting the attractiveness of trade unions to workers and did not question the emergence of a permanent proletariat and the organizational separation of workers and employers, both of which were distinct departures from the 1850s. Banker Henry Bischoff, who saw the root of trade unions in the increasing social distance between workers and their employers, for example, expected relations to improve once employers found time for "a kind word" to their workers.[96] Machine builder John Roach similarly propagated the good effects of personal contact between employers and employees, yet asserted that his workers "must conform to my rules," which first and foremost included that "every man has got to speak for himself."[97]

While paternalism as a defensive strategy against unions and strikes would persist, the paternalism of free-labor times that had at its core a shared pride of labor and social mobility had vanished. In effect, the belief in social harmony had weakened. Moreover, the rhetoric of paternalism was much stronger than the reality as, for example, was the case with Andrew Carnegie, who shortly after the conflict at his Homestead mills asserted that labor and capital were "twin brothers."[98] William Graham Sumner was more hard-nosed in these matters, calling the argument "that employers and employed are partners in an enterprise . . . a delusive figure of speech."[99]

Ideologically, bourgeois New Yorkers reconciled harsh attacks against unions and strikes on the one side and limited paternalism on the other side by drawing a sharp distinction between the group of workers who were deserving of this paternalism and those who were not. "The majority of American workingmen are law-abiding citizens, but there is a violent class among them whose brutality leads them to jump at any chance to destroy property, and if needs be, to sacrifice life. . . . It is this class which can only be met with rifles," said *Iron Age*.[100] Often upper-class discourse presented these radical unionists, socialists, and anarchists as foreign and of inferior racial heritage, thus standing outside the Republic.[101]

As a result, many bourgeois New Yorkers combined their own sense of superiority with a disdain for immigrants. While in the early 1880s immigrants were still being lauded for bringing prosperity to the United States, the country "being enriched by the drafts we are making upon the population of the Old World," positive assessment of immigration shifted during the decade.[102] The *Financial and Commercial Chronicle*, for example, still had asserted in 1882 that "[e]very immigrant . . . adds to the wealth-producing capacity of the nation," but by 1887 saw "immigration [as] far more potent for evil than for good."[103] Immigrants allegedly brought anarchism, socialism, and "almost every danger to the organization of society peculiar to the present time."[104] By 1889, the journal even supported restrictions on immigration.[105] Because of "the race changes" of immigrants, they now saw them as "vicious, degraded, ignorant, amenable neither to law nor reason, [without] code of morals, know[ing] nothing about the theory of our government, and in fact abhor[ing] all government."[106] And *Iron Age* concurred: "How America shall protect itself from the invasion of dangerous and otherwise undesirable classes of immigrants is becoming more and more a burning question."[107] Because the majority of American workers were born overseas, many bourgeois New Yorkers combined their fears of Catholics, Jews, and African Americans with their anxiety about trade unions and radicalism. Racism, hence, became an important part of their class identity.

Merchants came to share industrialists' relationship to labor and view of the world. They, like manufacturers, accepted trade unions and strikes as legal and legitimate. They, again like manufacturers, increasingly limited what they saw as the rightful sphere of unions' and workers' collective action.[108] The "laws of supply and demand" structured their view of society and explained their own exhalted position within it. These laws, explained the merchants' *Journal of Commerce*, "cannot be repealed by legislation, by the tyranny of employers . . . or by combinations of the employed."[109] Consequently, merchants, like industrialists, saw the conflict between labor and capital as one "between two systems of management," one giving control over industry to owners, the other to workers. "[I]t is a mere issue of who shall rule," the *Commercial and Financial Chronicle* asserted.[110] And such a system of industrial relations had not come about by "mere accident. It is a result of the survival of the fittest. The fact of its survival is to a great extent its justification."[111]

The coalescence of views among bourgeois New Yorkers about labor in particular and the "laws of political economy" in general was probably the most clearly articulated element of their increasing class awareness.[112] Differences of emphasis of course remained, such as when Andrew Carnegie professed his deeply held beliefs in democracy and social mobility, but the foundations of their shared worldview were solid.[113] This coalescence was also a basis of their ability to confront labor and call upon the state in support of their interests. In 1887, when the Knights of Labor's strength had already passed its peak, the *Commercial and Financial Chronicle* explained the success of employers in dealing with the movement in exactly such terms: "As the Knights of Labor grew in membership, and the number of boycotts increased, merchants and manufacturers began to feel that they had a common interest in preventing the growth of any such irresponsible power; they had a common interest in maintaining industrial order and independence which was more important than any temporary advantage to be obtained over a commercial rival."[114] Working-class mobilization thus had engendered a greater sense of solidarity among bourgeois New Yorkers.

The jelling of a common position, in turn, enabled bourgeois New Yorkers to appeal to the state to intervene in the relationship between labor and capital. While they had political disagreements among one another and embraced different political parties, they widely agreed that the state must protect their vision of property rights. (For a discussion on their relationship to the state, the courts, and parties, see also Chapter 10). Once they had effectively narrowed the legitimate sphere of unions and strikes, and reified the laws of the market into laws of nature, it was consistent to call upon the state to step in against workers' collective action. The "state of lawlessness," which workers had presumably created, required a response by the government.[115] Clearly spelling out this demand, *Iron Age* asked in 1886 for legislation "to suppress violence and protect life and property, and to restrain within proper bounds the exercise of the power acquired by the working classes through organizations."[116] In 1894, on the occasion of the Pullman strike by the American Railway Union, the journal again requested "some effective remedial measure" to undercut the power of unions.[117] Merchants concurred, accusing "the authorities" of a "strange timidity."[118] These demands for swifter governmental response to workers' collective action increased in frequency during the 1880s and 1890s. Especially after the 1892 Homestead strike, employers called upon the state to defend their property rights. The *Manufacturer and Builder* asked for a "policy of stern repression and exemplary punishment. . . . If the existing machinery of the law is inadequate effectually to cope with and check at its fountain head this rising flood of disorder and crime, then other and more efficient machinery must be invented."[119]

The "authorities," altogether heeded these demands, especially the courts, whose "work," according to the *Commercial and Financial Chronicle,* had "the elements of permanence and of growth."[120] Industrialists, William Steinway among them, successfully sought court injunctions against their workers, a "very natural and commendable procedure" in the eyes of *Iron Age.*[121] Bourgeois New Yorkers also came to laud the use of the National Guard in the suppression of strikes.[122] Additionally, they claimed the right to use private police forces against striking workers. Between 1869 and 1892, groups of Pinkerton watchmen operated on the side of employers in 77 strikes.[123] In addition, Pinkerton detectives spied regularly on unions and workers, helping employers to undercut the power of unions, all under the banner of protecting "property."[124]

Considering the importance of the state in limiting the power of their workers, employers naturally wondered how dependably a democratically legitimized state would intervene on the side of capital. Although organized expressions of antidemocratic thought had peaked in the 1870s in the effort to reintroduce property qualifications in municipal elections, concerns about democracy remained on the agenda of bourgeois New Yorkers. The Republican Club of the City of New York, for example, called upon its members "to guard and defend the purity of the ballot box" and questioned if this was best to be done by "an educational or by a property qualification, or by a residence of twenty-one years to obtain the right to the elective franchise."[125] William E. Dodge expressed a similar anxiety when he argued that "we are still to test the problem of our republican form of government with a nation of one hundred millions, extending from ocean to ocean," many of whom were recent immigrants with their "peculiar habits and customs of their native lands." A situation such as this, he claimed, leads "the Christian patriot to fear."[126] The *Commercial and*

Financial Chronicle, in a more practical manner, suggested limiting presidential campaigns to once every six years, as the resulting stability would make politics "more responsive to the needs of commerce."[127]

While suspicion about the ability of a democratic state to protect the interests of the owners of capital remained, it did not lead to an organized effort to limit the franchise. E. L. Godkin, after two decades of struggle against municipal democracy, noted resignedly in 1890 that "universal suffrage has . . . 'come to stay,' and is so firmly lodged in the political arrangements of most civilized nations, that it is a mere waste of time to declaim against it."[128]

In an ironic twist, in their embrace of laissez-faire ideology, bourgeois New Yorkers called upon the state to enforce the laws of the market. Their own power depended on an institution that they saw at other times as an unnatural intervention into economic laws. In a further twist, while bourgeois New Yorkers called upon the state to defend their interests, they were hostile to efforts by the state to support those of workers. When Grover Cleveland mentioned the possibility of a federal arbitration board in April 1886, *Iron Age* feared that the federal government would get involved in labor relations, in effect recognizing "labor as an independent class."[129] Similarly, after the electoral successes of the Farmers' Alliance, New York's economic elite observed with great relief the Supreme Court decision that state regulations on railroads in regard to rates were subject to review by the Supreme Court, thus limiting the power of states.[130] Bourgeois New Yorkers saw laws "to protect labor" as outright dangerous, because they thought that it was "a bad symptom . . . when any class comes forward with a confession of inability to protect itself, and asks the State to undertake the duty."[131] The government, however, upon the urging of bourgeois New Yorkers, undertook faithfully the defense of a particular interpretation of property rights.

≈ ≈ ≈

The need to call upon the state, however, was not the only tension in the upper class's ideology. As significant were their efforts at organizing employers' associations, which again violated the "iron law of the market." It was in these efforts to organize that their greater awareness of class gained another expression. Typically, when the National Association of Builders constituted itself in 1887, the delegates rejected the proposal of one of their own to change the name of the association to "National Association of Building Trades," arguing that only the term "builder" would clearly identify them as employers.[132] No one was to confuse them with the old-fashioned trade organizations that had included workers among their members.

In the late 1870s and early 1880s, employers' associations sprang up in most New York industries, and such industry journals as the *Oil and Paint Manufacturer* did not tire of calling for further efforts at organizing. This was the age of organization, and a prominent New York lawyer, John Bleecker Miller, expressed the spirit of the age when he called for the association of "men with common material interests" in the "Business, Trade, Professional and Property-Owners Associations of the City of New York."[133] This was a stunning departure from earlier times, as before the 1870s, most New York manufacturers had remained unorganized. By the eighties, however, all important industries, such as printing, metal, construction, furniture, and apparel, counted an employers' association, as did the carriage makers, the chandelier manufacturers, and brewers.[134] There was the United States Bottlers' Protective Association (including the Bottlers' Protective Association of New York and Vicinity), the Boss Piano Makers of New York, the Hat and Cap Manufacturers' Association of New York, the Manufacturing Furriers' Exchange of New York, the Iron League of New York, the Shoe Manufacturers of the United States, the Iron Founders' Association, the National Association of Stove Manufacturers, and the Real Estate Owners and Builders' Association.[135] The "employing printers" got together in 1887 and formed the United Typothetae of New York.[136] Hardware manufacturers and dealers organized in the Hardware Club of New York "in the name of a common business interest," and by 1894, its 585 members could even sport their own clubhouse.[137] The "temper of employers" had changed, one historian has noted aptly.[138]

The genealogy of manufacturers' organizations followed a rather uniform trajectory: First, employers organized in the narrow segments of their specific industries on a local or regional basis. Then, they broadened their organizations to a national scope, such as among builders, manufacturers of furniture, carriages, stoves, sheet iron, steel, and boilers. In a next step, organizations joined together several smaller trade organizations under a large umbrella organization, such as the Building Trades Employers' Association of the City of New York, which brought together thirty-two trade organizations upon its founding in 1903.[139] Eventually, some of them formed even more inclusive national organizations, such as the National Metal Trades Association and the Manufacturers' Association of Kings and Queens Counties, to represent "the great industrial interests of a locality."[140] In January 1895, the level of organization increased even further when 583 manufacturers from throughout the United States met to organize the National Association of Manufacturers (NAM).

Not only did most industries sport one or more employers' association, but the degree of organization also seems to have been quite high. In 1887, for example, 29 percent of all brewers in the United States were members of the United States Brewers' Association, producing 81 percent of all beer output in the United States.[141]

One important motive driving industrialists toward combination was their effort to deal with the cutthroat competition brought on by the deflationary crisis of the 1870s and 1880s. The National Stove Association, for example, was mostly obsessed with limiting "needless competition."[142] In similar ways, the *National Bottlers' Gazette* advocated a "union of business interests for self-protection," arguing that "it is an absolute necessity that any considerable trade be banded . . . into a common and effective solidarity."[143] Solidarity to maintain prices, however, was difficult to sustain and often broke down.[144] Efforts at combination to raise prices were extremely vulnerable to pressures from outsiders and from those members who abandoned the organization, the latter of which some associations tried to counter by forcing members to forfeit a bond in case they violated collective agreements.[145] Altogether, efforts to set prices more than temporarily were not successful, the centrifugal forces of competition proving too great to effect permanent organization.[146]

What really drove these associations into action, therefore, were confrontations with labor.[147] "Organization on the part of employers is rendered compulsory, because of organization on the part of employes [sic]," asserted the National Founders' Association.[148] The *Manufacturer and Builder*, a monthly journal published out of New York, agreed, arguing that "the only practical way of countermining the secret plottings of such irresponsible bands of brigands as the Knights, is by counter-organization on the part of employers, for mutual support and effective opposition."[149] According to the National Association of Manufacturers, "it was time that the manufacturing interests of this country should be organized and consolidated. Labor was already united. . . . Capital was disorganized, had no coherent force, had no definite, united policy to interpose against the aggressions that might be made upon its interests."[150] Effective resistance against the Knights would only be possible if employers united, a goal *Iron Age* believed to be within reach because "nothing so quickly quells civil strife and unifies a people as a common danger."[151] In some sense, the desires of employers to defend themselves against competition and to keep workers at bay were related because both were made that much more urgent by the crisis of profitability that derived from the deflationary pressures of the last decades of the nineteenth century. But it was workers in particular who "crystallized the combative sentiment of the manufacturers."[152]

And, indeed, the "common danger" did unite employers. The Boss Piano Makers of New York, the Hat and Cap Manufacturers' Association of New York, and the Manufacturing Furriers' Exchange of New York, among others, germinated directly out of strikes.[153] Even organizations that did not grow directly out of a specific strike saw among their most important tasks the unification of employers against union demands.[154] The National Association of Stove Manufacturers spent its 1882 meeting discussing "how to circumvent, encompass and suppress" labor organizations, and in June 1886, in response to the growing strength of the Knights, organized the Stove Founders' National Defense Association for the purpose of "the unification of its members for protection and defense against unjust, unlawful and unwarranted demands of labor," partly by collectively supporting those members who were hit by strikes.[155] In a similar fashion, the American Iron and Steel Association, supported by the editors of *Iron Age,* urged other associations in the iron and steel industry to close ranks with them so "[t]hey could then advance in solid column, with an unbroken front, without the fear of danger from external opposing force."[156] Indeed, *Iron Age* favored a National Federation of Employers for mutual protection against trade unions, hoping that such an organization would help to "root out" the "trade union evil."[157]

Although such plans came to naught, employers' associations involved themselves frequently in labor conflicts. The carriage makers, Furniture Manufacturers' Association, the Bowery merchants, and others coordinated their actions during the 1886 strikes, as did the Iron League of New York, which was engaged in a bitter strike with 15,000 construction workers in the summer of 1892.[158] Similarly, the national organization of employing printers, the United Typothetae of America, sought collective responses to labor demands, not least in order to preserve a level playing field for all companies.[159] Quite typical was the response of piano manufacturers. If workers of one of the member firms of the Piano Manufacturers' Association struck, the organization helped employers react collectively (albeit, at times, solidarity broke down).[160] During the 1880 strike, for example, the piano manufacturers resolved that "every piano manufacturer in the city of New York should inform his workers that, if the workers of Steinway & Sons will not return to work on Saturday March 13, 1880, the factory owners will close all factories next Monday."[161] William Steinway's efforts to strengthen his Boss Piano Makers of New York now paid off.

The capacity of New York's industrialists to organize was extraordinary. One historian, aptly, has termed it the "organized revolt" of employers.[162] This capacity to organize, along with a government that was unusually hostile to trade unions, explains to a significant degree the defeat of the powerful movement of the Knights of Labor in 1886, a defeat that arguably set the conditions for the unusually weak and exclusive style of American trade unions in the decades to come.[163] Employers' capacity to act collectively, together with their access to private and public repressive bodies, proved sufficient to weaken the labor movement in a fundamental way. It was a capacity, however, that they only enjoyed because of the state's support. It was, hence, ultimately the access to state power that helped secure and expand bourgeois power in civil society.

10

The Power of Capital
and the Problem of Legitimacy

On December 15, 1880, the gates of the new armory of the 7th New York Regiment swung open. After years of fund-raising, the armory of New York's elite regiment had finally been finished. To mark the occasion, "fashionable and distinguished" guests ventured to the sparkling new building on Manhattan's Upper East Side to join in the festivities of the New Armory Inauguration Ball. They ate and danced till late at night, examining "with deep interest the elaborate furniture, . . . the prizes in silver and bronze won by the company in various contests, and the splendid trophies of armor and arms, ancient and modern." Dinner, as always, was served by the caterer of choice – Delmonico's.[1]

This sunny December day was the culmination of an eight-year struggle by upper-class New Yorkers to give a new home to the 7th Regiment. As early as 1873, the "tax payers and business men" had disseminated a petition in elite circles for the construction of a new armory.[2] In the circular they had urged the city to pay for the construction, yet when adequate funds were not forthcoming, the regiment and its supporters, undeterred, appealed to "the active and veteran members of the Regiment," and to "the liberal citizens, business men, and tax-payers of the city of New York" to support the endeavor out of their own purses.[3] The response was overwhelming: Merchant Royal Phelps sent in a check for $500 the very same day he received the appeal, and by May 1, 1875, $80,000 had come in from such illustrious bourgeois New Yorkers as the Astors, Browns, Dodges, Singers, and Vanderbilts.[4] The efforts received another boost in 1877, when William W. Astor took over the leadership of the New Armory Fund, raising sufficient funds to begin construction in October of that year, hardly three months after the uprising of railroad workers that had so concerned the city's economic elite.[5] Euphemistically, Secretary of State William Evarts expressed at this occasion his hope that the regiment would help see that "the war between capital and labor . . . may be kept within the bounds of peace."[6] Two years later, President Rutherford B. Hayes opened a fair on the grounds of the new armory to help raise funds.[7] A ball at the Academy of Music the following year attracted "the best society of the city," and further lined the coffers of the regiment.[8]

The persistent efforts of bourgeois New Yorkers for a new armory eventually paid off, and in late 1880 the new structure sat on the corner of Lexington Avenue and 66th Street on the Upper East Side of Manhattan. The armory was unlike any the regiment had inhabited before. In contrast to armories built before the 1870s, the architecture of which did not clearly indicate their purpose and instead was often reminiscent of commercial buildings, the new structure was an enormous fort, sporting a "defensible structure" with walls "pierced with loop-holes for muskets."[9] Indeed, the new armory of New York's 7th Regiment was built, like so many others of the era, with major urban battles in mind, "so constructed as to be defensible from all points against mobs."[10]

Expectations of urban conflict had also dictated the location of the armory. The old armory of the 7th Regiment had been in close proximity to the working-class districts of downtown Manhattan, whereas the new one towered over the most exclusive of the city's homes around the upper reaches of Fifth Avenue. Relocation, members of the regiment argued, was essential, as they could not reach the old armory fast enough "when called upon to aid the city authorities in preserving the peace and good order of the city, and in protecting public and private property."[11] The *New York Times* grasped the need for the move best when it asserted that "a majority of the men live above Thirty-Fifth Street, and their rallying-point must be readily accessible in case of sudden calls."[12]

Convenience was important not solely at times of crisis but also during times of quiet, when the building served as an elaborate social club for its members, a venue for male social bonding under the banner of the martial arts. None other than Louis C. Tiffany had designed its decorations, furniture, and fixtures, and the building sported such militarily useless installations as "reception rooms," a library "done in old mahogany," and a colonel's room furnished with "polished French black walnut."[13] Although the armory was the place of assembly for the members of one of the military arms of the State of New York, in practical terms it found more frequent use as a place to "entertain," to engage in athletic practice, and to converse with fellow members about business and politics in much the same way as in the halls of the Union Club.[14]

So much did socializing dominate the regiment that instruction in the martial arts was a distinctly secondary concern, most of these gentlemanly soldiers training "only a few hours each year."[15] If they ventured outside the confines of the city on military practice, they stayed frequently in hotels, not in tents. The official historian of the regiment remarked with great honesty that "[t]here had certainly been too many general officers for the small number of troops, while the host of staff-officers of high rank, a majority of whom were destitute of any special military training or knowledge, and who received their appointments only from personal and social considerations, were an incubus, which depreciated the value of military commissions to those who earned and deserved them."[16]

Without doubt, then, the 7th Regiment was no ordinary regiment; it was the most elite of the state's fighting forces. Its members came almost exclusively from the city's upper class, some of whom had already marched in April 1861 to the defense of Washington, D.C.[17] In its day, the regiment was considered "one of the commands toward which the sons of good families in this town turn instinctively."[18] Indeed, the 1st Company of the 7th Regiment included among its ranks numerous brokers, lawyers, builders, and real estate speculators, as well as a dock builder, a furniture manufacturer, and an importer.[19] Bourgeois New Yorkers played such a dominant role in the "rich men's regiment" that it might be better characterized as an armed version of the Union Club than as an institution of the state.[20] It represented, in exaggerated form, the tight relationship between the state and the bourgeoisie, blurring the boundaries between the two.

Although the 7th Regiment was unusual for its elite social status, it was not the only regiment of the New York National Guard in Manhattan that fortified its armories and its links to the city's economic elite during the 1880s and 1890s. New armories went up also for the 9th and 71st Regiments.[21] Both of these regiments, though slightly less elite than the 7th, were also tightly linked to the city's upper class. Jay Gould's son Edwin was "inspector of rifle practice" of the 71st Regiment, a National Guard unit that sported among its "patronesses" the wives of Abram S. Hewitt, Seth Low, and J. P. Morgan.[22] When the 71st published its history, the book sported numerous ads from banks, as well as from Rockefeller's Standard Oil Company. Similarly, the published history of the 9th Regiment carried a plethora of advertisements from New York companies, with nearly every other page devoted to praising new pianos, carriages, or steamship lines.[23] The armory construction boom, such ads indicated, was of the bourgeoisie's making.

Insecure about the future and increasingly aware of the "danger" to their property engendered by rising inequality, upper-class New Yorkers saw new armories as a guarantee of their safety. Especially after the 1877 railroad strike they understood that at times, only military power could defeat workers' collective action. The *New York Times* made this point succinctly when it remarked in the wake of the 1892 Homestead strike that "in a State where vast manufacturing interests are liable to lead to disturbances of the sort now seen, the need of having a numerous and competent militia force to rely upon for the preservation of public order and the execution of the laws is obvious, and other communities may well take to heart the lesson taught by the present experience in Pennsylvania."[24] Indeed, so great was the reliance on the repressive capacities of the state that *Iron Age* expressed concern when Nebraska's People's Party advocated the abolition of militias.[25]

This dependence on force was a true departure, as only thirty years earlier, bourgeois New Yorkers had largely agreed with Henry Ward Beecher, that the United States did not rely upon its soldiers for safety but instead upon "[v]igorous, well-educated families . . . intelligent laboring man." These, Beecher had argued, are "our armories."[26] Now, however, prominent figures among New York's upper class, such as Theodore Roosevelt, suggested that the Populists be handled "as the Commune in Paris was suppressed, by taking ten or a dozen of their leaders out, standing them . . . against a wall and shooting them dead."[27] And preparing for battle went well beyond rhetoric: When the 71st Regiment's new armory opened in 1894, it featured a "Signal Corps," which, "in case of riot or insurrection in the city, should ordinary communication be cut off . . . would be able to communicate with either flag or torch with the Armories of the Seventh, Twelfth and Twenty-second Regiments and of the Eight Battalion."[28] Altogether, the armories stood as symbolic tombstones of the paternalism, optimism, and universalism that had flourished in earlier times.

Now that the federal and state governments had made their repressive power available to employers engaged in labor conflicts, the National Guard units housed in the new armories were decisively altering the balance of social power.[29] Nationwide, it has been estimated that the National Guard's approximately 100,000 soldiers were deployed more than 700 times between 1877 and 1903 (328 of these instances falling into the decade between 1886 and 1895 alone), with one-third of these mobilizations officially listed as "labor troubles."[30] Other historians have counted 150 deployments of state militias against striking workers between 1877 and 1900.[31] As America was "becoming a mighty armed camp, with enormous armories," military force played a major role in challenging the collective action of workers.[32] During the 1890s, American strikers were killed at a rate of 2 per 100,000 and injured at a rate of 140 per 100,000, contrasting with France's rate of no killings and only 3 injuries per

100,000.[33] Arrest rates diverged in a similarly dramatic fashion: It was ten times more likely that a striker would get arrested in Illinois than in France.[34] The cumulative results of such an embrace of violence were dramatic: As Richard Oestreicher has pointed out, "[a]t the beginning of the era has of mass production, the American labor movement was among the strongest in the world." By the 1920s, however, American unions had become considerably weaker than their counterparts abroad.[35]

While bourgeois New Yorkers, thanks to the national reach of their interests, benefited from National Guard mobilizations anywhere, close to home, several regiments of the New York National Guard were actively involved in the suppression of labor unrest. The 9th Regiment proudly saw as its duty "to hold in check, kill, if forced to . . . the disorderly people to be found in all large cities" and, indeed, internal policing against workers had become the principal function of the regiment.[36] Similarly, the 71st Regiment focused in the postwar decades on keeping striking workers in check, lavishly illustrating its history with pictures of the "Buffalo's Switchmen Strike" in 1892.[37] And even the elite 7th Regiment, despite its members' intense dislike of fighting, was called out onto the streets on at least two occasions, most dramatically, as we have seen, during the 1877 railroad strike.[38] In the winter of 1895, it again moved to help break the Brooklyn trolley workers strike. Though "[n]early all the militiamen complain that they are subjected to heavy business losses by the present strike" because of their time away from work, wrote the *New York Times* on the occasion, these bourgeois citizen soldiers helped the companies to persist against the strikers.[39]

The armory construction boom that swept Manhattan and the rest of the nation during the 1880s and 1890s, however, pointed not only to the increasing class awareness of bourgeois New Yorkers, but also to their enormous power over the institutions and policies of the state. After all, the National Guard was an institution of the state and the frequent use of military force against striking workers, as well as the ability to subvert the state's monopoly on violence by engaging private police forces such as the Pinkertons, was extraordinary. It pointed to a number of peculiarities of the American state and its relationship to the economic elite: By deploying the state's military, the guard units stood as symbols of the activist state in the age of laissez-faire. Moreover, the history of the 7th Regiment attests to the weak autonomy of the Gilded Age state, which essentially let one of its military arms become a class organization to be deployed in the narrow interests of its immediate members.

It was during the 1880s and 1890s that businessmen exerted unprecedented influence over the policies and institutions of the state, leading a French observer to remark in 1896 that in America, great capitalists "have more power than the czar of Russia."[40] Their power sprang from the absence of formidable elite competitors, as well as their agreement on the main outlines of the nation's political economy. After decades of struggle, and not always intentionally, bourgeois New Yorkers had helped to remove the once mighty southern slaveholders from the national political scene and, as political scientist Richard Bensel has remarked, strengthened the "colonial" character of the economic relationship between North and South.[41] Moreover, for the first time in three decades, no major political challenge faced the city's economic elite: Sectional crisis, Civil War, and Reconstruction – all of which had created significant conflicts and had made the city's merchants, industrialists, and bankers, to some degree, dependent on the mobilization of other social groups – had been safely left behind. Now, there was no elite opposition to the project of continental expansion on the basis of free labor and domestic industrialization. Altogether, the Chamber of Commerce made a reasonable assessment when it reported in 1880 that its influence "was never greater than it is now."[42]

The political strength of the city's upper class rested on three main pillars: First, the absence of powerful competing elites, namely an aristocracy, made its visions uncontested among Americans who controlled capital and social influence. The importance of this is illustrated by looking at France or Germany, both of which saw an emerging bourgeoisie whose power was more constrained due to the persistence of an aristocracy deeply rooted in state institutions.[43] Second, the comparatively small scale and scope of the American state left the structuring of social relations largely to civil society, and it was here that economic and social power gave upper-class New Yorkers their clearest advantage. The structure of the state also supported their political claims because one of the two strongest institutions of the American state – the courts – was ideologically close to the major concerns of the nation's bourgeoisie, in effect limiting the popular political power exerted via the other important institution of the American state – parties. Third, the political power of the city's economic elite rested on the absence of any substantial conflicts about the political economy of the United States among bourgeois New Yorkers, such as those that had characterized the Civil War years, giving them the political muscle to safeguard the parameters of this political economy while pursuing numerous specific and often competing demands on the state. Altogether, these structural and institutional characteristics, which in effect made the American state truly "exceptional," bestowed enormous power on the owners of capital.[44] And in all of this, New York and its upper class played a particularly exalted role because of the city's prominent position in the national hierarchy of cities.[45]

During the 1880s and 1890s, no other factor was more decisive for bourgeois political power than the absence of formidable competing elites in American national politics. This absence was partly the result of the particular development of the United States. Unlike in Europe, there was no aristocracy entrenched in the institutions of the state and, indeed, these institutions themselves were largely free from the historical baggage of feudalism.[46] Until 1865, however, southern slaveholders had formed a competing elite, an elite aligned with northern (mostly New York City) merchants and one that made distinctly different demands on the federal government than did the up-and-coming industrialists of the North. The clash between these two elites and the different political economies they embraced had come to its height during the Civil War, a clash that had ended in the decisive defeat of southern slaveholders and their allies.[47] While this conflict had effectively removed the one and only elite competitor to national political power, it had only been effected thanks to widespread popular mobilization – especially of workers and farmers in the North and of freedpeople in the South – all of whom were subsequently able to translate their importance in this struggle into political power. It was only after 1873, in the wake of the depression, that northern as well as southern elites had been able to reassert their authority and influence, and by the late 1870s, both had found a modus vivendi that brought them together under the banner of the defense of property rights. This was, as Barrington Moore has pointed out, "the classic conservative coalition," though one in which the national political agenda was decisively dominated by only one of the partners.[48]

If no deep split divided southern elites from those of the North, and the city's merchants from its manufacturers, there was even less of a divide between bourgeois New Yorkers and upper classes of other cities. Though disagreements about such issues as the regulation of railroads emerged, they were minor compared to the cleavages that had characterized the economic elites' divergent developmental visions during the age of the Civil War.[49]

Symbolic signs abounded that the deep divisions of antebellum times had been left behind, especially during the 1880s and 1890s, when reconciliation between the sections animated quite a few bourgeois New Yorkers. In 1881, for example, the elite 71st Regiment of the New York

National Guard ventured south, saluting fallen soldiers of the Confederacy in New Orleans in an expression of its desire to end sectional tensions.[50] Five years later, the New-England Society of the City of New York invited Atlanta journalist and "pacificator" Henry W. Grady to give a speech on the "New South," and the upper-class audience responded enthusiastically to his call for an end to sectional distrust.[51] And in 1895, on the occasion of "Manhattan Day" at the Atlanta Cotton States and International Exposition, a New York City delegation of bankers, industrialists, and merchants, among them the merchant James Talcott and the banker Levi P. Morton, both Republicans, celebrated at a banquet with the "leading citizens of Atlanta and their wives," extolling the benefits of ever growing economic relations between the cities.[52] Reconciliation was clearly the order of the day.[53]

Burying the conflicts that had given rise to the Civil War, northern economic elites and their junior partners in the South found common ground in their shared concern with property rights and the political power of lower-class citizens.[54] Unsurprisingly, when Jim Crow and disenfranchisement swept through the South, bourgeois New Yorkers cared little. Instead, they stressed the "nominal equality but . . . actual inferiority" of African Americans, a notion that went well with the belief in their own social or even racial superiority.[55] The southern elite thus gained a free hand in silencing expansive claims of citizenship rights, as well as demands for the redistribution of property.

The power of the former war enemy, however, remained strictly regional and subordinate to that of northern economic elites. The emergent "New South" was largely characterized by its total dependence on northern capital and expertise.[56] Northern capitalists accepted the regional political resurgence of southern elites, so long as southern elites could not effectively resist a political economy resting on a hard currency, high tariffs, and state support for internal improvements.[57] Though conflicts flared up, southern planters and industrialists could not muster sufficient political strength to challenge the northern bourgeoisie. In effect, the southern upper class's once-powerful divergent vision for the country's future had run out of steam.

The hampering of competing economic elites went hand in hand, by the late 1870s, with a coalescence of views on the broad outlines of the American political economy among bourgeois New Yorkers, giving them an enormous advantage in shaping the institutions and politics of the state. The sharp conflicts that had characterized the 1850s and 1860s had diminished. The city's upper class had overcome old frictions over free labor versus slave labor, and over the political economy of Atlantic trade versus domestic industrialization, replacing them with a broad and consistent commitment to the ideology and institutions of free labor and domestic industrial development, combined with a staunchly held belief in the primacy of property rights.[58] The industrialists' political economy of continental industrialization had triumphed, and even bankers, once closely aligned with merchants, now derived most of their profits by steering the domestic industrial economy.[59]

This coalescence, substantially rooted in the subsuming of merchant capital under industrial capital, was extraordinary and partly accounts for the absence of substantial disagreements in party politics during the 1880s.[60] Even reformers, who had some misgivings about the all-too-obvious moral shortcomings of certain businessmen, were reluctant to attack them, because they saw these robber barons as heroes of the capitalist marketplace and the defenders of property rights that they also held to be sacred.[61] The core of the newly solidified conceptions of the political economy of the United States was reified into laws of nature, though "laws" that were hardly legitimate in the eyes of many Americans.[62]

⌐ ⌐ ⌐

This weakening of divisions between different factions of the upper class, along with the absence of competing elites, both of which were substantial departures from prior decades, enabled bourgeois New Yorkers to shape the state in ways conducive to their interests and inclinations. Their particular political strength lay in their broad agreement in doing two things that at first glance seemed contradictory: on the one hand, to limit the scale and scope of the state so as to preserve their power in civil society; on the other hand, to mobilize the state against threats to what they considered to be the proper economic, social, and political order of the United States.[63] Ironically, therefore, those bourgeois New Yorkers who by inclination and temperament leaned toward a weak state became more dependent on it. Laissez-faire's defense rested on the state's might; laissez-faire itself became an ideological construct endowed with flexible meaning.

Throughout the 1870s, bourgeois New Yorkers had called for "less government" and, in many ways, they had been quite successful. Federal involvement in the South declined precipitously, forming the basis for the reassertion of the former slave-owning elite. In the North, the federal government did little to address the problems created by rising social inequality. It did not provide for the mediation of social conflict; no federal legislation was passed that would have extended or even defined the rights of workers and their unions.[64] Furthermore, by the mid-1880s, the Fourteenth Amendment to the Constitution was employed to safeguard the rights of employers against regulation. Locally, public relief remained unavailable to the poor outside of elite philanthropic organizations.[65] During the 1880s and 1890s, in effect, the scale and scope of the state had emerged in a configuration extremely beneficial for those with great power in civil society.

The particular character of the American state was conducive to such politics. The absence of feudal state traditions, the lack of a strong military contender on the North American continent, and the early industrialization of the United States had made for an American state that was exceptionally weak and fragmented. It was a state small in scale and scope, lacking the capacity as well as the desire to involve itself deeply in society. Moreover, the fragmentation of the state, most particularly the dispersal of authority on the different levels of government, and the limited number of state managers who could pursue their own state building projects, left the state a weak institution vis-à-vis those who dominated markets and civil society. The French, German and British states, in contrast, involved themselves to a much greater degree in the regulation of class relations (especially on the level of the central state) and were much less inclined to side only with employers in times of labor conflicts.[66] In western Europe, the strength of nonbourgeois elites in the institutions of the state left the state on the side of order, but not necessarily on the side of capital.[67]

In the United States, courts were the most important institution in the defense of the limited scale and scope of the state, an involvement, as we have seen in Chapter 9, that was broadly welcomed by the city's economic elite.[68] Courts, "the American surrogate for a more fully developed administrative apparatus," represented both the activist government (by formulating specific policies) and the principle of the state's retreat (by striking down laws and regulations).[69] They became so powerful because they self-consciously occupied a political space left open by a weak legislative branch and executive. One student of the courts has found that "common law judges proved vigorous and self-conscious policymakers, presiding over social and economic development for much of the nineteenth century."[70] And indeed, their power in regulating labor relations, for example, derived partly from the fact that the federal government remained quiet on these issues.[71] In the eyes of capital-owning New Yorkers, court-made policies had the great advantage of being removed from popular pressures. Moreover, it was in the courts that employers found strong allies in their efforts to define unfettered property rights as the central right of American citizenship.[72]

Courts intervened in social relations in a number of distinct ways. For one, they frequently invalidated legislation protecting workers' safety and health that local and state legislatures sympathetic to the concerns of labor had passed.[73] This fundamentally undermined the political influence of workers as it lodged policy-making authority in an institution removed from popular political pressures. Moreover, courts used injunctions (about 4,300 between 1880 and 1930) to curb the might of unions directly.[74] Altogether, courts fundamentally undermined the collective power of workers.[75]

These policy-making efforts of judges were set in an ideology validated by the Supreme Court, which saw "the protection of the rights of property holders against unwarranted invasion," as the central "credo . . . of the democratic state."[76] Towering over these efforts was Judge Stephen J. Field, who had argued influentially in the Slaughterhouse cases brought in front of the court in 1873 that the Fourteenth Amendment not only protected freedpeople but protected every American against "unreasonable regulation or molestation."[77] Field saw few, if any, public obligations of private property and defined its attendant rights as "rights which are the gift of the Creator, which the law does not confer, but only recognizes."[78]

Such thinking, dominating the court during the 1880s and 1890s, codified economic liberty as the highest value of the Republic, a notion that corresponded well with ideas of bourgeois New Yorkers, such as Andrew Carnegie, who insisted that "upon the sacredness of property civilization itself depends."[79] Furthermore, in 1886, the Supreme Court facilitated new organizational forms of business by transforming corporations into legal "persons," giving them the protection originally conceived for freedpeople. By 1895, the Supreme Court had expanded the power of the federal judiciary in effecting injunctions, limited the regulatory and taxing powers of Congress, embraced segregation, and forwarded a narrow interpretation of the Sherman Anti-Trust Act.[80] Altogether, the judiciary limited and expanded the scope of government simultaneously, actively formulating a response to the social conflicts of the age, while limiting the power of elected bodies. It legitimated and protected power exercised in civil society, giving upper-class New Yorkers a towering position in the American political landscape.

During the 1880s and 1890s, hence, courts bridged in an innovative way the contradictions between laissez-faire ideology and the sharpening social conflicts of the time. It was indeed these conflicts that forced bourgeois New Yorkers again and again to negotiate flexibly their approach toward the state, shying away from any ideological consistency. Loudly proclaiming the need for "less government," they simultaneously embraced greater state activism – ranging from the use of the military and policing power of the state to quell domestic dissent to the restriction of such fundamental rights as the freedom of movement, by successfully advocating the passage of antitramping legislation in New York State.[81] The city's economic elite's claims on the state meshed well with the developmental visions of state managers themselves who also believed in the need for "order."[82]

Although the conflict with labor made calls for the increasing activism of the state for the protection of private property compelling, another conflict, that with western and southern farmers, generated a broad political sentiment in exactly the opposite direction. In the eyes of the city's upper class, the core threat of the Populist Movement that swept through the South and West during the 1880s and 1890s was its demand to use monetary politics to ignite inflation in order to increase prices for agricultural commodities, while diminishing the value of debts held by farmers.[83] Organized in the Populist Movement, and by 1896 also supported by strong forces in the Democratic Party around William Jennings Bryan, these farmers hoped to reach their goals by monetizing silver. Indeed, monetary politics was a potentially powerful tool for regulating economic activity, and it was for this reason that bourgeois New Yorkers loudly and persistently voiced their opposition.[84]

Bourgeois New Yorkers of all political preferences and economic sectors were united in their opposition to the Populists' monetary politics, emphasizing that "[w]e must have a currency system which will not be threatened by every biennial election of a House of Representatives."[85] After all, in 1879 they had won the battle in favor of returning to the gold standard, and were quite content to leave the determination of money's value to markets in general and the Bank of England in particular, limiting the power of legislative intervention so susceptible to democratic popular influences.[86] Indeed, concerns about the Populists' monetary politics were so great that in 1896, when the Democratic Party adopted some of the Populists' demands, the Democratic elite of New York deserted their party to support Republican presidential candidate William McKinley.

Though in these conflicts with farmers and labor, upper-class New Yorkers presented laissez-faire as a cohesive ideology, it was at its roots a political matter, defending the interests of its protagonists. And these needs, as we have seen, were quite contradictory: On the one hand, only a strong state could guarantee property rights against challengers, while on the other hand, only a weak state would leave the prerogatives of capital in civil society largely untouched. It speaks to the tremendous political power of bourgeois New Yorkers that they successfully shaped policies forwarding both these goals.

≈ ≈ ≈

Upper-class power had another face, however, one that is more familiar and one that is at the center of classic accounts of Gilded Age politics: the power to effect numerous, very specific policies, the "spoils." These interests could be so specific that they were only to the benefit of one small industry or even just one firm, and they could be effected through numerous channels, including bribery. Because the institutions of the state enjoyed only limited autonomy, these specific claims on state power were extraordinarily successful. Power such as this, of course, generated substantial conflicts among the city's economic elite, conflicts that animated Gilded Age party politics. While these struggles often seemed to suggest that specific business interests were hostile to the state as such, the relationship between state and business is much better characterized as one in which numerous specific economic interests, rooted in specific firms or specific sectors of the economy, fought against one another over the formulation of state policies to advance their competitive position.[87]

To illustrate these conflicts, two examples should suffice: the debates on tariffs and those on railroad regulation. Probably most important here was the guiding theme of the politics of the 1880s and 1890s – the tariff.[88] Individual upper-class New Yorkers, but also organizations such as the American Protective Tariff League and the American Free Trade League, mobilized around this issue during the 1880s and 1890s to an extent unknown before.[89] Because tariffs affected different businessmen differently, the discussions on tariffs went into minute details, and tariff bills usually brought with them hundreds of amendments, favoring this or that specific industry or company.[90] The Wilson-Gorman tariff bill of 1894, for example, sported more than 600 amendments.

The relationship between economic interest and position on tariffs (which the Republican majority had increased to the highest levels ever) was straightforward: A steelmaker like Andrew Carnegie, a clothing merchant and manufacturer like James Talcott, a shipbuilder like John Roach, and a piano manufacturer like William Steinway were ardent protectionists, while many merchants (though by no means all) favored tariff reform, which mostly meant reduced tariff rates on either all or a number of specific goods they happened to be trading in.[91] The business press split along similar lines, with the merchants' *Commercial and Financial Chronicle* agitating for lower tariffs, while *Iron Age*, the journal of iron and steel manufacturers, unceasingly arguing for protectionism, seeing it as the guarantor of American industrialization and workers' well-being.[92] The debate on tariffs continued to be framed in reference to the fate of American workers, but it is safe to say that a tariff of $28 per ton of steel convinced steel manufacturers to support import duties for their own reasons.[93] But there were also numerous complications that cut across these tidy divides, as in the case of the carriage builders, who demanded higher tariffs on carriage imports and lower tariffs on the importation of materials necessary to build carriages.[94]

Even though tariff conflicts were noisy, the debate demonstrates that the boundaries of bourgeois conflict were quite narrow and seldom, if ever, left the confines of the political economy of domestic industrialization they all had come to share. The tariff agitation was not in general opposition to the policy of protectionism that had brought such rapid development of industry after the Civil War. As early as 1865, merchants had begun to retreat from their antebellum political economy of free trade, the Chamber of Commerce resolving that the "protection and encouragement which our manufactures needed and sought in vain before the war, the war has necessitated; and, henceforth, a high tariff may be regarded as the accepted policy of our country."[95] Not only did the merchants acknowledge their diminished power, but they themselves also began to embrace a trajectory of economic development that favored domestic industrial production over international trade.[96]

Though public debate on the tariff was frequently framed in terms of "protectionism versus free trade," the spectrum of tariff politics was much narrower. Tariff revenues were crucial for the maintenance of low taxation, and upper-class New Yorkers rarely disputed the need for some form of protection of American industry from foreign competitors. Indeed, even a tariff "for revenue only" would have been an effectively high protectionist barrier. Therefore, free traders, in contrast to the label that they gave themselves, did not expect to remove all trade barriers.[97] Even the New York Chamber of Commerce admitted in 1880 that it had "abandon[ed] hope of any radical change in the tariff system," and found that "a general tariff agitation is undesirable for the country."[98] Instead, they preferred stability, arguing that a "complete revision [of tariffs] is a work not lightly to be undertaken."[99] In such a world, the *Commercial and Financial Chronicle* editorialized, "there is no absolute free trade," and insisted that "[h]owever desirable a simple revenue tariff may be, it is quite generally believed to be unsuited to our present conditions."[100]

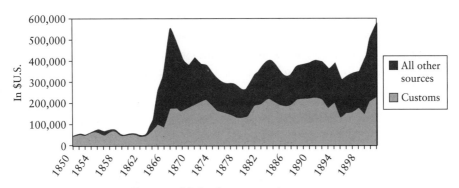

Sources of federal revenue, 1850–1900.
Source: United States Bureau of the Census, *Historical Statistics of the United States, Colonial Times to the Present* (New York: Basic Books, 1976), p. 1106.

Truly abandoning the system of protectionism and fully embracing laissez-faire capitalism was never at stake in these debates. What some merchants desired was a reform of the tariff, not free trade, which is why many of them focused their demands on the duty-free import of raw materials.[101] Although they appealed to manufacturers to join in the struggle for lower tariffs, they assured them that "it is not proposed by the conservative classes that industries which have been nurtured for years by fostering legislation, should be left to stand alone at once."[102] The industrialists' *Iron Age* returned the favor, arguing that both "[m]anufacturers and merchants all pray for stability" in the tariff.[103] Similarly, manufacturer John Roach, though demanding higher duties on the products of his industry, also saw that "some modifications [to tariff laws] . . . would be wholly reasonable," if only to end the "continued agitation."[104] Thus, conflicts over tariffs were less about a fundamental reorientation of American economic policy than about very specific benefits accruing to very specific interests to the exclusion of others. And it was framed by a generalized support of an industrial policy favoring domestic economic development.

The conflicts over tariffs pointed, on the one hand, to the enormous access of very specific "interests" to the political decision-making process, eventually producing a widely complicated, possibly irrational, system of tariff legislation, though one that was firmly based in the political economy of continental industrialization.[105] On the other hand, however, these conflicts demonstrated the inability of the American state to transcend in some fashion the multitudinous interests that created such a chaotic system in the first place. This, indeed, was the cornerstone of the critique by elite Mugwumps of the politics of Gilded Age America: Specific interests had captured small segments of policy making. And for them, as well as for others, tariff legislation was not the only case of an insufficiently developed autonomy of the state. The failure to regulate railroads effectively was another example, perhaps even the most blatant one, as American railroads remained locked in a largely unregulated environment at a time when some European countries had already put railroads under strict state supervision.[106]

Throughout the 1880s and 1890s, the central position of railroads in the economy, as well as their tendency toward monopoly, had created conflicts over rates and competition, thus encouraging numerous interest groups, from shippers to western farmers, from New York merchants to the railroads themselves, to pressure for regulation.[107] Some complained about exceedingly high charges by railroads, others about the roads' discrimination against New York City vis-à-vis other ports, and again others, such as J. Pierpont Morgan, tried to limit competition between different roads in which they had invested considerable sums.[108] Members of New York's Chamber of Commerce summarized these complaints by arguing that because of the "great importance" of railroads to "the industrial, commercial and real estate interests of the state, we cannot uphold a system of operating public highways . . . which is controlled absolutely by a few individuals who tax production and commerce at will, and who practically dictate what reward the producer, manufacturer and merchant shall receive for his labor."[109] The wholesale grocer Robert F. Austin agreed with such sentiments, complaining that "[o]ne cannot buy a piece of pie or a cup of coffee between New-York and Chicago without paying a profit to the railroad company."[110] Upper-class New Yorkers, in general, found that without federal regulation of railroads, their interests would not be well served, a belief strengthened even further by their desire to protect themselves from state regulation.[111] Though these calls contradicted their widely embraced laissez-faire liberalism ("the freer you allow things to be the better," said Jay Gould),[112] the city's economic elite saw no such contradiction, *Banker's Magazine* arguing that "[w]e are not aware that there is the slightest principle involved in the question; it is one purely of self-interest."[113]

In 1887, giving in to the myriad demands, Congress finally passed the Interstate Commerce Act, creating federal regulatory oversight of railroads.[114] The bill, however, was so weak and the opposition to it by the courts so virulent that it was virtually without teeth; Rhode Island Senator Nelson Aldrich characterized it as an "empty menace to great interests, made to answer the clamor of the ignorant and the unreasoning."[115] Its "supervision," claimed Attorney General Richard Olney, "is almost entirely nominal."[116] Railroad regulation, like tariff legislation, thus stumbled because it, according to political scientist Stephen Skowronek, "ventured into inconsistency and ambiguity by failing to choose among the interests."[117]

For upper-class New Yorkers, the combination of weak state autonomy and the broad agreement among themselves about the outline of the nation's political economy suggested particular ways to exert their influence. First and foremost, it allowed them to pursue their numerous interests through a densely knit network of personal relations. Such contacts secured them significant influence over Congress and the executive, leading a foreign visitor to comment that "the Senate of the Union . . . became not more than a few years ago a congress of millionaires; to-day, it is a gathering of thrifty business promoters."[118]

Numerous institutional connections facilitated this relationship: Bourgeois organizations, for example, counted many influential politicians among their members. The New-England Society in the City of New York in 1894 proudly proclaimed that one of its members had just been elected mayor of New York (William L. Strong) while another had been elected governor of New York State (Levi P. Morton).[119] Similarly, the elite Union Club counted among its members a president (Ulysses S. Grant), a secretary of state (William M. Evarts), an attorney general (Edwards Pierrepont), two secretaries of war (Robert T. Lincoln and Daniel S. Lamont), two secretaries of the navy (William C. Whitney and Benjamin F. Tracy), two senators (William Evarts and Edward O. Wolcott), an associate justice of the U.S. Supreme Court (Samuel Blatchford), two governors of New York State (Samuel Tilden and Levi P. Morton), and two mayors of the city (Edward Cooper and Abram S. Hewitt).[120] Some of these members were Democrats, others Republicans, but they all were part of the dense social networks of the city's bourgeoisie. Such institutional connections were further facilitated by contacts of a more immediately political nature: Banker August Belmont, for instance, nurtured a close relationship with Thomas F. Bayard, a member of the Senate Finance Committee, and Belmont's adult sons both became active in Democratic party politics, Perry Belmont joining the House as chairman of the Committee on Foreign Relations.[121] Of President James Garfield's six major cabinet officials, five enjoyed close links to railroads, as did the cabinet members of his successor, Chester Arthur.[122]

Consequently, businessmen and political leaders enjoyed a close and intimate relationship, often moving from one field of activity to the next without much of a break. When William R. Grace, for example, invested in the early eighties in a rubber plantation in the Brazilian Amazon region, he sought an appointment for a trusted friend to the consulship in Pará, Brazil, writing to Perry Belmont, the chair of the Committee on Foreign Relations, to suggest one of his employees, William Scott, for the post. Scott was made vice-consul.[123] Grace also proceeded with his own foreign policy in the region, selling arms to the Peruvian government in support of its conflict with Chile over Peru's nitrate-rich southernmost province, which was mined by Grace.[124] It was then that the political connections he had made while mayor of New York in the early 1880s paid off.[125]

Grace was certainly no exception and numerous similar stories could be told, for example, that of Democratic Party activist Samuel Barlow who employed his political connections to aid the Santo Domingo Improvement Company in acquiring huge tracts of land in the Dominican Republic.[126] Or that of Chauncey Depew, one of the big railroad men of the 1880s, who shifted comfortably throughout his life between the world of politics and the world of business. Active in Republican state politics since 1856 and a central figure during the Civil War years, he became an attorney for Vanderbilt's New York Central Railroad, rising through its ranks until he assumed its presidency in 1885. All the while, Depew continued to enjoy access to leading politicians of both parties, from Horace Greeley to General Grant, from Chester Arthur to Samuel Tilden.[127] But most promising was his relationship to Grover Cleveland. Years before Grover Cleveland won the presidency in 1884, Depew had offered him a position as a railroad councillor in Buffalo, New York, for $15,000 a year. Cleveland later repaid the offer by helping to break the railroad strike of 1894.[128] Cleveland himself, indeed, was closely tied to the city's bourgeoisie, and during his second administration, filled most important government posts with lawyers, especially railroad lawyers who often had sat on the boards of roads.[129] Not surprisingly, when Cleveland lost his reelection in 1888, he began working for the New York law firm of Bangs, Stetson, Tracy and MacVeagh, a move facilitated by Depew.[130] MacVeagh, after all, had been a personal friend of Depew's ever since their days at Yale in the 1850s.[131] While Depew, Barlow, and Grace had developed intense personal networks with people in office, others engaged in more questionable practices, such as when the American ambassador to London, Robert C. Schenk, promoted the sale of shares in a failing Utah mine to unsuspecting British investors, or when John D. Rockefeller bribed the Pennsylvania State legislature.[132]

Bourgeois New Yorkers who entered politics directly enjoyed even better access to governmental decision making. Though such involvement was untypical, there are a number of examples of bourgeois officeholders. Paper manufacturer George West was elected to Congress on the Republican ticket three times between 1880 and 1892.[133] Abram Hewitt joined the House of Representatives in 1874, where he stayed nearly continously until 1886. Banker Levi Parsons Morton ran for a seat in Congress in 1878 on the Republican ticket on a pro-specie and resumption platform for the elite eleventh district in New York City. As he was a dealer in government bonds, his restrictive monetary policies, his protectionism, and his ardent opposition to "free silver" brought him under attack as the "bondholders' representative."[134] Still, in 1888 he was elected vice president and in 1894 he became governor of the Empire State.[135]

In these close-knit networks of political and economic elites, lawyers played a particularly important role. As before, their parents tightly linked them to the city's upper class, whose increasingly numerous legal dealings they facilitated.[136] "The bar has usually been very powerful in America," observed the nineteenth-century British historian James Bryce, "not only as being the only class of educated men who are at once men of affairs and skilled speakers, but also because there has been no nobility or territorial aristocracy to overshadow it."[137] Joseph H. Choate symbolized this connection: He represented New York's wealthy in business conflicts and inheritance fights, was also a member of the Union League Club and the New-England Society, spoke at Harvard alumni meetings, and was invited to the Astors' famous Patriarchs' Dinners.[138] Lawyers such as Choate, in turn, were deeply involved in politics, the Association of the Bar of the City of New York proudly counting among its members "one president of the United States; one Governor of New York; two Lieutenant Governors; two United States Senators; 23 members of Congress; two Chief Justices and five associate judges of the Court of Appeals; twelve justices of the New York Supreme Court; three attorney-generals; one Secretary of the Navy; and one Postmaster General."[139]

Lawyers, of course, were particularly prominent in the nation's judiciary, and thus the nation's courts were deeply rooted in the concerns of the business community. Supreme Court Justice Stephen J. Field practiced law in New York City until 1848 and was friends with Leland Stanford and Collis P. Huntington, the California railroad magnates.[140] Other Supreme Court justices came from similar backgrounds. Samuel Blatchford had practiced law in New York City since 1854, enjoyed close family connections to the New York and Boston bourgeoisie, and, tellingly, died while summering at Newport, Rhode Island.[141] His colleague on the bench, Joseph P. Bradley, had been a counsel to railroads since the 1840s and had advanced to corporation director of the United Canal and Railway Company of New Jersey. Not surprisingly, Bradley saw the safeguarding of property rights as one of his most important tasks as a judge.[142] Morison R. Waite, who had been appointed chief justice in 1877, was a former Toledo railroad lawyer; Melville W. Fuller, appointed to the court in 1888, had as a lawyer represented Marshall Field, as well as the Chicago, Burlington and Quincy Railroad, among others; and both Stanley Matthews and David. J. Brewer had major corporate ties.[143] As a result of these links, lawyers frequently transmitted bourgeois political interests and beliefs into the institutions of the state and especially into the judiciary.

If lawyers linked the world of business to the world of politics like no other segment of the city's upper class, bourgeois New Yorkers further strengthened their considerable influence through party organizations. Parties, so central an institution of the American state, were private institutions supported in their work by private contributions. It was here that bourgeois New Yorkers had something to offer to politicians: money.[144] Electoral campaigns were expensive; Grover Cleveland's election campaign in 1884 alone cost the New York Democratic party an estimated $1 million dollars, of which Abram Hewitt single-handedly contributed $25,300.[145] Politicians leaned on the material support of the wealthy, many of whom were to be found in New York City.[146] Republican presidential candidate James A. Garfield, for example, during his 1880 campaign engaged the services of banker and fellow Republican Levi Parsons Morton as a fund-raiser, hoping that "our friends in the East will give all the help they can to make a fair fight."[147] This dependence of parties on the financial support of businesspeople had two effects: It made the parties less likely to be outspoken critics of bourgeois economic and political power, and more importantly, it created a nearly insurmountable barrier to the creation of competing political organizations that lacked such financial prowess.[148] As a result, bourgeois New Yorkers enjoyed enormous influence over both political parties, especially on the federal level, without turning either into a class organization.[149]

Agreeing on the fundamental outlines of the nation's political economy, and without having to face elite competitors, bourgeois New Yorkers related to the two major political parties with great flexibility.[150] They easily transcended party loyalties, probably more easily than at any other moment during the nineteenth century.[151] This flexibility explains to some extent why stasis characterized the politics of the 1880s. Now there were "no principles dividing parties," and, thus, "little to hold them together."[152] What drove them into competition, instead, were the spoils accessible to the governing party, especially the nomination of party loyalists to governmental jobs. By the 1880s, these spoils were as sharply contested as larger issues of political economy had been contested during the late 1850s.[153]

The striking similarity between both parties, as well as the broad agreement of bourgeois New Yorkers on the political economy of the United States, enabled them to support both parties throughout the 1880s and 1890s, though manufacturers were more likely to be Republicans, while New York's merchants became the northern power base of the Democratic Party.[154] Manufacturers knew that Republicans more reliably guaranteed high tariffs. But allegiance to the Democrats or Republicans was as often rooted in loyalties that had emerged in the conflicts of the Civil War era, loyalties that now guaranteed continued influence over the party and over policy making.

Twice during the last two decades of the century, however, bourgeois New Yorkers left prior party affiliations behind in national elections to support the candidate of "property" – in 1884 and again in 1896. In 1884, the Republicans had nominated as their presidential candidate James G. Blaine, whose unpredictability and questionable honesty drove many of the city's elite Republicans into the arms of Democrat Grover Cleveland. Cleveland and the Democratic Party embraced a clear pro-business platform, which was attractive to many bourgeois New Yorkers. Indeed, Cleveland himself was so attuned to the interests of capital-owning Americans that he has been characterized by historians as the "[b]usinessmen's President," and "a taxpayer's dream, the ideal bourgeois statesman for his time."[155] Upper-class Republicans, such as J. Pierpont Morgan, Chauncey Depew, James J. Hill, E. L. Godkin, George William Curtis, Henry Ward Beecher, and Horace B. Claflin, organized an "Independent Republican Committee" to support him, as did the New York Merchants' and Business Men's Association.[156] With the "solid backing of New York's biggest bankers and industrialists," Cleveland was elected the first Democratic president in thirty years.[157] So great was the support among bourgeois New Yorkers that Jay Gould allegedly congratulated Cleveland after the election with the words: "I feel . . . that the vast business interests of the country will be entirely safe in your hands."[158]

And, indeed, Cleveland turned out to be an articulate defender of the free market, seeing little reason to alter the scale and scope of the state.

He supported lower tariffs (but not free trade), signed the Interstate Commerce Act in 1887, worked toward a mild reform of the nation's civil service, and opposed free silver. A firm believer in states' rights, he encouraged a further retreat from the accomplishments of Reconstruction.[159] During his second term from 1893 to 1897, Cleveland also presided over one of the most violent episodes of labor conflict, in July of 1894 dispatching federal troops to break the strike of Pullman workers.[160] Nearly forty years later, Chauncey Depew, president of the New York Central, still remembered fondly that "Cleveland used the whole power of the federal government to keep free the transportation on the railways and to punish as the enemies of the whole people those who were trying to stop them. It was a lesson which has been of incalculable value ever since."[161]

Whereas in 1884 and 1892 many elite Republicans supported Democrat Cleveland, in 1896, many upper-class Democrats closed ranks behind Republican William McKinley. Fearful of the Populist-supported Democratic presidential candidate William Jennings Bryan, and sensing an acute crisis in the wake of a serious economic depression and widespread popular mobilization, bourgeois New Yorkers campaigned vigorously for McKinley.[162] The "merchants in the whole-sale dry goods district" held daily meetings, and "[m]any leading wealthy dry goods merchants have pledged their financial support to the backing of this movement," reported the *New York Times*.[163] McKinley organizations multiplied: There were, among others, the "Hat Trade McKinley and Hobart Sound Money and Sound Government League," the "Lawyers' Sound Money Campaign Club," and a "Real Estate Sound Money Club."[164] New York's Democratic Swallowtails jumped on the bandwagon, as did avid Democrats Abram Hewitt, Perry Belmont (the son of the former head of the Democratic National Committee, August Belmont), and William Steinway, who argued that "it would be foolish to deny that we are confronted with a crisis that threatens our very existence as a recognized great and honored Nation."[165] Indeed, support for McKinley was so widespread that it can be considered one of the few classwide mobilizations of bourgeois New Yorkers in national politics. And despite McKinley's victory, a bitter aftertaste remained since "Bryan got altogether more votes in the City of New-York than he ought to have received," not least because "appeals were made to workingmen on the score of their supposed grievances against the power of capital."[166]

The election of 1896, along with those of 1884 and 1892, however, also demonstrated that the relationship of the city's bourgeoisie to political parties in many ways paralleled their relationship to the state in general: Parties could serve them as instruments to effect very specific policy demands ("spoils"), often in conflict with one another. On the other hand, if any of the parties threatened to leave the widely embraced parameters of the nation's political economy, bourgeois New Yorkers closed ranks and supported the candidates of property, irrespective of their own party affiliation. In effect, political parties, especially on the national level, served as another institutional connection between economic and political elites, solidifying the power of the city's upper class over the institutions and politics of the state.

❧ ❧ ❧

Local politics turned out to be more complicated for bourgeois New Yorkers. In New York City, the dependence of political parties on elite support was waning, not least because these parties found access to resources outside of elite channels. Workers as well as lower-middle-class citizens mobilized politically, at times with great success. As a result, upper-class New Yorkers moved uneasily between, on the one side, continued efforts to influence party organizations and, on the other side, the creation of independent political movements that were class-based. Ironically, the creation of class-based political movement by the city's economic elite was a sign of their relative political weakness – and not their strength.

Throughout the 1870s and the first half of the 1880s, merchants, industrialists, bankers, and elite professionals had retained great influence in municipal affairs.[167] After defeating William Tweed in 1871, they clearly dominated both parties, and all mayors between 1872 and 1886 were of elite heritage: William F. Havemeyer was a sugar merchant, William H. Wickham traded in diamonds, Smith Ely dealt in leather, Edward Cooper manufactured iron goods, William R. Grace was a merchant as well as shipowner, and Abram Hewitt, an iron manufacturer.[168]

Though the alliance between the upper-class Swallowtail Democrats and Tammany Hall, resulting from the overthrow of Tweed, had disintegrated after 1878, bourgeois Democrats had regrouped first by taking control of another Democratic party faction, Irving Hall, and subsequently – in late 1880 – by forming the "County Democracy," a faction whose leadership included Abram Hewitt, William C. Whitney, Oswald Ottendorfer, Robert B. Roosevelt, Edward Cooper, William R. Grace, and E. Elley Anderson.[169] These Swallowtails, now organized in the County Democracy, were by far the most important political force in the city, not least because many elite Republicans supported their projects.[170] "These factions were as successful as Tammany in electing their candidates to the Board of Aldermen, the mayoralty, and to lesser city offices, and in gaining the recognition of the state party apparatus," finds a leading expert on local New York City politics.[171] In effect, Tammany's power to act, as historian David Hammack has remarked, depended on support from the Swallowtails.[172]

Although their influence on municipal affairs at times seemed threatened, often involved costly compromises with Tammany, and demanded great exertions and vigilance on their part (such as in 1871 and 1877), up until the mid-1880s bourgeois New Yorkers retained significant local political power thanks to their towering sway over some party organizations. After Henry George challenged the city's political arrangements in 1886, however, things were to change – albeit in ways neither upper-class New Yorkers frightened by a politically mobilized working class, nor New York workers, who challenged the entrenched party organizations, had anticipated. After 1886, local politics would never be the same again.

The results of the defeat of George's challenge to the power of New York's economic elite in local politics were twofold: First, the fiscal retreat, initiated in the early 1870s, continued. The political goals of the Swallowtails, and with them of most bourgeois New Yorkers – including lower taxes and the improvement of the city's infrastructure for commerce – were all, to some degree, implemented.[173] Projects that they considered to be nonessential, like Central Park, fell into neglect.[174] Municipally financed outdoor relief, similarly, was unavailable for the city's poorest and would remain so until the 1930s, instead replaced by what one advocate termed "the voluntary system."[175] And, notoriously, property remained assessed far under its market value[176]

Secondly, however, in the long term the defeat of George opened space for the political resurgence of Tammany. Because Hewitt, once mayor, ignored Tammany's patronage claims and turned against labor by removing peddlers and cartmen from the streets, the elite County Democracy lost much of its influence.[177] In 1888, as a result, Tammany was able to recapture the ethnic working-class votes that had propelled George's campaign, not least because such competing factions as Irving Hall and the County Democracy collapsed in 1887 and 1892 respectively.[178] The elite form of politics had finally come to an end, and the new political space was conclusively filled by the machine politicians of Tammany, whose policy of trade-offs with the immigrant working and lower middle class gave it a base of power that had eluded the elite challengers in the Democratic and Republican parties.[179]

The secret of Tammany's success was its ability to draw the immigrant vote away from the elite-led Democratic factions, as well as from George's movement, building a tightly run political organization able to

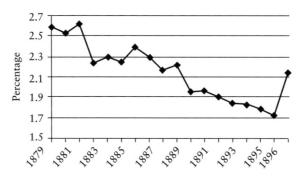

New York City tax rate, 1879–1896.
Source: Edward Dana Durand, *The Finances of New York City* (New York: The Macmillan Company, 1898), p. 373.

mobilize voters through a network of political clubs, newspapers, festivals, and social support.[180] With a large number of voters at Tammany's disposal, its endorsement became critical for aspiring politicians, and in turn Tammany could finance its operations by receiving financial support from officeholders elected with its backing.[181] As a result, Tammany dominated the Democratic Party after 1890.[182] Elite New Yorkers had lost their long-term dominant position in municipal politics – yet without surrendering it to a class-based political force.[183] Workers, in turn, had gained a political voice, albeit one they shared with a broad coalition of social forces. Thus George, while losing, had created the space for a municipal politics less dominated by elites, though scarcely one "radical" in its new tendencies.

It would be a mistake, however, to see this changing form of municipal politics as equivalent to a retreat of the city's upper class from local politics. Republican lawyer Joseph H. Choate objected in 1888 to what he called the widespread belief that "all the best men kept aloof from [politics]," and future historians would have done well to heed his wisdom.[184] Indeed, bourgeois New Yorkers did continue to engage in local politics.

For one, the well-to-do citizens of the metropolis succeeded in translating their market power over credits and public information, as well as their high degree of organization, into the ability to shape some elements of municipal politics, such as the consolidation of Greater New York and the construction of the city's subway system.[185] Incorporating Brooklyn and Queens into a "Greater New York" promised to allow for municipal planning that encompassed the metropolitan area as a whole, securing the position of the city in the nation's economy into the twentieth century. The idea for such drastic reorganization had germinated at the Chamber of Commerce, and though the precise structure of the new metropolitan area's government remained controversial among the upper class, elite New Yorkers decisively shaped its emergence. Indeed, a leading historian of consolidation has concluded that "[t]he poor, even the respectable workingmen and clerks . . . , had no direct voice in the matter."[186] The city's economic elite played a similar role in the building of a subway system that promised to overcome bottlenecks in the urban infrastructure.[187] Under the leadership of the Chamber of Commerce, they succeeded in wresting control over the construction of the subways from city government, creating a Rapid Transit Commission dominated by upper-class New Yorkers. (As one result, the first subway was built by none other than August Belmont, Jr.)[188]

Second, the dominance of Tammany Hall in local politics led to a resurgence of bourgeois collective mobilization outside the party system, in self-styled "reform movements." These reform organizations multiplied by the 1880s, among them the New York City Reform Club (founded in 1886), the City Club (active during the 1890s), the Citizens' Union Club, the New York Tax Reform Association, and a (new) Committee of Seventy (formed in September of 1894).[189] Through these organizations, upper-class New Yorkers, along with a select group of intellectuals, mobilized around a program of government efficiency, low taxes, and limitation of the role of parties in local politics. At the core of this project, however, was their effort to weaken the institutional underpinnings of political mobilizations independent of elite support. The machine stood as the symbol of this ability, and bourgeois New Yorkers set out with singular determination to undermine it. As Simon Sterne argued, "[t]he next revolt must be against this political class."[190]

Because resources were crucial to political mobilization and Tammany had managed to gain access to such means outside of upper-class channels, the reform movement worked to undermine this particular system of party financing. Local elections, just like statewide and national contests, were enormously expensive, and political machines had been able to gain access to money by "taxing" officeholders elected with their support. Now, bourgeois reformers wanted to take away this source of party funds, effectively making parties more dependent on elite resources.[191] Civil-service reform was central to this effort, as a professionalization of the civil-service system could undermine the patronage capacity of parties and thus their success in binding officeholders politically and financially to the party organization.[192] Upper-class New Yorkers, moreover, worked on bureaucratizing and professionalizing the police in order to isolate it from local politics and thus weaken the rule of political machines.[193]

Moreover, the city's economic elite, through the reform movement, aimed at structural changes in municipal government, centralizing power and limiting the influence of elected officials. The *motif* of taxpayers as the only legitimate rulers of the city, that they had so prominently embraced in the 1870s, remained high on their agenda, though proposals for suffrage restrictions had run out of steam.[194] Instead, upper-class activists wanted to break the hegemony of party organizations on municipal politics in order to create a "non-partisan city government."[195] To effect such an outcome, they successfully advocated structural changes in the organization of the municipal administration. As a result of their exertions, from the early 1880s, local political power was ever more concentrated in the hands of the mayor, as well as in the Board of Estimate and Apportionment, indeed so much so that according to a knowledgeable contemporary observer, "words can hardly express the ridicule which is heaped upon the mere shreds of governmental control which remain to [the common council], this once honorable and powerful body."[196] The Common Council once had been the part of city government most responsive to grassroots concerns at the neighborhood level, yet by 1884 it had even lost its erstwhile power to confirm the mayor's appointments, a step celebrated by the editor of *The Nation,* E. L. Godkin, who hoped that this would "reduce them [the aldermen] to insignificance."[197] Furthering this concentration of political power, by 1893, the mayor was nominating three of five members of the Board of Estimate and Apportionment, effectively taking the control of the city's finances out of the hands of its legislature.[198] At the end of the century, according to one historian, the council "did little more than grant permits for peanut stands and confirm the tax rate computed by the comptroller."[199]

When in 1894 another constitutional convention was convened, bourgeois New Yorkers took the initiative to further reform municipal government. The *Commercial and Financial Chronicle* clearly set out the agenda: Constitutional changes were to reduce the partisan character of local politics. This lofty goal, however, was largely a code for limiting the power of politicians elected independently of elite control.[200] And indeed, the new constitution did strengthen the civil service and, moreover, the state's militias.[201] It also reapportioned the state legislature, purposefully limiting the representation of New York City.[202] Although suffrage restrictions were once more on the table (various members of the committee on suffrage suggested educational qualifications), they came to naught, lacking the broad-based political support they had enjoyed in 1877.[203] Women's suffrage, on the other hand, emerged as a dominant theme (albeit without immediate effect). Even in this debate, however, some members of the committee suggested that suffrage should be limited to women who owned real estate, picking up on an important strand of thinking among elite suffrage activists, who increasingly justified their own claims to the vote as a way of increasing the influence of the "better classes," the New York Woman Suffrage Association, for example, hoping for a property-based suffrage in local elections.[204]

While some of the goals of upper-class reformers came to fruition, altogether they failed in their efforts to break Tammany.[205] Only once, in 1894, did a bipartisan campaign, led by reformers under the direction of the Committee of Seventy succeed in electing merchant William Strong to the position of mayor against a Tammany candidate.[206] Political machines remained firmly entrenched in New York City politics, a legacy of the failed class politics of 1886.

Consequently, by the 1890s, bourgeois New Yorkers were experiencing a fully articulated crisis in municipal politics. Having lost control over crucial political institutions, they were forced to resort to class mobilizations in order to advance their interests. While their persistent power in setting the boundaries of the nation's political economy limited the significance of this crisis, their local political challenges still pointed toward much deeper problems.

꘎ ꘎ ꘎

By the 1880s and 1890s, the political discourse of the city's economic elite was often characterized by anxiety, not triumphalism.[207] This was surprising, considering that bourgeois New Yorkers, as a result of their greater cohesion, the absence of major competing elites, and the specific structure of the state, had succeeded in shaping a political environment that was extraordinarily responsive to their interests and inclinations.[208] Despite the numerous challenges to their power, they enjoyed an unprecedented degree of control, as well as an unprecedented ability to accumulate ever-increasing amounts of capital.

Yet despite this new level of influence and wealth, pessimism seeped into upper-class discourse. As manufacturer John Roach put it, "there are few persons who know the excitement and the fear that exists among capitalists to-day."[209] Why? Why did "undercurrents of doubt and even despair" pervade this "age of confidence"?[210] The reason for what amounted at times to the outright pessimism of bourgeois New Yorkers at century's end had its roots in a paradox, namely the very extent of bourgeois power created a deep crisis for this power. From today's vantage point this is difficult to understand because the crisis did find a resolution. Yet looking forward from 1890, numerous instabilities appear, instabilities that cumulatively darkened the outlook of people who were at the height of their power.

At the root of bourgeois New Yorkers' problems was that already by the mid-1880s, the model of social relations of competitive capitalism – unregulated industries, a peculiar form of state intervention into the economy, and the enormous political power held by the holders of capital – had lost its viability. Economically, the structure of businesses and their relationships to one another resulted in relentless competitive pressures and a downward spiral of prices, accompanied by a decline in profitability.[214] Periodic depressions, with their devastating impact on many businesses and workers, further pointed toward the instability of existing arrangements, especially in 1893, when an unprecedented downturn hit the economy. Economic instabilities led to the deterioration of social relations, while this deterioration, in turn, further undermined economic stability. As the Chamber of Commerce remarked quite correctly, "labor troubles . . . checked . . . returning prosperity."[212] Although the political power of bourgeois New Yorkers gave them the ability to confront the labor movement, in particular via the courts and the National Guard, the persistent workplace struggles, especially with skilled workers, proved to be disruptive.[213] Moreover, these conflicts decreased the legitimacy of the lopsided distribution of wealth and power among many workers and even segments of the lower middle classes, which, in turn, led to political challenges.[214] Indeed, the new ideas upper-class New Yorkers embraced, ideas that validated large-scale capital accumulation, new forms of private property (such as the corporation), massive proletarianization, and a state essentially unresponsive to the social dislocations of industrialization, lacked legitimacy in the eyes of many Americans. While bourgeois economic and political power was tremendous, bourgeois hegemony proved to be elusive.

At the core of this crisis of legitimacy was the overwhelming power of bourgeois New Yorkers, as well as the particular structure of this power. As we have seen, the effects of proletarianization moved to the center of upper-class discourse during the 1880s and 1890s. The large and frequent strike waves and their militant and militarized character, along with the emergence of powerful political mobilizations outside of elite control, hinted at social and political instability. Movements ranging from Henry

George's mayoral campaign in 1886 to Tammany Hall to the electoral successes of the Farmers' Alliance in the early 1890s further challenged the enormous political power of the owners of capital.[215] At times, even small shopkeepers and artisans lent their support to striking workers, weakening the former economic and ideological proximity between them and large merchants, industrialists, and bankers.[216] Thus, the close coalition between bourgeois economic and state power eventually delegitimized both in the eyes of many Americans. "This is a government of the people, by the people and for the people no longer. It is a government of corporations, by corporations, and for corporations," stated John Hay, a state department official, summarizing this sentiment in the mid-1880s.[217]

Not only did the particular structure of the power of the city's economic elite create disruptive social conflicts whose outcomes were unpredictable and, therefore, generated significant anxiety over the future; it also limited the autonomy of the state and with it the ability of the government to find remedies to such economic and political upheavals. As we have seen, during the 1880s and 1890s, small government bureaucracies, dwarfed by huge business organizations, were accommodating to even the most particular interests of businesspeople.[218] Consequently, the American state of the 1880s and 1890s lacked the institutional capacity to act at a distance from society, a capacity that it had enjoyed to a substantial degree during the Civil War and Reconstruction and would enjoy again during the Progressive Era. As Stephen Skowronek has pointed out, this lack of autonomy was directly rooted in the structure of the nineteenth-century American state, a structure that increasingly became anachronistic in the world of modern capitalism.[219] The ability of upper-class New Yorkers to translate their numerous interests into governmental policies, in effect, damaged not only the political legitimacy of the state (thus creating the potential for political upheaval) but also the regulatory needs of an increasingly corporate economy.

Ironically, the great power enjoyed by bourgeois New Yorkers had helped create a state that eventually did not serve their interests very well.[220]

Epilogue

The broadening gap between bourgeois New Yorkers and other social groups, and the economic elite's ever-tightening relationship to the state, gave them an unprecedented hold over the American economy, society, and politics. Looking back from the 1890s to the antebellum decades, the accumulated power that came to reside in the hands of a few was indeed enormous. Single families controlled economic resources on a scale unimaginable for even the most successful merchants of the 1850s. Numerous and flamboyant social institutions knit tight networks among upper-class New Yorkers, and allowed them to display their prominence. A reformulated liberal legacy validated both large-scale capital accumulation and massive proletarianization. And the state was configured in a way that strongly privileged power emanating from civil society.

Enjoying this degree of prominence, power, and control was a departure for New York's merchants, industrialists, and bankers. In the 1850s, the economic elite had been socially, ideologically, and politically fragmented, articulating various universalist beliefs in free labor, in the absence of fundamental social conflicts, and asserting the duties of stewardship and responsibility for the community. By the 1880s, as this book has shown, upper-class New Yorkers found themselves in a tense, even antagonistic, relationship with workers and, increasingly, the lower middle class. Moreover, the ideological, social, and political projects of manufacturers on the one hand and the mercantile elite on the other hand, which had been so sharply divided in the 1850s and earlier, had merged into a common agenda, one centered on the matrix of domestic industrial development. The once small and relatively marginal group of manufacturers had carried this new political economy to the center of the discourse of the city's economic elite, effectively superseding the formerly dominant traders in agricultural commodities and imported manufactured goods.

All segments of the bourgeoisie now built common cultural and social institutions, institutions that upper-class New Yorkers defined as part of a conscious effort at stabilizing their own class. The ever-growing economic, social, and ideological distance from wage workers furthered this process. Since manufacturers and bankers, now dominant, experienced the conflict with workers much more directly than the antebellum merchants had, concerns about proletarianization took center stage, moving upper-class New Yorkers ever closer together under the banner of the defense of property rights, even as those rights became ever more abstract. By the 1890s, New York's economic elite had changed fundamentally, so much so that one observer found it to be the only class with a "politically effective or mobilizable class consciousness."[1]

Yet, as we have seen, the enormous economic, social, and political power of upper-class New Yorkers created in itself a crisis.[2] By the 1890s, the model of social relations of competitive capitalism – largely unregulated industries and the acquisition of enormous social power by the holders of capital – had come to an impasse.[3] This impasse was economic, ideological, and political.[4]

Economically, the structure of industry led to relentless competitive pressures and a downward spiral of prices, hurting profits.[5] Businessmen complained ever more vocally about "excessive" and "wasteful" competition, as well as overinvestment in industries as diverse as iron and steel, oil, and railroads.[6] A pattern of downturns shook the economy violently in frequent intervals during the 1870s, 1880s, and 1890s, creating high levels of uncertainty. Efforts to contain these upheavals, such as the forming of pools and trusts, often failed in the extremely competitive environment of the Gilded Age and, moreover, increasingly came under political and judicial attack. Shippers complained about monopolistic practices by railroads, while railroads chafed under a chaotic system of state regulations. Persistent workplace struggles, partly resulting from economic uncertainty, also proved to be disruptive.[7] When, during the depression of the mid-1890s, these economic instabilities came to a boil, calls for change became more insistent than ever before.

The nature of this crisis, however, was not only economic but also ideological and political:[8] Many workers, farmers, and segments of the lower middle classes refused to accept the legitimacy of an economic order in which an ever-larger percentage of Americans were unable to become economically "independent." The spreading dependence on wage work, according to them, threatened the very foundations of a republic of small producers. The unprecedented concentration of economic assets and the new organizational forms of property similarly lacked acceptance among people reared on a belief in the centrality of productive labor, and the importance of proprietorship to republican independence. Moreover, the frequency of economic downturns, along with their severe dislocations, unemployment, and plain misery, made an ever-larger number of Americans feel themselves to be victims of the whims of remote markets over which they lacked control. The economic order seemed to threaten their cherished, if partly imaginary, autonomy. As a result, the enormous economic and political power of bourgeois Americans, along with their refashioned liberal legacy, remained illegitimate in the eyes of many citizens.[9] Persistent and violent confrontations in the nation's factories, political challenges such as Henry George's mayoral campaign in New York, the continued embrace of republican and communitarian traditions as exemplified by the Knights of Labor, and, by the nineties, an unprecedented agrarian insurgency, all added up to a sense of instability for the city's economic elite. While upper-class New Yorkers' political influence gave them access to resources controlled by the state, as well as the means to confront the labor movement through repressive measures, such policies undermined even further the legitimacy of their power, along with that of the state, in the eyes of workers, farmers, and the urban lower middle classes.[10] Hegemony thus proved to be elusive. As the cultural authority of the northern bourgeoisie diminished, they reasserted their "power with rifles and bayonets."[11] It was, as T. Jackson Lears has argued, a "bourgeoisie under siege." Tellingly, the decadent costume ball that Cornelia and Bradley Martin had staged in 1897 led to such public outrage that the Martins decided to leave New York and resettle in Great Britain.[12]

By the 1890s, the Gilded Age state thus neither guaranteed legitimacy to this reformulated liberal legacy and this lopsided distribution of economic and political power, nor provided the conditions for accumulation preferred by many capitalists. This impasse effectively undermined the selective antistatist liberalism that most of the city's merchants, industrialists, and bankers had embraced for so long, and enabled the emergence of a recast bourgeois politics.[13] Trying to secure legitimacy as well as more favorable conditions for accumulation, bourgeois New Yorkers formulated new political preferences, preferences rooted in an awareness of the systemic nature of the crisis.[14] It was a reorientation that would reshape modern America.

This reorientation would eventually be particularly meaningful because it went hand in hand with the persistent reform pressures emanating from farmers, workers, and – most particularly – the urban lower middle classes. These groups exerted considerable pressure toward curbing the excesses of bourgeois power and demanding the regulation of industries, as well as the intervention of the state to ameliorate the social consequences of industrialization.[15] Indeed, these popular mobilizations had created the sense of crisis among bourgeois New Yorkers in the first place, by challenging the legitimacy of the new economic order.[16] The outcome of these diverse impulses was what historians have called "progressivism," a period in which relations between state and society would be significantly reshaped, a new foreign policy would emerge, and new ways of legitimizing a corporate economic order would evolve. This is not the place to review the complicated trajectory of progressivism, except to note that it was deeply rooted in the political and economic crisis of the Gilded Age, and with it, New York's economic elite.

Bourgeois New Yorkers and their counterparts in other cities retained enormous influence in shaping the precise outcomes of these turn-of-the-century reforms. They did so because they had forged social, cultural, and economic institutions that enabled them to act collectively. Perhaps even more importantly, the turmoil of the Gilded Age had encouraged them to clamor for reform themselves.[17] At first, only a few upper-class New Yorkers were aware of the depth and extent of the crisis. However, the most perceptive observers – Theodore Roosevelt and J. Pierpont Morgan prominent among them – saw in the 1880s that new approaches to politics and economic regulation would serve their interests well. They anticipated new ways in which the emerging economic order could be legitimated. Together with a group of national intellectuals, they supported far-reaching changes in the structure of the state, most importantly, by giving it greater administrative capacity, and a greater ability to regulate society at some distance from the manifold interests that pressured its institutions. Simon Sterne, for example, the rabid antisuffrage advocate of the 1860s and 1870s, while still pushing for his "minority representation" schemes in the last years of the century, also advocated that "[s]tate power . . . be better consolidated."[18] His concern about pervasive "private legislation" (legislation pushed through by particular private interests) now led him to cry out for greater protection of the institutions of the state from particularistic interests.[19] Other bourgeois reform initiatives articulated similar concerns.[20] The owners of the rapidly expanding corporations desired new and different policies from the state, demands hospitable to a greater expansion of bureaucracy and, hence, a greater regulatory capacity of the state.[21] They understood that unfettered markets, especially under the conditions of an increasing concentration of capital, resulted in economic and social conflicts that could only be addressed by the state itself. Making the point succinctly, *Banker's Magazine* editorialized in 1888 that "[e]xcessive competition is [one] of the reasons why profits are so small."[22] In a first step, the 1890 Sherman Antitrust Act and the 1889 New Jersey incorporation law securely established and legitimized the corporation as a form of business organization that would internalize markets and diminish competition, thus adding to economic stability. Furthered by this reorientation, by the time of World War I, the Hepburn Act had significantly strengthened the Interstate Commerce Commission, the Pure Food and Drug Act was protecting consumers and creating a level playing field for companies in the industry, and the Federal Reserve Act had established greater federal regulation of the banking industry.[23]

The Federal Reserve Act, indeed, illustrates well the dynamics of Progressive Era reforms. Demands for monetary reform had been at the core of the populist upheavals of the 1890s. They also had been high on the agenda of bourgeois Americans who were concerned that the regulatory deficiencies of the monetary system created economic instabilities, such as a deflationary environment, and with them, an unacceptable level of social conflict.[24] Although, as we have seen, the 1896 election once more drew bourgeois New Yorkers together in defense of the monetary status quo, in the two decades that followed, an increasing number of them sought change.

As historian James Livingston has demonstrated, the Federal Reserve Act resulted from an emerging awareness among many upper-class Americans that the monetary and banking system needed to be stabilized, as well as legitimated.[25] The Federal Reserve Act, largely penned by prominent bourgeois New Yorkers (notably the banker Paul Warburg), crafted an institution that could stabilize the banking system independent of the short-term interests of individual bankers, and at the same time insulate it from day-to-day politics.[26] And indeed, the Federal Reserve throughout the twentieth century played an important role in stabilizing the economy and, at the same time, decisively moved monetary politics out of the center of political discourse, where it had been for much of the nineteenth century. By taking up the political challenge of the Populists and others, and by focusing their attention on persuading Americans that their approach to the problems at hand was the only reasonable one, bourgeois Americans succeeded in forging a banking and monetary system that served their interests well, and allowed them to regain "cultural and ideological authority" in the eyes of farmers, the lower middle classes, and workers.[27]

Although pressures for reform came from many different social groups, as the example of the Federal Reserve Act shows, upper-class Americans retained a considerable degree of control over the final shape these reforms would take.[28] This was also the case concerning social reform. By the 1880s and 1890s, some upper-class New Yorkers foresaw an expanded role for the state in the regulation of social relations, pointing the way toward a less confrontational and more "progressive" resolution of social crises.[29] Indeed, some among the economic elite understood, according to Charles F. Phillips of the Delaware Trust Company of New York, that "the social problem cannot be divided from the economic."[30] Abram Hewitt called in 1888 for "legislation . . . to regulate the relations of employers and employees to each other," because "[a]t present we are all at sea," and Theodore Roosevelt, who had a distinguished record of hostility toward unions as well as workers, saw by 1884 that the "courts were not necessarily the best judge of what should be done to better social and individual conditions."[31] Andrew Carnegie agreed, expecting that "we shall have more and more occasion for the State to legislate on behalf of workers."[32] Even *The Nation,* no friend of labor, argued during an exceptional moment of faintheartedness that "the claims of labor must now be attended to."[33]

Change, indeed, did take place, though at a slow pace. Immediately after Henry George's narrow defeat in 1886, for example, a number of settlement houses in the city's poorer districts were set up by the college-educated daughters of wealthy bourgeois families. Inquiries into the status of tenements in the city led to changed building codes.[34] Eventually, progressive reforms of the early twentieth century, such as the Clayton Act, which specified the rights of trade unions, the passage of child labor laws, and the legal limitation of working hours for women, expanded this legacy. This kind of legislation, based on vigorous demands by workers, farmers, and middle-class reformers alike, expressed a new willingness to address some of the social effects of industrialization, while not substantially threatening the profitability of capital, or rearranging the distribution of social power in American society.

For upper-class New Yorkers, both political and social reform had very similar goals: to overcome the economic instabilities of the 1870s, 1880s, and 1890s and to create a legitimate form of bourgeois political and economic power, by mitigating the stark class polarization of New York City and the nation, while expanding the autonomy of the state, and enabling it to regulate a corporate economy. They were aided in this project by their sharpened sense of themselves as a class, and by the social and organizational ties that they had forged in the prior decades, which now enabled them to act collectively. While a "progressive" solution was not the necessary outcome of this crisis, it is true, as political scientist Stephen

Skowronek has argued, that "it is difficult to imagine how corporate capitalism could have thrived in America without an alteration of the preestablished institutional supports for American democracy."[35] At least in the beginning, however, this reform was to be the result of a crisis of political rule and economic regulation, not of a fundamental ideological reorientation of the city's upper class: Typically, when J. Bleecker Miller in 1887 called for reform, he argued that on the one hand, "no one can pretend that the condition of the working classes in our great cities is a satisfactory one," but added that on the other hand, "the rise and fall of individuals and races must continue."[36] Perhaps unbeknownst to its protagonists, Progressive Era reforms allowed bourgeois New Yorkers to preserve their power under radically new circumstances.

If reform and regulation were to strengthen the autonomy of the state, increase the legitimacy of bourgeois power, and limit social upheavals, a new orientation in foreign policy would support this political departure. Upper-class nationalism sharpened discernibly by the end of the century, most clearly articulated in the drive for the expansion of overseas markets. This reorientation, in the eyes of some business people, was intended to solve two problems: It would increase the legitimacy of the state and its elite (what some historians have termed the "reinvigoration" of the bourgeoisie), and it would point a way out of the serious economic depressions of the late nineteenth century.[37]

This was a subtle but powerful shift. While during the first half of the century, the city's merchants, in particular, had expressed their interest in gaining access to new markets and securing the routes of commerce, their free-trade internationalism had been averse toward military means of securing expansion.[38] Beginning in the 1880s, however, upper-class New Yorkers were increasingly confronted with a world divided into protectionist colonial blocs that limited access to foreign markets. And here it was mainly, though not exclusively, the world's industrialists who called for protectionism – not least in the United States. Simultaneously, the persistent depression of the 1870s, 1880s, and 1890s made some of these industrialists envision a way out of the crisis by gaining access to new markets, though not all of them thought of military acquisitions as the best way to secure them.

This departure, with some bourgeois New Yorkers now embracing market expansion through military means, was clearly reflected in their discourse. In earlier decades, for example, the business press was distinctly antimilitaristic, looking down upon the "appalling" arms races of European nations that "have neutralized the vast benefit to society arising from the past forty years of unparalleled material progress."[39] Such armaments "make the taxpayer shudder," they asserted.[40] The *Commercial and Financial Chronicle* saw "armaments . . . as Europe's curse," while *Scientific American* even understood the root of America's economic success to be in the absence of "the terrible war-burdens of Europe even in times of peace."[41]

By the 1880s, and especially during the 1890s, however, a more militarized foreign policy found its elite supporters: Abram Hewitt, quite typically, expected that "[o]ur relief . . . must come from the outside, and not the inside. It must come from securing foreign markets for our merchandise."[42] Unsurprisingly, Hewitt was an enthusiastic supporter of war with Spain.[43] Similarly, *Banker's Magazine* saw the securing of foreign markets as of "pressing importance," agreeing with the editors of the *Commercial and Financial Chronicle,* who looked upon Latin America as "our best prospective foreign markets for manufacturers."[44] Now, that "[t]he earth, is becoming in a sense somewhat crowded," the *Chronicle* expected even Africa to become an important market and supplier of raw materials for American industry.[45] Theodore Roosevelt, the future president, brought these attitudes to their most pointed formulation, by applying the social Darwinist lessons learned at home to international politics, appealing to the "global mission of the Anglo-American race."[46] Consequently, when the United States occupied Cuba, Puerto Rico, and the Philippines in 1898, the New York City Chamber of Commerce enthusiastically backed the move, with William E. Dodge Jr. arguing that the United States would have to be "part of the police of the world. . . ."[47]

Strengthened American military forces had laid the basis for the assertion of imperial power, with significant backing from the economic elite. Most prominently, during the 1880s, members of the New York City Chamber of Commerce, like Theodore Roosevelt, had demanded the reinforcement of the U.S. Navy. In 1880, the Chamber of Commerce was still limiting its interest in the military to an improvement of the defenses of the harbor of New York City, but by 1884, S. S. Cox of the Committee on Naval Affairs reasoned during the Chamber's annual banquet that the United States needed a large navy. For him, a strong navy and strong commerce were "the correlative of the other."[48] Indeed, so powerful was the call for increased military spending that in 1898 the Chamber of Commerce was celebrating its earlier support for a strengthened navy as one of the reasons for rapid success in the Spanish-American war.[49]

Commercial interests certainly strengthened such a reorientation. Some businessmen, like former mayor William R. Grace, easily translated their various interests in Latin American railroads, plantations, and mines into support for a more aggressive American foreign policy that would protect their claims throughout the hemisphere.[50] Other upper-class New Yorkers, most particularly the industrialists, also saw huge new markets emerging, if expenditures on armaments, especially the navy, were to increase. Consequently, by the 1880s and 1890s the pages of *Iron Age* and *Scientific American* were filled with discussions of new military technologies.[51] Though there was never agreement among bourgeois New Yorkers about foreign policy, and indeed quite a few businessmen remained opposed to military expansion overseas, the more virulent and at times aggressive nationalism some of them articulated represented a decisive departure.[52]

In 1896, however, the full unfolding of this important reorientation in foreign policy, as well as newly emerging preferences about the scale and scope of the state, still lay in the future. Solutions to the problems of legitimacy and of economic regulation could be anticipated, but their success, in the eyes of even the most forward-looking bourgeois New Yorker, was in no way assured. Still, out of the messy conflicts of the Progressive Era a different world did eventually arise, a world that has been called "corporate capitalism."[53]

The responses of bourgeois New Yorkers to the economic and social crisis of the end of the nineteenth century would, in effect, also remake the city's economic elite. Although the story of this change is beyond the scope of the present book, its broad outlines are clear. Proprietary capitalists merged their firms in a wave of consolidation: In the years between 1895 and 1904, 1,800 firms disappeared into newly formed corporations.[54] The economic and political impetus of the rising corporate capitalists brought them at first into conflict with the numerous proprietary capitalists, not only on issues of regulation but also on issues such as the nature of labor relations.[55] Eventually, however, proprietary capitalists, now in a clearly subordinate position, accepted the newly emerging order, just as the cultural preferences of those bourgeois New Yorkers who sought to reinvigorate their own class through their militaristic and "heroic defenses of property at home and imperialist crusades abroad" were assimilated into bourgeois culture more generally.[56] And economically, the beleaguered proprietary capitalists in time adjusted to the new corporate order, as their capital became socialized, its managerial jobs opened up to the sons of the old small-scale manufacturers, and many proprietary capitalists themselves joined the ranks of the new corporate order.[57] Corporate capitalism, in effect, helped consolidate, and eventually also legitimize, the power of an economic elite, who looked back on a long and distinguished history.

Thus, in a surprising twist, bourgeois New Yorkers mastered the crisis of the closing century and retained their enormous economic, social, and political power, even though its forms changed decisively.[58] The new economic and political arrangements gained legitimacy.[59] No competing elite arose. And, perhaps most importantly, alternative ways of thinking about labor, capital, and the state, which had been such a powerful force throughout the nineteenth century, crumbled in the ideologically reconfigured modern America, which legitimized not only bourgeois New Yorkers' exalted position but also their way of thinking about the new society.

To be sure, upper-class power continued to be challenged throughout the twentieth century – especially during the New Deal. But it was no small measure of the economic elite's emerging hegemony that discourses on the bourgeoisie as a social class became increasingly muted as the century went on, until in the post-World War II years even sharp-eyed historians came to see the bourgeoisie as part of a poorly-defined but all-encompassing middle-class. By then, nothing spoke more eloquently of the might of upper-class Americans than their ability to remove themselves from public discourse, and to make their vision of the world "common sense." It might have been just this ability of bourgeois Americans, to shape change and gain legitimacy, that eventually led the United States to take such a different road into the "Age of Extremes."[60]

～ ～ ～

Seven decades earlier, Alexis de Tocqueville had anticipated the possibility of such an outcome. Like few others, he had grasped the bourgeois nature of nineteenth-century United States society, including the possibility that the emancipatory and universal promises of such a society could narrow, once the wielders of capital accumulated fortunes, institutions, and positions of power.[61] It is an irony of American history that Tocqueville's basic insight often has been ignored. Tocqueville could see so much better because he knew another world – a world of courts and mutual obligations – a benefit that eludes those who live in a world in which bourgeois society and the bourgeoisie are ubiquitous, and seem natural.

This book, however, has shown that behind the camouflage of familiarity lurks the history of a social class that can be identified and observed in action, a class that had developed a distinctive sense of itself by the end of the nineteenth century, and that was able to mobilize on that basis. And though it has become fashionable of late to de-emphasize questions of social power in order to celebrate a whole range of presumably autonomous cultural worlds, crafted by diverse ethnic, social, and gender groups, a sustained look at the history of bourgeois New Yorkers shows that, for better or for worse, the dramatically uneven distribution of economic resources allowed this small group of Americans to exercise an expanding power over the way people lived and worked in the United States and beyond. Their access to capital, their ability to forge dense social networks, their influence on the state, and their capacity to formulate ideas explaining the world to themselves and others have stamped the lives of all Americans, independent of race, class, and gender, along with our natural and built environment. Indeed, the wielders of capital have played an extraordinarily important role in American society. And though they have been challenged on numerous occasions, they have mastered every crisis that has threatened their power or developmental vision, and have remained, to this day, at the pinnacle of United States society.

This power was exceptional, both in comparison to other United States cities and to the economic elites of other countries. As the nineteenth century went on, economic, social, and political power concentrated ever more in New York, decisively leaving behind the upper classes of such former powerhouses as Boston and Philadelphia. Chicago and, in the twentieth century, Los Angeles rose in importance, and their economic elites wielded considerable influence; yet, in one way or another, this influence remained subordinate to that of New York City, and their elites were subsumed into a national upper class dominated by the city on the Hudson. By 1945, New York even dethroned cities such as London, Paris, and Berlin to become the "capital of the world." It speaks to the enormous power of New York capitalists to have facilitated this ascendancy.

The nineteenth-century economic elite abroad looked with envy at the enormous power accumulated by New York City's bourgeoisie. With few exceptions (such as Switzerland), the European bourgeoisie by century's end still had to contend with an older aristocratic elite, who at times resisted (largely unsuccessfully) bourgeois advances in economics, social life, and politics. While they often denigrated the allegedly coarse and materialistic habits of their American counterparts (not least because the European bourgeoisie included among its ranks a much broader group of educational and cultural experts, bureaucrats, and professionals), they also admired the regulatory freedom, the political breathing space, and the sheer ability to reinvent ways of producing, marketing, and consuming goods that stood at the heart of American capitalism.

By late century, in short, the United States was the most bourgeois of all nineteenth-century societies.

No ideas of this kind crossed the minds of the hundreds of upper-class New Yorkers who had assembled in the fall of 1897 for Cornelia and Bradley Martin's costume ball. They celebrated the most bourgeois of all centuries, a century whose history, despite all its economic and social tensions, still allowed for unbounded optimism about the possibilities of modernity. They celebrated the ascendancy of the United States as a world economic power, as well as their prominent position within it. Indeed, so confident were these merchants, bankers, manufacturers, and professionals that they donned the costumes of the ruling elite of earlier times, of kings, counts, and warriors. By far the favorite historical figure to emulate was one who had not fared very well: Marie Antoinette.[62] Fully fifty women attending the ball dressed up as the queen whose life found a premature end on the guillotine. By symbolically appropriating the once-towering social position of the French aristocracy, they made clear that it was they who now were at the pinnacle of society. And Marie Antoinette's fate, they confidently believed, would not be theirs.

Notes

Introduction

1 *NYT,* 11 February 1897, p. 1.

2 *NYT,* 11 February 1897, p. 2. On Ruth Hoe see *NYT,* 14 October 1909, p. 2.

3 For a description of the event see Allen Churchill, *The Upper Crust: An Informal History of New York's Highest Society* (Englewood Cliffs, N.J.: Prentice-Hall, 1970), pp. 186–192.

4 *NYT,* 7 February 1897, p. 10.

5 *NYT,* 11 February 1897, p. 2.

6 *NYT,* 11 February 1897, p. 1. On the Bradley Martin ball in general see Robert Muccigrosso, "New York Has a Ball: The Bradley Martin Extravaganza," in *New York History* 75 (July 1994): 297–320.

7 *NYT,* 11 February 1897, p. 1.

8 See *NYT,* 4 February 1897, p. 11. For a more extensive discussion of this rationale see Muccigrosso, "New York Has a Ball," pp. 304–305. A lecturer at the "School of Social Economics" seconded Cornelia Bradley's notion, emphasizing that it is "[b]etter forty times [to] spend $300,000 on a ball than to distribute the money among the poor and thereby encourage pauperism."

9 *NYT,* 11 February 1897, p. 2. See also *NYT,* 9 February 1897, p. 3.

10 *Brooklyn Eagle,* 10 February 1897, p. 1.

11 "The fashionable world of thirty years ago," commented the *NYT,* was "decidedly more restricted than it is to-day." *NYT,* 7 February 1897, p. 10. See also *NYT,* 11 February 1897, p. 1.

12 Alexis de Tocqueville, *Democracy in America,* ed. Phillips Bradley (New York: Vintage Books, 1945), vol. 2, p. 111.

13 *NYT,* Sunday Magazine Supplement, 21 February 1897, p. 5.

14 The presence of old and new wealth is also noted by Muccigrosso, "New York Has a Ball," p. 309.

15 The power of capital to reshape nature and human relationships is effectively argued by William Cronon, *Nature's Metropolis: Chicago and the Great West* (New York: W. W. Norton, 1991).

16 Labor historians, such as Leon Fink, have pointed toward the importance of employers' tactics, power, and ideas in explaining the trajectory of the American labor movement, especially in the wake of the defeat of the Knights of Labor in 1886. See Leon Fink, "The New Labor History and the Powers of Historical Pessimism: Consensus, Hegemony, and the Case of the Knights of Labor," in *JAH* 75 (June 1988): 129.

17 M. Rainer Lepsius, "Zur Soziologie des Bürgertums und der Bürgerlichkeit," in Jürgen Kocka, ed., *Bürger und Bürgerlichkeit im 19. Jahrhundert* (Göttingen: Vandenhoeck & Ruprecht, 1987), p. 85.

18 On the bourgeois character of the United States, see Tocqueville, *Democracy in America*. For the importance of the absence of an aristocracy see also C. Wright Mills, *The Power Elite* (New York: Oxford University Press, 1956), p. 12.

19 Most historians of the Gilded Age agree that businesses and entrepreneurs deserve a central place. Charles A. Beard and Mary R. Beard, *The Rise of American Civilization*, vol. 2, *The Industrial Era* (New York: Macmillan, 1937), pp. 383–479; Richard Hofstadter, *The American Political Tradition and the Men Who Made It* (New York: A. A. Knopf, 1948), pp. 162–182; Robert Wiebe, *The Search for Order, 1877–1920* (New York: Hill and Wang, 1967), passim; Alan Trachtenberg, *The Incorporation of America: Culture and Society in the Gilded Age* (New York: Hill and Wang, 1982), passim.

20 The U.S. bourgeoisie also acquired a truly exceptional degree of power by the late nineteenth century, as it was unusually united, and did not know of elite competitors who could have challenged it in the economic, social, or political realm. A similar argument is made by Mills, *The Power Elite*, pp. 12–13.

21 "Cities," Charles Tilly has remarked, "offer privileged sites for study of the interaction between large social processes and the routines of social life." See Charles Tilly, "What Good Is Urban History?" (Center for Studies of Social Change, New School for Social Research, New York, 1990, Working Paper 99), p. 2.

22 For the central position of New York in the United States' hierarchy of cities see Cronon, *Nature's Metropolis*, p. 283.

23 New York's bourgeoisie, for example, had significant influence over Chicago's development. See Cronon, *Nature's Metropolis*, pp. 291–292.

24 The very centrality of the city, as well as its extraordinary diversity, of course, also made it in some ways "untypical." There is, however, no "typical" site, and New York's importance makes it the logical starting point for an inquiry into the nineteenth-century American bourgeoisie.

25 For the general point see Peter Gay, *The Bourgeois Experience*, 5 vols. (New York: Oxford University Press and Norton, 1984–1998); Eric Hobsbawm, *The Age of Capital, 1848–1875* (New York: Scribner, 1975); Jürgen Kocka, "Bürgertum und bürgerliche Gesellschaft im 19. Jahrhundert: Europäische Entwicklungen und deutsche Eigenarten," in Jürgen Kocka, ed., *Bürgertum im Neunzehnten Jahrhundert* (Munich: dtv, 1988), pp. 11–76.

26 This book, however, is not an argument for American exceptionalism. My aim is to situate the United States in the larger context of the emergence of bourgeois society and capitalism in the Western world. Such an approach also requires an emphasis on the particular historical trajectory of the United States bourgeoisie, which was, in particular ways, different from that of other countries.

27 By far the best account of the emergent economic, social, ideological, and political universe of the artisans-turned-manufacturers is Sean Wilentz, *Chants Democratic: New York City and the Rise of the American Working Class, 1788–1850* (New York: Oxford University Press, 1984), especially pp. 271–294. On the

world of merchants in eastern seaboard cities see Thomas M. Doerflinger, *A Vigorous Spirit of Enterprise: Merchants and Economic Development in Revolutionary Philadelphia* (Chapel Hill: University of North Carolina Press, 1986); Robert F. Dalzell, *Enterprising Elite: The Boston Associates and the World They Made* (Cambridge, Mass.: Harvard University Press, 1987); Robert Greenhalgh Albion, *The Rise of New York Port, 1815–1860* (New York: Charles Scribner's Sons, 1939); Bernard Bailyn, *The New England Merchants in the Seventeenth Century* (Cambridge, Mass.: Harvard University Press, 1955).

28 For the general point see Eric Foner, *Free Soil, Free Labor, Free Men: The Ideology of the Republican Party before the Civil War* (New York: Oxford University Press, 1970).

29 Some historians of the United States, however, do employ the term bourgeoisie in similar ways. The most prominent use of the term can be found in T. Jackson Lears, *No Place of Grace: Antimodernism and the Transformation of American Culture, 1880–1920* (Chicago: University of Chicago Press, 1994), especially p. xvi. See also David Scobey, "Anatomy of the Promenade: The Politics of Bourgeois Sociability in Nineteenth-Century New York," in *Social History* 17 (May 1992): 203–227.

30 For uses of the term "elites" see Frederic Cople Jaher, *The Urban Establishment: Upper Strata in Boston, New York, Charleston, Chicago and Los Angeles* (Urbana: University of Illinois Press, 1982). For a defense of such a profoundly ahistorical category see, for example, Edward Pessen, "The Social Configuration of the Antebellum City: An Historical and Theoretical Inquiry," in *Journal of Urban History* 2 (May 1976): 267–306. Elites, it is important to keep in mind, can base their claims to status on wealth, heritage, and education or even on the central roles they played in working-class organizations. For a sharp and useful distinction between upper class and elite see Richard Trainor, "Urban Elites in Victorian Britain," in *Urban History Yearbook 1983–1985* (1985): 1–2.

31 Even Ronald Story, who uses the term "aristocracy" in the title of his book, admits that the "United States has had no aristocracy." Ronald Story, *The Forging of an Aristocracy: Harvard & The Boston Upper Class, 1800–1870* (Middletown, Conn.: Wesleyan University Press, 1980), p. xiii.

32 For the use of the term "plutocracy" see, for example, Gabriel Almond, "Plutocracy and Politics in New York City" (Ph.D diss., University of Chicago, 1938).

33 Although this study is not concerned with the middle class, it is in the last sense that some historians of the nineteenth century, such as Stuart Blumin, Robert Johnston, and Mary Ryan, have begun to use the term successfully. See Stuart Blumin, *The Emergence of the Middle Class: Social Experience in the American City, 1760–1900* (New York: Cambridge University Press, 1989), pp. 8, 12; Robert Johnston, "Middle-Class Political Ideology in a Corporate Society: The Persistence of Small-Propertied Radicalism in Portland, Oregon, 1882–1923" (Ph.D. diss., Yale University, 1993); Mary P. Ryan, *Cradle of the Middle Class: The Family in Oneida County, New York, 1780–1865* (New York: Cambridge University Press, 1981).

34 For the terminological confusion that reigns supreme in studies on the bourgeoisie see, for example, the categories used in the titles of the following books:

Story, *The Forging of An Aristocracy;* Betty G. Farrell, *Elite Families: Class and Power in Nineteenth Century Boston* (Albany: State University of New York Press, 1993); E. Digby Baltzell, *Philadelphia Gentlemen: The Making of a National Upper Class* (Glencoe, Ill.: The Free Press, 1958); E. Digby Baltzell, *The Protestant Establishment: Aristocracy and Caste in America* (New York: Random House, 1964); John N. Ingham, *The Iron Barons: A Social Analysis of an American Urban Elite, 1874–1965* (Westport, Conn.: Greenwood Press, 1978); Almond, "Plutocracy and Politics in New York City"; Mills, *The Power Elite*, pp. 47–70; Nicola Kay Beisel, *Upper Class Formation and the Politics of Censorship in Boston, New York, and Philadelphia, 1872–1892* (Ph.D. diss., University of Michigan, 1990).

35 I borrowed these terms from David Blackbourn, "The German Bourgeoisie: An Introduction," in David Blackbourn and Richard J. Evans, eds., *The German Bourgeoisie: Essays on the Social History of the German Middle Class from the Late Eighteenth to the Early Twentieth Century* (London: Routledge, 1991), p. 7, and Theodore Koditschek, *Class Formation and Urban-Industrial Society: Bradford, 1750–1850* (New York: Cambridge University Press, 1990), p. 19.

36 This definition is also used by Eric Hobsbawm, "Die englische middle class, 1780–1920," in Kocka, ed., *Bürgertum im Neunzehnten Jahrhundert*, pp. 89–99. For a thoughtful definition of middle class that draws a clear distinction between middle class and bourgeoisie, see the *Encyclopedia of the Social Sciences*, vol. 10 (New York: The Macmillan Company, 1933), pp. 407–415. For a very similar definition of bourgeoisie see also Kocka, "Bürgertum und bürgerliche Gesellschaft im 19. Jahrhundert," p. 60. Such a definition works well with Max Weber's definition of class as shared market relations. In Weberian terms, the project this book engages in is to understand how, when, and why a class based on shared market interests turned into a status group. See also Edmond Goblot, *La Barrière et le Niveau* (Paris: Librairie Félix Alcan, 1925), p. 27.

37 For a discussion and definition of the lower middle class see Arno J. Mayer, "The Lower Middle Class As Historical Problem," in *Journal of Modern History* 47 (September 1975): 409–436.

38 The term "educational capital" is from Pierre Bourdieu, *Distinction: A Social Critique of the Judgment of Taste* (Cambridge, Mass.: Harvard University Press, 1984), pp. 12–14.

39 The openness of the bourgeoisie as one of its defining characteristics is also emphasized by Goblot, *La Barrière et le Niveau*, p. 1.

40 Here my argument follows Kocka, "Bürgertum und bürgerliche Gesellschaft im 19. Jahrhundert," p. 20. See also Albert Tanner, *Arbeitsame Patrioten, Wohlanständige Damen: Bürgertum und Bürgerlichkeit in der Schweiz, 1830–1914* (Zürich: Orell Fussli, 1995), pp. 16–17. Though Peter Gay looks at a much broader social stratum than I do, he also emphasizes the importance of culture and conflict in creating a "bourgeoisie." See especially Peter Gay, *The Naked Heart* (New York: Norton, 1995), p. 7, and Peter Gay, *Pleasure Wars* (New York: Norton, 1998), pp. 3–23.

41 Bourdieu, *Distinction*, p. 102. See also Kocka, ed., *Bürgertum im Neunzehnten Jahrhundert*.

42 The sense of class identity generated by the conflict with labor developed only later in the nineteenth century, setting New York's bourgeoisie apart from its European counterparts, who had already developed a sense of shared identity as a result of their conflict with the aristocracy earlier in the century. The importance of the conflict with workers to the development of collective identities is also emphasized by Philip Hills, "Division and Cohesion in the Nineteenth-Century Middle Class: The Case of Ipswich" (Ph.D. diss., University of Essex, 1988), p. 315.

On the relationship between interests and identities see Charles Tilly, "Citizenship, Identity, And Social History" (Center for Studies of Social Change, New School for Social Research, New York, 1994, Working Paper 205), especially pp. 3–4. On the formation of political identities see Charles Tilly, "Political Identities" (Center for Studies of Social Change, New School for Social Research, New York, 1995, Working Paper 212), especially pp. 4–6.

In this specific way, my approach is similar to the one embraced by E. P. Thompson, *The Making of the English Working Class* (London: V. Gollancz, 1963).

43 An argument also made by observers of the European bourgeoisie, such as Jürgen Kocka and David Blackbourn. See Kocka, "Bürgertum und bürgerliche Gesellschaft im 19. Jahrhundert," pp. 11–76; Blackbourn, "The German Bourgeoisie: An Introduction," passim. See also Goblot, *La Barrière et le Niveau*.

44 The importance of a shared culture to bourgeois citizens' sense of their collective self is emphasized by historians of the European bourgeoisie as well. See, among many others, Blackbourn, "The German Bourgeoisie: An Introduction," pp. 9–10. The case for the importance of culture to bourgeois class formation (in this case in regard to Great Britain) is also made powerfully by Janet Wolff and John Seed, eds., *The Culture of Capital: Art, Power and the Nineteenth-Century Middle Class* (Manchester: Manchester University Press, 1988), especially pp. 8–11, as well as by Jürgen Kocka.

45 On the importance of tastes and manners as markers of class, see the brilliant work by Bourdieu, *Distinction*, especially p. 2. See also Norbert Elias, *Über den Prozeß der Zivilisation: Soziogenetische und Pychogenetische Untersuchungen* (Frankfurt: Suhrkamp Verlag, 1976). On women's separate sphere see especially Nancy Cott, *The Bonds of Womanhood: "Woman's Sphere" in New England, 1780–1835* (New Haven: Yale University Press, 1977). On the emergence of bourgeois "high culture" see Lawrence Levine, *Highbrow/Lowbrow: The Emergence of Cultural Hierarchy in America* (Cambridge, Mass.: Harvard University Press, 1988).

46 Gabriel Almond emphasized in 1938 that a number of events mobilized bourgeois New Yorkers politically: "Three types of crisis are shown to have resulted in increased plutocratic political activity – political corruption, war, and lower class unrest." See Almond, "Plutocracy and Politics in New York City," p. 11.

47 For the general point, see Thompson, *The Making of the English Working Class,* pp. 8–11.

48 For a powerful teleological conception of history see Georg Wilhelm Friedrich

Hegel, *Reason in History: A General Introduction to the Philosophy of History* (1837; reprint Indianapolis: Bobbs-Merrill Company, 1953), passim, especially p. 48. Hegel would later inform Karl Marx's view of history, which put classes, including the bourgeoisie, at the center of the historical narrative. See, for example, Karl Marx, *Manifest der Kommunistischen Partei* (London: J. E. Burghard, 1848), passim, especially pp. 3–11.

49 Ryan, *Cradle of the Middle Class;* John S. Gilkeson, Jr., *Middle Class Providence, 1820–1940* (Princeton: Princeton University Press, 1986); Paul E. Johnson, *A Shopkeeper's Millennium: Society and Revivals in Rochester, New York, 1815–1837* (New York: Hill and Wang, 1978); Alexander Irwin Burckin, "The Formation and Growth of an Urban Middle Class: Power and Conflict in Louisville, Kentucky, 1828–1861" (Ph.D. diss., University of California, Irvine, 1993); David A. Gerber, *The Making of an American Pluralism: Buffalo, New York, 1825–1860* (Urbana: University of Illinois Press, 1989); Story, *The Forging of An Aristocracy;* Farrell, *Elite Families.* An exception to this focus on small cities, social life, and social networks is James Livingston's brilliant but short account of the United States bourgeoisie. See James Livingston, *Pragmatism and the Political Economy of Cultural Revolution, 1850–1940* (Chapel Hill: University of North Carolina Press, 1994), especially pp. 35–39. See also Christopher Lasch, "The Moral and Intellectual Rehabilitation of the Ruling Class," in Christopher Lasch, ed., *The World of Nations: Reflections on American History, Politics, and Culture* (New York: Knopf, 1973), and Lears, *No Place of Grace.* Read together, these three last-mentioned books provide the most intelligent view of the Gilded Age bourgeoisie.

Others have also noticed the striking absence of sustained discussions on the bourgeoisie. See, for example, a discussion on h-labor in 1996. The discussion can be found at http://www.h-net.msu.edu/logs/showlog.cgi?ent=0&file=h-labor.log9607d/36&list=h-labor.

50 For a different trajectory in twentieth-century Europe see Charles S. Maier, *Recasting Bourgeois Europe: Stabilization in France, Germany, and Italy in the Decade After World War I* (Princeton: Princeton University Press, 1975), pp. 6–21.

51 Wilentz, *Chants Democratic;* Christine Stansell, *City of Women: Sex and Class in New York, 1789–1860* (Urbana: University of Illinois Press, 1987); Elizabeth Blackmar, *Manhattan for Rent, 1785–1850* (Ithaca, N.Y.: Cornell University Press, 1989); Johnson, *A Shopkeeper's Millennium;* Pessen, *Riches, Class, and Power before the Civil War* (Lexington, Mass.: D. C. Heath, 1973); Alan Dawley, *Class and Community: The Industrial Revolution in Lynn* (Cambridge, Mass.: Harvard University Press, 1976).

52 The best of their works demonstrated the importance of examining class relations, the totality of different spheres (economics, culture, ideas, and politics), and the family, as well as politics and power. Beyond the works cited in note 51 see also Thompson, *The Making of the English Working Class;* Eric Hobsbawm, *Workers: World of Labor* (New York: Pantheon Books, 1984); Anthony C. Wallace, *Rockdale: The Growth of an American Village in the Early Industrial Revolution* (New York: Norton, 1972); Bruce Laurie, *Artisans Into Workers: Labor in Nineteenth-Century America* (New York: Hill and Wang, 1989); Gareth Stedman Jones, "Working-Class Culture and Working-

Class Politics in London, 1870–1900," in Gareth Stedman Jones, *Languages of Class: Studies in English Working-Class History, 1832–1932* (Cambridge: Cambridge University Press, 1983); Lizabeth Cohen, *Making a New Deal: Industrial Workers in Chicago, 1919–1939* (New York: Cambridge University Press, 1990); Dawley, *Class and Community;* Walter Rodney, *A History of the Guyanese Working People, 1881–1905* (Baltimore: Johns Hopkins University Press, 1981).

For historians paying attention to class relations see also Wilentz, *Chants Democratic;* David Montgomery, *The Fall of the House of Labor: The Workplace, the State, and American Labor Activism, 1865–1925* (New York: Cambridge University Press, 1987); and the essays in Michael H. Frisch and Daniel J. Walkowitz, eds., *Working-Class America: Essays on Labor, Community, and American Society* (Urbana: University of Illinois Press, 1983). For a good example of social history that is attentive to the bourgeoisie see Gutman, *Work, Culture and Society in Industrializing America: Essays in American Working-Class and Social History* (New York: Knopf, 1976), pp. 209–292.

Furthermore, historians of the middle class, especially Stuart M. Blumin and Mary Ryan, have pointed to the value of a close reading of class cultures, while numerous studies on women's history have illuminated bourgeois gender relations. Blumin, *The Emergence of the Middle Class;* Ryan, *Cradle of the Middle Class,* for example p. 15; Karen Halttunen, *Confidence Men and Painted Women: A Study of Middle-Class Culture in America, 1830–1870* (New Haven: Yale University Press, 1982); Lori D. Ginzberg, *Women and the Work of Benevolence: Morality, Politics, and Class in the 19th-Century United States* (New Haven: Yale University Press, 1990); Stansell, *City of Women.*

Ryan's pathbreaking study, however, leaves the question of agency in the process of the "making of the middle class" unresolved. See Ryan, *Cradle of the Middle Class,* p. 12. Like Ryan's, Blumin's work does not explicitly address the formation of a bourgeoisie; instead he is interested in the "formation, and the elevation, or rise, of the American middle class," a group he defines as "middling folk" – neither upper class nor workers. Blumin, *The Emergence of the Middle Class,* pp. 2, 12.

53 This was most particularly the case for the postbellum years, as Stuart Blumin shows for the middle class. Blumin, *The Emergence of the Middle Class,* p. 13. Mary Ryan agrees. See Ryan, *Cradle of the Middle Class,* p. 239. An excellent example for attending to the history of the bourgeoisie while writing a labor biography is Nick Salvatore's *Eugene V. Debs: Citizen and Socialist* (Urbana: University of Illinois Press, 1982), especially pp. 7–8, 12–17.

54 The quote is from Mills, *The Power Elite,* p. 30. Complaints along the same lines have been made by British and French historians, despite a much more distinguished tradition of scholarship on the bourgeoisie. For Britain, see Wolff and Seed, eds., *The Culture of Capital,* p. 8. For France, see John Merriman, ed., *Consciousness and Class Experience in Nineteenth Century Europe* (New York: Holmes & Meier Publishers, 1979), p. 8.

55 For the infatuation with oppositional culture see, for example, the pathbreaking works of Roy Rosenzweig, *Eight Hours for What We Will: Workers and*

Leisure in an Industrial City, 1870–1920 (New York: Cambridge University Press, 1983); Thomas Dublin, *Women at Work: The Transformation of Work and Community in Lowell, Massachusetts, 1826–1860* (New York: Columbia University Press, 1979); Gutman, *Work, Culture and Society in Industrializing America.*

56 For a similar critique see Peter Way, "Labor's Love Lost: Observations on the Historiography of Class and Ethnicity in the Nineteenth Century," in *Journal of American Studies* 28 (1994): 1–22; as well as Patricia Limerick, "Has 'Minority' History Transformed the Historical Discourse?" in *Perspectives* 35 (November 1997): 1, 32–36.

57 Writing on entrepreneurs, at first, was dominated by nineteenth-century businessmen themselves, who penned accounts of their lives, accounts that were often superficial and self-serving, but could nevertheless prove insightful about the inner mechanisms of their class. See, for example, John Crosby Brown, *A Hundred Years of Merchant Banking: A History of Brown Brothers and Company, Brown Shipley & Company and the Allied Firms* (New York: [privately printed], 1909); Marcellus Hartley, *A Brief Memoir* (New York: [privately printed], 1903); Thomas Mellon, *Thomas Mellon and His Times* (Pittsburgh: W. G. Johnston, 1885; reprint, Pittsburgh: University of Pittsburgh Press, 1994); Henry Wyshan Lanier, *A Century of Banking in New York, 1822–1922* (New York: The Gilliss Press, 1922).

Later professional business historians, whose insights, though often gained with more rigorous methods, frequently failed to go much beyond the self-promotions of the actors themselves, complemented these efforts. However, the lasting contribution of this generation of historians are scores of biographies and industry studies, which often painstakingly assemble information about individual bankers, industrialists, and merchants. See, for example, Maxwell Whiteman, *Copper for America: The Hendricks Family and a National Industry, 1755–1936* (New Brunswick, N.J.: Rutgers University Press, 1971); William Hurd Hillyer, *James Talcott: Merchant and His Times* (New York: Charles Scribner's Sons, 1937); Leonard Alexander Swann, Jr., *John Roach, Maritime Entrepreneur: The Years as Naval Contractor, 1862–1886* (Annapolis: United States Naval Institute, 1965); Edward C. Mack, *Peter Cooper: Citizen of New York* (New York: Duell, Sloan and Pearce, 1949); John A. Kouwenhoven, *Partners in Banking: An Historical Portrait of a Great Private Bank, Brown Brothers Harriman & Co., 1818–1968* (New York: Doubleday & Company, 1968); Allan Nevins, *Abram S. Hewitt: With Some Account of Peter Cooper* (New York: Harper, 1935).

While this school of historical inquiry elevated the entrepreneur, mostly portrayed in isolation from society, another group of historians set out to condemn them. Following the progressive historians, a number of Marxist scholars, among them Matthew Josephson and Gustavus Myers, wrote popular accounts of the "robber barons," which zealously condemned a few families. Matthew Josephson, *The Robber Barons: The Great American Capitalists, 1861–1901* (New York: Harcourt, 1934); Gustavus Myers, *History of the Great American Fortunes* (Chicago: Kerr, 1907–1910). See also Anna Rochester, *Rulers of America: A Study of Finance Capital* (New York: International Publishers, 1936).

By the late 1960s, however, both adulation and vilification of American entrepreneurs had reached an intellectual dead end. Although these genres did not die out, they turned stale, and, not surprisingly, once a new generation of historians focused attention on other social groups, few lamented that the dreaded entrepreneurial biographies had fallen by the wayside. Only social-mobility studies continued to show an ephemeral interest in the country's bourgeoisie, mostly by repetitious demonstrations that social mobility was the exception and not the rule. Once these studies had made their point, the upper class as a multifaceted social group was all but ignored. For the general argument see Tilly, "What Good is Urban History?" p. 4; for New York, see Pessen, *Riches, Class, and Power before the Civil War.* For studies that demonstrate that the "rags-to-riches" myth is just that, a myth, see Frances W. Gregory and Irene D. Neu, "The American Industrial Elite in the 1870s," in William Miller, ed., *Men in Business: Essays in the History of Entrepreneurship* (Cambridge, Mass.: Harvard University Press, 1952), pp. 193–211; Ingham, *The Iron Barons.*

58 More recently, however, business historians have made profitable use of the methodological insights of the social and political history of the last three decades. For an example of this new approach see Conrad Edick Wright and Katheryn P. Viens, eds., *Entrepreneurs: The Boston Business Community, 1700–1850* (Boston: Massachusetts Historical Society, 1997).

59 See Louis Hartz, *The Liberal Tradition in America: An Interpretation of American Political Thought Since the Revolution* (New York: Harcourt, Brace, 1955), pp. 7, 51, 52.

60 See, for example, Hofstadter, *American Political Tradition.*

61 See, for example, Charles A. Beard and Mary R. Beard, *A Basic History of the United States* (New York: Doubleday, Doran & Company, 1944), passim. Dixon Ryan Fox, *The Decline of Aristocracy in the Politics of New York State* (New York: Columbia University Press, 1919) also fell into the mold of their explanatory framework, explaining New York State's party politics in the first four decades of the nineteenth century as a narrow expression of class conflict.

62 Though there are some exceptions. See, for example, the work by Frederic Cople Jaher, who wrote a voluminous study on the economic elite of a number of American cities, including New York City. This broad study focuses on economic and social life, largely neglecting ideology and politics. In particular, it does not set the city's elite in the context of the social structure of the city or the nation, failing to take into account the dynamics of class relations as well as politics. Jaher, *The Urban Establishment.* Jaher also concludes wrongly that New York's elites possessed "neither solidarity nor community." See Frederic Cople Jaher, "Style and Status: High Society in Late Nineteenth-Century New York," in Frederic Cople Jaher, ed., *The Rich, the Well Born and the Powerful: Elites and Upper Classes in History* (Urbana: University of Illinois Press, 1973), p. 259. Less ambitious works by Ronald Story, Betty G. Farrell, E. Digby Baltzell, and John Ingham, concentrating on single cities, have been content to sketch bourgeois social networks, all but ignoring the importance of ideology and politics in the articulation of upper-class identities. See, for example, Story, *The Forging of an Aristocracy;* and Farrell, *Elite Families,* esp. pp. 3–19; Baltzell, *Philadelphia Gentlemen,* and Baltzell, *The Protestant Establishment;*

Ingham, *The Iron Barons*. Much more attentive to the importance of politics was an earlier study by Almond, "Plutocracy and Politics in New York City." The importance of social networks is also emphasized by Mills, *The Power Elite*, pp. 47–70. In a similar mold, sociologist Nicola Beisel, in her important work on anti vice societies, emphasized the centrality of the transmission and reproduction of class cultures to class formation, especially in and through the family. Nicola Kay Beisel, *Imperiled Innocents: Anthony Comstock and Family Reproduction in Victorian America* (Princeton: Princeton University Press, 1997), pp. 5–6.

From the perspective of this book, the history of New York's economic elite looks very different from the way it is presented in earlier writings. Most importantly, I believe it is essential to delineate the relationship among economics, social life, and ideas, as well as politics. It is only at this intersection that one can understand the history of a social class and its relevance for nineteenth-century United States history. Attention to these relationships is fruitful as the broad studies by Sean Wilentz, David Hammack, and Iver Bernstein on New York City, Anthony Wallace on Rockdale, and Paul Johnson on Rochester show. Though none of these works is solely concerned with bourgeois class formation, they all address the emergence of a bourgeoisie: Wilentz emphasized the emergence of a socially and ideologically distinct group of artisans-turned-entrepreneurs in the second quarter of the nineteenth century; Hammack analyzed the distribution of political power in Gilded Age New York; Bernstein sketched the response of different segments of New York City's upper class to the draft riots of 1863; Wallace stressed the volatility of manufacturing and the dependence of industrialists on merchants in the early Industrial Revolution; and Johnson delineated the role of religious revivals in the formulation of a shared identity among Rochester's manufacturers. Wilentz, *Chants Democratic;* David Hammack, *Power and Society: Greater New York at the Turn of the Century* (New York: Russell Sage Foundation, 1982); Iver Bernstein, *The New York City Draft Riots* (New York: Oxford University Press, 1990); Wallace, *Rockdale;* and Johnson, *A Shopkeeper's Millennium*. The most sustained and successful effort to integrate the history of the bourgeoisie into the larger history of New York City is Edwin G. Burrows and Mike Wallace, *Gotham: A History of New York City to 1898* (New York: Oxford University Press, 1999), drawing in their discussion of the nineteenth-century upper class on my Ph.D. dissertation, "The Making of New York City's Bourgeoisie" (Columbia University, 1995).

Ironically, new works in the genre of business biographies have perhaps best caught up with the need to integrate these different levels of analysis. See David Black, *The King of Fifth Avenue: The Fortunes of August Belmont* (New York: Dial Press, 1981); Ron Chernow, *The House of Morgan: An American Banking Dynasty and the Rise of Modern Finance* (New York: Simon & Schuster, 1990); Ron Chernow, *Titan: The Life of John D. Rockefeller, Sr.* (New York: Random House, 1998); Jean Strouse, *Morgan: American Financier* (New York: Random House, 1999).

63 To some extent, Ernest Labrousse's 1955 call urging historians to engage in comparative research on the bourgeoisie has been heeded. See Ernest Labrousse,

"Voies Nouvelles Vers une Histoire de la Bourgeoisie Occidentale aux XVIIIième et XIXième Siècles," in *Relazioni del X. Congresso Internazionale di Scienze Storiche*, vol. 4, *Storia Moderna* (Florence: G. C. Sansoni, 1955).

By far the largest comprehensive research effort was accomplished in the context of the University of Bielefeld's project on the European bourgeoisie. See, for the results, Kocka, *Bürgertum im Neunzehnten Jahrhundert*; Kocka, ed., *Bürger und Bürgerlichkeit im 19. Jahrhundert*; Hans-Jürgen Puhle, ed., *Bürger in der Gesellschaft der Neuzeit: Wirtschaft, Politik, Kultur* (Göttingen: Vandenhoeck & Ruprecht, 1991). For Germany see also the innovative conceptualization in Hartmut Zwahr, *Proletariat und Bourgeoisie in Deutschland: Studien zur Klassendialektik* (Cologne: Pahl-Rugenstein-Verlag, 1980); David Blackbourn and Geoff Eley, *The Peculiarities of German History: Bourgeois Society and Politics in Nineteenth-Century Germany* (New York: Oxford University Press, 1984); Blackbourn and Evans, eds., *The German Bourgeoisie* (especially Blackbourn's introduction); Maier, *Recasting Bourgeois Europe*; Marion Kaplan, *The Making of the Jewish Middle Class: Women, Family, and Identity in Imperial Germany* (New York: Oxford University Press, 1991); Thomas Mergel, *Zwischen Klasse und Konfession: Katholisches Bürgertum im Rheinland, 1794–1914* (Göttingen: Vandenhoeck & Ruprecht, 1994). On specifc cities see Thomas Weichsel, *Die Bürger von Wiesbaden* (Munich: R. Oldenbourg, 1997); Ralf Zerback, *München und sein Stadtbürgertum* (Munich: R. Oldenbourg, 1997); Birgit-Katharine Seeman, *Stadt, Bürgertum und Kultur: Kulturelle Entwicklung und Kulturpolitik in Hamburg von 1839 bis 1933 am Beispiel des Museumswesens* (Husum: Matthiesen Verlag, 1998); Ralf Roth, *Stadt und Bürgertum in Frankfurt am Main: Ein besonderer Weg von der ständischen zur modernen Bürgergesellschaft, 1760–1914* (Munich: R. Oldenbourg, 1996); Dolores L. Augustine, *Patricians and Parvenus: Wealth and High Society in Wilhelmine Germany* (Oxford and Providence: Berg, 1994).

For the Habsburg bourgeoisie see Ernst Bruckmüller et al., eds., *Bürgertum in der Habsburgmonarchie*, vol.1 (Wien: Böhlau Verlag, 1992); Hannes Stekl et al., eds., *Durch Arbeit, Besitz, Wissen und Gerichtigkeit: Bürgertum in der Habsbugmonarchie*, vol. 2 (Wien: Böhlau Verlag, 1992).

For the French bourgeoisie see the work of Adeline Daumard, for example Adeline Daumard, *Les Bourgeois et la Bourgeoisie en France depuis 1815* (Paris: Aubier, 1987). See also Theodore Zeitlin, *France, 1845–1945: Ambition & Love* (Oxford: Oxford University Press, 1973); Michael B. Miller, *The Bon Marche: Bourgeois Culture and the Department Store, 1869–1920* (Princeton: Princeton University Press, 1981); Bonnie G. Smith, *Ladies of The Leisure Class: The Bourgeoisie of Northern France in the Nineteenth Century* (Princeton: Princeton University Press, 1981); Richard Holt, "Social History and Bourgeois Culture in Nineteenth-Century France," in *Comparative Studies in Society and History* 27 (October 1985): 713–726; David Garrioch, *The Formation of the Parisian Bourgeoisie, 1690–1830* (Cambridge, Mass.: Harvard University Press, 1996).

For Great Britain see especially the work of W. D. Rubinstein, for example W. D. Rubinstein, "Wealth, Elites and the Class Structure of Modern Britain," in *Past and Present* 76 (August 1977): 99–126. See also Leonore Davidoff and Catherine Hall, *Family Fortunes: Men and Women of the English Middle Class,*

1780–1850 (London: Hutchinson, 1987); Peter Earle, *The Making of the English Middle Class: Business, Society and Family Life in London, 1660–1730* (London: Methuen, 1989); R. J. Morris, *Class, Sect, and Party: The Making of the British Middle Class, Leeds, 1820–1850* (Manchester: Manchester University Press, 1990); G. R. Seale, *Entrepreneurial Politics in Mid-Victorian Britain* (Oxford: Oxford University Press, 1993); Hills, "Division and Cohesion in the Nineteenth-Century Middle Class"; Charles A. Jones, *International Business in the Nineteenth Century: The Rise and Fall of a Cosmopolitan Bourgeoisie* (Brighton: Wheatsheaf Books, 1987); Richard H. Trainor, *Black Country Élites: The Exercise of Authority in an Industrialized Area, 1830–1900* (Oxford: Clarendon Press, 1993); Eleanor Gordon and Richard Trainor, "Employers and Policymaking: Scotland and Northern Ireland, c. 1880–1939," in S. J. Connolly, R. A. Houston, and R. J. Morris, eds., *Conflict, Identity and Economic Development: Ireland and Scotland, 1600–1939* (Preston, Eng.: Carnegie Publishing, 1995), pp. 254–267.

For Italy see Marco Meriggi, "Italienisches und deutsches Bürgertum im Vergleich," in Kocka, ed., *Bürgertum im 19. Jahrhundert,* pp. 141–159; Francesco Volpe, *La Borghesia di Provincia Nell'Eta Borbonica* (Naples: Edizioni Scientifiche Italiane, 1991). See also Daniela Luigia Caglioti, "Voluntary Societies and Urban Elites in Nineteenth-Century Naples," (paper presented at the Fourth International Conference on Urban History, Venice, 1998).

For the Netherlands see Boudien de Vries, *Electoraat en Elite: Sociale Structuur en Sociale Mobiliteit in Amsterdam, 1850–1895* (Amsterdam: Bataafsche Leeuw, 1986). It is striking how similar the social and cultural conflicts between merchants and industrialists were in Amsterdam and New York.

For Switzerland see the excellent study by Tanner, *Arbeitsame Patrioten.*

For a perspective on less industrialized countries and a very different set of problems, see the essay collection by Enrique Florescano, ed., *Origenes y Desarrollo de la Burguesia en America Latina, 1700–1955* (Mexico: Editorial Nueva Imagen, 1985), and Marie-Claire Bergère, *The Golden Age of the Chinese Bourgeoisie, 1911–1937* (New York: Cambridge University Press, 1989). It is noteworthy, however, that many of the issues and debates on the European and North American bourgeoisie have relevance to developments in the rest of the world, especially during the twentieth century.

64 In turn, it is my hope that this study will contribute to bridging the gap between historiographical concerns on both sides of the Atlantic.

65 How promising such attention could be is amply demonstrated by the scholarship on the Progressive Era. Both Martin Sklar and James Livingston emphasize capitalists' role as active participants in shaping the economic and political transition from competitive to corporate capitalism. See James Livingston, "The Social Analysis of Economic History and Theory: Conjectures of Late Nineteenth-Century American Development," in *AHR* 92 (February 1987): 69–95; James Livingston, *Origins of the Federal Reserve System: Money, Class, and Corporate Capitalism, 1890–1933* (Ithaca, N.Y.: Cornell University Press, 1986); Livingston, *Pragmatism and the Political Economy of Cultural Revolution;* Martin J. Sklar, *The Corporate Reconstruction of American Capitalism, 1890–1916: The Market, the Law, and Politics* (New York: Cambridge Univer-

sity Press, 1988), pp. 2–14. Alfred Chandler focuses less on the political and more on the organizational changes effected by the nation's entrepreneurs, but also sees them as agents of change. See Alfred Chandler, *The Visible Hand: The Managerial Revolution in American Business* (Cambridge: Belknap Press, 1977).

66 Barrington Moore, *Social Origins of Dictatorship and Democracy: Lord and Peasant in the Making of the Modern World* (Boston: Beacon Press, 1966), p. 125. There are, however, a few exceptions. See Philip Foner, *Business and Slavery: The New York Merchants and the Irrepressible Conflict* (Chapel Hill: University of North Carolina Press, 1941); Moore, *Social Origins of Dictatorship and Democracy;* Eric Foner, *Reconstruction: America's Unfinished Revolution, 1863–1877* (New York: Harper & Row, 1988); Peter Kolchin, "The Business Press and Reconstruction, 1865–1868," in *Journal of Southern History* 33 (May 1967), 183–196. For the Gilded Age, see also Trachtenberg, *Incorporation of America;* Richard Oestreicher, "Two Souls of American Democracy," in George Reid Andrew and Herrick Chapman, eds., *The Social Construction of Democracy, 1870–1990* (New York: New York University Press, 1995), p. 119. In the context of postwar southern policies, the power of the northern bourgeoisie is also emphasized by Lawrence Goodwyn, *The Populist Moment* (New York: Oxford University Press, 1978), p. 6.

67 See Ira Katznelson, "Working-Class Formation: Constructing Cases and Comparisons," in Ira Katznelson and Aristide R. Zolberg, eds., *Working-Class Formation: Nineteenth Century Patterns in Western Europe and the United States* (Princeton: Princeton University Press, 1986), pp. 3–4; Kocka, *Bürger und Bürgerlichkeit im 19. Jahrhundert,* p. 41.

68 My understanding of class in the nineteenth century in the widest sense is informed by a reading of Karl Marx, Max Weber, Anthony Giddens, E. P. Thompson, Pierre Bourdieu, and Antonio Gramsci. More particularly, I agree with Marx on the importance of relationship to the means of production in structuring social relations, but disagree with his teleological assumptions about the forming of classes and the trajectory of historical change. Max Weber, E. P. Thompson, Pierre Bourdieu, and Anthony Giddens emphasize the historically contingent nature of class, and their thinking has profoundly shaped this book. Weber usefully explores the tensions between class and status group, and the possibility (but not the certainty) that both can merge. Weber thus saw classes as "possible communities." Giddens, in turn, helps bridge the gap between class as a structural category and class as a relational category by emphasizing the different pays in which class can articulate itself, ranging from class awareness to class consciousness. His notion that classes become social realities once people embrace shared habits and views is important to my work. Thompson, in ways quite compatible with Giddens, powerfully emphasizes the historical nature of class, an insight that is at the center of this book. How to disentangle the emergence of class identities is most persuasively conceptualized by Pierre Bourdieu, who puts cultural and symbolic capital alongside economic capital in his analysis of the distribution of power and the emergence of collective identities. His approach suggests two insights: First, culture and symbols can bring together people with diverse economic interests – as was typical for the nineteenth-centuruy bourgeoisie. And, second,

it suggests that conflicts over the control of culture and symbols are important to the distribution of social power – and not ephemeral, as a reductionist view of class would suggest.

While my work embraces the emphasis on culture and ideas in the emerging of collective identities, I disagree with fashionable notions that it is culture alone that makes a class. Class cultures, I argue instead, are predicated on specific ways of gaining access to specific kinds of resources and, therefore, cannot be understood without an analysis of social structures and economic change. Last but not least, Anthony Gramsci's suggestive comments on the importance of legitimacy in maintaining social power in bourgeois societies is important to this book, especially for my thinking about the transition to progressivism at the end of the nineteenth century.

See Max Weber, "Class, Status, Party," in H. H. Gerth and C. Wright Mills, eds., *From Max Weber, Essays in Sociology,* pp. 181–195; Max Weber, *Wirtschaft und Gesellschaft: Grundriss der verstehenden Soziologie* (1922; reprint Tübingen: J. C. B. Mohr, 1985), pp. 177–180, 531–540; Karl Marx, "Wage Labor and Capital," in Robert C. Tucker, ed., *The Marx–Engels Reader* (2d ed.), pp. 203–217; Marx, *Das Kapital,* vol. 3 (Berlin: Dietz, 1975), pp. 892–893; E. P. Thompson, *The Making of the English Working Class,* pp. 9–14; Anthony Giddens, *The Class Structure of the Advanced Societies* (London: Hutchinson University Library, 1973), p. 111 and passim; Bourdieu, *Distinction;* Antonio Gramsci, "Political Struggle and Military War," in Quintin Hoare and Geoffrey N. Smith, eds., *Selections from the Prison Notebooks of Antonio Gramsci* (New York: International Publishers, 1987), pp. 229–238.

69 An emphasis on ideology and politics, moreover, will help us explore the relationship between bourgeoisie and bourgeois society. It is a relationship wrought with complications. For these complications see, among others, Blackbourn and Eley, *The Peculiarities of German History,* p. 164; Madeleine Hurd, "In Search of the Bourgeois Liberal" (paper presented at the Proseminar on State Formation and Collective Action, New School for Social Research, New York, 1991), p. 9; Dietrich Rueschemeyer, Evelyn Huber Stephens, and John D. Stephens, *Capitalist Development and Democracy* (Chicago: University of Chicago Press, 1992); Charles Tilly, "Of Oil Fields, Lakes, and Democracy" (Center for Studies of Social Change, New School for Social Research, New York, 1992, Working Paper 152), pp. 14–16; Gareth Stedman-Jones, "Society and Politics at the Beginning of the World Economy," in *Cambridge Journal of Economics* 1 (March 1977): 77–92.

70 The importance of change is also stressed by Hobsbawm, "Die englische middle-class, 1780–1920," pp. 89–99. See also Immanuel Wallerstein, "Bourgeois(ie): Begriff und Realität," in Etienne Balibar and Immanuel Wallerstein, *Rasse, Klasse, Nation: Ambivalente Identitäten* (Berlin: Argument, 1990), pp. 177–178. On the multiple dimensions of class and class formation see especially Weber, *Wirtschaft und Gesellschaft,* p. 27; Bourdieu, *Distinction,* p. 175; Giddens, *The Class Structure of the Advanced Societies,* especially pp. 99–138; Jürgen Kocka, *Arbeitsverhältnisse und Arbeiterexistenzen: Grundlagen der Klassenbildung im 19. Jahrhundert* (Bonn: J. H. W. Dietz, 1990).

71 Although collective political mobilizations, for example, are more likely once a shared class culture and class ideology had been formulated.

72 See Claus Offe, "Two Logics of Collective Action," in *Disorganized Capitalism: Contemporary Transformations of Work and Politics* (Cambridge, Mass.: MIT Press, 1985).

73 Such as Hammack, *Power and Society*, passim, especially pp. 65–79. Although Hammack's book has opened important new vistas on New York City history, I am not persuaded by his insistence on the existence of five distinct upper-class groups in New York. I am also not persuaded by his notion that the economic elite, lacking cultural and organizational resources and deeply fragmented by cultural preferences as well as ethnic heritage, experienced a relative loss in power. The weakest part of his argument, so it seems to me, is that he does not effectively show the connection between the cultural divisions he depicts and the political conflicts over consolidation, subway construction, and school centralization.

74 *NYT*, 11 February 1897, p. 1.

1. Accumulating Capital

1 Frances M. Wolcott, *Heritage of Years: Kaleidoscopic Memories* (New York: Minton, Balch and Company, 1932), pp. 28–32.

2 For an account of these dinners see David Black, *The King of Fifth Avenue: The Fortunes of August Belmont* (New York: Dial Press, 1981), pp. 169–172. For an account of his art gallery see August Belmont to Commodore Perry, December 21, 1856, quoted in Black, *King*, p. 170.

3 In the fall of 1857, this expansion had just come to a sudden but temporary halt.

4 Exports rose to $134 million, exports to $236 million. The increase is calculated in real 1857 dollars. Robert Greenhalgh Albion, *The Rise of New York Port, 1815–1860* (New York: Charles Scribner's Sons, 1939), pp. 390, 391.

5 Albion, *The Rise of New York Port*, p. 386. By 1860, nearly half (45.3 percent) of America's foreign commerce passed through the city's port. Jean Heffer, *Le Port de New York et le Commerce Extérieur Américain, 1860–1900* (Paris: Publications de la Sorbonne, 1986), p. 22. In 1859, more than 10 percent of goods manufactured in the United States, 62 percent of imports, and 24 percent of exports went through the ledgers of Manhattan's wholesalers. See Samuel Schoenberg, "An Historical Analysis of the Changing Business Life of New York City: A Study of Industrial and Occupational Trends for the Purpose of Determining the Probable Future Need for Business Workers in New York City" (Ph.D. diss., New York University, 1940), pp. 72, 75.

6 Precisely 24.17 percent. The exports of Baltimore, Boston, and Philadelphia taken together amounted to 21 percent of those of New York City, their imports to 29 percent. Albion, *The Rise of New York Port*, pp. 390–391. Export and import statistics are for 1860.

7 In real 1860 dollars. United States Census Office, *Twelfth Census of the United States Taken in the Year 1900*, vol. 8, *Manufactures*, Part II, "States and Territories" (Washington: U.S. Census Office, 1902), p. 580.

8 Paul Bairoch, Jean Batou, and Pierre Chèvre, *La Population des Villes Européennes, 800–1850* (Geneva: Librairie Droz, 1988), pp. 4, 33.

9 On the earlier world of merchants see Richard Bushman, *The Refinement of America: Persons, Houses, Cities* (New York: Knopf, 1992); Charles Sellers, *The Market Revolution: Jacksonian America, 1815–1846* (New York: Oxford University Press, 1991); Bernard Bailyn, *The New England Merchants in the Seventeenth Century* (Cambridge, Mass.: Harvard University Press, 1955); Thomas Doerflinger, *A Vigorous Spirit of Enterprise: Merchants and Economic Development in Revolutionary Philadelphia* (Chapel Hill: University of North Carolina Press, 1986).

10 Allan Pred, *Urban Growth and City-Systems in the United States, 1840–1860* (Cambridge, Mass.: Harvard University Press, 1980), pp. 143, 144, 159. See also Albion, *New York Port*, p. 94.

11 Wage laborers, who accounted for more than two out of three citizens (about 67 percent), owned next to no capital, and artisans (12 percent), small proprietors, and professionals (17 percent) owned the remaining amount. See Amy Bridges, *A City in the Republic: Antebellum New York and the Origins of Machine Politics* (New York: Cambridge University Press, 1984), p. 46. These numbers should be taken only as rough approximations, which help us understand the social structure of the city.

12 The number of individuals assessed on real and personal wealth is derived from *Boyd's New York City Tax Book*. The work force in New York City in 1855 encompassed, according to Amy Bridges, 191,059 individuals. See Bridges, *A City in the Republic*, p. 46. Bridges counts 6,398 "capitalists" (here defined as financiers, manufacturers, and merchants) in New York City in 1855 (or 3.4 percent of the "gainfully employed"). However, this category excludes professionals (among them lawyers and doctors), as well as small proprietors (among them clothiers and dry goods dealers, as well as builders and contractors), some of whom undoubtedly were among the city's economic elite. See Bridges, *A City in the Republic*, p. 56. The term "gainfully employed" is taken from Robert Ernst, who compiled the data on which Amy Bridges's estimation is based. Ernst counted all New Yorkers who were listed with an occupation in the 1855 state census. For his methods and results see Robert Ernst, *Immigrant New York*, pp. 206–219.

13 In 1856, the total assessed real and personal wealth in the city of New York equaled $527,945,713. If we calculate the total real and personal wealth for all 9,000 New Yorkers assessed at $10,000 or more, we come to an amount of $374,866,24, which equals 71 percent of the total assessed real and personal wealth in the city of New York in 1856. The average amount of real and personal wealth for people included in the 1855 sample (see footnote 15) was $41,651. The average real and personal wealth of the 20,748 people who were assessed on real and personal wealth of less than $10,000 was $7,378. For the names and numbers, see *Boyd's New York City Tax Book Being a List of Persons, Corporations and Co-Partnerships, Resident and Nonresident, who were taxed according to the Assessor's Books, 1856 & 1857* (New York: William H. Boyd, 1857).

Another historian has calculated that in 1845, the richest 1 percent of New York's families owned 47 percent of the city's noncorporate wealth, with the next 3 percent controlling another 32 percent. Edward Pessen, *Riches,*

Classes, and Power before the Civil War (Lexington, Mass.: D. C. Heath, 1973), p. 34.

14 A total of 29,748 New Yorkers were listed in Boyd's tax directory, some with as little as $100 in real and personal wealth. This group leaves out 84 percent of the economically active population of New York City in 1856 (which consisted of 191,059 individuals). See Bridges, *A City in the Republic,* p. 46. If we take the city's population as a whole into account (630,000 in 1855), 95.28 percent of all New Yorkers did not own sufficient wealth to be included on the tax lists.

15 These statistics are derived from a sample of 498 randomly selected taxpayers in New York City whose combined real estate and personal wealth was assessed at more than $10,000 in the tax year 1856 (hereafter cited as "1855 sample"). Their names were published in 1857 in *Boyd's New York City Tax Book,* which lists in alphabetical order on 222 pages "resident persons, corporations and co-partnerships." Each page is divided into two columns. The first person (excluding institutions and corporations) in each column showing a combined real estate and personal wealth of more than $10,000 was included in the sample. To bring the sample size close to 500, the 444 individuals thus incorporated were supplemented with the last individual in every fourth column with an assessed wealth of more than $10,000. This brought the total sample size to 498.

Not all individuals listed in the tax book paid taxes on $10,000 or more of assessed wealth. The cut-off point was chosen because the likelihood of bourgeois individuals being assessed on lesser wealth was small. It can hence be assumed that most bourgeois individuals in New York City were included in the group from which the sample was constructed. This inclusiveness also guaranteed that those bourgeois whose wealth was significantly under-assessed would still show up in the sample, as indeed was the case.

In a next step, the names derived from the tax book were linked to the city directory. Because city directories were often rather incomplete, three editions were used – published for the years 1855, 1856, and 1857 (H. Wilson, *Trow's New York City Directory For 1854–1855* [New York: John F. Trow, 1854]; H. Wilson, *Trow's New York City Directory for the Year Ending May 1, 1856* [New York: John F. Trow, 1855]; H. Wilson, *Trow's New York City Directory for the Year Ending May 1, 1857* [New York: John F. Trow, 1856]). Individuals not located in the 1856 edition were searched for in the 1855 and 1857 volumes. Great care was taken to include only individuals who could clearly be identified. If there was more than one person with the same name, and occupational categories did not clearly indicate that only one of them could have paid taxes on the wealth listed (laborers, for example, could principally be omitted), the directories' information was excluded. For all individuals who could be clearly identified, the home address and occupation were added to the sample.

Next, the residences of all individuals who were identified in the directories and had a street address for their home in Manhattan were located on a street map. The ward and election district in which their home was found were included in the sample.

In a subsequent research step, all individuals located in the city directories were searched for in the original census returns for the New York State Census of 1855. See 1855 New York State Census for the City and County of New York, Division of Old Records, New York County Clerk, New York, New York. For those who were identified, their place of birth, age, length of stay in New York City, marital status, and number of children and servants were added to the sample.

In the final step, *New York Times* obituaries were located for individuals in the sample. Information on individuals who could not be located in the census was included in the sample.

To analyze the sample, the wide variety of occupations specified in the city directories and census had to be categorized. The 108 occupations listed were divided into six major and two minor groups. The major groups were classified according to the kind of capital they controlled – trade, production, finance, professions, rentiers, and real estate. The minor groups are subdivisions of trade and production and help distinguish retail trade from commerce and manufacturing from craft production.

It is important to note that the sampling technique employed here should not suggest that I define "bourgeois" as owning combined real and personal property worth $10,000 or more. This sample is only a tool that allows us to get an idea of the structural characteristics of the city's bourgeoisie, one that is quite accurate. It does not serve as a definition of "bourgeois."

16 1855 sample.

17 Pessen, *Riches*, pp. 48–49, 323–326.

18 Albion, *The Rise of New York Port*, pp. 400, 401.

19 Albion, *The Rise of New York Port*, p. 116.

20 Glenn Porter and Harold C. Livesay, *Merchants and Manufacturers: Studies in the Changing Structure of Nineteenth Century Marketing* (Baltimore: Johns Hopkins Press, 1971), p. 8.

21 Albion, *The Rise of New York Port*, p. 266.

22 Leverich Family Papers, NYHS; "Leverich & Co.," New York, vol. 340, p. 17; Dun & Co. Collection, Baker Library, Harvard Business School; Albion, *The Rise of New York Port*, p. 250.

23 After 1818, regularly scheduled ships shuttled between New York and Liverpool. See Ernst, *Immigrant New York*, p. 14.

24 Albion, *The Rise of New York Port*, p. 75.

25 Albion, *The Rise of New York Port*, p. 61.

26 This account is based upon Albion, *The Rise of New York Port*, pp. 275f.

27 Marcellus Hartley, *A Brief Memoir* (New York: [privately printed], 1903), p. 18; "Schuyler, Hartley & Graham," New York, vol. 317, p. 204, Dun & Co. Collection, Baker Library, Harvard Business School.

28 Albion, *The Rise of New York Port*, p. 411.

29 Albion, *The Rise of New York Port*, p. 283.

30 Albion, *The Rise of New York Port*, p. 173.

31 A. A. Low, Miscellaneous Manuscripts, NYHS; *The National Cyclopedia of American Biography, Being the History of the United States* (New York: James T. White & Company, 1893), vol. 3, p. 355.

32 Stewart also served as a director of a bank, and invested in street railways. Bridges, *A City in the Republic,* p. 47; Schoenberg, "An Historical Analysis of the Changing Business Life of New York City," p. 100.

33 Ralph Hower, *The History of Macy's of New York, 1858–1919* (Cambridge, Mass.: Harvard University Press, 1943).

34 Albion, *The Rise of New York Port,* p. 284; Porter and Livesay, *Merchants and Manufacturers,* p. 71.

35 Alan Lester Olmstead, "New York City Mutual Savings Banks in the Ante-Bellum Years, 1819–1861" (Ph.D. diss., University of Wisconsin, 1970), p. 16; Henry Wyshan Lanier, *A Century of Banking in New York, 1822–1922* (New York: The Gilliss Press, 1922), p. 212; Edward K. Spann, *The New Metropolis: New York City, 1840–1857* (New York: Columbia University Press, 1981), p. 411; *Annual Report of the Chamber of Commerce of the State of New York, for the Year 1858* (New York: Wheeler and Williams, 1859), pp. 252–253.

36 Lanier, *A Century of Banking,* p. 212.

37 Porter and Livesay, *Merchants and Manufacturers,* p. 78.

38 Ernst, *Immigrant New York,* p. 216. See also 1855 sample.

39 1855 sample.

40 Black, *The King of Fifth Avenue,* p. 20; *The National Cyclopedia of American Biography,* vol. 5, p. 558; "August Belmont," in Larry Schweikart, ed., *Encyclopedia of American Business History and Biography, Banking and Finance to 1913* (New York: Facts on File, 1990), pp. 37–38. "August Belmont," New York, vol. 350, p. 1137, entry of February 13, 1872, Dun & Co. Collection, Baker Library, Harvard Business School.

41 John A. Kouwenhoven, *Partners in Banking: An Historical Portrait of a Great Private Bank, Brown Brothers Harriman & Co., 1818–1968* (New York: Doubleday & Company, 1968), and John Crosby Brown, *A Hundred Years of Merchant Banking: A History of Brown Brothers and Company, Brown Shipley & Company and the Allied Firms* (New York: [privately printed], 1909).

42 "Moses Taylor," in Schweikart, ed., *Encyclopedia of American Business, Banking to 1913,* p. 463. As Naomi Lamoreaux has shown for New England, it was indeed quite typical that banks served as a vehicle for making loans available to the directors of banks and their relatives. See Naomi R. Lamoreaux, *Insider Lending: Banks, Personal Connections, and Economic Development in Industrial New England* (New York: Cambridge University Press, 1994), p. 4. Harold van B. Cleveland, *Citibank, 1812–1970* (Cambridge, Mass.: Harvard University Press, 1985), pp. 17–23. On Taylor, see also Daniel Hodas, *The Business Career of Moses Taylor, Merchant, Finance Capitalist, and Industrialist* (New York: New York University Press, 1976).

43 Hodas, *The Business Career of Moses Taylor,* pp. 272–273.

44 Robert McElroy, *Levi Parsons Morton, Banker, Diplomat, and Statesman* (New York: Putnam, 1930), pp. 26–43; "Junius S. Morgan," in Schweikart, ed., *Encyclopedia of American Business, Banking to 1913,* p. 349; "Joseph Seligman," in Schweikart, ed., *Encyclopedia of American Business, Banking*

to 1913, pp. 421–430; *In Memoriam, Jesse Seligman* (New York: Press of Philip Cowen, 1984), p. 13.

45 McElroy, *Levi Parsons Morton*, pp. 44–69.

46 Lanier, *A Century of Banking*, p. 209.

47 Frederic Cople Jaher, *The Urban Establishment, Upper Strata in Boston, New York, Charleston, Chicago and Los Angeles* (Urbana: University of Illinois Press, 1973), p. 196f; Philip H. Burch, Jr., *Elites in American History*, vol. 2 (New York: Holmes & Meier Publishers Inc., 1981), p. 176.

48 Ron Chernow, *The House of Morgan: An American Banking Dynasty and the Rise of Modern Finance* (New York: Simon & Schuster, 1990), p. 10.

49 R. C. Michie, *The London and New York Stock Exchanges, 1850–1914* (London: Allen & Unwin, 1987), p. 181.

50 Lanier, *A Century of Banking*, p. 20.

51 Lanier, *A Century of Banking*, p. 21; J. F. D Lanier, *Sketch of the Life of J. F. D. Lanier* (New York: [printed for the use of his family only], 1877), p. 65.

52 Douglas T. Miller, *Jacksonian Aristocracy: Class and Democracy in New York, 1830–1860* (New York: Oxford University Press, 1967), p. 124.

53 *Third Annual Report of the Chamber of Commerce of the State of New-York for the Year 1860–61* (New York: John W. Amerman, 1861), pp. 313–316.

54 *Third Annual Report of the Chamber of Commerce*, p. 312.

55 Shepard B. Clough, *A Century of American Life Insurance, A History of the Mutual Life Insurance Company of New York, 1843–1943* (New York: Columbia University Press, 1946), pp. 3, 371.

56 Albion, *The Rise of New York Port*, p. 270.

57 Such as the Jones family, who dominated the Atlantic Mutual. Jaher, *The Urban Establishment*, pp. 193, 194.

58 On Astor see Albion, *The Rise of New York Port*, p. 236. Tom Shachtman, *Skyscraper Dreams: The Great Real Estate Dynasties of New York* (New York: Little, Brown and Company, 1991), pp. 9–44. On William E. Dodge's real estate investments see Richard Lowitt, *A Merchant Prince of the Nineteenth Century: William E. Dodge* (New York: Columbia University Press, 1954), p. 182.

59 Philip L. White, *The Beekmans of New York in Politics and Commerce* (New York: The New-York Historical Society, 1956), p. 619.

60 William Cronon, *Nature's Metropolis: Chicago and the Great West* (New York: W. W. Norton, 1991), pp. 28–46.

61 Daniel James to William E. Dodge, May 23, 1835, quoted in Lowitt, *A Merchant Prince*, p. 62.

62 Miller, *Jacksonian Aristocracy*, p. 122.

63 Daniel James to William E. Dodge, May 23, 1835, quoted in Lowitt, *A Merchant Prince*, p. 62; Porter and Livesay, *Merchants and Manufacturers*, p. 73.

64 Maxwell Whiteman, *Copper for America: The Hendricks Family and a National Industry, 1755–1936* (New Brunswick, N.J.: Rutgers University Press, 1971).

65 *NYT*, 2 June 1871, p. 5; "Jeremiah Milbank," New York, vol. 343, p. 400/RR, entry of August 28, 1874, Dun & Co. Collection, Baker Library, Harvard Business School.

66 According to his own calculations, annual profits from the production of Montgomery's sheet metal beams amounted to 25 percent of his costs. This story is fully elaborated in the papers of Richard S. Buchanan at the NYHS.

67 William Hurd Hillyer, *James Talcott: Merchant and His Times* (New York: Charles Scribner's Sons, 1937), pp. 52–55.

68 These calculations are based on a sample of 191 New York City taxpayers assessed at more than $10,000 in real estate and personal wealth in 1856.

69 1855 sample. See also Albion, *The Rise of New York Port,* p. 241. These immigrants often arrived later in their lives (on average, at ages twenty-seven and twenty-six, respectively) and were relatively recent arrivals to the city. In contrast, migrants from upstate New York and immigrants from Ireland arrived, on average, at a much younger age (twenty and twenty-one, respectively) and earlier in time, in 1825. By 1856, they were mainly concentrated in New York's retail trade and the professions, suggesting that they arrived with less capital and either marketed goods produced at their place of birth or took advantage of New York's greater possibilities for professional advancement.

70 For examples see Albion, *The Rise of New York Port,* pp. 236ff.

71 Albion, *The Rise of New York Port,* pp. 241–245.

72 These numbers are very similar to those calculated by Amy Bridges. According to Bridges, among her 6,398 "capitalists" in New York City in 1855, 77 percent were born in the United States and 23 percent abroad. See Bridges, *A City in the Republic,* p. 56.

73 Since 1832, however, the New York legislature also had allowed for "silent partners" who did not share in the work and were only liable to the limit of the capital they had invested with the firm.

74 See Albion, *The Rise of New York Port,* p. 263.

75 Albion, *The Rise of New York Port,* p. 264.

76 Albion, *The Rise of New York Port,* p. 267. (A few merchants, however, owned vessels without the involvement of any partners, Cornelius Vanderbilt prominent among them.)

77 The importance of family to business activities is also stressed by Barry E. Supple, "A Business Elite, German-Jewish Financiers in Nineteenth-Century New York," in *Business History Review* 31 (Summer 1957), especially p. 509.

78 Amy Bridges, *A City in the Republic,* p. 47.

79 Lowitt, *A Merchant Prince of the Nineteenth Century,* pp. 5, 6, 10, 11, 12, 13, 20, 40, 91, 95, 106, 139, 153, 181. On Dodge, see also "Phelps, Dodge & Co.," New York, vol. 316, p. 35, Dun & Co. Collection, Baker Library, Harvard Business School.

80 Elizabeth Blackmar, *Manhattan for Rent, 1785–1850* (Ithaca, N.Y.: Cornell University Press, 1989), pp. 141–142.

81 For an extended analysis of these marriage patterns see Edward Pessen, "The Marital Theory and Practice of the Antebellum Urban Elite," in *New York History* 53 (October 1972), esp. pp. 396–399.

82 Carlos Martyn, *William E. Dodge: The Christian Merchant* (New York: Funk & Wagnalls, 1890), p. 64.

83 See Timothy J. Gilfoyle, *City of Eros: New York City, Prostitution, and the Commercialization of Sex, 1790–1920* (New York: W. W. Norton, 1992), p. 103.

84 Walt Whitman, "On Vice," in *Brooklyn Daily Times*, 20 June 1857.

85 Albion, *The Rise of New York Port*, p. 249.

86 Martyn, *William E. Dodge*, p. 63; H. Wilson, *Trow's New-York City Directory for 1854–1855* (New York: John F. Trow, 1855), and H. Wilson, *Trow's New-York City Directory for the Year Ending May 1, 1858* (New York: John F. Trow, 1858). Another sister, Harriet, married Charles F. Pond, whose occupation cannot be established.

87 Whiteman, *Copper for America*, pp. 152f, 169, 171, 182, 283.

88 Allen Churchill, *The Upper Crust: An Informal History of New York's Highest Society* (Englewood Cliffs, N.J.: Prentice-Hall, 1970), pp. 50, 54.

89 See, for example, "Anson G. Phelps Dodge," entry of October 15, 1859, New York, vol. 345, p. 600 (N), Dun & Co. Collection, Baker Library, Harvard Business School.

90 Robert S. Buchanan, entry of April 1, 1851, New York, vol. 340, p. 56, Dun & Co. Collection, Baker Library, Harvard Business School.

91 Charles Haynes Haswell, *Reminiscences of an Octogenarian of the City of New York* (New York: Harper & Brothers, 1896), p. 514.

92 Jaher, *The Urban Establishment*, p. 206. These people were related by blood or kinship. For the general point see also Albion, *The Rise of New York Port*, p. 254.

93 Testifying to their efforts are the often substantial collections of family letters that they wrote and which are now housed with their partners' business papers in archives.

94 Brown, *A Hundred Years of Merchant Banking*, p. 24.

95 Hillyer, *James Talcott*, pp. 52–55.

96 *NYT*, 24 February 1875, p. 5.

97 Schweikart, ed., *Encyclopedia of American Business History and Biography, Banking and Finance to 1913*, pp. 462, 463.

98 Allan Stanley Horlick, *Country Boys and Merchant Princes: The Social Control of Young Men in New York* (Lewisburg, Pa.: Bucknell University Press, 1975), pp. 78–79. The firm remained a family enterprise until the 1880s. See Lowitt, *A Merchant Prince*, p. 19.

99 Jaher, *The Urban Establishment*, p. 203.

100 *NYT*, 17 December 1891, p. 5; Albion, *The Rise of New York Port*, p. 246.

101 1855 sample.

102 Allan Nevins and Milton H. Thomas, eds., *Diary of George Templeton Strong*, vol. 2 (New York: Octagon Books, 1952), p. 478. On physicians see Paul Starr, *The Social Transformation of American Medicine* (New York: Basic Books, 1982), pp. 81–88. On lawyers, albeit for an earlier time period, see also Michael Mann, *The Sources of Social Power*, vol. 2, *The Rise of Classes and Nation-States, 1760–1914* (New York: Cambridge University Press, 1982), p. 146.

103 Annual Commencement of Columbia College, Wednesday, July 30, 1851, SY 1851–41, NYHS; Miller, *Jacksonian Aristocracy*, p. 77.

104 Malone, ed., *Dictionary of American Biography,* vol. 8, p. 405; *NYT,* 17 December 1889, p. 5; Family of Hamon and Frances (Isaacs) Hendricks, Case 21, Hendricks Family Papers, NYHS; Edward C. Mack, *Peter Cooper: Citizen of New York* (New York: Duell, Sloan and Pearce, 1949), p. 173; Brown, *A Hundred Years of Merchant Banking,* p. xxiii; *A History of Columbia University, 1754–1904* (New York: The Columbia University Press, 1904), p. 135.; Hodas, *The Business Career of Moses Taylor,* pp. 163–164. See also Lawrence Arthur Cremin, *American Education: The National Experience, 1783–1876* (New York: Harper and Row, 1980), p. 448.

105 *Hunt's* 35 (1856), p. 56; *Hunt's* 28 (1853), p. 28.

106 See also Starr, *The Social Transformation of American Medicine,* pp. 81, 84.

107 A similar argument about lawyers can be found in Mann, *The Sources of Social Power,* vol. 2, p. 146.

108 *Tribute of the Chamber of Commerce of the State of New-York to the Memory of Samuel B. Ruggles, November 3, 1881* (New York: Press of the Chamber of Commerce, 1881), p. 7.

109 "William Peet and Charles A. Nicholas," entry of October 7, 1853, New York, vol. 374, p. 61, Dun & Co. Collection, Baker Library, Harvard Business School.

110 Samuel S. Howland to Frederic DePeyster, New York, August 15, 1851, DePeyster Papers, NYHS; "Frederick DePeyster," entry of 1874, New York, vol. 384, p. 808, Dun & Co. Collection, Baker Library, Harvard Business School.

111 Edward F. DeLancey, *Memoir of James William Beekman: Prepared at the Request of the St. Nicholas Society of the City of New York* (New York: St. Nicholas Society, 1877), p. 8.

112 Starr, *The Social Transformation of American Medicine,* p. 81.

113 *NYT,* 3 December 1886, p. 4.

114 "Horace Green," New York, vol. 224, p. 001/F, Dun & Co. Collection, Baker Library, Harvard Business School.

115 Box 1, Beekman Papers, NYHS.

116 For information on their family backgrounds see the relevant entries in John A. Garraty and Mark C. Carnes, *American National Biography* (New York: Oxford University Press, 1999).

117 Kenneth Myers, *The Catskills: Painters, Writers, and Tourists in the Mountains, 1820–1895* (Yonkers, N.Y.: The Hudson River Museum of Westchester, 1987), pp. 109, 133; *NYT,* 26 November 1877, p. 8; Raymond Jackson Wilson, *Figures of Speech, American Writers and the Literary Marketplace, From Benjamin Franklin to Emily Dickinson* (New York: Knopf, 1989), pp. 72, 76, 82, 88.

118 Bayard Tuckerman, *The Diary of Philip Hone, 1828–1851* (New York: Dodd, Mead and Company, 1889), entry of April 8, 1850, vol. 2, p. 378.

119 On this point see also Edmond Goblot, *La Barrière et le Niveau* (Paris: Librairie Félix Alcan, 1925), p. 23.

120 For the notion of separate spheres see especially Nancy Cott, *The Bonds of Womanhood: "Woman's Sphere" in New England, 1780–1835* (New Haven: Yale University Press, 1977). For explorations of the class-specific nature of

this notion see Carol Lasser, "Gender, Ideology, and Class in the Early Republic," in *Journal of the Early Republic* 10 (1990): 334.

121 See John A. Kouwenhoven, *Partners in Banking: An Historical Portrait of a Great Private Bank, Brown Brothers Harriman & Co., 1818–1968* (New York: Doubleday & Company, 1968), p. 85.

122 See, for example, "A Parlor View in a New York Dwelling House," 1854, reprinted in Churchill, *The Upper Crust,* p. 46. For illustrations of typical bourgeois furniture, see Eileen and Richard Dubrow, *American Furniture of the 19th Century* (Exton, Pa.: Schiffer Publishing Ltd., 1983); Elan and Susan Zingman-Leith, *The Secret Life of Victorian Houses* (Washington, D.C.: Elliott & Clark Publishing, 1993).

123 See also Katherine C. Grier, "The Decline of the Memory Palace, The Parlor After 1880," in Jessica H. Foy and Thomas J. Schlereth, eds., *American Home Life, 1880–1930: A Social History of Spaces and Services* (Knoxville: University of Tennessee Press, 1992), p. 51.

124 John Crosby Brown, *Reminiscences of the Early Life* (New York: n.p., n.d.), p. 24.

125 Brown, *Reminiscences of the Early Life,* p. 18.

126 1855 sample. Bankers employed, on average, 4.2 servants, professionals 2.8, people active in commerce 2.7, and manufacturers 2.3. Only the extraordinarily wealthy, such as James Brown and Sheppard Knapp, a banker on Washington Square, employed eight servants. See also Brown, *Reminiscences,* p. 26.

127 See, among others, Nicola Beisel, "Upper Class Formation and the Politics of Censorship in Boston, New York, and Philadelphia, 1872–1892" (Ph.D. diss., University of Michigan, 1990), p. 45.

128 See Beisel, "Upper Class Formation," p. 2.

129 Norbert Elias, *Über den Prozeß der Zivilisation: Soziogenetische und Psychogenetische Untersuchungen* (Frankfurt: Suhrkamp Verlag, 1976), passim.

130 *Hunt's* 41 (1859): 644; *Hunt's* 39 (1859): 140.

131 Hodas, *The Business Career of Moses Taylor,* p. 10.

132 Hodas, *The Business Career of Moses Taylor,* p. 37.

133 In the words of his biographer, Robert McElroy. See McElroy, *Levi Parsons Morton,* p. 40.

134 *Hunt's* 32 (1855): 522.

135 *American Merchant* 1 (June, 1858): 56.

136 Henry Moore Diary, entry of September 30, 1857, Rutgers University, New Brunswick, N.J.

137 Anna Robeson Burr, *The Portrait of a Banker: James Stilman, 1850–1918* (New York: Duffield, 1927), p. 42; John Ward Diary, April 1–April 20, 1864, NYHS; Benjamin Franklin, *The Autobiography of Benjamin Franklin,* reprinted in J. A. Leo Lemay and P. M. Zall, eds., *Benjamin Franklin's Autobiography* (New York: Norton, 1986), p. 54.

138 Martyn, *William E. Dodge,* p. 156.

139 Martyn, *William E. Dodge,* pp. 156–161.

140 *Hunt's* 35 (1856): 388; *Hunt's* 31 (1854): 263; *Hunt's* 34 (1856): 60; *Hunt's* 31 (1854): 59; *Hunt's* 41 (1859): 644; *Hunt's* 34 (1856): 59.

141 *Hunt's* 37 (1857): 515.

142 See, for example, New York, vol. 374, pp. 35, 41, 61, 63, 71, 75, 117, Dun & Co. Collection, Baker Library, Harvard Business School.

143 *Hunt's* 33 (1855): 390.

144 For a discussion of the recent literature on the bourgeois culture of consumption, see Lisa Tiersten, "Redefining Consumer Culture, Recent Literature on Consumption and the Bourgeoisie in Western Europe," in *RHR* 57 (Fall 1993), pp. 116–159. See also William Leach, *True Love and Perfect Union: The Feminist Reform of Sex and Society* (New York: Basic Books, 1980), pp. 222–226.

145 *NYH,* 18 September 1846, p. 2.

146 Christine M. Boyer, *Manhattan Manners: Architecture and Style, 1850–1900* (New York: Rizolli, 1985), p. 90.

147 *Hunt's* 31 (1854): 61; *Hunt's* 33 (1855): 558; *Hunt's* 30 (1854): 649. Calls against "extravagances" can also be found in the *USEconomist* 13 (18 June 1853): 18.

148 Karen Halttunen, *Confidence Men and Painted Women, A Study of Middle-Class Culture in America, 1830–1870* (New Haven: Yale University Press, 1982), pp. 163, 196.

149 Halttunen, *Confidence Men and Painted Women,* p. 162.

150 See Stella Blum, *Fashions and Costumes from Godey's Lady's Book* (New York: Dover Publications, 1985).

151 As wonderfully described by Karen Halttunen, *Confidence Men and Painted Women,* p. 167–174.

152 The concept of "social capital" is derived from Pierre Bourdieu's work. Pierre Bourdieu, *Distinction: A Social Critique of the Judgment of Taste* (Cambridge, Mass.: Harvard University Press, 1984), p. 114.

153 August Belmont, for example, regularly summered in Saratoga Springs. See "August Belmont," in Schweikart, ed., *Encyclopedia of American Business History and Biography, Banking and Finance to 1913,* p. 38; Betsy Blackmar, "Going to the Mountains, A Social History," in The Architectural League of New York, *Resorts of the Catskills* (New York: St. Martin's Press, 1979), pp. 71–98.

154 See also Churchill, *The Upper Crust,* p. 43.

155 Robert B. Minturn, *From New York to Delhi: By Way of Rio de Janeiro, Australia and China* (New York: D. Appleton & Co., 1858); *NYT,* 17 December 1889, p. 5.

156 Robert Bowne Minturn, *Memoir of Robert Bowne Minturn* (New York: Anson D. F. Randolph & Company, 1871), pp. 154, 157.

157 Letters to his mother, Box 1, Theodore Roosevelt Family Papers, LDC.

158 Letters to his mother, Box 1, Theodore Roosevelt Family Papers, LDC.

159 Beekman Family Papers, NYHS; Philip L. White, *The Beekmans of New York in Politics and Commerce* (New York: The New-York Historical Society, 1956), pp. 618–619.

160 David Scobey, "Anatomy of the Promenade: The Politics of Bourgeois Sociability in Nineteenth-Century New York," in *Social History* 17 (May 1992): 203–227.

161 The first quote is from *Appleton's Directory of New York and Vicinity* (1884), p. 8, the second quote from Walt Whitman, "Broadway," in *Life Illustrated* (9 August 1856).

162 Scobey, "Promenade," p. 213.

163 Brown, *Reminiscences,* p. 28.

164 Susan E. Lyman, "New Year's Day in 1861," in *NYHSQ* 28 (January 1944): 21–28.

165 See, for example, visiting list of Frederic DePeyster for 1857, DePeyster Papers, NYHS; and List of New Year's Calls, Jan 1, 1860, in 1860 Folder, Low Family Papers, 1850–1869, NYHS.

166 May King Van Rensselaer, *The Social Ladder* (New York: Henry Holt and Company, 1924), p. 31.

167 *The Laws of Etiquette, or Short Rules and Reflections for Conduct in Society* (Philadelphia: Carey, Lea, and Blanchard, 1836), p. 10.

2. Navigating the New Metropolis

1 Robert Ernst, *Immigrant Life in New York City, 1825–1863* (New York: King's Crown Press, 1949), p. 20.

2 Lydia Child, *Letters from New York, Second Series* (New York: C. S. Francis & Co., 1846), pp. 279–280.

3 *NYH,* 15 July 1850, p. 2.

4 Mary P. Ryan, *Civic Wars: Democracy and Public Life in the American City during the Nineteenth Century* (Berkeley: University of California Press, 1997), p. 37. A good survey of New York's cultural history during those years is Thomas Bender, *New York Intellect: A History of Intellectual Life in New York City, From 1750 to the Beginnings of Our Own Time* (New York: Knopf, 1987), especially pp. 66, 75.

5 For a persuasive account of the fluid nature of public spaces in antebellum cities see Ryan, *Civic Wars,* pp. 22–93.

6 Alexis de Tocqueville, *Democracy in America,* ed. Phillips Bradley (New York: Vintage Books, 1945), vol. 1, p. 198; vol. 2, p. 114. For a discussion that focuses on New York City see Ryan, *Civic Wars,* pp. 74–75.

7 For the concept of the public sphere see Jürgen Habermas, *The Structural Transformation of the Public Sphere: An Inquiry into a Category of Bourgeois Society* (Cambridge, Mass.: MIT Press, 1989), especially pp. 31–43.

8 Andrew Stulman Dennett, *Weird and Wonderful: The Dime Museum in America* (New York: New York University Press, 1997), pp. 18, 26.

9 Dennett, *Weird and Wonderful,* p. 27.

10 Dennett, *Weird and Wonderful,* p. 30. Rossiter Raymond, *Peter Cooper* (Boston: Houghton, Mifflin, 1901), p. 69. For the general point see also Ryan, *Civic Wars,* p. 38.

11 Douglas T. Miller, *Jacksonian Aristocracy: Class and Democracy in New York, 1830–1860* (New York: Oxford University Press, 1967), p. 162; Calvin Tomkins, *Merchants and Masterpieces: The Story of the Metropolitan Museum of Art* (New York: Henry Holt, 1989), pp. 22, 27.

12 Tomkins, *Merchants and Masterpieces,* pp. 26–27.

13 New-York Historical Society, *Proceedings at the Dedication of the Library, Tuesday, November 3, 1857* (New York: [printed for the society], 1857), p. 6.

14 Henry Edward Krehbiel, *The Philharmonic Society of New York* (New York and London: Novello, Ewer & Co., 1892), p. 28.

15 Krehbiel, *The Philharmonic Society of New York*, p. 65.

16 Krehbiel, *The Philharmonic Society of New York*, pp. 28–29.

17 John Warren Frick, Jr., "The Rialto: A Study of Union Square, The Center of New York's First Theatre District, 1870–1900" (Ph.D. diss., New York University, 1983), pp. 72, 151.

18 Salomon Rothschild to his brother-in-law, New York, February 10, 1860. Reprinted in Sigmund Diamond, *A Casual View of America: The Home Letters of Salomon de Rothschild, 1859–1861* (Stanford, Calif.: Stanford University Press, 1961), p. 31.

19 Salomon Rothschild to his brother-in-law, New York, February 10, 1860. Reprinted in Diamond, *A Casual View of America*, p. 31.

20 Peter George Buckley, "To the Opera House: Culture and Society in New York City, 1820–1860" (Ph.D. diss., SUNY Stony Brook, 1984), p. 9. For an excellent analysis of all these process see Paul DiMaggio, "Cultural Entrepreneurship in Nineteenth-Century Boston: The Creation of an Organizational Base of High Culture in America," in *Media, Culture and Society* (1982): 33–50.

21 See Roy Rosenzweig and Elizabeth Blackmar, *The Park and the People: A History of Central Park* (Ithaca, N.Y.: Cornell University Press, 1992), pp. 16–27.

22 *New York Evening Post*, 10 July 1851, as quoted in Rosenzweig and Blackmar, *The Park and the People*, p. 27.

23 Rosenzweig and Blackmar, *The Park and the People*, p. 23. On the Mercantile Library see *Appeal to the Merchants of New York in Behalf of the Mercantile Library Association* (New York: Baker & Godwin, 1855).

24 Alexis de Tocqueville, *Democracy in America*, vol. 2, p. 36.

25 See also, Tompkins, *Merchants and Masterpieces*, p. 27.

26 Ernst, *Immigrant Life in New York City*, p. 17.

27 See also Sean Wilentz, *Chants Democratic: New York City and the Rise of the American Working-Class, 1788–1850* (New York: Oxford University Press, 1984), pp. 107–142.

28 Ernst, *Immigrant Life in New York City*, p. 17.

29 1855 sample.

30 Wilentz, *Chants Democratic*, p. 107.

31 Thomas C. Cochran, *Frontiers of Change: Early Industrialism in America* (New York: Oxford University Press, 1981): 112.

32 United States, Secretary of the Interior, *Census of the United States in 1860, Compiled from the Original Returns of the Eighth Census* (Washington: G.P.O., 1865), pp. 379, 380, 382, 384; Carl Neumann Degler, "Labor in the Economy and Politics of New York City, 1850–1860" (Ph.D. diss., Columbia University, 1952), p. 9.

33 Degler, "Labor in the Economy," p. 8. On the Allaire Works (builder of steam engines) see H. T. Madison, "The Growth of New York City as a Manufacturing Center" (Ph.D. diss., New York University, 1914), n.p. Other iron manu-

facturers also employed more than a 1,000 workers each, such as the Delamater Iron Works. Other large employers included the Cornell Iron Works (500 workers), the John Stephenson Car Works, the William Tilden Varnish Works, and Robert Hoe and Company, as well as Steinway & Sons. Large employers in the clothing industry included P. L. Rogers, Hanford Brothers, and S. Chambers. See Patricia Evelyn Malon, "The Growth of Manufacturing in Manhattan, 1860–1900," p. 98. See also Robert Ernst, *Immigrant New York,* p. 18.

34 Merchants, however, were reluctant to provide capital for manufacturing purposes, preferring investment in real estate and the expansion of trade. See Allan R. Pred, *The Spatial Dynamics of U.S. Urban-Industrial Growth, 1800–1914: Interpretative and Theoretical Essays* (Cambridge, Mass.: MIT Press, 1966), p. 153. For the close connection between trade and the specific kinds of industries emerging in New York City, see especially p. 168.

35 United States, Secretary of the Interior, *Census of the United States in 1860,* pp. 379, 380, 382, 384; Degler, "Labor in the Economy," p. 49.

36 See, for example, the reports on Cornelius Delamater. "Cornelius Delamater," entry of September 14, 1857, New York, vol. 316a, p. 185, and entry of October 9, 1869, New York, vol. 411, p. 100L, Dun & Co. Collection, Baker Library, Harvard Business School.

37 Wholesale merchants controlled the largest share of the nation's capital; they maneuvered – according to Allan Pred – into a position of a "virtual monopoly" on the outside financing of manufacturing. Pred, *Urban-Industrial Growth,* p. 128.

38 "Novelty Iron Works," New York, vol. 368, pp. 400, 431, 440, 441, Dun & Co. Collection, Baker Library, Harvard Business School.

39 *The National Cyclopedia of American Biography, Being the History of the United States* (New York: James T. White & Company, 1897), vol. 7, p. 320.

40 *The National Cyclopedia of American Biography,* vol. 7, p. 68; Irene Tichenor, "Theodore Low De Vinne, 1828–1914, Dean of American Printers" (Ph.D. diss., Columbia University, 1983).

41 Fred Dietz, *A Leaf from the Past, Dietz Then and Now* (New York: R. E. Dietz Company, 1914), pp. 60, 74, 77, 94.

42 *The National Cyclopedia of American Biography,* vol. 30, p. 544.

43 Ernst, *Immigrant Life in New York City,* p. 93.

44 "Richard Hoe," entry of May 1851, New York, vol. 360, p. 5, Dun & Co. Collection, Baker Library, Harvard Business School; Iver Bernstein, *The New York City Draft Riots* (New York: Oxford University Press, 1990), p. 165. In 1859 George Quintard mortgaged his land and buildings to the Bowery Savings Bank and the Dry Dock Savings bank. See "George Quintard," entry of December 10, 1859, New York, vol. 316, p. 1/G, Dun & Co. Collection, Baker Library, Harvard Business School.

45 "His prospects are very good." "John Roach," entry of August 31, 1854, New York, vol. 317, p. 229, Dun & Co. Collection, Baker Library, Harvard Business School.

46 Leonard Alexander Swann, Jr., *John Roach, Maritime Entrepreneur: The Years as Naval Contractor, 1862–1886* (Annapolis: United States Naval Institute, 1965), pp. 12–16.

47 Peter Cooper quoted in Allan Nevins, *Abram S. Hewitt, With Some Account of Peter Cooper* (New York: Harper, 1935), p. 55.

48 Raymond, *Peter Cooper*, p. 69f.

49 Nevins, *Abram S. Hewitt*, p. 59. The capital for his venture very likely came from his family and personal savings.

50 Nevins, *Abram S. Hewitt*, p. 59–61.

51 Edward C. Mack, *Peter Cooper: Citizen of New York* (New York: Duell, Sloan and Pearce, 1949), pp. 35, 40, 44, 69, 204, 205; Nevins, *Abram S. Hewitt*, p. 46.

52 Elizabeth Blackmar, *Manhattan for Rent, 1785–1850* (Ithaca, N. Y.: Cornell University Press, 1989), pp. 40, 106.

53 Blackmar, *Manhattan for Rent*, p. 251.

54 Robert S. Buchanan Papers, NYHS. He also owned seventy lots outside of Manhattan, two houses on West 25th Street, a farm on Todt Hill, and another building whose location he did not specify.

55 Peter S. Hoe to Robert Hoe, New York, June 3, 1856, Hoe Papers, Library of Congress. The Hoes followed real estate prices with great attention. See, for example, Peter S. Hoe to Robert Hoe, New York, May 10, 1859, Hoe Papers, Library of Congress.

56 Indeed, a small but significant number of New York's wealthy (about 5 percent) based their fortunes entirely on this sector. 1855 sample.

57 Especially after 1852, when the city began to pay contractors before assessments were collected. See Eduard Durand, *The Finances of New York City* (New York: The Macmillan Company, 1898), p. 107.

58 John D. Crimmins, *The Diary of John D. Crimmins from 1878 to 1917* (n.p.: [privately printed], 1925), p. 1058.

59 Eugene P. Moehring, *Public Works and the Patterns of Urban Real Estate Growth in Manhattan, 1835–1894* (New York: Arno Press, 1981), pp. 256, 257, 264. On Masterson see also Robert Ernst, *Immigrant Life*, p. 75.

60 "William S. Dudley & Co.," New York, vol. 374, p. 200, Dun & Co. Collection, Baker Library, Harvard Business School.

61 Robert Greenhalgh Albion, *The Rise of New York Port, 1815–1860* (New York: C. Scribner's Sons, 1939), p. 259.

62 For the earlier proximity of counting houses and living quarters see Albion, *The Rise of New York Port*, p. 254.

63 Blackmar, *Manhattan for Rent*, pp. 149–212.

64 John Crosby Brown, *Reminiscences of the Early Life* (New York: n.p., n.d.), p. 16.

65 Charles Howland Russell, *Memoir of Charles H, Russell, 1796–1884* (New York: n.p., 1903), p. 52.

66 See, for this point, Amy Bridges, *A City in the Republic: Antebellum New York and the Origins of Machine Politics* (New York: Cambridge University Press, 1984), p. 43. These findings are supported also by the extremely thorough and detailed study of Kenneth A. Scherzer, *The Unbounded Community: Neighborhood Life and Social Structure in New York City, 1830–1875* (Durham, N.C.: Duke University Press, 1992). Scherzer finds that "social rank was emerging as the most important – and only distinct – determinant of residential choice" (p. 36).

67 *Annual Report of the Chamber of Commerce of the State of New York, for the Year 1858* (New York: Wheeler and Williams, 1859), pp. 340–350.

68 Albion, *The Rise of New York Port,* p. 265.

69 These numbers are derived from an analysis of the primary economic activities of all members of the Chamber of Commerce in the year 1858.

70 Francis Gerry Fairfield, *The Clubs of New York* (New York: H. L. Hinton, 1873), p. 59. See also Reginald Townsend, *Mother of Clubs: Being the History of the First Hundred Years of the Union Club of the City of New York, 1836–1936* (New York: William Edwin Rudge, 1936). On Belmont see David Black, *The King of Fifth Avenue: The Fortunes of August Belmont* (New York: Dial Press, 1981), p. 60.

71 Fairfield, *The Clubs of New York,* p. 64.

72 Townsend, *Mother of Clubs,* p. 57.

73 Townsend, *Mother of Clubs,* pp. 2, 84–87. See also Bender, *New York Intellect,* p. 135. For the Century Club, the members listed are for 1873.

74 The numbers are based on an analysis of a sample of 65 members of the New York Club, 1862, of which 43 could be located in the *City Directory* of 1862 and an analysis of a sample of 316 members of the Union Club who had joined the club before 1860, of whom 169 could be identified in Trow's city directory. For the members of the New York Club, see *Constitution of the New York Club, with a List of Members, May 1862* (New York: Charles O. Jones, Stationer and Printer, 1862); for the Union Club members see Townsend, *Mother of Clubs.*

75 Maxwell Whiteman, *Copper for America: The Hendricks Family and a National Industry, 1755–1936* (New Brunswick, N.J.: Rutgers University Press, 1971), pp. 292f. The Hendricks family also joined the St. Nicholas Society. See Whiteman, *Copper for America,* p. 218. Upper-class anti-Semitism, so important in the 1880s and 1890s, had not yet pervaded the thinking of the city's wealthy. See Frederic Cople Jaher, *A Scapegoat in the New Wilderness: The Origins and Rise of Anti-Semitism in America* (Cambridge, Mass.: Harvard University Press, 1994), pp. 5, 181.

76 Carl Lamson Carmer, *The Years of Grace, 1808–1958* (New York: Grace Church, 1958), p. 5; Elizabeth Blackmar, *Manhattan for Rent,* pp. 30–33, 210; Daniel Hodas, *The Business Career of Moses Taylor, Merchant, Finance Capitalist, and Industrialist* (New York: New York University Press, 1976), p. 162. For the social exclusiveness of churches, see also Scherzer, "The Unbounded Community," p. 196.

77 Townsend, *Mother of Clubs,* pp. 60–61.

78 Daniel Hodas, *The Business Career of Moses Taylor,* pp. 7–8.

79 Edward F. DeLancey, *Memoir of James William Beekman: Prepared at the Request of the St. Nicholas Society of the City of New York* (New York: St. Nicholas Society, 1877), p. 17.

80 "August Belmont," in Larry Schweikart, ed., *Encyclopedia of American Business History and Biography, Banking and Finance to 1913* (New York: Facts on File, 1990), p. 39.

81 See, for example, Miller, *Jacksonian Aristocracy,* p. 76.

82 Henry Anstice, *History of St. George's Church in the City of New York, 1752–1911* (New York: Harper & Brothers, 1911), p. 168.

83 Anstice, *History of St. George's Church,* p. 179. Trinity's congregation sent its rector to Europe in 1853, endowed with $1,500. See Morgan Dix, ed., *A History of the Parish of Trinity Church in the City of New York* (New York: G. P. Putnam's Sons, 1906), p. 379.

84 *NYH,* 8 March 1846, quoted in William R. Stewart, *Grace Church and Old New York* (New York: E. P. Dutton & Company, 1924), p. 161.

85 Philip Hone, diary entry of February 5, 1846, cited in Stewart, *Grace Church and Old New York,* p. 157.

86 Miller, *Jacksonian Aristocracy,* p. 158; Jaher, *The Urban Establishment,* pp. 230–231; Brown, *Reminiscences,* p. 22; Carl Carmer, *The Years of Grace, 1808–1958* (New York: Grace Church, 1958), p. 2.

87 Howard Crosby, *Sketch of the Fourth Avenue Presbyterian Church* (New York: E. French, 1864), pp. 8–9.

88 Anstice, *History of St. George's Church,* p. 168.

89 Anstice, *History of St. George's Church,* p. 198.

90 Its minister, William Berrian, happily noted that "I see the old and familiar faces of many to whom I had ministered in the outset of life." Dix, ed., *A History of the Parish of Trinity Church,* p. 413.

91 Anstice, *History of St. George's Church,* p. 195; William Berrian, *The Rector Rectified, In Reply to Facts Against Fancy* (New York: Anson D. F. Randolph, 1856), p. 44.

92 During the 1850s, Trinity Church counted 34 vestrymen and churchwardens. Twenty-five of these could be located in *Trow's City Directory.* Of those, 24 percent were engaged in trade, 20 percent in finance, 44 percent as professionals (mostly lawyers), and 8 percent as rentiers. See James Boorman, *A Letter from Mr. James Boorman to the Rector, Church Wardens and Vestrymen of Trinity Church in the City of New-York* (New York: n. p., 1855), p. 3; Dix, ed., *A History of the Parish of Trinity Church,* pp. 580–581; H. Wilson, *Trow's New-York City Directory, For 1854–1855* (New York: John F. Trow, 1855), pp. 580–581.

93 Analysis of the vestrymen and wardens of St. George's Church who served during the 1850s. Of the thirteen persons thus engaged, all could be located in *Trow's City Directory.* For their names, see Anstice, *History of St. George's Church,* pp. 442–453.

94 James J. Mapes, *Inaugural Address Delivered Tuesday Evening, January 7, 1845, Before the Mechanic's Institute of the City of New York* (New York: Institute Rooms, 1845), p. 11.

95 *SciAm* (29 March 1879): 193.

96 Mack, *Peter Cooper,* p. 165.

97 Nevins, *Hewitt,* p. 144.

98 Nevins, *Hewitt,* p. 268.

99 Mack, *Peter Cooper,* p. 182.

100 Horace Greeley, *Recollections of a Busy Life, Including Reminiscences of American Politics and Politicians, From the Opening of the Missouri Contest to the Downfall of Slavery* (New York: J. Ford and Company, 1868), p. 148.

101 Nevins, *Hewitt,* p. 147.

102 For Singer, see Charles M. Eastley, *The Singer Saga* (Braunton, Eng.: Merlin Books Ltd., 1983), passim.

103 1855 sample. Twenty-six and 30 percent, respectively, of all industrialists lived in these two wards.

104 *SciAm* (10 January 1880): 17; Richard K. Lieberman, *Steinway & Sons* (New Haven: Yale University Press, 1995), p. 21.

105 Allan Nevins and Milton Halsey Thomas, eds., *The Diary of George Templeton Strong* (New York: Macmillan, 1952), vol. 3, p. 52. Entry for October 22, 1860.

106 *NYT,* 17 October 1860, p. 3.

107 "John Roach," entry of June 4, 1860, New York, vol. 317, p. 229, Dun & Co. Collection, Baker Library, Harvard Business School.

108 "John Roach," entry of November 28, 1865, New York, vol. 317, p. 300 (p), Dun & Co. Collection, Baker Library, Harvard Business School.

109 "Richard Hoe," entry of May 1851, New York, vol. 360, p. 51, Dun & Co. Collection, Baker Library, Harvard Business School. One of the owners of the Novelty Iron Works was similarly scorned as "given to politics and big talk and . . . not in good standing. See "Novelty Iron Works," entry of April 10, 1855, New York, vol. 124, p. 285, Dun & Co. Collection, Baker Library, Harvard Business School.

110 Swann, Jr., *John Roach,* p. 23.

111 Peter S. Hoe to Robert Hoe, New York, October 20, 1857, Hoe Papers, Library of Congress.

112 Peter S. Hoe to Richard Hoe, New York, September 1, 1857, Hoe Papers, Library of Congress.

113 Raymond, *Peter Cooper,* p. x; Mack, *Peter Cooper,* pp. 164–165.

114 Mack, *Peter Cooper,* p. 166.

115 Nevins, *Hewitt,* p. 138.

116 See letter by Peter S. Hoe to Robert Hoe, New York, November 25, 1868, Hoe Papers, Library of Congress. Also letter by Peter S. Hoe to Robert Hoe, Brightside, June 7, 1858, in Hoe Papers, Library of Congress.

117 Alexander D. Bache, *Anniversary Address Before the American Institute, Of the City of New-York, at the Tabernacle, October 28, 1856, During the Twenty-Eighth Annual Fair* (New York: Pudney & Russell, 1857), p. 32. Both institutions were clearly dominated by manufacturers, as an analysis of the officers of the Mechanics' Institute demonstrates. For the names of members, see *Catalog of the Library of the Mechanics' Institute, of the City of New-York; Regulations of the Reading Room and Library; and Circular to the Public* (New York: A. Baptist, Jr., Printer, 1844).

118 *Catalogue of the Library of the Mechanics' Institute of the City of New York,* p. 63. For the composition of the leadership of the Mechanics' Institute, see James Mapes, *Inaugural Address Delivered Tuesday Evening, January 7, 1845, Before the Mechanic's Institute of the City of New York* (New York: Institute Rooms, 1845), p. 2, and *Catalogue of the Library of the Mechanics' Institute of the City of New York,* p. 64. Most of the institute's activists were in one way or another engaged in manufacturing, with the remainder working as professionals or in white-collar occupations. No merchants served in the leadership of the institute.

119 See *Catalogue of the Library of the Mechanics' Institute of the City of New*

York; Mapes, *Inaugural Address Delivered Tuesday Evening, January 7, 1845,* p. 9.

120 Mapes, *Inaugural Address Delivered Tuesday Evening, January 7, 1845,* p. 9.

121 Oakey A. Hall, *Anniversary Address Before the American Institute, at Palace Garden, October 29, 1859* (New York, n.p., 1859), p. 22. For the list of trustees and committee members of the American Institute, see *Transactions of the American Institute of the City of New-York for the Year 1855* (Albany, N.Y.: C. Van Benthuysen, 1856).

122 *Transactions of the American Institute of the City of New-York for the Year 1855,* p. 7; Hall, *Anniversary Address Before the American Institute,* p. 29; *Transactions of the American Institute of the City of New-York for the Year 1856* (Albany, N.Y.: C. Van Benthuysen, 1857), p. 9.

123 For a discussion of the concept of "gentlemanly capitalism" (for Great Britain), see P. J. Cain and A. G. Hopkins, "Gentlemanly Capitalism and British Expansion Overseas: The Old Colonial System, 1688–1850," in *Economic History Review* 39 (1986): 501–525. For the industrialists' sense of distance, see Mapes, *Inaugural Address Delivered Tuesday Evening, January 7, 1845,* p. 11.

124 *Hunt's* 33 (1855): 557.

125 Mapes, *Inaugural Address Delivered Tuesday Evening, January 7, 1845,* p. 11.

126 *Hunt's* 31 (1854): 518, 649; *Hunt's* 34 (1856): 58–59; *Hunt's* 35 (1856): 56.

127 *Hunt's* 30 (1854): 390.

128 *Hunt's* 37 (1857): 703; *Hunt's* 35 (1856): 54–55.

129 On the St. Andrew's Society see Ernst, *Immigrant Life in New York City,* p. 92.

130 Albion, *The Rise of New York Port,* p. 255; DeLancey, *Memoir of James William Beekman,* p. 16; *Charter, Constitution, By-Laws and List of Members of the St. Nicholas Society of the City of New York* (New York: [privately printed for the society], 1907).

131 By running social services and labor exchanges, the German-American bourgeoisie tried to gain a leadership role in the larger German-American community, a role they successfully transformed into political power. The German Society, for example, had a permanent seat on the Emigration Board, which played an important role in regulating the processing of immigrants in New York. See Dieter Plehwe, "The German Society of New York" (New York, unpublished paper, 1986), and Klaus Wust, *Guardian on the Hudson, The German Society of the City of New York, 1784–1984* (New York: German Society, 1984), pp. 28–42. For the names of the society's members in 1857 see the "Liste der Mitglieder," in the archives of the German Society of New York. Despite the diversity of its membership, however, the overwhelming majority were still engaged in trade, a full 76 percent.

132 Richard C. Murphy and Lawrence J. Mannion, *The History of the Society of the Friendly Sons of Saint Patrick in the City of New York, 1784 to 1955* (New York: J. C. Dillon Company, 1982), p. 260. On the Sons of St. Patrick see also Ryan, *Civic Wars,* p. 82. I analyzed the occupations of the members present at the meeting of March 6, 1851. Of the thirty members present, twenty-two could

be identified in the city directory. For their names, see Murphy and Mannion, *The History of the Society of the Friendly Sons of Saint Patrick,* pp. 281–282. See also pp. 290, 295. It is important to keep in mind that during the 1850s, the Irish-American bourgeoisie was still quite weak. It would not really develop until the last quarter of the century, when the Murray, Butler, McDonnell, and Cuddihy families came into their own. See Stephan Birmingham, *Real Lace: America's Irish Rich* (New York: Harper & Row, 1973), pp. 41, 51, 62, 78.

133   Cohen, *Encounter with Emancipation,* p. 124. *Annual Report of the Hebrew Benevolent Society and Orphan Asylum of the City of New York* (New York: S. Benedicks & Co., Stationers, 1863).

In the 1850s, the African American bourgeoisie was so small and weak that it could not sustain organizations on a par with those of other groups. Only a few African Americans managed to accumulate some capital, and although these successful black businessmen would come to play an important role in their community and link that community to upper-class New Yorkers with abolitionist sentiments, they remained largely isolated from the bourgeois world of the city – from the family networks and cultural institutions. It is important to note that because they lacked easy access to wider bourgeois social networks, they lacked access to capital and business contacts and, thus, found many fewer opportunities for capital accumulation than did their white counterparts. See George E. Walker, *The Afro-American in New York City, 1827–1860* (New York: Garland Publishing, 1993), pp. 36–37; J. H. Harmon, Jr., Arnett G. Lindsay, and Carter G. Woodson, *The Negro as a Business Man* (1929; reprint College Park, Md.: McGrath Publishing Company, 1969), pp. 5–8. See also Lindsay, "The Economic Conditions of Negroes in New York Prior to 1861," in *Journal of Negro History* 6 (1921): 197. On black organizations see especially C. Peter Ripley, *The Black Abolitionist Papers,* vols. 1–5 (Chapel Hill: University of North Carolina Press, 1986–1991).

134   Ernst, *Immigrant Life in New York City,* p. 94.

135   DeLancey, *Memoir of James William Beekman,* p. 6.

136   *Transactions of the American Institute of the City of New-York for the Year 1855,* p. 15.

137   Speech by John Ward, 1857, "John Ward," Box 1, Ward Family Papers, NYHS.

138   New-York Historical Society, *Proceedings at the Dedication of the Library, Tuesday, November 3, 1857* (New York: [printed for the society], 1857), p. 11.

139   *Transactions of the American Institute of the City of New-York for the Year 1856,* p. 32.

140   *Transactions of the American Institute of the City of New-York for the Year 1857* (Albany, N.Y.: C. Van Benthuysen, 1858), p. 25.

141   See, for example, George Opdyke, *Treatise on Political Economy* (New York: G. P. Putnam, 1851), pp. 59–140.

142   E. P. Hurlbut, *Essays on Human Rights and Their Political Guaranties, with A Preface and Notes by George Combe* (Edinburgh: Maclachlan, Stewart & Co., 1847), pp. 11–15.

143 For an elaboration of this argument, see L. Ray Gunn, *The Decline of Authority, Public Policy and Political Development in New York, 1800–1860* (Ithaca, N.Y.: Cornell University Press, 1988), pp. 1ff. See also Bridges, *A City in the Republic,* p. 143. The ideological commitment to unregulated markets was often contradicted by the desire for protectionism and infrastructure improvements. See also *The Ninth Annual Report of the New-York Association for Improving the Conditions of the Poor, For the Year 1852* (New York: John F. Trow, 1852), p. 16.

144 *Hunt's* 37 (1857): 702.

145 *Fifteenth Annual Report of the New-York Association for Improving the Conditions of the Poor* (New York: John F. Trow, 1858), p. 32.

146 For a comprehensive discussion of these different positions, see Martin J. Burke, *The Conundrum of Class, Public Discourse on the Social Order in America* (Chicago: The University of Chicago Press, 1995), pp. 76–132.

147 Howard Furer, *William Frederick Havemeyer: A Political Biography* (New York: The American Press, 1965), p. 94; Charles Haynes Haswell, *Reminiscences of an Octogenarian of the City of New York* (New York: Harper & Brothers, 1896), p. 474.

148 Charles Haswell, *Reminiscences,* p. 472.

149 Thomas R. Whitney, *A Defense of the American Policy as Opposed to the Encroachments of Foreign Influence and Especially to the Interference of the Papacy in the Political Interests and Affairs of the United States* (New York: De Witt & Davenport, 1856), pp. 126, 128.

150 New York Journal of Commerce, *Corruption of the City Government, Reprint from the New York Journal of Commerce, of a Series of Unanswered and Unanswerable Editorials showing Deep Abuses in the New York City Government* (New York: Wm. C. Bryant & Co., 1853), p. 5. See also *JoC,* 12 November 1857, p. 2.

151 Alexis de Tocqueville, *Memoir, Letters, and Remains* (London: Macmillan and Co., 1861), vol. 1, p. 309. For the overwhelming support for universal male suffrage see also Chilton Williamson, *American Suffrage: From Property to Democracy, 1760–1860* (Princeton: Princeton University Press, 1960), pp. 260–280, 281, 288.

152 Letter of Salomon Rothschild, New York, December 19, 1859, and January 16, 1860, in Diamond, *A Casual View of America,* pp. 20, 27.

153 *Sixth Annual Report of the Chamber of Commerce of the State of New-York, For the Year 1863–64* (New York: John W. Amerman, 1864), p. 37.

154 Chamber of Commerce, *Proceedings of the Chamber of Commerce of the State of New York at the Opening of their New Rooms, June 10, 1858* (New York: John A. Douglas & Co., 1858), p. 10.

155 See in *Hunt's* 33 (1855): 555.

156 *Hunt's* 28 (1853): 24–25.

157 *Hunt's* 40 (1859): 518.

158 Speech by Charles King, President of Columbia College, at the New York Chamber of Commerce. Reprinted in *American Merchant* 1 (July 1858): 124.

159 Tom Paine, *The Rights of Man* (Harmondsworth, Eng.: Pelican Books, 1969), p. 99; Immanuel Kant, "Idea for a Universal History with a Cosmopolitan

Purpose," in Hans Reiss, ed., *Kant's Political Writings* (Cambridge: Cambridge University Press, 1970), p. 50.

160 Chamber of Commerce, *Proceedings of the Chamber of Commerce of the State of New York at the Opening of their New Rooms, June 10, 1858*, p. 8.

161 Chamber of Commerce, *Proceedings of the Chamber of Commerce of the State of New York at the Opening of their New Rooms, June 10, 1858*, p. 20.

162 Charles Sumner, "Past and Present Position of the Merchant," as quoted in *Hunt's* 32 (1855): 136. For similar statements, see *Hunt's* 33 (1855): 552; *Hunt's* 28 (1853): 676; *Hunt's* 30 (1854): 518; *Hunt's* 36 (1857): 219; *Hunt's* 40 (1859): 518–519; *USEconomist* 13 (30 April 1853): 19.

163 *American Merchant* 2 (November 1858): 35.

164 See, for example, Charles F. Hoffman, *The Pioneers of New-York: An Anniversary Discourse Delivered Before the St. Nicholas Society of Manhattan, December 6, 1847* (New York: Stanford and Swors, 1848), p. 14.

165 *Hunt's* 28 (1853): 36; Paul Migliore, "The Business of Union: New York's Business Community and the Civil War" (Ph.D. diss., Columbia University, 1975), p. 315; *Hunt's* 30 (1854): 392.

166 *Hunt's* 28 (1853): 135; *Hunt's* 34 (1856): 63.

167 *Hunt's* 34 (1856): 65, 645.

168 Alan Lester Olmstead, "New York City Mutual Savings Banks in the Ante-Bellum Years, 1819–1861" (Ph.D. diss., University of Wisconsin, 1970), pp. 25, 272, 273; *Hunt's* 33 (1855): 559. See also *Sixth Annual Report of the Chamber of Commerce of the State of New-York*, p. 37; Allan Stanley Horlick, *Country Boys and Merchant Princes: The Social Control of Young Men in New York* (Lewisburg, Pa.: Bucknell University Press, 1975), p. 67; *Fifteenth Annual Report of the New-York Association for Improving the Conditions of the Poor*, p. 34; William Betts, *The Causes of the Prosperity of New-York, An Anniversary Address delivered before the St. Nicholas Society of New-York, December 3d, 1850* (New York: Stanford and Swords, 1851), p. 27; Albion, *The Rise of New York Port*, p. 258; letter from Mary DePeyster to James W. Beekman, New York, February 8, 1855, Folder 8, Box 1, Beekman Papers, NYHS; Wilson, *Trow's New York City Directory for the Year Ending May 1, 1856*, pp. 48–51; *Annual Report of the Hebrew Benevolent Society and Orphan Asylum of the City of New York* (New York: S. Benedicks & Co., 1863).

169 See, for example, *Hunt's* 31 (1854): 265; *Hunt's* 34 (1856): 61, 63.

170 *Hunt's* 38 (1858): 405; *Hunt's* 35 (1856): 54; *Hunt's* 34 (1856): 64.

171 See *JoC*, 4 November 1857, p. 2; 7 November 1857, p. 2; 10 November 1857, p. 3; 12 November 1857, p. 1; 13 November 1857, p. 3.

172 *JoC*, 7 November 1857, p. 2.

173 *NYCA*, 18 February 1854, p. 2.

174 *Hunt's* 31 (1854): 265.

175 Betts, *The Causes of the Prosperity of New-York*, p. 23.

176 *Speech of Hon. Edwards Pierrepont, Delivered at a Meeting of the Judges and Lawyers of New York on the Occasion of the Death of Hon. Theodore Sedgwick, December 14, 1959* (New York: Wm. C. Bryant, 1864), pp. 10–11.

177 Wilentz, *Chants Democratic*, pp. 377, 380; On the strike, see *JoC*, 30 July 1850, p. 2; *NYCA*, 29 July 1850, p. 2.

178 Hall, *Anniversary Address Before the American Institute*, p. 24.

179 *Transactions of the American Institute of the City of New-York for the Year 1857*, p. 44; Hall, *Anniversary Address Before the American Institute*, pp. 24–27.

180 Wilentz, *Chants Democratic*, p. 17.

181 *Hunt's* 30 (1854): 390.

182 *Transactions of the American Institute of the City of New-York for the Year 1855*, p. 7.

183 "Address Delieverd at the Opening of the Twenty-Third Annual Fair," reprinted in *Transactions of the American Institute of the City of New-York for the Year 1850* (Albany, N.Y.: C. Van Benthuysen, 1851), p. 273. See also Hall, *Anniversary Address Before the American Institute*, p. 29; Bache, *Anniversary Address Before the American Institute*, p. 4.

184 *Transactions of the American Institute of the City of New-York for the Year 1856*, p. 30.

185 *Transactions of the American Institute of the City of New-York for the Year 1856*, pp. 29, 37.

186 Nevins, *Hewitt*, p. 73.

187 Raymond, *Peter Cooper*, p. xi.

188 Nevins, *Hewitt*, pp. 135, 441.

189 Peter S. Hoe to Robert Hoe, New York, October 20, 1857, in Hoe Papers, Library of Congress.

190 Wilentz, *Chants Democratic*, pp. 373, 377.

191 Degler, "Labor in the Economy," pp. 14, 15, 16, 18.

192 See also Anthony F. C. Wallace, *Rockdale, The Growth of an American Village in the Early Industrial Revolution* (New York: Alfred A. Knopf, 1978), passim.

193 See Eric Foner, *Free Soil, Free Labor, Free Men: The Ideology of the Republican Party before the Civil War* (New York: Oxford University Press, 1970).

194 *NYDT*, 2 May 1846, p. 3.

195 At least no able-bodied paupers. Greeley, *Recollections of a Busy Life*, p. 147.

196 *NYDT*, 7 November 1857, p. 4.

197 *NYDT*, 11 November 1857, p. 5.

198 Bernstein, *New York City Draft Riots*, p. 173.

199 Bernstein, *New York City Draft Riots*, pp. 172–173.

200 Mack, *Peter Cooper*, p. 245.

201 Mack, *Peter Cooper*, p. 252; Cooper Papers, "Address to Students," 1871, cited in Mack, *Peter Cooper*, p. 250.

202 Mack, *Peter Cooper*, p. 244.

203 Peter Cooper quoted in "Peter Cooper," in *The Encyclopedia of American Business History and Biography*, p. 106.

204 On Central Park, see Rosenzweig and Blackmar, *The Park and the People*, pp. 22–25.

205 Wilson, *Trow's New York City Directory for the Year Ending May 1, 1856*,

Appendix, pp. 44–47; Leonard I. Sweet, "Nineteenth-Century Evangelism," in Charles H. Lippy and Peter W. Williams, eds., *Encyclopedia of the American Religious Experience: Studies of Traditions and Movements* (New York: Charles Scribner's Sons, 1988), p. 876.

206 William Gerald McLoughlin, *The Meaning of Henry Ward Beecher: An Essay on the Shifting Values of Mid-Victorian America, 1840–1870* (New York: Knopf, 1970), p. 21.

207 Bernstein, *New York City Draft Riots,* pp. 155, 156; Jeanne Boydston, Mary Kelley, and Anne Margolis, *The Limits of Sisterhood: The Beecher Sisters on Women's Rights and Woman's Sphere* (Chapel Hill: University of North Carolina Press, 1988), pp. 4–5; Catherine E. Beecher, *Treatise on Domestic Economy for Use of Young Ladies at Home and at School,* rev. ed. (Boston: Thomas H. Webb & Co., 1842); McLoughlin, *The Meaning of Henry Ward Beecher,* p. 132.

208 Clifford S. Griffin, *Their Brothers' Keepers: Moral Stewardship in the United States, 1800–1865* (Westport, Conn.: Greenwood Press, 1960), p. xi.

209 James Beekman, in *Proceedings of the New-York Historical Society* (October-December, 1849), p. 254.

210 See also Theda Skocpol, *Protecting Soldiers and Mothers* (Cambridge, Mass.: Harvard University Press, 1992), p. 51; Lori D. Ginzberg, *Women and the Work of Benevolence: Morality, Politics, and Class in the 19th-Century United States* (New Haven: Yale University Press, 1990), pp. 41, 56, 60, 62; for organizations led by women see Wilson, *Trow's New York City Directory for the Year Ending May 1, 1856,* Appendix, pp. 47–48.

211 *The Tenth Annual Report of the New-York Association for the Improvement of the Conditions of the Poor, for the Year 1853* (New York: John F. Trow, 1853), p. 17.

212 Bernstein, *New York City Draft Riots,* p. 177.

213 Analysis of a sample of 87 donors of the AICP in the year 1855.

214 *The Ninth Annual Report of the New-York Association for Improving the Conditions of the Poor, For the Year 1852,* p. 16; *Eleventh Annual Report of the New-York Association for the Improvement of the Conditions of the Poor, for the Year 1854* (New York: John F. Trow, 1854), p. 18.

215 Wilson, *Trow's New York City Directory for the Year Ending May 1, 1856,* Appendix, pp. 48–57; DeAlva Stanwood Alexander, *A Political History of the State of New York* (Port Washington, N.Y.: I. J. Friedman, 1969); Jack S. Blocker, *American Temperance Movements: Cycles of Reform* (Boston: Twayne Publishers, 1989), p. 57; James Beekman, in *Proceedings of the New York Historical Society* (October-December, 1849), p. 254; *Fortieth Annual Report of the American Bible Society, Presented May 8, 1856* (New York: American Bible Society, 1856), pp. 2, 17, 52; *Thirty-Seventh Annual Report of the American Bible Society, Presented May 12, 1853* (New York: American Bible Society, 1853), p. 16.

3. The Politics of Capital

1 For this argument see, among many others, Charles C. Bright, "The State in the United States During the Nineteenth Century," in Charles Bright and Susan Harding, eds., *Statemaking and Social Movements: Essays in History*

and Theory (Ann Arbor: University of Michigan Press, 1984), pp. 121–158. On the "weakness" of the antebellum state see also Theda Skocpol, *Protecting Soldiers and Mothers: The Political Origins of Social Policy in the United States* (Cambridge, Mass: Harvard University Press, 1992); Stephen Skowronek, *Building a New American State: The Expansion of National Administrative Capacities, 1877–1920* (New York: Cambridge University Press, 1982); and Richard Franklin Bensel, *Yankee Leviathan: The Origins of Central State Authority in America, 1859–1877* (New York: Cambridge University Press, 1990).

2 For the importance of the institutional-legal context of the state, see Roger Benjamin and Raymond Duvall, "The Capitalist State in Context," in Roger Benjamin and Stephan Elkin, eds., *The Democratic State* (Lawrence: University of Kansas Press, 1985), pp. 36–37.

3 Letter of June 12, 1860, reprinted in Sigmund Diamond, *A Casual View of America: The Home Letters of Salomon de Rothschild, 1859–1861* (Stanford, Calif.: Stanford University Press, 1961), p. 46.

4 U.S. Bureau of the Census, *Historical Statistics of the United States, Colonial Times to 1970* (Washington: U.S. Department of Commerce, 1975), vol. 2, p. 1106.

5 Amy Bridges, *A City in the Republic: Antebellum New York and the Origins of Machine Politics* (New York: Cambridge University Press, 1984), pp. 110, 115. See also Mary P. Ryan, *Civic Wars: Democracy and Public Life in the American City during the Nineteenth Century* (Berkeley: University of California Press, 1997), p. 308.

6 Bridges, *A City in the Republic*, p. 116.

7 Bridges, *A City in the Republic*, p. 123.

8 Eugene Moehring, *Public Works and Urban History: Recent Trends and New Directions* (Chicago: Public Works Historical Society, 1982), p. 265.

9 Gabriel A. Almond, *Plutocracy and Politics in New York City* (1938; reprint Colorado: Westview Press, 1998), pp. 59–70.

10 Amy Bridges, "Another Look at Plutocracy in Antebellum New York City" in *Political Science Quarterly* 97 (1982): 62.

11 Anthony Boleslaw Gronowicz, "Revising the Concept of Jacksonian Democracy" (Ph.D. diss., University of Pennsylvania, 1981), p. 49.

12 Reginald Townsend, *Mother of Clubs: Being the History of the First Hundred Years of the Union Club of the City of New York, 1836–1936* (New York: William Edwin Rudge, 1936), p. 136.

13 Edward K. Spann, "Gotham in Congress: New York's Representatives and the National Government, 1840–1854" in *New York History* 67 (1986): 308, 315, 318, 319.

14 Both are quoted in Bridges, *A City in the Republic*, p. 126.

15 See Bridges, *A City in the Republic*, p. 137.

16 Henry Nicoll quoted in *NYH*, 15 November 1857, p. 1. See also *JoC*, 21 November 1857, p. 2; *JoC*, 25 November 1857, pp. 2–3.

17 See, for example, Gabriel Almond, "Plutocracy and Politics in New York City" (Ph.D. diss., University of Chicago, 1938), pp. 52–53; Edward Pessen, *Riches, Classes, and Power Before the Civil War* (Lexington, Mass.: D. C. Heath, 1973); Spann, "Gotham in Congress," p. 319.

18 Bridges, *A City in the Republic,* p. 125, and Bridges, "Another Look at Plutocracy," pp. 63, 67.

19 Irving Katz, *August Belmont: A Political Biography* (New York: Columbia University Press, 1968), pp. 11–22, 23–49.

20 Bridges, "Another Look at Plutocracy," p. 63.

21 Philip L. White, *The Beekmans of New York in Politics and Commerce* (New York: The New-York Historical Society, 1956), p. 610.

22 Edgar Ketchum to James Beekman, March 3, 1852, in B. V. Sec. Beekman, Letterbook 2, NYHS.

23 See A. Munson to James Beekman, Utica, June 14, 1853, Letterbox, vol. 3, B. V. Sec. Beekman, James W. Beekman Papers, NYHS.

24 J. W. Chauler to Frederick DePeyster, Albany, February 14, 1858, vol. 3, p. 29, B. V. DePeyster, Frederick, NYHS.

25 Eben Meriam to Beekman, April 1, 1850, Beekman Box 25, Beekman Papers, NYHS.

26 D. Francis Bacon to James W. Beekman, New York, April 8, 1851, Folder 10, Beekman Box 25, Beekman Papers, NYHS.

27 G. Tucker to Isaac Sherman, Albany, February 8, 1859, Isaac Sherman Papers, Huntington Library, Pasadena, Calif.

28 Edward K. Spann, *The New Metropolis: New York City, 1840–1857* (New York: Columbia University Press, 1981), p. 323; *NYDT,* 7 March 1853, p. 5; Edward Durand, *The Finances of New York City* (New York: The Macmillan Company, 1898), p. 372. William E. Dodge thundered that "as merchants" they needed to secure "an honest, economical city government." Speech by William E. Dodge, reprinted in Carlos Martyn, *William E. Dodge: The Christian Merchant* (New York: Funk & Wagnalls, 1890), p. 149. In the meeting, among others, Peter Cooper and shipbuilder William H. Webb represented the manufacturers, Henry Grinnell and George Griswold the merchants, and Moses Taylor the bankers.

29 Bridges, "Another Look at Plutocracy," p. 64.

30 The charter strengthened the mayor's veto, removed aldermen from their position as city judges, and put the police under the control of a Board of Commissioners consisting of the mayor, the city recorder, and the city judges. Spann, *The New Metropolis,* pp. 324, 331; Durand, *The Finances of New York City,* p. 73.

31 See *JoC,* 21 November 1857, p. 2; *JoC,* 25 November 1857, pp. 2–3; *NYH,* 15 November 1857, p. 1; *NYH,* 15 November 1857, p. 1; Peter S. Hoe to Robert Hoe, New York, September 29, 1857, Hoe Papers, Library of Congress; *Fifteenth Annual Report of the New-York Association for Improving the Conditions of the Poor for the Year 1858* (New York: John F. Trow, 1858), p. 19; Allan Nevins and Milton Halsey Thomas, eds., *The Diary of George Templeton Strong* (New York: Macmillan Company, 1952), vol. 2, p. 369. Entry of November 10, 1857. *The New York Times* is quoted in Spann, *The New Metropolis,* p. 395. See also Bridges, "Another Look at Plutocracy," p. 68.

32 Spann, *The New Metropolis,* p. 395; Melvin Holli and Peter Jones, eds., *Biographical Dictionary of American Mayors, 1820–1980* (Westport, Conn.:

Greenwood Press, 1981), p. 363. Wood, however, retained some bourgeois support, for example, from Augustus Shell and Moses Taylor. See *JoC*, 26 November 1857, pp. 2–3.

33 This argument also has been made by Bridges, *A City in the Republic*, pp. 140–145.

34 See, among many others, *NYT*, 14 September 1860, p. 1; *NYDT*, 5 November 1860; *JoC*, 6 November 1860, pp. 2–3.

35 Bridges, "Another Look at Plutocracy," p. 64.

36 Bridges, *A City in the Republic*, p. 139; Spann, *The New Metropolis*, p. 376.

37 Joseph Alfred Scoville, *The Old Merchants of New York City*, Walter Barret, pseud. (New York: George W. Carleton, 1862), as quoted in Robert Greenhalgh Albion, *The Rise of New York Port, 1815–1860* (New York: Scribner's Sons, 1939), p. 258.

38 Bridges, "Another Look at Plutocracy," pp. 62–63. John Ashworth has argued that Whiggery "reflected . . . the older paternalism associated with the dominance of merchant capital." John Ashworth, *Slavery, Capitalism, and Politics in the Antebellum Republic: Commerce and Compromise, 1820–1850* (New York: Cambridge University Press, 1995), vol. 1, p. 365.

39 See for example *NYH*, 1 October 1859, p. 4.

40 Spann, *The New Metropolis*, pp. 384–395.

41 On the Compromise of 1850, see *NYCA*, 13 June 1850, p. 1f; *NYCA*, 26 June 1850, p. 1; *NYCA*, 24 October 1850, p. 2. On the Kansas-Nebraska controversy see *JoC*, 3 February 1854, p. 2; *JoC*, 6 February 1854, p. 2; *JoC*, 9 February 1854, p. 2; *JoC*, 14 February 1854, p. 2. Although in 1854 many bourgeois New Yorkers at first protested the Kansas-Nebraska Act, arguing that it would repudiate the Compromise of 1850, they eventually acceded to it. For protests against the Kansas-Nebraska Act see, for example, *NYDT*, 31 January 1854, p. 5; *NYDT*, 15 March 1854, p. 7.

42 *JoC*, 1 November 1860, p. 2.

43 See, for example, *JoC*, 24 October 1860, pp. 1–3.

44 Isaac Sherman, for example, came to be as much interested in politics as in trade: "I presume . . . you are still staving away down on Water Street + philosophizing at the New York Hotel," a friend wrote to him in 1857. See O. G. Steele to Isaac Sherman, Buffalo, January 24, 1857, Isaac Sherman Papers, Huntington Library. Isaac Sherman was a dealer in staves, the "narrow strips of wood or narrow iron plates placed edge to edge to form the sides, covering, or lining of a vessel." (According to *Merriam Webster's Dictionary*, 10th ed., 1993.)

45 *JoC*, 21 June 1850, p. 2.

46 *JoC*, 18 October 1860, p. 3.

47 Friedrich Kapp, *Geschichte der Sklaverei in den Vereinigten Staten von Amerika* (Hamburg: Otto Meißner, 1861), p. 6, quoted in Karl Walter Hickel, "The Response of German Forty-Eighters to the Reconstruction of the American South, 1861–1871: Liberal Ideology, Slave Emancipation, and the Concept of Citizenship," (unpublished paper in author's possession, 1992), p. 11.

48 For their efforts see the *Journal of Commerce* throughout June 1850 and Foner, *Business and Slavery*, pp. 27, 35–43.

49 Among many others, A. A. Belknap, Hiram Ketchum, Robert Wetmore, and J. DePeyster Ogden to Beekman, all February 1851, "Political Correspondence, Misc. Mss. Beekman," Box 25, James W. Beekman Papers, NYHS.

50 See *JoC*, 24 October 1850, p. 2.

51 See *JoC*, 24 October 1850, p. 2.

52 Foner, *Business and Slavery*, pp. 74–78, 84–86.

53 *JoC*, 6 November 1860, pp. 2–3. Another example was the Union "mass meeting" on December 19, 1859, chaired by James Beekman and attended by many important merchants. James W. Beekman to Hon. Fernando Wood, December 14, 1859, Box 1, Beekman Papers, NYHS; see also Foner, *Business and Slavery*, pp. 26, 43, 55.

54 *Proceedings of the Merchant's Great Democratic Meeting* (New York: John F. Trow, 1856).

55 As quoted in the *NYCA*, 23 October 1850, p. 1.

56 Henry V. Booraem, *The Formation of the Republican Party in New York: Politics and Conscience in the Antebellum North* (New York: New York University Press, 1983), p. 82; Karen Fox Markoe, "The Origins of the Republican Party in the State of New York" (Ph.D. diss., Columbia University, 1971), p. 146.

57 Foner, *Business and Slavery*, pp. 119f. For the (unusually) high percentage of well-to-do Know Nothing legislators in the New York Assembly, see Tyler Anbinder, *Nativism and Slavery: The Northern Know Nothings and the Politics of the 1850s* (New York: Oxford University Press, 1992), p. 131. In 1855, 39 percent of Know Nothing legislators were manufactures and merchants, compared to 22 percent in other parties.

58 Foner, *Business and Slavery*, p. 19; Thomas Prentice Kettell, *Eighty Years' Progress of the United States* (New York: L. Stebbins, 1861), pp. 119–121.

59 Nevins and Thomas, eds, *The Diary of George Templeton Strong*, vol. 2, p. 275. Entry of 29 May 1856. Foner, *Business and Slavery*, p. 45.

60 Quoted in Richard Lowitt, *A Merchant Prince of the Nineteenth Century: William E. Dodge* (New York: Columbia University Press, 1954), p. 204.

61 Martyn, *William E. Dodge*, p. 128.

62 See, for example, on August Belmont, "August Belmont," in Larry Schweikart, ed., *Encyclopedia of American Business History and Biography, Banking and Finance to 1913* (New York: Facts on File, 1990), p. 40.

63 Quoting the *Richmond [Virginia] Dispatch*. See also *Hunt's* 32 (1855): 264. *Hunt's Merchants' Magazine* tended to reprint, approvingly, southern justifications of slavery. See also *Hunt's* 28 (1853): 326–327; *Hunt's* 39 (1858): 523; *Hunt's* 41 (1859): 129–130. See also Kettell, *Eighty Years' Progress of the United States*, pp. 119–121.

64 *JoC*, 2 July 1850, p. 2. For similar statements see also *JoC*, 25 October 1850, p. 1; and the *JoC* throughout October 1860.

65 See *JoC*, 24 October 1860, p. 1–3; *JoC*, 3 November 1860, p. 3.

66 Foner, *Business and Slavery*, pp. 4–13, 143.

67 Chamber of Commerce, *Proceedings of the Chamber of Commerce of the State of New York at the Opening of their new Rooms, June 10, 1858* (New York: John A. Douglas * Co., 1858), p. 11.

68 *JoC*, 11 November 1857, p. 3.

69 See for example *JoC*, 18 June 1860, p. 3; *JoC*, 4 July 1850, pp. 3, 4.

70 *Hunt's* 40 (1859): 519. They shared this vision with southern planters, who conceptualized the U.S. economy as fundamentally based on agricultural commodities produced by slave labor. *Hunt's* 41 (1859): 129–130.

71 Iver Bernstein, *The New York City Draft Riots: Their Significance for American Society and Politics in the Age of the Civil War* (New York: Oxford University Press, 1990), pp. 133–134.

72 Bernstein, *The New York City Draft Riots*, p. 133.

73 As visible, for example, in the appeal to workers to vote against Republicans in the *JoC*, 5 November 1860, p. 3.

74 Kettell, *Eighty Years' Progress of the United States*, p. 122.

75 Thomas P. Kettell, *Southern Wealth and Northern Profits, As Exhibited in Statistical Facts and Officials Figures: Showing the Necessity of Union to the Future Prosperity and Welfare of the Republic* (New York: George W. & John A. Wood, 1860), pp. 3, 19, 34, 60, 172, 173.

76 Kettell, *Southern Wealth and Northern Profits*, p. 98.

77 Kettell, *Southern Wealth and Northern Profits*, p. 50.

78 Kettell, *Southern Wealth and Northern Profits*, p. 10.

79 See *JoC*, 4 July 1850, p. 2. On the abolitionists and their relationship to the bourgeoisie and bourgeois society in general, see Ashworth, *Slavery, Capitalism, and Politics in the Antebellum Republic*, vol. 1, pp. 125–191.

80 *NYDT*, 31 May 1856, p. 8. For the connection made between land reform, tariffs, and the limitation of the expansion of slavery, see also *NYDT*, 11 June 1850, p. 4.

81 See also Barrington Moore, *Social Origins of Dictatorship and Democracy: Lord and Peasant in the Making of the Modern World* (Boston: Beacon Press, 1966), pp. 111–155; James Livingston, *Pragmatism and the Political Economy of Cultural Revolution, 1850–1940* (Chapel Hill: University of North Carolina Press, 1994).

82 *NYDT*, 7 November 1857, p. 2.

83 For a concise statement to this effect see *NYDT*, 7 November 1857, p. 2.

84 Cited in Edward Mack, *Peter Cooper: Citizen of New York* (New York: Duell, Sloan and Pearce, 1949), p. 191.

85 Nevins and Thomas, eds., *The Diary of George Templeton Strong*, vol. 2, pp. 282, 287–288, 303–305, 480–481. Entries of 26 June 1856, 5 August 1856, 19 October 1856, 22 December 1859.

86 Foner, *Business and Slavery*, p. 141.

87 *NYT*, 14 September 1860, p. 1.

88 George Opdyke, *Treatise on Political Economy* (New York: G. P. Putnam, 1851), pp. 327, 330, 331.

89 G. Tucker to Isaac Sherman, Albany, February 28, 1859, Isaac Sherman Papers, Huntington Library; Isaac Sherman to Thurlow Weed, Champlain Arsenal, Vermont, March 22, 1861, copy in Isaac Sherman papers, Huntington Library, original in Rochester University Library. Though Sherman was not among the wealthiest New York merchants, his holdings had by 1860 surpassed $1.3 million. See "Transfer Balance for the Year 1860," Isaac Sherman Papers, Huntington Library.

90 American society and the American state were, of course, already by the

1850s largely "bourgeois." Yet this bourgeois revolution was incomplete. It was only in the 1850s, as a direct result of rapid industrialization and territorial expansion, that prebourgeois forms of social organization and political power became problematic for some – but not all – bourgeois northerners.

91 Horace Greeley, *Recollections of a Busy Life, Including Reminiscences of American Politics and Politicians, From the Opening of the Missouri Contest to the Downfall of Slavery* (New York: J. Ford and Company, 1868), pp. 311, 354, 397. For the newly emerging political economy of domestic industrialization, see Livingston, *Pragmatism and the Political Economy of Cultural Revolution*, pp. 25–35.

92 For the importance of agricultural implements, see *Transactions of the American Institute of the City of New-York for the Year 1853* (Albany, N.Y.: C. Van Benthuysen, 1854), p. 8; *Transactions of the American Institute of the City of New-York for the Year 1850* (Albany, N.Y.: C. Van Benthuysen, 1851), p. 7; *Transactions of the American Institute of the City of New-York for the Year 1858* (Albany, N.Y.: C. Van Benthuysen, 1859), p. 51.

93 *Transactions of the American Institute of the City of New-York for the Year 1850*, p. 7; *Transactions of the American Institute of the City of New-York for the Year 1856* (Albany, N.Y.: C. Van Benthuysen, 1857), pp. 7–8.

94 *Transactions of the American Institute of the City of New-York for the Year 1850*, p. 9; *Transactions of the American Institute of the City of New-York for the Year 1851* (Albany, N.Y.: C. Van Benthuysen, 1852), p. 11.

95 *NYCA*, 4 October 1860, p. 2.

96 The party organization in the city remained weak because it had to contend with the local Whigs, who, in contrast to all other Whig organizations in the state, refused to fuse with them.

97 Foner, *Business and Slavery*, p. 114.

98 Booraem, *The Formation of the Republican Party*, pp. 157–163.

99 For the names see *NYH*, 30 October 1856, p. 8, and "Printed Letter to Francis Spinner," New York, April 10, 1856, Box 1, Francis G. Spinner Papers, H. K. Crofoot Collection, Library of Congress.

100 *NYT*, 26 November 1877, p. 8; Foner, *Business and Slavery*, pp. 117, 126. Also joining were James B. Taylor, John A. King, shipping merchant Charles H. Marshall, auctioneer Anthony J. Bleecker, merchant Charles Ely, auctioneer Charles W. Ogden, salt merchant Samuel Hotaling, and merchant H. McCurdy, as well as lawyers, such as Henry Townsend and Edgar Ketchum, and physicians, such as Samuel L. Griswold.

101 *NYH*, 30 October 1856, p. 8.

102 The importance of support from manufacturers for New York's early Republican Party is also argued by Bernstein, *The New York City Draft Riots*, pp. 184f.

103 For the composition of the city's bourgeoisie at large, see 1855 sample. For the vice presidents and secretaries of the "Great Republican Rally" in New York City on September 13, 1860 see *NYT*, 14 September 1860, p. 1.

104 *NYCA*, 24 October 1860, p. 2; *NYCA*, 1 November 1860, p. 2.

105 "Wall Street for Lincoln, Mass Meeting of Merchants," in *NYDT*, 5 November 1860. Among the signers of this particular circular were also manufactur-

ers, bankers, and professionals. Information about some of the merchants who signed the petition has been culled from Henry Hall, ed., *America's Successful Men of Affairs, An Encyclopedia of Contemporaneous Biography*, vol. 1 (New York: *The New York Tribune*, 1895).

106 Foner, *Business and Slavery*, pp. 44f.

107 Both gave speeches at the "Great Republican Rally" on September 13, 1860. See *NYT*, 14 September 1860, p. 1.

108 Lowitt, *A Merchant Prince*, p. 31.

109 Richard Lathers to Henry Gourdinet, New York, November 28, 1860, vol. 1, Richard Lathers Papers; see also Foner, *Business and Slavery*, p. 226.

110 Printed circular, vol. 1, 1826–1863, Richard Lathers Papers, Library of Congress.

111 Howard Furer, *William Frederick Havemeyer: A Political Biography* (New York: American Press, 1965), pp. 118, 119. See also *JoC*, 5 October 1860; *JoC*, 8 October 1860; *JoC*, 9 October 1860, p. 2.

112 "Call for Meeting," New York, December 10, 1860, vol. 1, Richard Lathers Papers, Library of Congress.

113 Letter by Samuel Barlow to [illegible], New York, November 5, 1860, Letterbooks, BW 1, Samuel Barlow Papers, Huntington Library.

114 Hallock, *Life of Gerard Hallock*, p. 91.

115 William H. Hallock, *Life of Gerard Hallock, Thirty-Three Years Editor of the New York Journal of Commerce* (New York: Oakley, Mason & Co., 1869), p. 85. *NYDT*, 9 October 1860, p. 5.

116 Foner, *Business and Slavery*, pp. 248, 251, 255, 258, 263.

117 *JoC*, 1 February 1861, pp. 1–3; Foner, *Business and Slavery*, pp. 238, 302, 400.

118 Foner, *Business and Slavery*, p. 274.

119 Foner, *Business and Slavery*, p. 277.

120 For an excellent discussion of federal government bond purchases by New York City merchants just before the war, see Michael Zakim, "Capital Divided: New York City Merchants and Manufacturers on the Eve of the Civil War" (Master's thesis, Columbia University, 1992), pp. 35–44. The quotation is on page 37.

121 Quoted in Zakim, "Capital Divided," p. 37.

122 Loyal Publication Society of New York, *Loyal Reprints No. 3: The Great Mass Meeting of Loyal Citizens, at Cooper Institute, Friday Evening, March 6, 1863* (New York: n.p., 1863), p. 8.

4. Bourgeois New Yorkers Go to War

1 *NYT*, 21 April 1861, p. 1.

2 McKay, *The Civil War*, p. 62.

3 *NYT*, 21 April 1861, p. 1.

4 *NYT*, 21 April 1861, p. 8.

5 *NYT*, 21 April 1861, p. 1.

6 *Fourth Annual Report of the Chamber of Commerce of the State of New-York for the Year 1861–62* (New York: John W. Amerman, 1862), p. 9.

7 *Fourth Annual Report of the Chamber of Commerce of the State of New-York for the Year 1861–62,* p. 8.

8 Letter to his mother, New York, April 22, 1861, reprinted in Edwin S. Martin, *The Life of Joseph Hodges Choate as Gathered Chiefly from his Letters* (New York: Scribner, 1920), p. 220. For a similar statement see also *ARJ* 34 (1 June 1861): 417.

9 *NYT,* 21 April 1861, p. 1.

10 *NYT,* 21 April 1861, p. 1.

11 *NYT,* 21 April 1861, p. 8.

12 Joseph H. Choate to his mother, New York, May 6, 1861, reprinted in Martin, *The Life of Joseph Hodges Choate,* p. 221.

13 John L. Graham to William Crabell Rives, May 1, 1861, GM 175, Box 8, Graham Papers, Huntington Library.

14 Senator James Dixon to James Beekman, June 8, 1861, Box 2, "Letters to James W. Beekman, 1850–1877," Beekman Papers, NYHS.

15 Note by Peter Cooper, undated, letters, misc. mss., Abram S. Hewitt, NYHS. The context of the letter suggests that it was written in the spring of 1861.

16 Cited in Philip Foner, *Business and Slavery: The New York Merchants and the Irrepressible Conflict* (Chapel Hill: University of North Carolina Press, 1941), p. 289; Ernest A. McKay, *The Civil War and New York City* (Syracuse, N.Y.: Syracuse University Press, 1990), p. 58.

17 Belmont, for example, helped raise and supply the first German-American regiment. See "August Belmont," in Larry Schweikart, ed., *Encyclopedia of American Business History and Biography, Banking and Finance to 1913* (New York: Facts on File, 1990), p. 41.

18 Foner, *Business and Slavery,* p. 276f.

19 *NYT,* 21 April 1861, p. 8.

20 Howard Potter to John Crosby Brown, New York, May 25, 1861, "Extracts from Brown Family Letters, 1860–1865," Brown Brothers Harriman and Company Papers, NYHS.

21 J. Cooper Lord to John Crosby Brown, New York, September 10, 1861, "Extracts from Brown Family Letters, 1860–1865," Brown Brothers Harriman and Company Papers, NYHS.

22 The Boston bourgeoisie's mobilization occurred exactly along the same lines; they were "united in their support of the war," but they did not "wish it conducted on an antislavery basis." Richard Abbott, *Cotton & Capital: Boston Businessmen and Antislavery Reform, 1854–1868* (Amherst: University of Massachusetts Press, 1991), p. 75.

23 For the centrality of slavery to the southern political economy see, for example, Eugene Genovese, *The Political Economy of Slavery, Studies in the Economy & Society of the Slave South* (New York: Pantheon Books, 1965).

24 Barrington Moore termed the Civil War the "last bourgeois revolution." See Barrington Moore, *Social Origins of Dictatorship and Democracy: Lord and Peasant in the Making of the Modern World* (Boston: Beacon Press, 1966), pp. 111–155. See also John Ashworth, *Slavery, Capitalism, and Politics in the Antebellum Republic,* vol. 1, *Commerce and Compromise, 1820–1850* (New

York: Cambridge University Press, 1995), p. ix. That bourgeois revolutions were fought with only reluctant support by the bourgeoisie is not unique to the United States. See, for example, David Blackbourn and Geoff Eley, *The Peculiarities of German History: Bourgeois Society and Politics in Nineteenth Century Germany* (Oxford: Oxford University Press, 1984), p. 82; Hartmut Zwahr, *Proletariat und Bourgeoisie in Deutschland: Studien zur Klassendialektik* (Cologne: PRV, 1980).

25 McKay, *The Civil War*, p. 64.

26 J. F. D. Lanier, *Sketch of the Life of J. F. D. Lanier*, 2d ed. (n.p.: [printed for the use of the family only], 1877), p. 35.

27 Richard Lowitt, *A Merchant Prince of the Nineteenth Century: William E. Dodge* (New York: Columbia University Press, 1954), p. 213.

28 Foner, *Business and Slavery*, p. 311.

29 Minutes of the Union Defense Committee, April 1861, B. V. Section "W," Union Defense Committee, NYHS.

30 John Perry Pritchett, Frances Katzman, and Howard Dellon, "The Union Defense Committee of the City of New York During the Civil War," *NYHSQ* 30 (1946): 142–160; McKay, *The Civil War*, p. 84.

31 Ledger B, Union Defense Committee, NYHS; Pritchett, Katzman, and Dellon, "The Union Defense Committee," p. 156; James J. Heslin, "Peaceful Compromise in New York City, 1860–1861," *NYHSQ* 44 (1960): 341–352.

32 Pritchett, Katzman, and Dellon, "The Union Defense Committee," p. 153.

33 Charles Howland Russell, *Memoir of Charles H. Russell, 1796–1884* (New York: n.p., 1903), p. 89; Pritchett, Katzman, and Dellon, "The Union Defense Committee," p. 151.

34 Irving Katz, *August Belmont, A Political Biography* (New York: Columbia University Press, 1968), pp. 100–103.

35 August Belmont to S. P. Chase, October 31, 1861, Box 1, Belmont Papers, Library of Congress; see also A. Belmont to Chase, Newport, July 3, 1861, and A. Belmont to S.P. Chase, Schlangenbad, August 15, 1861, Box 1, Belmont Papers, Library of Congress.

36 For a general discussion of the relationship between capitalists, war, and the state, see especially Charles Tilly, "Cities and the Rise of States in Europe, A.D. 1000 to 1800," in Charles Tilly and Wim P. Blockmans, eds., *Cities and the Rise of States in Europe, A.D. 1000 to 1800* (Boulder, Colo.: Westview Press, 1994), pp. 10–12.

37 As quoted in Phillip Shaw Paludan, *"A People's Contest," The Union and Civil War, 1861–1865* (New York: Harper and Row, 1988), p. 108.

38 Paludan, *A People's Contest*, p. 108.

39 Paludan, *A People's Contest*, pp. 113–114.

40 Salmon P. Chase to John A. Stevens, Sr., Washington, June 26, 1861, in John Niven, ed., *The Salmon P. Chase Papers*, vol. 3, 1858–March 1863 (Kent, Ohio: Kent State University Press, 1996), p. 70; McKay, *The Civil War*, pp. 94, 95.

41 On the negotiations, see Daniel Hodas, *The Business Career of Moses Taylor: Merchant, Finance Capitalist and Industrialist* (New York: New York University Press, 1976), pp. 180–181. See also Elbridge Gerry Spaulding, *A*

Resource of War: The Credit of the Government Made Immediately Available, A History of the Legal Tender Paper Money Issued During the Great Rebellion, Being a Loan Without Interest and a National Currency (Buffalo, N.Y.: Express Printing Company, 1869), p. 7; McKay, *The Civil War*, p. 95. On the conflict between Chase and New York's banking community, see also Heather Richardson, *The Greatest Nation on Earth, Republican Economic Policies During the Civil War* (Cambridge, Mass.: Harvard University Press, 1997), pp. 36–47.

42 Paludan, *A People's Contest*, p. 118. For the acceptance of taxation see also *ARJ* 35 (13 December 1862): 978.

43 McKay, *The Civil War*, p. 67.

44 McKay, *The Civil War*, p. 68.

45 John F. Carroll, *A Brief History of New York's Famous Seventh Regiment and the Events Surrounding its March to the Defense of the National Capital* (New York: Veterans of the Seventh Regiment, Civil War Centennial Committee, 1961), p. 1. The "Roll of Honor of the Seventh Regiment" lists 662 veterans of the Civil War of which 556 were officers. For the names see Emmons Clark, *History of the Seventh Regiment of New York, 1806–1889* (New York: Seventh Regiment, 1890), vol. 2, pp. 479–487.

46 John A. Kouwenhoven, *Partners in Banking, An Historical Portrait of a Great Private Bank, Brown Brothers Harriman & Co., 1818–1968* (New York: Doubleday & Company, 1968), p. 124; "New Year's Day in 1861," in *NYHSQ* 28 (1944): 21; James A. Rawley, *Edwin D. Morgan, 1811–1883: Merchant in Politics* (New York: Columbia University Press, 1955), p. 163. See also *A History of Columbia University, 1754–1904* (New York: Columbia University Press, 1904), p. 137; Lowitt, *A Merchant Prince of the Nineteenth Century*, p. 218. Richard K. Lieberman, *Steinway & Sons* (New Haven: Yale University Press, 1995), p. 35. For a list of members of the Union Club who joined the Union army, see Reginald Townsend, *Mother of Clubs: Being the History of the First Hundred Years of the Union Club of the City of New York, 1836–1936* (New York: William Edwin Rudge, 1936), pp. 70f.

47 Allen Churchill, *The Upper Crust, An Informal History of New York's Highest Society* (Englewood Cliffs, N.J.: Prentice-Hall, 1970), p. 68.

48 *Sixth Annual Report of the New-York Chamber of Commerce of the State of New-York for the Year 1863–64* (New York: John W. Amerman, 1864), p. 38.

49 *ARJ* 34 (19 October 1861): 729. For a similar statement see *ARJ* 35 (12 April 1862): 280–281. The close link between the need to uphold the union and the future of American business was also expressed in the pages of the *United States Insurance Gazette and Magazine of Useful Knowledge*. See, for example, *United States Insurance Gazette and Magazine of Useful Knowledge* 15 (1862): iii–vi.

50 Charles C. Bright, "The State in the United States During the Nineteenth Century," in Charles Bright and Susan Harding, eds., *Statemaking and Social Movements: Essays in History and Theory* (Ann Arbor: University of Michigan Press, 1984), p. 145.

51 See also Bright, "The State in the United States During the Nineteenth Cen-

tury," p. 144. Richard Bensel, *Yankee Leviathan, The Origins of Central State Authority in America, 1859–1877* (New York: Cambridge University Press, 1990), pp. 173, 174. For an explicit statement of this alliance, see *Bulletin of the American Iron and Steel Association*, Supplement (6 February 1867): 185.

52 Ross L. Muir and Carl J. White, *Over the Long Term: The Story of J. & W. Seligman & Co., 1864–1964* (New York: J. & W. Seligman & Co., 1964), p. 46.

53 *ARJ* 35 (18 January 1862): 33.

54 However, for most of them the main goal of the war was still the reunification of the United States and not the destruction of slavery.

55 *ARJ* 34 (5 October 1861): 696–698.

56 *ARJ* 34 (24 August 1861): 601; *ARJ* 34 (5 October 1861): 696; Robert Hoe II to John Mac Donald, New York, February 17, 1862, reel 6, Hoe Papers, Library of Congress.

57 J. Laurence Laughlin, "Political Economy and the Civil War," *Atlantic Monthly* 55 (April 1885): 446.

58 *ARJ* 34 (6 July 1861): 489; *ARJ* 34 (13 July 1861): 505–506. For the argument that the Civil War policies favored the specific political economy of industrial capital, see for example Charles Post, "The American Road to Capitalism," *New Left Review* 133 (May 1982): 50–51. He also mentions the Homestead Act as an important element in building this political economy, for it helped provide huge land grants to railroads and created a tremendous market of prospering farmers.

59 Bensel, *Yankee Leviathan*, pp. 163, 172. On the process of selling government bonds see Hodas, *The Business Career of Moses Taylor*, pp. 178–192.

60 In an entirely different context, this problem has been discussed by Marjolein 't Hart, *The Making of a Bourgeois State: War, Politics, and Finance During the Dutch Revolt* (New York: Manchester University Press, 1993), especially p. 216.

61 Chase to John A. Stevens, Sr., Washington, D.C., January 17, 1862, printed in Niven, ed., *The Salmon P. Chase Papers*, vol. 3, p. 119.

62 David M. Gische, "The New York City Banks and the Development of the National Banking System, 1860–1870," *American Journal of Legal History* 23 (1979): 33; Eugene Spaulding to Isaac Sherman, Washington, D.C., January 8, 1862, reprinted in Spaulding, *A Resource of War*, p. 17; James Willard Hurst, *A Legal History of Money in the United States, 1774–1970* (Lincoln: University of Nebraska Press, 1973), p. 178. Speech of Eugene Spaulding in the Committee of Ways and Means, February 19, 1862, reprinted in Spaulding, *A Resource of War*, p. 132.

63 They instead suggested new excise taxes, duties, and loans. Spaulding, *A Resource of War*, pp. 19, 20.

64 As did New York City Mayor George Opdyke, *Tribune* editor Horace Greeley, and the Chamber of Commerce. See Moses H. Grinnell to Spaulding, New York, January 30, 1862, cited in Spaulding, *A Resource of War*, p. 23 and John A. Stevens to Spaulding, New York, January 29, 1862, cited in Spaulding, *A Resource of War*, p. 47. The Chamber of Commerce resolved

that "the present financial condition of the government . . . requires the immediate passage of the bill." See Joseph Bucklin Bishop, *A Chronicle of One Hundred & Fifty Years, The Chamber of Commerce of the State of New York, 1768–1918* (New York: Scribner's, 1918), p. 76. On the same theme see also Chase to George Opdyke, Washington, D.C., November 11, 1862, reprinted in Niven, ed., *The Salmon P. Chase Papers,* vol. 3, p. 315; Horace Greeley to Chase, New York, January 31, 1863, reprinted in Niven, ed., *The Salmon P. Chase Papers,* vol. 3, p. 376; Hodas, *The Business Career of Moses Taylor,* p. 187.

65 Gische, "The New York City Banks," p. 36f. Speech by Eugene Spaulding in the Committee of the Whole, December 12, 1862, reprinted in Spaulding, *A Resource of War,* p. 169.

66 To groups of at least five individuals who provided $30,000 or one-third of their capital in federal bonds.

67 Paludan, *A People's Contest,* pp. 123–124.

68 Gische, "The New York City Banks," p. 41.

69 Gische, "The New York City Banks," p. 45; *Proceedings of the Meeting in Relation to the Establishment of a Large National Bank in this City* (New York: Wm. C. Bryant, 1863); "George F. Baker," in Schweikart, ed., *Encyclopedia of American Business History and Biography, Banking and Finance to 1913,* p. 26.

70 Gische, "The New York City Banks," pp. 49–50.

71 Gische, "The New York City Banks," p. 54.

72 Russell, *Memoir of Charles H. Russell,* p. 100.

73 Gische, "The New York City Banks," pp. 56, 57.

74 Hurst, *A Legal History of Money,* pp. 176, 190.

75 Indeed, as Richard Bensel has argued, because of the war large segments of finance capital won their autonomy from British influence. Bensel, *Yankee Leviathan,* p. 364.

76 The impact of New York City on federal banking policy is well documented in the correspondence of Lincoln's secretary of the treasury, Salmon P. Chase. See, for example, Chase to George Opdyke, Columbus, January 9, 1861; Chase to John Austin Stevens, Sr., Washington, D.C., June 26, 1861; Chase to John Austin Stevens, Sr., January 17, 1862; Chase to Opdyke, Washington, D.C., November 11, 1862; Opdyke to Chase, New York, December 14, 1862; Chase to Horace Greeley, Washington, January 28, 1863; letter from Opdyke to Chase, New York, February 27, 1863; Opdyke to Chase, New York, March 20, 1863 (and postscript by Morris Ketchum); Chase to William H. Aspinwall and John M. Forbes, March 30, 1863, reprinted in Niven, ed., *The Salmon P. Chase Papers,* vol. 3, pp. 44–46, 69–70, 119–120, 315, 338–340, 375–377, 392–393, 397–402, 408–411.

77 See James Livingston, *Pragmatism and the Political Economy of Cultural Revolution, 1850–1940* (Chapel Hill: University of North Carolina Press, 1994), p. 36.

78 "Joseph Seligman," in Schweikart, ed., *Encyclopedia of American Business History and Biography, Banking and Finance to 1913,* pp. 424–426.

79 *Fifth Annual Report of the New-York Chamber of Commerce of the State of*

New-York for the Year 1862–63 (New York: John W. Amerman, 1862), p. 2; Bishop, *A Chronicle of One Hundred & Fifty Years,* p. 83; Jean Heffer, *Le Port de New York et le Commerce Extérieur Americain, 1860–1900* (Paris: Publications de la Sorbonne, 1986), p. 83.

80 *Fifth Annual Report of the New-York Chamber of Commerce of the State of New-York for the Year 1862–63,* p. 3; *Sixth Annual Report of the New-York Chamber of Commerce of the State of New-York for the Year 1863–64,* p. 8

81 Lowitt, *A Merchant Prince of the Nineteenth Century,* p. 227; William E. Dodge, speech on July 10, 1866, in United States House of Representatives Thirty-Ninth Congress, First Session, *Congressional Globe,* p. 3720.

82 Iver Bernstein, *The New York City Draft Riots, Their Significance for American Society and Politics in the Age of the Civil War* (Oxford: Oxford University Press, 1990), pp. 222–223.

83 *Sixth Annual Report of the New-York Chamber of Commerce of the State of New-York for the Year 1863–64,* pp. 7–8.

84 McKay, *The Civil War,* p. 80.

85 See August Belmont to Samuel Barlow, Nice, December 10, 1861, BW 37, Samuel Barlow Papers, Huntington Library.

86 *Sixth Annual Report of the New-York Chamber of Commerce of the State of New-York for the Year 1863–64,* p. 53.

87 Dumas Malone, ed., *Dictionary of American Biography* (New York: Charles Scribner's Sons, 1953), vol. 8, p. 405; Rejean Attie, "A Swindling Concern, The United States Sanitary Commission and the Northern Female Public, 1861–1865" (Ph.D. diss., Columbia University, 1987), p. 78; Paul Migliore, "The Business of Union" (Ph.D. diss., Columbia University, 1975), p. 323; Howard Furer, *William Frederick Havemeyer: A Political Biography* (New York: The American Press, 1965), p. 121; Loyal Publication Society of New York, *Loyal Reprints No. 3,* p. 9.

88 August Belmont to Samuel Barlow, Newport, August 1862, BW 40, Samuel Barlow Papers, Huntington Library.

89 Sheridan Logan, *George F. Baker and His Bank, 1840–1955, A Double Biography* (n.p.: [privately printed], 1981), p. 41.

90 Nevins and Thomas, *The Diary of George Templeton Strong,* vol. 3, p. 267.

91 Frémont to Isaac Sherman, August 12, October 9, and November 20, 1861, Isaac Sherman Papers, Huntington Library.

92 Report of the Proceedings of the National War Committee of the Citizens of New York, No. 3, September 22, 1862, pp. 8–9, B. V. Sec. National War Committee, NYHS. For an account of the meeting see *NYH,* 28 August 1862, p. 1.

93 George Opdyke, *Official Documents, Addresses etc. of George Opdyke: Mayor of the City of New York During the Years 1862 and 1863* (New York: Hurd and Houghton, 1866), p. 223.

94 *NYH,* 8 August 1862, p. 1.

95 *Fifth Annual Report of the New-York Chamber of Commerce of the State of New-York for the Year 1862–63,* p. 45.

96 Moses H. Grinnell to National War Committee, September 6, 1861, B. V. Sec. National War Committee, NYHS.

97 National War Committee to August Belmont, September 11, 1862, B. V. Sec. National War Committee, NYHS. See also *JoC*, 8 September 1862, p. 2.

98 William B. Astor to National War Committee, New York, September 1862, B. V. Sec. National War Committee, New-York Historical Society; Minutes of Meeting, September 9, 1862, National War Committee, NYHS.

99 David Black, *The King of Fifth Avenue: The Fortunes of August Belmont* (New York: Dial Press, 1981), pp. 205–209. Support for McClellan also came from the *JoC*. See, for example, *JoC*, 3 September 1862, p. 2.

100 Samuel Barlow to August Belmont, New York, November 12, 1861, Letterbook, BW 1, Samuel Barlow Papers, Huntington Library.

101 Migliore, "The Business of Union," p. 323; Black, *The King of Fifth Avenue*, p. 217; McKay, *The Civil War*, pp. 132, 144.

102 August Belmont to Samuel Barlow, Newport, October 17, 1862, BW 40, Samuel Barlow Papers, Huntington Library.

103 *JoC*, 3 November 1862, p. 2. The *Journal of Commerce* consistently gave voice to this position.

104 *JoC*, 13 January 1863, p. 2.

105 For the fear that emancipation would increase labor costs in the South, see *JoC*, 13 January 1863, p. 2.

106 See especially the correspondence in the Samuel Barlow Papers, Huntington Library, especially BW 50, Samuel Barlow Papers, Huntington Library.

107 August Belmont to Samuel Barlow, Nice, December 10, 1861, BW 37, Samuel Barlow Papers, Huntington Library. See also *JoC*, 6 November 1862, p. 2.

108 August Belmont to Lionel de Rothschild, November 25, 1862, cited in Black, *The King of Fifth Avenue*, p. 222.

109 Black, *The King of Fifth Avenue*, pp. 241–242.

110 Loyal Publication Society, Pamphlet 28, *The Death of Slavery, Letter from Peter Cooper to Governor Seymour* (New York: n.p., 1863), p. 9.

111 See for this point also Ira Berlin et al., *Slaves No More, Three Essays on Emancipation and the Civil War* (New York: Cambridge University Press, 1992), especially pp. 1–76.

112 Samuel Barlow to [illegible], New York, November 16, 1860, "Letterbooks," BW 1, Samuel Barlow Papers, Huntington Library.

113 *Proceedings of the Union State Convention*, Box E5, Hamilton Fish Papers, NYHS; Migliore, "The Business of Union," p. 325; *NYT*, 17 June 1887, p. 8; McKay, *The Civil War*, p. 157.

114 Letter to his father, November 19, 1861, cited in Logan, *George F. Baker*, p. 48; Henry Anstice, *History of St. George's Church in the City of New York, 1752–1911* (New York: Harper & Brothers, 1911), p. 221f.

115 Cited in McKay, *The Civil War*, p. 143. See also Edward C. Mack, *Peter Cooper, Citizen of New York* (New York: Duell, Sloan and Peance, 1949), p. 278; Rossiter W. Raymond, *Peter Cooper* (New York: Houghton, Mifflin and Company, 1901), p. 99.

116 Beecher is quoted in John Harvey Gossard, "The New York City Congregational Cluster, 1848–1871: Congregationalism and Antislavery in the Careers of Henry Ward Beecher, George B. Cheever, Richard S. Storrs and Joseph P. Thompson" (Ph.D. diss., Bowling Green State University, Bowling Green, Ohio, 1996), p. 147.

117 Robert Hoe to Robert Hoe II, New York, August 11, 1863, reel 4, Hoe Papers, Library of Congress.

118 Migliore, "The Business of Union," p. 325. On his opinions on slavery before the war, see Nevins and Thomas, *The Diary of George Templeton Strong,* vol. 3, p. 478–480, entries of December 19 and December 22, 1859.

119 Migliore, "The Business of Union," p. 327

120 George Opdyke, Speech at the New England Dinner, December 22, 1863, reprinted in Opdyke, *Official Documents, Addresses etc. of George Opdyke, Mayor of the City of New York During the Years 1862 and 1863,* p. 354; J. W. Phelps to Prosper Wetmore, May 22, 1863, cited in Migliore, "The Business of Union," p. 335.

121 Plan of Operation of the Loyal Publication Society (February 14, 1863), cited in McKay, *The Civil War,* p. 175. For the different pamphlets see Loyal Publication Society, *Pamphlets issued by the Loyal Publication Society* (New York: Loyal Publication Society, 1864).

122 Loyal Publication Society, Pamphlet 23, *Letter from Peter Cooper on Slave Emancipation* (New York: Wm. C. Bryant & Co., 1863), p. 6.

123 Loyal Publication Society, Pamphlet 28, *The Death of Slavery, Letter from Peter Cooper to Governor Seymour,* p. 5.

124 Loyal Publication Society, Pamphlet 28, *The Death of Slavery,* p. 4.

125 Salmon P. Chase to William H. Aspinwall and John M. Forbes, March 30, 1863, reprinted in Niven, ed., *The Salmon P. Chase Papers,* vol. 3, p. 409.

126 *JoC,* 16 January 1863, p. 2; JoC, 3 August 1863, p. 2.

127 See Wolcott Gibbs, Frederick Law Olmsted, George Templeton Strong, and others who debated the merits of founding an organization to represent pro-war sentiments among the elite. Migliore, "The Business of Union," p. 176; Nevins and Thomas, *The Diary of George Templeton Strong,* vol. 3, p. 276, entry of December 2, 1862.

128 Confidential Circular, Union League Club, New York, January 15, 1863, cited in Henry Bellows, *Historical Sketch of the Union League Club of New York: Its Origin, Organization, and Work, 1863–1879* (New York: Club House, 1879), p. 21.

129 Sister organizations were also set up in Boston and Philadelphia.

130 Migliore, "The Business of Union," pp. 15, 181, 186, 189, 191.

131 Migliore, "The Business of Union," p. 194.

132 Bellows, *Historical Sketch of the Union League Club,* p. 64.

133 Migliore, "The Business of Union," pp. 195–197, 200. The Loyal Publication League was led by Columbia College President Charles King, John A. Stevens, Jr., Moses Taylor, Judge James A. Roosevelt, James McKaye, and William Blodgett. On the Loyal League of Union Citizens (which organized parts of the Democratic elite of the city), see *NYT,* 7 March 1863, p. 1; Loyal Publication Society of New York, *Loyal Reprints No. 3,* p. 1; *NYT,* 21 April 1863, p. 8. On the Loyal National League (which attracted mostly Republicans to its ranks), see Migliore, "The Business of Union," p. 204; *NYT,* 21 March 1863, p. 9; *NYT,* 21 March 1863, p. 9; *NYT,* 12 April 1863, p. 8.

134 Loyal Publication Society, *Character and Results of the War, A Thrilling and Eloquent Speech by Mayor-General B. F. Butler* (New York: Wm. C. Bryant, 1863), p. 2.

135 Henry Hall, *America's Successful Men of Affairs: An Encyclopedia of Contemporaneous Biography* (New York: New York Tribune, 1896), pp. 648–649.

136 *MMCR* 46 (January 1862): 64.

137 Hodas, *The Business Career of Moses Taylor,* pp. 169–176.

138 See William E. Dodge's speech in a Baltimore church in 1865, reprinted in Carlos Martyn, *William E. Dodge, the Christian Merchant* (New York: Funk and Wagnalls, 1890), pp. 217–222.

139 George Fredrickson, *The Inner Civil War: Northern Intellectuals and the Crisis of the Union* (New York: Harper and Row, 1965), p. 115.

140 Loyal Publication Society, Pamphlet 28, *The Death of Slavery, Letter from Peter Cooper to Governor Seymour,* p. 6.

141 See, for example, the publications of the Loyal Publication League, which did not discuss either.

142 McKay, *The Civil War,* p. 165.

143 For Barlow's position see Samuel Barlow to J. Barnet, New York City, June 1864, "Letterbook," BW 1, Samuel Barlow Papers, Huntington Library. August Belmont to Lord Rokeby, May 7, 1863, cited in Black, *The King of Fifth Avenue,* p. 226; Black, *The King of Fifth Avenue,* p. 231; McKay, *The Civil War,* p. 144.

144 Black, *The King of Fifth Avenue,* p. 220.

145 *World,* 14 October 1862, p. 2.

146 Society for the Diffusion of Political Knowledge, *Reply to President Lincoln's Letter of 12th June, 1863* (New York: n.p., 1863); Society for the Diffusion of Political Knowledge, *To Churchmen* (New York: n.p., 1863).

147 See, for example, *Papers From the Society for the Diffusion of Political Knowledge* 18 (n.d.).

148 *NYT,* 4 June 1863, p. 1

149 Katz, *August Belmont,* p. 36; *NYH,* 2 July 1862, p. 5.

150 *NYH,* 2 July 1862, p. 5; *Democratic Anti-Abolition State Rights Association of New York* (New York: n.p., 1863), pp. i, 4, 5, 8, 9; Bernstein, *The New York City Draft Riots,* p. 222; Richard C. Murphy and Lawrence J. Mannion, *The History of the Society of the Friendly Sons of Saint Patrick in the City of New York, 1784 to 1955* (New York: J. C. Dillon Company, 1982), p. 303.

151 *NYT,* 4 June 1863, p. 4; Bernstein, *The New York City Draft Riots,* p. 146. Alvin W. Lookwood from New York City also attended, but his occupation could not be identified.

152 Especially Samuel Barlow actively handled McClellan's political career. See, among many others, letter of McClellan to Barlow, August 4, 1863, BW 47, Samuel Barlow Papers, Huntington Library, and Barlow's letters of July to November 1864, in "Letterbooks," BW 1, Samuel Barlow Papers, Huntington Library.

153 See the correspondence in the Samuel Barlow Papers, for example, Samuel Cox to Barlow, Columbus, Ohio, November 21, 1863, BW 46, Samuel Barlow Papers, Huntington Library. Black, *The King of Fifth Avenue,* p. 244. For a critique of the platform see Samuel Barlow to John Doyle, New York City, November 11, 1864, "Letterbooks," BW 1, Samuel Barlow Papers, Huntington Library.

154 Letter from August Belmont to McClellan, September 3, 1864, McClellan Papers, cited in Black, *The King of Fifth Avenue*, p. 252.

155 Black, *The King of Fifth Avenue*, pp. 252, 255.

156 Hodas, *The Business Career of Moses Taylor*, p. 191.

157 Robert Hoe II to Richard Hoe, February 22, 1864, Reel 11, Hoe Papers, Library of Congress.

158 Migliore, "The Business of Union," p. 335.

159 *New York Tribune*, 7 March 1864, p. 8.

160 Migliore, "The Business of Union," p. 345.

161 Bellows, *Historical Sketch of the Union League Club of New York: Its Origin, Organization, and Work, 1863–1879*, p. 56f; *New York Tribune*, 7 March 1864, p. 8.

162 Address to the 20th Regiment U.S. Colored Troops on the Occasion of the Presentation of a Stand of Colors by the Ladies, March 5, 1864, cited in Bellows, *Historical Sketch of the Union League Club*, p. 187.

163 Robert Hoe II to Richard Hoe, February 22, 1864, Reel 11, Hoe Papers, Library of Congress.

164 Maxwell Whiteman, *Copper for America: The Hendricks Family and a National Industry, 1755–1939* (New Brunswick, N.J.: Rutgers University Press, 1971), pp. 192–199.

165 Marcellus Hartley, *A Brief Memoir* (New York: [privately printed], 1903), pp. 26–49.

166 *The National Cyclopedia of American Biography, Being the History of the United States* (New York: James T. White & Company, 1921), vol. 2, p. 262; "George Quintard," New York, vol. 316, p. 1 (W), Dun & Co. Collection, Baker Library, Harvard Business School.

167 *ARJ* 34 (6 July 1861): 489.

168 Heffer, *Le Port de New York et le Commerce Exterieur Americain*, pp. 59, 64; *ARJ* 35 (4 January 1862): 1.

169 Hodas, *The Business Career of Moses Taylor*, p. 186.

170 Robert Hoe II to John Mac Donald, New York, February 17, 1862, Reel 6, Hoe Papers, Library of Congress; McKay, *The Civil War*, p. 98; Swann, *John Roach*, p. 23; Frederic Cople Jaher, *The Urban Establishment: Upper Strata in Boston, New York, Charleston, Chicago and Los Angeles* (Urbana: University of Illinois Press, 1973), p. 258; Ron Chernow, *The House of Morgan: An American Banking Dynasty and the Rise of Modern Finance* (New York: Simon & Schuster: 1990), p. 22; Lowitt, *A Merchant Prince of the Nineteenth Century*, p. 23.

171 Leonard Alexander Swann, *John Roach: Maritime Entrepreneur, The Years as Naval Contractor, 1862–1886* (Annapolis: U.S. Naval Institute, 1965), pp. 19, 20, 23. On the boom among apparel manufacturers see Patricia Evelyn Malon, "The Growth of Manufacturing in Manhattan, 1860–1900: An Analysis of Factoral Changes and Urban Structure" (Ph.D. diss., Columbia University, 1981), p. 100.

172 "Novelty Iron Works," entry of June 2, 1866, New York, vol. 386, p. 401, Dun & Co. Collection, Baker Library, Harvard Business School. Abram Hewitt used wartime government contracts to invest in the production of new kinds of iron. Allan Nevins, *Abram S. Hewitt, With some Account of*

Peter Cooper (New York: Harper, 1935), p. 206. See also Edwin Stanton to Abram S. Hewitt, September 10, 1862, "Letters," Abram S. Hewitt Papers, NYHS.

173 William Hurd Hillyer, *James Talcott: Merchant, and His Times* (New York: Scribner's, 1937), pp. 68, 70. For other evidence of war profits see "Schuyler, Hartley & Graham," New York, vol. 317, p. 30 (H), Dun & Co. Collection, Baker Library, Harvard Business School.

174 Hillyer, *James Talcott,* p. 71.

175 Heffer, *Le Port de New York et le Commerce Exterieur Americain,* pp. 131, 133.

176 Glenn Porter and Harold C. Livesay, *Merchants and Manufacturers: Studies in the Changing Structure of Nineteenth Century Marketing* (Baltimore: Johns Hopkins Press, 1971), p. 124.

177 "George Quintard," entry of October 21, 1860, New York, vol. 316, p. 1 (W), Dun & Co. Collection, Baker Library, Harvard Business School.

178 Porter and Livesay, *Merchants and Manufacturers,* p. 126.

179 See also *ARJ* 36 (3 January 1863): 1.

180 Swann, *John Roach,* p. 23.

181 McKay, *The Civil War,* pp. 225, 226.

182 *JoC,* 6 November 1862, p. 2.

183 Cited in Martin, *The Life of Joseph Hodges Choate,* vol. 1, pp. 240–241.

184 William E. Dodge to William B. Kinney, March 9, 1863, Stedman Mss., Columbia University, quoted in Migliore, "The Business of Union," p. 90.

185 Eric Foner, *Reconstruction: America's Unfinished Revolution, 1863–1877* (New York: Harper & Row, 1988), p. 31. While the currency depreciated between 1860 and 1863 by 43 percent, wages increased by only 12 percent. McKay, *The Civil War,* p. 216. Food prices rose dramatically – beef, for example, nearly doubled in price – while rents went up 15 to 20 percent. McKay, *The Civil War,* p. 216.

186 Karl Wesslau to his family, New York, May 28, 1864. See also letter to his parents, New York, July 28, 1863. A copy of these letters is in the holdings of the University of Bochum's research project on German immigrants in the United States. The author thanks Wolfgang Helbich for making these documents available.

187 Foner, *Reconstruction,* p. 31; Bernstein, *The New York City Draft Riots,* pp. 104–114; Lieberman, *Steinway & Sons,* p. 38.

188 Bernstein, *The New York City Draft Riots,* p. 9.

189 See Anstice, *History of St. George's Church,* p. 227.

190 For a detailed account see Bernstein, *The New York City Draft Riots,* pp. 17–42.

191 *ARJ* 36 (18 July 1863): 681–682. Among other reactions, the *NYT* headlined the following day: "Crush the Mob!" and the *JoC* appealed to "sustain the law." See *NYT,* 14 July 1863, p. 4; *JoC,* 14 July 1863, p. 2.

192 Morgan Dix, ed., *A History of the Parish of Trinity Church in the City of New York* (New York: Putnam's Sons, 1906), p. 50. "We had four days of great anxiety," noted Maria Lydig Daly in her diary on July 23. "Colonel O'Brian was murdered by the mob in such a brutal manner that nothing in

the French Revolution exceeded it." Maria Lydig Daly, *Diary of a Union Lady, 1861–1865* (New York: Funk & Wagnalls, 1962), p. 249.

193 Nevins and Thomas, *The Diary of George Templeton Strong,* vol. 3, p. 337.

194 Steinway Diary, entries of July 13 and July 15, 1863, NYHS. John Ward also noted in his diary the "fearful riot." John Ward Diary, entry of Jan. 8, 1864, NYHS.

195 John A. Parker to Richard Lathers, New York City, July 13, 1863, vol. 2, 1863–1901, Richard Lathers Papers, LDC. See also Migliore, "The Business of Union," p. 256.

196 J. T. Headley, *The Great Riots of New York, 1712–1873, Including a Full and Complete Account of the Four Day's Draft Riot of 1863* (New York: E. B. Treat, 1873), pp. 18–19.

197 Samuel Barlow to "My dear," July 18, 1863, "Letterbook," BW 1, Samuel Barlow Papers, Huntington Library.

198 Joseph H. Choate to his mother (Mrs. George Choate), New York, July 14, 1863. Reprinted in Martin, *The Life of Joseph Hodges Choate,* vol. 1, p. 256. See also Joseph H. Choate to his mother, New York, July 15, 1863. Reprinted in Martin, *The Life of Joseph Hodges Choate,* vol. 1, p. 256.

199 McKay, *The Civil War,* p. 205; Bernstein, *The New York City Draft Riots,* p. 55.

200 *NYT,* 30 August 1863, pp. 4–5.

201 Nevins and Thomas, *The Diary of George Templeton Strong,* vol. 3, p. 336, entry of July 13, 1863.

203 Nevins and Thomas, *The Diary of George Templeton Strong,* vol. 3, p. 337.

203 Already on Monday night George T. Strong had "begged that martial law might be declared." Nevins and Thomas, *The Diary of George Templeton Strong,* vol. 3, p. 337, entry of July 13, 1863. David Dudley Field and William Hall wanted to put the city under military administration. William E. Dodge, Prosper Wetmore, John A. Stevens, and William M. Vermilye demanded the mobilization of federal troops at a meeting at the Merchants Exchange. Bernstein, *The New York City Draft Riots,* pp. 55–56.

204 George T. Strong was "sorry to find that England is right about the lower class Irish. They are brutal, base, cruel, cowards, and as insolent as base. . . . For myself, personally, I would like to see war made on Irish scum as in 1688." Nevins and Thomas, *The Diary of George Templeton Strong,* vol. 3, p. 337, entry of July 13, 1863. In the Union League Club a sign went up suggesting "Sam, Organize" – a direct connection to the nativist traditions of the 1850s. Migliore, "The Business of Union," p. 256. On African Americans see Nevins and Thomas (abridged by Thomas J. Pressly), *The Diary of George Templeton Strong,* p. 244. Joseph Choate rescued blacks by taking them into his house. Martin, *The Life of Joseph Hodges Choate,* vol. 1, pp. 255–256. A committee of merchants, industrialists, and bankers "for the Relief of Colored People Suffering from the late Riots in the City of New York" was formed only three days after the suppression of the riots to aid black victims. Jonathan Sturges legitimized this aid as being in the tradition of New York's merchant community: "Those who know the colored people of this city, can testify to their being peaceable, industrious people." *Report of the Committee of Merchants for the*

Relief of Colored People Suffering from the late Riots in the City of New York (New York: G. A. Whitehorne, 1863). p. 4.

205 For this position, see also the *JoC*, 20 July 1863, p. 2; *JoC*, 24 July 1863, p. 2.

206 Daly, *Diary of a Union Lady*, p. 251.

207 Bernstein, *The New York City Draft Riots*, pp. 44, 47.

208 Even August Belmont expressed his relief that the "schemes have been foiled by the bravery of our army." August Belmont to the Hon. W. H. Seward, Newport, July 20, 1863, reprinted in August Belmont, *A Few Letters and Speeches of the Late Civil War* (New York: [privately printed], 1870), pp. 89–90. For a similar sentiment from a manufacturer, see Robert Hoe II to Robert Hoe, Jr., New York, August 24, 1863, Reel 4, Hoe Papers, Library of Congress.

209 Bernstein, *The New York City Draft Riots*, pp. 50, 51, 60, 64.

210 Headley, *The Great Riots of New York*, p. 19.

211 See, for example, *ARJ* 36 (26 September 1863): 918.

212 *NYT*, 1 November 1864, p. 8.

213 On Taylor see Hodas, *The Business Career of Moses Taylor*, p. 191. For the others see *NYH*, 2 November 1864, p. 5. Republican Peter Hoe also actively campaigned for Lincoln's reelection. See letter to his "brother" (either Robert Hoe II or Richard Hoe), October 10, 1864, Reel 11, Hoe Papers, Library of Congress.

214 Samuel Barlow to [illegible], November 1, 1864, BW 1, Samuel Barlow Papers, Huntington Library.

215 Nevins and Thomas, *The Diary of George Templeton Strong*, vol. 3, p. 580, entry of April 11, 1865.

216 *JoC*, 27 April 1865, p. 2. This article indeed summarizes the development of elite discourse during the war in a way quite similar to this chapter.

217 Among the speakers were S. B. Chittenden, Columbia College Law Professor Dr. Francis Lieber, Honorable John Van Buren, and Oakey Hall. *NYT*, 6 March 1865, pp. 1, 8.

218 Nevins and Thomas, *The Diary of George Templeton Strong*, vol. 3, p. 560, entry of March 6, 1865.

219 Mass Meeting at Union Square, B. V. War, Union Defense Committee, NYHS.

220 See, for example, Daly, *Diary of a Union Lady*, entry of April 15, 1865, p. 348.

221 Daly, *Diary of a Union Lady*, p. 349, entry of April 15, 1865. See also Nevins and Thomas, *The Diary of George Templeton Strong*, vol. 3, pp. 573–576, entry of April 3, 1865.

222 Nevins and Thomas, *The Diary of George Templeton Strong*, vol. 3, pp. 573–576, entry of April 3, 1865.

223 Robert Hoe II to Richard M. Hoe, New York, April 11, 1865, Reel 11, Hoe Papers, Library of Congress.

224 Nevins and Thomas, *The Diary of George Templeton Strong*, vol. 3, pp. 573–576, entry of April 3, 1865.

225 *Seventh Annual Report of the Chamber of Commerce of the State of New-York, for the Year 1864–65* (New York: John W. Amerman, 1865), p. 94.

226 Cited in McKay, *The Civil War*, p. 303.

227 Nevins and Thomas, *The Diary of George Templeton Strong*, vol. 3, pp. 578–579, entry of April 10, 1865.

228 Hellen Grinnell Diary, entry of April 15, 1865, NYPL, cited in McKay, *The Civil War*, p. 305.

229 Nevins and Thomas, *The Diary of George Templeton Strong*, vol. 3, pp. 582–585, entry of April 15, 1865.

230 B. V. Ward, John; Diary, Jan. 1–Dec. 31, 1865; April 15, 1865, NYHS.

231 Samuel Barlow to [illegible], New York City, April 15, 1865, in "Letterbook," Samuel Barlow Papers, BW 1, Huntington Library.

232 *Seventh Annual Report of the Chamber of Commerce*, p. 97.

233 *ARJ* (15 April 1861): 361.

234 Loyal Publication Society, *Proceedings at the Second Anniversary Meeting* (New York: Loyal Publication Society, 1865), p. 10.

235 A. A. Low Diary, entry of April 19, 1865, Low Family papers, NYHS.

236 *Centennial Celebration of the Chamber of Commerce of the State of New-York at Irving Hall, April 6th, 1868, Report of Proceedings* (New York: John W. Amerman, 1868), p. 20.

237 *ARJ* 38 (15 April 1865): 362.

5. The Spoils of Victory

1 *Annual Report of the American Institute of the City of New York For the Years 1867 & 8* (Albany, N.Y.: Charles Van Benthuysen & Sons, 1868), p. 133.

2 In 1859 there had been 140,433 factories in the United States, in 1869, 252,148. In constant 1958 dollars. "Capital in Manufacturing Industries, 1863 to 1970," in *Historical Statistics of the United States, Colonial Times to 1970* (Washington, D.C.: U.S. Department of Commerce, 1975), vol. 2, p. 683.

3 "Total Horsepower of All Prime Movers, 1849 to 1970," in *Historical Statistics of the United States*, vol. 2, p. 818.

4 Chamber of Commerce, *The Atlantic Telegraph, Report of the Proceedings at a Banquet given to Mr. Cyrus W. Field, by the Chamber of Commerce of New York, November 15th, 1866* (New York: n.p., 1866).

5 David Whitten, *Handbook of American Business History* (New York: Greenwood Press, 1990), vol. 1, p. 177.

6 "Railroad Mileage and Equipment: 1830 to 1890," in *Historical Statistics of the United States*, vol. 2, p. 731.

7 "Miles of Railroad Built: 1830 to 1925," in *Historical Statistics of the United States*, vol. 2, p. 732.

8 Patrick O'Donnell, "Industrial Capitalism and the Rise of Modern American Cities," in *Kapitalstate* 6 (1977): 106.

9 "Population by Age, Sex, Race, and Nativity, 1790 to 1970," in *Historical Statistics of the United States*, vol. 1, p. 15; "Immigrants by Country, 1820–1870," in *Historical Statistics of the United States*, vol. 1, p. 106.

10 1870 sample. In a sample of one of eight New Yorkers who appeared in the

1870 federal census, 1,571 individuals were listed with a combined real and personal wealth of $15,000. That suggests that the total number of New Yorkers who fell into this category was 12,568. This, however, is a conservative estimate since the census takers did not record the real and personal wealth of all the people they visited. Even if they are imprecise, the numbers suggest that New York City's upper class grew rapidly in the postwar years. (See also note 11.)

11 See 1870s sample. Most notably, the share of bourgeois New Yorkers born in Germany increased from 6 percent to 23 percent. While the percentage of bourgeois New Yorkers born in Manhattan remained approximately constant (32 percent in 1870 versus 31 percent in 1855), the importance of those born in New York State fell (from 16 percent to 6 percent), as did those born in New England (from 15 percent to 10 percent).

These numbers are derived from a sample of 1,571 New Yorkers who appear in the 1870 federal census. The sample included every eighth person assessed by the census taker as owning more than $15,000 in combined real and personal wealth. Since each census sheet contained forty entries, the people listed in the first five rows of each sheet were considered for inclusion in the sample. I chose $15,000 as the cut-off point because I wanted to make the 1855 and 1870 samples roughly comparable. For the 1855 sample, the cut-off point had been a combined real and personal wealth of $10,000. The rate of inflation between 1855 and 1870 was approximately 35.8 percent. (See "Consumer Price Index [Hoover], 1851–1880," in *Historical Statistics of the United States,* vol. 1, p. 212.) Thus $10,000 in 1855 equalled about $13,580 in 1870. As the reporting of real and personal wealth in both the 1855 tax list and the 1870 census was notoriously inaccurate, and because it was easier to use a round sum as a cut-off point in order to speed the sampling process, I chose the minimum combined real and personal wealth required for inclusion in the sample as $15,000. There might hence be a very slight bias toward a slightly better-off group in the 1870 sample, compared to that of the 1855 sample. It should also be noted that I used tax lists for the 1855 sample, and these lists might have been slightly more accurate in their estimates of wealth than the census. Unfortunately, no comparable tax lists for 1870 exist today. Moreover, the census takers in 1870 were not consistent in their recording of real and personal wealth and omitted to record the results of their inquiries in a number of areas of the city. Despite these unavoidable shortcomings, the numbers still allow us to establish some general points about the structure of New York City's bourgeoisie in 1870, including its economic activities, the social geography of Manhattan, and the breathtaking diversity of the city's upper class.

12 *CFC* (10 September 1870): 328.

13 See 1870 sample.

14 Secretary of the Interior, *Ninth Census, The Statistics of the Wealth and Industry in the United States* (Washington, D.C.: GPO, 1875), vol. 3, p. 550. In real dollars.

15 Patricia Evelyn Malon, "The Growth of Manufacturing in Manhattan, 1860–1900, An Analysis of Factoral Changes and Urban Structure" (Ph.D. diss., Columbia University, 1981), pp. 6, 59.

16 In Manhattan, the capital invested per worker (in real dollars) stayed nearly constant during the 1860s. Secretary of the Interior, *Ninth Census,* vol. 3, p. 550.

17 Malon, "The Growth of Manufacturing in Manhattan," p. 98; Iver Bernstein, *The New York City Draft Riots* (New York: Oxford University Press, 1990), p. 213.

18 Malon, "The Growth of Manufacturing in Manhattan," p. 233.

19 Malon, "The Growth of Manufacturing in Manhattan," p. 280.

20 Speech by Horace Greeley at the Thirty-seventh Annual Exhibition of the American Institute, reprinted in *Annual Report of the American Institute of the City of New York For the Years 1867&8* (Albany, N.Y.: Charles Van Benthuysen & Sons, 1868), p. 126.

21 Philip H. Burch, Jr., *Elites in American History* (New York: Holmes & Meier Publishers Inc., 1981), p. 16.

22 Burch, Jr., *Elites in American History,* p. 15.

23 Chamber of Commerce, *Address of the Hon. William Bross, Lieutenant-Governor of Illinois, on the Resources of the Far West and the Pacific Railway, Before the Chamber of Commerce of the State of New York, At a Special Meeting, Thursday, January 25, 1866* (New York: John W. Amerman, 1866), pp. 13, 14.

24 Burch, Jr., *Elites in American History,* pp. 27, 36, 44.

25 Charles Barber, Jr., "Joseph Seligman," in Larry Schweikart, ed., *Encyclopedia of American Business History and Biography, Banking and Finance to 1913* (New York: Facts on File, 1990), pp. 421–430.

26 David M. Gische, "The New York City Banks and the Development of the National Banking System, 1860–1870," in *American Journal of Legal History* 23 (1979): 54, 60. In contrast, the city next in importance for its banks, Philadelphia, employed only one-fifth as many bankers as New York City. For the numbers, see Samuel Schoenberg, "An Historical Analysis of the Changing Business Life in New York City" (Ph.D. diss., New York University, 1940), p. 139.

27 Peter J. Buckley and Brian R. Roberts, *European Direct Investment in the U.S.A. before World War I* (New York: St. Martin's Press, 1982), pp. 26, 30.

28 John Crosby Brown, February 17, 1871, as quoted in John A. Kouwenhoven, *Partners in Banking, An Historical Portrait of a Great Private Bank, Brown Brothers Harriman & Co., 1818–1968* (New York: Doubleday & Company, 1968), p. 143.

29 Bourgeois New Yorkers engaged in finance had on average 2.99 servants, compared to 2.21 for people engaged in commerce and 1.34 for manufacturers. The average real and personal wealth by 1870 was $137,065 for financiers, $108,084 for people engaged in commerce, and $61,935 for manufacturers. The absolute amount of these numbers can not be considered accurate as they notoriously underreported their wealth. However, they give a good estimation of their relative wealth. See 1870 sample.

30 Rom Chernow, *The House of Morgan: An American Banking Dynasty and the Rise of Modern Finance* (New York: Simon & Schuster, 1990), p. 30.

31 The Fourth National Bank, the Bank of New York, the Central National

Bank, the Importers and Traders National Bank, and the Mechanics National Bank. See Gische, "The New York City Banks," p. 63.

32 Chernow, *The House of Morgan*, p. 32.

33 Christine M. Boyer, *Manhattan Manners, Architecture and Style, 1850–1900* (New York: Rizzoli, 1985), p. 31.

34 Eugene P. Moehring, *Public Works and the Patterns of Urban Real Estate Growth in Manhattan, 1835–1894* (New York: Arno Press, 1981), p. 302; Rosenzweig and Blackmar, *The Park and the People: A History of Central Park* (Ithaca, N.Y.: Cornell University Press, 1992), p. 272.

35 Moehring, *Public Works*, p. 306.

36 Moehring, *Public Works*, p. 314.

37 Exports increased from $178,626,599 (1865) to $300,245,405 (1873), while imports increased from $222,619,138 (1865) to $379,960,225 (1873). The percentage calculations are based on constant 1873 dollars. William Nelson Black, *Storage and Transportation in the Port of New York* (New York: Putnam, 1884), pp. 2–3. Merchants also managed to capitalize on the rise of the West as their trade increasingly consisted of grain and beef, not cotton. Jean Heffer, *Le Port de New York et le Commerce Extérieur Americain* (Paris: Publications de la Sorbonne, 1986), p. 185.

The analysis of the economic structure of New York City's bourgeoisie is based on the 1870 sample.

38 Heffer, *Le Port de New York*, pp. 337, 409.

39 Glenn Porter and Harold C. Livesay, *Merchants and Manufacturers, Studies in the Changing Structure of Nineteenth Century Marketing* (Baltimore: Johns Hopkins Press, 1971), pp. 129–132; *Centennial Celebration of the Chamber of Commerce of the State of New-York at Irving Hall, April 6, 1868, Report of the Proceedings* (New York: John W. Amerman, 1868), pp. 33, 34.

40 Kouwenhoven, *Partners in Banking*, pp. 129, 144.

41 Marcellus Hartley, *A Brief Memoir* (New York: [privately printed], 1903), pp. 50, 52.

42 James A. Rawley, *Edwin D. Morgan: Merchant in Politics* (New York: Columbia University Press, 1955), p. 233.

43 Frank S. Winchester to Horace Greeley, New York, June 20, 1872, Box 7, Greeley Papers, Library of Congress; Matthew Josephson, *The Robber Barons: The Great American Capitalists, 1861–1901* (New York: Harcourt, Brace and Co., 1934), p. 95.

44 Josephson, *The Robber Barons*, p. 95.

45 E. Riggs Ledger Balances, March 31, 1872, Box 56, Riggs Family Papers, Library of Congress.

46 For examples of diversification see Abiel Abbot Low, "Correspondence and Papers, Low Family, 1870–1899," NYHS. When Clarence Brown thought about leaving the banking house of Brown Brothers in the late 1860s, he was content to fall back on "his fortune & his Novelty Works . . . & his underground railroad, & his Pacific Mail." Letter from Howard Potter to John Crosby Brown, July 3, 1868, as cited in Kouwenhoven, *Partners in Banking*, p. 143.

47 Allen Churchill, *The Upper Crust, An Informal History of New York's Highest Society* (Englewood Cliffs, N.J.: Prentice-Hall, 1970), p. 201.

48 Chamber of Commerce, *Address of the Hon. William Bross,* pp. 3–4.

49 Chamber of Commerce, *Address of the Hon. William Bross,* pp. 17, 19, 22.

50 *Centennial Celebration of the Chamber of Commerce,* 1868, p. 21.

51 *Third Annual Report of the Chamber of Commerce of the State of New-York for the Year 1860–'61* (New York: John W. Amerman, 1861), p. 327. See also *Eleventh Annual Report of the Chamber of Commerce of the State of New-York for the Year 1868–'69* (New York: John W. Amerman, 1869), p. 25.

52 *Sixth Annual Report of the Chamber of Commerce of the State of New-York for the Year 1863–'64* (New York: John W. Amerman, 1864), p. 67.

53 See *International Relations with Brazil, Proceedings of the Reception of H.E. Senator D'Azambuja by the Chamber of Commerce of the State of New-York, November 2, 1865* (New York: John W. Amerman, 1865); Chamber of Commerce of the State of New-York, *Ninth Annual Report for the Year 1866–'67* (New York: John W. Amerman, 1867), p. 28; Chamber of Commerce of the State of New-York, *Thirteenth Annual Report of the Corporation of the Chamber of Commerce of the State of New-York for the Year 1870–'71* (New York: Press of the Chamber of Commerce, 1871), pp. 105–106; Chamber of Commerce, *Fifteenth Annual Report of the Corporation of the Chamber of Commerce of the State of New-York for the Year 1872–'73* (New York: Press of the Chamber of Commerce, 1873), p. 10.

54 Citizens' Association of New-York, *Report of the Executive Council to the Honorary Council of the Citizens' Association of New-York, November 7, 1866* (New York: Association of New York, 1866), p. 18.

55 *Entertainment given to A. A. Low by Members of the Chamber of Commerce on his Return from A Voyage Round the World, Fifth Avenue Hotel, October 8, 1867* (New York: Press of the Chamber of Commerce, 1867), p. 9.

56 *Entertainment given to A. A. Low, 1867,* p. 32. In January of 1872, a traveller reported glowingly to Augustus A. Low from Japan that "they are buying a good quantity of merchandise at good prices and selling their products at fair rates." Particularly tea and silk could be bought there. R. G. Walsh to A. A. Low, Yoka, Japan, January 23, 1872, "Correspondence and Papers, 1870–1899," Low Family, NYHS.

57 David Black, *The King of Fifth Avenue, The Fortunes of August Belmont* (New York: Dial Press, 1981), p. 272.

58 Churchill, *The Upper Crust,* p. 95.

59 Churchill, *The Upper Crust,* p. 198.

60 Black, *The King of Fifth Avenue,* pp. 275, 276.

61 Churchill, *The Upper Crust,* p. 199.

62 May King Van Rensselaer, *The Social Ladder* (New York: Henry Holt and Company, 1924), p. 169.

63 Ruth Brandon, *The Dollar Princess, Sagas of Upward Nobility, 1870–1914* (New York: Alfred A. Knopf, 1980), p. 19.

64 Boyer, *Manhattan Manners,* p. 141.

65 Black, *The King of Fifth Avenue,* p. 275.

66 Boyer, *Manhattan Manners,* p. 88.

67 Boyer, *Manhattan Manners,* p. 116.

68 Boyer, *Manhattan Manners,* pp. 116, 118.

69 Clarence Cook, *The House Beautiful: Essays on Beds and Tables, Stools and Candlesticks* (New York: Scribner, Armstrong and Co., 1878), p. 319.

70 Robert Hoe II to Richard M. Hoe, March 2, 1872, Reel 6, Hoe Papers, Library of Congress. His brother instead suggested an oil painting by a Parisian painter.

71 Churchill, *The Upper Crust*, p. 185.

72 John Crosby Brown, *Reminiscences of the Early Life* (New York: n.p., n.d.), p. 20.

73 Henry Collins Brown, *Delmonico's: A Story of Old New York* (New York: Valentine's Manual, 1928), p. 59.

74 1870 sample.

75 1870 sample.

76 Brandon, *The Dollar Princess*, p. 19. Van Rensselaer, *Social Ladder*, p. 33. Maureen E. Montgomery, *Gilded Prostitution: Status, Money, and Transatlantic Marriages, 1870–1914* (London: Routledge, 1989), p. 38.

77 Van Rensselaer, *Social Ladder*, p. 37.

78 Brandon, *The Dollar Princess*, p. 43.

79 Van Rensselaer, *Social Ladder*, p. 53.

80 Gail MacColl and Wallace, *To Marry an English Lord* (New York: Workman, 1989), p. 14.

81 Van Rensselaer, *Social Ladder*, p. 36.

82 Rosenzweig and Blackmar, *The Park and the People*, p. 218.

83 Churchill, *The Upper Crust*, p. 169.

84 James E. Montgomery, Office of the Executive Committee for the Reception of H.J.H. The Grand Duke Alexis of Russia, New York, to the Reception Committee, May 9, 1871, Isaac Sherman Papers, Huntington Library.

85 *NYT,* 27 November 1871, p. 1.

86 *NYT,* 30 November 1871, p. 1.

87 *NYT,* 30 November 1871, p. 1

88 *NYT,* 30 November 1871, p. 1.

89 On the desire to keep former slave owners subordinate see, for example, *NYCA,* 8 September 1865, p. 2. See also New York Chamber of Commerce, *Eight Annual Report* (New York: John W. Amerman, 1866), p. 4. On the embrace of emancipation see *CFC* (23 December 1865): 803.

90 *Sixtieth Anniversary Celebration of the New England Society, In the City of New York, At Delmonico's, December 22, 1865* (New York: John F. Trow, 1866), p. 15. The merchants' *NYCA* concurred, explaining that it "cannot be too strongly impressed upon the South that slavery is actually dead and gone." *NYCA,* 25 July 1865, p. 2.

91 *USEconomist* (25 March 1865): 4.

92 *Report of the Special Committee of the Chamber of Commerce of the State of New-York on the Confiscation of Cotton in the Southern States by the Government* (New York: John W. Amerman, 1865); Richard Bensel, *Yankee Leviathan: The Origins of Central State Authority in America, 1859–1877* (New York: Cambridge University Press, 1990), p. 331. On their concern about antebellum southern state debts see *MMCR* 53 (December 1865): 409–412. For the quotation see "Report submitted by Walter S. Griffith,

Chairman of the Committee of Arbitration," reprinted in *Seventh Annual Report of the Chamber of Commerce of the State of New York for the Year 1864–1865* (New York: John W. Amerman, 1865), p. 76.

93 *ARJ* (8 July 1865): 651. For the success of free labor see also *ARJ* (7 October 1865): 949; *NYCA*, 11 October 1865, p. 2; *NYCA*, 2 September 1865, p. 249; *USEconomist* (30 June 1865): 4; *USEconomist* (23 September 1865): 4; *USEconomist* (11 November 1865): 4; *ARJ* (7 October 1865): 949; *MMCR* (October 1868): 290; *Sixtieth Anniversary Celebration of the New England Society in the City of New York at Delmonico's, December 22, 1865* (New York: John F. Trow, 1866), p. 61.

94 *NYDT*, 21 February 1862, p. 8.

95 *NYDT*, 21 February 1862, p. 8.

96 Paul Migliore, "The Business of Union" (Ph.D. diss., Columbia University, 1975), p. 351.

97 *NYDT*, 21 February 1862, p. 8. This was an opinion also shared (at first) by the *CFC*. *CFC* (23 December 1865): 803. For more evidence, consult Willie Lee Rose, *Rehearsal for Reconstruction, The Port Royal Experiment* (New York: Oxford University Press, 1964), pp. 333–336. They had actively worked for the improvement of southern schools for former slaves by supporting the National Freedmen's Association (a delegation to the association included international trader Jonathan Sturges, banker George Cabot Ward, and industrialist Peter Cooper) and by managing the New York branch of the American Freedmen's Union Commission, which sent 150 teachers into the South. Henry Bellows, *Historical Sketch of the Union League Club of New York: Its Origin, Organization, and Work, 1863–1879* (New York: Club House, 1879), pp. 87, 90.

98 *MMCR* (September 1867): 177.

99 *CFC* (1 July 1865): 3.

100 The importance of cotton production for some merchants is illustrated in *NYCA*, 26 August 1865, pp. 258–279; *NYCA*, 11 November 1865, pp. 611–612; *NYCA*, 26 January 1867, pp. 103–104; *NYCA*, 6 February 1869, pp. 167–168. See also *MMCR* (December 1866): 409–411.

101 *NYCA*, 1 July 1865, p. 3; Peter Kolchin, "The Business Press and Reconstruction, 1865–1868," *Journal of Southern History* 33 (May 1967): p. 185. See also Eric Foner, *Reconstruction, America's Unfinished Revolution, 1863–1877* (New York: Harper & Row, 1988), p. 220

102 This point is well taken by Peter Kolchin and Stanley Coben against the progressive view that Radical Republicans were the political representatives of the northeastern bourgeoisie. For the progressive view, see Howard K. Beale, "On Rewriting Reconstruction History," *AHR* 45 (July 1940): 807–827. In response, see Stanley Cohen, "Northeastern Business and Radical Reconstruction: A Re-examination," *Mississippi Valley Historical Review* 46 (June 1959): 67–90, and Kolchin, "The Business Press and Reconstruction," 184. Stripped of some of its simplifying rhetoric, the most intelligent discussion about the relationship between northern capitalists and reconstruction is still W. E. B. DuBois, *Black Reconstruction in America, 1860–1880* (1935; reprint New York: Touchstone, 1995), especially pp. 182–236, 580–634. For an interest in stability and peace see, for example, *ARJ* (14 April 1866): 1.

103 See, for example, *NYCA*, 8 July 1865, p. 3; *NYCA*, 23 September 1865, p. 388; *NYCA*, 9 December 1865, p. 740; *NYCA*, 17 February 1866, pp. 197–198. Also *USEconomist* (7 April 1866): 4.

104 *NYCA*, 23 September 1865, p. 388. See also *NYCA*, 26 August 1865, p. 260.

105 *MMCR* (March 1866): 169–174; *NYCA*, 1 July 1865, p. 5.

106 Joseph Bucklin Bishop, *A Chronicle of One Hundred & Fifty Years, The Chamber of Commerce of the State of New York, 1768–1918* (New York: Scribner's, 1918), pp. 90–91.

107 *NYT*, 30 August 1866, p. 1.

108 Irving Katz, *August Belmont, A Political Biography* (New York: Columbia University Press, 1968), p. 157; Coben, "Northeastern Business and Radical Reconstruction," p. 88; Daniel Hodas, *The Business Career of Moses Taylor, Merchant, Finance Capitalist, and Industrialist* (New York: New York University Press, 1976), p. 193.

109 *NYT*, 30 August 1866, p. 8.

110 See Cohen, "Northeastern Business and Radical Reconstruction," p. 88, and *NYT*, 23 February 1866, pp. 4–5.

111 *CFC* (17 February 1866): 198; *ARJ* (7 October 1865): 949.

112 *MMCR* 53 (July 1865): 19–30.

113 New York Chamber of Commerce, *Eighth Annual Report* (1866), p. 4. See also Chamber of Commerce of the State of New-York, *Ninth Annual Report* (1867), p. 6.

114 For their concern to receive payment on outstanding antebellum debts (including interest accrued during the war) see, for example, New York Chamber of Commerce, *Eighth Annual Report* (1866), p. 121. See also *MMCR* (December 1865): 409–412. The concern about the resumption of cotton production can be seen in the attention the Chamber of Commerce lavished on the subject. See New York Chamber of Commerce, *Eighth Annual Report* (1866), pp. 69, 94; New York Chamber of Commerce, *Ninth Annual Report* (1867), pp. 12, 36.

    Cotton production in the southern states increased rapidly, from an estimated 300,000 bales in the last year of the war (1864/65) to 4,347,006 bales in 1870/71. Chamber of Commerce of the State of New-York, *Fourteenth Annual Report of the Corporation of the Chamber of Commerce of the State of New-York for the Year 1871–'72* (New York: Press of the Chamber of Commerce, 1872), pp. 100, 102. Of this output, more than 1 million bales were spun by northern industries and more than 3 million bales were exported.

    New York's merchants profited greatly from this expansion: While in 1865 they had exported only about 6 million pounds of cotton, in 1873 they exported more than 300 million pounds – nearly two and a half times the amount exported from New York City in 1861. Chamber of Commerce of the State of New-York, *Fourteenth Annual Report*, p. 146.

115 *JoC*, 27 April 1865, p. 2.

116 The centrality of this struggle to Reconstruction policies is argued by Foner, *Reconstruction*, especially pp. 50–60, 153–170, and Barbara Fields, "Freedom," in Ira Berlin et al., *Slaves No More: Three Essays on Emancipation and the Civil War* (New York: Cambridge University Press, 1992), pp. 1–76.

117 George H. Brown to John Crosby Brown, Mobile, Alabama, May 22, 1865, in "Side Lights on the Civil War" from "Family Letters, Extracts, Brown Family Letters, 1860–1865," Brown Brothers Harriman and Company Papers, NYHS.

118 "Charles" to "My dear Sir," Charleston, S.C., February 12, 1866, Tobias, Hendricks & Co, Case 25, Hendricks Papers, NYHS.

119 "Conner" to Tobias, Hendricks & Co., New Orleans, January 8, 1866, Tobias, Hendricks & Co., Case 25, Hendricks Papers, NYHS. Similarly, a South Island planter, writing in September 1866 to Richard Lathers in New York to solicit his help in finding investors for his rice plantation, stressed, after lamenting the loss of his slaves, that the main problem for any future undertaking would be labor. S. Deas [name unclear] to Richard Lathers, South Island, September 26, 1866, Lathers Papers, vol. 2, Library of Congress.

120 Diverse letters, Leverich Papers, NYHS. The plantation they owned and managed was the Oaklawn Plantation in Louisiana.

121 *USEconomist* 10 (23 September 1865): 4; *CFC* (6 February 1869): 167.

122 *NYCA*, 11 November 1865, p. 611.

123 *USEconomist* 10 (23 July 1865): 4.

124 *NYCA*, 20 January 1866, p. 68.

125 *MMCR* (October 1869): 271–274. The journal advised planters, however, that "until labor in the cotton districts should be more abundant, . . . [to] make the best of the present condition of affairs," since no alternative source of labor was available.

126 See also David Montgomery, *Beyond Equality: Labor and the Radical Republicans, 1862–1872* (Urbana: University of Illinois Press, 1981), pp. 238, 338. For the relationship between cotton exports and monetary policy see *CFC*, 6 November 1869, pp. 582–583.

127 *JoC*, 27 April 1865, p. 2.

128 This is also argued by Stanley Cohen, "Northeastern Business and Radical Reconstruction," p. 86.

129 See, for example, James Robb to Isaac Sherman, February 29, 1868, or Isaac Sherman to John S. Ryan, June 22, 1868, Isaac Sherman Papers, Huntington Library. Isaac Sherman to the Governor of Tennessee, May 17, 1870, Isaac Sherman Papers, Huntington Library.

130 Cohen, "Northeastern Business and Radical Reconstruction," p. 87; Richard Lowitt, *A Merchant Prince of the Nineteenth Century: William E. Dodge* (New York: Columbia University Press, 1954), p. 264.

131 See John Brown Gordon to Samuel Barlow, Atlanta, June 13, 1877, Barlow Papers, BW 113, Folder 12, Huntington Library. See "Declaration regarding title of certain Virginia property," January 16, 1872, Samuel Barlow Papers, Box 208, Huntington Library. Samuel Barlow was also invited in December of 1865 to purchase cotton plantations in Georgia. William Montague Browne to Samuel Barlow, Macon, Georgia, December 4, 1865, Barlow Papers, Huntington Library, Box 56, Folder 376.

132 Hodas, *Taylor*, p. 238.

133 *JoC*, 27 April 1865, p. 2.

134 *CFC* (16 November 1867): 615.

135 *MMCR* (January 1868): 32; *CFC* (11 November 1865): 613.

136 *CFC* (9 December 1865): 740.

137 *CFC* (7 July 1866): 3.

138 Bensel, *Yankee Leviathan*, p. 348.

139 *The Finances of the United States, An Address Delivered by A. A. Low, Esq. 1868*, p. 8. See also *Eleventh Annual Report of the Chamber of Commerce of the State of New-York for the Year 1868–'69* (New York: John W. Amerman, 1869), p. 47.

140 New York Chamber of Commerce, *Tenth Annual Report* (1867), p. 51. *The Finances of the United States, An Address Delivered by A. A. Low, Esq., At the Centennial Celebration of the Chamber of Commerce of the State of New-York, At Irving Hall, New-York, April 6, 1868* (n.p.: n.p., n.d.), p. 4.

141 *Entertainment given to A. A. Low*, p. 28.

142 *The Finances of the United States, An Address Delivered by A. A. Low, Esq. 1868*, p. 10. Resumption was also of particular importance to the *ARJ* (18 March 1865): 265, the *NYCA*, 15 May 1866, p. 2; *NYCA*, November 14, 1866, p. 2 and the *CFC* (23 September 1865): 386. The repeal of the legal tender act, according to the *USEconomist*, was "one of the greatest misfortunes growing out if the war." *USEconomist* (18 February 1865): 4. See also *USEconomist* (11 March 1865): 4. See also *USEconomist* (19 August 1865): 4.

143 *USEconomist* (2 September 1865): 4.

144 Robert P. Sharkey, *Money, Class, And Party, An Economic Study of Civil War and Reconstruction* (Baltimore: Johns Hopkins Press, 1959), pp. 241, 243. New York City bankers applauded the passage of the Resumption Act in 1865, which allowed for a slow contraction of greenbacks. Irwin Unger, *The Greenback Era: A Social and Political History of American Finance, 1865–1879* (Princeton, N.J.: Princeton University Press, 1964), p. 159.

145 See Bensel, *Yankee Leviathan*, pp. 254, 264, 272.

146 See for this point also James Willard Hurst, *A Legal History of Money in the United States, 1774–1970* (Lincoln: University of Nebraska Press, 1973), pp. 176, 178. On p. 178, he concludes that "the years 1878 and 1884 brought the truly drastic change affecting the distribution of power between the government and the market over the place of money in the economy."

147 Edward C. Mack, *Peter Cooper, Citizen of New York* (New York: Duell, Sloan and Pearce, 1949), p. 363.

148 Frank W. Taussig, *The Tariff History of the United States* (New York: Putnam's, 1888), pp. 142–144; Montgomery, *Beyond Equality*, p. 343. See also American Industrial League, *Protection of Our Industry, Development of our Resources: American Labor* (Detroit: American Industrial League, 1870); Sharkey, *Money, Class, and Party*, p. 272. Railroad investors opposed tariffs on iron because of the resulting increase in the prize of rails. For opposition to high tariffs see also *USEconomist* (7 July 1868): 3 and *CFC* (16 November 1867): 615.

149 *Eighth Annual Report of the Chamber of Commerce of the State of New York for the Year 1865–'66* (New York: John W. Amerman, 1866), p. 4; Chamber of Commerce of the State of New-York, *Ninth Annual Report,*

p. 29. Francis Lieber, *Notes on the Fallacies Peculiar to American Protectionists, Or Chiefly Resorted to in America* (New York: American Free Trade League, 1869), p. 41. Its president was David Dudley Field, and among its leaders were Stewart Brown, Samuel J. Tilden, Frederick DePeyster, and Robert B. Minturn. Edward Atkinson, *On the Collection of Revenue* (New York: American Free-Trade League, 1869), p. 1.

150 *USEconomist* (7 April 1866): 4.

151 *NYCA*, 17 October 1867, p. 2.

152 *USEconomist* (11 May 1867): 4.

153 *CFC* (11 November 1867): 681.

154 William E. Dodge, *Speech of Hon. William E. Dodge, on Reconstruction* (Washington: Congressional Globe Office, 1867), p. 7.

155 Dodge, *Speech of Hon. William E. Dodge, on Reconstruction*, p. 7.

156 Dodge, *Speech of Hon. William E. Dodge, on Reconstruction*, p. 4. See also Lowitt, *Merchant Prince*, p. 237.

157 *NYCA*, 19 August 1865, p. 2; *NYCA*, 25 August 1865, p. 2; *NYCA*, 29 January 1866, p. 2; *NYCA*, 7 April 1865, p. 2; *NYCA*, 30 April 1866, p. 2; *NYCA*, 14 May 1867, p. 2.

158 See also George Roble Woolfolk, *The Cotton Regency, The Northern Merchants and Reconstruction, 1865–1880* (New York: Octagon Books, 1979), pp. 53, 56. This sense of losing influence is also reflected in the *CFC* (18 January 1868): 71.

159 Chamber of Commerce of the State of New-York, *Ninth Annual Report*, p. 7.

160 Foner, *Reconstruction*, p. 337; *NYCA*, 14 August 1868, p. 2.

161 Wheaton J. Lane, *Commodore Vanderbilt, An Epic of the Steam Age* (New York: Knopf, 1942), p. 305; Lowitt, *Merchant Prince*, p. 322. According to Black, *The King of Fifth Avenue*, pp. 300, 328, 343, 304–307; Lane, *Commodore Vanderbilt*, p. 306; Hodas, *Moses Taylor*, p. 193. *NYCA* (14 August 1868): 2. For the general support of Grant see *Reception of Lieutenant Grant by the Citizens of New York: November 16, 1865, 1864/65* Folder, Low Family, 1850–1889, NYHS.

163 See also *NYCA*, 9 April 1869, p. 2. Johnson also helped to recapture the New York State Republican Party from the Radicals. James C. Mohr, ed., *Radical Republicans in the North, State Politics During Reconstruction* (Baltimore: Johns Hopkins University Press, 1976), p. 77.

164 Foner, *Reconstruction*, pp. 446, 447.

165 See, for example *NYCA*, 1 November 1869, p. 2. For the first years after the war, most wealthy New Yorkers had warned consistently of the danger of enfranchising freedmen. The *USEconomist* had warned that suffrage increased the "ability for inflicting wrongs upon the propertied classes." *USEconomist* (3 August 1867): 4. John Jay directly linked the expansion of suffrage rights in the South to the dangers of democracy in the North, arguing, "We of New York know by daily experience the evils that result from the exercise of the suffrage among a population uninstructed in the elements of American freedom and unable to read the Constitution and the laws of the country." Speech at the Union League Club (June 23, 1866), pp. 54–55, cited in Migliore, "The Business of Union," p. 352. See also Foner, *Reconstruc-*

tion, p. 412; *NYCA,* 23 September 1867, p. 2. The *NYCA* also editorialized in support of the enfranchisement of southern African Americans on December 10, 1868, p. 2.

166   Montgomery, *Beyond Equality,* p. 352, 355.

167   Lowitt, *Merchant Prince,* p. 326.

168   The expectation that a more substantial reconstruction of the southern states would bring stability is, for example, articulated in the *NYCA,* 2 December 1870, p. 2.

169   See also Foner, *Reconstruction,* pp. 224f; *NYCA,* 24 January 1866, p. 2.

170   *NYCA,* 2 February 1867, p. 2. See also *NYCA,* 17 October 1867, p. 2; *NYCA,* 31 March 1868, p. 2; *NYCA,* 20 April 1872, p. 2.

171   *NYCA,* 10 December 1866, p. 2. For examples of such thinking see also *Report Read Before the Chamber of Commerce of the State of New-York on the Introduction of Capital and Men, From the Northern States and From Europe into the Southern States of the Union, By Thomas W. Conway* (New York: John W. Amerman, 1866), pp. 9, 12.

172   Robert Hoe to Robert Hoe II, New York, September 3, 1867, Hoe Papers, Reel 4, Library of Congress.

173   W. E. B. DuBois brilliantly accounts for this changing position of segments of the northern bourgeoisie towards Reconstruction. See DuBois, *Black Reconstruction,* pp. 212–213.

174   On *Iron Age* see Kolchin, "The Business Press and Reconstruction," p. 184; letter of Peter Cooper, August 23, 1872, cited in Mack, *Peter Cooper,* p. 289.

175   Robert Hoe to Robert Hoe II, New York, September 3, 1867, Hoe Papers, Reel 4, Library of Congress.

176   Bellows, *Historical Sketch of the Union League Club, 1863–1879,* pp. 87, 89; Migliore, "The Business of Union," pp. 347, 348.

177   Bellows, *Historical Sketch of the Union League Club,* p. 101.

178   *Thirty-First Annual Report of the American Institute of the City of New York For the Year 1870–71* (Albany, N.Y.: The Argus Company, 1871), pp. 107–108.

179   Speech by Massachusetts lawyer and Republican politician Dr. George B. Loring as quoted in *Thirty-First Annual Report of the American Institute of the City of New York, 1870–71,* p. 109.

180   The picture is reprinted in John Kouwenhoven, *The Columbia Historical Portrait of New York* (Garden City, N.Y.: Doubleday, 1953), p. 309.

181   Hurst, *Legal History of Money,* p. 188

182   Sharkey, *Money, Class, and Party,* p. 156.

183   Sharkey, *Money, Class, and Party,* pp. 149, 153.

184   George Opdyke, *Letter on National Finances* (New York: The Sun, 1869), p. 20; Opdyke also led the opposition in the Chamber of Commerce against resumption. See Unger, *The Greenback Era,* p. 154; New York Chamber of Commerce, *Eleventh Annual Report* (1869), p. 52–53.

185   Peter Cooper, *Ideas for a Science of Good Government, in Addresses, Letters and Articles on a Strictly National Currency, Tariff and Civil Service* (New York: Trow's Printing and Bookbinding Co., 1883), p. 341.

186   Unger, *The Greenback Era,* pp. 53–67.

187   See *IA* (March 22, 1867); *NYT,* 29 May 1868, p. 5.

188 *Thirty-First Annual Report of the American Institute of the City of New York For the Year 1870–71* (Albany, N.Y.: The Argus Company, 1871), p. 107.

189 The radicalization was partly a result of the fact that an ever-increasing number of bourgeois New Yorkers were rooted in the political economy of Atlantic trade. This is also an argument James Livingston makes. See James Livingston, *Pragmatism and the Political Economy of Cultural Revolution, 1850–1940* (Chapel Hill: University of North Carolina Press, 1994), p. 37.

190 *NYCA*, 10 December 1866, p. 2; *NYCA*, 3 December 1868, p. 2.

191 Unger, *The Greenback Era*, p. 166.

192 Quoted in Unger, *The Greenback Era*, pp. 166–167. See also speech by Chittenden at the meeting of the National Board of Trade. *Proceedings of the Fifth Annual Meeting of the National Board of Trade, Held in New York, October, 1872* (Boston: James F. Cotter, 1872), p. 195.

193 New York Chamber of Commerce, *Thirteenth Annual Report* (1871), p. 90.

194 *CFC* (23 March 1867): 358. Similarly see *NYCA*, 26 October 1871, p. 2.

195 *CFC* (20 February 1869): 232. See also *CFC* (26 February 1870): 261, calling for "Congressional inaction." See also the call for "stability" in the *CFC* (9 July 1870): 37.

196 William E. Dodge on July 10, 1866. For the complete speech see "Thirty-Ninth Congress, First Session," *Congressional Globe*, part 4, p. 3720.

197 Lowitt, *Merchant Prince*, p. 262.

198 August Belmont, "An Address of the National Committee to the Democracy of the U.S.," cited in Black, *The King of Fifth Avenue*, p. 279.

199 August Belmont to Samuel Barlow, Newport, June 26, 1865, in Barlow Papers, Folder 7, Box 61, Huntington Library.

200 Black, *The King of Fifth Avenue*, p. 362; See Bernstein, *The New York City Draft Riots*, p. 218. $250 equaled the amount black voters had to be assessed in order to vote in New York State since 1821.

201 *Speech of Hon. E. Pierrepont, delivered before The Republican Mass Meeting at Cooper Institute, September 25, 1872* (New York: Evening Post Steam Presses, 1872), p. 23; Katz, *August Belmont*, p. 196; Stanwood, *American Tariff Controversies*, p. 175; Foner, *Reconstruction*, p. 510. Grant defeated the opposing fusion ticket of Liberal Republicans and Democrats, which had at first attracted some merchants and bankers to its ranks. On Vanderbilt see Lane, *Commodore Vanderbilt*, p. 307; Hodas, *Moses Taylor*, p. 193. Taylor gave $5,000 to the Grant campaign.

202 White, *Beekman*, p. 626.

203 For this argument see David Montgomery, *Beyond Equality*. See also Foner, *Reconstruction*, p. 497. Concern about eight-hour legislation by Radical Republicans is expressed, for example, in the *CFC* (13 April 1867): 455, and *MMCR* (August 1868): 91.

6. Reconstructing New York

1 Such as Peter Cooper, who advocated in 1868 that "paupers" be shipped to the "fertile lands in the West." Peter Cooper, *Philanthropic and Charitable Relief* (New York: Citizens' Association, 1868), p. 4.

2   On migration to New York, see Robert Ernst, *Immigrant Life in New York City* (New York: King's Crown Press, 1949). For a survey of the processes that brought workers from the European countryside to the United States see John Bodnar, *The Transplanted, A History of Immigrants in Urban America,* (Bloomington: Indiana University Press, 1985).

3   *NYT,* 18 June 1871, p. 4.

4   Lawrence Costello, "The New York City Labor Movement, 1861–1873" (Ph.D. diss., Columbia University, 1967), p. 4.

5   Costello, "The New York City Labor Movement," p. 194.

6   Costello, "The New York City Labor Movement," pp. 351, 379. For the reactions among merchants to the strike see *MMCR* (August 1868): 91–94.

7   Which, however, could be overridden by "private contracts."

8   Albeit without long-lasting success. See Costello, "The New York City Labor Movement," p. 238. On the power of workers vis-à-vis their employers see also Robert Hoe II to Richard M. Hoe, New York, July 12, 1871, Reel 6, Hoe Papers, Library of Congress. Hoe decided against lowering wages on account of the danger of creating "a good deal of dissatisfaction."

9   John W. Pratt, "Boss Tweed's Public Welfare Program," *NYHSQ* 45 (October 1961): 399.

10   Eduard Durand, *The Finances of New York City* (New York: The Macmillan Company, 1898), p. 376. The sum in 1860 was $12.14.

11   See *HW* (24 June 1871): 570. Allan Nevins and Milton Halsey Thomas, eds., *The Diary of George Templeton Strong,* vol. 4, *Post-War Years, 1865–1875* (New York: Macmillan, 1952), p. 171, entry for December 3, 1867.

12   For the importance of this support see also Martin Shefter, "The Emergence of the Political Machine: An Alternative View," in Willis Hawley, ed., *Theoretical Perspectives on Urban Politics* (Englewood Cliffs, N.J.: Prentice-Hall, 1976), p. 21.

13   Iver Bernstein, *The New York City Draft Riots, Their Significance for American Society and Politics in the Age of the Civil War* (New York: Oxford University Press, 1990), p. 201; Daniel Hodas, *The Business Career of Moses Taylor: Merchant, Finance Capitalist and Industrialist* (New York: New York University Press, 1976), p. 196. Hodas makes the point that Taylor's interest in two New York utility companies kept him in political proximity to Tweed until early 1871.

14   *CFC* (12 January 1867): 43.

15   Bernstein, *The New York City Draft Riots,* p. 205.

16   Cited in Bernstein, *The New York City Draft Riots,* p. 206.

17   Bernstein, *The New York City Draft Riots,* p. 207.

18   Hodas, *The Business Career of Moses Taylor,* p. 195.

19   The piano manufacturers of Steinway & Sons, for example, confronted strikes frequently – in 1863, 1864, twice in 1865, and again in 1869. See diary of William Steinway, NYHS.

20   Letter from [unreadable] in Riggs letter book to Superintendent, New York, May 12, 1865; Elisha Riggs, Jr., to Benjamin Peer, New York, May 27, 1865, Box 50, Riggs Family Papers, Library of Congress.

21   See "Speech by Horace Greeley at the 36th Annual Fair of the American Insti-

tute," *Annual Report of the American Institute of the City of New York for the Years 1865–66* (Albany, N.Y.: C. Wendell, 1866), pp. 68–74.

22 See "Speech by Daniel E. Sickles at the 36ᵗʰ Annual Fair of the American Institute," *Annual Report of the American Institute of the City of New York for the Years 1865–66*, pp. 52–60.

23 See "Speech by Horace Greeley at the 36ᵗʰ Annual Fair of the American Institute," p. 74; *Manufacturer and Builder* 6 (January 1874): 1.

24 *Thirty-First Annual Report of the American Institute of the City of New York For the Year 1870–71* (Albany, N.Y.: The Argus Company, 1871), p. 109.

25 *IA* (31 July 1873): 16.

26 See "Speech by John W. Draper at the 36ᵗʰ Annual Fair of the American Institute," *Annual Report of the American Institute of the City of New York for the Years 1865–66*, p. 66. Indeed, industrialists made great efforts to integrate farmers into their political economy of domestic industrialization. Speech by John L. Hayes, *Thirty-First Annual Report of the American Institute of the City of New York For the Year 1870–71*, p. 118.

27 *Thirty-First Annual Report of the American Institute of the City of New York For the Year 1870–71*, p. 108.

28 Horace Greeley, "Capital and Labor," in *Wood's Household Magazine* (November 1871): 211.

29 See, for example, *USEconomist* (15 July 1865): 4.

30 *IA* (13 February 1873): 16; *NYCA*, 9 May 1872, p. 2.

31 Robert Hoe II to Richard M. Hoe, New York, June 25, 1872, Reel 6, Hoe Papers, Library of Congress.

32 Robert Hoe II to Richard M. Hoe, New York, June 17, 1872, Reel 6, Hoe Papers, Library of Congress.

33 Robert Hoe II to Richard M. Hoe, New York, July 8, 1872, Reel 6, Hoe Papers, Library of Congress.

34 *USEconomist* (5 September 1868): 4.

35 Speech by A. A. Low at the Chamber of Commerce, reprinted in Chamber of Commerce of the State of New-York, *Ninth Annual Report for the Year 1866–67* (New York: John W. Amerman, 1867), p. 6.

36 In 1871 they still called for the formation of a board of arbitration to resolve labor conflicts. *CFC* (30 September 1865): 419; *CFC* (31 March 1866): 387; *CFC* (23 June 1866): 773; *MMCR* (July 1866): 63–65. For their position toward strikes see also *USEconomist* (23 September 1865), 4.

37 *CFC* (8 April 1871): 422.

38 *CFC* (13 July 1872): 38.

39 See among many others *NYCA*, 20 April 1871, p. 2; *NYCA*, 8 August 1871, p. 2.

40 *MMCR* (April 1868): 249–251.

41 *Twenty-Fourth Annual Report of the New York Association for the Improvement of the Conditions of the Poor for the Year 1867* (New York: Trow, 1867), p. 69.

42 *NYT*, 25 June 1871, p. 4.

43 *Twenty-Third Annual Report of the New York Association for the Improvement of the Conditions of the Poor* (New York: John F. Trow, 1866), pp. 28ff.

44 *Atlantic Monthly* 27 (May 1871): 544–559.

45 Elliot C. Cowdin, *France in 1870–71, An Address Delivered Before the Cooper Union for the Advancement of Science and Art, New-York, February 10, 1872* (New York: Printed for the Cooper Union, 1872), p. 25.

46 *NYT,* 31 May 1871, p. 4. See also *NYH,* 20 March 1871, p. 3; *NYDT,* 28 March 1871, p. 1. For surveys of American reactions to the Paris Commune see Philip M. Katz, *From Appomattox to Montmartre: Americans and the Paris Commune* (Cambridge, Mass.: Harvard University Press, 1998); George L. Cherry, "American Metropolitan Press Reaction to the Paris Commune of 1871," *Mid-America* 32 (January 1950): 3–12; Samuel Bernstein, "American Labor and the Paris Commune," *Science and Society* 15 (Spring 1951): 144–162.

47 See, for example, *NYT,* 25 March 1871, p. 4.

48 *Nation,* (18 May 1871): 334.

49 Nevins and Thomas, eds., *The Diary of George Templeton Strong,* vol. 4, p. 351, entry for April 15, 1871.

50 *Nation* (25 May 1871): 351.

51 *NYT,* 31 May 1871, p. 4.

52 *NYH,* 29 May 1871, p. 8.

53 Cowdin, *France in 1870–71,* pp. 25, 34, 59. The *NYH* similarly trusted that the "power . . . [of] the free and independent press" as well as the diffusion of religion would prevent the occurrence of a Commune in New York. *NYH,* 28 May 1871, p. 8; *NYH,* 29 May 1871, p. 8. This was the more important, as Henry Ward Beecher and Father Hewitt had preached in June 1871 that communism would have its roots in "infidelity" and "the want of education." See *NYH,* 4 June 1871, p. 6. This argument was also made by *Scribner's Monthly* 2 (June 1871): 206.

54 *NYT,* 17 April 1871, p. 4; *NYT,* 31 May 1871, p. 4.

55 *Twenty-Eighth Annual Report of the New York Association for the Improvement of the Conditions of the Poor, ending in the Year 1871* (New York: Office of the Association, 1871), p. 53.

56 *NYT,* 7 June 1871, p. 4.

57 *NYT,* 7 June 1871, p. 4. See also *NYT,* 18 June 1871, p. 4. For comparison with the Draft Riots see also *Nation* (1 June 1871): 374.

58 J. T. Headley, *The Great Riots of New York, 1712–1873, Including a Full and Complete Account of the Four Day's Draft Riot of 1863* (New York: E. B. Treat, 1873), p. 17.

59 Nevins and Thomas, eds., *The Diary of George Templeton Strong,* vol. 4, pp. 362, 363, entries for May 31, 1871, and June 7, 1871.

60 *NYDT,* 17 April 1871, p. 4.

61 Bernstein, *The New York City Draft Riots,* p. 229; Michael A. Gordon, *The Orange Riots: Irish Political Violence in New York City, 1870 and 1871* (Ithaca, N.Y.: Cornell University Press, 1993), pp. 79–81; *HW* (July 29, 1871): 691.

62 For the Orange Riots in general see Gordon, *The Orange Riots,* passim; Bernstein, *The New York City Draft Riots,* p. 231.

63 For an account of the meeting see *NYT,* 4 September 1871, p. 4; *NYT,* 5 September 1871, p. 4; *NYDT,* 5 September 1871, p. 1. On Robert Hoe II see

Robert Hoe II to Richard M. Hoe, New York, September 13, 1871, Reel 6, Hoe Papers, Library of Congress.

64 *NYT,* 5 September 1871, Supplement, p. 2.

65 See John A. Kouwenhoven, *Partners in Banking: An Historical Portrait of a Great Private Bank, Brown Brothers Harriman & Co., 1818–1968* (New York: Doubleday & Company, 1968), p. 132.

66 They did so most successfully with the help of judicial injunctions. See Mary P. Ryan, *Civic Wars: Democracy and Public Life in the American City during the Nineteenth Century* (Berkeley: University of California Press, 1997), p. 279.

67 See Ryan, *Civic Wars,* p. 279.

68 Citizens' Association of New-York, *To Honorary Council of the Citizens' Association of New York* (New York: Printed by the Association, 1866), p. 16.

69 Citizens' Association, *To the Honorary Council of the Citizens' Association of New-York,* p. 16.

70 Kouwenhoven, *Partners in Banking,* p. 132. See, for example, Citizens' Association, *An Appeal to the Iron-Trade of New-York* (New York: Citizens' Association, n.d), which lists a number of foremen of large iron manufacturing enterprises as supporters of the association.

71 Citizens' Association of New-York, *Report of the Citizens' Association of New York, New York, December 1, 1868* (New York: Published by the Citizens' Association, 1868), p. 1.

72 Citizens' Association of New-York, *Report, How our Taxes may be Reduced, our Resources Developed, and the Local Government Improved* (New York: Citizens' Association, 1868), p. 3.

73 Citizens' Association of New-York, *Report of the Citizens' Association, Our Taxes, Markets, Streets and Sanitary Condition, Public Improvements, Public Institutions, &c., &c., What New-York might be with a Good Government, Reading for Every Citizen* (New York: George F. Nesbitt & Co., 1865), p. 16.

74 Citizens' Association, *Report of the Executive Council to the Honorary Council of the Citizens' Association of New-York, November 17, 1866* (New York: Published by the Citizens' Association, 1866), p. 17.

75 Citizens' Association, *Report of the Executive Council, 1866,* p. 18.

76 Citizens' Association, *To Honorary Council,* p. 16.

77 There had always been a weak current of antidemocratic thought in the North, yet it was marginal and remained unorganized. See Chilton Williamson, *American Suffrage: From Property to Democracy, 1760–1860* (Princeton, N.J.: Princeton University Press, 1960), p. 282.

78 Samuel P. Dinsmore, *Suggestions Touching the Municipal Government of New York* (New York: Hilton & Co., 1860), p. 8. Dinsmore joined the Citizens' Association. Citizens' Association of New-York, *Report of the Executive Council, 1866,* p. 6.

79 Citizens' Association of New-York, *Wholesale Corruption! Sale of Situations in Fourth Ward Schools, The Evidence in the Case* (New York: Citizens' Association of New-York, 1864); Citizens' Association of New-York, *Report of the Citizens' Association, Our Taxes, Markets, Streets and Sanitary Condition,* p. 16.

80 Citizens' Association of New-York, *Items of Abuse in the Government of the City of New-York, Tax-Payers, Citizens, Read! Read! Read!, The First and Highest Duty of every State is to Protect the Homes and Rights of All its Citizens* (New York: Citizens' Association of New-York, 1866), p. 3.

81 Citizens' Association of New-York, *Report of the Executive Council, 1866*, p. 21.

82 *CFC* (25 March 1871): 353.

83 Citizens' Association of New-York, *The Constitutional Convention, The Basis or General Plan for the Government of the City of New-York* (New York: George F. Nesbitt & Co., 1867), pp. 26, 10.

84 Citizens' Association, *Report of the Executive Council, 1866*, p. 22.

85 Citizens' Association of New-York, *The Constitutional Convention, Alterations in the Fundamental Law of the State, Proposed by the Citizens' Association of New-York* (New York: G. F. Nesbitt, 1867), pp. 2, 5.

86 Citizens' Association, *The Constitutional Convention*, pp. 3, 4.

87 Citizens' Association of New York, *Report, How our Taxes may be Reduced*, p. 19. These demands were formulated and approved by a special committee of the Citizens' Association, which counted among its members James Brown, Peter Cooper, Moses H. Grinnell, Horatio Allen, and fifty-seven others. Citizens' Association, *The Constitutional Convention*, p. 22. This was the more remarkable as the convention decided to remove property qualifications for African Americans (an amendment that was turned down by the voters of New York State), and discussed the enfranchisement of women. On efforts to extend the franchise to women see *Equal Rights for Women: A Speech by George William Curtis In The Constitutional Convention of New York at Albany, July 19, 1867* [Woman's Suffrage Tracts, No. 2] (Boston: C. K. Whipple, 1869); *MMCR* (August 1867): 122. On another occasion, the Citizens' Association proposed the creation of a Board of Councilmen, consisting of members assessed on at least $3,000 and elected by all taxpayers assessed on at least $5,000. The Board was to be the sole institution that could approve all city expenditures. The profoundly antidemocratic thrust of the Citizens' Association's reform ideas was shared by other organizations. The Union League Club's Committee on Municipal Reform, for example, demanded a "limitation of the absolute supremacy of numerical majorities in city affairs." Citizens' Association, *The Constitutional Convention*, pp. 3–4. Union League Club, *Committee on Municipal Reform, 1867*, p. 21.

88 On the downfall of the Citizens' Association see also Edward C. Mack, *Peter Cooper: Citizen of New York* (New York: Duell, Sloan and Pearce, 1949), pp. 344–354.

89 Bernstein, *The New York City Draft Riots*, p. 190; Citizens' Association, *Report of the Citizens' Association, Our Taxes, Markets, Streets and Sanitary Condition*, p. 28.

90 Citizens' Association, *Reform in New-York City, Address to the People of the City of New-York* (New York: Citizens' Association, 1870), p. 6; Citizens' Association of New-York, *Address to the People of the City of New-York by the Citizens' Association of New-York, Adopted at a General Meeting Held May 9th, 1871* (New York: Published by the Association, 1871), p. 12.

91 The reasons for this rapprochement are somewhat unclear, but it seems that Tweed and the Citizens' Association both shared an interest in the concentration of power. In addition, Tweed had succeeded in infiltrating the management of the Citizens' Association. Citizens' Association of New-York, *Memorial of the Citizens' Association of New-York, And Petition of Taxpayers in Favor of the New Charter for that City, as Passed by the Assembly* (New York: George F. Nesbitt & Co., 1870), p. 5. See also Durand, *The Finances of New York City*, p. 126.

92 See *The Annual Report of the New York City Council of Political Reform, Presented at the First Annual Meeting of the Council, November 27th, 1871* (New York: John P. Prall Printer by Steam, 1872), p. 3.

93 *The Annual Report of the New York City Council of Political Reform*, p. 1

94 Citizens' Association, *Report, How our Taxes may be Reduced*, p. 3.

95 Among the precursors of the Committee of Seventy was also the Personal Representation Society of New York. See Simon Sterne, *Report to the Constitutional Convention of the State of New-York on Personal Representation, Prepared at the Request, and Printed under the Auspices of the Personal Representation Society* (New York: A. Simpson, 1867).

96 Nevins and Thomas, eds., *The Diary of George Templeton Strong*, vol. 4, p. 381, entry for September 4, 1871.

97 Analysis of the vice presidents and secretaries of the Committee of Seventy. Of 239 individuals who were members, 191 individuals (80 percent) could be identified. For the names see *NYT*, 15 September 1871, Supplement, p. 1, and H. Wilson, *Trow's New York City Directory for the Year Ending May 1, 1872* (New York: John F. Trow, 1872).

98 See diary of William Steinway, entries for November 28, 1871, December 5, 1871, January 19, 1871, January 23, 1871, April 1, 1871, NYHS.

99 For the characterization of lawyers as "practical theorists," see Michael Mann, *The Sources of Social Power*, vol. 2, *The Rise of Classes and Nation-States, 1760–1914* (New York: Cambridge University Press, 1993), p. 146.

100 *NYDT*, 4 September 1871, p. 1; *Nation* (7 September 1871): 158.

101 See, for example, Union League Club, *The Report of the Committee on Municipal Reform, Especially in the City of New-York* (New York: John W. Amerman, 1867). For opposition to suffrage restrictions see also *Real Estate Record and Builders' Guide* (20 January 1872): 25.

102 Hardly six weeks after the forming of the committee, they had raised $52,000, of which $26,000 had already been spent. See Committee of Citizens and Taxpayers for the Financial Reform of the City and County of New York, Minute Book, 1871–1873, entry for October 24, 1871, Manuscript Division, The New York Public Library, Astor, Lenox, and Tilden Foundations.

103 Durand, *The Finances of New York City*, p. 151. Havemeyer's administration in general, however, was not characterized by success. See Howard B. Furer, *William Frederik Havemeyer: A Political Biography* (New York: The American Press, 1965), 155–178.

104 Robert Hoe II to Richard M. Hoe, New York, November 10, 1871, Reel 6,

Hoe Papers, Library of Congress. For a similar statement see also *Dry Goods Economist* (11 November 1871): 4.

105 Committee of Citizens and Taxpayers for the Financial Reform of the City and County of New York, Minute Book, entry for December 5, 1871, Manuscript Division, NYPL; Citizens' Association of New-York, *Argument upon the Charter of the Committee of Seventy, Made before the Committee on the Affairs of Cities of the Senate of the State of New-York by Mr. Stephen H. Olin on Behalf of the Citizens' Association of New-York, March 6, 1872* (New York: Headquarters of the Association, 1872).

106 See Committee of Seventy, *Address to the Citizens of New York* (New York: Union Printing Company, 1872), pp. 2–3.

107 See Committee of Seventy for Financial Reform, New York, at a meeting of the Committee of Seventy, December 17, 1872, a circular issued by the committee, "Strictly Private," p. 6, General Research Division, The New York Public Libray, Astor, Lenox, and Tilden Foundations.

108 Committee of Seventy, "Strictly Private," p. 1.

109 It counted among its members David Dudley Field, Robert B. Minturn, and Edward Cooper. See Simon Sterne, *Report to the Constitutional Convention of the State of New York, on Personal Representation; Prepared at the Request, and Printed Under the Auspices of the Personal Representation Society* (New York: A. Simpson, 1867), p. 2; John Foord, *The Life and Public Services of Simon Sterne* (London: Macmillan and Co., 1903), pp. 267, 268.

110 For the governor's reasoning see *Governor Hoffman's Veto of New York Charter* (n.p.: n.p., 1872). The charter was also strongly opposed by the CFC. See *CFC* (18 May 1872): 647. For a statement of support for the charter see Robert Hoe to Hon. E. M. Madden, New York, February 2, 1872, Reel 6, Hoe Papers, Library of Congress.

111 Committee of Citizens and Taxpayers for the Financial Reform of the City and County of New York, Minute Book, entry for April 15, 1873, Manuscript Division, NYPL. See also Chester, *Courts and Lawyers*, pp. 725–726.

112 See Committee of Citizens and Taxpayers for the Financial Reform of the City and County of New York, Minute Book, entry for December 5, 1871, Manuscript Division, NYPL; Committee of Seventy, *Address by the Chairman, Hon. Wm. F. Havemeyer at the Meeting of the Committee of Seventy in the Rooms of the Chamber of Commerce* (New York: n.p., 1872), p. 3. See Committee of Citizens and Taxpayers for the Financial Reform of the City and County of New York, Minute Book, entries for March 9, 1872, and March 11, 1872, Manuscript Division, NYPL.

113 Stephen H. Olin, *Argument Upon the Charter of the Committee of Seventy, Made Before the Committee on the Affairs of Cities of the Senate to the State of New-York, On Behalf of the Citizens' Association of New-York, March 6, 1872* (n.p., n.p., 1872). The quotation is from page 3.

114 *Nation* (September 7, 1871): 158, 159.

115 See Committee of Citizens and Taxpayers for the Financial Reform of the City and County of New York, Minute Book, entry for December 20, 1872, Manuscript Division, NYPL.

116 See Committee of Citizens and Taxpayers for the Financial Reform of the City and County of New York, Minute Book, entry of January 14, 1873, Manuscript Division, NYPL.

117 See Committee of Citizens and Taxpayers for the Financial Reform of the City and County of New York, Minute Book, entry for October 21, 1873, Manuscript Division, NYPL.

118 See for this argument also David Montgomery, *Citizen Worker: The Experience of Workers in the United States with Democracy and the Free Market During the Nineteenth Century* (New York: Cambridge University Press, 1993), p. 143. For employers' criticism of the activist state see *Dry Goods Economist* (16 September 1871): 4.

119 New York Council of Political Reform, *Report for The Year 1875* (New York: Evening Post Steam Presses, 1876), p. 24.

120 John G. Sproat, *"The Best Men," Liberal Reformers in the Gilded Age* (New York: Oxford University Press, 1968), p. 226.

121 Kouwenhoven, *Partners in Banking*, p. 132; Thomas Bender, *New York Intellect: A History of Intellectual Life in New York City* (New York: Knopf, 1987), p. 183; See also Katharine Neilley Villard, "Villard: The Years of Fortune" (Ph.D. diss., University of Arkansas, 1988), pp. ii, 56.

122 For Samuel Tilden see Furer, *William Frederick Havemeyer*, p. 128.

123 For the concept of "organic intellectuals" see Antonio Gramsci, *'The Modern Prince' and Other Writings* (London: Lawrence & Wishart, 1957), pp. 118–120.

124 Sproat, *"The Best Men,"* p. 253.

125 Robert Green McCloskey, *American Conservatism in the Age of Enterprise, 1865–1910* (New York: Harper & Row, 1964), p. 169.

126 See also Eric Foner, *Reconstruction: America's Unfinished Revolution, 1863–1877* (New York: Harper & Row, 1988), pp. 492–493.

127 Roy Rosenzweig and Elizabeth Blackmar, *The Park and the People: A History of Central Park* (Ithaca, N.Y.: Cornell University Press, 1992), p. 266.

128 Sproat, *"The Best Men,"* pp. 146, 152, 158.

129 E. L. Godkin, "Criminal Politics," in Morton Keller, ed, *Problems of Modern Democracy: Political and Economic Essays* (Cambridge, Mass.: Belknap Press, 1966), pp. 128–130. Accepting inequality as a fact of life, Beecher became the favorite cleric of New York's bourgeoisie. He was never far from public meetings, demonstrations, or reform efforts. Beecher, a brilliant speaker, could also articulate a moral legitimation for the harsh world of economics. See William Gerald McLoughlin, *The Meaning of Henry Ward Beecher, An Essay on the Shifting Values of Mid-Victorian America, 1840–1870* (New York: Knopf, 1970), pp. 35, 38, 39.

130 For the general point see Jackson Lears, *No Place of Grace: Antimodernism and the Transformation of American Culture, 1880–1920* (New York: Pantheon Books, 1981), p. 24. Beecher is quoted in Lears, *No Place of Grace,* p. 24.

131 *Nation* (22 June 1871): 429.

132 *The Twenty-Seventh Annual Report of the New York Association for the Improvement of the Conditions of the Poor* (New York: Trow & Smith,

1870); *Twenty-Fourth Annual Report of the New York Association for the Improvement of the Conditions of the Poor*, pp. 39, 69; *Twenty-Ninth Annual Report of the New York Association for the Improvement of the Conditions of the Poor* (New York: Office of the Association, 1872), p. 32.

133 The *Twenty-Seventh Annual Report of the New York Association for the Improvement of the Conditions of the Poor*, p. 42.

134 The *Twenty-Seventh Annual Report of the New York Association for the Improvement of the Conditions of the Poor*, p. 45.

135 Citizens' Association of New-York, *Philanthropic and Charitable Relief* (New York: n.p., 1868), p. 2.

136 McCloskey, *American Conservatism*, pp. 15, 20. Most specifically on legal doctrine, courts became central to securing the rights of property against interventionist political bodies. See McCloskey, *American Conservatism*, p. 73.

137 Costello, "The New York City Labor Movement," p. 375.

138 *NYT*, 20 May 1872, p. 4.

139 *NYT*, 20 May 1872, p. 8.

140 *NYT*, 28 May 1872, p. 8.

141 *NYT*, 28 May 1872, p. 8; *NYT*, 14 June 1872, p. 8.

142 On John Roach see Leonard Alexander Swann, *John Roach, Maritime Entrepreneur, The Years as Naval Contractor, 1862–1886* (Annapolis: U.S. Naval Institute, 1965); Costello, "The New York City Labor Movement," p. 363; *NYT*, 9 June 1872, p. 1.

143 *NYT*, 16 June 1872, p. 1. The quotation is from the *CFC* (1 June 1872): 719.

144 *NYT*, 6 June 1872, p. 4.

145 Steinway Diary, entries for May 28 and May 29, 1872, NYHS.

146 Steinway Diary, entries for May 31 and June 1, 1872, NYHS.

147 See, for example, *NYT*, 9 June 1872, p. 1, and *NYT*, 16 June 1872, p. 1.

148 Steinway Diary, entry for June 5, 1872, NYHS.

149 Steinway Diary, entry for June 15, 1872, NYHS.

150 Richard K. Lieberman, *Steinway & Sons* (New Haven: Yale University Press, 1995), p. 75.

151 *NYT*, 13 June 1872, p. 8.

152 For the importance of the police see also Robert Hoe II to Richard M. Hoe, New York, June 17, 1872, Reel 6, Hoe Papers, Library of Congress.

153 *NYT*, 18 June 1872, p. 8.

154 Clarence E. Bonnett, *History of Employers' Associations in the United States* (New York: Vintage Press, 1957), pp. 106–110.

155 *NYT*, 19 June 1872, p. 8; *NYDT*, 19 June 1872, p. 5.

156 *NYCA* (19 June 1872): 2. For the total number of workers see Bureau of the Census, *Ninth Census*, vol. 3, *Statistics of the Wealth and Industry of the United States* (Washington, D.C.: Government Printing Office, 1870), p. 550.

157 *CFC* (22 June 1872): 815. For the names see *IA* (15 May 1873): 16. For their lines of business see *Trow's New York City Directory 1871–1872*, (New York: J. F. Trow, 1872).

158 *NYT*, 19 June 1872, p. 8. While the *NYT* had at first restrained itself from rhetorical attacks on the strikers, its position changed by mid-June. On June 17, it warned of Communists who "disseminated their ideas advocating an

equal division of the wealth of the country, and attempted to spread dissatis-faction." *NYT,* 17 June 1872, p. 8.

159 *NYT,* 19 June 1872, p. 8
160 *NYT,* 19 June 1872, p. 8
161 *IA* (15 May 1873): 16.
162 *CFC* (1 June 1872): 719–720.
163 *CFC* (1 June 1872): 815.
164 *NYDT,* 19 June 1872, p. 5.
165 Irene Tichenor, "Theodore Low De Vinne, 1828–1914, Dean of American Printers" (Ph.D. diss., Columbia University, 1983), p. 76; Theodore Low De Vinne, in *Printer* (September 1864), cited in Tichenor, *Theodore Low De Vinne,* p. 82.
166 Tichenor, "Theodore Low De Vinne," p. 8; letter to Francis Hurt, September 22, 1872, cited in Tichenor, "Theodore Low De Vinne," p. 95.

7. Democracy in the Age of Capital

1 James Livingston, "The Social Analysis of Economic History and Theory: Conjectures of Late Nineteenth-Century American Development," *AHR* 92 (February 1987): 72.
2 Allan Nevins and Milton Halsey Thomas, eds., *The Diary of George Temple-ton Strong,* vol. 4, *Post-War Years, 1865–1875* (New York: The Macmillan Company, 1952), p. 495; Ron Chernow, *The House of Morgan: An Ameri-can Banking Dynasty and the Rise of Modern Finance* (New York: Simon & Schuster, 1990), p. 36.
3 Livingston, "The Social Analysis of Economic History and Theory," p. 73.
4 David Black, *The King of Fifth Avenue: The Fortunes of August Belmont* (New York: Dial Press, 1981), p. 420.
5 *Seventeenth Annual Report of the Corporation of the Chamber of Commerce of the State of New York for the Year 1874–'75* (New York: Press of the Chamber of Commerce, 1875), part 2, p. 218.
6 "Railroad Mileage and Equipment: 1830 to 1890," in *Historical Statistics of the United States, Colonial Times to 1970* (Washington, D.C.: U.S. Depart-ment of Commerce, 1975), vol. 2, p. 731.
7 Eric Foner, *Reconstruction: America's Unfinished Revolution, 1863–1877* (New York: Harper & Row, 1988), p. 512.
8 The numbers refer to the years between 1872 and 1874. See "Physical Out-put of Selected Manufactured Commodities, 1860 to 1970," in *Historical Statistics of the United States,* vol. 2, p. 694.
9 Foner, *Reconstruction,* p. 512.
10 Even in the late 1890s, each of the nation's twelve largest railroad companies had assets in excess of even the largest industrial enterprise, the Standard Oil Company. Philip H. Burch, Jr., *Elites in American History,* vol. 2, *The Civil War to the New Deal* (New York: Holmes & Meier Publishers Inc., 1981), pp. 69–70.
11 August Belmont to Manton Marble, October 30, 1873, quoted in Black, *The King of Fifth Avenue,* pp. 419–420; August Belmont to August Belmont, Jr.,

February 4, 1874, quoted in Black, *The King of Fifth Avenue*, p. 422. Banker J. Pierpont Morgan also had to call in loans. See Chernow, *The House of Morgan*, p. 37. See also Nevins and Thomas, eds., *The Diary of George Templeton Strong*, vol. 4, p. 493, entry of 19 September 1873.

12 *Seventeenth Annual Report of the Corporation of the Chamber of Commerce of the State of New-York for the Year 1874–'75*, p. 11.

13 *Seventeenth Annual Report of the Corporation of the Chamber of Commerce*, part 2, p. 52. Trade in textiles and metallurgic goods dropped off sharply while coffee and sugar traders were somewhat better off. See Jean Heffer, *Le Port de New York et le Commerce Extérieur Americain, 1860–1900* (Paris: Publications de la Sorbonne, 1986), p. 177.

14 Simon Sterne, *The Railway in Its Relation to Public and Private Interests: Address of Simone Sterne, Before the Merchants and Business Men of New York, at Steinway Hall, April 19, 1878* (New York: Press of the Chamber of Commerce, 1878), p. 8. For other statements on the impact of the crisis see Maxwell Whiteman, *Copper for America: The Hendricks Family and a National Industry, 1755–1936* (New Brunswick, N.J.: Rutgers University Press, 1971), p. 212; Uriah Hendricks to "My Dear Martindale," February 7, 1874, "Uriah Hendricks Letterbook," Case 17, Hendricks Papers, NYHS; *Real Estate Record and Builders' Guide* (4 December 1875): 762; *Real Estate Record and Builders' Guide* (2 December 1876): 887.

15 Peter S. Hoe to Robert Hoe, New York, October 24, 1873, Box 1, Hoe Papers, Library of Congress.

16 William Steinway Diary, October 1, October 6, October 17, and October 20, 1873, Steinway Papers, NYHS.

17 Steinway Diary, October 24, 1873, Steinway Papers, NYHS. In May 1876, Steinway & Sons was formed. See Steinway Diary, May 17, 1876, Steinway Papers, NYHS. For another reaction to the depression see Samuel Barlow to Bacon, New York, October 4, 1873, "Letterbooks," BW 1, Samuel Barlow Papers, Huntington Library. On the Hoes' business problems see, for example, Robert Hoe III to Robert Hoe II, New York, December 1, 1874, Reel 5, Hoe Papers, Library of Congress.

18 *Thirty-First Annual Report of the New York Association for the Improvement of the Conditions of the Poor for the Year 1875* (New York: Office of the Association, 1874), p. 29.

19 Between 1873 and 1879 wages fell by approximately 4 percent (in real terms). See "Average Annual and Daily Earnings of Nonfarm Employees, 1860 to 1900," in *Historical Statistics of the United States*, vol. 1, p. 185. There were some differences among economic sectors. While New York City textile and iron workers experienced a decline below the levels of the 1860s, printers, who managed to maintain their unions, gained a slight wage increase. Patricia Evelyn Malon, "The Growth of Manufacturing in Manhattan, 1860–1900: An Analysis of Factoral Changes and Urban Structure" (Ph.D. diss., Columbia University, 1981), pp. 213, 240, 270.

20 *Manufacturer and Builder* 6 (December 1874): 275.

21 *NYT*, 12 January 1876, p. 8.

22 Herbert G. Gutman, "The Tompkins Square 'Riot' in New York City on Jan-

uary 13, 1874: A Re-Examination of Its Causes and Its Aftermath," *Labor History* 6 (Winter 1965): passim, esp. 53–55.

23 *IA* (30 October 1873): 18.

24 Sheridan Logan, *George F. Baker and His Bank, 1840–1955: A Double Biography* (n.p.: [privately printed], 1981), pp. 96–99.

25 Chernow, *The House of Morgan*, p. 40.

26 Chernow, *The House of Morgan*, p. 44.

27 Chernow, *The House of Morgan*, p. 79.

28 Chernow, *The House of Morgan*, p. 38.

29 Alfred Chandler, *The Visible Hand: The Managerial Revolution in American Business* (Cambridge, Mass.: Belknap Press, 1977), pp. 256–258; Chernow, *The House of Morgan*, p. 90.

30 Foner, *Reconstruction*, p. 513.

31 Nevins and Thomas, eds., *The Diary of George Templeton Strong*, vol. 4, p. 496, entry of October 2, 1873.

32 Black, *The King of Fifth Avenue*, p. 491.

33 John Michael Kennedy, "Philanthropy and Science in New York City: The American Museum of Natural History, 1868–1968" (Ph.D. diss., Yale University, 1968), p. 70.

34 Nevins and Thomas, eds., *The Diary of George Templeton Strong*, vol. 4, p. 498, entry of October 21, 1873.

35 Henry Edward Krehbiel, *The Philharmonic Society of New York* (New York: Novello, Ewer & Co., 1892), p. 175.

36 Nevins and Thomas, eds., *The Diary of George Templeton Strong*, vol. 4, p. 501, entry of November 10, 1873.

37 Nicola Beisel, "Upper-Class Formation and the Politics of Censorship in Boston, New York, and Philadelphia, 1872–1892" (Ph.D. diss., University of Michigan, 1990), p. 5.

38 Beisel, "Upper-Class Formation and the Politics of Censorship in Boston, New York, and Philadelphia," p. 5.

39 Henry Bellows, *Historical Sketch of the Union League Club of New York: Its Origin, Organization, and Work, 1863–1879* (New York: Club House, 1879), p. 135.

40 See Frederic Cople Jaher, "Style and Status: High Society in Late Nineteenth-Century New York," in Frederic Cople Jaher, ed., *The Rich, The Well Born and the Powerful: Elites and Upper Classes in History* (Urbana: University of Illinois Press, 1973), p. 279; John Ward Diary, January 1, 1874, to December 31, 1875, NYHS.

41 Black, *The King of Fifth Avenue*, pp. 444–445.

42 Robert T. Davis, "Pauperism in the City of New York," *Journal of Social Science* 6 (1874): 74.

43 Bellows, *Historical Sketch of the Union League Club of New York*, p. 132.

44 Allan Nevins, ed., *Selected Writings of Abram S. Hewitt* (New York: Columbia University Press, 1937), p. 277.

45 Antonio Gramsci, *Il Risorgimento* (Turin: Einaudi, 1949), pp. 199–200.

46 John G. Sproat, *"The Best Men:" Liberal Reformers in the Gilded Age* (New York: Oxford University Press, 1968), p. 206.

47 Richard Hofstadter, *Social Darwinism in American Thought* (Philadelphia: University of Pennsylvania Press, 1945), p. 6.

48 Chauncey Depew, *My Memories of Eighty Years* (New York: Charles Scribner's Sons, 1922), p. 384.

49 James J. Hill, *Highways of Progress* (New York: Doubleday, Page & Company, 1910), p. 126. The *Manufacturer and Builder* called Darwin's theory of the survival of the fittest "self-evident." See *Manufacturer and Builder* 8 (March 1875): 99.

50 For Carnegie see Robert McCloskey, *American Conservatism in the Age of Enterprise, 1865–1910: A Study of William Graham Sumner, Stephen J. Field and Andrew Carnegie* (New York: Harper & Row, 1964), pp. 134, 158–159, 160–163, 166. For Rockefeller see Hofstadter, *Social Darwinism in American Thought*, p. 31.

51 As quoted in Joseph Frazier Wall, *Andrew Carnegie* (New York: Oxford University Press, 1970), p. 381.

52 Lawrence S. Benson, "Philosophic Reviews: Darwin Answered, or Evolution a Myth," in *Manufacturer and Builder* 8 (January 1875): 20.

53 *NYDT*, 10 November 1882, pp. 1–2; Hofstadter, *Social Darwinism in American Thought*, p. 34.

54 John Foord, *The Life and Public Services of Simon Sterne* (London: Macmillan and Co., 1903), p. 4; "Andrew Carnegie," in *The Encyclopedia of American Business History and Biography* (New York: Facts on File, 1988), p. 60.

55 Iver Bernstein, *The New York City Draft Riots: Their Significance for American Society and Politics in the Age of the Civil War* (New York: Oxford University Press, 1990), pp. 239–241.

56 Edward C. Mack, *Peter Cooper: Citizen of New York* (New York: Duell, Sloan and Pearce, 1949), pp. 363, 365.

57 Mack, *Peter Cooper*, p. 74; Peter Cooper, "An Open Letter to the Hon. President and Gentlemen of the Tariff Commission" (1883), cited in Mack, *Peter Cooper*, p. 375.

58 Mack, *Peter Cooper*, p. 375.

59 Peter Cooper, quoted in Mack, *Peter Cooper*, p. 375.

60 Mack, *Peter Cooper*, pp. 376–377.

61 Mack, *Peter Cooper*, pp. 378–380.

62 See, for example, *CFC* 18 (14 February 1874): 157.

63 For this attitude see in general *NYCA*, 22 October 1873, p. 2.

64 *Nineteenth Annual Report of the Corporation of the Chamber of Commerce of the State of New York For the Year 1876–'77* (New York: Press of the Chamber of Commerce, 1877), p. 13; *Eighteenth Annual Report of the Corporation of the Chamber of Commerce of the State of New York For the Year 1875–'76* (New York: Press of the Chamber of Commerce, 1876), p. 18.

65 *Eighteenth Annual Report of the Corporation of the Chamber of Commerce*, p. 33.

66 Samuel J. Tilden, *The Writings and Speeches of Samuel J. Tilden*, ed. John Bigelow (New York: Harper and Brothers, 1885), vol. 2, p. 58.

67 *NYT*, 9 June 1875, p. 4; *NYT*, 30 November 1876, p. 7; *NYT*, 31 January 1877, p. 8; *NYT*, 28 February 1877, p. 5.

68 *Real Estate Record and Builders' Guide* 17 (1 January 1876): 2.

69 Jeffrey Sklansky, "The War on Pauperism: Responses to Poverty in New York City During the Depression, 1873–1978" (Master's thesis, Columbia University, 1990), p. 17.

70 Martin Shefter, "The Emergence of the Political Machine: An Alternative View," in Willis Hawley, ed., *Theoretical Perspectives on Urban Politics* (Englewood Cliffs, N.J.: Prentice-Hall, 1976), p. 32; Eric Foner, *Politics and Ideology in the Age of the Civil War* (New York: Oxford University Press, 1980), p. 165.

71 Shefter, "The Emergence of the Political Machine," p. 27; Seymour J. Mandelbaum, *Boss Tweed's New York* (New York: John Wiley & Sons, 1965), p. 177.

72 John C. Teaford, *The Unheralded Triumph: City Government in America, 1870–1900* (Baltimore: Johns Hopkins University Press, 1984), p. 188.

73 Edward Dana Durand, *The Finances of New York City* (New York: Macmillan Company, 1898), p. 373.

74 Teaford, *The Unheralded Triumph*, pp. 288, 293.

75 Jerome Mushkat, *The Reconstruction of New York Democracy: 1861–1874* (Rutherford, N.J.: Fairleigh Dickinson University Press, 1981), p. 215.

76 *Sixteenth Annual Report of the Commissioner of Public Charities and Correction, New York, For the Year 1875* (New York: Bellevue Press, 1876). The total sum expended rose only minimally from $42,797 in 1871 to $48,231 in 1875, while the number of people receiving aid skyrocketed from 19,157 to 51,758.

77 Barry J. Kaplan, "Reformers and Charity: The Abolition of Public Outdoor Relief in New York City, 1870–1898," in *Social Service Review* (June 1978): 202–203, 207. This retreat was supported by the city's economic elite.

78 See Gutman, "The Tompkins Square 'Riot' in New York City on January 13, 1874," pp. 45, 67.

79 *NYT,* 22 November 1873, p. 2.

80 *Sixteenth Annual Report of the Commissioner of Public Charities and Correction,* pp. viii–ix.

81 Sklansky, "The War on Pauperism," p. 19.

82 Robert T. Davis, "Pauperism in the City of New York," *Journal of Social Science* 6 (1874): 77.

83 Bellows, *Historical Sketch of the Union League Club of New York,* p. 137.

84 See also Theda Skocpol, *Protecting Soldiers and Mothers* (Cambridge, Mass.: Harvard University Press, 1992), p. 95.

85 *NYT,* 21 November 1873, p. 8.

86 *NYT,* 21 November 1873, p. 8; Davis, "Pauperism in the City of New York," p. 78.

87 Davis, "Pauperism in the City of New York," p. 78.

88 *SciAm* (19 October 1878): 241.

89 New York State Board of Charities, *Tenth Annual Report* (1877), p. 287, as quoted in Marvin E. Gettleman, "Charity and Social Classes in the United States, 1874–1900," part 1, in *American Journal of Economics and Sociology* 22 (April 1963): 327.

90 *Thirty-First Annual Report of the New York Association for Improvement of the Condition of the Poor, For the Year 1874,* p. 59.

91 *Thirty-First Annual Report of the New York Association for the Improvement of the Conditions of the Poor,* p. 59.

92 *Twenty-Seventh Annual Report of the Association for the Improvement of the Conditions of the Poor* (New York: Trow & Smith, 1870), p. 39.

93 Daniel Hodas, *The Business Career of Moses Taylor: Merchant, Finance Capitalist, and Industrialist* (New York: New York University Press, 1976), p. 198. *NYT,* 21 November 1873, p. 8.

94 *Thirty-First Annual Report of the New York Association for the Improvement of the Conditions of the Poor,* p. 52.

95 *Thirty-First Annual Report of the New York Association for the Improvement of the Conditions of the Poor,* p. 58; *Thirty-Second Annual Report of the New York Association for the Improvement of the Conditions of the Poor for the Year 1876* (New York: Office of the Association, 1875), p. 51.

96 Lori D. Ginzberg, *Women and the Work of Benevolence: Morality, Politics, and Class in the Nineteenth-Century United States* (New Haven: Yale University Press, 1990), pp. 5, 177, 198. For the general point see also Gettleman, "Charity and Social Classes in the United States," pp. 317–321.

97 J. K. Paulding, "Democracy and Charity," in *Charities Review* 4 (April 1895): 287; Lori D. Ginzberg, *Women and the Work of Benevolence,* p. 200.

98 Gutman, "The Tompkins Square 'Riot' in New York City on January 13, 1874," passim, esp. pp. 53–55.

99 "Certificate for the Incorporation of the Society for the Prevention of Crime," October 29, 1878, Oversize No. 1, Records, 1878–1973, Society for the Prevention of Crime, Rare Books Collection, Columbia University.

100 Cited in M. J. Heale, *American Anti-Communism: Combating the Enemy Within, 1830–1970* (Baltimore: The Johns Hopkins University Press, 1990), p. 27.

101 The connection between retrenchment and social conflict is also made by William E. Forbath, "The Ambitious of Free Labor: Labor and the Law in the Gilded Age," in *Wisconsin Law Review* (1985), p. 770.

102 Sproat, *"The Best Men,"* p. 253; *HW* (7 April 1877): 263.

103 C. K. Yearly, *The Money Machines: The Breakdown and Reform of Governmental and Party Finance in the North, 1860–1920* (Albany: State University of New York Press, 1970), p. 118.

104 Foord, *The Life and Public Services of Simon Sterne,* p. 5.

105 Simon Sterne, "The Administration of American Cities," in *International Review* 4 (1877): 632.

106 Sterne, "The Administration of American Cities," pp. 635, 637.

107 McCloskey, *American Conservatism in the Age of Enterprise,* pp. 3, 15, 18.

108 Sproat, *"The Best Men,"* p. 252. W. E. B. DuBois also emphasized the ambivalent relationship of the northern bourgeoisie to democracy in the North and South. See W. E. B. DuBois, *Black Reconstruction in America, 1860–1880* (1935; reprint New York: Touchstone, 1995), p. 584.
   Women's suffrage amendments were introduced in the New York State legislature in 1878, 1880, 1882, 1883 and 1885, but to no avail. See Charles Z.

Lincoln, *The Constitutional History of New York* (Rochester, N.Y.: The Lawyers Co-Operative Publishing Company, 1906), vol. 2, p. 660. However, there was a group of women in the suffrage movement who demanded the right of suffrage in order to balance the influences of undesirable male voters. See Ellen Carol DuBois, *Feminism and Suffrage: The Emergence of an Independent Women's Movement in America, 1868–1869* (Ithaca, N.Y.: Cornell University Press, 1978); Paula Giddings, *When and Where I Enter* (New York: Bantam, 1986).

109　Francis Parkman, "The Failure of Universal Suffrage," in *North American Review* 127 (1878): 8.

110　*Nation* (7 September 1871): 158. See also Jonathan Baxter Harrison, "Limited Sovereignty in the United States," in *Atlantic Monthly* 43 (February 1879): 186; Sproat, *Best Men*, p. 250.

111　Parkman, "The Failure of Universal Suffrage," p. 20.

112　*NYT,* 4 August 1878, p. 6.

113　Samuel Tilden, "Municipal Reform Message" (Address to the Legislature), Albany, May 11, 1875, reprinted in John Bigelow, ed., *The Writings and Speeches of Samuel J. Tilden* (New York: Harper and Brothers, 1885), vol. 2, pp. 119–137.

114　*Report of the Commission to Devise a Plan for the Government of Cities in the State of New York: Presented to the Legislature, March 6th, 1877* (New York: Evening Post Steam Press, 1877), p. 3. For a more detailed discussion of the amendment see Sven Beckert, "Democracy in the Age of Capital," in Meg Jacobs et al., eds., *Democracy in America* (forthcoming).

115　*Report of the Commission to Devise a Plan,* pp. 4–10.

116　*Report of the Commission to Devise a Plan,* pp. 10, 13, 15.

117　*Report of the Commission to Devise a Plan,* pp. 21–27.

118　*Report of the Commission to Devise a Plan,* p. 28.

119　*Report of the Commission to Devise a Plan,* p. 40.

120　*Report of the Commission to Devise a Plan,* p. 43.

121　*Report of the Commission to Devise a Plan,* pp. 41–42.

122　*Report of the Commission to Devise a Plan,* p. 42.

123　*Report of the Commission to Devise a Plan,* p. 48.

124　*Report of the Commission to Devise a Plan,* p. 42.

125　*NYT,* 21 October 1877, p. 7.

126　For the number of males age twenty-one or older, see Department of the Interior, Census Office, *Statistics of the Population of the United States at the Tenth Census, June 1, 1880* (Washington, D.C.: GPO, 1883). There were also other estimates about the percentage of voters who would be disenfranchised. The *Sun* estimated that 50,000 voters would lose their suffrage rights, or about one-third of the total number of voters as estimated by the *New York Times.* See the *Sun,* 22 October 1877, p. 2. On another occasion, the *Sun* estimated that 92,000 out of 190,000 voters would be disenfranchised, slightly less than 50 percent. See the *Sun,* 14 April 1877, p. 3.

127　*NYT,* 30 March 1877, p. 3.

128　*Nineteenth Annual Report of the Corporation of the Chamber of Commerce,* pp. 96–97, 99.

129 Meyer Stern, as quoted in *Nineteenth Annual Report of the Corporation of the Chamber of Commerce,* p. 100.

130 *Nineteenth Annual Report of the Corporation of the Chamber of Commerce,* p. 104.

131 *NYDT,* 5 April 1877, p. 2; *NYDT,* 13 April 1877, p. 8; *NYT,* 25 April 1877, p. 8; *NYT,* 31 January 1873, p. 3; New York Council of Political Reform, *Report for the Year 1875* (New York: Evening Post Steam Press, 1876), p. 231; *NYT,* 30 November 1876, p. 7; *NYT,* 31 January 1877, p. 8; *NYT,* 28 February 1877, p. 5; *NYT,* 25 April 1877, p. 8; *NYT,* 30 March 1877, p. 3; Richard Lowitt, *A Merchant Prince of the Nineteenth Century, William E. Dodge* (New York: Columbia University Press, 1954), p. 285.

132 The quotation is from *NYT,* 17 April 1877, p. 1. Mandelbaum, *Boss Tweed's New York,* p. 171.

133 The *Nation* stressed that the limitation of suffrage was "the most important" part of the reform plan. *Nation* (19 April 1877): 288. See also *NYT,* 7 April 1877, p. 4; *NYH,* 8 April 1877, p. 10; *NYDT,* 7 April 1877, p. 4; *CFC* 24 (17 March 1877): 237–238. *Harper's Weekly* called up the ghost of the Paris Commune to justify the amendments. *HW* (10 November 1877): 879.

134 *NYH,* 28 March 1877, p. 4.

135 *CFC* 24 (31 March 1877): 285.

136 *Twentieth Annual Report of the Corporation of the Chamber of Commerce of the State of New York for the Year 1877–'78* (New York: Press of the Chamber of Commerce, 1878), pp. 9–10.

137 The meeting's backers also included lawyer Joseph H. Choate, glass importer James A. Roosevelt, leather manufacturer Jackson S. Schultz, future governor of New York, Levi P. Morton, metal dealer William E. Dodge, Jr., and banker Morris K. Jessup, as well as Thurlow Weed and Abram S. Hewitt. *NYH,* 8 April 1877, p. 7. See also Michael McGerr, *The Decline of Popular Politics: The American North, 1865–1928* (New York: Oxford University Press, 1986), pp. 49, 50; *NYT,* 8 April 1877, p. 1.

138 *NYT,* 8 September 1877, p. 4.

139 *NYT,* 8 April 1877, p. 7; *NYH,* 8 April 1877, p. 1.

140 *NYH,* 8 April 1877, p. 7.

141 *NYDT,* 9 April 1877, 3.

142 *NYT,* 8 April 1877, p. 1.

143 *NYT,* 11 October 1877, p. 8.

144 *NYT,* 13 October 1877, p. 2.

145 *NYT,* 9 October 1877, p. 5.

146 *NYDT,* 23 October 1877, p. 2; *NYT,* 8 April 1877, p. 1.

147 *NYT,* 8 April 1877, p. 1.

148 *NYT,* 23 October 1877, p. 1.

149 *NYT,* 6 November 1877, p. 5.

150 McGerr, *The Decline of Popular Politics,* p. 50; Foner, *Politics and Ideology in the Age of the Civil War,* p. 165.

151 *NYDT,* 23 October 1877, p. 2.

152 *Labor Standard,* 14 April 1877, p. 1.

153 *Labor Standard,* 4 November 1877, p. 2. For working-class opposition, see

also the speech by J. W. Maddox at the Cosmopolitan Conference on April 22, 1877. Reprinted in *NYT,* April 23, 1877, p. 8.

154 *Sun,* October 22, 1877, p. 2; see also *CFC* 24 (17 March 1877): 238.

155 McGerr, *The Decline of Popular Politics,* p. 51.

156 McGerr, *The Decline of Popular Politics,* p. 51.

157 Speech by Simon Sterne in front of the German-American Citizens' Association, 1887, quoted in Foord, *The Life and Public Services of Simon Sterne,* p. 289.

158 *NYDT,* 7 April 1877, p. 4.

159 Foner, *Reconstruction,* p. 544.

160 Foner, *Reconstruction,* p. 523.

161 Foner, *Reconstruction,* p. 528.

162 Foner, *Reconstruction,* p. 529.

163 Foner, *Reconstruction,* p. 556.

164 Foner, *Reconstruction,* p. 562.

165 *CFC* (28 April 1877): 383.

166 Nevins, ed., *Selected Writings of Abram S. Hewitt,* p. 403.

167 Nevins and Thomas, eds., *The Diary of George Templeton Strong,* vol. 4, p. 517, entry of March 11, 1874.

168 Nevins and Thomas, eds., *The Diary of George Templeton Strong,* vol. 4, p. 538, entry of September 16, 1874.

169 *Sixteenth Annual Report of the Corporation of the Chamber of Commerce of the State of New York For the Year 1873–'74* (New York: Press of the Chamber of Commerce, 1874), p. 87.

170 *Eighteenth Annual Report of the Corporation of the Chamber of Commerce,* p. 89.

171 In 1876, the American Bankers Association began lobbying for the restoration of the gold standard. "American Bankers Association," in *The Encyclopedia of American Business History and Biography,* p. 11.

172 See, for example, the *CFC* 21 (21 August 1875): 172; *CFC* 17 (6 December 1873): 750. By late December 1873 the *CFC* reversed some of its earlier acceptance of paper currency arguing that the "derangement of currency . . . is of a very serious character, and forcibly illustrates the mischiefs of quitting the solid anchorage of specie payments for the treacherous quicksands of irredeemable issues." *CFC* 17 (27 December 1873): 854.

173 *CFC* 27 (26 February 1876): 193. "[T]he panic, on balance had strengthened hard money opinion among the merchants," writes one historian. Irwin Unger, *The Greenback Era: A Social and Political History of American Finance, 1865–1879* (Princeton, N.J.: Princeton University Press, 1964), p. 239.

174 Robert Hoe II to Robert Hoe Jr., Paris, February 26, 1875, Reel 14, Hoe Papers, Library of Congress. For his opposition to paper currency see also Robert Hoe II to Robert Hoe III, Paris, January 10, 1874, Reel 4, Hoe Papers, Library of Congress. "When the dollar appreciated to par the troubles were over." *Shoe and Leather Reporter* (2 September 1880): 385.

175 On *Iron Age,* see Unger, *The Greenback Era,* p. 284. On the general point see Unger, *The Greenback Era,* p. 326.

176 See *Proceedings at the Mass Meeting of Citizens in the Cooper Institute, New York, Tuesday Evening, March 24, 1874 on National Finances* (New York: Comes, Lawrence & Co., 1874). Grant eventually vetoed the bill.

177 For the negligible support that greenbacks still received from elite New Yorkers, see *NYT*, 24 September 1875, p. 8, which reported on a meeting of "the inflationists," which few attended. However, Peter Cooper, as always was present.

178 Robert McElroy, *Levi Parsons Morton, Banker, Diplomat, and Statesman* (New York: Putnam, 1930), pp. 74, 76, 79. This was in 1878.

179 *CFC* 20 (2 January 1875): 3.

180 *Nation* (1 October 1874): 212.

181 See, among many examples, speech by Richard Lathers, *South Carolina: Her Wrongs and The Remedy, Remarks of Col. Richard Lathers, Delivered at The Opening of the Taxpayers' Convention, in Columbia, S.C., Tuesday, February 17, 1874* (Charleston, S.C.: n.p., 1874).

182 Mary P. Ryan, *Civic Wars: Democracy and Public Life in the American City During the Nineteenth Century* (Berkeley: University of California Press, 1995), p. 272.

183 *NYDT*, 12 May 1871, p. 5.

184 *NYDT*, 1 May 1871, p. 1.

185 *NYDT*, 1 May 1871, p. 1.

186 *NYDT*, 3 May 1871, p. 4.

187 *NYDT*, 3 May 1871, p. 4.

188 *NYDT*, 5 March 1872, p. 2. For similar statements see *The Nation* (16 April 1874): 247–248; *Dry Goods Economist* (5 September 1868): 4.

189 *NYT*, 14 November 1866, p. 2.

190 *NYT*, 25 January 1867, p. 2.

191 *NYT*, 25 January 1867, p. 2.

192 See the reports on South Carolina by "Our special correspondent" published in the *NYDT* in May of 1871.

193 *CFC* (18 January 1868): 71.

194 James S. Pike, *The Prostrate State: South Carolina Under Negro Government* (1874; reprint New York: Harper & Row, 1968), p. 12.

195 Pike, *The Prostrate State*, pp. 58–65.

196 *CFC* (28 April 1877): 383.

197 See, for example, *CFC* (23 October 1869): 518. They favored a general retrenchment of the state and lower state expenditures. *CFC* 4 (23 March 1867): 359.

198 Nevins and Thomas, eds., *The Diary of George Templeton Strong*, vol. 4, p. 524, entry of April 28, 1874; Gerald Carson, *The Golden Egg, The Personal Income Tax, Where it Came from, How it Grew* (Boston: Houghton Mifflin Company, 1977), p. 40; Clarkson N. Potter to Sherman, New York, August 23, 1870, Isaac Sherman Papers, Huntington Library; Martin Bradley to Isaac Sherman, Albany, June 20, 1870, and January 3, 1871, Isaac Sherman Papers, Huntington Library; *ARJ* (8 July 1865): 633; *CFC* (23 April 1870): 518.

199 See letters to Sherman received in July of 1870, Isaac Sherman Papers, Huntington Library.

200 Henry Hitchock to Sherman, January 13, 1874, Isaac Sherman Papers, Huntington Library. Espen Miller to Isaac Sherman, Philadelphia, August 27, 1870, Isaac Sherman Papers, Huntington Library.

201 Jonathan Sturges to Isaac Sherman, New York, March 21, 1871, as well as "List of Officers of the Association," Isaac Sherman Papers, Huntington Library.

202 M. Winslow to Sherman, New York, April 8, 1871, Isaac Sherman Papers, Huntington Library.

203 Document signed by Isaac Sherman and a number of prominent politicians and citizens, December 1871. Among them were Jackson Schultz, Isaac Sherman, William Dennistoun, Russell Sage, S. Chamberlain, James Robb, Charles Cobb, J. S. Ward, Astor and Brown Brothers. Isaac Sherman Papers, Huntington Library.

204 Carson, *The Golden Egg*, p. 41; Thomas Cochran to Isaac Sherman, Philadelphia, August 16, 1870, Isaac Sherman Papers, Huntington Library; note by Isaac Sherman, January 1872, Isaac Sherman Papers, Huntington Library; Durand, *The Finances of New York City*, p. 373.

205 He opposed Thaddeus Stevens's bill for the creation of military districts in the South. William Earl Dodge, *Speech of Hon. William E. Dodge, on Reconstruction, Delivered in the House of Representatives, January 21, 1867* (Washington, D.C.: Printed at the Congressional Globe Office, 1867), pp. 5–6.

206 Dodge, *Speech of Hon. William E. Dodge, on Reconstruction*, pp. 5–6. Dodge was widely praised for this speech by New York's merchants. Lowitt, *Merchant Prince*, p. 241.

207 This, at least, was an argument that William E. Dodge made. See Lowitt, *Merchant Prince*, p. 239.

208 Foner, *Reconstruction*, p. 554; *NYT*, 8 January 1875, p. 1.

209 *NYT*, 8 January 1875, p. 1; *NYT*, 9 January 1875, p. 5.

210 *NYT*, 12 January 1875, p. 2.

211 *NYT*, 12 January 1875, p. 2.

212 Both candidates, Tilden and Hayes, had wealthy backers in New York City: Tilden relied on the resources of Abram Hewitt and August Belmont, while Hayes counted, for instance, on the former governor of New York and merchant banker, E. D. Morgan. Circular letter of E. D. Morgan, New York, October 24, 1876, Box 1, Papers of Francis E. Spinner, LDC; Irving Katz, *August Belmont: A Political Biography* (New York: Columbia University Press, 1968), p. 221.

213 Foner, *Reconstruction*, p. 574.

214 Henry V. Boynton to James M. Comly, January 25, 1877, cited in Foner, *Reconstruction*, p. 579.

215 Nevins, ed., *Selected Writings of Abram S. Hewitt*, p. 177. On New York City see *Nineteenth Annual Report of the New-York Chamber of Commerce of the State of New-York* p. 73. For the desire for compromise see also Samuel Barlow to Bayard, New York City, January 10, 1877, "Letterbooks," Samuel Barlow Papers, Huntington Library.

216 Foner, *Reconstruction*, p. 582.

217 Samuel Barlow to General Richard Taylor, New York City, January 19, 1877, "Letterbooks," BW 1, Samuel Barlow Papers, Huntington Library; Samuel Ward to Samuel Barlow, March 23, 1877, Folder 23, BW 116, Samuel Barlow Papers, Huntington Library.

218 William Shipman to Samuel Barlow, New York, March 9, 1877, Folder 36, BW 115, Samuel Barlow Papers, Huntington Library.

219 *Twentieth Annual Report of the Corporation of the Chamber of Commerce of the State of New York*, p. 12.

220 See also Foner, *Reconstruction*, p. 582.

221 Steinway Diary, July 23, July 24, July 25, July 26, and July 27, 1877, Steinway Papers, NYHS. On the fear among bourgeois New Yorkers see also Randolph T. Percy, *Who was G.W? Being a Truthful Tale of the Seventh Regiment in the Armory During the Railroad Strikes in July, 1877* (New York: n.p., 1879), pp. 9–11.

222 *NYDT,* 24 July 1877, p. 5; *NYDT,* 25 July 1877, p. 4.

223 *NYT,* 25 July 1877, p. 1.

224 Elliot C. Cowdin, *Capital and Labor: An Address Delivered Before the American Institute of the City of New York, In Celebration of Its Semi-Centennial Anniversary, on Thursday Evening, October 11, 1877* (New York: Printed for the Institute, 1877), p. 9. *RW* (28 July 1877): 700. For similar reaction see *NYDT,* 24 July 1877, p. 5; *NYDT,* 25 July 1877, p. 4; *CFC Investors' Supplement* (28 July 1877): 1.

225 *Nation* (26 July 1877): 3ff; *HW* (18 August 1877): 638; *HW* (18 August 1877): 631.

226 *HW* (18 August 1877): 638

227 See, for example, *NYT,* 26 July 1877, p. 4.

228 *NYDT,* 3 August 1877, p. 4.

229 *RW* (28 July 1877): 698.

230 *RW* (21 July 1877): 675.

231 *RW* (28 July 1877): 699; *RW* (18 August 1877): 772. On the endorsement of repression see also *Real Estate Record and Builders Guide* (2 June 1877): 440; August Belmont to August Belmont, Jr., July 25, 1877, cited in Black, *The King of Fifth Avenue*, p. 522; *NYDT,* 24 July 1877, p. 4.

232 New York State Adjutant General's Office, National Guard, Ninth Regiment, *Souvenir of the Opening of the Armory, Ninth Regiment, N. G. N. Y., New York, February 22d, 1897* (New York: n.p., 1897), n.p.

233 Percy, *Who was G.W?* p. 22.

234 Emmons Clark, *History of the Seventh Regiment of New York, 1806–1889* (New York: The Seventh Regiment, 1890), vol. 2, p. 258.

235 Percy, *Who was G.W?* p. 19.

236 Percy, *Who was G.W?* p. 28; Clark, *History of the Seventh Regiment of New York*, vol. 2, p. 258.

237 Percy, *Who was G.W?* p. 36.

238 Percy, *Who was G.W?* p. 13.

239 *NYT,* 26 July 1877, p. 4. See also *RW* (28 July 1877): 700.

240 J. T. Headley, *The Great Riots of New York, 1712–1873, Including a Full and Complete Account of the Four Day's Draft Riot of 1863* (New York: E. B. Treat, 1873), p. 21.

241 *NYT,* 28 July 1877, p. 4.
242 *Nation* (2 August 1877): 1.
243 Stephen Skowronek, *Building a New American State: The Expansion of National Administrative Capacities, 1877–1920* (New York: Cambridge University Press, 1982), p. 87.
244 *CFC* (2 July 1877): 74.
245 See Foner, *Reconstruction,* p. 585
246 The importance of the militarization of the bourgeoisie's outlook on society is also emphasized by T. Jackson Lears, *No Place of Grace: Antimodernism and the Transformation of American Culture, 1880–1920* (New York: Pantheon Books, 1981), pp. 111–112.
247 See Robert M. Fogelson, *America's Armories: Architecture, Society and Public Order* (Cambridge, Mass.: Harvard University Press, 1989).
248 *NYT,* 22 November 1877, p. 8.

8. The Culture of Capital

1 See for example Richard Hofstadter, *The American Political Tradition and the Men Who Made It* (New York: Knopf, 1948), p. 162.
2 It is unfortunately impossible to estimate the precise number of people who can be considered bourgeois in 1880 or 1890. Neither tax lists nor census returns allow for an estimate along the lines of those done for 1855 and 1870. (See in Chapter 1, footnotes 12 and 15, and Chapter 5, footnotes 10 and 11.)
3 Here I disagree with the argument made by Frederic Cople Jaher, *The Urban Establishment: Upper Strata in Boston, New York, Charleston, Chicago, and Los Angeles* (Urbana: University of Illinois Press, 1982), pp. 254–255. Jaher argues that the "superior commercial vitality of the Brahmins" is shown by their greater persistence among the upper echelons of the wealthy between mid- and late-nineteenth century. However, the opposite is true – the much more limited commercial dynamics of Boston put the city and its economic elite increasingly into a subordinate position to New York capital and capitalists. This, it seems, hardly testifies to the "commercial impotence of New York's Old Guard." Jaher, *The Urban Establishment,* p. 257.
4 This number is the more impressive as New York City accounted for only about 2 percent of the nation's population. For the list of millionaires see "American Millionaires. The Tribune's List of Person's Reputed to be Worth a Million or More," in *Tribune Monthly* 4 (June, 1892).
5 Jaher, *The Urban Establishment,* p. 253.
6 Jaher, *The Urban Establishment,* p. 255.
7 David C. Hammack, *Power and Society: Greater New York at the Turn of the Century* (New York: Columbia University Press, 1982), p. 51. It was indeed this process of successful adaptation that gave the old elites the power to shape the institutions and ideas of the nation's bourgeoisie as a whole. Christopher Lasch, *The World of Nations: Reflections on American History, Politics, and Culture* (New York: Knopf, 1973), pp. 80, 82, 88, 89.
8 Henry Hall, ed., *America's Successful Men of Affairs: An Encyclopedia of*

Contemporaneous Biography (New York: The New York Tribune, 1895), vol. 2, pp. 75–77; *The National Cyclopedia of American Biography* (New York: J. T. White, 1898), vol. 1, p. 13.

9 Hammack, *Power and Society*, p. 48.

10 Allen Churchill, *The Upper Crust: An Informal History of New York's Highest Society* (Englewood Cliffs, N.J.: Prentice-Hall, 1970), pp. 108, 147; Hammack, *Power and Society*, pp. 44, 46; Matthew Josephson, *The Robber Barons: The Great American Capitalists, 1861–1901* (New York: Harcourt, 1934), pp. 326, 328; Harvey O'Connor, *The Guggenheims: The Making of an American Dynasty* (New York: Covici, Friede, 1937), p. 70; Allan Nevins, *Study in Power: John D. Rockefeller, Industrialist and Philanthropist* (New York: Charles Scribner's Sons, 1953), vol. 2, pp. 80, 81.

11 Hall, ed., *America's Successful Men of Affairs*, vol. 1, pp. 668–670.

12 Hall, ed., *America's Successful Men of Affairs*, vol. 1, p. 241.

13 See John N. Ingham, *The Iron Barons: A Social Analysis of an American Urban Elite, 1874–1965* (Westport, Conn.: Greenwood Press, 1978), p. 216.

14 The relationship between private schools as well as universities and the increasing nationalization of the bourgeoisie is also stressed by E. Digby Baltzell, *Philadelphia Gentlemen: The Making of a National Upper Class* (Glencoe, Ill.: The Free Press, 1958), p. 302.

15 Ronald Story, *The Forging of An Aristocracy: Harvard and the Boston Upper Class, 1800–1870* (Middletown, Conn.: Weslyan University Press, 1980), p. 179. See also Peter Dobkin Hall, *The Organization of American Culture, 1700–1900: Private Institutions, Elites, and the Origins of American Nationality* (New York: New York University Press, 1982), p. 262.

16 Ron Chernow, *The House of Morgan: An American Banking Dynasty and the Rise of Modern Finance* (New York: Simon & Schuster, 1990), p. 62.

17 Jaher, *The Urban Establishment*, p. 266.

18 Edward Sanford Martin, *The Life of Joseph Hodges Choate* (New York: Charles Scribner's Sons, 1920), vol. 1, p. 359.

19 Baltzell, *Philadelphia Gentlemen*, p. 302; William G. Roy, "Institutional Governance and Social Cohesion: The Internal Organization of the American Capitalist Class, 1886–1905," in *Research in Social Stratification and Mobility* 3 (1984): 156.

20 Baltzell, *Philadelphia Gentlemen*, p. 305. See also Hall, *The Organization of American Culture*, p. 264.

21 See *Hardware Club of New York, April, 1897* (New York: n.p., 1897), pp. 83–94.

22 *Annual Report of the American Institute of the City of New York For the Years 1866&7* (Albany, N.Y.: Charles Van Benthuysen & Sons, 1867), p. 32.

23 Hall, *The Organization of American Culture*, p. 247.

24 See National Municipal League, *Publications of the National Municipal League*, No. 4 (Philadelphia: The League, 1895).

25 Alfred Chandler, *The Visible Hand: The Managerial Revolution in American Business* (Cambridge, Mass.: Belknap Press, 1977), pp. 285–287.

26 Chernow, *The House of Morgan*, pp. 29–45, especially p. 42.

27 Chandler, *The Visible Hand*, pp. 240–241.

28 Chandler, *The Visible Hand*, pp. 240, 249, 256, 257, 259, 287, 290–291.
29 Chandler, *The Visible Hand*, pp. 137–143.
30 Chandler, *The Visible Hand*, pp. 148–159.
31 Chernow, *The House of Morgan*, pp. 53–54; Chandler, *The Visible Hand*, p. 167.
32 See Hammack, *Power and Society*, p. 37. It is important to keep in mind not only that the importance of merchants in the economy as a whole diminished, but also that merchants attached themselves to the political economy of industrialists in a subordinate position. Merchant capital as such is of course compatible with industrial capital.
33 Jean Heffer, *Le Port de New York et le Commerce Extérieur. Americain, 1860–1900* (Paris: Publications de la Sorbonne, 1986), p. 93.
34 William Dodge, *Old New York: A Lecture Delivered at Association Hall April 27th 1880, Upon the Invitation of Merchants and Other Citizens of New York* (New York: Dodd, Mead & Company, 1880), p. 11.
35 Dodge, *Old New York*, p. 56.
36 Frederic J. DePeyster, "Speech at the St. Nicholas Society Dinner," in *New American Gazette* 7 (30 November 1891–7 January 1892): 2, quoted in Jaher, *The Urban Establishment*, p. 276.
37 Jaher, *The Urban Establishment*, p. 252.
38 Hammack, *Power and Society*, p. 43. See also the history of Chemical Bank, which under the direction of the Roosevelts moved away from its earlier dependence on the financing of trade. William T. Cobb, *The Strenuous Life: The "Oyster Bay" Roosevelts in Business and Finance* (New York: William E. Rudge's Sons, 1946), p. 44. See also Chandler, *The Visible Hand*, p. 146; Jaher, *The Urban Establishment*, p. 252.
39 Francis L. Eames, *The New York Stock Exchange* (New York: T. G. Hall, 1894); Hammack, *Power and Society*, p. 41. See also Hall, *The Organization of American Culture*, p. 249; Chernow, *The House of Morgan*, pp. 54, 55, 56.
40 Nevins, *Study in Power: John D. Rockefeller*, p. 197.
41 Nevins, *Study in Power: John D. Rockefeller*, p. 197.
42 He also played an important role in Republican Party politics. See Hall, ed., *America's Successful Men of Affairs*, vol. 2, pp. 416–417.
43 *Shoe and Leather Reporter* (16 December 1880): 1045.
44 This is a process also described by John Ingham for the nation's iron and steel manufacturers. Ingham, *The Iron Barons*, p. 6.
45 Forty-three percent of all industrialists who were members of the Chamber of Commerce in 1886 had joined after 1881. In contrast, only 32 percent of all merchants had joined during the same time period. For the members of the Chamber of Commerce see New York Chamber of Commerce, *Twenty-Ninth Annual Report of the Corporation of the Chamber of Commerce, of the State of New York, for the Year 1886–1887* (New York: Press of the Chamber of Commerce, 1887), pp. 139–156.

To find out who among the members was active in which economic sectors, the names were correlated to entries in H. Wilson, *Trow's New York City Directory For 1886–87* (New York: John F. Trow, 1887); Hall, ed., *America's Successful Men of Affairs*; Moses King, *Notable New Yorkers of*

1896–1899 (New York: Bartlett & Co., The Orr Press, 1899); *Phillips' Business Directory of New York City* (New York: J. T. White, 1886).

46 For a list of the wardens and vestrymen of St. George's Church see Henry Anstice, *History of St. George's Church in the City of New York* (New York: Harper & Row, 1911), pp. 442–453.

47 Reginald T. Townsend, *Mother of Clubs: Being the History of the First Hundred Years of the Union Club of the City of New York, 1836–1936* (New York: The Printing House of W. E. Rudge, 1936).

48 Harold C. Livesay, *Andrew Carnegie and the Rise of Big Business* (Boston: Little, Brown and Company, 1975), p. 126. May King Van Rensselaer, *The Social Ladder* (New York: Henry Holt and Company, 1924), p. 172.

49 *NYT*, 23 September 1909, p. 11. On Peter Cooper Hewitt see *Who Was Who in America,* vol. 1, *1897–1942* (Chicago: A. N. Marquis Company, 1943). On Frank Work, see Hall, ed., *America's Successful Men of Affairs,* p. 743.

50 Chernow, *The House of Morgan,* p. 90.

51 See Hall, ed., *America's Successful Men of Affairs.* Hall's book includes the biographies of 143 New York manufacturers, 43 of whom list their club affiliations.

52 See *SciAm* (6 August 1881): 80.

53 See *SciAm* (6 August 1881): 80.

54 "John Roach," entry of June 4, 1860, New York, vol. 317, p. 229, Dun & Co. Collection, Baker Library, Harvard Business School. For a description of the dinner at Delmonico's see Leonard Alexander Swann, *John Roach, Maritime Entrepreneur, The Years as Naval Contractor, 1862–1886* (Annapolis: U.S. Naval Institute, 1965), p. 196, and *NYT,* 30 October 1884, p. 2.

55 Van Rensselaer, *Social Ladder,* pp. 163, 186.

56 Van Rensselaer, *Social Ladder,* p. 58.

57 Jack W. Rudolph, "Launching the Met," in *American History Illustrated* 18 (1983): 21.

58 John Warren Frick, "The Rialto: A Study of Union Square, The Center of New York's First Theatre District, 1870–1900" (Ph.D. diss., New York University, 1983), p. 57; Rudolph, "Launching the Met," p. 21; Steinway also acquired a box. See William Steinway, diary, October 12, 1883, Steinway Papers, NYHS.

59 Lloyd R. Morris, *Incredible New York* (New York: Random House, 1951), p. 192.

60 Quoted in John Frederick Cone, *First Rival of the Metropolitan Opera* (New York: Columbia University Press, 1983), p. 21. See J. J. Astor, note, October 11, 1886, "Letterbook, 1884–1890," John Jacob Astor Papers, NYHS.

61 Apparently, it was the Astors who made the first overtures toward the Metropolitan Opera. After the opening of the Metropolitan Opera, the stockholders of the Academy of Music slowly withdrew their funds from the enterprise. See Cone, *First Rival of the Metropolitan Opera,* pp. 87, 85.

62 Irving Kolodin, *The Metropolitan Opera, 1883–1966* (New York: Alfred A. Knopf, 1966). For the history of the Metropolitan Opera see also Paul E. Eisler, *The Metropolitan Opera: The First Twenty-Five Years, 1883–1908* (Croton-On-Hudson, N.Y.: North River Press, 1984); Calvin Tomkins, *Mer-*

chants and Masterpieces: The Story of the Metropolitan Museum of Art (New York: Henry Holt, 1989), p. 19.

63 Churchill, *The Upper Crust*, p. 126.

64 Churchill, *The Upper Crust*, p. 133.

65 For an account of the ball see *NYDT*, 27 March 1883, p. 5; Van Rensselaer, *Social Ladder*, pp. 171, 172.

66 Hammack, *Power and Society*, p. 37.

67 Chandler, *The Visible Hand*, p. 233.

68 Nevins, *Study in Power: John D. Rockefeller*, p. 113.

69 Livesay, *Andrew Carnegie*, p. 164.

70 *IA* (28 April 1892): 843; *IA* (27 April 1893): 976; *IA* (20 April 1893): 927; *IA* (9 February 1893): 334; *IA* (1 October 1896): 651.

71 *NYT*, 17 December 1889, p. 5.

72 Chamber of Commerce, *Tribute of the Chamber of Commerce of the State of New-York to the Memory of Horace B. Claflin, Adopted January 7, 1886* (New York: Press of the Chamber of Commerce, 1886), pp. 68–69.

73 Cobb, *The Strenuous Life*, pp. 49, 51.

74 O'Connor, *The Guggenheims*, pp. 61, 62, 73, 78, 89.

75 Moreover, many factories were located just outside the island of Manhattan, where real estate was cheaper. See *SciAm* (6 August 1881): 80.

76 Bureau of the Census, *Report of the Manufacturing Industries in the United States at the Eleventh Census, 1890:* Part 2, "Statistics of Cities," prepared by the Department of the Interior, Bureau of the Census (Washington, D.C.: GPO, 1895), pp. xxxi, 391.

77 Bureau of the Census, *Report of the Manufactures of the United States at the Tenth Census (June 1, 1880), Embracing General Statistics and Monographs,* prepared by the Department of the Interior, Bureau of the Census (Washington, D.C.: GPO, 1883), pp. 19, 427.

78 1850 = 100. The numbers are derived from Bureau of the Census, *Twelfth Census of the United States Taken in 1900: Manufactures,* Part 2, "States and Territories" (Washington, D.C.: GPO, 1902), p. 580. Capital intensity is calculated as the average amount of capital invested per worker in a given year. The numbers have been adjusted for inflation.

79 Bureau of the Census, *Report of the Manufactures of the United States at the Tenth Census (June 1, 1880),* pp. 389, 390. While a capital investment of $69.39 was needed to produce an object valued at $100 in Pittsburgh, in New York City $38.34 sufficed.

80 Hammack, *Power and Society*, p. 39.

81 Two sectors of the local manufacturing industry, in particular, had drawn large amounts of new capital since the mid-1850s: apparel and chemicals. The metals and machinery industries, though growing in absolute numbers, had lost some of their importance. In 1890, 17 percent of all capital invested in manufacturing in Manhattan was invested in the apparel industry, compared to only 5 percent in 1855. Chemicals had increased from 7 percent to 16 percent, while the metals and machinery industries declined from a share of 25 percent to 10 percent. See *First Annual Report of the Chamber of Commerce of the State of New York for the Year 1858* (New York: Wheeler and

Williams, Stationers, 1859), pp. 160–167, and the 1890 federal census. Bureau of the Census, *Eleventh Census of the United States, 1890* (Washington, D.C.: GPO, 1892). Industries are arranged by the "Standard Industrial Classifications." See Executive Office of the President, U.S. Office of Management and Budget, *Standard Industrial Classification Manual* (Washington, D.C.: GPO, 1972).

82　On the growth of the women's ready-made industry see Patricia Evelyn Malon, "The Growth of Manufacturing in Manhattan, 1860–1900: An Analysis of Factoral Changes and Urban Structure," (Ph.D. diss., Columbia University, 1981), p. 300.

83　See Malon, "The Growth of Manufacturing," p. 308.

84　"Manufactures in 165 Principal Cities by Specified Industries – NY, NY," United States, Bureau of the Census, *Eleventh Census of the United States, 1890*, vol. 12, *Manufacturing Industries*, Part 2 (Washington, D.C.: GPO, 1895), p. 390. The number for the metalworking industry includes the industry groups Primary Metals Industry, Fabricated Metals Industry, Machinery, Electrical Machinery, and Transportation Equipment. The printing and publishing industry in particular flourished in the city, thanks to the availability of a large market and its closeness to the economic, technical, and cultural expertise of the metropolis.

85　On the decline of the heavy iron industry see Malon, *The Growth of Manufacturing*, p. 231.

86　Importantly, its workers were on average more highly skilled, were often unionized, and experienced better and improving working conditions and wages. Malon, *The Growth of Manufacturing*, p. 270.

87　*NYT*, 23 September 1909, p. 11.

88　Robert Wiebe, in contrast, argues that the national elite emerged later, between 1900 and 1925, and that it stayed in ideological, social, and political distance from local elites. While this might be the case for cities other than New York, in New York itself a dynamic national bourgeoisie, quite apt at "class formation," had already emerged during the 1880s and 1890s, partly out of an earlier local bourgeoisie. See Robert Wiebe, *Self-Rule: A Cultural History of American Democracy* (Chicago: University of Chicago Press, 1995), pp. 139–141.

89　See Wiebe, *Self-Rule*, p. 115.

90　*Manufacturer and Builder* 24 (August 1892): 185.

91　Mona Domosh, "Imagining New York's First Skyscrapers, 1875–1910," in *Journal of Historical Geography* 13 (1987): 233, 235.

92　See also Hammack, *Power and Society*, p. 49.

93　Chandler, *The Visible Hand*, pp. 218, 219; Shepard B. Clough, *A Century of American Life Insurance: A History of the Mutual Life Insurance Company of New York, 1843–1943* (New York: Columbia University Press, 1946), p. 164.

94　The persistent control of a large share of capital by a small number of families well into the twentieth century is documented by Maurice Zeitlin, "Corporate Ownership and Control: The Large Corporation and the Capitalist Class," in *American Journal of Sociology* 79 (March 1974): 1073–1119.

95　Chandler, *The Visible Hand*, p. 132. On physicians see Paul Starr, *The Social*

Transformation of American Medicine (New York: Basic Books, 1982), pp. 93–145.

96 David F. Noble, *America By Design: Science, Technology and the Rise of Corporate Capitalism* (New York: Knopf, 1979), pp. xxiv–xxv.

97 Chandler, *The Visible Hand*, p. 132. For the expansion of this white-collar middle class see also Stuart Blumin, *The Emergence of the Middle Class: Social Experience in the American City, 1760–1900* (New York: Cambridge University Press, 1989), especially pp. 259–297.

98 The percentages have been derived from a sample of the 732 professionals listed in *King's Notable New Yorkers*. About one in four names were chosen, all those whose last names started with the letters A, C, F, N, S, Z.

99 For a list of members see New York Genealogical and Biographical Society, *Twenty-Fifth Anniversary of the New York Genealogical and Biographical Society* (New York: Printed for the Society by T. A. Wright, 1895), pp. 49–72.

100 For the general point of the greater currency of class in American discourse, see Martin J. Burke, *The Conundrum of Class: Public Discourse on the Social Order in America* (Chicago: Chicago University Press, 1995), pp. 133–158. See also Alan Trachtenberg, *The Incorporation of American Culture: Culture and Society in the Gilded Age* (New York: Hill and Wang, 1982), especially p. 79.

101 Grover Cleveland's message to Congress, December 1888. Quoted in Richard Welch, Jr., *The Presidencies of Grover Cleveland* (Lawrence, Kans.: University Press of Kansas, 1988), p. 17.

102 Wiebe, *Self-Rule*, p. 127; Blumin, *The Emergence of the Middle Class*, p. 258. See also Neville Kirk, "The Limits of Liberalism: Working-Class Formation in Britain and the United States," in Rick Halpern and Jonathan Morris, eds., *American Exceptionalism: US Working-Class Formation in an International Context* (New York: St. Martin's Press, 1997), p. 126. See also Karen Haltunnen, *Confidence Men and Painted Women: A Study of Middle-Class Culture in America, 1830–1870* (New Haven: Yale University Press, 1982), p. 206.

103 John R. Commons, *Social Reform and the Church* (New York: T. Y. Crowell, 1894), p. 34.

104 Lydia Maria Childs to Sarah Blake Shaw, July 31, 1877, quoted in Blumin, *The Emergence of the Middle Class*, p. 288.

105 Albert S. Bowles, *The Conflict between Capital and Labor* (Philadelphia: Lippincott, 1876), p. vii.

106 William Graham Sumner, *What Social Classes Owe to Each Other* (New York: Harper and Brothers, 1883), p. 13.

107 See, for example, Junius H. Browne, *The Great Metropolis: A Mirror of New York* (Hartford, Conn.: American Publishing Co., 1869); James Dabney McCabe, *The Secrets of the Great City: A Work Descriptive of the Virtues and Vices, the Mysteries, Miseries, and Crimes of New York City* (Philadelphia: Jones, 1868).

108 For a description of these events see David Traxel, *1898: The Birth of the American Century* (New York: Knopf, 1998), p. 306; Stephen Nissenbaum, *The Battle for Christmas: A Cultural History of America's Most Cherished Holiday* (New York: Vintage, 1997), p. 252.

109 Richard L. Rapson, *Britons View America: Travel Commentary, 1860–1935* (Seattle: University of Washington Press, 1971), p. 164.

110 James Bryce, *The American Commonwealth*, 2d rev. ed. (New York: The Commonwealth Publishing Company, 1908), vol. 2, p. 701.

111 See Rapson, *Britons View America*, p. 165.

112 Anonymous, *Sozialistische Briefe aus Amerika* (Munich: Carl Merkhoffs Verlag, 1883), pp. 35, 81.

113 Friedrich Engels to Friedrich Adolph Sorge, London, November 29, 1886, cited in *Marx and Engels on the United States* (Moscow: Progress Publisher, 1979), p. 312.

114 Stuart Blumin correctly critiques this literature as ignoring the emergence of a middle class. See Blumin, *The Emergence of the Middle Class*, pp. 14–16.

115 For the use of the term "capitalist" see, for example, *Manufacturer and Builder* 12 (April 1880): 90. For the use of "business men and capitalist," see, among many others, National Commercial Convention, *Proceedings of the National Commercial Convention of 1885* (Atlanta, Ga.: W. H. Scott, 1885), p. ix.

116 See Mark Twain and Charles Ardley Warner, *The Gilded Age: A Tale of To-Day* (Hartford, Conn.: American Publishing Co., 1874), p. 527; Wendell Philips, "The Outlook," in *North American Review* 127 (1878): 109; J. Lawrence Laughlin, "Political Economy and the Civil War," in *Atlantic Monthly* 55 (April 1885): 448; Clare Virginia Eby, "Representative Men: Businessmen in American Fiction, 1875–1914" (Ph.D. diss., University of Michigan, Ann Arbor, 1988), p. 16.

117 See, for example, *CFC* 32 (26 March 1881): 325; *CFC* 33 (21 September 1881): 316; *CFC* 33 (8 October 1881): 370.

118 As in the publications of the Citizens' Association, the Committee of Seventy, and other reform organizations. See also the frequent use of these terms in *Nation, HW,* and the *NYT*.

119 While the word "bourgeois" did not enter the American vocabulary in any major way (in contrast to *bürgerlich* in German and *bourgeois* in French), and Noah Webster in his dictionary of 1857 had noted that bourgeois "appears to be a French word, but I know not the reason of its application to types"; by 1881, bourgeoisie was clearly identified in the dictionary as the "middle classes of a country." Noah Webster, *An American Dictionary of the English Language* (Springfield, Mass.: George and Charles Merriam, 1857), and Noah Webster et al., *An American Dictionary of the English Language* (Springfield, Mass.: G. & C. Merriam, 1881).

120 The importance of access to resources is also emphasized by Edmond Goblot, *La Barrière et le Niveau* (Paris: Librairie Félix Alcan, 1925), p. 22. See also Nicola Beisel, *Imperiled Innocents: Anthony Comstock and Family Reproduction in Victorian America* (Princeton, N.J.: Princeton University Press, 1997), p. 5.

121 Edmond Goblot, *La Barrière et le Niveau*, p. 9.

122 Quoted in "Andrew Carnegie," in *The Encyclopedia of American Business History and Biography* (New York: Facts on File, 1988), p. 50.

123 Chernow, *The House of Morgan*, pp. 46–47.

124 Churchill, *The Upper Crust,* p. 121. See also William Hurd Hillyer, *James Talcott: Merchant and His Times* (New York: Charles Scribner's Sons, 1937), p. 120.

125 Katherine Howe et al., *Herter Brothers: Furniture and Interiors for a Gilded Age* (Houston: Museum of Fine Arts, 1994), p. 53.

126 Churchill, *The Upper Crust,* p. 124.

127 Churchill, *The Upper Crust,* pp. 140, 141.

128 See David Marck Wheeler, "Perceptions of Money and Wealth on Gilded Age Stages: A Study of Long Run Production in New York City" (Ph.D. diss., University of Oregon, Eugene, 1986), p. 222.

129 Maureen E. Montgomery, *"Gilded Prostitution": Status, Money, and Transatlantic Marriages, 1870–1914* (London: Routledge, 1989), p. 48.

130 Churchill, *The Upper Crust,* p. 196; Gail MacColl and Carol McD. Wallace, *To Marry an English Lord* (New York: Workman Publishing, 1989), p. 31.

131 In 1871 the publisher of the *NYH,* James Gordon Bennett, Jr., together with General Phil Sheridan, Leonard Jerome, John G. Hecksher, Carrol Livingston, and J. Schuyler Crosby, ventured on one of these expeditions. Churchill, *The Upper Crust,* p. 167.

132 Van Rensselaer, *Social Ladder,* pp. 177, 219.

133 David Black, *The King of Fifth Avenue: The Fortunes of August Belmont* (New York: Dial Press, 1981), p. 284; Robert McElroy, *Levi Parsons Morton: Banker, Diplomat and Statesman* (New York: G. P. Putnam's Sons, 1930), p. 167

134 Roy Rosenzweig and Elizabeth Blackmar, *The Park and the People, A History of Central Park* (Ithaca, N.Y.: Cornell University Press, 1992), p. 212.

135 Rosenzweig and Blackmar, *The Park and the People,* p. 216.

136 Churchill, *The Upper Crust,* pp. 162, 165; Black, *The King of Fifth Avenue,* p. 284.

137 *NYT,* 2 June 1872, p. 8.

138 Black, *The King of Fifth Avenue,* p. 289.

139 Pierre Bourdieu, *Distinction: A Social Critique of the Judgment of Taste* (Cambridge, Mass.: Harvard University Press, 1984), p. 55.

140 Quoted in James A. Rawley, *Edwin D. Morgan, 1811–1883: Merchant in Politics* (New York: Columbia University Press, 1955), p. 265.

141 Rawley, *Edwin D. Morgan, 1811–1883,* p. 265. The items were sold for $79,013.

142 Churchill, *The Upper Crust,* p. 122.

143 Churchill, *The Upper Crust,* p. 150.

144 Josephson, *The Robber Baron,* p. 345.

145 Montgomery, *"Gilded Prostitution,"* passim.

146 Ruth Brandon, *The Dollar Princesses: Sagas of Upward Nobility, 1870–1914* (New York: Knopf, 1980), p. 1.

147 MacColl and Wallace, *To Marry an English Lord,* p. 39.

148 MacColl and Wallace, *To Marry an English Lord,* p. 44.

149 In a European context it has been argued that the "aristocratization" of the bourgeoisie was a sign of its weakness. See, for example, Hans Ulrich Wehler, *Das Deutsche Kaiserreich, 1871–1918* (Göttingen: Vandenhoeck &

Ruprecht, 1980), esp. pp. 129ff; G. N. Izenberg, "Die 'Aristokratisierung' der bürgerlichen Kultur im 19. Jahrhundert," in P. U. Hohendahl and P. M. Lützeler, eds., *Legitimationskrisen des deutschen Adels* (Stuttgart: Metzler-sche Verlagsbuchhandlung, 1979): 233–244. The case of New York, however, shows that the appropriation of cultural norms of another elite is first and foremost a sign of the strength and historical confidence of the bourgeoisie.

150 Katherine C. Grier, "The Decline of the Memory Palace: The Parlor After 1880," in Jessica H. Foy and Thomas J. Schlereth, eds., *American Home Life, 1880–1930: A Social History of Spaces and Services* (Knoxville: The University of Tennessee Press, 1992), p. 59.

151 Arnold Lewis, James Truner, and Steven McQuillin, *The Opulent Interiors of the Gilded Age* (New York: Dover Publications, 1987), p. 28; *American Architect and Building News* (9 August 1884), p. 63.

152 Elan Zingman-Leith and Susan Zingman-Leith, *The Secret Life of Victorian Houses* (Washington, D.C.: Elliott & Clark Publishing, 1993), p. 35; Katherine C. Grier, *Culture and Comfort: People, Parlors, and Upholstery, 1850–1930* (Amherst, Mass.: University of Massachusetts Press, 1988), p. 81.

153 *Scribner's Monthly* 11 (February 1876), p. 503.

154 Lewis, Truner, and McQuillin, *The Opulent Interiors of the Gilded Age,* p. 27.

155 L. Marcotte & Co. to Bradley Martin, bill, April 2, 1883, Isaac Sherman Papers, Huntington Library.

156 Bourdieu, *Distinction,* p. 71.

157 Grier, *Culture and Comfort,* p. 13.

158 Churchill, *The Upper Crust,* p. 184.

159 See also Susan Williams, *Savory Suppers and Fashionable Feasts: Dining in Victorian America* (New York: Pantheon Books, 1985), pp. 7, 17, 21, 37; Lewis, Truner, and McQuillin, *The Opulent Interiors of the Gilded Age,* p. 9.

160 *Proceedings of the First Convention of the United Typothetae of America Held in Chicago, Ill., October 18th, 19th and 20th, 1887* (Richmond, Va.: Everett Waddey Co., 1887), p. 339; *Eighty-first Anniversary Celebration of the New-England Society in the City of New York at Delmonico's, December 22, 1886* (New York: Wm. C. Bryant & Co., 1886), pp. 18–19; *IA* (27 February 1896): 551.

161 Williams, *Savory Suppers and Fashionable Feasts,* p. 46.

162 The classic statement here is by Thorsten Veblen, *The Theory of the Leisure Class: An Economic Study in the Evolution of Institutions* (New York: The Macmillan Company, 1899), pp. 81–83. The quote is from Rosenzweig and Blackmar, *The Park and the People,* p. 220.

163 Beisel, *Imperiled Innocents,* p. 13.

164 Montgomery, *"Gilded Prostitution,"* pp. 51–52, 64.

165 Nevins, *Study in Power: John D. Rockefeller,* p. 88.

166 O'Connor, *The Guggenheims,* p. 70.

167 *A Handbook of the Best Private Schools of The United States and Canada* (Boston: Porter E. Sargent, 1915), pp. 120–123. See also Baltzell, *Philadelphia Gentlemen,* pp. 293, 296.

168 Van Rensselaer, *Social Ladder,* p. 16.

169 Nevins, *Study in Power: John D. Rockefeller,* vol. 2, pp. 85–86, 91.

170 Letter by Joseph Choate to his son George, Stockbridge, July 21, 1882. Reprinted in Edward Sanford Martin, *The Life of Joseph Hodges Choate,* vol. 1, p. 354.

171 Nicola Beisel, "Upper Class Formation and the Politics of Censorship in Boston, New York, and Philadelphia, 1872–1892" (Ph.D. diss., University of Michigan, Ann Arbor, 1990), p. 2. See also Chernow, *The House of Morgan,* p. 38. J. Pierpont Morgan also supported the YMCA and revival meetings.

172 Beisel, *Imperiled Innocents,* pp. 9, 51; Beisel, "Upper Class Formation," p. 81.

173 Townsend, *Mother of Clubs,* p. 72.

174 *Galaxy Magazine* 22 (August 1876): 231.

175 On the importance of institution building to class formation in late nine-teenth-century America, see William G. Roy, "Institutional Governance and Social Cohesion: The Internal Organization of the American Capitalist Class, 1886–1905," in Donald J. Treiman and Robert V. Robinson, eds., *Research in Social Stratification and Mobility* (Greenwich, Conn.: JAI Press, 1984), vol. 3, pp. 147–171. He concludes from an analysis of the associational ties of 778 officers and directors of corporations, as well as owners and partners of nonincorporated firms, that the years between 1886 and 1905 were decades of "class formation," during which "the emerging corporate class segment adopted a strategy of class cohesion as the first priority" (p. 162). Because Roy's perspective is limited to relatively few years and his evidence focused on his quantitative analysis, he fails to note how the older merchant families joined into the associational networks of the "corporate segment." Starting one's analysis from the associations themselves, instead of from a list of corporation officers and proprietors, it is striking to note how much these organizations integrated not only the corporate segment of the nation's bour-geoisie but also older mercantile elites.

176 See Hall, ed., *America's Successful Men.*

177 See Hall, ed., *America's Successful Men.*

178 Of those people whose club affiliation could be identified, 77 were members of the Union Club, 69 of the Knickerbocker Club, 62 of the Country Club, 17 of the Union League, and 10 of the Century Club. For the names, see "List of Young People Invited to Mrs. Havemeyer's Dance, February 2, 1891," "Misc. Manuscripts, Mrs. Theo A. Havemeyer, 1891," NYHS. Of 301 guests invited to the dance, 230 could be clearly identified. Of these 230 guests, 64 were not listed in the *Social Register;* 38 others were listed in the *Social Register,* though without club affiliations. See *Social Register New York,* No. 6 (New York: Social Register Association, 1892). For 128 guests of Mrs. Havemeyer, club affiliations were found in the New York *Social Register.*

179 In contrast to what David Hammack has argued. Hammack, *Power and Soci-ety,* p. 75.

180 Henry Collins Brown, *Delmonico's: A Story of Old New York* (New York: Valentine's Manual, 1928), p. 59.

181 *The Season – An Annual Record of Society in New York, Brooklyn, and Vicinity, First Year, 1882–1883* (New York: White, Stokes, & Allen, 1883), p. 9. Social life and social institutions did not, as David Hammack has

argued, sharply set apart families who emphasized "wealth," "ancestry," or "culture." Hammack, *Power and Society*, pp. 72–77.

182 The larger theoretical implications of this point are drawn out by Bourdieu, *Distinction*, esp. p. 23. See also Goblot, *La Barrière et le Niveau*, p. 11.

183 For a statement of purpose, see *The Season – An Annual Record of Society in New York, Brooklyn, and Vicinity, First Year, 1882–1883*, p. 5.

184 Churchill, *The Upper Crust*, p. 157; Social Register Association, *Social Register, New York, 1886–1900* (New York: Social Register Association, 1886–1900).

185 *Eighty-First Anniversary Celebration of the New-England Society in the City of New York at Delmonico's, December 22, 1886; One Hundred Years, 1852–1952: The Harmonie Club* (New York: The Harmonie Club, 1952), p. 20.

186 *The Season – An Annual Record of Society in New York, Brooklyn, and Vicinity, First Year, 1882–1883*, p. 276.

187 See also T. Jackson Lears, *No Place of Grace: Antimodernism and the Transformation of American Culture* (1981; reprint Chicago: University of Chicago Press, 1994), p. 108.

188 Hammack, *Power and Society*, pp. 66–67; Baltzell, *Philadelphia Gentlemen*, p. 285. For an account of upper-class anti-Semitism (at Bryn Mawr College), see also Helen Lefkowitz Horowitz, *The Power and Passion of M. Carey Thomas* (New York: Knopf, 1994), pp. 230–231. For the social clubs considered by the *Social Register* as sufficiently select, see the Social Register Association, *New York Social Register 1900*, vol. 14 (New York: Social Register Association, 1900).

189 For a comparative assessment of anti-Semitism in Europe and the United States, see Frederic Cople Jaher, *A Scapegoat in the New Wilderness: The Origins and Rise of Anti-Semitism in America* (Cambridge, Mass.: Harvard University Press, 1994), pp. 1, 5, 6, 8, 9, 181, 204, 243. The quotation is on page 9.

190 The possibility of a positive relationship between ethnic and religious identities and working-class identities has long been established. The same is true for bourgeois identities.

191 See also Barry E. Supple, "A Business Elite: German-Jewish Financiers in Nineteenth-Century New York," in *Business History Review* 31 (Summer 1957): 166.

192 *The Season – An Annual Record of Society in New York, Brooklyn, and Vicinity, First Year, 1882–1883*, p. 276.

193 *The Season – An Annual Record of Society in New York, Brooklyn, and Vicinity, First Year, 1882–1883*, p. 239.

194 *Proceedings at the Mass Meeting of Citizens in the Cooper Institute, New York, Tuesday Evening, March 24, 1874 on National Finances* (New York: Comes, Lawrence & Co., 1874), pp. 5–9.

195 See *Hardware Club of New York, April, 1897*, pp. 31–94; *Proceedings at the First Annual Dinner of the Republican Club of the City of New York, Held at Delmonico's, February 12, 1887* (New York: Mercantile Printing and Stationary Co., 1887), pp. 73–79. This aspect is also emphasized by Supple, "A Business Elite," p. 166.

196 Lawrence A. Clayton, *Grace: W. R. Grace & Co., The Formative Years, 1850–1930* (Ottawa: Jameson Books, 1985), p. 83.

197 For a more detailed discussion of this process see also Sven Beckert, "Die Kultur des Kapitals," in Warburg-Haus, ed., *Vorträge aus dem Warburg-Haus* 4 (Berlin: Akademie-Verlag, 2000), pp. 139–173.

198 For a brilliant analysis of Boston's cultural history and its relationship to bourgeois class formation, see Paul DiMaggio, "Cultural Entrepreneurship in Nineteenth-Century Boston: The Creation of an Organizational Base of High Culture in America," in *Media, Culture and Society* (1982): 33–50. For a discussion of the emergence of stratified cultural spheres in the course of the nineteenth century, see Lawrence W. Levine, *Highbrow, Lowbrow: The Emergence of Cultural Hierarchy in America* (Cambridge, Mass.: Harvard University Press, 1988), especially pp. 17, 208, 231.

199 Chernow, *The House of Morgan*, pp. 50–51. For the division of high and low culture, see Levine, *Highbrow, Lowbrow*, passim.

200 On Riggs, see "Note on William Riggs," Box 118, Riggs Family Papers, Library of Congress. Bourgeois New Yorkers dominated among the museum's visitors. See *NYT*, 26 May 1872, p. 4.

201 This argument, in reference to Boston, has also been made by Paul DiMaggio, "Cultural Entrepreneurship in Nineteenth-Century Boston," in Paul DiMaggio, ed., *Nonprofit Enterprise in the Arts* (New Haven: Yale University Press, 1986), pp. 33–50. The classification of art, argues Pierre Bourdieu, is the "forgotten dimension of the class struggle." Bourdieu, *Distinction*, p. 483.

202 Quoted in Tompkins, *Merchants and Masterpieces*, p. 75. See also Tompkins, *Merchants and Masterpieces*, pp. 17, 30, 47, 68, 73, 78.

203 For a list of trustees of the Metropolitan Museum, see Tompkins, *Merchants and Masterpieces*, pp. 395–399. See also Jaher, *The Urban Establishment*, p. 270; Rosenzweig and Blackmar, *The Park and the People*, pp. 357–358. Joseph Choate is quoted in Tompkins, *Merchants and Masterpieces*, p. 23.

204 I disagree here with Beisel, *Imperiled Innocents*, p. 194; Jaher, *The Urban Establishment*, pp. 270–271. For members of the NYHS, see *The Charter and By-Laws of the New-York Historical Society, With a List of Members* (New York: Printed for the Society, 1862, 1875); "Resident Members of the New-York Historical Society," (March 1866, March 1884, January 1892, February 1895, February 1904), NYHS.

205 Henry Edward Krehbiel, *The Philharmonic Society of New York* (New York and London: Novello, Ewer & Co., 1892), p. 7.

206 Krehbiel, *The Philharmonic Society of New York*, p. 83.

207 Krehbiel, *The Philharmonic Society of New York*, pp. 16, 28.

208 Krehbiel, *The Philharmonic Society of New York*, pp. 168–169.

209 Krehbiel, *The Philharmonic Society of New York*, pp. 59–60.

210 Krehbiel, *The Philharmonic Society of New York*, pp. 68, 175–176.

211 Krehbiel, *The Philharmonic Society of New York*, pp. 177–183.

212 M. J. Heale, *American Anti-Communism: Combating the Enemy Within 1830–1970* (Baltimore: Johns Hopkins University Press, 1990), p. 36;

Michael Wallace, "Visiting the Past: History Museums in the United States," in Susan Porter Benson, Stephen Brier, and Roy Rosenzweig, eds., *Presenting the Past: Essays on History and the Public* (Philadelphia: Temple University Press, 1986), p. 140.

213   "Genealogy of the Morton Family," Box 8, Levi Parsons Morton Papers, NYPL; *Memoir of the Gibbs Family of Warwickshire, England and United States of America* (Philadelphia: Press of Lewis & Greene, 1879); "Genealogy," Box 2, Astor Family Papers, Manuscript Division, NYPL, Astor, Lenox, and Tilden Foundations; "Diverse Genealogical Research," Box 2, Supplemental, Belknap Family Papers, NYHS.

214   Wallace, "Visiting the Past," p. 141.

215   New York Genealogical and Biographical Society, *Twenty-Fifth Anniversary, February 27, 1864* (New York: T. A. Wright, 1895), pp. 10, 23.

216   Sherman to [illegible], August 19, 1878, Isaac Sherman Papers, Huntington Library.

217   *NYH,* 21 April 1871, p. 6; Donna Haraway, *Primate Visions, Gender, Race, and Nature in the World of Modern Science* (New York: Routledge, 1989), p. 56; John Michael Kennedy, "Philanthropy and Science in New York City, The American Museum of Natural History, 1868–1968" (Ph.D. diss., Yale University, 1968), pp. 13, 38.

9. The Rights of Labor, The Rights of Property

1   Robert Wiebe, *Self-Rule: A Cultural History of American Democracy* (Chicago: University of Chicago Press, 1995), pp. 122–123.

2   See *IA* (23 November 1893): 932f. See also *CFC* 59 (14 July 1894): 44.

3   *IA* (12 March 1896): 652.

4   *Nation* (6 May 1886): 376.

5   Among many others, see Moses Bruhl, *Our Finances: A Plan for Building up the Country's Credit and to Conciliate Capital and Labor* (New York: n.p. 1898); John Stolze, *The Wage-Workers of America and the Relation of Capital to Labor* (Reading, Pa.: Eagle Book and Job Print, 1893); John Vernon, *Labor, Capital and a Protective Tariff* (Chicago: Rand, McNally & Company, 1888); Robert Ellis Thompson, *The Duty of the Church in the Conflict Between Capital and Labor* (Philadelphia: Presbyterian Board of Publication, 1887); John Philip Phillips, *Social Struggles: The Fundamental Facts and Principles Relative to Values, Prices, Money and Interest: National Banks, Franchises, the Silver Question, Socialism, Capital and Labor, and Business Derangement* (New Haven: Tuttle, Morehouse & Taylor, 1888).

6   See testimony of Charles Lenz, editor of *Capital and Labor* on August 15, 1883, before the Senate Committee on Education and Labor. See U.S. Senate Committee on Education and Labor, *Report of the Committee of the Senate Upon the Relations Between Labor and Capital, and Testimony Taken by the Committee* (Washington, D.C.: GPO, 1885), vol. 1, p. 237.

7   *NYT,* 2 November 1886, p. 4.

8   See, for example, David Montgomery, *The Fall of the House of Labor: The*

Workplace, the State, and American Labor Activism, 1865–1925 (New York: Cambridge University Press, 1987), p. 121.

9 Harvey O'Connor, *The Guggenheims: The Making of an American Dynasty* (New York: Covici, Friede, 1937), pp. 56–57. Guggenheim relied eventually on the deployment of light cavalry against his striking employees, teaching him and others once more that, in the end, it was the power of the state that guaranteed their property rights.

10 Eric Foner and John A. Garraty, *The Reader's Companion to American History* (New York: Houghton Mifflin, 1991), p. 632.

11 Sidney Harring, *Policing a Class Society: The Experience of American Cities, 1865–1915* (New Brunswick, N.J.: Rutgers University Press, 1983), p. 102.

12 P. K. Edwards, *Strikes in the United States, 1881–1974* (New York: St. Martin's Press, 1981), p. 94.

13 William Steinway diary, November 14, 1878; September 11, 1879; February 12–March 26, 1880; October 23–November 22, 1882; May 3–May 9, 1886, Steinway Papers, NYHS.

14 Steinway diary, March 15, 1880, Steinway Papers, NYHS.

15 Steinway diary, October 23, 1882, Steinway Papers, NYHS.

16 Steinway diary, November 10, 1882, Steinway Papers, NYHS.

17 As quoted in Richard K. Lieberman, *Steinway & Sons* (New Haven: Yale University Press, 1995), pp. 94–95.

18 Steinway diary, May 1, 1886, Steinway Papers, NYHS.

19 Steinway diary, October 24, 1882, Steinway Papers, NYHS.

20 *Report of the Committee of the Senate Upon the Relations Between Labor and Capital*, vol. 2, p. 1086. Testimony by William Steinway.

21 *Report of the Committee of the Senate Upon the Relations Between Labor and Capital*, vol. 1, p. 255.

22 *Report of the Committee of the Senate Upon the Relations Between Labor and Capital*, vol. 1, p. 1013. Testimony by John Roach.

23 *NYT*, 7 August 1878, p. 2.

24 Allan Nevins, ed., *Selected Writings of Abram S. Hewitt* (New York: Columbia University Press, 1937), pp. 409–419, especially p. 412; *NYT*, 2 August–29 August 1878. On Hewitt's hopes for cooperation in the future, see Abram S. Hewitt, "Speech at the Church Congress, Cincinnati, October 18, 1878," reprinted in Nevins, *Selected Writings of Abram S. Hewitt*, p. 277–289. Hewitt himself turned against strikers when walkouts in his own factory occurred in 1902.

25 *Proceedings, Second Annual Meeting of the United Typothetae of America, Held on September 18, 19 and 20, 1888 in New York* (New York: Lockwood Press, 1888), p. 12.

26 See, for example, Leon Fink, *Workingmen's Democracy: The Knights of Labor and American Politics* (Urbana: University of Illinois Press, 1983).

27 *Nation* (13 May 1886): 392; *Nation* (22 April 1886): 330; Steinway diary, April and May 1886, Steinway Papers, NYHS; Sarah M. Henry, "The Strikers and their Sympathizers: Brooklyn in the Trolley Strike of 1895," in *Labor History* 32 (Summer 1991): 331.

28 *Twenty-Eighth Annual Report of the Corporation of the Chamber of Com-*

merce of the State of New-York for the Year 1885–86 (New York: Press of the Chamber of Commerce, 1886), p. 117.

29 *Twenty-Eighth Annual Report of the Corporation of the Chamber of Commerce*, p. 119.

30 *NYT*, 14 May 1886, p. 3.

31 T. Jackson Lears, *No Place of Grace, Anti-Modernism and the Transformation of American Culture, 1880–1920* (1981; reprint Chicago: Chicago University Press, 1994), p. 29.

32 *CFC* 45 (8 October 1887): 459; David Scobey, "Boycotting the Politics Factory: Labor Radicalism and the New York City Mayoral Election of 1886," in *RHR* 28–30 (1984): 282, 295.

33 The best treatment of the Knights' entry into politics is Fink, *Workingmen's Democracy.*

34 Martin Shefter, "The Electoral Foundations of City Machines: New York City, 1884–1897," in Joel Silbey, Allan Bogue, and William Flanigan, eds., *The History of American Electoral Behavior* (Princeton: Princeton University Press, 1978), p. 290; Scobey, "Boycotting the Politics Factory," pp. 282, 283.

35 On the breadth of support for George, see David Hammack, *Power and Society: Greater New York at the Turn of the Century* (New York: Russell Sage Foundation, 1982), pp. 174–175. On the affinities between the lower middle classes and George, see also the forthcoming work by Robert Johnston, "The Radical Middle Class: Popular Democracy and Anti-Capitalism in Progressive Era Portland, Oregon" (unpublished manuscript, in author's possession).

36 Roy Rosenzweig and Elizabeth Blackmar, *The Park and the People: A History of Central Park* (Ithaca, N.Y.: Cornell University Press, 1992), p. 286.

37 For the crisis of legitimacy see also Mary O. Furner, "The Republican Tradition and the New Liberalism: Social Investigation, State Building, and Social Learning in the Gilded Age," in Mary O. Furner and Michael Lacey, eds., *The State and Social Investigation in Britain and the United States* (Washington, D.C.: Woodrow Wilson Center Press, 1993), p. 201; Stephen Skowronek, *Building a New American State: The Expansion of National Administrative Capacities, 1877–1920* (New York: Cambridge University Press, 1982), p. 165.

38 *NYT*, 4 November 1886, p. 4; see also *NYDT*, 22 October 1886, p. 4.

39 *CFC* 42 (30 October 1886): 517.

40 *Bradstreet's* 14 (6 November 1886): 1.

41 "Resolution of Union League Club," reprinted in *NYDT*, 22 October 1886, p. 1.

42 J. Bleecker Miller, *Progress and Robbery and Progress and Justice: An Answer to Henry George, The Demi-Communist* (New York: The Baker & Taylor Co., 1887), p. 6.

43 *HW* (30 October 1886): 694.

44 *Nation* (30 September 1886): 265. See also *Nation* (14 October 1886): 300.

45 Samuel Barlow to Doyle, October 27, 1886, "Letterbooks," Barlow Papers, BW 1, Huntington Library. See also Samuel Barlow to [illegible], New York City, October 25, 1886, "Letterbooks," Barlow Papers.

46 *NYH*, 28 October 1886, p. 4; *NYH*, 30 October 1886, p. 3; *NYT*, 22 October 1886, p. 1; Steinway diary, October 29, 1886, Steinway Papers, NYHS.

47 See Scobey, "Boycotting the Politics Factory," p. 285; Hammack, *Power and Society*, p. 135; Nevins, *Selected Writings of Abram S. Hewitt*, p. 461; Condon, "Politics, Reform and the New York City Election of 1886," in *NYHSQ* 44 (1966): 378; *NYH*, 9 October 1886, p. 4.

48 *Nation* (4 November 1886): 361.

49 Scobey, "Boycotting the Politics Factory," p. 284; Condon, "Politics, Reform and the New York City Election of 1886," p. 382; *Nation* (11 November 1886): 386.

50 Hammack, *Power and Society*, p. 137.

51 W. R. Grace to Abram Hewitt, November 3, 1886, "Private Letterbook 11, 1886–1887," Box 64, W. R. Grace and Company Papers, Rare Books and Manuscript Library, Columbia University.

52 W. R. Grace to President Grover Cleveland, November 3, 1886, "Private Letterbook 11, 1886–1887," Box 64, W. R. Grace and Company Papers, Rare Books and Manuscript Library, Columbia University.

53 Miller, *Progress and Robbery*, p. 53.

54 The "mood of panic among the 'comfortable classes'" is also invoked by Walter Dean Burnham, "The System of 1896: An Analysis," in Paul Kleppner et al., eds., *The Evolution of American Electoral Systems* (Westport, Conn.: Greenwood Press, 1981), p. 162.

55 *CFC* 41 (21 November 1885): 575.

56 *IA* (22 July 1880): 14.

57 See, for example, the long discussion on labor in *IA* (21 July 1892): 110f, which does not discuss social mobility or mutuality of interests in the old free-labor sense.

58 *IA* (21 July 1886): 110; *Report of the Committee of the Senate Upon the Relations Between Labor and Capital*, vol. 2, p. 1071. Testimony by Danford Knowlton.

59 *IA* (2 February 1893): 251.

60 Elliot C. Cowdin, *Capital and Labor: An Address Delivered Before the American Institute of the City of New York, In Celebration of Its Semi-Centennial Anniversary, on Thursday Evening, October 11, 1877* (New York: Printed for the Institute, 1877), p. 12.

61 Cowdin, *Capital and Labor*, p. 14.

62 William Forbath, *Law and the Shaping of the American Labor Movement* (Cambridge, Mass.: Harvard University Press, 1991), p. 129; *Twenty-Eighth Annual Report of the Corporation of the Chamber of Commerce of the State of New York for the Year 1885–1886*, p. xxiii.

63 *IA* (7 September 1882): 21; Mary H. Blewett, *Men, Women, and Work: Class, Gender, and Protest in the New England Shoe Industry, 1780–1910* (Urbana: University of Illinois Press, 1988), p. 166.

64 *Nation* (2 September 1886): 191.

65 Joseph Frazier Wall, *Andrew Carnegie* (New York: Oxford University Press, 1970), p. 379f.

66 *Farm and Fireside*, 6 January 1917.

67 See Clyde Ferguson, "The Political and Social Ideas of John D. Rockefeller and Andrew Carnegie: A Study of Conservatism" (Ph.D. diss., University of

Illinois, Urbana, 1951), pp. 1–6. This hostility to unions was partly the result of the competitive disadvantages any firm which did negotiate with trade unions experienced. This also accounts for the fact that some employers preferred an industry-wide organization. See, for example, the testimony of Thomas M. Miller, general manger of the Pittsburgh Atlas Works before the Senate Committee on Education and Labor. *Report of the Committee of the Senate Upon the Relations Between Labor and Capital,* vol. 2, p. 20.

68 As summarized by James Livingston, *Origins of the Federal Reserve System* (Ithaca, N.Y.: Cornell University Press, 1986), p. 53.

69 *IA* (1 June 1882): 15.

70 See, for example, *Report of the Committee of the Senate Upon the Relations Between Labor and Capital,* vol. 1, p. 1080. Testimony by Jay Gould.

71 *IA* (21 July 1892): 110; *IA* (16 September 1886): 17.

72 See, for example, Edwards, *Strikes in the United States,* p. 238. See also Sanford Jacoby, "American Exceptionalism Revisted," in Sanford Jacoby, ed., *Masters to Managers: Historical and Comparative Perspectives on American Employers* (New York: Columbia University Press, 1991), p. 187; Gerald Friedman, "The State and the Making of the Working Class: France and the United States, 1880–1914," in *Theory and Society* 17 (1988): 416. See also Colin Gordon, "Why No Corporatism in the United States? Business Disorganization and its Consequences" (paper presented at the Business History Conference, College Park, Md., 1998), p. 9.

73 For such statements see also *Manufacturer and Builder* 10 (July 1875): 154; *Manufacturer and Builder* 10 (July 1875): 16.

74 *IA* (24 August 1882): 14.

75 *IA* (24 March 1882): 14.

76 *Report of the Committee of the Senate Upon the Relations Between Labor and Capital,* vol. 1, p. 1090. Testimony by Jay Gould.

77 *IA* (23 March 1882): 14.

78 *NYT,* 15 July 1892, p. 4.

79 Cowdin, *Capital and Labor,* p. 16. For a similar argument see *Manufacturer and Builder* 12 (April 1880): 90.

80 *Twenty-Eighth Annual Report of the Corporation of the Chamber of Commerce,* p. 118. Of the 57 people who signed the letter to call the meeting, 39 were identified in the city directory, of whom 14 were listed as dry goods merchants. Another 12 were merchants who seem to have engaged in trading dry goods. The others were listed as "president," "manager," "woolens," "broker," "coal," and "treasurer." It is interesting to note that only one banker and no lawyers were present at the meeting. See also *Manufacturer and Builder* 18 (May 1886), p. 98.

81 *IA* (21 July 1892): 110.

82 *IA* (29 August 1895): 433. Similar arguments were made in the context of the 1892 Homestead conflict. See *NYDT,* 9 July 1892, p. 6; *NYDT,* 13 July 1892, p. 6.

83 *NYT,* 7 July 1892, p. 4. For the theme of the "laws of supply and demand," see also *CFC* 30 (28 July 1877): 73; *NYDT,* 24 July 1877, p. 4; *NYT,* 9 April 1877, p. 4; *Nation* (9 August 1877): 85.

84 *IA* (21 July 1892): 111.

85 *IA* (21 July 1892): 111. For a discussion of what iron manufacturers saw as the appropriate sphere of action for trade unions see also *IA* (25 August 1892): 335.

86 *IA* (12 March 1896): 652; *IA* (7 September 1882): 21.

87 *Nation* (11 August 1892): 99.

88 *NYDT,* 23 July 1877, p. 4; *NYT,* 24 July 1877, p. 4; *Nation* (30 August 1877): 13; *Nation* (2 August 1877): 68; see also Herbert G. Gutman, "The Tompkins Square 'Riot' in New York City on January 13, 1874: A Re-examination of Its Causes and Its Aftermath," in *Labor History* 6 (Winter 1965), pp. 68–69; *IA* (26 July 1877): 15.

89 *IA* (22 April 1886): 14.

90 *IA* (29 August 1886): 15.

91 *Report of the Committee of the Senate Upon the Relations Between Labor and Capital,* vol. 1, p. 238. Testimony by Charles Lens.

92 Similarly, Philip Scranton argues that the textile manufacturers of Philadelphia felt "extreme antagonism" toward the Knights because they violated the culture of the proprietary workshop. Philip Scranton, *Proprietary Capitalism: The Textile Manufacture at Philadelphia, 1800–1885* (New York: Cambridge University Press, 1983), p. 389.

93 *IA* (4 March 1880): 14. See also *IA* (6 May 1880): 15; *IA* (1 April 1880): 3; *IA* (10 June 1880): 14; *IA* (4 December 1884): 22; *IA* (1 April 1886): 29. See also *SciAm* (2 October 1880): 208, which asserts that "American working-men . . . are better behaved" than their European counterparts. *CFC* 34 (8 April 1882): 389. See also *CFC* 41 (21 November 1885): 576. The *Manufacturer and Builder* editorialized that "cooperation between capital and labor must . . . take the place of competition in this country, or social anarchy is inevitable." *Manufacturer and Builder* 10 (July 1876): 190.

94 *Report of the Committee of the Senate Upon the Relations Between Labor and Capital,* vol. 2, p. 1085. Testimony by William Steinway.

95 *IA* (13 February 1896): 441; *IA* (1 February 1894): 210. Paternalism as an antiunion strategy is also discussed in *SciAm* (25 August 1883): 116.

96 *Report of the Committee of the Senate Upon the Relations Between Labor and Capital,* vol. 2, p. 896. Testimony by Henry Bischoff.

97 *Report of the Committee of the Senate Upon the Relations Between Labor and Capital,* vol. 1, p. 1004. John Roach.

98 Quoted in *IA* (3 February 1893): 245.

99 William Graham Sumner, *What Social Classes Owe to Each Other* (New York: Harper & Brothers, 1883), p. 85.

100 See, for example, *IA* (25 May 1893): 1179; *IA* (16 February 1893): 371. See *NYT,* 15 May 1886, p. 2; *NYT,* 14 May 1886, p. 3; M. J. Heale, *American Anti-Communism: Combating the Enemy Within, 1830–1970* (Baltimore: Johns Hopkins University Press, 1990), p. 29; *HW* (15 May 1886): title page; *Nation* (22 April 1886): 330.

101 See, for example, a letter to the editor of *IA* by "B.D.," referring to "Italians, Poles, and other common laborers" as "Europe's worst element" and as "labor pests." *IA* (19 October 1893): 711.

102 See, among others, *Shoe and Leather Reporter* (16 December 1880): 1046, from which the quote is taken; also *SciAm* (20 November 1880): 329.

103 *CFC* 35 (19 August 1882): 201. Similarly, *CFC* 36 (21 July 1883): 63; *CFC* 44 (28 May 1887): 669.

104 *CFC* 44 (28 May 1887): 669.

105 *CFC* 48 (2 February 1889): 142–143.

106 *CFC* 55 (30 July 1892): 163.

107 *IA* (12 May 1892): 928; *IA* (12 January 1893).

108 Especially during the 1890s, in the wake of Homestead and Coxey's Army, the *CFC* voiced increasing concern about labor. *CFC* 58 (5 May 1894): 753; *CFC* 58 (19 May 1894): 836.

109 *JOC*, 15 August 1883.

110 *CFC* 51 (16 August 1890): 185.

111 *CFC* 48 (15 June 1889): 780.

112 Leon Fink also emphasizes the "growing ideological conservatism of America's industrialists and their steady merger into older socioeconomic elites." See Fink, *Workingmen's Democracy*, p. 3.

113 Robert McCloskey, *American Conservatism in the Age of Enterprise: A Study of William Graham Sumner, Stephen J. Field, and Andrew Carnegie* (Cambridge, Mass.: Harvard University Press, 1951), pp. 160–161.

114 *CFC* 45 (8 October 1887): 459.

115 See, among others, *HW* (16 July 1892): 674–675.

116 *IA* (29 April 1886): 16.

117 *IA* (12 July 1894): 64. Pullman's factory and town were held up as "exemplifications of practical philanthropy based upon business sagacity," which is why the shock about the strike was that much greater. See *SciAm* (23 July 1881): 52.

118 *CFC* 41 (1 August 1885): 118. Beginning in the late 1880s, the journal reported frequently and with great enthusiasm of court cases that served to contain the rights of labor. See *CFC* 44 (5 March 1887): 288; *CFC* 45 (8 October 1887): 458.

119 *Manufacturer and Builder* 24 (July 1892): 161.

120 *CFC* 48 (15 June 1889): 781. See also *CFC* 56 (8 April 1893): 560.

121 Steinway diary, November 12 and November 15, 1882, Steinway Papers, NYHS; see Forbath, *Law and the Shaping of the American Labor Movement*, p. 61; *IA* (29 July 1884): 14.

122 *CFC* 55 (20 August 1892): 272, 276.

123 James D. Horan, *The Pinkertons: The Detective Dynasty That Made History* (New York: Crown Publishers, 1967), p. 329.

124 *Pinkerton's National Detective Agency, And its Connection with The Labor Troubles at Homestead, Penn, July 6, 1892* (New York: n.p., 1893), pp. 1, 25. *IA* (February 16, 1893), p. 371. For a similar argument see *Manufacturer and Builder* 24 (July 1892): 161.

125 *Proceedings at the First Annual Dinner of the Republican Club of the City of New York, Held at Delmonico's, February 12, 1887* (New York: Mercantile Printing and Stationary Co., 1887), p. 7.

126 William Dodge, *Old New York: A Lecture Delivered at Association Hall,*

April 27th, 1880, Upon the Invitation of Merchants and Other Citizens of New York (New York: Dodd, Mead & Co., 1880), pp. 56–58.

127 *CFC* 38 (7 June 1884): 657.

128 E. L. Godkin, "Criminal Politics," in *North American Review* 150 (June 1890): 719.

129 *IA* (29 April 1886), p. 16.

130 *CFC* 51 (15 November 1890): 658.

131 *CFC* 45 (20 August 1887): 228.

132 *Official Report, First Annual Convention of the National Association of Builders of the United States of America, Held at Chicago, Illinois, March 29, 30th and 31st, 1887* (Boston: Press of Rockwell and Churchill, 1887), pp. 23–24.

133 John Bleecker Miller, *Trade, Professional, and Property-Owners' Organizations in Public Affairs* (New York: H. Cherouny, 1884), pp. 5, 45. See also *IA* (28 December 1882): 14. See also Claus Offe, "Two Logics of Collective Action," in *Disorganized Capitalism: Contemporary Transformations of Work and Politics* (Cambridge, Mass.: MIT Press, 1985), pp. 170–220.

134 On the American Brewers' Association see *SciAm* (19 June 1880): 384.

135 *National Bottlers' Gazette* (1 March 1886): 15; *Shoe and Leather Reporter* (23 November 1886): 902; Miller, *Trade, Professional, and Property-Owners' Organizations in Public Affairs*, p. 42.

136 Malon, "The Growth of Manufacturing," p. 370.

137 *IA* (15 September 1892): 499; *NYT,* 1 June 1894, p. 8; *IA* (27 February 1896): 551. The membership statistics are as of 1897. *Hardware Club of New York, April, 1897* (New York: n.p., 1897), p. 95.

138 Clarence E. Bonnett, *History of Employers' Associations in the United States* (New York: Vintage Press, 1957), p. 112; Clarence E. Bonnett, *Employers' Associations in the United States: A Study of Typical Associations* (New York: The Macmillian Co., 1922).

139 Bonnett, *History of Employers' Associations in the United States,* pp. 119, 153.

140 See *IA* (24 May 1894): 1012; *IA* (19 April 1894): 774; *IA* (22 March 1894): 571. The Manufacturers' Association of Kings and Queens Counties modeled themselves after the Manufacturers' Club of Philadelphia. See *IA* (8 March 1894): 477. About 130 manufacturers attended its March 1894 meeting. The information on employers' associations is derived from Bonnett, *History of Employers' Associations in the United States.* The Foundrymen's Association in 1893 also called upon employer organizations to unite. See *IA* (15 June 1893): 1340.

141 *IA* (7 June 1888): 929. They organized against "union dictation." See *IA* (5 April 1888): 569.

142 *Report of the First National Convention of Carriage-Builders of the United States, Held at the St. Nicholas Hotel, New York, November 19, 1872* (New York: Hub Publishing Company, 1873). See also *IA* (12 February 1880): 7, 11; *IA* (9 February 1888): 234.

143 *National Bottlers' Gazette* (1 July 1886): 16; *National Bottlers' Gazette* (1 August 1886): 51.

144 *National Bottlers' Gazette* (1 November 1886): 45.

145 Such as, for example, the Sash and Blind Manufacturers' Association. See *IA* (5 April 1888): 569.

146 For a theoretical conceptualization of the problems of employers' collective action, see John R. Bowman, *Capitalist Collective Action: Competition, Cooperation, and Conflict in the Coal Industry* (New York: Cambridge University Press, 1989).

147 *Oil and Paint Manufacturer* (20 October 1886): 6; *Oil and Paint Manufacturer* (17 November 1886): 6.

148 See *Reports of Officers, National Founders' Association, Sixth Annual Convention, November 19–20, 1902, Detroit, Michigan* (Detroit: Speaker Printing Company, n.d.), p. 17.

149 *Manufacturer and Builder* 22 (October 1890): 233.

150 *Proceedings of the Annual Convention of the National Association of Manufacturers* 9 (1904), pp. 243–244, quoted in Bonnett, *Employers' Associations in the United States: A Study of Typical Associations*, p. 300; *IA* (31 January 1895): 216. The NAM, in response to the serious economic crisis, at first focused its attention mostly on the restoration of a high protective tariff and the opening of foreign markets, but by 1903 it increasingly shifted its attention toward labor conflict. See National Association of Manufacturers, *Significant Highlights of the Organization and History of the National Association of Manufacturers, 1895–1948* (New York: National Association of Manufacturers, 1948), pp. 2, 4.

151 *IA* (1 April 1886): 25.

152 *National Bottlers' Gazette* (1 September 1886): 15.

153 See Lieberman, *Steinway & Sons*, p. 38; Bonnett, *Employers' Associations in the United States: A Study of Typical Associations*, pp. 371, 374.

154 Bonnett, *Employers' Associations in the United States: A Study of Typical Associations*, pp. 265, 267, 278, 292, 339, 346, 349, 347, 371.

155 *Stove Founders' National Defense Association, Manual* (1920), pp. 27–28, quoted in Bonnett, *Employers' Associations in the United States: A Study of Typical Associations*, p. 40; *IA* (17 June 1886): 17. The association battled with the Iron Molders' Union of North America and allegedly defeated it consistently until 1891. See Bonnett, *Employers' Associations in the United States: A Study of Typical Associations*, p. 40. By the late 1890s, however, unable to defeat the union, the National Founders' Association negotiated directly with the Iron Molders' Union, searching for stable labor relations. See "Existing Conference Agreement, Conference Agreement in Force and Ruling between the International Molders' Union of N.A. and the Stove Founders' N.D.A.," in "Constitution, Agreements, 1891–1928," Stove Founders' National Defense Association, "Records of Labor Union Locals, 1891–1928," Baker Library, Harvard Business School. Among its members were such New York firms as Ely & Ramsay, Richardson & Boynton Co., Boynton Furnace Co., and Eugene Munsell & Co. *IA* (17 June 1886): 17.

156 *NYT*, 21 November 1873, p. 5. See also "American Iron and Steel Association," in *The Encyclopedia of American Business History and Biography* (New York: Facts on File, 1988), p. 2023. For calls by *IA* that employers in

the iron industry should combine, see *IA* (5 March 1874): 14; *IA* (16 July 1874): 14.

157 *IA* (16 July 1874): 14.

158 *New-Yorker Staats-Zeitung*, 7 May 1886, p. 5; *NYT*, 15 May 1886, p. 2; *IA* (4 August 1892): 199.

159 Confronted with an unusually well-organized trade, they reported in 1889 some willingness to accede to the eight-hour day if it would be uniformly enforced in all of North America. See *Proceedings, Third Annual Meeting of the United Typothetae of America, Held on October 8, 9 and 10, 1889 in Saint Louis*, p. 10. The United Typothetae of America, a national organization of local employing printers' associations, convened for its first national convention in 1887, in response to their workers' demand for the nine-hour day. *Proceedings of the First Convention of the United Typothetae of America Held in Chicago, Ill., October 18th, 19th and 20th, 1887* (Richmond, Va.: Everett Waddey Co., 1887), p. 3.

160 See Steinway diary, February 27, 1880, and March 15, 1880, Steinway Papers, NYHS.

161 "Jeder Pianofabrikant in der Stadt New-York die Arbeiter seiner Fabrik benachrichtigt, dass, wenn die Arbeiter von Steinway & Sons nicht bis zum Samstag den 13. März 1880 ihre Arbeit wieder aufnehmen, die Fabrikanten am folgenden Montag . . . ihre Fabriken schliessen werden." *New-Yorker Staats-Zeitung*, 28 February 1880, p. 1.

162 Sidney Fine, "*Without Blare of Trumpets*": *Walter Drew, The National Erectors' Association, and the Open Shop Drive, 1903–57* (Ann Arbor: University of Michigan Press, 1995), p. 1.

163 This argument is eloquently made by Kim Voss, *The Making of American Exceptionalism: The Knights of Labor and Class Formation in the Nineteenth Century* (Ithaca, N.Y.: Cornell University Press, 1993), esp. pp. 202–228, 237–240. For similar arguments, see also Jacoby, "American Exceptionalism Revisited," passim, and James Holt, "Trade Unionism in the British and U.S. Steel Industries, 1880–1914, A Comparative Study," in Daniel J. Leab, *The Labor History Reader* (Urbana: University of Illinois Press, 1985), pp. 166–196.

10. The Power of Capital and the Problem of Legitimacy

1 The quotation is from the *NYT*, 16 December 1880, p. 5.

2 *The New Armory of the Seventh Regiment, National Guard, State of New York* (New York: n. p., 1875), p. 9.

3 Emmons Clark, *History of the Seventh Regiment of New York, 1806–1889* (New York: The Seventh Regiment, 1890), vol. 2, pp. 229–239.

4 Clark, *History of the Seventh Regiment*, pp. 229–240.

5 Clark, *History of the Seventh Regiment*, p. 261.

6 *NYT*, 14 October 1877, p. 12.

7 Clark, *History of the Seventh Regiment*, p. 275.

8 Clark, *History of the Seventh Regimen*, p. 264; *NYT*, 16 December 1880, p. 5.

9   Robert M. Fogelson, *America's Armories: Architecture, Society and Public Order* (Cambridge, Mass.: Harvard University Press, 1989), p.11; Clark, *History of the Seventh Regiment*, p. 291.

10 *Army and Navy Journal* (1 May 1889): 769. The quotation refers to armories in general, not to that of the 7th Regiment in particular.

11 *The New Armory of the Seventh Regiment*, p. 4.

12 *NYT,* 4 October 1877, p. 4.

13 Clark, *History of the Seventh Regiment*, pp. 285, 295.

14 Clark, *History of the Seventh Regiment*, pp. 307, 313.

15 Clark, *History of the Seventh Regiment*, p. 386.

16 Clark, *History of the Seventh Regiment*, p. 369.

17 For a detailed description of this mobilization, see Chapter 4.

18 Henry Hall, ed., *America's Successful Men of Affairs: An Encyclopedia of Contemporaneous Biography* (New York: *The New York Tribune*, 1895–96), vol. 1, p. 415.

19 The names of the members of the 7th Regiment are listed in Clark, *History of the Seventh Regiment*, pp. 435–445; forty-two out of one hundred and four members could be located in the 1890 city directory. See *Trow's New York City Directory for the Year Ending May 1, 1891* (New York: The Trow City Directory Company, 1891).

20 For the characterization as the "rich men's regiment," see B. O. Flower, "Plutocracy's Bastille: Or Why the Republic is Becoming an Armed Camp," in *Arena* 10 (October 1894): 618, 619.

21 Fogelson, *America's Armories*, p. i.

22 *Official Souvenir, Celebration of the Opening of the New Armory, 71st Regiment, National Guard, New York State, April 20, 1894* (New York: n.p., 1894), p. 31.

23 New York (State) Adjutant General's Office, National Guard, 9th Regiment, *Souvenir* [of the] *Opening of the Armory, Ninth Regiment, National Guard, New York State, February 22d, 1897* (New York: Freytag Press, 1897), n.p.

24 *NYT,* 12 July 1892, p. 4.

25 *IA* (11 August 1892): 244.

26 *Brooklyn Eagle,* 6 July 1858, as quoted in Fogelson, *America's Armories,* p. 19.

27 As quoted in Fogelson, *America's Armories,* p. 27.

28 *Official Souvenir, Celebration of the Opening of the New Armory,* p. 105.

29 Sanford Jacoby, "American Exceptionalism Revisited: The Importance of Management," in Sanford Jacoby, ed., *Masters to Managers: Historical and Comparative Perspectives on American Employers* (New York: Columbia University Press, 1991), p. 182.

30 Robert Reinders, "Militia and Public Order in Nineteenth Century America," in *Journal of American Studies* 2 (1977): 98. For the importance of the National Guard, see also David Montgomery, *Citizen Worker: The Experience of Workers in the United States with Democracy and the Free Market During the Nineteenth Century* (New York: Cambridge University Press, 1993), pp. 89, 95. On the number of soliders, see Stephen Skowronek, *Building A New American State, The Expansion of National Administrative*

Capacities, 1870–1920 (New York: Cambridge University Press, 1982), p. 105.

31 Jacoby, "American Exceptionalism Revisited," p. 183.

32 Flower, "Plutocracy's Bastille," p. 606.

33 These statistics and others are quoted in Richard Oestreicher, "Two Souls of American Democracy," in George Reid Andrew and Herrick Chapman, eds., *The Social Construction of Democracy, 1870–1990* (New York: New York University Press, 1995), p. 128.

34 Oestreicher, "Two Souls of American Democracy," p. 128.

35 Oestreicher, "Two Souls of American Democracy," p. 123.

36 *Souvenir* [of the] *Opening of the Armory, Ninth Regiment,* n.p. The regiment was also called to duty in early 1895 on the occasion of the Brooklyn trolley strike.

37 *Official Souvenir, Celebration of the Opening of the New Armory,* pp. 5–13.

38 Clark, *History of the Seventh Regiment of New York,* p. 267.

39 *NYT,* 24 January 1895, p. 2. See also *NYT,* 19 January 1895, pp. 2, 4; *NYT,* 20 January 1895, p. 4; *NYT,* 22 January 1895, p. 3; *NYT,* 23 January 1895, p. 2.

40 Jacoby, "American Exceptionalism Revisited," pp. 180–181, 184; S. C. de Soissons [Guy Jean Raoul Eugène Charles Emmanuel de Savoie-Carignan, Comte de Soissons], *A Parisian in America* (Boston: Estes and Lauriat, 1896), p. 74.

41 Richard Bensel, *Yankee Leviathan: The Origins of Central State Authority in America, 1859–1877* (New York: Cambridge University Press, 1990), pp. 418–419.

42 *Twenty-Second Annual Report of the Corporation of the Chamber of Commerce of the State of New York, For the Year 1879–'80* (New York: Press of the Chamber of Commerce, 1880), p. xiii. Contemporary observers and later historians have widely commented upon the unusual degree of political power enjoyed by the late nineteenth-century American bourgeoisie. See, for example, Gerald Friedman, "The State and the Making of the Working-Class, France and the United States, 1880–1914," in *Theory and Society* 17 (1988): 424.

43 Gerald Friedman argues similarly that in France, the persistent power of a landed aristocracy "limited the influence that middle-class employers could exert over [the] . . . state apparatus." Gerald Friedman, "The Decline of Paternalism and the Making of the Employer Class: France, 1870–1914," in Jacoby, ed., *Masters to Managers,* p. 157. The relative weakness of the bourgeoisie vis-à-vis the state apparatus has also been a theme in German historiography, albeit one that has been challenged. For the statement itself see Hans Ulrich Wehler, *Das Deutsche Kaiserreich, 1871–1918* (Göttingen: Vandenhoeck & Ruprecht, 1980), esp. pp. 129ff. For the challenge see David Blackbourn and Geoff Eley, *The Peculiarities of German History: Bourgeois Society and Politics in Nineteenth-Century Germany* (New York: Oxford University Press, 1984).

44 For the concept of the American state as exceptional, see Skowronek, *Building A New American State,* pp. 4–9. This particular combination of "exceptional-

ist" factors is also emphasized by C. Wright Mills, *The Power Elite* (New York: Oxford University Press, 1956), p. 12. The political power of business interests is also argued for by Colin Gordon, "Why No Corporatism in the United States? Business Disorganization and its Consequences" (paper presented at the Business History Conference, College Park, Md., 1998), pp. 3, 9.

45 On the central position of New York in the nation's system of cities see, among others, Martin Shefter, "New York City and American National Politics," in Martin Shefter, ed., *Capital of the American Century: National and International Influence of New York City* (New York: Russell Sage Foundation, 1993), pp. 95–115.

46 For this argument see also Jacoby, "American Exceptionalism Revisited," p. 184. See also Dietrich Rueschemeyer, "Bourgeoisie, Staat und Bildungsbürgertum," in Jürgen Kocka, ed. *Bürger und Bürgerlichkeit im 19. Jahrhundert* (Göttingen: Vandenhoeck & Ruprecht, 1987), p. 107.

47 This argument is also made by Barrington Moore, *Social Origins of Dictatorship and Democracy: Lord and Peasant in the Making of the Modern World* (Boston: Beacon Press, 1966), p. 141.

48 Moore, *Social Origins of Dictatorship and Democracy,* p. 149; Steven Hahn, "Class and State in Postemancipation Societies: Southern Planters in Comparative Perspective," in *AHR* 95 (February 1990): 92–93.

49 For this argument see also Martin Shefter, "Trade Unions and Political Machines: The Organization and Disorganization of the American Working Class in the Late Nineteenth Century," in Ira Katznelson and Aristide R. Zolberg, eds., *Working-Class Formation: Nineteenth-Century Patterns in Western Europe and the United States* (Princeton: Princeton University Press, 1986), p. 246.

50 John F. Cowan, *A New Invasion of the South, Being a Narrative of the Expedition of the Seventy-First Infantry, National Guard, Through the Southern States in New Orleans, February 24–March 7, 1881* (New York: Board of Officers Seventy-First Infantry, 1881), pp. 7, 79.

51 New-England Society in the City of New York, *Eighty-First Anniversary Celebration of the New-England Society of New York at Delmonico's (December 22, 1886)* (New York: William C. Bryant & Co., 1886), esp. p. 50. "Pacificator" is the characterization used by the *National Cyclopedia of American Biography* (New York: J. T. White, 1898).

52 William Hillyer, *James Talcott, Merchant and His Times* (New York: C. Scribner's Sons, 1937), p. 137.

53 See also the *Proceedings of National Commercial Convention of 1885* (Atlanta, Ga.: W. H. Scott, 1885), which emphasized the overcoming of tensions between the sections and invited businesspeople from all over the United States. For the general point see also Lawrence Goodwyn, *The Populist Moment: A Short History of the Agrarian Revolt in America* (New York: Oxford University Press, 1978), p. 5.

54 As discussed in detail in Chapter 7. See also C. Vann Woodward, *The Strange Career of Jim Crow* (New York: Oxford University Press, 1955), p. 52. See also *Atlanta Constitution,* 25 November 1895, pp. 7–8; *Atlanta Constitution,* 26 November 1895, pp. 1–2, 5.

55 *CFC* 52 (25 April 1891): 626.
56 For this point see also Steven Hahn, *The Roots of Southern Populism: Yeoman Farmers and the Transformation of the Georgia Upcountry, 1850–1890* (New York: Oxford University Press, 1983), p.169; Edward Ayers, *The Promise of the New South: Life after Reconstruction* (New York: Oxford University Press, 1992); Barbara Jeanne Fields, "The Advent of Capitalist Agriculture: The New South in a Bourgeois World," in Thavolia Glymph, ed., *Essays on the Postbellum Southern Economy* (Arlington: Texas A&M University Press, 1985), pp. 73–94.
57 For this argument see also Hahn, "Class and State in Postemancipation Societies," esp. pp. 83, 86, 92, 93, 98. Charles C. Bright, "The State in the United States During the Nineteenth Century," in Charles Bright and Susan Harding, eds., *Statemaking and Social Movements, Essays in History and Theory* (Ann Arbor: University of Michigan Press, 1984), p. 145. Reflecting this relationship, the business press put special emphasis on the resource endowment of the South. *CFC* 43 (25 December 1886): 761; *CFC* 33 (3 September 1881): 237.
58 See also James Livingston, *Pragmatism and the Political Economy of Cultural Revolution, 1850–1940* (Chapel Hill: University of North Carolina Press, 1994), p. 39.
59 As exemplified by National City Bank, which focused its business relations on domestic industries, especially railroads. "George F. Baker," in *The Encyclopedia of American Business History and Biography* (New York: Facts on File, 1988), p. 27.
60 On the character of politics, see Morton Keller, *Affairs of State: Public Life in Late Nineteenth Century America* (Cambridge, Mass.: Belknap Press of Harvard University Press, 1977), pp. 547, 561.
61 John G. Sproat, *The Best Men: Liberal Reformers in the Gilded Age* (New York: Oxford University Press, 1968), p. 152.
62 On the "naturalness" of political economy, see also Sproat, *Best Men*, p. 145. The power of businesspeople to set the boundaries of debate on economic issues is also emphasized by R. Jeffrey Lustig, *Corporate Liberalism: The Origins of Modern American Political Theory, 1890–1920*, (Berkeley: University of California Press, 1982), especially p. 304, and Robert Wiebe, *Businessmen and Reform: A Study of the Progressive Movement* (Cambridge, Mass.: Harvard University Press, 1962), especially pp. 212, 214.
63 See also Montgomery, *Citizen Worker*, p. 114.
64 The Labor Department, created in 1888, had no representation in the Cabinet, and its task was limited to the collection of statistics, again testifying to the unwillingness of the state to involve itself in the regulation of relations between employers and employees. The government played virtually no role in arbitrating conflicts between labor and capital. See Keller, *Affairs of State*, pp. 315, 400.
65 Barry J. Kaplan, "Reformers and Charity: The Abolition of Public Outdoor Relief in New York City, 1870–1898," in *Social Service Review* 52 (June 1978): 202–203, 207.
66 On France see Friedman, "The State and the Making of the Working-Class,"

p. 419. On Great Britain see Jacoby, "American Exceptionalism Revisited," p. 191, and Ira Katznelson, "Working-Class Formation and the State: Nineteenth Century England in American Perspective," in Peter Evans, Dietrich Rueschemeyer, and Theda Skocpol, eds., *Bringing the State Back In* (New York: Cambridge University Press, 1985), p. 274. On Britain, see also Neville Kirk, "The Limits of Liberalism: Working-Class Formation in Britain and the United States," in Rick Halpern and Jonathan Morris, eds., *American Exceptionalism? U.S. Working-Class Formation in an International Context* (New York: St. Martin's Press, 1997), p. 126. Germany's earlier efforts at building a welfare state attracted the scorn of *Scientific American,* which argued that it undermined "[t]he manliness of the laboring class of Germany." See *SciAm* (11 December 1880): 369.

67 Jacoby, "American Exceptionalism Revisited," pp. 180–181.

68 On the courts' role in redefining the republican legacy and the meaning of "free labor," see William E. Forbath, "The Ambitions of Free Labor: Labor and the Law in the Gilded Age," in *Wisconsin Law Review* (1985): 768–817.

69 The importance of courts as policy-making institutions is also stressed by Keller, *Affairs of State,* pp. 342, 358. The quotation is from Skowronek, *Building a New American State,* p. 28.

70 William Forbath, *Law and the Shaping of the American Labor Movement* (Cambridge, Mass.: Harvard University Press, 1991), p. 26.

71 Jacoby, "American Exceptionalism Revisited," p. 184.

72 See also Forbath, *Law and the Shaping of the American Labor Movement,* p. 26.

73 Montgomery, *Citizen Worker,* p. 150–151; for numbers of state laws struck down by courts, see Keller, *Affairs of State,* p. 362; Bright, "The State in the United States," p. 147. One student of these decisions has found that the vast majority of such cases were decided against labor. Forbath, *Law and the Shaping of the American Labor Movement,* p. 38.

74 Forbath, *Law and the Shaping of the American Labor Movement,* p. 61.

75 Friedman, "The State and the Making of the Working-Class," pp. 413, 417.

76 Robert Green McCloskey, *American Conservatism in the Age of Enterprise: A Study of William Graham Sumner, Stephen J. Field and Andrew Carnegie* (Cambridge, Mass.: Harvard University Press, 1951), pp. 73, 75.

77 George C. Gorham, *Some Account of the Work of Stephen J. Field* (n.p.: n.p., 1895), p. 155; for an extended evaluation of Field's thinking, see Paul Kens, *Justice Stephen Field: Shaping Liberty From the Gold Rush to the Gilded Age* (Lawrence: University Press of Kansas, 1997).

78 Quoted in McCloskey, *American Conservatism in the Age of Enterprise,* p. 113.

79 Andrew Carnegie, *The Gospel of Wealth and Other Timely Essays* (New York: Century, 1900), p. 6.

80 Richard E. Welch, Jr., *The Presidencies of Grover Cleveland* (Lawrence, Kans.: The University of Kansas Press, 1988), p. 151.

81 Military Association of the State of New York, *Proceedings of the Military Association of the State of New York* (New York: George F. Nesbitt and Co., 1867), pp. 46–47; Paul T. Ringenbach, *Tramps and Reformers, 1873–1916:*

The Discovery of Unemployment in New York (Westport, Conn.: Greenwood Press, 1973), p. 23. In New York City alone, more than 1 million people were arrested as early as 1877 for "vagrancy." Ringenbach, *Tramps and Reformers*, p. 11. For bourgeois support see *NYT*, 3 June 1875, p. 6; *NYT*, 24 August 1877, p. 4; *NYT*, 9 July 1879, p. 5; *NYT*, 11 July 1879, p. 3; *Nation* (24 January 1878): 50; *NYT*, 3 June 1875, p. 6; Francis Wayland, *Papers on Out-Door Relief and Tramps, Read at the Saratoga Meeting of the American Social Science Association before the Conference of State Charities, September 5th & 6th, 1877* (New Haven, Conn.: Hoggson & Robinson, 1877), p. 10. On tramps in the 1890s see Sidney L. Harring, "Class Conflict and the Suppression of Tramps in Buffalo, 1892–1894," in *Law and Society Review* 2 (1977): 873–911.

82 See also Colin Gordon, "Does the Ruling Class Rule?" in *Reviews in American History* 25 (June 1997): 289; Theda Skocpol, "Bringing the State Back In: Strategies of Analysis in Current Research," in Evans, Rueschemeyer, and Skocpol, *Bringing the State Back In*, p. 15.

83 On the populist movement and the divergence of its ideological agenda from that of the northern bourgeoisie, see Hahn, *The Roots of Southern Populism*, especially pp. 282–284.

84 The *CFC* had already warned much earlier that bimetallism would lead to a drain of the country's gold reserves to Europe. *CFC* 32 (10 March 1881): 299; *CFC* 52 (17 January 1891): 97; *CFC* 38 (8 March 1884): 274; *CFC* 38 (17 May 1884): 582; *CFC* 56 (11 March 1893): 390; *CFC* 60 (20 April 1895): 684. See also Joseph Bishop, *A Chronicle of One Hundred and Fifty Years: The Chamber of Commerce of the State of New York, 1768–1918* (New York: C. Scribner's Sons, 1918), p. 116; *IA* (14 March 1895): 550; *IA* (29 October 1896): 824; *IA* (12 November 1896): 897.

85 *IA* (12 November 1896): 897.

86 See also Keller, *Affairs of State*, p. 383. See James Willard Hurst, *A Legal History of Money in the United States, 1774–1970* (Lincoln: University of Nebraska Press, 1973), p. 176.

87 See also David Vogel, *Kindred Strangers: The Uneasy Relationship Between Business and Politics in America* (Princeton: Princeton University Press, 1996), p. 130.

88 On the importance of tariff politics for the 1880s, see also Keller, *Affairs of State*, p. 376.

89 In 1882, some of them organized the New York Free Trade Club, which agitated for an end to duties on raw materials, as well as "to effect the gradual reduction of duties upon manufactured articles." New York Free Trade Club, *Organization of the New York Free Trade Club* (New York: Putnam's Sons, 1882), p. 2.

90 Keller, *Affairs of State*, pp. 377, 378.

91 Allan Nevins, *Abram S. Hewitt: With Some Account of Peter Cooper* (New York: Harper, 1935), p. 421; Hillyer, *James Talcott*, pp. 128, 130, 133, 134; U.S. Senate, Committee on Education and Labor, *Report of the Committee of the Senate Upon the Relations Between Labor and Capital, and Testimony Taken by the Committee* (Washington, D.C.: GPO, 1885), vol. 2, p. 1095.

Testimony by William Steinway. For strong protectionist sentiments see *IA* (22 April 1880): 15; *SciAm* (17 June 1882): 380; *Manufacturer and Builder* 12 (November 1880): 242. The *CFC* favored lower tariffs. See *CFC* 58 (3 February 1894): 196; *CFC* 34 (8 April 1882): 391; *CFC* 36 (17 February 1883): 182. See also *Proceedings of National Tariff Convention Held at the Cooper Institute, New York, November 29 and 30, 1881* (Philadelphia: The American Iron and Steel Association, 1882), pp. 26–27. On John Roach see *Proceedings of National Tariff Convention Held at the Cooper Institute, New York, November 29 and 30, 1881*, p. 204. Surprisingly, even a number of New York shipowners signed a petition in 1882 demanding higher tariffs. *Proceedings of National Tariff Convention Held at the Cooper Institute, New York, November 29 and 30, 1881*, pp. 268–270.

92   *CFC* 30 (15 May 1880): 506; *IA* (13 July 1882): 15; *IA* (28 August 1884): 16; *IA* (17 July 1884): 16; *IA* (17 May 1888): 818; *IA* (29 March 1888): 527; *IA* (8 February 1894): 274.

93   Nevins, *Abram S. Hewitt*, pp. 421, 425. For the discussion of the tariff framed in terms of the fate of American labor, see for example *HW* (6 August 1892): 746; *NYDT*, 8 July 1892, p. 6; *NYDT*, 11 July 1892, p. 6; *Nation* (21 July 1892): 41. See also the testimony by manufacturers and merchants before the Senate Committee on Education and Labor in *Report of the Committee of the Senate Upon the Relations Between Labor and Capital*. For a free trader arguing for the beneficial effects on the working class of his suggested policy of low duties, see J. Schoenhof, *The Destructive Influence of the Tariff Upon Manufacture and Commerce and the Figures and Facts Relating Thereto* (New York: New York Free Trade Club, 1883), p. iv.

94   *Report of the Third Annual Meeting of the Carriage-Builders' National Association of the United States of America, Held at the St. Nicholas Hotel, New-York, October 21, 1874* (New York: Hub Publishing Company, 1875), p. 4.

95   *Report on Emigration By A Special Committee of The Chamber of Commerce of the State of New-York, January 5, 1865* (New York: John W. Amerman, 1865), p. 13.

96   William E. Dodge, *Old New York: A Lecture Delivered at Association Hall, April 27th, 1880 Upon the Invitation of Merchants and Other Citizens of New York* (New York: Dodd, Mead & Company, 1880), p. 11.

97   Sproat, *Best Men*, p. 177.

98   Nevins, *Abram S. Hewitt*, p. 419; *Twenty-Second Annual Report of the Corporation of the Chamber of Commerce*, p. xxii.

99   *CFC* 30 (15 May 1880): 507.

100   *CFC* 31 (18 December 1880): 640.

101   See, for example, *Report of the Committee of the Senate Upon the Relations Between Labor and Capital, and Testimony Taken by the Committee*, vol. 2, p. 1081. Testimony of Danford Knowlton.

102   *CFC* 38 (10 May 1884): 549.

103   *IA* (23 April 1896): 978; *IA* (April 30, 1896): 1019.

104   *Proceedings of National Tariff Convention Held at the Cooper Institute, New York, November 29 and 30, 1881*, p. 206.

105   The difficulty of creating "rational" regulatory policies at this point is also

emphasized by Gerald Berk, *Alternative Tracks: The Constitution of American Industrial Order, 1865–1917* (Baltimore: Johns Hopkins University Press, 1994), p. 10.

106 For Europe see Nicholas Faith, *The World The Railways Made* (London: The Bodley Head, 1990), pp. 60, 73, 74.

107 Thomas McCraw, *Prophets of Regulation: Charles Francis Adams, Louis D. Brandeis, James M. Landis, Alfred E. Kahn* (Cambridge, Mass.: Belknap Press of Harvard University Press, 1984), pp. 9–10. See also Gabriel Kolko, *Railroads and Regulation, 1877–1916* (New York: W. W. Norton, 1965); Lee Benson, *Merchants, Farmers and Railroads: Railroad Regulation and New York Politics, 1850–1887* (New York: Russell & Russell, 1969). For support from shippers, railroads, and investors in railroads, see *CFC* 40 (6 June 1885): 667. For support from merchants in general, see *MMCR* (December 1870): 464. The multiplicity of approaches to railroad regulation is also argued for by Berk, *Alternative Tracks*, p. 11.

108 Ron Chernow, *The House of Morgan: An American Banking Dynasty and the Rise of Modern Finance* (New York: Simon & Schuster, 1990), p. 56.

109 *Twentieth Annual Report of the Corporation of the Chamber of Commerce of the State of New York for the Year 1877–'78* (New York: Press of the Chamber of Commerce, 1878), p. 116.

110 *NYT,* 27 August 1878, p. 8.

111 Edward A. Purcell, Jr., "Ideas and Interests: Businessmen and the Interstate Commerce Act," in *JAH* 54 (June 1967): 578. See also Bright, "The State in the United States," p. 146.

112 *Report of the Committee of the Senate Upon the Relations Between Labor and Capital, and Testimony Taken by the Committee,* vol. 1, p. 1090. Testimony by Jay Gould.

113 *Banker's Magazine* 42 (March 1888): 660.

114 For its genesis see also Keller, *Affairs of State,* pp. 427–430.

115 Quoted in Nathaniel W. Stephenson, *Nelson W. Aldrich: A Leader in American Politics* (New York: Charles Scribner's Sons, 1930), p. 68.

116 Quoted in Lustig, *Corporate Liberalism,* p. 94.

117 Skowronek, *Building a New American State,* p. 149.

118 de Soissons, *A Parisian in America,* p. 92.

119 New-England Society in the City of New York, *Eighty-ninth Anniversary Celebration of the New-England Society in the City of New York (Saturday, December 22, 1894)* (New York: William C. Bryant & Co., 1894), p. 21.

120 Reginald Townsend, *Mother of Clubs: Being the History of the First Hundred Years of the Union Club of the City of New York, 1836–1936* (New York: The Printing House of W. E. Rudge, 1936), pp. 135–136. The Union Club also admitted a number of officers of the army and navy, exempting them from paying yearly dues. Townsend, *Mother of Clubs,* p. 75.

121 Irving Katz, *August Belmont: A Political Biography* (New York: Columbia University Press, 1968), pp. 235, 237, 245, 250, 255, 267, 274.

122 Philip H. Burch, Jr., *Elites in American History,* vol. 2, *The Civil War to the New Deal* (New York: Holmes & Meier Publishers Inc., 1981), pp. 80, 81, 82.

123 See W. R. Grace to Perry Belmont, May 19, 1881; W. R. Grace to F. Sears, Esq., April 28, 1882; W. R. Grace to Alvin Scott, April 28, 1882; "W. R. Grace Letterbook (Private), 1881–1884," Box 57, W. R. Grace and Company Papers, Rare Books and Manuscript Library, Columbia University.

124 See, for example, bill by W. R. Grace to the Supremeo Gobierno del Peru, 29 de Septembre 1883, p. 420f; and W. R. Grace to Providence Tool Co., September 26, 1882, both in "W. R. Grace Letterbook (Private), 1881–1884," Box 57, W. R. Grace and Company Papers, Rare Books and Manuscript Library, Columbia University.

125 Lawrence A. Clayton, *Grace: W. R. Grace & Co., 1850–1930* (Ottawa: Jameson Books, 1985), passim, but especially pp. 83, 141–225.

126 See William M. Gibb to Samuel Barlow, May 25, 1877; April 30, 1877; June 15, 1877; June 15, 1877 (II); September 1, 1877, all in Samuel Barlow Papers, Huntington Library. William M. Gibb, who represented the Improvement Company in Santo Domingo also bribed powerful Dominican politicians, including the president's private secretary, to favor the company. They also discussed the possibility of Barlow acquiring arms in New York for the Dominican president's war against insurgents.

127 Chauncey Depew, *My Memories of Eighty Years* (New York: Charles Scribner's Sons, 1924), pp. 70, 88, 101, 116.

128 Depew, *My Memories of Eighty Years*, pp. 124, 127.

129 Burch, Jr., *Elites in American History*, vol. 2, pp. 381–387.

130 Welch, Jr., *The Presidencies of Grover Cleveland*, p. 100.

131 Depew, *My Memories of Eighty Years*, p. 6; Burch, Jr., *Elites in American History*, vol. 2, p. 97. Chernow, *The House of Morgan*, p. 73.

132 See on this Abram Hewitt, "Speech in the House of Representatives," May 25, 1876, quoted in Nevins, *Abram S. Hewitt*, pp. 145–154. On Rockefeller see Ron Chernow, *Titan: The Life of John D. Rockefeller* (New York: Random House, 1998), p. 261.

133 Hall, ed., *America's Successful Men*, pp. 717–718.

134 Robert McElroy, *Levi Parsons Morton, Banker, Diplomat, and Statesman* (New York: Putnam, 1930), pp. 74, 79, 81, 95.

135 McElroy, *Levi Parsons Morton*, pp. 173, 219.

136 McCloskey, *American Conservatism in the Age of Enterprise*, p. 75; Jeffery B. Morris, *Federal Justice in the Second Circuit: A History of the United States Courts in New York, Connecticut & Vermont, 1787 to 1987* (New York: Second Circuit Historical Committee, 1987), pp. 70–71, 73, 75, 88.

137 James Bryce, *The American Commonwealth* (London: Macmillan and Co., 1889), vol. 1, p. 260.

138 Edward Sanford Martin, *The Life of Joseph Hodges Choate, As Gathered Chiefly from His Letters* (New York: Charles Scribner's Sons, 1920), vol. 1, pp. 348, 359, 384, 403, 432, 454.

139 Alden Chester, *Courts and Lawyers of New York: A History, 1609–1925* (New York: The American Historical Society, 1925), pp. 1323, 1328, 1330.

140 McCloskey, *American Conservatism in the Age of Enterprise*, pp. 91, 102.

141 Chester, *Courts and Lawyers of New York*, p. 1377; Burch, Jr., *Elites in American History*, vol. 2, p. 108.

142 *In Memoriam: Joseph P. Bradley* (Philadelphia: The Press of Allen, Lane & Scott, 1892), pp. 5, 13, 14, 16, 35, 85.

143 Association of the Bar of the City of New York, *Chief-Justice Waite, Memorial Before the Association of the Bar of the City of New-York, Proceedings at the Meeting of the Bar of the City of New-York, Held March 31, 1888* (New York: The Association, 1890). Burch, Jr., *Elites in American History*, vol. 2, pp. 104, 106–107. On Brewer see D. J. Brewer, "Address at the Yale Law School Commencement: Protection to Private Property from Public Attack," in *New Englander and Yale Review* (August 1891): 99.

144 Keller, *Affairs of State*, p. 562.

145 C. K. Yearly, *The Money Machines: The Breakdown and Reform of Governmental and Party Finance in the North, 1860–1920* (Albany: State University of New York Press, 1970), p. 105; Sproat, *Best Men*, p. 454.

146 Keller, *Affairs of State*, p. 543.

147 Garfield to Morton, Lawnfield, Mentor, Ohio, September 28, 1880, quoted in McElroy, *Levi Parsons Morton*, p. 116.

148 For the impact of this phenomenon on the trajectory of working-class political action in the United States, see Richard Oestreicher, "Urban Working-Class Political Behavior and Theories of American Electoral Politics, 1870–1940," in *JAH* 74 (1987): 1271.

149 For the power of economic elites over both parties, see also Walter Dean Burnham, "The System of 1896: An Analysis," in Paul Kleppner et al., eds., *The Evolution of American Electoral Systems* (Westport, Conn.: Greenwood Press, 1981), p. 165.

150 Neither the Republican Party nor the Democratic Party articulated sharply divergent views on the American political economy. See Richard Hofstadter, *American Political Tradition and the Men Who Made It* (New York: Knopf, 1948), pp. 167, 177.

151 For the absence of strong ideological disagreements between the parties, see also Keller, *Affairs of State*, p. 543.

152 *CFC* 43 (6 November 1886): 549.

153 See also Skowronek, *Building a New American State*, p. 39. This was especially the case for the presidency. See Keller, *Affairs of State*, p. 297.

154 Among a sample of 33 New York City manufacturers whose political affiliation could be established, 25 were Republicans. Manufacturers are listed with their political affiliation in Hall, ed., *America's Successful Men of Business*, passim. For Republican manufacturers, see also *Proceedings at the First Annual Dinner of the Republican Club of the City of New York, Held at Delmonico's, February 12, 1887* (New York: Mercantile Printing and Stationary Co., 1887).

155 Horace Samuel Merrill, *Bourbon Leader: Grover Cleveland and the Democratic Party* (Boston: Little, Brown and Company, 1957), p. 71; Hofstadter, *American Political Tradition*, p. 182.

156 See Sproat, *Best Men*, pp. 127, 129; New York Chamber of Commerce, *Tribute of the Chamber of Commerce of the State of New York to the Memory of Horace B. Claflin* (New York: Press of the Chamber of Commerce, 1886), p. 8; Katz, *August Belmont*, p. 271. Sproat, *Best Men*, p. 126.

157 Sproat, *Best Men,* p. 129. Hofstadter, *American Political Tradition,* p. 179. Cleveland's administration was closely linked to business interests, especially to railroads. Burch, Jr., *Elites in American History,* vol. 2, pp. 97–103.

158 Quoted in Hofstadter, *American Political Tradition,* p. 180.

159 Welch, Jr., *The Presidencies of Grover Cleveland,* pp. 12, 13, 48, 58, 68, 79, 81, 87.

160 Welch, Jr., *The Presidencies of Grover Cleveland,* pp. 141, 143, 145. His attorney general, Richard Olney, a railroad lawyer still on a railroad company's payroll while serving as a member of the Cabinet, cooperated with the General Managers' Association to break the strike. Welch, Jr., *The Presidencies of Grover Cleveland,* p. 143.

161 Depew, *My Memories of Eighty Years,* p. 127. Chauncey Depew approved of the government's repression of strikes; however, in front of the Republican Club of New York, he declared himself in favor of "harmonious relations between the employers and employees." See *Proceedings at the First Annual Dinner of the Republican Club of the City of New York,* p. 31.

162 See also Montgomery, *Citizen Worker,* pp. 144–145.

163 *NYT,* 13 September 1896, p. 17.

164 *NYT,* 16 September 1896, p. 9; *NYT,* 24 September 1896, p. 9; *NYT,* 23 September 1896, p. 6.

165 David Hammack, *Power and Society: Greater New York at the Turn of the Century* (New York: Russell Sage Foundation, 1982), p. 131; *NYT,* 16 October 1896, p. 8.

166 *NYT,* 5 November 1896, p. 4.

167 See, for example, Hammack, *Power and Society,* p. 139.

168 Hammack, *Power and Society,* pp. 132–133.

169 Nevins, *Abram S. Hewitt,* p. 438. On Grace see Clayton, *Grace: W. R. Grace & Co.,* p. 98.

170 Hammack, *Power and Society,* p. 140.

171 Shefter, "The Electoral Foundations of the Political Machine: New York City, 1884–1897," in Joel Silbey, Allen Bogue, and William Flanagan, eds., *The History of American Electoral Behavior* (Princeton: Princeton University Press, 1978), p. 264.

172 Hammack, *Power and Society,* p. 19.

173 Hammack, *Power and Society,* p. 131; Roy Rosenzweig and Elizabeth Blackmar, *The Park and the People: A History of Central Park* (Ithaca, N.Y.: Cornell University Press, 1992), p. 303.

174 Rosenzweig and Blackmar, *The Park and the People,* p. 287.

175 Kaplan, "Reformers and Charity," p. 207, 212; Wayland, *Papers on Out-Door Relief and Tramps,* p. 7.

176 Edward Dana Durand, *The Finances of New York City* (New York: The Macmillan Company, 1898), p. 373. Yearly, *The Money Machines,* pp. 41, 68, 69.

177 Hammack, *Power and Society,* pp. 137, 138.

178 Shefter, "The Electoral Foundations of the Political Machine," pp. 265, 290.

179 Shefter, "The Electoral Foundations of the Political Machine," p. 392.

180 Shefter, "The Electoral Foundations of the Political Machine," pp. 294–296.

For the integrative power of political machines, see also Oestreicher, "Urban Working-Class Political Behavior," p. 1272.

181 Shefter, "The Electoral Foundations of the Political Machine," p. 295; Yearly, *The Money Machines,* pp. 98, 108–109.

182 Shefter, "The Electoral Foundations of the Political Machine," p. 265.

183 For the division between workplace and community politics, see Ira Katznelson, "Working-Class Formation and the State: Nineteenth Century England in American Perspective," p. 259. Machine politics in general and Tammany in particular did not mobilize on the basis of class, but on that of neighborhood and cultural identifications, albeit both of which frequently corresponded with class.

184 Joseph Choate, "Speech at the Alpha Delta Phi Fraternity on May 3, 1888," quoted in Martin, *The Life of Joseph Hodges Choate,* vol. 1, p. 399.

185 Though they disagreed on some of the particulars. See Hammack, *Power and Society,* pp. 192, 228, 231.

186 Hammack, *Power and Society,* p. 214. The quotation can be found on p. 228.

187 See Hammack, *Power and Society,* especially p. 231.

188 On the history of the subway see Clifton Hood, *722 Miles: The Building of the Subways and How They Transformed New York* (New York: Simon & Schuster, 1993), esp. pp. 14, 21, 65.

189 The New York Tax Reform Association agitated against taxation based on "abilities [to pay]." Bolton Hall, ed., *Who Pays Your Taxes? A Consideration on the Question of Taxation* (New York: G. P. Putnam's Sons, 1892), p. 4. Yearly, *The Money Machines,* p. 173.

190 Simon Sterne, *Address Before the German-American Citizens' Association on the Proposed Constitutional Convention and the Work Before It* (New York: n.p., 1887), p. 38.

191 Yearly, *The Money Machines,* pp. 104, 106, 118, 129.

192 Skowronek, *Building a New American State,* p. 54.

193 Harring, "Class Conflict and the Suppression of Tramps in Buffalo, 1892–1894," p. 874; *Report of the Police Department of the City of New York For the Year Ending December 31, 1896* (New York: The Martin B. Brown Company, 1897), p. 21. For the general point, see Robert Wiebe, *Self-Rule: A Cultural History of American Democracy* (Chicago: University of Chicago Press, 1995), p. 126. Robert M. Fogelson, *Big-City Police* (Cambridge, Mass.: Harvard University Press, 1977), pp. 1, 3. On the theme of modernization and bureaucratization in the late nineteenth and early twentieth century, see Eric Monkkonen, *Police in Urban America, 1860–1929* (New York: Cambridge University Press, 1981), p. 153; Sidney Harring, *Policing a Class Society: The Experience of American Cities, 1865–1915* (New Brunswick, N.J.: Rutgers University Press, 1983), p. 248; Fogelson, *Big-City Police,* p. 42. The New York City Police force grew from 2,519 members in 1880 to 4,609 sixteen years later. *Report of the Police Department of the City of New York For the Year Ending December 31, 1896,* p. 26.

194 *Campaign Book of the Citizens' Union* (New York: Citizens' Union, n.d.), pp. 28–29.

195   For their ideas, see *Speeches by Ex-Judge Joseph F. Daly, Governor Theodore Roosevelt and Reverend Thomas R. Slicer, Delivered at the Dinner of the Citizens' Union Club of the 27th & 29th Assembly Districts at Tuxedo Hall, New York, March 24, 1899* (New York: n.p., 1899). See also CFC 59 (10 November 1894): 813.

196   Durand, *The Finances of New York City*, p. 164. Elite New Yorkers always played a central role in this reform of city government. Durand, *The Finances of New York City*, pp. 155–158, 159–160.

197   Durand, *The Finances of New York*, p. 164. *Nation* (21 February 1884): 159.

198   Joseph P. Viteritti, "The Tradition of Municpal Reform: Charter Revision in Historical Perspective," in Frank J. Mauro and Gerald Benjamin, eds., *Restructuring the New York City Government: The Reemergence of Municipal Reform* (New York: The Academy of Political Science, 1989), p. 19.

199   Frederick Shaw, *History of the New York City Legislature* (New York: Columbia University Press, 1954), p. 4.

200   CFC 58 (12 May 1894): 795.

201   Chester, *Courts and Lawyers of New York*, pp. 736f.

202   Burnham, "The System of 1896: An Analysis," p. 164.

203   Charles Z. Lincoln, *The Constitutional History of New York* (Rochester, N.Y.: The Lawyers Co-Operative Publishing Company, 1906), vol. 5, p. 79.:

204   See Lincoln, *The Constitutional History of New York*, p. 82. For an analysis of how elite women negotiated the treacherous terrain of class and gender, see Ellen Carol DuBois, "Working Women, Class Relations, and Suffrage Militance: Harriot Stanton Blatch and the New York Woman Suffrage Movement, 1894–1909," in *AHR* 71 (1987): 37–39, 51.

205   Skowronek, *Building a New American State*, p. 46.

206   Hammack, *Power and Society*, pp. 147–149. Considering Hammack's emphasis on the depth of the divisions among "five social elites," it is notable that the Committee of Seventy attracted all segments of the city's economic elite to its ranks.

207   The theme of bourgeois confidence and bourgeois anxiety also is emphasized by Peter Gay, *Pleasure Wars: The Bourgeois Experience, Victoria to Freud* (New York: Norton, 1998), pp. 3, 13.

208   See also Moore, *Social Origins of Dictatorship and Democracy*, p. 150.

209   *Report of the Committee of the Senate Upon the Relations Between Labor and Capital*, vol. 1, p. 1013. Testimony by John Roach.

210   T. Jackson Lears, *No Place of Grace: Anti-Modernism and the Transformation of American Culture, 1880–1920* (1981; reprint Chicago: Chicago University Press, 1994), p. xi; Burnham, "The System of 1896," p. 162.

211   This is the central argument of James Livingston, "The Social Analysis of Economic History and Theory: Conjectures of Late Nineteenth-Century American Development," in *AHR* 92 (February 1987): 69–95.

212   *Twenty-Eighth Annual Report of the Corporation of the Chamber of Commerce of the State of New-York for the Year 1885–'86* (New York: Press of the Chamber of Commerce, 1886), p. 118.

213   See also James Livingston, *Origins of the Federal Reserve System: Money,*

Class, and Corporate Capitalism, 1890–1933 (Ithaca, N.Y.: Cornell University Press, 1886), Chapter 1.

214 For the sense of distance between the lower middle class and the bourgeoisie, see, for example, *Report of the Committee of the Senate Upon the Relations Between Labor and Capital, and Testimony Taken by the Committee,* vol. 3, p. 487. Here, the owner of a small print shop in Fall River, Massachusetts, refused to characterize himself as a "capitalist," despite the steady prodding of the Senate investigators. For the comprehensive challenge by the Populists, see Burnham, "The System of 1896," p. 162.

215 See for concerns about the Farmers' Alliance, for example, *CFC* 51 (15 November 1890): 658.

216 Herbert Gutman, *Work, Culture and Society in Industrializing America* (New York: Vintage Books, 1977), p. 243. This distance between middle-class Americans and the bourgeoisie is also argued by Robert Johnston, "Middle-Class Political Ideology in a Corporate Society: The Persistence of Small-Propertied Radicalism in Portland, Oregon, 1883–1926" (Ph.D. diss., Rutgers University, 1993), passim.

217 Quoted in Walter LaFeber, *The New Empire: An Interpretation of American Expansion, 1860–1898* (Ithaca, N.Y.: Cornell University Press, 1963), p. 17.

218 See Thomas K. McCraw, "Business & Government: The Origins of the Adversary Relationship," in *California Management Review* 26 (1984): 45.

219 Skowronek, *Building a New American State,* p. 17.

220 This theme is also explored by Gordon, "Why No Corporatism in the United States?" p. 10.

Epilogue

1 Walter Dean Burnham, "The System of 1896: An Analysis," in Paul Kleppner et al., eds., *The Evolution of American Electoral Systems* (Westport, Conn.: Greenwood Press, 1981), p. 165.

2 For the crisis of legitimacy see also Mary O. Furner, "The Republican Tradition and the New Liberalism: Social Investigation, State Building, and Social Learning in the Gilded Age," in Mary O. Furner and Michael Lacey, eds., *The State and Social Investigation in Britain and the United States* (Washington, D.C.: Woodrow Wilson Center Press, 1993), p. 201. For the larger sense of crisis among the bourgeoisie, see T. Jackson Lears, *No Place of Grace: Antimodernism and the Transformation of American Culture, 1880–1920* (1981; reprint Chicago: University of Chicago Press, 1994), p. xii; Peter Gay, *Pleasure Wars: The Bourgeois Experience, Victoria to Freud* (New York: Norton, 1998), pp. 3, 13.

3 See, for example, Richard L. McCormick, *From Realignment to Reform: Political Change in New York State, 1893–1910* (Ithaca, N.Y.: Cornell University Press, 1981) p. 254.

4 For a discussion of this crisis see also James Livingston, *Origins of the Federal Reserve System: Money, Class, and Corporate Capitalism, 1890–1933* (Ithaca, N.Y.: Cornell University Press, 1986), pp. 33–48.

5 James Livingston, "The Social Analysis of Economic History and Theory:

Conjectures of Late Nineteenth-Century American Development," *AHR* 92 (February 1987): 69–95.

6   Livingston, *Origins of the Federal Reserve System*, p. 51ff.

7   See also Livingston, *Origins of the Federal Reserve System*, Chapter 1.

8   This notion of political crisis is also shared by McCormick, *From Realignment to Reform*, p. 266.

9   See, for a detailed discussion, Louis Galambos, *The Public Image of Big Business, 1880–1940* (Baltimore: Johns Hopkins University Press, 1975).

10 Among many authors who emphasize the crisis of legitimacy, albeit in different terms, see McCormick, *From Realignment to Reform*, p. 254.

11 Lears, *No Place of Grace*, p. 5, 111.

12 On the Martins' move to Great Britain in the wake of the costume ball, see Allen Churchill, *Upper Crust: An Informal History of New York's Highest Society* (Englewood Cliffs, N.J.: Prentice-Hall, 1970), p. 192.

13 On the importance of legitimacy and accumulation, see James O'Connor, *The Fiscal Crisis of the State* (New York: St. Martin's Press, 1973), p. 6.

14 And not the struggle for particular sets of narrow economic interests. Here I agree with Livingston, *Origins of the Federal Reserve System*, passim. Gabriel Kolko and others instead have emphasized sectoral economic interests as the moving force behind bourgeois embraces of progressivism. See Gabriel Kolko, *The Triumph of Conservatism: A Reinterpretation of American History, 1900–1916* (New York: The Free Press, 1963), passim.

15 McCormick, *From Realignment to Reform*, pp. 31, 256; David Montgomery, *The Fall of the House of Labor: The Workplace, the State, and American Labor Activism, 1865–1925* (New York: Cambridge University Press, 1987), pp. 420–424.

16 Livingston, *Origins of the Federal Reserve System*, p. 66.

17 Indeed, they were often among the first advocating such changes. See, for example, McCormick, *From Realignment to Reform*, p. 260.

18 Simon Sterne, *Address Before the German-American Citizens' Association on the Proposed Constitutional Convention and the Work Before It* (New York: n.p., 1887), p. 5. For an excellent account of discussions among national intellectuals, see James T. Kloppenberg, *Uncertain Victory: Social Democracy and Progressivism in European and American Thought, 1870–1920* (New York: Oxford University Press, 1986).

19 For this concern, see the elaborate statement by Simon Sterne, *Our Methods of Legislation and Their Defects* (New York: Published by Order of the Society, 1879), passim.

20 See Citizens' Union Club, New York, *Speeches by Ex-Judge Joseph F. Daley, Governor Theodore Roosevelt and Reverend Thomas R. Slicer Delivered at the Dinner of the Citizens' Union Club of the 27th and 29th Assembly Districts at Tuxedo Hall, New York, March 24, 1899* (New York: n.p., 1899), especially pp. 7–8.

21 Martin J. Sklar, *The Corporate Reconstruction of American Capitalism, 1890–1916: The Market, The Law, and Politics* (New York: Cambridge University Press, 1989), pp. 12, 17.

22 *Banker's Magazine* 42 (March 1888): 41.

23 McCormick, *From Realignment to Reform,* p. 266.

24 Livingston, *Origins of the Federal Reserve System,* p. 93.

25 Livingston, *Origins of the Federal Reserve System,* p. 21.

26 Livingston, *Origins of the Federal Reserve System,* pp. 73, 220.

27 Livingston, *Origins of the Federal Reserve System,* p. 232.

28 McCormick, *From Realignment to Reform,* p. 270.

29 Livingston, *Origins of the Federal Reserve System,* Chapter 1. For this point see also David Hammack, *Power and Society: Greater New York at the Turn of the Century* (New York: Russell Sage Foundation, 1982), p. 56.

30 Quoted in Livingston, *Origins of the Federal Reserve System,* p. 61.

31 Hewitt to E. Tracy, Esq., March 8, 1888, "Letter Press Book," "1888," BV Hewitt Abrams, NYHS; Roosevelt is quoted in G. Wallace Chessman, *Theodore Roosevelt and the Politics of Power* (Boston: Little, Brown and Company, 1969), pp. 37–38. Roosevelt referred to the Court of Appeals decision calling a law unconstitutional that would have made the production of cigars illegal in tenements.

32 As quoted in Joseph Frazier Wall, *Andrew Carnegie* (New York: Oxford University Press, 1970), p. 392.

33 *Nation* (11 November 1886): 386.

34 Hammack, *Power and Society,* p. 142

35 Stephen Skowronek, *Building a New American State: The Expansion of National Administrative Capacities, 1877–1920* (New York: Cambridge University Press, 1982), p. 17.

36 John Bleecker Miller, *Progress and Robbery and Progress and Justice: An Answer to Henry George, the Demi-Communist* (New York: Baker & Taylor, Co., 1887), pp. 56, 70. See also McCormick, *From Realignment to Reform,* p. 270.

37 Imperialism as a legitimizing strategy is especially emphasized by Hans Ulrich Wehler, *Der Aufstieg des Amerikanischen Imperialismus: Studien zur Entwicklung des Imperium Americanum, 1865–1900* (Göttingen: Vandenhoeck & Ruprecht, 1974), pp. 37–43. The problem is cast in a slightly different way, namely as a "crisis of manliness," in Kristin Hoganson, *Fighting for American Manhood: How Gender Politics Provoked the Spanish-American and Philippine-American Wars* (New Haven: Yale University Press, 1998).

38 They had followed with great interest the exploration of Africa as well as Latin America. See, for example, *Third Annual Report of the Chamber of Commerce of the State of New-York for the Year 1860–'61* (New York: John W. Amerman, 1861), p. 327; *Sixth Annual Report of the Chamber of Commerce of the State of New-York, for the Year 1863–'64* (New York: John W. Amerman, 1864), p. 67. They had also taken great interest in affairs relating to the building of a canal through Panama. (Though the *Commercial and Financial Chronicle* argued that the construction could be done by any nation and did not need direct U.S. government influence, as U.S. businesses would benefit anyhow.) *CFC* 33 (29 October 1881): 456; *SciAm* (21 June 1879): 385.

39 *IA* (25 March 1880): 8.

40 *IA* (8 April 1880): 14. For a similar statement see *IA* (23 June 1874): 14.

41 *CFC* 30 (31 January 1880): 104; *SciAm* (3 April 1880): 208.

42 Hewitt, "The True Road to Prosperity," Speech in the House of Representatives, February 21, 1878, in Allan Nevins, ed., *Selected Writings of Abram S. Hewitt* (New York: Columbia University Press, 1937), p. 199.

43 Joseph Bucklin Bishop, *A Chronicle of One Hundred and Fifty Years: The Chamber of Commerce of the State of New York, 1768–1918* (New York: Charles Scribner's Sons, 1918), p. 100.

44 *CFC* 39 (16 August 1884): 171.

45 *CFC* 50 (5 April 1890): 467.

46 Quoted in Christopher Lasch, "The Moral and Intellectual Rehabilitation of the Ruling Class," in Christopher Lasch, ed., *The World of Nations: Reflections on American History, Politics, and Culture* (New York: Knopf, 1973), p. 85. Even those opposing expansion nevertheless often embraced similar beliefs in natural racial hierarchies, though they concluded that Anglo-Saxons would never be able to adapt to rule in tropical climes. For the argument that imperialists and anti-imperialists shared a set of core beliefs focused on a critique of the universalist liberal tradition see Christopher Lasch, "The Anti-Imperialists, the Philippines, and the Inequality of Man," *Journal of Southern History* 24 (August, 1958): 319–331.

    The talk of expansion of foreign markets and strong naval forces was amplified by such increasingly popular writers as Josiah Strong, whose *Our Country: The Possible Future and Its Present Crisis* was first published in 1885. In it, he advocated the expansion of the American nation and the Anglo-Saxon race to other areas of the world, legitimized by an application of social Darwinism to the sphere of international politics. See Friedrich W. Horlander, "The Language of Late Nineteenth Century Expansionism," in Serge Ricard, ed., *An American Empire, Expansionist Cultures and Politics, 1881–1917* (Aix-En-Provence: Université de Provence, 1990), pp. 35–37.

47 William E. Dodge, Jr., "Speech at the Chamber of Commerce," reprinted in *Forty-First Annual Report of the New-York Chamber of Commerce of the State of New-York for the Year 1898–'99* (New York: Press of the Chamber of Commerce, 1899), p. 5.

48 *Twenty-Second Annual Report of the Corporation of the Chamber of Commerce,* 1880, pp. xviii–xix; *Twenty-Seventh Annual Report of the Corporation of the Chamber of Commerce of the State of New-York for the Year 1884–'85* (New York: Press of the Chamber of Commerce, 1884), p. 38.

49 *Forty-First Annual Report of the New-York Chamber of Commerce,* pp. 50–51.

50 See Lawrence A. Clayton, *Grace: W. R. Grace & Co., 1850–1930* (Ottawa: Jameson Books, 1985), pp. 141, 150, 181, 189, 224, 225.

51 *IA* (13 April 1893): 832; (21 September 1893): 514; (7 December 1893): 1021; (8 February 1894): 269; (5 July 1894): 3; (5 September 1895): 1; (24 October 1895): 849; (5 December 1895): 1159; (16 July 1896): 123. *SciAm* (3 December 1881): 352; (22 February 1879): 119; (10 June 1882): 368.

52 On opposition to imperialism see, for example, the *Commercial and Financial Chronicle,* which opposed the annexation of Hawaii. See *CFC* 57 (18 November 1893): 826ff. Also consult Ernest May, *Imperial Democracy: The*

Emergence of America As A Great Power (New York: Harcourt, Brace, Jovanovich, 1961), pp. 80–81, 90, 118, 139–140, 143–145. This is also noticeable in the discussions of the New York Chamber of Commerce. See Bishop, *A Chronicle of One Hundred and Fifty Years*, pp. 99–101.

53 See Sklar, *The Corporate Reconstruction*, passim, esp. pp. 4–5.

54 Naomi R Lamoreaux, *The Great Merger Movement in American Business, 1895–1904* (New York: Cambridge University Press, 1985), p. 2.

55 For a summary of this newly emerging outlook, see R. Jeffrey Lustig, *Corporate Liberalism: The Origins of Modern American Political Theory, 1890–1920* (Berkeley: University of California Press, 1982), especially pp. 113–115.

56 Lears, *No Place of Grace*, pp. 111–112, 116.

57 See Sklar, *The Corporate Reconstruction*, p. 16.

58 One of the few historians who also grasped this continuity is Lears, *No Place of Grace*, pp. xii, xviii. See also Lasch, "The Moral and Intellectual Rehabilitation of the Ruling Class," pp. 80–99; Maurice Zeitlin, "Who Owns America? The Same Old Gang," in Maurice Zeitlin, *The Large Corporation and Contemporary Classes* (Cambridge: Polity Press, 1989), pp. 142–161. In a different context, Charles Maier also emphasizes the continuity of bourgeois elites. See Charles Maier, *Recasting Bourgeois Europe* (Princeton: Princeton University Press, 1975), p. 4.

59 Importantly, however, they continued to be legitimized in liberal terms, unlike the outright rejection of liberalism by many among Europe's elites. For this argument see Lears, *No Place of Grace*, p. 6.

60 Eric Hobsbawm, *The Age of Extremes: A History of the World, 1914–1991* (New York: Pantheon Books, 1994).

61 Alexis de Tocqueville, *Democracy in America*, trans. Henry Reeve (1835; reprint Cambridge: Sever and Francis, 1863), vol. 2, pp. 193–197.

62 *NYT*, 7 February 1897, p. 10.

Index